The History
of Human Reason

RJ Robinson

Prometheus Research Group

The History
of Human Reason

Published by the Prometheus Research Group, 10-12 London Road, Alton, GU34 4EG, United Kingdom.

ISBN 0-9542168-5-7

British Library Cataloguing-in-Publication Data.

A CIP record for this book is available from the British Library.

The Prometheus Research Group:

- is an independent association of academics and other intellectuals interested in the problem of human intelligence and its place in nature.
- seeks to create an integrated account of all aspects of human nature, from the life of the newborn infant to the widest reaches of history and consciousness.
- is critical of the glib biologism and information processing metaphors of 'evolutionary psychology', 'cognitive science' and their allies.
- regards human creativity, originality and self-knowledge as real phenomena to be explained, not as illusions to be explained away.
- is sympathetic to a great traditions of structural, phenomenological and dialectical thought.
- seeks collaborators in all walks of academic and intellectual life.

If you would like to know more about the Prometheus Research Group, we can be contacted at:

www.prometheus.org.uk

Contents

Acknowledgements

This book owes a great deal to a many different people. Some debts arise from passing comments, others from systematic critiques. Both have been invaluable, the former because of the ideas and insights they have inadvertently supplied and the intellectual log jams they have cleared, the latter because of the generosity and acumen with which they were performed. Among the latter, I would especially like to thank Professor Leslie Smith of Lancaster University, Dr Ulrich Müller of Penn State University, and Dr Hsueh Yeh of the University of Memphis, all of whom kindly reviewed drafts. I would also like to thank my editor, Lindsey Brake, whose detailed reviews and very helpful explanations contributed greatly to the quality of the end result.

To all these individuals I give my thanks.

However, my greatest debt is without doubt to André Hopper. For two decades André has discussed the topics covered by this book with me, provided innumerable seminal ideas and examples, read more drafts than I can recall, and more than once saved me from major mistakes and misunderstandings. So if there are any mistakes left in here, they are his fault.

This book is dedicated to my children, although I
suspect they would have preferred chocolate.

...il est fort possible que la coordination générale des actions, dont l'équilibration progressive semble constitutive de la formation des opérations logiques ou logico-mathématiques, intéresse aussi bien les actions collectives ou interindividuelles que les actions individuelles. En d'autres termes, qu'il s'agisse des actions exécutées individuellement ou d'actions faites en commun avec échanges, collaborations, oppositions, etc., on retrouverait les mêmes lois de coordination et de régulation qui aboutiraient aux mêmes structures finales d'opérations ou de coopérations, en tants que coopérations; on pourrait ainsi considérer la logique, en tant que forme finale des équilibrations, comme étant simultanément individuelle et sociale, individuelle en tant qu'elle est générale ou commune à tous les individus, et également sociale en tant qu'elle est générale ou commune à toutes les sociétés.

Jean Piaget

Introduction

Time is awake, the Wheel is turning,
Lifting up and overthrowing.
Thunder in the roof of heaven!

Sophocles, *Oedipus at Colonus*

What is the problem?

This book is about the nature, development and significance of intelligence, in the individual and in history. Its main concerns are the basic properties of intelligence, the stages through which intelligence develops, the micro-developmental processes whereby each of the main stages unfolds, and the limits to intelligence, real and apparent. It draws on a wide range of social and psychic phenomena, from the functions of primitive exchange and children's strategies for solving jigsaw puzzles to the nature of happiness and the rise and fall of great social systems.

As this already implies, I do not define intelligence in the usual manner. This is not a book about IQ testing[1] and it is only partly an enquiry into the kinds of cognitive activity normally associated with the idea of intelligence. It does not privilege any particular kind or aspect of activity (language, tool-making, etc.) as quintessentially or primordially intelligent, and it is most certainly not about information processing, which seems to me to have literally nothing whatsoever to do with intelligence properly so called.

Instead, I use the term 'intelligence' to encompass all that is specifically human about human beings – and all that makes some other animals, including the great apes, dolphins and perhaps a few others, so very human too. Exactly what that means will emerge in the course of this book, but I can start by saying that, by this definition, intelligence is the central attribute of – dreadful but unavoidable phrase – human nature. Consequently, any credible theory of human nature must begin from the concept of intelligence, and any credible theory of intelligence must account for human nature in all its most complex, sophisticated and exceptional aspects.

---

[1] As John Dewy remarked (see also Richardson, 1999: Ch. 2 and *passim*):

> This intelligence-testing business reminds me of the way they used to weigh hogs in Texas. They would get a long plank, put it over a cross-bar, and somehow tie the hog on one end of the plank. They'd search all around till they'd found a stone that would balance the weight of the hog and they'd put that on the other end of the plank. Then they'd guess the weight of the stone.

That last point allows me to anticipate an important and usually quite legitimate criticism of allegedly new theories of human nature. That is, why do we need a new explanation anyway – and new not only in its detail or in its application of existing concepts but new in kind? Aren't allegedly 'new' theories of what it is to be human usually either the product of hyperbole and half-baked platitudes or disguised re-workings of long discredited ideas? Certainly in my experience they are. In particular we already have some extraordinarily powerful scientific explanations of basic biological processes and mechanisms, and if it must be admitted that biologists seldom address the specifically *human* features of human nature other than in the most general terms, then there is no shortage of knowledge, concepts, methods and theories in the humanities and the social sciences that are surely capable of filling in any important gaps. So why neglect the tried and tested tools we already possess?

A biology of human nature?

Regarding biology, my answer to this reasonable objection is quite straightforward. It is to say that human beings are not like other organisms, and that intelligence cannot be explained in biological terms. That is why the biology of human nature has so far remained at the most general level, without any biological account of, say, the specifics of history or consciousness: biology is incapable of going any further without exposing its own irrelevance.

This may seem to be an odd attitude: after all, what scientific alternative is there? There can be no doubt that our ancestry is exclusively biological, that everything we do relies on definite kinds of biological structure and function that are plainly the products of ordinary evolutionary and developmental processes, that human beings have to deal with biological demands and a biological environment, that human beings reside on the same biological continua as other organisms, and so on. To take only some of the most widely cited examples of our animal nature, if we share so much of our nervous systems and the vast majority of our genes with other primates, not to mention many other features (much of the structure of our haemoglobin, for example[1]), how can I argue that human beings demand a fundamentally different *kind* of explanation from other organisms?

But if I may reverse this conventional argument, even if human beings *had* developed out of, yet were now qualitatively different from, the general run of organisms, we would still share a good deal with them. After all, life is not a chemical reaction, but it does rely on chemical structures and their activity. So how much would have to be different for such a change to be considered qualitative? Plainly, if we limit the question to *strictly* quantitative terms, we do not know. In fact, it is intrinsically unlikely that any question about qualitative differences could ever be answered sensibly in quantitative terms – so many per cent difference in this factor or that, so much growth in our encephalisation index, and so on.

---

[1] Van Valen (1974); King and Wilson (1975).

So why should we assume that sharing 50 per cent of our genes, our nervous system or any other biological attribute with another species – or even or 90 per cent or 99.999 per cent – means that there are no qualitative differences between us? A pile of rocks might easily share practically *all* of its physical content with a Gothic cathedral, but one would surely question whether they were in any important sense the same! There may be some quantifiable sense in which more is better or worse, but even that would not tell me when it became qualitatively *other*. Conversely, were our encephalisation index twice – or a hundred times – that of our nearest relative, would that mean that we were qualitatively different? Why not conclude that we would still be essentially the same, only more so? In fact, on what grounds would *either* conclusion be justified? Such an argument would only make sense if one *assumed* that potential qualitative differences could be meaningfully investigated in quantitative terms. Yet it is precisely the validity of this approach that is in question here. To insist on a biological explanation of human nature solely on the grounds that human beings share many overt features with other organisms is quite empty, since it is not the things we share with sheep or artichokes that make human beings interesting (or indeed human) but rather the things that are different.

In summary, arguments from continuity, ancestry and similarity can tell us nothing about the qualitative relationship between human beings and other organisms. On the contrary, they assume that there is *no* qualitative difference here – otherwise what would be the point of the comparison? Perhaps we are just like other organisms, perhaps there is a critical sense in which we are quite different, and perhaps the answer lies somewhere in between. But there is nothing in biology that can tell us which is the case.

One assumption made by many claims for biology's precedence over any other approach is that, unlike the humanities, biology is scientific. It is a fair point – biology is indeed scientific (in general terms), whereas the alternatives are not. But it does not follow that if we apply biological methods to human beings, we will get scientific answers. After all, we plainly would not get a scientific account of life if we restricted ourselves to the methods of physics or chemistry: as far as I am aware, there is no chemical formula for territoriality. We would merely get a reductionistic trivialisation. Similarly, if biological concepts and methods are not capable of grasping what it means to be a human being, then the results of any would-be human biology must be equally trivial.

If, by contrast, we start from the assumption that the purpose of science is to provide a solution that is adequate to the problem at hand, then the assumption that biology is the right starting point is much less compelling. In particular, if we share a great deal with other organisms – a proposition I would not dream of contesting – the reverse is not true. Indeed, the things we share with or inherit from non-intelligent organisms seem to have very little to do with what it means to be human. In fact it is very hard to look at any aspect of human nature that human beings themselves consider important and *not* suspect that trying to explain such a thing in biological terms is a fool's errand.

To take only the most obvious way in which human beings differ from other organisms, any credible theory of human nature must explain why human beings have a history while other organisms – even our closest relatives –

do not. It is after all only by virtue of the historical dimension of human nature that I can have the same biology as a Cro-Magnon hunter or a medieval Javan peasant yet live a profoundly different life, and that human beings have moved from being a few thousand slow, weak scavengers to the single most important factor in the environment of practically every other large species on the planet. As I shall try to show in the main body of this book, all this follows from the specifically intelligent nature of human beings.

Other organisms have no history. It is true that they all organisms change over time, that many are altered in substantial yet reversible ways by the actions of their predecessors and contemporaries, that these changes can have a collective effect that is more than the sum of its parts, and that these are all features of historical change. Nevertheless, all changes to all non-human organisms seem to be explicable, without exception, in terms of changes to their biology, changes in the environment in which they live or (as in the case of social primates) completely localised, transient and contingent changes in relationships between particular organisms. In particular, there is no fundamental change to (and certainly no advance in) the social or practical conditions in which they collectively live and act (as there is in the case of human history), and as a result no changes of which the organisms in question could either take account or exploit in their own further development.

For example, for all their apparent capacity for mutual imitation, social facilitation and even intentional teaching,[1] not even the perfectly real differences in social organisation between chimpanzee troops seem to reflect much more than the accretion of accidental and incidental changes. So a given chimpanzee society may well be different from what it was a hundred years ago or from another chimpanzee society on the other side of Africa, but these changes could not be said to have come about by virtue of the self-development or restructuring of chimpanzee society. Nor are they actively constitutive of the development of the chimpanzees who live in such societies – there is no possibility of progress in the offing. Nor are they changes of which the chimpanzees involved seem capable of noticing, let alone fathoming. So they are not really *historical* changes at all.

Conversely, it seems unlikely that the changes that have taken place have systematically altered how chimpanzees inhabit and experience their environment, as historical changes in human societies have transformed not only the scope but also the nature of human activity, organisation and awareness. Finally, it certainly could not be said that chimpanzees are aware of their position in history – in relation to a cultural heritage or a family lineage, for example – or that they act as they do specifically in terms of that historical position. If they did, then chimpanzees too would be historical beings. But they don't, so they aren't. And even if there were hints of historicity among the primates, there is none at all elsewhere in the animal kingdom.

---

[1] For a summary of the evidence of teaching among chimpanzees, see Byrne (1995: 140ff). See also Boesch in Gibson and Ingold (1993: 171–83). For a sceptical review of both the evidence for and alleged mechanisms of tradition in animals generally, see Galef in Bekoff and Jamieson (1990: vol. I, pp. 74–95).

So, given the fundamental significance and consequences of human historicity, no explanation of human nature that does not also explain history could possibly be correct. Given both that human beings are above all else historical creatures and that biology has no concepts that are capable of dealing with history, then as soon as one accepts that human beings are historical beings, any appeal to biology is rendered futile.

Our consciousness also seems to set us apart from other organisms. Again, it does not seem to distinguish us absolutely from other primates and perhaps a few other species, but there seems to be very little reason to think that it is at all pervasive, even among the more sophisticated echelons of the animal kingdom. Yet the consequences of our consciousness are so vast that they leave even the most sophisticated primates lagging behind quite small children. As human beings, we have ways of structuring our consciousness of things and events, such as symbolism, metaphor, logic and mathematics, rules, science, ideology, imagination, values and even bureaucratic procedure, that are literally infinitely more powerful than anything other organisms have produced. Again, if other organisms showed any sign of such abilities it might be appropriate to compare them with human beings. But they don't, and given the radical importance of consciousness to human activity, and the lack of any explanation of consciousness in biological terms, it is again hard to see why one would even begin looking to biology for an explanation of human activity.

It is tempting for biologists to reply to this argument that consciousness is plainly highly adaptive. But then so is having a history, and so would being lucky or being able to perform miracles or having all your wishes come true, but that does not mean that, if an organism possessed such abilities, they would be open to biological *explanation*. Being adaptive is at best an explanation for why things that already exist persist. It is never an explanation for why they come into existence in the first place (that would be teleological), for their structure (adaptation is a wholly functional criterion) or for the processes and mechanisms through which they operate (which are all wholly transparent to the notion of adaptiveness). Since, as I shall argue in detail below, what is peculiar to intelligent activity is the special character that is conferred by its unique structures, processes and mechanisms, and indeed its ability to act in terms of, among other things, its expectations and plans for the future, plainly biology will have little to offer by way of an explanation.

This difference goes to the very heart of biology, even to the point where the mechanisms of evolution itself are overthrown. For what is the process of 'random variation and natural selection' but a process whereby the *functioning* of an organism is changed in some way that is not directed by any sense of that functioning's *functionality*; and the functionality of that functioning is determined by external factors (the forces of selection)? This is precisely the *opposite* of an intelligent action, for what could be more typical of intelligence than deciding in advance what it was trying to accomplish (reaching a goal, sustaining a value, realising a design, and so on), then defining the process, mechanisms and steps whereby this outcome can best be achieved (a plan, a tool kit, a resource list, a work environment, etc.), and then proceeding to work towards that outcome, all the while adjusting and re-adjusting one's actual actions to suit changes in effectiveness, circumstance, and so on? And even when we fail, is there any obstacle to learning directly from our mistakes, as there so obviously is for strictly biological adaptations?

Indeed, isn't all this indispensable to that most hallowed of intelligent actions – science itself? How, for example, would it be possible to 'do' evolutionary theory if one relied of the indirect methods of evolution itself? How does one construct and perform an experiment, if not by constructing a hypothesis, defining procedures for arriving at an outcome, and then evaluating what the outcome means in relation to the original hypothesis? Or does each new idea emerge at random, find itself emitted into an external environment with which it has no intrinsic connection, where it is then subjected to 'selection' by equally extraneous forces that deal solely in terms of reproductive efficiency and effectiveness, as opposed to truth or even empirical correctness? Do the scientists who initiated this process remain oblivious to the entire process and its outcome, as a non-intelligent animal is of the evolutionary origins, significance and consequences of its actions? Such would be the case if scientific knowledge were the product of natural selection.[1]

And so on, through every arena of human activity. Other organisms hunt and forage; we have a global economy. A few other organisms make elementary tools; we hunt quarks and quasars, create new elements, build complete artificial environments and write equations for the end of the universe. A few social insects apart, other organisms have relationships with a modest local group; we operate a global society with billions of members. The most advanced non-human organisms are capable of a level of representation broadly equal to that possessed by a small child; adult human beings have full-blown natural language, art, religion, philosophy, programming languages, logic and mathematics, science, law... And they all appeared in the twinkling of an eye, evolutionarily speaking – far too fast and far too precisely, in fact, for random variation and natural selection to have created them, or for them to have emerged from any known biological precursor, or for any organic structure or process to have directed their construction. Once one adds to this how extremely difficult it is to describe the formation, operation and change of human individuals and societies in biological terms – the one-sided, circular and self-serving arguments of the adaptationist lobby notwithstanding – it becomes difficult to draw any conclusion other than that, the frenetic attention biologists pay to human beings notwithstanding, seeking a biological account of the specifically human aspects of human nature is a futile quest.[2]

This still leaves that one tenuous link between biology and intelligence: the primates, dolphins and perhaps other species that can make a realistic claim to at least some of the tell-tale features of intelligence, such as language, self-awareness, and so on. Their claims are by no means universally accepted, but I have no doubt that human beings and chimpanzees have a good deal more in common than chimpanzees and ants. But in what way does that fact contradict

---

[1] A greatly expanded version of this argument can be found in Robinson (in preparation).

[2] Hallpike (1986) provides a very full critique of biological explanations of human activity and organisation.

the view that there is a qualitative difference between biology and intelligence? If there were such a difference and it was not brought about by fairy dust or a divine spark, then surely one would *expect* intermediate forms? After all, is a virus alive or is it, as Peter Medawar put it, 'simply a piece of bad news wrapped in protein'?[1] Clearly, it depends what you mean by 'alive'. In some circumstances, yes, a virus qualifies as alive, or at least as the kernel of a living thing; in others, certainly not. And likewise, whether a chimpanzee, a whale or a parrot is intelligent depends on what you mean by intelligent. By the criterion of consciousness, then yes, they probably are, to a limited extent, especially when provided with the right 'scaffolding'; but by the criterion of historicity or clear intelligence in the absence of any external support, then no, perhaps they aren't.[2] But that does not mean that the concept of intelligence is incoherent, that history and consciousness are not characteristic of intelligence or that a fully developed intelligence would not have both to the full. It means only that the different aspects of intelligence, like the different aspects of life, come into existence in a somewhat disorderly way.

And what if we were to discover that chimpanzee societies have a history after all, replete with highly structured social systems and major phases comparable to feudalism and the like? What should one infer from this fact? That human beings are just organisms after all? Or that chimpanzees have joined human beings on this side of the (broad and indistinct) divide that separates biology from intelligence? It is after all not the purpose of the present account to argue that *human* beings are different; rather, it is *intelligent* beings that stand apart, and if chimpanzees (or whales or grey parrots or even nematode worms) stand with us, then so be it.

One last point about the relationship between biology and intelligence. At present, the main non-human candidates for intelligence proper are the chimpanzee, the parrot and the dolphin. Note how unexpected this would be from a strictly evolutionary point of view. Primates are quite closely related to the one definitely intelligent species of which we know – ourselves – and it seems that the most intelligent primates are (with some notable exceptions) those closest to human beings. But primates, dolphins and parrots share no common ancestor that could possibly have been intelligent, so how do we explain the fact that such distantly related species share this common (yet most uncommon) feature? As far as we can tell, insofar as they are intelligent at all, dolphins, parrots, primates and human beings are all intelligent in the same sense, and their respective intelligences embody a case not of evolutionary *convergence* but of evolutionary *identity*. The resemblance between chimpanzee intelligence and dolphin intelligence is not like the similar streamlining of dolphins, sharks and ichthyosaurs: they are not merely structurally similar but structurally *identical*. Given that, from a biological point of view, such identities are completely inexplicable, plainly routine biology is not the answer. On the other hand, if intelligence is indeed a novel structure rather than the cumulative effect of

---

[1] Medawar and Medawar (1978: 8-9).

[2] For a comprehensive review of the evidence for intelligence in primates, see Parker and McKinney (1999). On grey parrots, see Pepperberg (1999).

strictly biological changes, then it is just as plausible that it could have arisen in parallel from many different biological ancestries as it is that life itself could have arisen from many different pre-biotic chemistries.[1]

In short, there may be other organisms that have also started to break away from the constraints of a strictly biological existence, but to argue that human beings have *not* done so would be preposterous in the extreme.

Intelligence and the humanities

If a strictly biological account will not do, do the humanities (in which, for present purposes, I include the social sciences) have the answer? Here the answer is still no, although for rather less direct reasons. As the reader will soon see, I have made great use of methods, findings and theories from the humanities. The humanities are, after all, of more obvious significance to human nature than biology, not only because of their self-evident relevance but also because, unlike most biological accounts of human nature, they do not usually completely ignore what it means to be a human being (although behaviourists, certain economists and evolutionary psychologists have made impressive attempts). On the contrary, they have collectively provided a wide range of profound insights into what being human is all about.

Yet, with few exceptions, the humanities have seldom produced a truly general account that is simultaneously capable of scientific assessment, comparable in scope and power to the contributions to biology made by Darwin and Mendel, and actually supported by empirical research. Almost all seem either far too narrow or hopelessly mired in ideological or metaphysical baggage. As a result, the humanities have always lacked a shared, integral conception of what it means to be human, around which they might organise themselves *as* 'the humanities', in the sense that physics is grounded in relativity and quantum theory or biology revolves around evolution, heredity and epigenesis. There is no central core to the humanities capable of grasping both the kernel and the full scope of what it means to be human, and they do not really account for anything quite as grand as 'human nature'.

As a result, not only are the major disciplines (psychology, history, literary theory, anthropology, aesthetics, sociology, economics, and so on) separated by great conceptual chasms, but each individual discipline is broken into a number of competing schools, each at least incommensurable with, and often bluntly contradictory to, its neighbours. And so it seems to have been since the beginning of modern intellectual life. Consequently, whereas biology is prone to reducing human nature to a quite inappropriate level of explanation, the humanities are more likely to dismember human beings into a range of unconnected 'dimensions', 'aspects', 'levels', and other apparently complementary but actually mutually indifferent components.

Various writers have noted this perennial crisis before, but that has not brought us any closer to solving it. So the humanities remain as helpless as bi-

---

[1] Kauffman (1993).

ology to supply a conceptual, methodological or theoretical framework within which any account of human nature could operate. Indeed, if that were not the case, the present book would be wholly unnecessary. So the humanities may well provide a huge amount of content for any systematic study of human nature, but they are just as incapable of supplying the framework needed to satisfy the requirements of a genuinely unified theory.

Nor should the importance of a *unified* account be underestimated. Of course, all disciplines aspire to unity, as do the sciences as a whole, not to mention all human existence. But only in human beings (which is to say, in human beings as specifically *intelligent* beings) is this unity a central feature of the object in question. To the extent that we are intelligent, to the extent that human beings are reasoning beings, we are undivided and indivisible. In that respect we are true individuals, although it must be emphasised that the real nature of our individuality is somewhat different from that imagined by bourgeois apologists. Most especially, our individuality can only be brought to full fruition through the equally full development of society – a state of affairs in which the modern world shows a singular, indeed historically unprecedented, lack of interest. Conversely, to the extent that we are divided – above all as fragmented individuals alienated even from the society that gave birth to us – we have failed to realise our potential, and so are doubly inexplicable. Firstly, if we have yet to complete our development, then it cannot yet be known what it is to be a fully mature human in the first place. Secondly, if we are only incompletely developed, we lack the maturity to make sense of ourselves.

An organism, by contrast, has no particular propensity for individuality, or indeed unity or wholeness of any kind. True, a horse and a starfish and an anemone all share structures serving to integrate, preserve and reproduce the whole, but unlike human beings, not even Clever Hans had any notion of individuality, wholeness or unity, aspired to any such condition, or would have been capable of it even if he did. As Konrad Lorenz once remarked:

> There is not one organism in existence in which the mutual causal coherence of all parts is… complete…, because every organic system contains unchangeable structures which, though certainly causally influencing the form and the function of the whole, are not appreciably influenced by it in turn.[1]

The same could hardly be said of human beings, notwithstanding their practical failure to reach this ideal state (so far). Hence the humanities' perennial crisis: they lack the ability either to account for or to unite the most essential of all features of human nature.

---

[1] Lorenz in Whyte (1968: 158). Paradoxically, elsewhere (eg, Lorenz, 1977) Lorenz includes key cognitive structures in the list of biological items, including the classic Kantian categories, to which any charge of intrinsic incoherence – precisely what he ascribes to all biological systems – would be completely fatal.

Synopsis

Hence this book. *Vis à vis* biology, it will present a view of human nature that is as natural, as material and as open to scientific investigation as any strictly biological alternative, yet is in no way biological in its character or assumptions. And *vis à vis* the humanities, it will present a view of human nature that is based on a single unitary structure, namely intelligence itself, by virtue of which all aspects of human nature, even the most lofty, can not only be explained but also be seen to point the way towards a practical resolution to its current conflicts, short-comings and immaturity. In the process of providing that view it aims to reach into the very heart of what it means to be a human being, yet also reaches out to the very edges of our experience and our aspirations.

What then does this book have to say? Perhaps the best way to explain it for now is to give a chapter-by-chapter summary. In general terms, the first chapter presents an analysis of intelligence as such. The next four chapters describe the main stages in the development of intelligence. These chapters vary in focus, each addressing different areas of experience that come to prominence at each stage. The next chapter sets out the detailed developmental process that takes place *within* each major stage, and the last chapter reviews the limits, real and apparent, of the human capacity for rationality.

In more detail:

Chapter 1: The Nature of Intelligence

The purpose of the opening chapter is to describe the conceptual framework within which this book operates. Intelligence is initially defined in terms of its internal structure, which consists of 'subject', 'object' and 'world'. These terms are used to refer not to purely philosophical or intellectual constructions but to structures that are every bit as material as 'organism' or 'planet'. They are certainly abstract structures, but in the present context describing a structure as 'abstract' will take on a rather unusual meaning.

Having established the basic structure of intelligence, the second section describes the basic forms of intelligent activity (including construction and production, which are contrasted with adaptation and other forms of biological activity), and the organisation of that activity (including social and symbolic relationships, the structure of culture and technology, and so on). The third section then reviews the radically new ways in which intelligence develops. Special attention is paid to how intelligence systematically produces its world, the role of rationality and reason's unprecedented ability to lift itself up by its bootstraps, and so to scale equally unprecedented heights.

Unlike later chapters, this opening chapter is rather abstract, and the reader who is not already well acquainted with recent conceptions of intelligence (especially Piaget's) may be better advised to read this chapter last.

Chapter 2: Intuitive Reason

The first major stage in the development of intelligence is that of *intuitive reason*.[1] The essential feature of this stage is that intelligence grasps objects on the empirical plane, but has no sense of the relationships that control their actions and collective forms. As a result, intuitive reason is restricted to the aspects of things and events that can be perceived and acted upon directly, but lacks any sense of any more abstract relationships. As a result, its horizons are very limited. A typical problem this creates on the cognitive level is the young child's inability to sustain a single abstract criterion of judgement across an empirically changing situation. In one of the classic formulations, a red triangle is like a blue triangle and a blue triangle is like a blue square – so a blue square, if not actually *like* a red triangle, is certainly a legitimate member of the same series.

The social analogue of this situation is the kind of simple society that lacks any explicit structure or relationships over and above those that arise between individuals. Even a sophisticated but still intuitively structured society relies entirely on organising itself in terms of empirically defined features of individuals such as gender or age group. Not only is such a society incapable of organising large-scale or sustained actions (again, apart from the rites and occasions that individual members are inclined to create and recreate) but it even lacks anything that could be considered a history. Of course, individuals may be well aware of their personal ancestry and they share memories in the form of myths and stories, but there is no explicit or objective lineage or heritage in terms of which individuals define and control their actions, beyond that which can be identified, organised and controlled in empirical terms.

Chapter 3: Concrete Reason

If intuitive reason is limited to the empirical surfaces of objects (tools, stories, people), the repetition of particular kinds of action on those objects will eventually turn these repetitions themselves into the objects of intelligence's attention. As the objectified forms of these repeated actions are gradually comprehended, they are internalised as a grasp of *relationships*. On the psychic level this enables concrete reason to navigate much more effectively around its world, especially because it creates what Piaget called 'operations'. That is, because concrete reason operates in terms of series, classes and other abstract structures, what can be done once can be done again, what was done can be undone, and so on. The result is not only greater flexibility but also greater rigour (due to this apprehension of enduring relationships) and, of course, a much increased range and scope of action. Perhaps most importantly of all, by organising action explicitly in terms of specific relationships, it becomes possible to identify independent criteria whereby action can be defined, organised and judged. Hence the most universal and enduring of concrete reason's accomplishments: the transformation of *intelligence* into *rationality*.

---

[1] This terminology is explained on page 5.

Socially the stabilisation of explicit relationships leads to the formation of the first truly historical societies and so a stabilisation of society itself. To a very great extent this is accomplished through the organisation of individuals and groups into chains of dependence and respect. Of these the best known is probably the European feudal system, but a similar logic informs such a huge range of social systems that concrete reason can be said to be the basis of *all* the main forms of large-scale social system right up until the predominance of industrial capitalism. Their consequences are immense: permanent and semi-permanent political systems, organised wars of conquest, and generally the intentional organisation of collective activity into specialised functions. With the rise of concrete social organisations, the quasi-natural structuring of age sets and men's houses is progressively replaced by – and, equally importantly, governed in terms of – groups such as craft guilds, soldiers (as distinct from warriors), merchants, and so on.

If concrete reason represents a considerable expansion of intelligence through rationality, the limits of a concrete reasoning are still very narrow. The relationships it can grasp stand in no clear relationship to one another, so, given that no real action can be carried out without a grasp of multiple connections, concrete reason is forced to continue relying on the ability of individuals to apply them. They in turn rely on their ability to interpret and manipulate empirical things and events, which remain the indispensable stepping-stones of real activity. Conversely, for lack of any structure integrating all relationships into a single whole, concrete reason frequently falls into contradictory or superficial actions and judgements, from astrology to pre-classical theories of money.

Chapter 4: Formal Reason

So the main shortcoming of concrete reason is its inability to extricate itself from the empirical conditions in which it operates. Being unable to extricate itself from the conditions in which it operates, for example by creating the kind of abstract principles that might support scientific method or bureaucratic administration or an engineering discipline, it can never make the transition from the pragmatic to the truly practical. The cure for this form of cognitive myopia is, in general terms, the same as that which intelligence applied to intuitive reason's shortcomings: the forms of outward activity that characterised the previous stage become the internalised structures of the next.

In other words, where concrete reason was able to master discrete relationships, it cannot grasp the relationships *between* relationships; that is why it cannot transcend the empirical. But by continually constructing and applying the whole gamut of relationships at its disposal, in different conditions and different combinations, they are variously joined, dismantled, differentiated and integrated. But that is only to say that the objects concrete reason constructs increasingly *consist of* the very relationships between relationships it originally found so hard to gasp. Hence the next stage in the development of intelligence, in which *systems* composed of just such relationships between relationships come into existence and are refined and elaborated. This is the stage of *formal reason*.

The strength of formalisation is obvious: not only would a comprehensive system of relationships between relationships become increasingly self-sufficient but its independence of local conditions would allow intelligence to pursue strategies of the most global and enduring nature. And we find ourselves surrounded by the results. Our logic and mathematics achieve unprecedented pinnacles not only of rigour but also of energy and creativity, matched only by the vigour and dynamism of our economies and political systems, the exponential growth of science and technology and the wealth and multiplicity of our cultures. Indeed, the rise of formalisation seems unstoppable.

Unfortunately, it may be unstoppable, but it is also inherently irrational, if not unintelligible. Not by the standards of intuitive or concrete reason, perhaps, but then their standards were always very meagre. From the point of view of formal reason's own inhabitants, its inherent propensities to crisis, its evident inability to avoid *reducing* things to mere formalities mean that the power of formal reason is never quite matched by its fidelity. Hence its fundamental failings and the direction of its own, equally inexorable self-transcendence.

Chapter 5: Dialectical Reason

Both the normal development and the crises of formal reason tend to push it further and further in two directions. On the one hand, just as concrete reason gradually constructed the relationships that would allow it to make sense of the relationships at its disposal, and so arrived at formal reason, so formal reason systematises and re-systematises the multiplicity of systems it constructs until it arrives at a single unified totality of structures. This process of totalisation eventually encompasses every structure and every system, from the mental capacities of individuals to global social and economic systems and the culture and technology needed to integrate them into that last, final, complete totality.

On the other hand, this same process brings individuals closer and closer to the unspoken grail of all rational activity, namely a true grasp of that last, unsuspected hiding place of value, meaning and significance, the here and now. Indeed, these are not two different processes, but a single process whereby reality is totally manifested in the most superficial appearances of things, where the opposition between self and others is demolished and where the scope of the present is expanded to embrace all that was once absent. At which point, the development of intelligence comes to a conclusion (if not quite to an end), for there is nothing left for it to make sense of, or which it has not made to make sense.

Chapter 6: The Developmental Process

One of the more serious complications that arise for any stage theory is the difficulty of reconciling the gradual changes and enhancements that occur within any given stage with the qualitative advance that each stage is supposed to represent. To take an example that has already been mentioned, I have claimed that an intuitive society lacks an explicit structure. However, I made this claim only to immediately add that structures such as age sets might play a role in social activity. Clearly there is a contradiction here. As it happens, the contradiction is more apparent than real, as I also noted that any social structuring that occurred in an intuitive society is limited to features that can be identified empirically – which, I think, age groups can, given only a very limited contribution from the individual participants' personal knowledge of when particular individuals were born. Conversely, it is striking that the societies that operate a more abstract age-set system, such as the *gada* system employed by certain East African peoples, also exhibit other social features that raise them above the purely intuitive level. That is, the age-based system is itself waning in the face of more concrete structures.[1]

A more generalised version of this process whereby stages pass into one another is advanced in this chapter. Six sub-stages are proposed, showing how the core structures of intelligence, namely subject, object and world, develop themselves into the new forms appropriate to each new stage. By this means the qualitative differences between stages are shown to be consistent with their progressive construction, and various apparently contrary phenomena, such as the way in which early versions of allegedly 'higher' systems appear seemingly too early, are shown not only to be compatible with the present account but also seem to be predicated by it.

Having presented an abstract model of the way in which stages succeed one another, a number of practical examples are then rehearsed. These include the way young children improve their strategies for solving jigsaw puzzles, the way management systems mature, the way the history of software engineering has unfolded, and a general synopsis of the history of capitalism – all of which reveal the same abstract logic.

Chapter 7: The Bounds of Reason?

The final chapter is concerned with some of the residual problems that face any theory of human nature as essentially intelligent – or, *a fortiori*, rational. The present account does not assume that human beings are never stupid or ignorant or wicked or immature, any more than the theory that animals are all alive assumes that they are never sick or immature or that they cannot be poisoned. The two sides are not contradictory, and in many respects the features that most seem to contradict any account of human nature as rational are disposed of simply by showing the length, complexity and generally fraught nature of the process whereby a *mature* intelligence comes into existence.

There are however various aspects of human irrationality that are not so easily brushed aside. This chapter deals with some of them. The first is what I term the 'infrastructure of intelligence'. This is the mass of structures a given intelligence has already constructed, and so can quite literally take for granted. These are significant because they explain how we can do so many things in a completely thoughtless, apparently non-rational manner, and yet do them su-

---

[1] Hallpike (1986).

perlatively well. Yet, as soon as their real status is recognised, they cease to be a mystery, and certainly do not lend any support to the idea that certain key talents and capabilities we all possess are either innate or (as some mathematicians persist in suggesting for their own field) exist as some kind of Platonic Form.

A second feature of human reality that causes problems for global theories is its unevenness. To take only a single example, Aristotle's logic stood for two millennia as a paragon of formal reasoning, yet his physics can be refuted by a pre-formal school child. Social systems are equally mixed bags. How can this obvious (and undisputed) fact be reconciled with the idea that intelligence is a unitary structure? The answer proposed here is that intelligence is indeed unitary, but that when a new structure comes into existence, it has to pass through the main phases defined for intelligence as a whole. Shortcuts are possible, but in general the actual maturity of any given structure depends heavily on the opportunities for development the structure in question has available to it, its relationship to surrounding structures, the conditions in which that development takes place, and so on. Hence the unevenness of many an actual intelligence. Indeed, given that intelligent beings rely on many structures, social and psychic, of varying levels of maturity, unevenness is exactly what one would expect.

A third feature of intelligence dealt with in this chapter is the profound irrationality of many of the reasons we offer for our own actions, institutions and world. The explanation offered here for this entirely real phenomenon is that intelligent beings are never relieved of the obligation to make sense of their worlds and themselves, even when they lack the talent, experience, resources or maturity to do so. Hence our propensity to rationalisation. Of course, this is understandable enough in those we consider less mature than ourselves – in children, for example – and then we take for granted their limitations. But the same limitation is less straightforward (or perhaps just less acceptable to us) when the same irrationality emerges in the actions of our fellow adults.

Finally, there is the (occasionally fashionable) problem of alienation – perhaps the most problematic of all aspects of intelligence. Through this most profoundly paradoxical expression of intelligence and rationality, it is the very processes and mechanisms we create to carry out our genuinely rational plans that rob us of the intelligibility and meaning to which all rational action aspires. Yet the final fruit of alienation is the finalisation of development itself.

Conclusion

The Conclusion derives two main points from this account of intelligence.

The first is that, in opposition to both biological and most humanistic accounts of what being human is all about, an account of human nature that is based on intelligence allows us to develop a 'strong' account of human nature – of human nature as specifically human – without having to accept any limiting set of concrete features of that nature. Human nature, like the nature of any intelligent being, is totally open, even though it develops through determinate stages. To say that the process whereby the development of intelligence takes place is determined in key ways is not to say that there is something unintelligent or irrational to which that process can be reduced, that it is an illusion or that intelligent beings are fated to turn out one way rather than another. To return to the very first chapter, this is because of the very abstractness by which intelligence is defined in the first place.

The second point the Conclusion makes is that, despite this inherent abstractness, despite this denial that human nature can be defined in terms of any particular concrete properties and despite the fact that the author of this book is transparently far from reaching any such result, it is still possible to say something positive (if not very substantive) about the final outcome of human development. The topic of this section is truth and freedom.

After Marx and Piaget

There is no standard terminology for the stages of human development, not least because there is no agreement that that development passes through stages or on what aspect of human nature any standard nomenclature for human development as a whole should be based. In this book I outline a sequence of four major stages, and then divide each major stage into six sub-stages, based in each case on known patterns in the development of intelligence. These stages and the logic that connects them to one another are supposed to apply to all aspects, not only of the development of intelligence, but also of human nature as a whole, including its social and psychic, phenomenal and historical aspects.

The structure, content and relationship between these major and minor sequences are set out in the main text, and I hope that the reader will quickly notice similarities with two very different precursors. These are the stage theories advocated by Karl Marx and Jean Piaget. This resemblance is far from accidental, but the model presented here is not simply an attempt to synthesise historical materialism with genetic epistemology. So it may be helpful to the reader to explain the relationship between the present account and these predecessors.

Marxist and Piagetian stages

The sequence of stages presented here was originally based on my reading of Piaget. Even though my own account soon came to diverge from Piaget's in many important ways, from a terminological point of view I was tempted to retain the standard Piagetian sequence of 'pre-operational', 'concrete operational' and 'formal operational' intelligence. But 'pre-operational' soon came to sound too negative, as though this stage were nothing but the anteroom to 'real' intelligence. In fact its achievements are as positive and substantial as those of any later stage, including the first full expressions of such essentials of human nature as intentionality, realism, symbolism and sociality. Hence the substitution of the more positive term 'intuitive', which, I think, captures the intelligent yet unarticulated and unreflective nature of activity at this stage.[1]

---

[1] Piaget also uses 'intuitive' for part of his pre-operational stage, and limits it to only

And at the other end of the process, I quickly realised that formal operations not only *is* not but *cannot* be the final stage, even by the criteria Piaget himself set for finality. Following from my own assessment of the underlying logic (and borrowing extensively from other sources), I began to construct a dialectical stage too.

I also quickly decided to discard the Piagetian term 'operation' in favour of the more comprehensive 'reason'. This was for two reasons. Firstly, the language of operations is highly technical, and I willingly concede it to specialists in cognitive theory. But secondly, and much more importantly, to give undue prominence to the term 'operation' in its well-defined Piagetian sense would be to suggest that intelligence's critical achievements are *essentially* or *primarily* cognitive. Although this would certainly be true for the psychological plane, it would be quite wrong for human nature as a whole. The real scope of intelligence is infinitely wider, to the extent that echoes of Hegel's Reason are neither unintentional nor inappropriate.

As for Marx's stages, the terminology used here may be unfamiliar, but the meaning and content of the main stages is somewhat clearer, especially when one rises above the psychological level. For example, the account I give of feudalism and capitalism will be at least moderately familiar to anyone acquainted with Marx's own, and I hope I have been able to say something new and interesting about these stages, about their underlying logic, about how and why they developed and about the transition between them. More generally, I hope I have made it much clearer why stages exist at all – an issue that has been neglected by Marxist orthodoxy – and why it is the particular stages we observe in history that occur and not others. Nor does insisting (quite rightly) on setting activity in its historical context really explain how history itself is possible. As with the question of why human history passes through stages, this issue has often been skirted around, but I have yet to see a credible Marxist account of what it is about human beings that makes them the creatures of history while sheep and ants and even other primates are not.[1]

But how is it possible to unite Marx and Piaget in a single theory? The fact that both define stages between which certain important analogies can be drawn is clearly not enough. But, although they are by no means perfect, the resemblances between Marx and Piaget are very close. Indeed, Piaget himself wrote that Marx's 'essentially concrete conception of the problem of ideologies and logic... fits exceptionally well with the actual facts of both psychology and

---

part with some justice. Nevertheless, in the absence of a better term, I shall persist with using it for the stage as a whole.

[1] Claims in the primatological literature that some apes exhibit 'culture' by virtue of their development of localised technologies, teaching of one kind and another and so on do not imply that apes have a history. Mere variation over time or between social groups is not enough: neither the social groups nor the culture in question amount to systems in their own right, which then impose themselves on future generations. So there may be good deal of change and variety, but not history properly so called. In the terminology of history itself, primates have neither lineage nor heritage (on which see 'The origins of history', p. 5ff). On the limits of primate intelligence, see Parker and McKinney (1999).

sociology', and explicitly approved of Marx's insistence on the 'sensuous' rather than merely 'contemplative' character of human activity (as Marx himself put it, when criticising Feuerbach and others), not to mention the irreducibly social and symbolic aspects of all human action.

Remaking the world

As far as the present account is concerned, there are many other ways in which Marx and Piaget converge. In particular, the process of development each describes is driven by changes in the ways in which human beings make their world. This is another of the features it shares with both Marx and Piaget – the idea that human beings are constantly making and remaking their world. More especially, they *produce* it: not only do they make *sense* of their world (the normal limit of cognitive models) but they make and remake the world *itself*, in the fullest sense. We do not merely understand our world in novel ways; the world itself is increasingly the product of our actions. To mention only one extreme consequence of this fact, it makes no difference to our non-intelligent neighbours how intelligent beings *think* about the wild or how we *name* its denizens, but it makes literally all the difference in the world to them that we, the only indisputably intelligent species on the planet, have created at least fifty dead zones in the seas, have raised the rate of extinctions to a thousand times the normal level, are busy punching holes in the ozone layer, and show little sign of getting ourselves under control.

Nor is this constant changing of the world a temporary blind spot or a passing spasm of species hubris: insofar as intelligence needs to make sense of its world if its own actions are to make sense, sometimes the world itself must be made to make sense. This cannot be avoided, as it is only through making their world that human beings themselves come into existence, endure and develop. In order to make our food, take shelter or organise our thoughts into religions and ideologies, our peculiar nature obliges us to do so by extracting resources from the world, processing them, disposing of the remains, and generally altering our natural environment. Ultimately, if that means the radical physical, chemical and biological transformation of the planet's entire surface until it accords with intelligence's requirements for intelligibility, then that is what will happen. So it is critical to see how the intelligence that will rationalise the world in this way accomplishes this feat, and Marx and Piaget are remarkable for their commitment to the idea that not only is human existence ultimately rational but also that existence must be made increasingly rational if we are to gain control of either our world or ourselves. Both are committed to the idea that raising the level of rationality demands that we get to grips with physical, chemical, biological and intelligent processes and mechanisms of literally global impact and significance. In short, understanding human nature is a function of history and consciousness, of culture and technology in their fullest senses, and demands that any explanation of the nature, development or likely outcome of human existence be couched in terms of the full range of social and psychic processes and mechanisms.[1]

There are other points of convergence. For example, Piaget applauded Marx's distinction between the appearances of things, activity and events and the realities underpinning these appearances, and although his own account did not extend to a full appreciation of such powerful notions as alienation, he fully understood the developmental significance of this relationship and the struggles to which it gives rise.[2] Hence the importance each attached to science and ideology as forces for both stability and change. This connection is further reinforced by the fact that both of their accounts of human activity assume that the most 'materialistic' of actions and interests are always and inherently imbued with what Piaget terms 'operatory' factors, namely systems of implication and meaning, through which human activity becomes both intelligent and intelligible.[3]

The developmental process

Nor is there any great disparity between Marx and Piaget's accounts of the developmental process. Both are pre-eminently constructivists, in the sense that the higher forms of human activity are regarded as syntheses of lower forms, rather than mechanical result of the unrolling of a pre-existing nature, the expression of underlying forces or the accumulation of empirical experience. Neither seems to have felt any need for innate programmes, inherent tendencies or other ahistorical mechanisms to explain why human beings are as they are, or to seek motivation in specific 'deficits' in the human condition that our activity development serves to meet. In fact exogenous drivers in general seem to be all but completely disregarded. At the same time, for both Marx and Piaget the *transition* between stages is truly revolutionary. Not only does human development mean the development of human nature in its entirety, without any fixed point (although abstract structures apply throughout), but that development is also the product of the *mutual* reconstruction of the pre-existing parts, albeit often by violent means and with mutually destructive results. So each new stage is both a beginning and an end in a far more fundamental sense than for other theories of development.

Of course, their respective interests in and uses of the stage concept were very different. However, although I suspect that Marx would have found Piaget's model of stages unacceptably formal – hardly a criticism to trouble Piaget himself – he would certainly have appreciated Piaget's view of stages as 'equilibrium structures' – in Marxist terms, as the resolution of the contradictions that plagued (and largely defined) the previous stage and the bearers of yet higher forms of contradiction. Their stages also share an all-encompassing character: nothing escapes the transformation each new stage initiates. Incidental, isolated and unimportant residues apart, each stage is a

---

[1] Piaget (1995: 154–5).

[2] Piaget (1995: 77).

[3] Piaget (1995: 281–2).

tal, isolated and unimportant residues apart, each stage is a complete, integral, systematic and self-consolidating replacement for its predecessor. Once a system such as capitalism or formal operations has superseded its immediate predecessor, there is no going back. That is why capitalism in crisis does not revert to feudal forms, and even the most severe psychopathology does not really turn adults back into children. In addition, the interests (in every sense) that typify each new stage are qualitatively different from those of their predecessors. They are moreover intrinsically more advanced: although neither Marx nor Piaget would have suggested that progress or even normalcy is inevitable, there is nothing that an earlier stage could manage that a later stage cannot manage better, there are many previous misunderstandings and prejudices that are now dropped, and there are innumerable things the new stage can manage that would have been unthinkable before.

Note the paradox this creates for the development of intelligence. On the one hand, it is unconstrained, but on the other, not only is it always progressive but the specific stages through which it passes are always the same. How is this to be explained? If the course of human development is neither contingent nor predestined, yet still comes to necessary conclusions, it must have a logic that is both determinate and compelling without being either our fate or our compulsion. And again Marx and Piaget share the distinction of having devised theories of human nature that meet all these apparently contradictory criteria. This is achieved by insisting on a profoundly original approach to activity and development. This is the idea that the abstract can also be the real.

The meaning and significance of this idea will become apparent in the next few chapters, but a typical example can be given here. In this view of the abstract as the real, one of the most critical aspects of development is the formation of new forms of necessity, possibility and contingency and of new forms of 'modal' activity that are expressed in terms like 'could', 'should', 'must', 'might', and so on.[1] Be they imposed by new ethical systems, new levels of logico-mathematical structure or new modes of economic production, all more concrete forms of and products of activity are subordinated to the entirely real abstractions inherent in thought, social regulation and other, more worldly systems and processes. Money, roles, commodities, bureaucracy, scientific method, and formal logic and mathematics all provide instances. But this does not imply the elimination of everything *but* the abstract: the possession of specific logico-mathematical structures could scarcely be said to define the details of one's psyche, any more than (to adopt for one moment a particularly deplorable metaphor) the economic base on which society rests defines its social superstructure in all its cultural, technological, legal, religious and other richness. For neither Marx nor Piaget is the explanation of human nature to be accomplished through either reductionism or fatalism, and just as Piaget always battled against both logicism and psychologism with equal vehemence, so Marx fought economism and historicism.

Of course, there are also many contrasts to be found between Marx and Piaget, over and above the very different topics they addressed. Not the least of

---

[1] For a Piagetian view of necessity and modality see, see Smith (1993: 167ff).

these is their all but opposite interpretations of contradiction and dialectic. For Piaget, dialectic is a tool of thought, not a property of things,[1] whereas for Marx dialectic is out there in the world, and defines the essential logic of thought and things alike. The reason for this conflict may be connected to another difference, namely the absence in Piaget's work of any clear connection between the structure of activity and the motivation to act in the first place. As Hopper has argued,[2] by resting his account on the idea of contradiction within the structures of activity themselves (and hence of the shifting bases of power, class struggle, revolution, and so on), Marx treats action, values and motivation as merely difference facets of a single structure. It might even be argued that the only motive for action is the resolution of contradiction. It is far less clear that Piaget's analysis provides anything comparable. They would also have disagreed vigorously about the nature of the final stage of human development, disputing not only its content but also the criterion by which its final equilibrium should be judged. Still, it is clear that they can be regarded as potential allies in any serious attempt at making sense of human nature.

Departures from Marx

Of course, if I have made use of Marx' and Piaget's ideas, that does not mean that the result would have met with either's approval. Perhaps they would have agreed with me, perhaps not. On the other hand, to the extent that the ideas presented in this book are right or wrong in their own right, what difference would anyone else's approval make? And in fact this book diverges from both its illustrious predecessors in many important respects.

Despite the fact that its links with Piaget's genetic epistemology are far more obvious than those with Marxism, the main reason why Marx does not figure more prominently in this book is that I see little need to revise his ideas. If quasi-Piagetian concepts and methods seem to be more to the fore, it is because I take Marx for granted: it is much more likely that Marx would have disagreed with me than that I would disagree with him. As far as I am concerned, he has more or less solved the fundamental problem of the underlying drivers of human development, and to a very large extent the problem of the relationship between those drivers and their expression in history and consciousness.

Yet agreeing with Marx that the reproduction of society is the *sine qua non* of social (and so human) existence, and that (therefore) the analysis of this process of reproduction is the first task facing any theory of human nature, is not the same as agreeing that this problem figures overtly in most people's existence or shapes their lives at all directly. Certainly Marx denied that it did, and developed the theory of alienation to explain why not. Nor does even the most enthusiastic analysis of the economic determination of social systems entail any kind of economic reductionism or economic fatalism. Indeed, it is one of the

---

[1] Piaget (1971a, 1980).

[2] Hopper, pers. comm.

great strengths of Marx's method that the difference between what ultimately *determines* the structure of human existence and the forms that actually *dominate* social activity is inherent in the different modes of production themselves.[1] So some of the main structures through which human beings act (individually and collectively) can operate at a considerable distance from Marx's economic forces and relations. Hence one of the main topics of this book: the analysis of the shapes in which human activity confronts not only the analyst but also the inhabitant of each successive form of 'everyday life'. Since it is on this level that individual human beings actually live their lives, this is at least as important a question as that of modes of production. Or at least, it is when one is concerned with how the development of individual human beings comes about and where individual human beings imagine they are going, so to speak.

There is also a second problem (if not fault) with Marx's account: that, although quite rightly couched in terms of production, it does not actually explain how production itself is possible. The capacity for production (as opposed to adaptation or construction in the Kantian sense) is a central feature of human ontology. It is also central to Marxism, because it is through production that human beings break free of the fetters of their biology. More generally still, not only do human beings as producers inhabit a world with unique properties – an increasingly permanent, autonomous and universal world of factories and ideas and space ships and hopes and anxieties – but they are the very creators of that world.[2] Given that this world is (for Marxism) the very basis of being a human being – for we are its creatures as well as its creators – it is surely indispensable for Marxism to establish what kind of being human beings actually are that they are capable of this, and so how production itself is possible. But as far as I can see, Marxism offers no such explanation.

There is yet a third weakness that I feel haunts Marxism, to which I have already alluded. Although it is intuitively plausible that a combination of social structure and economic production will lead to the systematic mutual restructuring of both economy and society, it is not at all clear that the specific sequence of *stages* we see acted out in history makes any particular sense or whether there is any particular logic to it. In fact it is not even clear what the sequence is. Even where specific historical links can be traced fairly easily (as in the transition from feudalism to capitalism), neither the *necessity* for such a transformation nor its necessary start and end points is at all clear; and in other cases (such as the notorious 'Asiatic mode of production') Marx's original hypothesis is scarcely intelligible.[3]

So the present account operates at both a higher and a lower level than Marx's own: on the one hand, it skims the surface of social life as superficially as the most innocent sociologist (because that is, after all, where people actually live most of the time); but on the other, it attempts to account for the fun-

---

[1] On the contrast and relationship between structures that are determinant and structures that are dominant, see Godelier (1972). Hallpike (1986) presents a strong case for a very considerable latitude for social indeterminacy in simple societies.

[2] Marx and Engels (1976: 31).

[3] Anderson (1974: 462–549).

damental processes and mechanisms that even Marx took for granted. To apply a potentially treacherous biological analogy, the process of evolution relies of four apparently equipotent forces: adaptation, which steers evolution on the widest scale; molecular drive and its non-genic analogues, which generate spontaneous change within the genome and other organic structures;[1] genetic drift, which introduces an element of chance; and structural equilibrium,[2] which imposes a necessary order on life, regardless of the exact functioning and functionality in which a given organic structure may be engaged. On the intelligent plane, a similar array of factors interacts: the forces and relations of production and the labour process on which Marx focused; the autonomous functioning of non-economic structures, operating on both social and psychic planes; the indeterminacy and chance that oblige us to treat human existence by means of history as well as science; and the forces of historical equilibrium, acting through social structures of all kinds and all but forcing human existence into certain systematic arrangements that express themselves in the form of developmental stages. It is largely this final factor, which is, as I have already observed, left largely unexplained by Marxism, that this book addresses.

As I hope the reader will agree by the end of my argument, the concept of intelligence is certainly capable of explaining how production is possible and what stages should be expected in the development of production in particular and history in general. So in that respect I hope the present work not only rests on but also makes a positive contribution to the Marxist canon.

Departures from Piaget

My dispute with Piaget revolves around four issues. The first, although fundamental to both Piaget and myself, does not impinge directly on the present account. Jean Piaget spent his life trying to show that even the loftiest aspects of human nature could be accommodated by biology.[3] The interpretation of intelligence on which the present account is based is exactly the opposite.[4] The second area of disagreement is the topic of Chapter 5, which shows that a post-formal stage in the development of intelligence – which is to say, a stage coming after Piaget's own final stage of 'formal operations' – is not only possible but necessary, and that a dialectical stage would be truly final. I also disagree with his criteria for identifying the final stage in the development of intelligence as a whole, but this issue is neither particularly significant in the present context nor especially interesting unless one has a specialist interest in Piaget.[5]

---

[1] Summarised in Dover (2000).

[2] Kauffman (1993).

[3] Eg, Piaget (1971b).

[4] An account of the biological origins of intelligence and the subsequent, strictly post-biological relationship between the two can be found in Robinson (in preparation).

[5] For those who do have such an interest, my recollection is that his works on infancy argue that intelligence cannot be stable until it has achieved equilibrium both internally and externally. There must be equilibrium not only between thought and thought but also between thought and things. When dealing with formal operations, however, Pia-

My other criticisms are more important but also more doubtful. Although I have argued above that Piaget shared the view that intelligence was inherently social, I cannot find any account of this social nature that shows how far this idea can be taken in the directions I propose. My impression is that Piaget might not have disagreed with what I have written below, but such thoughts would have been rather a long way from his mind! First and foremost, there seems to be little evidence that Piaget took account of any level of social organisation above that of values or interactions between individuals.[1] So I have no positive reason to believe that he would have agreed with anything that follows. Given my admiration for Piaget's other achievements, this is a genuine disappointment.

Beyond that, and notwithstanding the epigraph of this book, I have no positive reason to say that Piaget would have agreed with the proposition that the stages through which social structures develop are not only the same as those through which individuals grow but also follow the same sequence for the very same reasons. That is, the stages in human history are not the same as the stages in individual development because it is individual human beings who build society but because any intelligent structure, social or psychic, will undergo the same developmental process and follow the same developmental sequence. Shortcuts, derailments and reversals are possible, and they are sometimes caused by individuals; nevertheless, social and other supra-individual structures develop according to the logic of intelligence as such, which is by no means the exclusive province of the individual.

Finally, another equivocal criticism. I have said that intelligence not only comes to grips with the world by means of its growing prowess but also transforms the world to match its own idea of a rational order. Again, I have claimed that Piaget would have agreed with this view, but in fact, insofar as he wrote on such topics, he neither states the case with anything like the vehemence the reader will find below nor draws anything like the conclusions that will be drawn here. But as readers will realise before they reach the end of this volume, this single, rather grandiose claim is perhaps the most important thing that can be said about human beings. It also follows from what is, I think, one of the flaws in Piaget's explanatory methods, namely that he *tends* to treat activity as the action of a subject on an object (whose net effect can never be more than experience for the subject and superficial rearrangements of its objects), whereas the present account takes all activity to consist of interactions between objects, and the effects of this activity include radical transformations of the objects in question, and with them the world they constitute.

This appears to follow from the fact that, in Piaget's analysis of the child's activity, the relationship between the subject and the body (ie, of the subject and the key object mediating early activity) is more or less transparent, and in

---

get seems to neglect external equilibrium, focussing solely on the internal consistency of formal structures. As I argue below, if one applies both Piaget's criteria, formal reasoning ceases to seem very stable. For a summary of Piagetian views on post-formal cognition, see Marchand (2002).

[1] Based primarily on Piaget (1995).

later activity, Piaget, like almost all psychologists, was more interested in cognitive and intellectual activity (eg, the development of logic, scientific method, moral values, and so on) than in supra-psychological activities such as the creation and control of great organisations or the unfolding of history. The consequences of this narrowness are considerable, not least because it means that the forms of cognitive and intellectual activity on which Piaget and his colleagues have concentrated represent a special case rather than the norm. Being a scientist is important and in some ways emblematic of a certain level of reasoning, but it remains an unusual occupation, whereas playing roles or using money (of one kind or another) are all but universal experiences. Conversely, changing the world (and with it the conditions for all future action) is, in however small a way, the rule, not the exception. So, reluctant though I am to join the foolish chorus of critics who attack Piaget for not attending to their personal hobbyhorses, I must say that this is a severe criticism. But then it is hardly one to be levelled against Piaget alone.

1. The Nature of Intelligence

The science of human nature

Intelligence is widely cited as one of the defining attributes of human nature. And rightly so: it is plainly implicated in a vast range of characteristically human propensities, capacities and modes of activity, many central to any definition of humanity. In the present context, it is especially telling that an account of intelligence is essential to any possible explanation of our ability to explain ourselves and our place in the universe, for if it takes intelligence to explain what it means to be human, and the ability (or at least the need) to explain ourselves is one of our defining features, then our intelligence must one be too. Conversely, not only would any account of human nature that failed to assign intelligence a pivotal role be palpably inadequate, but such an omission would leave the would-be explanation in the invidious position of explaining human nature in terms that left the explanation itself unexplained.

Hence the various paradoxes that so often bedevil theories of human nature: that they assume the very intelligence that is to be explained; that they require the intervention of crypto-rational forces, be they orthogenesis, entelechy, divinity, or whatever; or they tacitly assume that scientists possess an Olympian vision, rationality and detachment that is wholly antithetical to the altogether more parochial, pragmatic or even base motives and capacities in terms of which they pretend to explain the human nature of others. In short, despite its centrality, intelligence remains one of the great unexplained concepts. Of course, there are plenty of would-be 'explanations', but far too often they are extraordinarily thin. Even where a Kant or a Piaget manages to lift our intelligence onto the plane on which it evidently belongs, they almost always seem to limit their notion of intelligence to the intellectual or psychological sphere.

There are notable exceptions, most remarkably Hegel, whose concepts of Spirit and Reason[1] are infinitely more comprehensive and much more closely allied to the notion of intelligence to be presented here. Yet I would not agree with Hegel's concepts either, impressive though they undoubtedly are. So, before launching into my own account of the role intelligence plays in the history of human nature, it behoves me to say just what *I* mean by this elusive term. That is what the present chapter strives to do: to define intelligence, and to do so in terms that are capable of supporting the widest possible conception of human nature. It does this in three steps: by describing the basic structures of

---

[1] Hegel (1977).

intelligence; by analysing the kinds of activity through which those structures function; and by setting out the process of development that follows from that activity. This serves a threefold purpose: to define intelligence, to explain how it relates to itself and to the universe around it, and to outline the potential that is revealed in more detail in the remainder of this book.

First, however, some preliminary comments about what exactly a science of human nature presupposes.

Intelligence is a form of matter in exactly the same sense as an atom or an organism. It is harder to detect than a rock or a fish, but no harder than a quark or an ecosystem. Intelligence is also a structure in its own right, in the sense that it always consists of its own special elements – subject, object and world – set in the same regular relationships, and the functioning of this structure creates consistent forms of specifically intelligent activity. For example, all intelligences are capable of reflexivity, means–end relationships, or experimentation. So intelligence is as suitable a topic for scientific study as any of its physical, chemical and biological precursors.

But even this simple assurance contains its own immediate qualification, if not contradiction. For although it may be possible to define intelligence in terms of 'subject', 'object' and 'world', exactly how a structure composed of such extraordinary elements could be studied is a quite different issue. An organic structure such as 'the nervous system' at least has a characteristic form for any given species, which can be observed, measured, manipulated, and so on. But 'subject'? 'Object'? 'World'? Not only do these terms emerge from a quite different discourse to that of science as it is presently conceived, but they possess an abstractness that is surely completely alien to science's insistence on grasping things and events in concrete terms. How could we possibly observe a subject or experiment on 'the object'?

Yet it is important to insist on such a starting point, for although intelligence always has, at any given moment, a definite content and context, which in turn ensures that its subjectivity, objects and world are wholly concrete, there is no precise content or context to which it may be reduced, by which it is bound or through which it may be empirically studied. While non-intelligent structures like an atom of carbon or a fish are invariably limited to a definite range of contents and contexts – a chemical element can only interact with suitable reagents, the most sensitive and flexible organic structure is still inherently limited to a definite range of states and stimuli, and so on – there is literally no limit to the content and context to which intelligence can be applied, through which it can express itself or in terms of which it could operate.

From a scientific point of view, this peculiar status has clear repercussions. Most especially, it makes it logically impossible to answer the question 'What is intelligence?' in purely empirical terms. Any given intelligent being always has an observable form – a distinct personality, a definite economic and political organisation, a particular language, a unique history, a more or less explicit ideology, and so on – but there is no form of concrete existence to which intelligence in general, any individual intelligent being in particular or any of the vast array of supporting structures of which intelligence is the author, is inevitably predestined or by which it is consistently represented. Intelligence isn't like that.

Of course, much the same could be said of matter generally. All forms of matter are more or less abstract. That is why a biology that did not tease out the universal formula of random variation and natural selection from the existence of particular species, organisms, and so on, would have so little to say about the nature of evolution, life in general or even particular organisms. Nor has anyone ever actually *observed* gravity, acidity or adaptation, as opposed to inferring their existence (if that is the word) from the activity of various kinds of matter in motion. Nor is the abstractness of matter limited to theory: any visual system can detect many things of no interest to its possessor, and any atom or molecule can enter into whole classes of chemical reaction and structure (acids, alcohols, organisms) without special 'programming'. Yet the radical – and potentially complete – dissociation of the abstract from the concrete that characterises intelligence cannot help but make a certain kind of scientific disposition rather queasy. To put this crucial point as concisely as possible, the abstractness of concepts like 'subject', 'object' and 'world' reflects not the vagueness of the present theory but a unique property of subjects, objects and worlds themselves: that whatever their concrete manifestations, they are, in themselves, wholly and exclusively abstract. Hence the uncomfortable corollary that, when it comes to understanding what intelligence is and what its actions signify, there is no particular empirical content that has an unequivocal significance, and it is always unwise to treat outward appearances as decisive.

Despite the difficulties this creates for science, it is just as well that intelligence is so entirely abstract. For it is just this abstractness, this freedom from any inescapable interests, predispositions or circumstances, that is the main motor of intelligence's amazing ability to transcend all limitations, and so to encompass all aspects of existence. In particular, it is only by virtue of its abstractness that intelligence can be equal to any possible content and can work in any possible context, yet be bound to none in particular. That is not to say that the content and context of intelligent activity should be treated as ephemeral. After all, it is only through this content and context that we have any access to the underlying abstractions. What is more, the concrete structures that inform any given intelligence at any given moment also have a life of their own, which must also be comprehended if we are to grasp human nature in its broadest sense. That is after all what being a structure – abstract or concrete – means: to have a life of its own. That is why it takes such effort to change an organisation or abandon a prejudice or change your mind or discard a religion or revise a plan: minds, plans, faiths, and so on all have logics of their own, which operate quite independently not only of our purely subjective intentions and desires but also of their own superficial appearances. There are also cases (such as the formal procedures for amending many political constitutions) where we intentionally encumber the process of development precisely in order to give our systems an enduring reality that is independent of our immediate intentions or will, and so protect ourselves from (overly-hasty) change.

Yet none of this implies that there is anything to which we are *irrevocably* committed, unless we are in the grip of some kind of pathological condition. What is more, such changes come about without any apparent change in the nature of intelligence as such: any genuinely intelligent structure seems to be capable of comprehending any kind of thing or event, given only time, motive and opportunity, and of making use of an indefinitely large range of cultural and technical forms, expressions and artefacts in the process. In that respect, intelligence plainly bursts the bounds of any previous form of matter. In biological terms, intelligence is adapted to nothing, and that is precisely why it is capable of literally anything.

This contrary relationship to any preceding form of adaptation should not be taken to mean that intelligence has no biological origins or substrate. On the contrary, it is inconceivable that a natural intelligence should either arise or operate on any other basis. But just as there is no chemical formula for any biological process or mechanism and an organism's structure and functioning is irreducible to its chemical states, so intelligence, once it has come into existence, supersedes its organic origins and substrate completely. Just as it comes to be the organism that recruits chemical structures to its processes rather than the reverse, so an intelligent organism's biology is always at least partially subordinated to its intelligence, and the more that intelligence develops, the more complete that subordination becomes. Ultimately – when we finally manage to make an entirely artificial intelligence of ourselves – our biology may even be completely replaced by a more suitable collection of artefacts and prostheses that exceed the powers of any possible biology.

Nor is the abstractness of intelligence limited to its independence of any particular empirical appearance or situation. Just as intelligence always has a definite concrete content and context, so it is always structured in specific ways that are far more concrete than 'subject', 'object' and 'world'. This can also easily give the incautious observer the impression of a predetermined and fixed concrete structure, and so a restricted range of functioning. In particular, our intentionality as subjects and the reality of our objects invade all aspects of intelligent action, and our actions and our worlds are always organised in terms of social and symbolic relationships. So it is tempting to identify intelligence and human nature with particular forms of sociality, symbolism, and so on. But is the sociality of action and experience a form of activity in the same sense as, say, an instinct to nest in the spring? Not at all, for however concrete notions such as intentionality, reality, sociality and symbolism may be relative to subject, object and world, they are also so abstract and so universal, so *entirely* open to different contents and context and to future enrichment and subversion, that it is impossible not to regard them as part of the definition of intelligence as such, rather than as special or localised limits on its scope or range, or as predispositions that bias intelligence towards certain kinds of motivation, action, experience, and so on. They may be *modes* of intelligent activity, but they are neither methods nor biases. Or at least, so I shall argue shortly.

Taken together with the previous point about the treacherousness of any empirical study of intelligence, this makes any science of human nature doubly complex. For example, it means that there is nothing in any particular form of human social behaviour that is irreducibly a sign of human sociality. That makes it hard to spot someone being unequivocally social, except in the general sense that all human activity is social. But the persistent abstractness that creates this difficulty is also the reason why the human capacity for social (or intentional, symbolic, or realistic) activity and relationships makes it unnecessary for human beings to undergo irreversible changes in order to make the most astonishing progress. As I have already said, it is intelligence's very abstractness that makes it equal to any form of concreteness. That is why, had there ever been a first intelligent being, the only impediment to him or her also living in an industrial society such as our own would be the limitations imposed, not by their intelligence as such but by the physical, chemical and biological natures out of which intelligence emerges and on whose continuing activity intelligence relies. At the very least it is unlikely that a mature adult kidnapped from some Neolithic savannah would live long enough to learn a completely new way of life. But these limitations are imposed not by intelligence as such, but by the contingent (and potentially transient) conditions imposed by human biology.

At the moment, readers may well regard all this as nothing but empty speculation, but I hope that they will have changed their minds by the end of this book. By then I shall have described a great variety of structures and functions, all of which have been produced and then surpassed by this single invariant form of matter, intelligence. To mention only a few highlights, it was the very children who once struggled to solve the simplest jigsaw puzzle who grew up to create industrial societies of global proportions, who penetrated interplanetary space and who will soon build the first artificial intelligences. In what way does this extraordinary range resemble the narrowness and rigidity of any of intelligence's predecessors, even the most flexible?

Nor is this infinite range the only mark of intelligence's unprecedented abstractness. Even within a single action, intelligence is perfectly capable of matching completely contrary appearances to the same reality, as *vice versa*. For example, it is well established that there are universal forms of human facial expression such as smiling and frowning, apparently based on universal biological structures. This fact is generally taken to indicate that such a form of activity has a definite biological basis. Yet it is exactly this universality that reveals how *little* such a biological 'universal' really signifies from the point of view of understanding what human actions *mean*: as Shakespeare's Duke of Gloucester observes, can we not smile – and murder whiles we smile?[1] Now, which is the more telling – the fact that smiling has a universal biological substrate, or the fact that we can all manipulate a smile to mean infinitely many, infinitely contradictory things, independently of its biological moorings? Is it the mechanics of smiling that tell us what it means to be human, or the ability to subordinate the most open and pleasing of expressions to the most insidious of purposes?

Likewise for frowning and grimacing and all manner of threatening and welcoming gestures: unlike the signals emitted by a strictly non-intelligent organism, which always take more or less the same forms and are always more or less directly bound to particular states, particular patterns of activity, particular stimulus conditions, and so always 'mean' much the same thing, the expression on a human face can never be taken for granted. Often we rely on particular gestures and expressions to mean just what they say, of course, not only at the level of facial expressions but also for the efficacy of rituals, social

---

[1] Shakespeare, *Henry VI*, III. ii. 182.

graces and the like, and we would do very well to acknowledge this fact rather than writing off such very concrete actions as 'merely' ritual (or 'merely' anything else).[1] In fact, we would be incapable of hypocrisy and deception if we did not know exactly what a given expression is *supposed* to mean in *normal* circumstances. That is why we feel so ambivalent about such mechanisms, and why they reveal both the importance we attach to particular concrete forms and how little any such form can convince us, once our suspicions have been aroused.

In short, in the case of true organic structures and functioning, it is the sheer complexity of biological activity that makes it wise to distinguish between surface appearances and the deeper reality: there may be many possible links between the two poles of action. For intelligence too we should take the same precautions, but in this case, not only may appearance and reality stand in an objectively complex and ambiguous relationship to one another, but appearance and reality may be made contradictory *intentionally*, and the contradiction may be both intentionally maintained and intentionally obfuscated by the intelligence in question. Hence the importance when studying human nature of distinguishing between what human beings do and what they mean, what they seem to be and what they are, and so of approaching any claim as to the naturalness or observability of any kind of human activity with the utmost caution.

But how then can it ever be possible for any would-be scientific account to centre on an intrinsically deceptive expression like 'human nature'? The answer is that I am objecting to the term 'nature' here only in its almost automatic biological interpretation. Where human nature is taken to be determined by biological structures and forces outside intelligence itself (adaptation, genes, etc.) and fundamentally beyond rational control, this appears to be an entirely gratuitous assumption, which only someone singularly unacquainted with human history could possibly make. However, insofar as 'human nature' is taken to mean 'whatever nature human beings really have, regardless of our current prejudices about its ultimate biological, theological, existential, ideological, historical or other bases', then I have no objection to the term 'human nature' at all. On the contrary, I positively insist on it.

This approach to the concept of human nature has a serious bearing on what a science of human nature should be like. On the other hand, it is only a repetition on the human level of the more general postulate that we should define scientific method generally as any method that is adequate to its object. That is, rather than assuming *a priori* that a scientific explanation of human nature *must* be couched in terms of our biology – or history or geography or our existential 'thrownness' or the will of the gods or any other *a priori* – we should assume only that it could take any form that made it possible to grasp all the irreducibly human attributes of human nature. That does not mean confirming every prejudice about human nature anyone has ever held, but it does mean that any prejudice that is to be ejected must be specifically refuted in terms of its demonstrable incoherence, inconsistency, incompleteness or incorrectness *vis à vis* the real actions, real relationships and real products of real human be-

---

[1] Douglas (1996).

ings, regardless of whether it has a biological (historic, theological...) basis. Fortunately many such prejudices have already been refuted by history, and no one is around to suggest that there might be a Great Chain of Being or that heavenly bodies do naturally move in circles after all. But where other views prevail, it is scarcely 'scientific' simply to dismiss them on the grounds that they do not conform to present prejudices about scientific method itself.

Of course, in this book I am assuming that human nature is best explained in terms of intelligence. In a sense that is simply the assumption from which I proceed. However, unlike the rampant biologism with which we have all become unpleasantly acquainted in the last few decades, which has concentrated on reducing human beings to biological proportions, I shall offer a range of empirical and theoretical arguments for believing not only that human nature is every bit as big as human beings have long suspected it to be, but also that *everything* about human beings is capable of scientific explanation, including all those phenomena such as consciousness and morality that anti-scientific thinkers hold up as unassailably beyond science, and that biologism, historicism, phenomenology, theology, and so on pretend to address but only abuse. Not that I shall try to explain everything about human beings here, but to the extent that the present account is correct, it will make it very hard in future to declare any aspect of human nature off-limits. What is more, the kernel of the science of human nature will not be drawn from the biological (or humanistic or metaphysical) concepts with which we are familiar now. But then, given how poorly science has dealt with human beings so far, how could things be otherwise?[1]

The structure of intelligence

The next task is to explain what I mean by what I have taken to be the central terms in any theory of intelligence, namely 'subject', 'object' and 'world', and in particular what it means to describe them as abstractions.

The subject

The abstractness of the subject is most distinctively expressed in its functional *autonomy* and its structural *intentionality*.

The subject's autonomy is most clearly and directly expressed by the fact that it is the same 'I' that is the subject of all my actions, regardless of the particular activity in which I happen to be involved at any given moment. I may

---

[1] There have been many expositions of the irreducibility of human nature to biological categories. Many were written at the dawn of Darwinism (see R.J. Richards, 1987), but such is the impetus of neo-Darwinism that their long-term impact has been slight. Although the social sciences and humanities have sometimes been rather supine in the face of biologism, social and cultural anthropologists have often been more robust (eg, Hallpike, 1986, or Montague, 1962 or 1976). A good deal of criticism of specific forms of biological reductionism has also arisen from within biology itself, notably from Gould (1984), Lewontin (1991, 2000) and Rose *et al.* (1984).

become distracted or inattentive, I may be confused or fooled or just plain bored, but there never seems to be a point at which a distinctly different subject takes over or a profoundly and irremediably different point of view is adopted. Even where I contradict myself from one moment to the next, there remains enough continuity for me to be able to sense this conflict, even if I do have to be forced to acknowledge it. At least at that very abstract level, there seem to be no structural gaps in my subjective experience, even in the face of quite radical functional leaps.

The basis of this remarkable integrity is the subject's status as the synthesis of all the structures of which the intelligence in question is composed.[1] That is why it is the subject and the subject alone that structures a given intelligence's activity. It is certainly the case that action is influenced by the conditions in which the subject finds itself, but even the most overpowering or insidious force must be mediated by the subject before it can enter into its actions. This in turn depends exclusively on the extent to which the subject in question is able to make sense of that which influences it: like nature (and any other structure), the subject, to be commanded, must be obeyed, and the central demand of subjectivity is that things make sense. Even when the subject is at its most careless and uncritical about things and events, it is still only its careless and uncritical view of them that actually enters into its actions, not the things and events themselves.

Hence the other side of the subject's autonomy: its striking and unique independence, both of any particular kind of activity in which it may engage and of any particular content or context in terms of which it may act. If our subjectivity is capable of an unprecedented involvement in things and events, that is not to say either that it is wedded to any particular kinds of functioning or that its functioning depends on its possession of any particular structures. On the contrary, we can always do the same thing another way, and always redeploy the means we created to achieve one end for other, quite different purposes. That is why, even when most completely embroiled in the here and now, we never quite lose the ability to step back from our actual experience and subject it to the most disparate and abstruse considerations. In short, the subject possesses but, unlike non-intelligent structures, it is not ultimately possessed by its own actions. On the contrary, what was lovingly and painstakingly crafted yesterday may be rejected in disgust tomorrow, and *vice versa*. Hence the extreme facility (especially by pre-intelligent standards) with which intelligence proliferates new interests, skills, powers, artefacts, organisations and insights, and the equally dramatic abandon with which it discards them as new experiences and opportunities indicate.

Clearly this autonomy of any concrete content or context is a direct expression of the subject's possession of an abstract and invariant internal structure. The subject remains the highest-level structure of intelligent activity, no matter what activity it is engaged in or, therefore, the lower level structures through which it acts. It gathers experience, constructs new knowledge, hones new

---

[1] The preconditions for this synthesis and the exact process through which it comes about are the central topics of the author's forthcoming *Birth of Reason* (in preparation).

skills, adopts new points of view, builds new systems and institutions, raises itself to new levels of development; but even as it internalises and incorporates each new element, it also preserves itself as *that* subject. Conversely, there are no aspects of intelligent activity that are not determined by the current nature of its subjectivity taken as a whole.

Or again, the subject may be rather shallow and disjointed, but even at the outset this reflects a lack of articulation and experience rather than genuine fragmentation. As it matures, an undivided, indivisible individuality comes to prevail, not *against* a multitudinous and disparate network of structures but *through* it. That is how intelligence can put the most obscure and abstruse knowledge and abilities to such new and fruitful uses. But it is also why any sclerosis or shattering of this internal structure is so dangerous, be it on the epic scale of ossifying social systems or in the most intimate personality disorder. In the latter case, it is universally recognised that there is something extraordinary about the possession of fragmented or multiple subjectivities, although different cultures deal with this fact in quite different ways – as blessedness, as pathology, and so on.[1] The social version is perhaps less extraordinary or celebrated, but it is equally the source of conflict and inhumanity.

Although the subject possesses an autonomy that is unprecedented among forms of matter, clearly it is not indifferent to other structures. Indeed, the converse of its autonomy is its *intentionality*, in the sense that, as the structure of *activity*, its activity consists of structuring the content and context on and through which it acts. In other words, the activity through which the subject establishes and maintains its independence is also the channel through which it engages things and events.

Intentionality has many aspects, such as the attitudes a subject brings to bear on things, from liking or loathing to testing them against previous experience, to relating the current content and context of its activity to its current goals. And insofar as the idea of intentionality can be freed from a narrowly phenomenological definition, *social* structures can also be said to embody intentionality, from the rituals of primitive religion to the command structure of a Roman legion, from the great principles of due process and equality before the law to the national and global political institutions that regulate our own world.

As well as this external orientation towards things and events, intentionality also operates internally, actively generating new networks and structures of activity out of the mutual implications of existing structures. By this means the subject binds its various actions and experiences into a progressively more intelligent and intelligible totality. However, this is not only a crucial component of its remarkable capacity for self-development but also the source of many problems, dead ends and dilemmas. For the internal nature of this activity means that increasingly many of the things and events it encounters are *purely* intentional, in the sense that they originate solely within the subject and its internal actions. This is not always a shortcoming: on the contrary, not only is this the origin of at least the principles governing the great institutions and

---

[1] Cohen and Rapport (1995).

ideals through which human beings comprehend their world, but such a re-working of its internal structure is absolutely central to the development of intelligence as a whole. Nevertheless, it can equally easily generate any number of rather less justifiable fantasies such as epicycles, Eldorado, N-rays[1] and free market economics.

The significance of the subject's intentionality follows from the same features that give it its autonomy. To the extent that it has achieved the integrity and independence autonomy implies, any action will bring to bear all the structures at the subject's disposal, independently of any previous experience or supposed suitability. Conversely, the subject's ability to do this – the central measure of its autonomy – is proportionate to the breadth, depth, articulation and maturity of its intentions. Of course, a growing structural complexity and functional distance from any fixed content or context can sometimes confuse the subject by offering an unmanageably vast range of ill-defined options, among which it is forced to choose without any reliable guide. Nevertheless, it is also a great liberation, since it ensures that the subject is never completely constrained by its previous life or the prescriptions of biology, history or immediate experience. As will become clearer in later chapters, not only does this lead to some of intelligence's most radical departures from all previous forms of matter, but it also leads the development of intelligence itself to startling yet instantly recognisable conclusions.

The object

If the subject comprises the entire internal structure of intelligent activity, then it must be the subject whose functioning (modulated by innumerable substructures) bears ultimate responsibility for intelligence's external embodiment, namely its *objects*. Hence the reciprocity between the two sides, for if subjects are autonomous and intentional, objects are characterised first and foremost by what Piaget called their functional *permanence* and by what I would term their structural *reality*.

Objects are permanent in the sense that they exist independently of our consciousness of them. What is more, we are conscious of this independence of our consciousness in proportion to the development of our intelligence as a whole. Nor is its independence merely one fact among many others we know about a given object, analogous to its properties, its location in time and space, or even the role it plays in our activity; rather, the very way in which we are conscious of an object declares its independence of our consciousness. The permanence of objects has nothing to do with the way we think *about* them, after the event as it were: we do not construct an object and then discover that it is permanent. Rather, its permanence is intrinsic to the way in which we construct it in the first place, and so to any consciousness of an object *as* that object, before any question of 'aboutness' arises.[2]

---

[1] On N-rays, see Gratzer (2000).

[2] This is, I think, the reason why Piaget was right to proceed as he did, since his method obliges us to infer the kind of object our interlocutors' words and deeds imply, inde-

So a sense of our objects' permanence informs all our relationships with those objects, regardless of exactly which particular relationships and which particular objects may be involved. Conversely, object permanence is present in some form from the very start of intelligence properly so called, but it also develops as intelligence itself develops. Indeed, it is the emergence of object permanence and its progress through various kinds of relationship and system that provide the single most widely used measure of intelligence's maturity.[1] It is very difficult to explain this permanence, but it is in the explaining that the problem lies, not in deciding whether we experience our objects as existing independently of ourselves. There is always a sense in which the very way in which we construct our objects declares that they are not 'our' objects at all.

Objects are real as well as permanent. If, as its permanence entails, an object exists independently of its subject, that is only to say that, looked at from its own point of view, it exists at least as much 'in itself' as 'for us'. That existence 'in itself' naturally implies that each object has its own structure, independent of (but not necessarily different from) the structure with which we are subjectively acquainted. In other words, every object has its own realm of action, its own substance and causality, its own location in time and space, its own processes and mechanisms, independently of the actions we perform on and through it. That is why, when I throw a ball against a wall, I expect it to come back, and why, if I do not turn off the taps, I expect the bath to overflow: not only do the objects involved exist independently of my consciousness of them, but I have positive expectations about what they are likely to get up to while they are outside my control. That is why I involve them in the first place.

Likewise, when I make a new object, I make it in such a way that it will be a stable entity in its own right, remaining itself through a predictable range of real transformations, with predictable consequences. The slings and arrows of outrageous fortune are not problems for subjects alone, and as intelligent beings we make sure that our objects will overcome their own trials in much the same sense that we would wish to overcome them as subjects. Conversely, just as my intentionality places me in a vigorous, dynamic and self-directing relationship to my objects, so the reality of my objects places them in a vigorous, dynamic and self-directing relationship to, amongst other things, me.

The fact that we construct our objects as really existing in their own right has some unprecedented consequences. For example, even when I construct an object as *expressly* imaginary (an idea, an ideal, a possibility, a plan, and so on) its objectivity ensures that I still treat it as having an existence and enduring significance of its own, even though it exists solely in my mind, needs to be continually constructed and re-constructed, and this constructing is consciously done by me within my own mental 'space'. That is how I am able to

---

pendently of (though in conjunction with) what they actually say and do, and so to infer from their explicit words and deeds the basic logic they attribute to objects themselves.

[1] Piagetians who consider that intelligence begins at the *start* of sensorimotor development will notice a significant departure from convention here. My own view is that subject, object and world are *products* of the sensorimotor phase, and that intelligence proper does not begin until all three are in place.

address, analyse, share and discuss an idea like any other object. We may well know that an idea is imaginary, but once imagined, its implications can no more be avoided than a runaway truck. At least, not if we are sincere in our intentions.

On the other hand, the fact that strictly intentional objects have their own objective reality has many less attractive consequences. When I believe whole-heartedly in the reality of entirely imaginary concepts, ideals, deductions, and so on (the public spiritedness of global corporations, the leading role of the Communist Party, the Protocols of the Elders of Zion, and so on) and start to confuse their real existence within my mind with a reality in the world, there is ample opportunity for me not merely to set off on a private wild-goose chase but also to inflict incalculable damage on myself, my world and millions of in-nocent human beings.

Despite their eminently practical, even overpowering reality, the apparently contradictory claim that objects are only as real as they are abstract can be veri-fied from their most basic properties. Indeed, an object's abstractness is the precondition of its reality. To be real, an object must retain its identity through all transformations, even though its every concrete element and every empiri-cal appearance may have been changed in the process.[1] To stay real, an object must handle complex relationships with its neighbours and itself, must change and develop and present many different faces, yet never cease to be that object. Even in the most magical tale an object seldom simply disappears; rather, it is transmuted into a different *kind* of thing, while its 'real' identity endures. And conversely, where an object does finally lose its distinct identity, there are al-ways successor objects standing in intelligibly real relationships to their prede-cessor. So what are these many forms of constantly inconstant concreteness, if not the practical expressions of the fact that any object's identity is ultimately

---

[1] It must be emphasised that the validity of the distinction between an object's identity and its embodiment depends on the material level of the object itself. Or rather, the dis-tinction is always valid, but it does not always reflect the same difference. A strictly physical object is itself only to the extent that its content (if not its context) remains the same: change even a single atom and its identity is called into question. In the case of a chemical object, it remains the same only for as long as one part is replaced by any other of the same type. For example, it makes reasonably good sense to say that a molecule remains the same molecule if one of its atoms is replaced by another atom of the same element. However, as this equivocation shows, even at this level the link between iden-tity and content is almost inextricably close, even if there is a difference in principle. In the case of organic structures, by contrast, it is perfectly clear that an organism main-tains its identity itself despite changes in its chemical constituents. Indeed, it is only because the organism is constantly making such changes (through feeding, metabolism, and so on) that it remains the same organism. Yet there are still limits to how much an organism of a given species can change and still remain itself. At the very least, it will eventually change enough to die. In the case of intelligence, however, there seems to be no such limit, and were natural intelligence not always embodied in physical, chemical and biological structures of doubtful durability, it would be both universal and immor-tal.

an abstraction, existing independently of, though never separately from, any particular embodiment?

So the object is just as abstract a structure as the subject. In the course of this book it will be shown how objects embody structures, relationships and systems operating increasingly far above the empirical level, including classes, series, hierarchies, networks, totalities and beyond. These are by no means simply intellectual or cognitive structures: the same logic applies to the formation of real social systems, from age sets and feudal dependencies to money, bureaucracies, commodities and global economies. On the other hand, an object is an object *only* to the extent that it participates in more concrete realms, in which all objects of a given kind participate, regardless of their particular empirical form. Yet it is still the case that, for many cultural and technological objects of the most practical kind, such as laws or currencies or engineering disciplines, their *significance*, and so their impact, depends solely on the abstractions they realise. It is true that any object also has an empirical content, but that content is often only an indicator that the object in question is indeed the structure we are interested in, and it is only by virtue of our ability to abstract its proper identity as that object from the empirical content and context with which we are presented that we can apprehend its identity in the mobile, stable way that rational knowledge and action demand. Ultimately it is only because of the process of abstraction that we find even the most empirical object intelligible.

The world

Taken together with the subject's autonomy and intentionality, the permanence and reality of objects underpin all of intelligence's most fundamental innovations. For example, it is only through them that technology is possible. On the one hand, we can translate our plans and purposes (ie, our intentions) into products, results and other real things; and on the other, we can rely on these products and results (as real entities in their own right) to go on realising our intentions and serving as our proxies long after we have quit the scene. Hence tools, machines, automation and, one day, artificial intelligence. Likewise for culture: because the objects I construct exist 'out there', many of them as practical, sensuous realities in their own right, they can be shared by any number of other intelligences, and the intentionality (values, meanings, significance, and so on) they embody for me can be appreciated, analysed, applied, criticised and developed further by my fellow subjects. Hence also our collective ability both to internalise and to elaborate ever more powerful systems of knowledge and values about things and events, quite independently of any direct acquaintance with or interest in them; our ability to create systems and devices capable of operating in corners of the universe to which we, as organisms, have no natural access; and so on.

So the autonomy and intentionality of the subject and the permanence and reality of the object take intelligence far beyond subjects and objects themselves. In fact every intelligent being is constantly embroiled in a great network of other subjects and objects. Moreover, this network includes a huge and growing realm of entities that owe their existence solely to an interplay of structures that was intended by no one, whose reality is under no one's control and whose independence may even enable it to subordinate individual intelligences to its own demands. Again this follows from the fact that subjects and objects are as material as any other structures, and the fact that, like all other structures, they are structures of *activity*. So in proportion to the success with which an object possesses the integrity a permanent existence requires, it must be composed of materials and informed by structures that continue to operate not only *independently* of our intentions (which was, of course, precisely what we intended when we created them) but also at least partially *regardless* both of our intentions and of any future guidance or intervention on our part. That is after all what the permanence of objects means: that they go their own way, guided not only by the direction and impetus we impart to them at their creation but also by the logic inherent in their own substance and causality and under the direction of their own proper processes and mechanisms.

But if the permanence of objects implies that they will continue to travel under their own steam, so to speak, then they will also enter into relationships with one another, not only because we designed them to but because they are capable of it anyway: as physical, chemical, biological and even intelligent structures in their own right, they could scarcely do otherwise. So our objects create relationships, systems and totalities among themselves, to which we have no privileged access and over which we exercise no special control. Very often we do not even recognise that such structures are of our own making, or even that they exist at all.

The same is equally true of the structures that make up our subjectivity. Again intentions are structures of subjective *activity*, and although we sometimes have more direct access to them, they are intrinsically difficult to control. After all, isn't that what is entailed by saying that intentional objects are just as real as objects of any other kind? If my intentions are the constituents of my subjectivity, in what sense am I, as that subject, in a position to bring them under control? Clearly only to the extent that I have achieved a high degree of reflexivity. And even when I am in a position to reflect on them fully, the very intentionality of my assumptions, analyses and arguments entails that their implications will foist themselves upon me, regardless of whether I like them or intended them when I started out. So again, just as the permanence and reality of objects allows them to generate vast and growing structures over which I have no direct control, so my very autonomy and intentionality as a subject can impel me to draw conclusions of the most unpalatable kind.

Multiplied on every side by subject and object's innumerable interactions with innumerable neighbours, it is hard to see how an individual intelligence could conceivably imagine, let alone keep control of, the resulting whole. Conversely, it is easy to see that any individual intelligence will soon find itself besieged by an array of subjects and objects over which it exercises no effective control. But even if such control were possible, it is clear that, as soon as the first subject and objects come into existence, so too does a wider domain within which the logic of subjects and objects will play itself out. In short, the most general and sweeping consequence of the organisation of intelligence in terms of subjects and objects is their joint creation of a true *world*.

Or rather, it is a plethora of worlds, each one centred on a single system of intentions yet also intermingled with those of their neighbours. To the extent that my fellow subjects and I are able to make sense of (ie, reconstruct on our own terms) one another's objects as they were originally constructed, we can be said to share the same world and can thenceforth act jointly within it. Thus, we can sit and admire the sunset, hand in hand, agree to drive on the right instead of the left, and gyrate around the dance floor in the most intricately entwined manner. And to the extent that sharing is impossible or we fight over whose world it really is, uncertainty and conflict inevitably follow. Thus again, you may not quite agree with me when I denounce the sunset's pastiche of sky blue and salmon pink as an extraordinary failure of taste on Nature's part, I may veer into the opposite lane or prove beyond all doubt to you that I have two left feet. Again this is clearly not merely a cognitive issue, a question of whether we agree how the world works in theory or whether your *qualia* are the same as mine. To put the matter very clumsily, the world is full of prizes more than one subject is prepared to fight for, and of contending systems that would place those prizes in the hands of quite different groups of subjects. Why else have we arrived at rules, conventions and agencies for everything from property to argument to forming an orderly queue? And conversely, why else does intelligence differ from its non-intelligent predecessors by its propensity not only for philosophical speculation but also for civil war?

Of course, there are endless subtleties to this, such as the difficulty of deciding whether our respective objects are the same or merely equivalent, what the criteria are for preferring one object to another, how to handle conflicts between contending subjects, and so on. There are contradictions in objects themselves and in the relationships we each have with the objects we share, and so with each other. Nevertheless, this sharing, exchange and joint construction of objects are all absolutely crucial to the relationship between subjects and absolutely central to the special status of intelligence. For to the extent that we have objects in common, they become the vehicles – the only vehicles – of our *social* relationships. Conversely, the possibility that an object can *symbolise* another object depends on the ways in which these objects are mediated to one another in the actions of the subjects who act on, with and through them.

That is not to say that the world that arises out of relationships between subjects and objects is exclusively or even primarily social or symbolic. On the contrary, there is the rest of the universe too, making its own demands, operating by its own rules and seldom contenting itself with a subsidiary role. At the very least, a surgical operation no more saves lives by virtue of the social relationships it creates than being sent to an extermination camp is primarily a symbolic experience. The world cannot be grasped without also seeing how it is constructed out of, but also exceeds, the initial intentionality and reality of subjects and objects and the social and symbolic relationships through which intentionality and reality are expressed. Although even the universe enters into the world only to the extent that it is constructed as an object, it is always extremely peremptory in its demand to be constructed. After all, the only alternative to objectifying everything about the universe that impinges on our actions and our world is accepting that our actions and our world will inevitably fail.

So the world is clearly more than the sum of subjects and objects. Whatever a given intelligence is doing, it is always embedded in, and at least implicitly informed by, a much greater totality of things and events, subjects and objects, including many with no connection to me at this moment but whose actions will one day have a bearing on the things I do. Still more importantly, subjects and objects come to be organised into larger systems, structures and totalities with processes and mechanisms of their own, not only larger and more powerful than any study of their component subjects and objects might lead one to expect but also often acting in direct contradiction to the intentions of the subjects who created them and in quite different ways from the intrinsic properties of their individual elements.

Clearly then, when trying to account for human nature, we would do well to take into account all the unintended but perfectly real properties of the world. In fact, just as the subject has its autonomy and the object its permanence, so one can say that the fundamental functional property of the world is its very *worldliness*. This worldliness of the world expresses the extent to which the world stands outside our subjective autonomy and our intentions – not necessarily opposed to us, but certainly beyond. As such, it obliges us to develop a degree of worldliness too: a sense of the unreliability of even the best-laid plans, an appreciation of myriad perspectives and subtleties, a grasp of the imponderability of things and the constant need to adjust our expectations to accord more closely with what the world is willing and able to support.

Likewise, the worldliness of the world always places it above any particular object, in the sense that there will always be more to things and events than the objects of which they are apparently composed. However well we may grasp the permanent character of particular objects, the worlds of which they are part cannot be expected to show a comparable consistency or predictability. Nor, conversely, does the consistency or predictability of the world entail that it is made of consistent or predictable objects. There is a very necessary relationship between the nature of subjects and objects on the one hand and the world on the other, so it is conceivable that we might one day grasp everything about the world, and with that comprehend even the most intractable agents, things and events. But that day is still a long way off, not only because the tools we have for understanding the world are so limited but also because the world itself is so vast, contradictory and immature.

So our worldliness should recognise that there is a reality to things that extends beyond any particular objects we may be able to grasp. It is not this, not this, not that, not that. In one direction, as the totality of current things and events, the world incorporates any number of actual structures we have yet to grasp; and in the other, as the totality of *all possible* objects, including the objective forms of all those things and events we have yet to encounter or comprehend, it quite probably embodies any number of structures of whose very existence we currently have *no idea*. And in both cases, these structures continue to function, perhaps with immense consequences for ourselves, regardless of our ignorance of or impotence before them. Or to put all these points more concisely, the *ideal* form of the world is that it should encompass the entire universe, whereas the only thing we know for sure about its *actual* form is that it does not.

We can adopt any number of attitudes to this demand for worldliness. We may become pragmatists, cheerfully setting out to do battle with the world, or idealists seeking hidden meanings and divine Forms in everyday things. Like

Heidegger, we may develop profoundly worldly philosophies of *Dasein*, 'thrownness' and 'care'. We may resign ourselves to never finding the world intelligible, and so *expect* to be surprised and mystified and disappointed by existence. We may conclude that the world is not only stranger than we know but stranger than we *can* know, or even be astonished that we can know anything at all. Conversely, we may treat this lack of ultimate intelligibility as a sign that worldliness is a snare, and retreat into a devout un- or other-worldliness. But the world will not go away, so in the long run these are inherently unsustainable positions.

Worldviews that try to force reality into a straitjacket are equally notorious for their rigidity, instability and irrationality – all the things that intelligence is not, in fact. Indeed, a fixed position is made doubly unsustainable by the fact that, as ever, we are dealing with a structure of activity. The world does not stand aloof from subjects or objects, leaving us alone while we make up our mind about things one way or the other. On the contrary, the world engages us actively. Nor is it particular about how it does this; in fact, to the extent that we have successfully constructed subjective and objective relationships, systems and totalities, their wider implications arm the world with a vastly increased potential for intruding in our activity. What is more, there is no simple recipe, no end and no limit to how this interference will come about.

But the richness of the world is as much to be treasured as feared: because it is everywhere, so potentially are we. To the extent that we can grasp how the world works (which is tantamount to saying, to the extent that we are able to objectify the world) we can make use of its own relationships, systems and totalities. So the world is not only constantly intruding on us, but also constantly providing us with new avenues for action. And these avenues are as boundless as the ways in which our intelligence exposes us to action from without. In short, just as the subject is characterised by intentionality as well as autonomy and objects are characterised by reality as well as permanence, so the world is characterised not only by its worldliness but also by its *universality*.

As I shall argue throughout this book, the nature, range and scope of the world develop just like every other aspect of intelligence. But in what sense is the world abstract? Surely the picture just painted suggests an irreducible concreteness, a barely comprehensible *mélange* of mutually interpenetrating subjects and objects, things and events that resist all attempts to create a credible abstract picture that would be valid independently of any particular content or context? The answer is the same for the world as for subject and object, whose abstractness may be much more apparent but is no more real. The key to our worlds' abstractness is also the key to the completion of the subject and object's acquisition of this magical property. Just as it is the mark of intelligence's abstractness that its subjectivity be totally intentional and its objects totally real, so its world abstractness is signalled by its total universality. A totally intentional subject would be absolutely free to construct and discard structures of activity as and when they were needed, and so sustain its autonomy in the face of every vicissitude; and a totally real object would be one that retained exactly the kind and degree of permanence we intended for it, regardless of (because both truly independent of and truly sensitive to) the circumstances in which it existed. With that, subject and object would achieve complete abstractness as well as complete concreteness. Similarly, a truly universal world would be one in which all possible relationships, systems and totalities had been developed and comprehended by the intelligence at its heart, and the nature of this world would guarantee that intelligence's independence of any particular concrete content or context. With that that world would achieve its final abstraction from – because of its total command over – any concrete existence.

Intelligent activity

If subject, object and world are indeed fundamentally abstract structures and it is only by virtue of this abstractness that intelligent beings are liberated from the constraints of a biological existence, this creates a paradox as soon as the question of intelligent *activity* is raised. For how is it possible for *abstract* structures to relate to one another, or indeed to any aspect of the universe? An abstract structure is by definition independent of any content or context, but how is such a structure then able to act on things and events? In a sense the paradox is not especially profound, as we already know how subject, object and world arise and acquire their abstract character.

First and foremost, 'independent' of any content or context does not mean 'isolated'. What is more, we know that it is the very mechanism whereby this abstractness arose that ensures that contact, far from being relinquished, becomes far closer than anything achieved by any organic structure. As Piaget showed, the newborn infant is equipped with a number of innate sensorimotor reflexes out of whose structural and functional overlaps, coordination and synthesis the simplest forms of subject, object and world emerge, without however taking leave of the original bodily forms.[1] It is true that the higher forms of intelligence that are constructed on the basis of these preliminary structures render this relationship so tenuous that it becomes almost invisible, to the point where philosophers and psychologists have found it all but impossible to fathom. All the same, the link remains as real as either intelligence on the one side or biology on the other.

But this link must be understood properly. For if the child's link with the world is through its body, and all later means of action arise from or substitute for the organs and organisation out of which intelligence arose in the first place, that is not to say that the link between the abstract structures of intelligence and the universe it inhabits is a *natural* one. For it is not with the organs and reflexes with which the infant is born that intelligence engages the world. On the contrary, the formation of intelligence is also the reformation of the body. Whether it be through the articulation of reflex activity (eg, sucking, visual tracking, bodily stilling) into functional units of behaviour (eg, feeding), the inculcation of regular patterns of perception, the creation of typical body

---

[1] Piaget (1953, 1955). Piaget does not describe this process in terms of subject, object and world, however, although they are plainly there. For an explicit restatement of sensorimotor development in these terms, and an extensive analysis of its implications, see the author's *Birth of Reason* (in preparation).

shapes and postures, the development of automatic gestures, or the elevation of the body and its functions to the level of symbolic objects, the body, when considered as the instrument of action, is the product of intelligent activity.[1] Although it has the merit of being all but universally available to human beings, the body still has to be shaped, trained, organised and generally developed before it can be used for even the most trivial purpose. Luckily for newborn babies and those abandoned to desert islands, it is enough for certain basic purposes, even without being supported by society's vast panoply of tools, facilities, institutions and vicarious experience. But there is no aspect of the body that enters into intelligent activity that is not itself the product of the social and psychic order within which the intelligence in question itself lives.

Furthermore, if subject, object and world are indeed abstract structures, then no matter what their concrete embodiment, they remain in themselves abstract. As a result, it is absurd to define activity in terms of direct relationships between, say, subject and object or object and object. We should especially not assume that, just because there is a direct link between intelligence and the body out of whose sensorimotor reflexes it grew, that that body is part of the subject rather than simply another object. No matter how pervasive and ubiquitous its presence, the body relates to the subject in just the same way as any other object: it is only by virtue of the direct connection between exercising a sensorimotor reflex such as auditory location and movements of the head, plus our subsequently developed grasp of its objective properties *as* a body, that we are able to act through it.

So when an infant acts on food or a toy, this is no direct action of a subject on an object, or *vice versa*: in both cases, the activity consists of the subject structuring the activity of one object (the body) on another (the toy, food, etc.) – a structuring activity that is only possible by virtue of the intelligence in question's inheritance of links to the body from the apprenticeship of its sensorimotor days, and the consequent dual nature of the body as both artificer and artefact. Likewise for the apparently direct relationship between subjects that arises out of apparently objectless actions such as speech. It is in fact only because words are physical objects as well as meaningful symbols that they permit individual subjects to communicate with one another. In short, subject–object relationships are really object–subject–object (O–S–O) relationships; and intersubjective relationships are really subject–object–subject (S–O–S) relationships. The significance of this complication will be made clearer shortly, when it will be argued that object–subject–object is the defining structure of a *symbolic* rela-

---

[1] See, for example, Bullinger, in Butterworth (1982). There have been innumerable analyses of the impact of culture and technology, skill and personality on our bodily competence, performance, posture and sensibility, and of course on what do and do not count as normal biological structures and functioning. As for the way intelligence as such dominates the body, perhaps the best known statement of this thesis is Engels' account of the role played by labour in the formation of the hand. As Aristotle put it:

Anaxagoras says that it is *because* Man has hands that he is the most intelligent of the animals. But the right account is the got hands *because* he is the most intelligent. for hands are a tool; and nature, just like an intelligent man, allots each tool to one who can make use of it (*de Partibus Animalium*, 4.10.687a6-11, quoted in by Furley in Frede and Striker, 1996: 59).

tionship, while subject–object–subject is the defining structure of a *social* relationship.

In the mean time, having insisted that intelligence is fundamentally different from its biological precursors, it may be helpful to start any account of the nature of intelligent activity by contrasting it with biological activity, especially adaptation. Even Piaget regarded intelligence as ultimately a biological in nature,[1] but a major point that will emerge in the chapters that follow is that the two are separated by a very wide gulf indeed. What is more, not even those who insist on the specialness of human nature always appreciate the size and nature of this gulf. This point can be made in two steps: first by distinguishing biological activity in general and adaptation in particular from *construction*, and then by distinguishing construction from the most powerful of all forms of material activity, namely *production*.

Adaptation, construction and production

> For specialised functions there must always exist specialised structures; but man through his consciousness has been able to put off the burden of them from his own substance on to the broader shoulders of inorganic nature.
>
> Julian Huxley[2]

> Men can be distinguished from animals by consciousness, by religion or anything else you like. They themselves begin to distinguish themselves from animals as soon as they begin to *produce* their means of subsistence…
>
> Karl Marx and Friedrich Engels[3]

Generally speaking, adaptation considered as a form of *activity* has two aspects: assimilation and accommodation. 'Assimilation' refers to the process whereby an external stimulus or aliment is transformed by the organism in the course of being incorporated, whereas 'accommodation' refers to the adjustments an organism makes while carrying out this assimilation. In the former case, it is an external structure that is changed by the act of adaptation, whereas in the latter it is the organism itself. Both assimilation and accommodation are involved in most, perhaps all, adaptive acts.

So when I see a squirrel eating in the garden, I watch it put a nut to its mouth and chew it; and I imagine its digestive system breaking the nut down into its chemical constituents and then re-assembling them into nourishment. In this way the nut is assimilated. Of course, the squirrel may only be able to assimilate this food successfully if it also makes certain accommodations. For example, how will it deal with something that is too large to be handled in the usual way? How will the squirrel adjust its usual jaw and tongue movements to chew it if it is exceptionally hard? And how will its blood supply adjust the

---

[1] This is a persistent theme in Piaget's works. A major statement can be found in Piaget (1971b).

[2] Huxley (1912: 13).

[3] Marx and Engels (1976: 31).

demands of digestion against all the other things this particular squirrel is do-ing at the same time? Indeed, doesn't even the most routine act require at least a functional accommodation of some kind, no matter how transient and how trivial?

To appreciate the difference between an intelligent action and its organic counterparts, it is important to notice that assimilation is first and foremost a process of reduction. Not only is the nut broken into its component parts but even the features the squirrel detects in the first place seem to depend on its own current state rather than on the intrinsic nature of the thing itself. In other words, the squirrel is neither interested in, nor capable of dealing with, the nut considered *as* that nut. If the squirrel hadn't been hungry or otherwise moti-vated to look for food, there is nothing in its activity to suggest that it would even have noticed the nut, and insofar as the nut is noticed when the squirrel is hungry, it seems to notice only the features that relate to that hunger and its satiation. It is for this reason that squirrels don't rhapsodise on the beauty of hazelnuts, and not because they have no language: because they are completely unaware of the hazelnuts' existence. Even in the case of a purely functional form of assimilation, such as climbing a tree (in which the tree is assimilated to the act of climbing), only those aspects of the tree that are relevant to the climb-ing are taken into account: it is extremely debatable whether any squirrel has any sense of a 'tree' as such.

For intelligence, by contrast, an object exists existentially, so to speak. As Dennett puts it:

> Many organisms 'experience' the sun, and even guide their lives by its passage. A sunflower may track the sun in a minimal way, twisting to face it as it crosses the sky, maximising its daily exposure to sunlight, but it can't cope with an interven-ing umbrella... But we human beings don't just track the sun, we make an onto-logical discovery about the sun: it's *the sun!*[1]

From which follows an altogether different view of things, and a totally un-biological mode of existence – one that is, to repeat, specifically existential. So, an animal is preyed on and killed. It is terrified, it runs, it fights, it will not ac-quiesce in its fate. But it has no sense of impending death, no existential crisis in the face of the inevitability of its demise. No animal ever said 'But touching my fate, silence and speech alike are unsupportable'.[2] But again this is not for want of a language through which it might discuss death or rituals through which to symbolise and tame it; organisms lack any sense of their death be-cause they lack any objective sense of existence in *any* sense of the word. Inso-far as they have any apprehension of their own existence, it seems to be solely from the point of view of its ongoing activity – an inherently shallow, transient, one-sided and partial perspective. From this difference there springs in turn the entire history of the human struggle with mortality.

All this explains why it is more proper for biologists, but not the human sci-ences, to speak of *stimuli* than *objects*: it is only by virtue of the stimulation the

---

[1] Dennett (1996: 43).

[2] Aeschylus, *Prometheus Bound*.

stimulant generates that the organism is interested in it, and the organism is only interested in the stimulus because it positively stimulates a currently sensitive structure of activity. Any other properties that may be possessed by the thing that created the original stimulation are of literally no consequence. So in assimilation the non-intelligent organism possesses the very opposite of objectivity, since it has no interest in or respect whatsoever for the object as an independent reality.

Accommodation is just as parochial. Even when it results in permanent structural changes to the organism, these changes are pragmatic and localised. Unlike a subjective act, from which the subject may draw truly abstract and universal conclusions, accommodation is limited to the concrete structures that happen to bear more or less directly on the stimulus. Consequently, accommodation neither has nor could have implications for the organism as a whole, in the sense of generating universal insights or being treated as a test of a hypothesis, a proposition, a principle, and so on (of which, of course, the non-intelligent organism has none – and for exactly the same reasons).

Plainly, the differences between biological and intelligent activity could hardly be greater. Yet, such is the authority of biological science, the two have been persistently confused, even by those with the greatest knowledge of both. Yet when searching for examples of intelligent activity that are clearly *not* forms of assimilation or accommodation, one need look no further than to two kinds of activity that have often been treated as forms of assimilation and accommodation, namely play and imitation.[1]

The aspect of play that seems most like assimilation is probably the primacy it accords to activity over content. Whether symbolic or imaginative, play consists of making use of things to act out being or doing something that isn't 'real' – or more precisely, where its reality is not relevant. However, one should not confuse 'making use' of something with its assimilation properly so called. If the biological definition of assimilation is to be taken seriously, then play is only assimilatory in the same metaphorical sense in which birds sing songs or ants fight wars. By contrast with assimilation properly so called, intelligent play does not consist of reducing things to their useful parts or subordinating them to one's needs. On the contrary, the dolls participating in a tea party and the rules and other players in a football match must be accorded the utmost respect for the game to succeed.

It is true that a great deal of imagination goes into play and that the toys 'assimilated' to the game are quite routinely forced into all kinds of novel shapes and positions (literally and metaphorically). In that respect the assimilatory quality of play seems to be quite clear. Nevertheless, the basic purpose of this process is not to reduce the playthings to the player's needs but, on the contrary, to enrich them and build them up so that they possess the (usually social or symbolic) properties needed to participate in an independent, objective manner. Of course, often these properties exist solely in the players' heads,

---

[1] The *locus classicus* of the interpretation of play and imitation as intelligent in the present sense is Piaget (1951). Piaget's views have been subjected to endless analysis and dispute, none of which will be addressed here.

but that only means that the objective nature of the plaything includes elements that are present not in the plaything itself but are conferred by its involvement in the game. And to a very great extent it is the careful arrangement of props and scenarios to mimic 'real life' that brings the toys to life too. In sum, the plaything is by no means assimilated to the game in anything like the sense that my food is assimilated by my digestive system when I eat it.

Likewise for imitation, which is commonly compared with pure accommodation. In imitating an action, a person or a thing, I am not adjusting my actions in order to 'deal with' the thing I am imitating. This is not *reculer pour mieux sauter*. That would require only that I make enough sense of the thing being imitated to assimilate it in the reductive sense just alluded to. This is plainly not what is happening in the case of imitation. On the contrary, when I imitate, my purpose is to reproduce the object of imitation as faithfully as possible, or at least as faithfully as is necessary (in the case of copying a purely functional action) to achieve equivalence. That is why imitation so often involves taking the perspective of what is imitated – again the very antithesis of accommodation. Frequently imitation will extend to asking profound questions as to the 'why' of an action, so that I may not only understand it better but also adjust other things appropriately and even derive the most general inferences from it. So again, the pragmatic and parochial focus that is so typical of accommodation is precisely what is missing from true imitation. As with assimilation, the resemblance between adaptation and truly intelligent imitation is real enough, but so are the differences.

Like all other forms of intelligent activity properly so called, play and imitation are forms not of *adaptation* but of *construction*. Of course, to the extent that an intelligent being is also an organism, the success of an intelligent action must comply with the demands of adaptation in the general biological sense. But that is like saying that all organic activity must respect the demands of the chemical reactions on which all organic activity relies – a true statement, but less than helpful about the nature of specifically organic activity! Likewise, even where a specifically intelligent act has biological implications, no intelligent action can be reduced to, say, its adaptive aspect. Partly this is because of the quartet of strictly intelligent concepts already referred to, namely intentionality, reality, sociality and symbolism, whose adaptiveness is plainly vast but whose immediate biological bases are, to say the least, difficult to pin down. But more generally, the results of an intelligent act can be contrasted with any adaptive act in that, whereas adaptation creates a result that is less than the sum of its parts, the result of an intelligent act is always a lot more.

For example, when we assimilate nourishment, what do we actually do? We take an existing structure (the food), break it down, digest the parts we can use and discard the parts we cannot. In other words, we begin with two complex structures – ourselves and the food – and end with one structure that is much the same as before (ourselves) and an excreted mess of less complex structures. Whether this outcome is literally less than the sum of the original parts depends on how you account for wholes and parts, but assuredly it is not more. In the case of the dolls' tea party, by contrast, we start with a collection of relatively simple structures – the dolls, a tea set, and so on – and end with all these structures still present, and something put together that exists and works only

at a higher level – the tea party itself. Again, in what sense a tea party is more than the sum of its parts depends on how you account for such things, but it certainly is not less. That is why, whereas eating is adaptation, playing is construction.

In a sense, this substitution of construction for adaptation is only intelligence making a virtue of its greatest weakness. After all, its lack of natural concrete embodiment – which is to say, its inherent abstractness – ensures that intelligence is denied any natural means of adaptation. So, not only *can* it construct things and events into objects that exceed its own local and temporary needs, but it absolutely must do so if it is to achieve any results at all – even the most local and temporary. Conversely, it is true that, at any given moment, every intelligence has a concrete embodiment through which it acts, and a great deal of its activity certainly does consist of breaking things down, adjusting itself to circumstances or both. Yet this is still not adaptation, if only because even the most flagrant act of destruction by an intelligent being generally serves some larger value or purpose. Even the Holocaust and the contemporary horrors of 'ethnic cleansing' were carried out for reasons, grotesque, repellent and ultimately irrational though those reasons were. In just the same way, a game is not a success because the players successfully adapt the playthings to organic purposes, but because they are able to inject the order into the relationships and actions of the playthings that is needed to achieve the game's larger goal – having a 'good' game. As for the creation of more obviously independent constructs (temples, housing estates, transistors, whaling ships), the distance between their construction and purpose and adaptation's accomplishments is even more obvious, even though their adaptiveness is as plain as day.

What is more, the activities needed to construct an intelligent end result are themselves subject to increasingly stringent, conscious and deliberate regulation on the part of the intelligence in question. This includes not only ever more elaborate rules and plans and designs and the incorporation of an ever wider and deeper content and context but also the ever more rigorous application of strictly non-functional criteria such as value and meaning, not to mention logical criteria such as coherence, consistency, completeness and correctness. Or, where these criteria are violated, their violation can only be intelligibly expressed in terms of the *purpose* of the action, its objective logic, and so on. From the point of view of adaptation, such issues are wholly irrelevant, yet for intelligence they stand at the centre of acceptable and intelligible activity.

Furthermore, such concerns necessarily stand in an inherently abstract relation to the activity in question, which allows the intelligence in question not only to have an independent criterion for judging the action but also to vary and substitute concrete actions indefinitely, without contravening the integrity and rationality of the action itself. Such criteria are moreover applied not only to the intelligence in question's own states, interests and changing point of view – the limits of an adaptive action – but also to the objective properties of the goals at which it is aiming, the things by which it is surrounded and the independent properties of the social and symbolic processes and mechanisms through which it acts. Indeed, an intelligent act is couched in an increasingly refined and all-embracing web of principles, goals and plans, each pursued as a means in its own right, to the point where the basic principle of adaptive activity – if it works then it is right – is turned completely on its head – if it is right, then it will work.[1]

It is tempting to try to eliminate this contradiction between adaptation and construction, and so between biology and intelligence, by claiming that perhaps construction is only adaptation taken to extremes. And that would be entirely correct. After all, where else could intelligence have sprung from, if not from the further evolution of adaptation itself?[2] However, once such an interpretation has been accepted, it is important to draw out *all* its implications. For once the logical and natural extreme of adaptation has been reached, is it still only adaptation? When physical particles that were previously free to interact in random ways were organised into standing patterns of interaction (ie, they formed atoms), it is true that what they did among themselves was still entirely physical. Nevertheless, a completely new order of structure and function, namely chemistry, emerged. And life itself was originally only an extraordinarily elaborate chemical reaction, but does it make sense to treat the new forms of activity that were unleashed as simply more chemical reactions? In what sense is adaptation a chemical reaction?

The same applies to the emergence of intelligence, construction and all the rest: they arise from taking adaptation, reproduction and epigenesis to their logical conclusion, but the conclusion nature actually draws from this process is to initiate yet another form of material structure and activity, namely intelligence. Intelligence has no origins other than its biological forebears, yet it is as irreducible to biological terms as evolution, metabolism, mating, hunting or any other strictly biological activity is irreducible to chemical terms. It is true that intelligent imitation and play have non-intelligent predecessors and (at least in natural intelligences) strictly biological substrates; yet, once intelligence has taken the stage, these activities acquire properties and features that are wholly unprecedented.

Of these novelties the replacement of adaptation by construction is undoubtedly one of the most important. But construction is by no means the last word in intelligence. At least in the very limited sense in which the term is used here, intelligence 'constructs' objects only in the sense of construing them or of placing a construction upon things that already exist. Beyond that, however, intelligence differs far more radically from any of its predecessors by virtue of its ability to *produce* completely *new* structures.[3] Not that other organisms

---

[1] The pragmatism of adaptive *activity* should be clearly distinguished from the criterion of *evolutionary* adaptiveness, namely reproductive fitness. But even in the latter case, the logical limitations inherent in the cycle of random variation and natural selection make it *intrinsically* impossible for evolution to step outside pragmatism, except by breeding hopeful monsters of various kinds.

[2] Although this point will not be pursued here, the evolution of intelligence requires the supersession not only of adaptation but also of all specifically organic forms of organisation. See the author's *Birth of Reason* (in preparation).

[3] Clearly there is a sense in which constructing an object shares all the essential features of 'production'. That is why we have a 'construction' industry that constructs bridges, houses, canals, and so on. My deliberately limited use of these terms follows from a

produce nothing. Beavers and birds and termites build nests of one kind or another, and as Darwin showed, corals and earthworms have had the most profound effect on their respective environments.[1] The natural world is anything but ready-made or fixed. Nevertheless, the effects of production proper are not only potentially still more vast and pervasive but they also arise from a quite different source and have quite different implications.

When a bird builds a nest, its activity is limited to the assimilation of very specific aspects of its environment to a nest-building instinct that is itself the temporary and localised expression of the organism's current state; and once the nesting season is over, the nest is simply abandoned. Beavers and termites build more permanently, but they work under comparably rigid controls and within comparably rigid constraints. Furthermore, the abilities nest-building deploys, if not entirely localised to that type of activity, are never free to be extended to any other form of activity they may happen to suit. Much the same seems to be true of animal tool-making and tool use, at least well into the era of birds and mammals (whose activity, though it cannot be considered narrowly instinctive, is still not strictly intelligent). The impact of earthworms on their respective environments is still more straightforward, in that it seems to be completely incidental and stands in no direct relationship whatever to the organism's activity.

Plainly much less is involved here than a true subject, object or world. Indeed, production is even more different from organic activity than construction. First and foremost, unlike the organism, for which the general ability (if not skilled performance) to build a nest or wield a tool requires only that it should possess the normal organs and attributes of its species, the abstractness of intelligence means that it has to produce literally everything it needs. Even the simplest items can only seldom be used as they are found in intelligence's natural environment. Usually they need cooking or shaping or preparing in some other way. The only exceptions are those items (such as certain raw foods, 'naturefacts', and so on) for which we are naturally prepared because we were organisms before we were intelligent beings, and can rely on organic processes and mechanisms to sort out this kind of thing for us. But even this is by no means a purely natural phenomenon: the human body may have an innate capacity for, say, digesting certain kinds of food, but it has none for manipulating even the simplest object: the reflexes with which the neonate is equipped are completely useless from any functional point of view. And as I have already argued, even the body, when considered as the instrument of action, is a product.

Hence not only the centrality of production to human activity but also its radical import. If intelligence can do nothing without first creating the means to do it, including reconstructing its own body into an instrument of the most elementary kind, then it can do nothing without producing something that was

more intellectual tradition and is designed to bring out important conceptual distinctions, even though there is undeniably something slightly artificial about foisting such stark distinctions upon what are really overlapping terms.

[1] On life's transformation of its environment, see Levins and Lewontin (1985).

not there before. Cumulatively this can only mean that intelligence as a whole, considered on a historical scale, cannot exist without also producing its entire world. So the apparently massive leap backwards in the human neonate's capabilities when compared with the most elementary instinct has completely the opposite effect to the one that might have been expected. Far from disabling human beings, placing this vast new burden on them is also a massive liberation. Naturally the production of the whole world is, from a historical point of view, a slow process, but from the evolutionary point of view, historical processes are practically instantaneous. And even if production changed the world at the same snail's pace as evolution, the fragmented, episodic and parochial changes wrought by organisms adapting themselves to their environments and their environments to themselves would soon lag behind the conscious and deliberate transformation of an environment that suited intelligence very little to one that was in complete harmony with it.

This advance from adaptation to production can be summarised in terms of a very commonplace idea that is nevertheless central to any understanding of the relationship between biology and intelligence and between intelligence and its world. This is the ambiguous idea of 'sense'. In the case of adaptation the situation is clear: although an organism senses things, it does not make sense of them. They have no meaning, no value, no nature and no significance that is independent of how they are engaged as part of an active instinct. Even when the non-intelligent organism appears to recognise a thing or event it has experienced previously, it is doubtful whether it experiences it *as* something it has 'experienced before', as opposed to its reaction this time resembling its previous reaction, and resembling it in a way that relates to the previous encounter. As a result, the non-intelligent organism feels no compulsion to look beyond the surface of things and events.

As organisms become more complex, their actions extend over broader swathes of time and space, and success demands a more precise attunement to the nuances of the current situation, the exact meaning of 'the surface of things and events' also becomes more complex and ambiguous, to the point where, with construction proper, the idea that things and events need to be made sense of starts to emerge. But as far as construction as such is concerned, making sense of things is still limited to deciding what sense they already make. This is to invite tragedy, of course, for if things simply do not make sense from the subject in question's point of view, then there is nothing that construction (in this limited sense) can do about it.

With production, by contrast, intelligence starts to look beyond construction's essentially epistemic view of sense, to see not only what sense things and events make now but also what sense *could* be made of them. If their current sense is lacking or contradictory or they do not fit my own values, meanings or intentions, then perhaps they can be changed until they make sense after all. In other words, unlike construction, production is quite capable of *making* things make sense. That is why the sense intelligence makes of things through production is so different from the way an organic structure senses its environment. No strictly non-intelligent organic structure has any interest in what things could or should be, or indeed in what they actually are, in themselves. Leaving aside for the time being the age-old question of whether human beings could ever answer such questions fully, the fact that they are capable of *asking* them, and then acting to change things into something else, is enough to place them in a quite different league from their non-intelligent predecessors and neighbours.

Nor should the consequences of this change be underestimated. As the entire history of humanity testifies, production leads directly to the transformation both of human beings and of the world itself. In fact (to complete the circle), the impact of production on adaptation could scarcely be more profound. For production's ability to change the world itself, not in the incidental and localised manner of a worm's activity but as the systematic and intentional action of intelligent beings operating over continental spaces and historical timescales, reverses the entire relationship between human beings and nature. With production, intelligence not only frees itself from the demands of a predefined environment and the limits of bodily organs and organic instincts, but makes human activity the main criterion of adaptation itself, not only for human beings but for every part of the organic world that crosses its path – for better or for worse.

All this is of course simply an elaboration of the notions of subject, object and world. After all, the reason we care about the environment is that, unlike any other organism, we can see the environment *as* an 'environment'. That is, we are capable of appreciating its role in life in general and life as a whole quite independently of any functional or instrumental interest we may have in it as organisms. But this capacity for objective awareness of the conditions of our own existence is also the reason why we have the ability not only to save the environment from our ravages but also to ravage it in the first place. To do either, we need the subjectivity, objectivity and worldliness to which I referred above. Conversely, it is precisely because they lack these things that non-intelligent organisms do not care about the environment, nor about the niche they inhabit, nor even about their own lives.

The social and the symbolic

As I have already mentioned in passing, subject–object and object–object relationships take two general forms. In social relationships, individuals are linked to one another through shared artefacts (words, plans, rites, bodily organs, machines, laws, organisations, and so on), which thereby create reciprocity, hierarchy, conflict, and so on. In more general terms, in social relationships, objects mediate the link between subjects (S–O–S). In symbolic relationships, the inverse relationship applies. That is, the very same artefacts that previously created the relationship between individuals are themselves related to one another by a common subjectivity, so creating values, purposes, ideals, goals, and so on. In other words, in symbolic relationships a subject mediates the relationship between two objects (O–S–O), one of which 'stands for' the other.

All intelligent activity takes one of these two forms: social or symbolic. As often as not, it will take both forms at the same time. There are no direct subject–subject or object–object relationships. Nor, given the basic character of intelligence's core elements, could there be. If the subject is indeed an abstract structure, clearly it cannot engage another subject except through a concrete medium, which is to say, through its objectification. That is, subjects must enter into social relationships mediated by shared objects if they are to relate to one another, and to the extent that an object is grasped in much the same way by all the subjects participating in this relationship, it can indeed be used to create a social relationship. Conversely, although objects, considered as concrete structures in their own right, may be able to engage one another directly, this cannot be of any significance or value to a subject, and neither can an object participate in intelligent activity unless it is informed by the kind of abstract values, meanings, purposes, and so on, through which subjects can make sense of them. So objects must be imbued with symbolic significance – a designation, a value, a purpose, and so on – before they can be incorporated in intelligent activity. Even an object's most direct impact is of no *significance* (though it may have the utmost *effect*) if it does not play a part in a larger stratagem or plan, does not support or contradict a value or purpose, or does not otherwise possess a more abstract meaning.

Hence the significance of objects, whose simultaneous existence *in* themselves and *for* all subjects provides a medium for both social and symbolic relationships. Unlike an organic stimulus, which is neither (deliberately) made nor (knowingly) shared by any of the organisms that have access to it, the very objectivity of an object makes it both accessible and intelligible to each individual subject. Hence the role objects play in both social and symbolic relations. Of course, no object will be able to perform this role perfectly until the intelligences involved are all fully developed – a state of affairs that necessarily lies a long way from the first intimations of intelligence. But even a limited capacity for objectivity clearly places intelligence in a far stronger position than even the most sophisticated non-intelligent organism. As for the equally critical role of subjectivity, neither social nor symbolic relationships would be possible between structures that were not as stable and mobile as the subject. In particular, non-intelligent organisms that cannot keep the same structures of activity in play from one state or situation to the next are hardly able to maintain social or symbolic relationships of any (non-metaphorical) kind, if only because it is a moot point whether so unstable an organism could be said to be present from one moment to the next.

It is, to repeat, only through our capacity for sharing objects that social or symbolic activity is possible or that different intelligences can relate to one another. Without the shared medium that objects afford, without a common space to inhabit and the common forms at the interstices of overlapping worlds, and more generally a shared method and system of making concrete the intrinsically abstract structures of subject and object as they enter the picture, it would be impossible for subjects even to recognise one another's existence, let alone establish any kind of relationship with one another, social, symbolic or otherwise. And conversely, the more subjects share objects the harder it becomes to avoid, ignore and resolve the relationships they create between different intelligences. After all, each social relationship (S–O–S) already contains two-thirds of a symbolic relationship (O–S–O), and *vice versa*. Furthermore, each subject and object brings with it its own baggage of previous, simultaneous and expected relationships with other subjects and objects, and so a whole panoply of assumptions, implications, obligations and claims.

So how can even the simplest action be extricated from a plethora of social and symbolic relationships? Clearly it cannot. And how can it be protected from conflict and contradiction? Clearly again, it cannot. And how can the ensuing mutual onslaught be terminated other than by raising both relationships to a higher, more stable level? And so the whole grows.

There are of course many complications to this rather simplistic formulation. In particular, it is only on the surface of intelligent actions that social and symbolic relationships prevail (although that is still quite enough). Beneath the strictly intelligent surface, objects must also retain their non-intelligent properties as physical, chemical and biological structures if they are to contribute to intelligence activity, especially if the activity in question is not in itself exclusively intelligent in character. It is clearly not purely by virtue of the social or symbolic properties of machines that we can use them to extract minerals, fly to the moon or communicate over vast distances!

Other hazards follow from the fact that many subject–object and object–object relationships fuse social and symbolic elements. For example, a flag both symbolises an ideal and unites many individual subjects for whom this ideal is vital. However, these are quite different relationships. On one side, a flag is able to symbolise an ideal because the subjects for whom it symbolises that ideal are able to 'see' the relationship between the two. This relationship is quite distinct from the flag's social power to unite the enthusiasts for that ideal in amity and its enemies in enmity, and to set its friends and enemies at each others' throats. What is more, it is far from unusual for both love and hatred to attach themselves to the symbol, even though they only properly belong to the ideal that the flag symbolises. Hence the innumerable individuals who have been willing to lay down their lives to defend their flag, even though their deaths do not advance the ideal for which the flag stands by one inch. But that is, I suspect, a comment on the individuals in question's confused and immature grasp of what they are fighting for (as a sociologist might put it, a rather radical case of goal displacement), rather than the plainly deranged act of an apparently intelligent being sacrificing themselves for a piece of cloth.

Still more complicated is the question of just how much of a social or symbolic relationship is created when subjects and objects are mediated by and to each other. It is after all not only when we mean to be social that social relationships are created. The possibility of a social relationship is automatically created by the creation of any object of any kind, regardless of its creator's intentions, merely by virtue of its objects' very objectivity. If, as I have just argued, objects provide a medium and nexus for social relationships simply because their objectivity allows them to be agreed by any number of individual subjects, then any object offers clues (and perhaps access) to the subject who created it, regardless of whether they intended it to be used in that way. These clues may well be used by other subjects, perhaps to identify, understand or communicate with the creator, but also, possibly, to manipulate or exploit them. So social relationships exist independently of the intentions of individual subjects (because the reality of objects necessarily expresses the intentions of their subjects, however indirectly), even though they only exist because of that intentionality (because, again, the reality of objects necessarily expresses the intentions of their subjects, however indirectly). Likewise for symbolic relationships.

The social and the psychic

> Human beings must therefore create their own social order, analogous to that which they find in nature, and can only co-operate on the basis of rules or conventions: for sharing and reciprocity, for the allocation of resources, and for defining notions of property and theft, for controlling competition and retaliation, establishing how to greet one another, how to behave to one's seniors and juniors, and how to treat different categories of kin and neighbours. Rules thus relate not only to behaviour but also to social categories, to roles, such as parent, child, debtor and creditor, noble and commoner, judge and policeman, and so on.[1]

If social and symbolic relationships follow directly from the nature of subject and object, the world also has a special role to play in intelligent activity. Not only does it provide the arena within which activity takes place, but it consists of larger structures of its own that inform individual activity, yet are largely beyond the ability of any individual subject or object to comprehend or control. So intelligent activity can be loosely divided between layers of activity over which the individual intelligence exercises direct control, layers that are composed of the higher and more remote relationships between subjects and objects, over which the individual intelligence has little control (and of which it often has no knowledge), and intermediate structures through which the individual can exercise at least some influence over these larger structures, and through which the individual is influenced in turn. Addressing for the moment only the two extremes, one of the fundamental contributions worlds make to the structure of intelligent activity is to engender a distinction between *psychic* and *social* forms.[2]

There are many points at which the social and the psychic merge: in glory, repute, justice, infamy, honour, deceit, work, rights, shame, law, love and hate. There are also many ways in which the relationship between the social and the psychic plays a vital role in the determination and development of the other: through education, ideology, leadership, power, due process, management, and so on. But what none of these factors explains is how it is possible for the social and the psychic to exist in the first place. Nor is it obvious that these terms mean the same for human beings as for non-intelligent creatures, so their existence cannot simply be taken for granted, as might digestion or vision (and even they are by no means the same for human beings as for other, non-intelligent creatures). At the far extreme of social organisms, it is clear that neither term has anything like the same meaning when applied to, say, ants or jellyfish as when we apply it to ourselves. On the contrary, it seems clear that an individual ant has no discrete psyche, to the point where the very term 'in-

---

[1] Hallpike (2004: 71).

[2] It is regrettable that what follows introduces a second, quite different meaning for the term 'social', as the complement to 'psychic' rather than 'symbolic'. However, that is how the term is used in ordinary language, and no sensible alternative seems to exist.

dividual ant' is probably quite meaningless. Nor can ant societies be said to be social in the same sense as human societies: they have no history, they are not self-organising at the social level, there is no social structure that arises from their character *as* that society, and so on. Rather, at both social and psychic levels, both the structure and the functioning of both an ant colony and the particular ant seem to be all but wholly inscribed in a collection of instincts operating on a strictly biological plane, with neither social nor psychic activity and experience playing any significant role in their genesis, their nature or their further development. In other words, for ants the social and psychic planes are completely the reverse of what they are for human beings.

It would be difficult to exaggerate the significance of this distinction. It is after all because of the ill-informed enthusiasm with which common social and psychic characters have been imputed to our respective biologies that terms like 'altruism' (when applied to non-human organisms) and 'social instinct' (when applied to human beings) have created so much confusion. Contrary to the belief of many respected scientists, these terms mean such radically different things when applied to intelligent and non-intelligent beings that their indiscriminate use tends to corrode knowledge rather than advance it. It is true that, as the focus shifts from highly instinctive species such as social insects to more flexible creatures such as birds and mammals, the flexibility of which the organism is capable, and therefore the extent to which it has a truly social and psychic existence, increase enormously. Partly this comes about through an increased capacity for learning – an all but universal biological faculty – but mainly it arises from the reorganisation of activity. That is, instinct's more or less rigid binding of discrete structures to discrete kinds of functioning (and *vice versa*) is gradually transformed into a radical differentiation of the kinds of functioning in which we engage from the structures through which that functioning is carried out. In Piaget's terms, the structure of activity changes from an instinctive amalgam of 'drive' and 'technique' to the infant's sensorimotor 'affects' and 'reflexes'.[1] It is out of this differentiation that not only the possibility but also the unique consequences of intelligence emerge.

But what has this to do with the kinds of social and psychic life that characterise intelligence? The answer lies in intelligence itself. The very presence of an integral subject planning, predicting and controlling activity of every kind, the very capacity for disinterestedly objectifying activity, its means and its results, and the very existence of an increasingly universal world, potentially containing not only all objects but also all other subjects, their actions and their worlds, implies two things. Firstly, all intelligent beings are capable of construing their relationships to other intelligent beings as objects in their own right. Once objectified, such relationships can be grasped on their own terms and for their own sake, like any other object, although extricating the relationship itself from its social and psychic baggage can be an extraordinarily fraught task. Consequently, the individual intelligence can grasp social relationships independently of its own perspectives, interests and needs. Secondly, once such relationships have been objectified, the intelligences involved in them can pro-

---

[1] Piaget (1971b).

duce yet further 'objects' based on these new object-relationships, including the organisations, procedures, institutions and other structures needed to inform, institutionalise, manage, sustain and enforce them. So not only is the possibility of social relationships open to all subjects for the reasons given in the previous section, but the ensuing social structures, unlike their instinctive counterparts, can be apprehended, comprehended and transformed by their participants.

But the fact that social and psychic relationships *can* be comprehended is no guarantee that, as far as any given action or situation is concerned, the social and psychic structures actually in play *will* be grasped by any of the participants. Like all other products of intelligence, social structures exist independently of how individuals are affected by them. And to the extent that a given

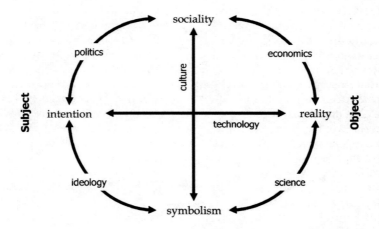

Figure 1: The social structure of intelligence

social structure is beyond either the understanding or the control of any single individual, it can persist and operate not only independently of but also despite the individuals in question. Perhaps, while 'society' is limited to a simple hunter-gatherer band, it is possible for individuals to shrug off its constraints; but when society comes equipped not only with laws, legal systems, police forces, prisons and armies but also ideologies, mass media and schools, not only resistance but even conceiving of resistance is difficult. Yet it is only through the need both to participate in and to resist the demands of social structures that stand apart from and even dominate the individual psyche that individuality itself becomes possible. After all, how else is one to comprehend both one's individual place and role in the world (historical as well as natural) and the nature, significance and value of one's personal existence, if not through one's relationships, be they of cooperation or conflict, with other intelligent beings faced with essentially the same conundrum? Hence the formation of an independent psyche is the corollary of the formation of an independent social system.

In terms of the history of human reason, it is clear that the relationship between the social and the psychic is both crucial and one of the great unsolved mysteries. Without true social systems, the historic progress since the Neolithic that has played such an obvious role in advancing human nature at every level would have been unthinkable. But social systems have been denounced as prisons of the psyche at least as often as they have been praised as its nurseries and its champions, so whatever their ability to create systems of greater and greater power, their role in the liberation of human reason is necessarily called into question.

As I hope will be clear by the end of this book, the exact process through which the social and the psychic emerge and mature contains large elements of both predictability and indeterminacy. Or rather, the entire process is deterministic, but the locus of determination constantly oscillates between different elements of the social system and the personal psyche. The balance of activity

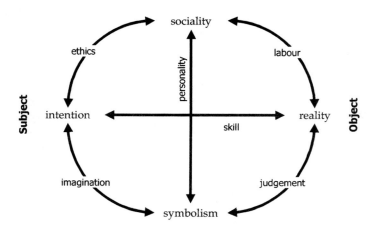

Figure 2: The psychic structure of intelligence

is constantly changing, without any unequivocal pattern or order. However, it is quite possible to describe in advance the main forms of intelligent activity, social and psychic, independently of their real history, based on nothing more than the subject's intentionality, the object's reality and the social and symbolic relationships that mediate between them. And although this is not always made explicit in the remainder of the text (whose purpose is somewhat different), it is actually the emergence and maturation of these forms through a succession of stages that explains above all else the history of human reason.

Given that, for reasons already mentioned, the social and the psychic part company quite early in this history and remerge only at its conclusion, there are in fact two quite different, if tightly interwoven planes and forms of intelligent activity to be produced and superseded by the history of human reason. The social and psychic series are inextricably bound to one another, but never is there any sense in which the social and the psychic can be reduced to one another, the one determines the other exhaustively, or the one provides an adequate model of the other. Thus, on the social plane, the following forms of activity are always present (see Figure 1). Firstly, the social structuring of intentions and the intentional structuring of the social comprise *politics*, while the symbolic structuring of intentions and the intentional structuring of symbols combine to create *ideology*. And whereas the symbolic structuring of reality and the real structuring of symbols (eg, through experiments) define *science*, the final pair, the social structuring of reality and the real structuring of society, makes up the *economic*. There are also two second-order forms of activity that have already been mentioned, operating at one remove from both the social and the symbolic and the intentional and the real. On the one hand, the social structuring of symbols and the symbolic structuring of the social jointly form *culture*, and on the other, where real objects are imbued with intentions, as when a non-intelligent object is injected with a structure of activity that allows it to simulate intelligent actions (eg, when designing and building a machine), and intentionality is thereby clothed in the form of the real, there is *technology*.

The same general kinds of activity are also to be found on the psychic plane (see Figure 2), although in somewhat different form. On this level, the social structuring of intentions and the intentional structuring of the social create the *ethical*, and the symbolic structuring of intentions and the intentional structuring of symbols create the *imagination*. Likewise, whereas the symbolic structuring of reality and the real structuring of symbols make up *judgement*, the final pair, the social structuring of reality and the real structuring of the social (eg, through organised work), combine to form *labour*. As for higher-order forms of activity akin to culture and technology, they also recur on the psychic plane: the social structuring of symbols and the symbolic structuring of the social jointly create *personality*, while the real structuring of intentions and the intentional structuring of reality define *skill*.

The dialectic of internalisation and externalisation

Given the terms in which I have outlined the overall character and organisation of intelligent activity, how can the activity itself be summarised at the highest level? The answer goes back to the most general of all forms of activity, intelligent or non-intelligent, namely the dialectic of internalisation and externalisation. Whether the general level of activity is physical, chemical, biological or intelligent, all forms of material activity, change and development can be analysed in terms of this super-dialectic.

The universality of this dialectic is not always apparent from the immediate forms of activity. A chemical reaction, for example, consists of the reciprocal internalisation and externalisation of the reagents' respective electrons, but it is far from obvious in what sense the specifically dialectical processes of contradiction, resolution and supersession enter into activity of this kind. And, insofar as one isolates chemical reactions from the remaining phases of material existence, this would be a valid criticism. However, as soon as the residual powers of physical matter operating on the astronomical scale are taken into account, and through them the stellar life histories and succession of the chemical elements as a whole, the problem largely evaporates.[1] Other forms of non-intelligent activity can be dealt with in analogous terms. For example, a good deal of organic evolution plainly consists of the acquisition and refine-

---

[1] Mason (1991).

ment of 'powers' and 'knowledge' that neutralise (and so effectively internal-ise) external forces of one kind or another. Thus, oxygen was by no means the only element that was poisonous to the earliest organisms that was later con-verted by evolution into a mainstay of life.[1]

But whatever its status as far as non-intelligent matter is concerned, the radical difference between the dialectic of internalisation and externalisation as it appears before intelligence and as it appears in intelligence itself is that, once intelligence emerges, this dialectic becomes completely overt. That is, not only is it present in intelligent activity but it is essential to the nature of that activity that the dialectic of internalisation and externalisation can be positively recog-nised and exploited by the intelligence in question. This is after all only the logical corollary of the processes of objectification, production and abstraction referred to above. Indeed, one can *define* intelligent activity in terms of this dia-lectic – as activity that knows itself to be that activity and is that activity by vir-tue of that knowledge. This recognition then allows intelligence to recognise, internalise and resolve the paradoxes and conflicts that govern its own imma-ture activity, and so advance the very dialectic that drives matter in general. So if matter follows a grand dialectic of internalisation and externalisation, the conclusion of that dialectic should surely be its positive recognition, comple-tion and embodiment in the highest form of matter, namely intelligence.

Within intelligence, the dialectic of internalisation and externalisation takes the form of three internally connected sub-dialectics: of present and absent, of appearance and reality, and of self and other.

The phrase 'dialectic of the present and the absent' refers to the constant in-terplay between the world as it exists for the subject and the totality of exis-tence that lies outside that presence. Until intelligence reaches the point where its direct reach extends to the remotest edges and the utmost depths of the uni-verse, the present will always be surrounded, informed and negated by ab-sences of one kind or another. This relationship is complicated by the fact that these absences include not only the parts of my world that lie beyond my im-mediate reach but also aspects of the universe that have never been part of my world but inform it anyway. However, intelligence differs from its predeces-sors in that its capacity to objectify its own experience (and so grasp conflicts, errors and omissions within that experience) allows it to notice that its world as it finds it – the present – is not the be all and end all of existence. Indeed, as the entire history of philosophy, politics, religion and art seems determined to demonstrate, intelligence is constantly seeking or postulating something that is currently absent (god, justice, revolution, enlightenment, and so on) that will complete or resolve the otherwise unintelligible incoherence, inconsistency, incompleteness and incorrectness of the present. In less optimistic times, it is equally capable of making a fetish of these shortcomings, as though the unin-telligibility of the world were an incurable symptom of the human condition.

But even if unintelligibility were our fate, the ability to grasp the situation in which we find ourselves with any degree of precision or detachment would still place intelligent beings in an intrinsically superior position to any non-

---

[1] Williams and Fraústo da Silva (1996: 475ff).

intelligent being. This can be illustrated by one of the most familiar of all forms of the dialectic of presence and absence, namely the means–end relationship. For the fact that we can postulate the existence of things that are not only absent from our present or from our experience but do not exist at all immediately sets the bounds of our existence infinitely more widely than those of any organism, for it leads intelligence out of the actual (the realm of all non-intelligent structures) and into the possible. What is more, by being able to define even the most abstract ideal or goal or hypothesis in objective terms, we can often work backwards from that point until we have constructed a sequence of actions that begins and is defined, regulated and justified by a figment of our imaginations! As Oscar Wilde remarked, 'A map of the world that does not include Utopia is not worth even glancing at, for it leaves out the one country at which humanity is always landing'.[1]

The dialectical nature of such a sequence is clear enough, given that the achievement of the desired end can only mean that the previously imaginary is made real and the previously real is reduced to a memory. The view from Utopia is necessarily very different from the view from the original point of departure, for even if it turns out not to be Utopia after all, one at least has a completely transformed view of where one came from. Action then finds itself at a quite new starting point, from which it can hypothesise and dream afresh. As Wilde went on to say: 'When Humanity lands there, it looks out, and seeing a better country, sets sail. Progress is the realisation of Utopias'. So the absent is made present, and the present is reconstructed on new and more complete terms. It is a startling achievement, and one that has led humanity to an amazing array of consequences.

Closely related to the dialectic of present and absent is that of appearance and reality. Because the perspective from which one engages them is more or less limited and one-sided, things are not, or at least need not be, what they seem. But it is only intelligent beings that can appreciate this fact. On the other hand, any incoherence, inconsistency, incompleteness and incorrectness in how things seem to be creates a contradiction that intelligence cannot help but try to eliminate. This is not the result of any epistemic instinct or metaphysical craving for truth (as I shall argue in the Conclusion, intelligence has a far more impressive form of truth up its sleeve) but the simple and direct consequence of its capacity for objectivity: by constructing its objects *as* objects, any hint of contradiction contradicts its claims to objectivity, and so to intelligibility. So whatever its interpretation of or response to contradictions in the appearance of things, intelligence cannot help recognising them.

For example, one straightforward way in which intelligence discovers the distance between the appearances of things and their reality is to approach a single object from a number of directions – an effect that can be achieved by simply rotating an object in one's hand. And that, of course, is the point: the link between appearance and reality is also the link between the different appearances of the individual object of which these are the appearances. If any contradictions emerge from either of these relationships, even if only of the

---

[1] Oscar Wilde, *The Soul Of Man Under Socialism*.

very shallowest kind (such as the subject's inability to keep track of a rapidly shifting sequence of appearances), then the object becomes overtly incoherent, inconsistent, incomplete or incorrect, and so begins to disintegrate. Consequently, it requires no more than an interest in the intelligibility of things to want to eliminate the difference between appearances and reality. What intelligence makes of this difference is another matter, of course. Does a single reality lie behind many appearances? Is reality the sum of appearances? Will reality come into existence only once all appearances have been transcended? And so on.

One of the most powerful and sophisticated forms of the dialectic of appearance and reality is the experiment. Generally speaking, an experiment is an attempt to test a claim about the real nature of an object by generating the corresponding appearances. Experimental method is a method for organising, executing and analysing this test and its outcome, and the results of applying experimental method provide us with new insights into the relationship between the two sides. Plainly experimentation is driven by the idea that there is a reality uniting an object's various appearances, and the need to experiment follows from intelligence's current inability to form an objective sense of that reality from the various appearances available. This is just as remarkable a departure from any pre-intelligent form of activity as the means–end relationship. As with the present and the absent, the consequences of this process are truly dialectical, since the result of the experiment is a new set of appearances that provokes new contradictions, be it between different appearances or between the new appearances and our hypotheses about other aspects of reality. So around goes the process once again.

Finally there is the dialectic of self and other (in the sense of self and not-self). My self consists of the structures that constitute me at any given moment. As the preceding account of how intelligence is organised suggests, this includes not only the structures that inform my subjectivity but also all the cultural and technological artefacts (such as languages, organisations, tools, and so on) that embody and represent me in the world or whose existence and operations I can command, or at least take for granted. As always, intelligence's interest in the other follows from its natural objectivity: the structures that make up its self could never be isolated from the rest of the universe (ie, the totality of others), so even the most routine or pragmatic interest in an object will all but directly reveal any otherness it harbours. As far as the subject is concerned, the persistence of this sense of otherness may be the source of the utmost pessimism or a thrilling sensation of worlds to conquer, but neither case requires any more than the most general capacities of intelligence.

As with the other dialectics, it is not only unconquered worlds that create the otherness of things. My self can only be said to consist of particular structures to the extent that I am developed enough to mobilise them as required. But while I am still too immature or inexperienced to have them completely at my disposal, many of the skills, relationships and other structures I have created in the past may not really operate as part of my self properly so called. What is more, some of the otherness even of things we take to be our own in fact springs from this very incomprehension of structures that actually reside within the self. And even though they must inform our subjectivity to some extent, the objects we produce may still not be fully taken into account by our actions. Indeed, our objects by definition operate independently of our awareness of them: they have their own laws and histories. Their activity is therefore determined by a whole range of factors and events that lie, at least as far as the immature intelligence is concerned, outside the sphere of the self. This is true even of the products of our imagination. For example, a hypothesis is obliged to meet certain logical norms, quite independently of our *desire* for it to be valid, correct or otherwise credible. There are moreover many structures with which I am embroiled but over which I exercise no real control. For example, it can take centuries, if not millennia, for the real potential and full implications of major social structures such as slavery or capitalism to surface and be dealt with.

Finally, at least some of the otherness of things is generated by the very immaturity of the self to which they are contrasted. Of course, this is not different from the situation with the other two dialectics mentioned above. As I shall argue when dealing with the topic of alienation, it is quite normal for the obtuseness and hostility of people, situations and things to be actively (though unintentionally) created by ourselves, rather than being the expression of any intrinsic limits of human abilities, of the 'human condition', of the intrinsically mysterious nature of the noumenon, and so on.

The development of intelligence

To put all this in more positive terms, it may be that much of the unintelligibility of things and events comes from our ignorance and impotence, but the development of intelligence consists precisely of overcoming these limitations. However, as will become clear as my arguments unfold, this overcoming consists of more than simply learning how to navigate the things and events we encounter. The unintelligible can be interpreted as either an obstacle or an opportunity, but in either case it has yet to be mastered. But even more radically, the unintelligible may also embody or possess powers that are different, contrary or simply greater than those I possess already. So, to the extent that I can make the unintelligible intelligible, and so make it more or less part of my self, I both acquire its powers and transform my outlook, perhaps even my nature, for better or worse. This transformation may sound somewhat mysterious, but in fact the reader is already surrounded by cultural and technical artefacts that exemplify it. After all, even the use of something as apparently ethereal as language requires that we internalise the acoustic properties of air for speech, the electromagnetic spectrum for visual signals such as writing, and any number of devices for transmitting these symbols from one place and one time to another. The command of the environment that is embodied in architecture and in industry is an equally important (and eve more neglected) expression of this process of internalisation.

As I have already said, the three dialectics of presence and absence, appearance and reality, self and other show how the universal dialectic of internalisation and externalisation is expressed in intelligence. One of the consequences of the three forms this dialectic takes at this level is that we are not only constantly reducing the distance between appearances and reality, presence and absence and selfhood and otherness, but in so doing we transform the very nature of self, appearance and the present to incorporate more and more of their erstwhile opposites. This has repercussions for any theory of human nature, not the least of which is that it explains why arguments for 'cognitive closure' are never valid. It may or may not be the case that human beings do not have the intelligence to comprehend the universe in all its depth and diversity, but we would certainly be aware of the contradictions that would inevitably be created by any discrepancy between the present and the absent, appearances and reality or self and other. After all, the very first thing such contradictions would do would be to diminish the coherence, consistency, completeness and correctness – and so the very objectivity – of our objects! Given that no one has yet proposed any specific limit that the full self-development of intelligence could not overcome, cognitive closure remains an unsubstantiated claim, powered more by pessimistic assumptions about human nature and by the intrinsic but quite possibly irrelevant limitations of biological models than by compelling arguments or examples.

Some much wider implications of this transformation will be suggested in the Conclusion, but in the mean time, this point leads me to the next aspect of the nature of intelligence, namely the unprecedented relationship between intelligence's activity and its *development*.

Activity and development

The organisation of intelligent activity in terms of an increasingly integral structure that operates in genuinely dialectical ways has innumerable striking consequences. For example, it means that *activity* and the further *development* of that activity, if not identical, are no longer separate, and that any given intelligence quickly becomes the main instigator, driver, vehicle and judge of its own advancement. In other words, intelligence is increasingly the author of its own development, and the process of development is increasingly a process of *self*-development.

Again the contrast with biology is as illuminating as it is stark. Among organisms there are three general levels on which activity develops: through evolution; through the epigenetic 'focusing' of inherited nervous structures according to the organism's actual activity; and through learning.[1] Although each

---

[1] Although evolution will need no explaining to non-biologists, epigenesis may be less familiar. For accessible reviews of epigenetic processes that emphasise their role in the development of key forms of intelligent activity, see Deacon (1997) or Edelman (1992). For a more technical view, see Goodwin and Saunders (1992). As for learning, the problem is more likely to be an over-familiarity that causes this complicated phenomenon to be treated too simplistically:

> Learning spans an enormous range of phenomena, from highly specific one-time learning through imprinting, to individual trial-and-error learning, to highly flexible forms of learning over prolonged periods through such sophisticated means as social imitation... Intelligent species are adept at learning a variety of means for solving problems, whereas unintelligent species learn a very narrow range of specific skills and associations. In other words, learning is not equivalent to intelligence. (Parker and McKinney 1999: 274)

of these processes contributes significantly to the organism's flexibility and versatility, all three remain limited in one simple yet profound way. For all biological structures, the processes and mechanisms of *development* are more or less divorced from those that control *activity*. The ability to learn is not much influenced by what the (non-intelligent) organism learns; the criteria of evolutionary selection have no direct bearing on the process of variation or *vice versa*; and so on. Given that, on the one hand, it is this very lack of integration between activity and development that limits biological structures to such shallow and hobbled forms of advancement and, on the other, it is their reconciliation within a single structure that unleashes construction and production alike, the importance of this change can scarcely be exaggerated.

One precondition for creating an internal connection between activity and development is the achievement of a certain level in the dialectic of internalisation and externalisation. If the activity that typifies each successive level of matter is indeed a dialectical supersession of its immediate predecessor, then it is no accident that physical structures and functioning are succeeded by chemical structures and functioning, that chemical structures and functioning are succeeded by biological structures and functioning, or that biological structures and functioning themselves are succeeded by intelligence. For what each new level embodies is precisely the coordination of entire sequences and patterns of lower level activity, and so the synthesis of the higher level structures that are needed to resolve the persistent conflicts and gaps that prevent the stabilisation of matter at the lower level. In other words, the essential precondition for the *development* of each higher form is the resolution of the contradictions that plague the *activity* of the lower. From this point of view at least, the sequence from physics, chemistry, biology and intelligence is not only successive but also progressive.

The contradiction within biological activity that is overcome in intelligence is that between the *functioning* of an organic structure and its *functionality*. To simplify the matter somewhat, evolutionary changes to how an organic structure operates – its *functioning* – are the product of random variations. In this case 'random' does not mean statistically random or uncaused so much as exogenous. That is, the sources of change to a structure (and so of changes in its functioning) are unrelated to that structure's own activity. On the other hand, the process of selection, which determines which particular evolutionary developments are actually reproduced in future generations, and so determines which structures are *functional* from an evolutionary point of view, is equally remote from the organism's functioning, being defined in terms of reproductive fitness rather than any specific evaluation of the activity itself.

In other words, taken as a whole, the evolutionary processes and mechanisms that determine a structure's functioning (what it does) are quite separate from those that decide its functionality (what it is worth), and so the development of the forms of activity characteristic of that species. For example, a variation may follow from a genetic mutation caused by cosmic rays and its selective benefits may only be determined after equally random mutations in a predator population that won't actually take place for some millennia yet. It is hard to see how activity and its development could become more completely disconnected, yet this is by no means a parody of everyday evolution.

So on the phylogenetic plane, the development of biological activity is clearly separated from the activity itself. As biologists have been keen to point out recently, both learning and epigenesis can be modelled in similar terms. What is more, this separation between functioning and functionality is fundamental to biological methodology, for if activity and its development were not at least partially separated in this manner, then many of the core methods of scientific biology would be irrelevant and most of its core findings demonstrably untrue. On the other hand, it is precisely the final overcoming of this separation that accompanies the emergence and development of intelligence. Although arising out of strictly biological structures and their functioning and supported by normal biological process and mechanisms, the functioning of intelligent structures and their functionality have indeed been organised into a single integral structure, in much the same way that life itself organised chemical reactions into self-replicating loops capable of adaptation and advanced self-organisation, and so initiated forms of specifically living activity, for which chemistry has no explanation at all, any more than the physics of stones explains the beauty of great architecture.

Hence the profound role played by intelligence in the development of matter. Once subject, object and world enter the scene, it becomes perfectly possible – as every single reader of these words demonstrates every day – to plan our actions in terms of increasingly exactly and explicitly anticipated consequences, to envisage and execute innumerable alternative courses of action, to design cultural and technical artefacts to take account of any number of eventualities (including evolutionary threats of all kinds), to transfer genuine insight from one area of activity to another, and so on. And in all these forms of activity, we are expressly structuring our functioning *in terms of* its functionality. Unlike non-intelligent organisms, we can establish specific criteria for the success of our actions (including their contribution to an exquisitely calculated reproductive fitness), we can organise, monitor and correct those actions in terms of those criteria, and we can tell whether or not we have achieved them. Of course, we are not as good at this as we might be, but the simple fact that we recognise the objective nature and properties of learning, evolution and epigenesis shows that we have already side-stepped most of the limitations placed on both the activity *and* the development of non-intelligent organisms.

In many respects, this change in the relationship between our structures' functioning and their functionality simply places intelligence in the same position as physics, chemistry and biology: a new and independent form of matter. However, the fact that intelligence not only resolves the contradiction created by the mutual indifference of biological functioning and its functionality but also does this by recognising just what the essential problem *is* places it in the enviable position (were mesons, molecules or molluscs capable of envy) of having resolved the fundamental problem of material activity and development once and for all. Or at least, that is what it would mean if intelligence could back up this general insight with the practical means to realise its potential in the real universe. What is more, the fact that intelligent activity has, by means of this insight and its practical applications, acquired the power of apprehending, articulating and resolving *directly* the contradictions that plagued all preceding form of matter also means that the relationship between our activity and our development is no longer the clouded and circuitous relationship it always was before. On the contrary, it is now direct and immediate in proportion to the maturity of intelligence's activity and development.

Abstraction and concretion

The ways in which intelligence acts and develops are the principal topic of this book, and it would be absurd to try to anticipate its conclusions before setting out the argument. However, for the moment their main outlines can be noted. Like any organism we are capable of learning, of course, although it is debatable whether any but the simplest form of learning in human beings is quite like learning in non-intelligent organisms. There are also the various forms of insight and criticism that are so characteristic of humanity and that make it especially easy for intelligence to identify threats and opportunities above the level of empirical errors and omissions: 'This action failed *because*...'; '*If* we did this *then*...'; '*Although* it is true that...'. If, then, because, although – words far more magical than *abracadabra* and *sesame* ever were. It is quite the norm for human beings to respond to what seems to be a perfectly successful action with the view that it could have been done better – more efficiently, more effectively, more precisely, more reliably, more easily, more fully, and so on. This would be quite unimaginable for a strictly biological activity, for which, for want of the autonomous subjectivity, permanent objectivity and universal worldliness that must underpin any independent standard, no such self-criticism either does or could take place. That is why it is only for intelligence that the best is the enemy of the good, or that the good exists in the first place. Conversely, only an intelligent being would ever admonish itself to not waste time 'reinventing the wheel'. And so on, up to the point where the entire logic of knowledge and power is reconstructed and a completely new stage begins. Hence again, on the most general level, the constant interplay between activity and development – and also its absence in non-intelligent organisms, to which such *aperçus* are wholly inaccessible.

The process whereby higher level ideals, concepts, goals, and so on are formulated – the process of *abstraction* – takes two quite different forms: the empirical and the reflective – although these forms are closely related and all the most powerful forms of human development, such as scientific method, the division of labour and political organisation, require both. Empirical abstraction consists of constructing insights into the nature of objects leading to hierarchies of concepts such as 'blue', 'colour', 'sensation', and so on. Reflective abstraction, on the other hand, builds its insights through its objectification of its actions on its objects, leading to concepts such as 'done', 'successful', 'right', and 'ideal'. In this way, as higher and higher forms of activity are constructed and recognised, intelligence constructs logic and mathematics and formulates views on the nature of subjectivity, objectivity and so on.[1] By a combination of

---

[1] Empirical and reflective abstraction are mentioned here primarily to provide a short-hand account of the links between intelligence's activity and its development. Readers interested in these concepts for their own sakes should consult any of Piaget's many

these means, intelligence comes to see not only how the world works but also how to work the world.

However, as the preceding comments on intelligence as a structure of *activity* (and more especially as a structure capable of *production* properly so called) should have made clear, this process of abstraction is only one side of a larger process, of which the natural complement are processes of 'concretion', which is to say, the subject's re-synthesis of abstractions in the form of new objects. By these means, intelligence expresses, extends and projects itself into the world, not only creating empirical objects but also, where necessary, imbuing them with the structures needed to ensure that they do intelligence's bidding of their own accord.

It is important to distinguish both abstraction and concretion from generalisation. Like learning, generalisation is a talent intelligence shares with organic structures of all kinds, although it is clear that an intelligent generalisation is quite unlike the kinds of generalisation with which learning theorists are typically concerned. For intelligent beings, to generalise is to summarise a collection of particular empirical experiences in broadly empirical terms. For example, the proposition that 'All generalisations are bad', if treated strictly as a generalisation, is not self-contradictory, since no generalisation, being only an induction from empirical experience, can ever claim either to be *absolutely* universal or to express a formal principle.

To *abstract* from experience, by contrast, is to construct forms that not only apply to any and all of the particular things or events from which they were abstracted (already a completeness and consistency to which generalisation does not aspire) but also apply to absolutely any object of the right kind with equal validity. Conversely, having been constructed through a process of objectification, abstractions and concretions not only have an objective order (again not the case for generalisations) but they can also be organised among themselves into new and original structures of activity, without further reference to the particular cases from which they were generalised. So the proposition that 'All generalisations are bad', if now treated strictly as an abstraction from the activity of generalising, *is* self-contradictory, since it is a claim about the intrinsic nature and logic of generalisations, and as such it *does* claim universal validity. The proposition that 'All generalisations are bad' would then be directly applicable to itself, with all its paradoxical consequences. What is more, this proposition can be fitted into (and in fact only makes sense in terms of) a larger system of epistemological abstractions, within which it is capable of generating yet deeper insights, but to which it is, in turn, rigorously subordinated. The same can hardly be said of generalisations.

All this reflects a critical and specifically intelligent feature of abstractions and concretions: that, once constructed, they exist independently of any particular experience. That is, they are objects in their own right. A generalisation, by contrast, always relies on the subjective element of experience, which is to say, on the unique empirical history and perspective of the person or culture making it. There is no inherent contradiction between me asserting something

---

discussions of this subject, most notably Piaget (1977, 1978, 2001).

to be generally true and you denying it; this may simply reflect our different experience, perspective or situation. But for me to assert that a particular abstraction is true *is* contradicted by your denying it, since the very fact of abstraction casts that which is abstracted onto the objective plane – as something that is true, independently of my (or your) experience, perspective or situation.

Conversely, the role played by abstractions and concretions, be they empirical or reflective, is that they not only extend but also transform the conditions (subjective as well as objective) in which intelligence operates. For example, it is our ability to abstract the properties and character of a form of activity from any particular instance of that activity that enables us to consider its utility, efficiency, effectiveness and reliability, to design, build and test methods, tools and techniques through which it might be better executed, to set criteria for its success, and so on. Thus, having built a machine, its operations can be observed and assessed from the point of view not only of, say, its physical efficiency but also of its more or less successful implementation of the sequence of actions needed to create the desired end product. The latter plainly demands an act of empirical abstraction. At the same time, the machine itself is an objectification (an equivalent rather than a copy) of the sequence of actions a skilled artisan would normally carry out when doing the same job. This in turn is plainly only possible by virtue of its makers' capacity for reflective abstraction.

A little less prosaically, the act of abstracting a principle or a procedure from action not only allows us to repeat it but also, by objectifying the principle that underlies that activity, lets us consider the intrinsic properties of that kind of act, as opposed to their outward effects and particular cases. That does not mean that abstraction enables us to step outside our personal or cultural perspectives, histories or experience, and many an alleged universal abstraction has turned out to be nothing of the kind. But it does mean that we can come to conclusions that are independent of our subjectivity, even though they never arise *regardless* of our subjectivity. Furthermore, until intelligence reaches the very highest levels of maturity, this independence is always conditioned by a larger context (cultural and technological) within which alone it makes sense. However, as the development of intelligence proceeds, the size and richness of the context that contains it and the content it contains grow greater and greater.

In short, by allowing us to reflect on the intrinsic nature of a thing or event, the ability to abstract lets us consider it *qualitatively*, which it to say, in terms of its intrinsic *logic*, including its own coherence, consistency, completeness and correctness. Indeed, once a structure has been abstracted from any particular exemplar, it is possible to compare its ideal form with its practical instantiation – which is to say, to compare what *is* the case with what *should* or *could* or (in the right conditions) *would* be the case. With that, not only does the *distinction* between fact and value come to be established, but so does the enduring *link* between them that makes principled action or the rational pursuit of an idea possible.

In its small way, this change of focus – again brought about by nothing more than the emergence of subject, object and world – is the starting point for the inextricable entanglement of intelligent activity and development. Given the analysis of activity already suggested, with its insistence on the production and reproduction of the world through the constant elaboration of social and psychic structures, it would be difficult to overstate the power at intelligence's command – if, that is, it can get it under control. But that can only happen through the maturation of intelligence itself, whereby intelligence is not only extended in knowledge, scope and power but also intensified by virtue of its increasing rationalisation and its elevation to higher and higher levels of structure and function.

Rationality

Fortunately, there is a much more concise way of putting all this. If objectification and abstraction are intelligence's normal route of development – its own peculiar version of the dialectic of internalisation and externalisation – then it will immediately begin to identify and internalise the basic structures of its own activity based solely on the various objectifications, deliberate or otherwise, of its own acts. From that point onwards, it will be able to reflect on the facts, the organisations, the tools, the rules, the concepts and all the other elements that *objectively* initiate, structure, motivate, comprise, guide and justify its own actions.

Conversely, in proportion to the level of maturity it has reached, intelligence will be able to determine the why, what and how of its actions – and, of course, re-externalise these conclusions and their implications in later rounds of activity. Which is to only say that intelligence will scarcely have begun before it begins to provide *reasons* (or at least excuses) for its actions.[1] And, to the extent that these reasons are truly what drives them and these reasons reflect the true subjective and objective conditions of its own activity, its actions will become *rational*. In terms of the closing paragraphs of the previous section, a rational act is one that is defined, executed and evaluated in terms of what it is supposed to be – what it could, should or would be. In other words, all rational acts are driven by values (in the most general sense of the word) as well as facts: they are all *for* something, be it a goal, a value or something else.[2]

That in turn means that the motivation, control, and so on of rational actions are increasingly endogenous to the agent, and that the agent can give reasons, be it in the form of explanations, bureaucratic procedures, professional codes of conduct, the rules of war, or whatever. Describing reasons as endogenous does not mean *exclusively* endogenous, of course, as though rationality were a form of navel-gazing or whim. However, it does mean that ultimately all aspects of the activity in question, unlike habit, tradition or even inspiration, are at the disposal of the agent. That is why, where the agent is unable to explain the relationship between these alleged 'reasons' and the action at hand, it is hard to avoid the conclusion that the action was in fact irrational.[3]

---

[1] As the next two chapters show, this is a slight understatement of the amount of development intelligence needs to go through before it can be said to have reached the point of reasoning properly so called.

[2] Hence Max Weber's emphasis on *Zweck-* and *Wertrationalität* – but hence also the inadequacy of his *opposition* of fact and value, in science, politics or anywhere else.

[3] On the role of justification in rationality, see Smith (1993). For further comments on the

Hence yet another critical feature of intelligence: that its reasons are indeed *its* reasons. Such an idea has no counterpart in biological activity, whose reasons are all causes and whose causes reside in the forces of evolution, in hereditary connections between states and stimuli, in epigenetic sequences and in the episodic learning of parochial contingencies. None of these could be said to be at the disposal of the organism, and in each case the structures that control action are either sub-organismic fragments or trans-organismic structures over which the participating organisms have little or no control. Indeed, in the absence of rationality properly so called, it is hard to see in what sense any organism could be described as the true agent of *any* action.

Among human beings, by contrast, an act is rational to the extent that we have effectively internalised the criteria for performing it. Fortunately, that is exactly what objectification, abstraction and internalisation give us. That is, they give us the distinction between an object and both its content and its context; modal reasoning; necessity, possibility and contingency; supra-empirical, supra-instrumental and supra-functional goals, values and principles; abstract criteria of rationality, such as coherence, consistency, completeness and correctness; and so on. Even on the instrumental and functional planes, they allow us to decide what we want to achieve, independently of our current appetites and perspective; to devise appropriate means for achieving our ends; to plan and pursue our goals intentionally and realistically; and decide objectively whether or not those goals have been achieved. And all this can be done in terms of appropriate ideals, standards and norms.

The converse of the objective origins and basis of our rationality is that a rational act is one for which the agent could legitimately be held responsible. After all, to the extent that my insights into my own actions are indeed objective and indeed under my control, it would be difficult to claim that I was unaware of their wider significance or unable to do anything about them. So I must be at least partially responsible for them. Indeed, as the preceding account of the forms of intelligent activity suggests, I am equally unable to escape from the specifically ethical and ideological dimensions of my actions: they are intrinsic to the very structure of my activity. So rationality is not only a force for the liberation of intelligence but also its own greatest burden: once one has the power to reason, one is also obliged to have good reasons for what one does. On the other hand, the same analysis of the forms of intelligent activity also shows just how complex the processes of arriving at and acting on a 'good reason' are, given that so many of the social and even the psychic conditions of activity are typically beyond the individual's control.

So reason and rationality are ambiguous concepts, being both obvious and obscure at the same time. This ambiguity largely follows from the fact that they are just as much subject to a progressive process of development and maturation as any other aspect of intelligence, and it happens that, as things presently stand, they are far from complete. So ambiguity is doubly expected: not only have reason and rationality yet to realise their potential and resolve their contradictions, but we are not mature enough yet to appreciate them fully. Or per-

---

relationship between the rational and the irrational, see Chapter 7.

haps, given that these are only two sides of the same coin, this is only one reason to expect reason to be ambiguous.

Reason could well be defined as the *normal* form of intelligence, in the sense that it is the way intelligence would always operate if it could overcome its inexperience, its immaturity, the social and psychic forces that bear down on it, its neuroses and its other contingent foibles. In this sense, pure rationality is to intelligence as perfectly healthy teeth are to real teeth: an ideal that is extremely unlikely to be realised under current circumstances, but an ideal to which one can meaningfully aspire and an ideal that future developments may yet make completely sensible in every sense. In other words, far from being ethereal or some kind of Platonic Form, rationality is the form that intelligence would take if it could realise its full potential. Such rationality is currently only a norm, but it could easily become a fact, and become a fact not least because of its status as an enduring ideal. Indeed, as I argue at length below, it is extremely likely to become much more of a fact than most theorists now seem to imagine possible.

Conclusions

Two things follow from this analysis of the nature of intelligence. All the many kinds of structure, functioning and functionality attributed to intelligence in this book follow directly from the analysis of intelligence into subject, object and world. The details have been omitted and many steps in the argument skipped but, at the highest level at least, no other concepts are called for. That is not to say that the account of the history of human reason offered in the remaining chapters flows directly from this account. In fact, as its purpose is to convince by its general plausibility rather than by deductive rigour, the story that follows must be connected to the notions of subject, object and world as much by the reader's imagination as by explicit analysis.

On the other hand, although this model takes full account of the social and symbolic forces bearing on intelligent activity and internalised in the course of its development, the restraining forces of history's irrefutable objective reality and consciousness's irreducibly subjective intentionality exclude the possibility that an arid sociologism or psychologism could account for human nature. Even if our social and symbolic systems press us to act in one way or another, the 'moment of ideality' in which the individual intelligence actually makes up its mind is no more reducible to the play of ethics and imagination, judgement and labour than the nexus of historical events can be inferred directly from an interaction of the scientific and the ideological or the political and the economic. Actuality is all.

Which brings me to the main problem addressed by this book: the problem of how to explain the development of human nature *as a whole* in terms of subject, object and world, without thereby reducing human nature or human existence to precisely this interplay of universal structures, but also without simply writing a catalogue or reducing it to a simplistic parody. The solution offered here (which is by no means exhaustive) is based on the concept of intelligence as outlined in this chapter, and the stages through which it develops, as outlined in the Introduction. These stages demonstrate intelligence's radical departure from and transcendence of any previous form of matter, physical, chemical or biological. To take only the two transitions that seem to be more or less complete, the historical form of the transition from intuitive to concrete reason was the Neolithic revolution, through which agriculture and large-scale settled communities first came into the world; and that from concrete to formal reason seems to have taken the form of the industrial revolution, which is surely the only event in human history of comparable significance. As for the transition from formal to what I call dialectical reason, there have been inklings of what that might mean, a few of which are considered below. But to grasp the scale, scope and profundity of the change intelligence has wrought in the world, it is necessary to step through each successive stage until we arrive at some kind of final resolution.

2. Intuitive Reason

Modern man is incapable of experiencing the sacred in his deal-
ings with matter; at most he can achieve an aesthetic experience.
He is capable of knowing matter as a 'natural phenomenon'. But
we have only to imagine a communion, no longer limited to the
eucharistic elements of bread or wine, but extending to every kind
of 'substance', in order to measure the distance separating a primitive religious experience from the experience of 'natural phenomena'.

Mircea Eliade, *The Forge and the Crucible*[1]

The standpoint of intuitive reason

Briefly, everything that exists contains force. Man and the spirits of his ancestors
can activate forces directly and consciously, or inadvertently and by accident.
Animals, plants and inanimate objects have forces too, but these can only be released by man and the spirits of man. The reason for man's eminence is mainly his
control over words, which themselves have force... and, because they are prime
movers of actions, transcend space and time and fuse space and time into a single
modality.

Mircea Eliade[2]

The earliest form of intelligence proper is intuitive reason, which inherits only
the most rudimentary forms of subject, object and world from its sensorimotor
predecessor. These structures are truly intelligent, but at this stage they exist
only in their shallowest form. Indeed, for all the implicit intelligence of its actions, intuitive reason's exploitation of its own subjectivity, objectivity and
worldliness is strangely blind, for of all the structures that make up its world,
intuitive reason is least capable of being intelligent about those of which it is
itself composed. Although it may act *by virtue* of the superior logic even the
most primitive forms of subjectivity, objectivity and worldliness afford, it is not
yet mature enough to act *in terms* of that logic. Although sensorimotor development creates true intelligence in the form of an autonomous subject and
builds it a universal world populated with permanent objects, it does not supply any yet higher perspective from which these structures can themselves be
grasped. As a result, although it can, say, tell good from bad, distinct forms of

---

[1] Eliade (1978: 143).
[2] Irvine in Berry and Dasen (1974: 255).

'badness' with radically different origins and natures such as pain, malice, misfortune, evil and sickness are only vaguely differentiated and are interpreted in essentially the same manner.

This lack of self-knowledge cannot be helped: intelligence has only just established these structures; indeed, in establishing them it was establishing itself. As with any other ability, one is intelligent before one knows what it means to *be* intelligent, before one becomes able to make use of that knowledge in an insightful, critical – and so intelligent – manner. This is only one more expression of the fact that, before it can make a correct and effective use of something – an idea, a tool, a resource, a process, a system – intelligence must first indeed make sense of it. To do this, it must construct it *objectively*, which is to say, as a object it can make sense of, since it can only make sense of something by making it sensible. Given that this is the rule for all 'somethings', subject, object and world included, how could intuitive reason comprehend itself *as* subject, object and world well enough to apply its intelligence intelligently?

Indeed, this blindness should apply *more* to intelligent nature than to all the other natures by which it is confronted. As luminaries and sages have repeated down the ages, nothing is more carefully hidden from us than our inmost selves. In the case of intelligence we know it is possible to transcend this dilemma, if only because we can produce luminaries of various stellar magnitudes capable of detecting, if not always revealing, this inmost self. Nevertheless, it is only with the last stage in the development of intelligence, whose peculiar origins, station and properties allow it to overcome this otherwise universal paradox, that we will finally overcome this primitive blindness. Until that point, the logic of subject, object and world is as much a given of activity as its content or context, and intuitive reason must make sense of it like any other condition of its activity. The special paradox of intuitive reason lies in the fact that at this point intelligence is so immature that the *givenness* of subject, object and world does not yet make them *data*. At least at the start of this stage, intelligence sees only the surfaces of things, and is as bereft of knowledge of its own internal abstractions – above all of subject, object and world – as it is of the physical, chemical and biological laws that govern the external things, events and circumstances on and in terms of which it acts.

But in that case, isn't 'intuitive *reason*' a contradiction in terms? In part it certainly is, for intuitive reason lacks the one critical attribute we might reasonably require of reason of any kind, namely a capacity for reasons and reasoning. Although it can *describe* its actions to a greater or lesser extent, only towards the end of intuitive reason can intelligence *explain* them even in the most superficial manner. Still less can it direct and control its own activity in terms of anything resembling a principle or a system. How then could intuitive reason's activity, aims (such as they are) or achievements be considered *rational*? Clearly the answer is, they cannot. The only thing that prevents 'intuitive reason' from being a total contradiction in terms (and the only reason I shall continue to use the term) is that, even at this stage, intelligence possesses all the right credentials for rationality *except* this last one. And even there rationality is potentially present, and the whole development of intuitive reason consists of the formation of this true rationality, albeit only in *its* most primitive form. So intuitive reason can at least claim a kind of honorary rationality, as it were.

This lack of explicit rationality explains intuitive reason's treatment of things and objects as facts of the most primitive sort, comprehended only to the extent that they can be handled on a pre-rational level, which is to say, only in terms of their empirical surfaces. In terms of the basic dialectic of internalisation and externalisation – all of whose aspects require a strictly rational dimension to be brought to fruition – the poverty and superficiality of intuitive reason's approach to the dialectic of self and other are rivalled only by its ineptitude in the face of the dialectics of present and absent and appearance and reality. That is why, just as intuitive reason initially lacks the reflexivity needed to know itself, so it lacks an explicit grasp of means–end relationships or the ability to conduct any but the most pragmatic investigation.

That is not to say that intuitive reason cannot intuit effective means to its intuitive ends or operate at least by trial and error. It is also perfectly capable of using basic tools, models, symbols, and so on. However, on the intuitive plane these are all far more fragmented and limited than anything any adult would now take for granted. For example, intuitive reason is initially incapable of incorporating unplanned contingencies or of handling more than one aspect of an object at a time, and its technical and conceptual resources have no penetration beneath the perceptible surface of things. The tools an early intuitive culture employs consist of irregularly shaped pots and measures, personally carved weapons and instruments, natural materials, communal dishes that defeat any notion of equal portions, and so on. As a result, standardisation is rare, objects are dealt with as isolated and static entities, measurement is seldom employed and invariably scalar. In all, it is an environment almost designed to defeat any notion of objectivity, comparison, analysis or enquiry.[1] Or again, intuitive reason can be *prompted* to remember and anticipate and generally behave as though it comprehended a much wider sphere than immediate appearances, but it can only do this when induced to by perceptible cues, under the direction of a more sophisticated intelligence or in a well-signposted setting.

So intuitive reason wanders around an impressively broad landscape, engaging in a sequence of seemingly interconnected episodes, but the links are pragmatic, eclectic and conventional, as are intuitive reason's own actions. Which is to say, from a strictly rational point of view, specious. Although it has crossed the threshold of intelligence proper, its acts embrace only those objects it can see, touch, move, hear, and so on, and the practical inertia the simple fact of direct perceptual or behavioural contact implies. Beyond that, intuitive reason lacks even the limited consistency of perspective, that precious persistence of vision, without which not even empirical data can really be managed effectively. And so, for want of either the capacity or the occasion to compare them, the various constructs intuitive reason applies to its objects and its world are subjectively quite unrelated. Thus intuitive reason wields truly intelligent constructs, but it wields them obliviously. They may constitute intuitive reason,

---

[1] Hallpike (1979).

but intuitive reason does not constitute them. Far from finding itself in a position of calm reflection or decisive action, as one might expect of a rational being, it is all intuitive reason can do to keep up a running battle with wilful, stubborn, uncooperative reality.

Hence the seemingly empiricist starting point to that most rational and rationalising of processes, the development of intelligence. The boundary intuitive reason sets between self and other is the boundary between touching bodies, not neighbouring selves and certainly not adjoining existences. That is why it communicates by means of injunctions to do this or that, rather than by arguments or explanations or requests or instructions.[1] Similarly, for intuitive reason appearance is distinguished from reality only in the sense that it eventually comes to realise that reality is not exhausted by its current appearances. However, explicit insights into the reality informing appearances remain beyond it until its development is all but complete. Finally, intuitive reason recognises the absent only insofar as the present is understood to continue over the horizon into other, presently absent presents.

It is a peculiar vision of the world, finite but boundless (or perhaps just interminable), grounded in endless pragmatic connections binding together disconnected things and events. Lacking both breadth and depth, the intuitive world is limited to an indefinite succession of things and events, beyond which it lacks any internal order. At least at its outset, intuitive reason operates on a purely phenomenal plane, without the least sense of an underlying noumenon.[2]

---

[1] Lindberg (1992: 10–3, 21–5).

[2] Lest this seem an unnecessary lapse into dualism, Kantianism or both, I should explain how the relationship between phenomenon and noumenon is interpreted from the present perspective. The universe of noumena consists of the totality of matter, including intelligence, as it exists *in itself*. But this existence of things in themselves consists precisely of their relating to one another and to themselves, which is to say, their existence *for one another* and *for themselves*. At pre-intelligent levels this 'existence for' other things takes the form of physical forces, chemical reactions, organic adaptations, and so on: chemical reaction is the mutual existence of two chemical structures *for* one another, adaptation is the mutual existence of two organic structures *for* one another, and so on. In this scheme, the world of phenomena – the world of history and consciousness – simply consists of noumena, including other intelligences, as they exist *for intelligence*.

Phenomena thus constitute a sub-set of noumena, not a separate or opposed class of entities existing on another plane. So intuitive reason's problem is not that it lacks either phenomena or noumena. That would contradict one of the elementary givens of intelligence of any kind, namely the mutual independence of even the intuitive subject from its objects. Intuitive reason's problem is more that it has yet to make any sense of the distinction between the two. It may operate on a purely phenomenal plane, but it has no sense of phenomena *as* phenomena, any more than it intuits the existence of noumena. That, again, is what makes it *intuitive* reason: a phenomenology lacking any sense of its phenomena *as* phenomena.

The logic of intuitive identity

It follows from this elementary pseudo-empiricism that intuitive reason's underlying logic represents a perfectly valid logic of *identity* – as even the lowliest objectivity entails – but also that this logic is so impoverished that it omits any positive sense of *non*-identity, of difference or otherness, not to mention active change processes such as negation or transformation, or relationships generally. These are not yet recognised as corollaries of identity, as they are for higher forms of intelligence and for all forms of reasoning properly so called. For intuitive reason they are simply a more mature intelligence's incomprehensible names for the equally incomprehensible vicissitudes of its own objects. In no way do they inform intuitive reason's sense of self and other, appearance and reality or present and absent.

This superficiality also accounts for the other crucial impoverishment of intuitive reason's logic of identity: its inability to grasp its objects' structures in the sense of what its objects consist of, how their parts relate to the whole, how they relate to one another, and so on. Even while retaining a clear and effective picture of the object itself, intuitive reason finds it impossible (initially at least) to sustain its grasp of one level when considering another. As a result, it has no sense of the *implications* the part has for the whole or *vice versa*. Intuitive reason can manage a succession of particular things and, to the extent that they can be relied on to behave themselves while intuitive reason's back is turned, it can handle continuous events, but it cannot cope with multiple, complexly related objects. Nor can it sustain a complex process or event as it unfolds in accordance with its own objective logic. Still less can it manage contradiction or dynamics or abstraction.

This impoverished logic of identity explains why intuitive reason sees no contradiction in citing a number of mutually exclusive 'explanations' for the same phenomenon. It is entirely characteristic of intuitive reason that most early mythologies are happy to explain death in terms of a curse or evil intent *and* as a quasi-poisonous substance *and* as the Grim Reaper, often in the same story. An intuitive child is likely to assemble an equally rich and inconsistent confabulation. This is not intellectual incompetence or artistic licence; on the contrary, these explanations are carefully constructed and sincere. The problem is that the level of explanation demanded by the intuitive nature of mythology sees no contradiction in this, and indeed takes no cognisance of contradiction as a category or a problem.[1] Neither does the intuitive child. This is why intuitive reason is content with simply asserting that this is the cause of that, without actually specifying any actual causal process or mechanism: the readers of this book may be inclined to take explanations as seriously than the facts they purport to explain, but intuitive reason is not. This sameness and difference of things are both well known to intuitive reason, but the contradiction between

---

[1] Frankfort *et al.* (1949: 11–36). This work provides an extraordinarily apposite account of intuitive reason as expressed in the myths and ideologies of early Mesopotamia and Egypt, their transition to a later concrete level and even some intimations of formal reason, at least on the intellectual and psychological levels.

them is not: they are 'divisions, distinctions of ideas, not schemes of classification'.[1] Instead of being subjected to objective categories, things and events are 'classified' in terms of their perceptual, functional and contextual resemblances and associations – rather than being objectively the same kind of objects, they 'go together' in various ways.[2]

This absence of a supra-empirical order explains why, as Darwin observed, 'Children like hearing a story told though they remember it so well that they can correct every detail, yet they have not imagination enough to recall up the image in their own mind'.[3] Although they are often far better acquainted with the details of the tale than the (adult) narrator, the totality of the story escapes them, and the parts are not experienced in terms of the whole. So there is no active anticipation of the ending, even if a few questions to the child will reveal that they know perfectly well what the ending is. The tension and anxiety the intuitive child shows in the face of a scary story has literally no connection with their knowledge that it has a happy ending. Of course, adults presented with a well-crafted fiction may respond no differently – but only while they are effectively insulated from any alternative 'reality' (in a darkened theatre, for example) and they willingly suspend their disbelief. These options are not open to intuitive reason: there is no capacity for scepticism for it to suspend.

Intuition and pragmatism

> This total process goes forward without reference to any explicit principles and without any planning... It is nonverbal and does not follow a coherent sequence of logical steps. As such it does not represent what we tend to value in our own culture as 'intelligent' behaviour... We might refer to this kind of ability as a 'knack', and respect a person for his competence, but we would not on these grounds qualify him as a profound thinker.[4]

For want of even an intimation of the inner nature of things and events or the absurdity of certain combinations of things (or indeed the *absurdity* of anything), intuitive reason certainly cannot reason *about* anything. That is why even the most elementary *method* is quite beyond it. That is, it is incapable of being intelligent for its own sake, which is to say, of being *intentionally* intelligent. True, it will soon start to devise a wide range of tools and techniques, which will provide it with regular (and so quasi-methodical) means of taking action, and a whole raft of decidedly *un*intuitive, supra-empirical notions, such as the idea that there might exist enduring relationships *between* its objects, will start to emerge in transient *ad hoc* forms. Nevertheless, once intuitive reason

---

[1] Durkheim and Mauss (1963: 82n).

[2] Hallpike (1979).

[3] Darwin (1974: 11). This phenomenon should be distinguished from the superficially similar way in which oral tradition uses repetition. Here the function of repetition seems to be mnemonic, ritual or stylistic.

[4] Gladwin, describing Trukese navigation methods, in Berry and Dasen (1974: 36).

turns away again, this higher complexity (or rather, this more profound simplicity) disappears and its object dissolves without its active intervention.

This ability to create higher structures by pragmatic means is not only
vulnerable to momentary distractions and minor changes in content or context,
but it is flawed in a more fundamental sense. No matter how much effort intuitive reason puts into identifying, organising and controlling things and events,
it lacks the capacity for insight and criticism that the possession of stable, mobile internal structures would confer and even the most superficial methodical-
ity assumes. So intuitive reason is obliged to find its own way from one object
to the next solely by means of the strictly empirical cues and measures offered
by its object and its transient feelings. There are no consistent goals or values
on which it can rely, no possibility of a pre-defined or sustained principle, no
constancy of purpose, integrity of method or consistency of perspective. Supra-
empirical constancies of the kind that will express themselves at later stages,
such as 'number', 'type', 'harmony', 'proportion', 'order' or 'law', are still conspicuous only by their absence. There is no explicit or articulated sense of the
result to be achieved by any given task, no sense of the proper procedure. So
intuitive activity proceeds by practical persistence until a more or less acceptable outcome is achieved: the identity of things and the continuity of events
remain merely brute facts, with which nothing more can be done.

Hence what Piaget, following Stern, called 'transductive' reasoning. Hence
also Vygotsky's 'unorganised congeries' or 'heap', with its associated 'chain
complex':

> For instance, if the experimental sample is a yellow triangle, the child might pick
> out a few triangular blocks until his attention is caught by, let us say, the blue col-
> our of a block he has just added; he switches to selecting blue blocks of any shape
> – angular, circular, semi-circular. This in turn is sufficient to change the criterion
> again; oblivious of colour, the child begins to choose rounded blocks. The decisive
> attribute keeps changing during the entire process. There is no consistency in the
> type of bonds or in the manner in which a link of the chain is joined with the one
> that precedes it and the one that follows it. The original sample has no central sig-
> nificance. Each link, once included in the chain complex, is as important as the
> first and may become the magnet for a series of other objects.[1]

For the intuitive child, a red triangle is like a blue triangle and a blue triangle is
like a blue square – so a blue square, if not actually *like* a red triangle, is still a
perfectly acceptable member of this sequence. If asked, the child is perfectly
aware that there is no resemblance between a red triangle and a blue square,
yet each shape and colour is inextricably yet formlessly linked with its immediate neighbour by their treacherously hypnotic empirical continuities.[2] Objects
are linked by perfectly real resemblances, but, for want of the ability to keep
the overall criterion before its mind's eye, the child loses track of exactly which
particular resemblance and which comparison is important. That is why intui-

---

[1] Vygotsky (1962: 64; and pp. 59ff generally). Vygotsky's explanation of this phenomenon diverges markedly from both Piaget's and my own.

[2] Vygotsky (1962: 64). See Wertsch (1985: 99–108) for further examples and references.

tive reason can never aspire to analysis properly so called; indeed, it can never transcend the 'incoherent coherence'[1] of syncretism.

Of course, the reader has only to imagine the inherent *in*constancy of organic functioning in the face of changing states and stimuli to see how great an advance even intuitive reason represents.[2] Even the least developed subjective autonomy, object permanence and worldly universality mark a huge improvement over any possible organic structure or functioning. Nonetheless, intuitive reason's version of constancy is as primitive as it could possibly be. In particular, its ability to identify a thing as the same does not presuppose any recognition of its constant identity *as* constant, and so as embodying a constant independent power capable of resisting intuitive reason. Intuitive reason certainly does not act as it does *because of* any such sense of its objects' constancy. Even in its most elaborately detailed and effective actions, early intuitive reason lacks any sense of its object's inner nature or potential or spontaneous tendency to change, or its inclination to resist intuitive reason's own initiatives. So, lacking any insight into the forces objectively in play, intuitive reason is doubly deceived as to the necessary constituents of a successful or satisfactory act.

Hence the characteristic plight of intuitive reason: it could only really work in a universe of truly isolated, atomic objects, and with objects whose internal structures are faithfully reflected in their external bearing. Unfortunately, there is no such thing as a truly isolated or atomic or superficial object. Even if an object could be isolated from other objects (not an altogether meaningful notion, given that even the simplest activity consists of the interaction of objects), not even a miracle could isolate it from itself. Yet intuitive reason cannot help acting as though its world really is made up of a series of snapshots. It lacks any method for pursuing even seemingly direct goals objectively, systematically or reliably, relying instead on the universe standing still and waiting for it to catch up. This, not unnaturally, the universe declines to do. So intuitive reason is left helpless in the face of disorder, and incapable of taking advantage of any intrinsic order.

If intuitive reason has so little sense of its object and itself, how can it be expected to notice either the connections or contradictions between any two objectively related but empirically different things, such as the different facets of a single thing or the successive moments of a single event? That would presuppose the organisation of the original objects – the facets or moments – into a higher object – the thing or event – whilst simultaneously respecting and controlling the differences between them, thereby sustaining the distinct identities of the things and events themselves. Or to put the same point in more abstract terms, how could intuitive reason ever grasp a *relationship*, given that a relationship, like a thing or an event, is a matter of sameness and difference *at the same time*. Indeed, a relationship, like an event, is nothing other than sameness *in* difference: the sameness it seeks to establish is only the sameness *of* a relationship or a single event because it expressly distinguishes the contrasting

---

[1] Blonsky, quoted in Vygotsky (1962: 60).

[2] On non-human animals' grasp of sameness and difference, see Thompson in Roitblat and Meyer (1995: 175–224). See also Vauclair (1996: 13–6).

identities of the objects and moments and facets related even as it comprehends them as elements of a single larger unity.

Of course, intuitive reason can manage sameness *or* difference, at least insofar as they are revealed by its objects' outward, empirical surfaces, but managing both at once is quite beyond it. It may not confuse them on the empirical *cum* phenomenal plane, but subjectively (which is to say, from intuitive reason's own point of view) they are neither one nor distinct nor even comparable. For example, notions such as 'long' or 'heavy' may be used, but concepts such as 'length' and weight' are not addressed explicitly, so heights and lengths cannot be systematically compared or related one another as distinct dimensions of objects, capable of being analysed for their own sakes or being used to conserve objects through their many otherwise unintelligible phenomenal shifts.[1]

Even when seemingly supra-empirical links can be established through painstaking, one-to-one connections (such as when working out family trees), the inferences intuitive reason draws are the result not of the true articulation and integration of these links but of pragmatically fusing those that are salient and ignoring those that are not. Similarly, although constructs such as 'animal', 'dog' and 'elephant' are routinely applied to the right object, often with astounding acuity, nothing can be deduced about a dog from the fact that it is an animal. And again, for want of the ability to coordinate the various dimensions of activity and objects on any but the pragmatic plane, intuitive reason has no sense of proportion in any sense of the word.

So although, abstractly speaking, intuitive reason possesses all the attributes of intelligence proper, its methods are naïve, banal and impulsive in the extreme. For example, although it can anticipate the *results* of quite complex activities (insofar as the results consist of another empirical situation), it is immediately defeated when required to describe the *process* that brings these results about. That is why, even if intuitive reason is genuinely sensible *of* things, it cannot yet be sensible *about* them. That would assume an explicit grasp of the *activity* as well as its *consequences*, which in turn would presuppose precisely the degree of abstraction and self-awareness that intuitive reason lacks. It cannot even focus properly on such objects as it *can* construct; it merely swallows and is swallowed up in them. The action and its immediate object become everything, the agent's larger circumstances and even the content of the action (considered as a complex structure in its own right) nothing.

And again, the possibility of identifying, organising and controlling groups of processes and products, or of comparing, sequencing or otherwise arranging objects systematically, are all extremely impoverished. So are its egocentric memory and its capacity to anticipate and plan. All are initially negligible, and none ever quite surpasses the limits of empirical knowledge and pragmatic control, even when intuitive reason reaches its zenith and stands on the verge of being superseded altogether. For all these abilities presuppose some command of the relevant dimensions or relationships or series – in short, the set of

---

[1] The Piagetian canon is awash with research on this topic; for the anthropological literature, see Hallpike (1979, *passim*).

independent abstractions – which are objectively necessary if intelligence is to make sense of these divergent empirical appearances.

Indeed, the methods intuitive reason uses to identify a given set of objects as being of the same kind are so conflated with the actual things and events to which they are applied that method and object lose their separate identities. As Robertson Smith put it:

> ... it is of the first importance to realise clearly from the outset that ritual and practical usage were, strictly speaking, the sum-total of ancient religions. Religion in primitive times was not a system of belief with practical applications; it was a body of fixed traditional practices, to which every member of society conformed as a matter of course.[1]

This is why intuitive reason is so prone to reifying once effective acts and intermediaries into fixed rituals and symbols, and forced to rely on makeshifts to achieve even the most pragmatic stability and mobility of action. At least at its birth, intuitive reason is entirely restricted to an undifferentiated symbolic, ritual level of activity that is simultaneously meant to have the most direct and practical effects, and is inimical to the insight and criticism required for genuine rationality. As Atran puts it:

> Any symbolic utterance is non-propositional, however one chooses to look at it: logically, no fixed meaning (not even a context-relative one) can be assigned that would permit a coherent evaluation of entailments; empirically, no determinate factual content can be attributed whose consequences experience might definitely confirm or disconfirm; and psychologically, no specific mnemonic structure can be accorded storage and recall of information. In multiplying senses and metaphor, symbolism leaves the interpretation of any utterance significantly 'open-ended'.[2]

So even the most developed and experienced intuitive reason can still be fooled as to the sameness and difference of the things about it, and its acts are readily distorted by any accidental interruption, by extraneous events, by unacknowledged or non-empirical subtleties in its objects or even by its own incidental actions. Ironically, it is always too busy doing something to have any sense of what it is doing. Consequently, intuitive processes and their results are in constant need of shoring up, of endless correction and adjustment. If intuitive reason knows where it is, it does not know where it is up to.

The natural corollary of this inarticulate notion of sameness is not that, as a subject, intuitive reason has no real objects, but rather that it projects its subjectivity onto its objects (and *vice versa*) without recognising what it has done.

---

[1] Quoted in Hallpike (1979: 46). As Hallpike goes on to note, far from being explicit, 'basic categories such as purity/impurity, order/disorder, culture/nature, sacred/secular, male/female, and so on have to be elicited by an examination of the total experience of the people, as represented by their institutions, customs, and symbolism' (1979: 78). For intuitive reason, language is an instrument for organising action, expressing emotion and coordinating social relationships. It may be used to communicate information, but it is neither an analytical tool nor required to exhibit the properties of coherence or consistency, completeness or correctness that would be demanded of the language of a culture operating at a higher developmental level.

[2] Atran (1990: 3–4). See also Hallpike (1979: 142–9 and *passim*).

There is no unconscious urge or mechanism for projection; rather, in the absence of yet higher structures capable of regulating its actions or differentiating their various elements from one another (including, of course, the subject–object boundary), intuitive reason cannot help constructing its *others* in terms that are directly familiar (intuitive, in fact) to its *self*. Initially at least, that other – mother, playmate, cat, toy, the weather, a fetish – is always 'thou' because there is no other option available.

> [T]he idea of chance is absent from child thought before the age of 7–8. Before this date, the world is conceived as an assemblage of willed and well-regulated actions and intentions, which leave no room for fortuitous and, as such, inexplicable events. Everything can be justified; we need only to appeal to an arbitrary factor, which is not the equivalent of chance but resembles rather the whim of all-powerful wills.[1]

Everything is of one substance, one order, one nature; or, if not *one*, everything certainly participates in a single fused sequence of substances, orders and natures that intuitive reason is incapable of distinguishing. That is why, in intuitive mythologies, the dead may need to be provided with bread for the afterlife, but symbols of bread – images and pictures of loaves on the walls of the tomb or a model loaf placed by the coffin – will not only do just as well as the real thing but are materially indistinguishable from the real thing.[2]

So intuitive activity is empirical, but it is so far from empiricist in any principled or methodological sense as to totally corrupt its objects and world with subjective prejudices. Not only are the things that surround intuitive reason and the events in which it is embroiled interpreted in very limited terms, but implicitly at least they are interpreted as though they possessed a subjectivity that is really proper to intelligence alone. Thus, intuitive cultures rest on superstition, talismans and ritual, traditional and charismatic authority prevails in intuitive political systems, and there is a general tendency for intuitive wisdom to express itself through a fusion of empirical and irrational (eg, mythic) elements. This places intelligence in a singularly precarious position:

> Magic on the ontological plane, and conviction without proof on the logical; participation in the realm of being, and 'transduction' in that of reasoning are thus the two converging products of the same phenomenon. At the root both of magic and conviction without proof lie the same egocentric illusions, namely confusion between one's own thought and that of others and confusion between the self and the external world.[3]

This tendency to project reveals a more subtle side when considered in terms of intuitive reason's corruption of the various dialectics of internalisation and externalisation that govern the development of intelligence as a whole. For example, one of the critical problems of self and other is the question of how one grasps one's own place in the universe. To answer this question it is helpful (although not necessary, as a certain breed of idealist would kindly remind us)

---

[1] Piaget (1928: 254). As always, specific dates have been qualified by later research. However, research continues to support Piaget's general point.

[2] Frankfort *et al.* (1949: 71ff).

[3] Piaget (1928: 168). See also Vygotsky (1962: 52ff).

to answer the question of where the boundaries between self and not-self actually lie. Intuitive reason's shortcomings lead it to mislocate these boundaries quite fundamentally, but even magic is still an earnest attempt to make sense of the universe.

> Among the Lobedu, just as of course among other Bantu people, witches and sorcerers, so far from playing the role of unreason, make a rational contribution to the fulfilment of men's need and purposes. This is almost immediately evident when we remember that witchcraft and sorcery are explanations of evil in the universe. They enable men to account for their failures and frustrations. Moreover, since the evil operates only through the medium of human beings, it can also be brought under human control. The parts assigned to these characters, the witches and sorcerers, presuppose a just world, ordered and coherent, in which the evil is not merely outlawed but can be overcome by man-made techniques. In the result men feel secure and the moral order is upheld.[1]

But, good intentions notwithstanding, the boundaries are still decidedly misplaced. For example, all magical activity seems to involve the replacement of a train of material causes capable of achieving a desired result by the 'modal' aspects of the same actions – with their 'could', 'should' and 'would'. That is, rather than achieving the desired result by objective means, a set of suitable 'intermediaries' – ie, ancillary subjects – equipped with the right powers and the right 'attitude' are called into action. Simplest of all, one may have no real sense of self, with the world a 'paradise of archetypes'. In the *Iliad*, for example, the elemental moods, experiences and actions that burgeon throughout are only knitted together by divinely inspired impulses: the Homeric individual is definitely not the captain of his soul.[2] Beyond that there is the identification of the individual subject with the objects with which they are directly associated:

> Of course, under simple economic conditions the articles thus owned by an individual were in most cases also made or collected by him or obtained by some simple form of exchange. They are in fact regarded as part of his personality and are quite naturally buried with him.[3]

Indeed, if 'know thyself' can be taken as one motto of reason as a whole (perhaps as the middle term between 'create thyself' and 'transcend thyself'), intuitive reasoning is as devoid of self-knowledge as an intelligent being can be. As

---

[1] Krige, 'The social function of witchcraft', in Marwick (1970: 237).

[2] Adkins in Strong (1992: 25–46); Snell (1960: 31–2). Snell tracks (in quite different terms, of course) the gradual transformation of intuitive reasoning among the Greeks (Snell, 1960: 227–30). However, note that, as Adkins puts it, 'a course of action said to be planned, caused, or instigated by a god, or prophesied by an oracle is nonetheless, when the actions are described in detail, and evaluated, attributed to the human being who performed it; and certainly no warrior society could afford to allow the excuse for cowardice that a god had caused it, or would wish to diminish the credit for success on these grounds' (Strong, 1992: 34). Magical beliefs are likewise often compatible with a straightforwardly naturalistic *how*, concentrating instead on *why* an action or event turned out as it did.

[3] Childe (1963: 70). See also Hewes in Quiatt and Itani (1994: 59–93) for instances and for the general level of social and economic organisation to which such activity corresponds.

with the tendency of young children to vest inanimate objects and favourite toys with a false subjectivity or the analogous tendency of undeveloped religions to treat inanimate forces (rivers, volcanoes, winds, the sea, and so on) as intelligent beings in their own right, it is a universal trend for intuitive reason to project an imaginary subjectivity onto the most diverse objects, up to and including mythological accounts of the universe as a whole.

It is important to be clear why this is happening. The key shortcoming of any immature form of intelligence is its inability to distinguish between the proper nature of an object and the incidental resemblances its appearances and actions create. Exactly what distinction it is that intelligence fails to make depends on its current stage of development. In the present case, it may well be that a storm is a meteorological process, not a moral agent, but intuitive reason, which is unable to articulate internal structures of *any* kind, rational *or* physical, is unlikely to draw any such distinction. On the other hand, when intuitive reason fails to make this distinction, it is not because it is mistaken about the facts or even that it *cannot* make such distinctions. Rather, in the absence of a more mature intelligence to make the necessary differences explicit, it simply does not realise that these differences mean anything.[1]

The consequences of this are familiar enough. For example, given that we cannot help but construct objects in terms of the structures in terms of which we ourselves act (for that is what acting is – constructing objects), the fact that intuitive reason does not even realise how its own activity is structured means that it can scarcely avoid attributing to all its objects a nature barely distinguishable from its own. Conversely, as far as intuitive reason is concerned, the human role in the universe is not to observe or even merely to take account of the forces which regulate natural events, but to play an active role in the drama, through prayer, ritual, sacrifice, and so on.

> It is one of the tenets of mythopoeic logic that similarity and identity merge; 'to be like' is as good as 'to be'. Therefore, by being like, by enacting the role of, a force of nature, a god, a man could in the cult enter into and clothe himself with the identity of these powers, with the identity of the gods, and through his own actions, when thus identified, cause the powers involved to act as he would have them act.[2]

Even time, space, substance and causality are interpreted in strictly personalised terms or in terms of the subject's own activity. On the purely cognitive plane, this is expressed by the topological nature of the space within which intuitive reason operates – a space determined in terms of proximity, order, inclusion, separation, continuity, discontinuity, and so on.[3] Such a space cannot account for or maintain distances, angles, or even shapes in the face of quite elementary distortions generated by changes of perspective or action. And on the social level, the anthropological literature makes its very clear that time,

---

[1] On the central role played by differentiation in the development of intelligence, see Smith (1993).

[2] Thorkild Jacobsen in Frankfort *et al.* (1949: 215).

[3] Eg, Cole, Gay and Glick in Berry and Dasen (1974: 159-195).

space, substance and causality are imbued with social and symbolic significance.

> Time is seen not so much as measuring the distance between past, present and future as, on the contrary, linking them all together in eternity. Continuity overrides succession. Thus on some occasions Dogon smiths work together in groups of three. A child, an old man and an adult belonging to the same caste each strike the anvil in turn. By these strokes they link together the present, the past and the future represented in each of them. This repetitive rhythm is that of the myth...[1]

Events are judged in terms of meanings and intentions, not their objective properties. That is why intuitive reason personalises the sun, the sky, the earth, and so on,[2] why simple societies construct time in terms of village layouts, tribal structures and practical routines rather than as an independent objective natural process, and so on. Ritual meaning – the meaning of projected but inarticulate subjectivity – is frequently the highest form of meaning available at this stage.

So it is unsurprising that all the main theories of prehistoric art – as totemic symbolism, as hunting magic, as props for rites of passage, as shamanic expressionism, and so on – assume this type of explanation. For example, the origins of the universe may be interpreted in terms of the sexual union of primeval deities and the causes of personal illnesses are sought in mysterious yet all too practical witchcraft.[3] On the pre-classical stage, mysterious places fall under the spell of their *genius loci*, natural forces are again personified, heroes and sprites frolic in the hills, and 'storms, lightning and earthquakes were not considered the inevitable outcome of impersonal, natural forces, but mighty feats, willed by the gods'.[4] Indeed, 'Every cave and mountain top was sacred; any snake could be a dead relative or a guardian, or bird a manifestation of a deity; every stream, river, copse and settlement had its presiding deity or deities – even individual trees and rocks could be sacred'.[5] Unless you are an Archimedes or an Anaxagoras, natural events are omens and cosmogony and cosmology are simply the family history of the gods.[6]

In summary, intuitive reason proceeds from – and never quite overcomes – the blandest notion of identity. Although it will elaborate this notion to the utmost, it will never quite shake off the limitations it imposes. If there are any 'higher' structures to the universe, intuitive reason can neither detect nor deal with them. It is equally helpless to grasp its own nature. Not only is it incapa-

---

[1] Rouland (1994: 155).

[2] Frankfort *et al.* (1949: 23–36; Hallpike (1979: Ch.7). See also Whitrow (1989) for the early development of temporal concepts.

[3] Lindberg (1992: 6–13).

[4] Lindberg (1992: 24). The main current theories of prehistoric art and religion are summarised in Dickson (1990: 123ff and *passim*). For the psychogenetic and cognitive aspects of animism, see any of countless Piagetian and post-Piagetian sources, beginning with Piaget (1928). For its anthropological expressions, see Douglas (1966), and again any of a wide range of texts on superstition, magic and ritual.

[5] Waterfield (1989: 20).

[6] Cassirer (1944: 3–4, 13).

ble of being fully effective even on its own terms but it cannot account for, judge or justify even the activities in which it does happen to succeed. So far are intuitive acts and objects from the organised complexity of the truly simple that they can only be described as trivial. Hence the excruciatingly prosaic nature of this most perfectly naïve of agency. And hence not only much of its charm but also the patronising attitude a more sophisticated intelligence is almost bound to adopt to an intuitive child: who could stand idly by and watch a 3-year-old flounder about putting on her socks and not lend a hand?

Before history

The social implications of these foibles are just as radical. In particular, the inability to locate things and events in terms of enduring or overt relationships entails that the very distinction between the social, the interpersonal and the psychic cannot be articulated. As a result, truly social structures cannot be assembled or managed. Nor can there be a balanced assessment of such relationships as do exist, for no matter how regular they may be in practice, they are typically eclectic, conventional, pragmatic and, of course, implicit.

For example, given intuitive reason's inability to manage either sameness or difference with any insight or intentionality, even in connection with a single object, how much less can it draw social distinctions like 'friend or foe' correctly, such that both terms retain a positive meaning and lead to opposite but appropriate and related responses. Instead it is limited to pseudo-pairs such as 'Greek' (ie, civilised) and 'barbarian' (ie, not civilised). Only one term has any substance or value, the other being used solely as a marker for something lacking. Likewise, in how many languages, from ancient Egyptian to various Amerindian tongues, is the name of my people also the word for 'human beings'? Perhaps that is why (as Benveniste claimed) the primary meaning of the concept 'free' in early Indo-European languages 'is not, as we might be tempted to imagine, "released from something"; it refers to membership of an ethnic stock described by a metaphor taken from plant growth. This membership confers a privilege which is unknown to the alien and the slave'.[1]

Hence also the lack of practical differentiation between social functions. Indeed, the simplest societies are not organised in terms of 'functions' at all: intentional organisation in terms of regular specialists, functionaries, mechanisms and processes only begins quite late in intuitive reason. In the simplest groups, not only are ritual, leadership, combat, economic activity and so on all the responsibility of individuals identified by very global empirical features such as membership of a particular age group or sex, but there is no real differ-

---

[1] Quoted in Meillassoux (1991: 23). Meillassoux observes that 'Because of their alien origins, slaves were permanently relegated to the category of beings of different and naturally inferior *species*: tolerated if they kept their distance, rejected if they showed the slightest desire to identify themselves with "humans"' (1991: 75) – or indeed to possess a positive status of any kind. This naturally made the status of educated slaves, particularly those with significant social roles and responsibilities (as teachers, administrators and so on), extremely equivocal and even threatening.

ence between art, war, religion and work themselves.[1] In both respects, little
specifically social definition or organisation of these 'functions' is discernible.

This is especially clear when a critical social activity such as warfare is analysed in any detail. Intuitive societies lack the ability to create an explicit and
objectively structured organisation for war, including an effective central
command, trained, specialised and disciplined troops, a plan of campaign organised into phased tactical movements and engagements, and logistical support. As a result, they are rarely capable of using war as an instrument for real
social or political policy or conducting extended campaigns aimed at objectives
more far-reaching and enduring than plunder, glory and vengeance.[2] Conversely, experts in seamlessly welding together the various elements are likely
to be looked upon as possessing magical powers.[3] Of course, more sophisticated social systems will also seek to obscure the boundaries between different
areas of activity and meaning – how else can we explain advertising's passion
for bogus associations? – and we still attribute genius to artists, scientists and
others whose talents we find baffling; but for intuitive reason, such fusions are
intrinsic to social activity of all kinds.

In summary, in the absence of well-defined, objective structures and controls, embodied in independent social roles, organisations and institutions, a
society can only exist to the extent that it is constantly created and re-created
by its members' personal actions. Under intuitive reason:

> ... the connection between material flow and social relations is reciprocal. A spe-
> cific social relation may constrain a given movement of goods, but a specific
> transaction... suggests a particular social relation. If friends make gifts, gifts make
> friends... Thus do primitive societies transcend the Hobbesian chaos. For the in-
> dicative condition of primitive society is the absence of a public and sovereign
> power: persons and (especially) groups confront each other not merely as distinct
> interests but with the possible inclination and certain right to physically prosecute
> those interests. Force is decentralised, legitimately held in severalty, the social
> compact has yet to be drawn, the state non-existent. So peacemaking is not a spo-
> radic, intersocietal event, it is a continuous process going on within society itself.
> Groups must 'come to terms' – the phrase notably connotes a material exchange
> satisfactory on both sides.[4]

---

[1] Hallpike (1986) provides examples and analysis.

[2] Hallpike (1986: 101ff).

[3] See, for example, Gell in Coote and Shelton (1992: 40–63).

[4] Sahlins (1974: 186–7). See Douglas and Isherwood (1996) and Appadurai (1986) for
further instances. Meillassoux (1981, 1991) provides a powerful materialist account of
the earlier steps and wider ramifications in the development of exchange. Hallpike
(1979, 2004) reviews the relationship between social and cognitive development of 'atomistic societies', while Crook (1980: especially ch. 8) gives a broad but concise account
of some of the main features of intuitive reason at the social and psychic levels, though
not presented in those terms. Rappoport (1967) provides a widely discussed case study
of the pragmatic control of social relationships through rituals of exchange. The parallel
embodiment of social relationships in cultural artefacts and the physical layout and
operation of villages has been a commonplace topic for anthropologists, especially
structuralists, ever since the classic work of Durkheim and Mauss (Durkheim and

Such a structure, by means of which the egalitarian ethos of hunter-gatherer societies is constantly replicated and enforced, uses overt and conspicuous exchange to embody in social practice the very regularity intuitive reason cannot take for granted. Conversely, unduly ostentatious or miserly individuals may be subject to personal sanctions, from ostracism to accusations of witchcraft.[1] However, because it relies on constant direct re-affirmation, it is extremely limited in its effectiveness, as the 'tragedy of the commons' illustrates: for want of a true system of authoritative checks and balances built into social relationships and standing over and above particular interests or local events, an intuitive 'system' is always liable to descend into exploitation, resentment, conflict and reprisal.[2] Hence the need for codes of politeness whereby peoples such as the !Kung San ask permission before using resources currently under others' control. That such codes exemplify an intuitive society's need for constant practical affirmation rather than the special social sensibility often attributed to simple societies is suggested by the fact that permission is always forthcoming. This shows that this is really a practical technique for organising how access is managed, not a test of whether one is polite enough to ask for or give permission or even a real occasion for deciding whether or not to grant access.

This lack of inherent social structure is expressed in the absence of even the most rudimentary political or administrative apparatus. To return momentarily to the topic of warfare, war in intuitive societies is *not* an extension of politics by other means, not least because they contain little we would call politics in the first place. Although there is no lack of social change, much of it quite intentional, the decision to effect a change does not rely on truly social instruments already present in the social structure, for there are none.[3] But then it needs none, since the level of organisation, of production especially, requires only the slightest degree of organisation, which individuals can debate and modify as they see fit through changes in their personal activity.

Other crucial elements of social activity are equally lacking in objective structure. If there is a division of labour it rests on individual differences in skill and personal cooperation, not on an analytical breakdown and organisation of work. Foraging may be done collectively, but it is seldom organised other than by sharing knowledge of where the best pickings are to be found. Even a chief is likely to be 'seen as the cause of the group's desire to exist as a group, and not as the result of the need for a central authority felt by some al-

---

Mauss, 1963). See also Lévi-Strauss' accounts of the Bororo (Lévi-Strauss, 1963, 1984). For a further summary of the economic order at the intuitive stage, see Dickson (1990: 160–180).

[1] Hallpike (2004) rehearses a wide range of evidence and the many subtleties of moral life in 'atomistic' societies.

[2] Pearce (1995: ch. 1) makes a similar point about the relationship between 'open access' and 'common property' resources and the impact of each for human and environmental welfare even at a much higher level of development. However, in that case the lack of social order follows from the presence of a highly organised system of private property.

[3] Redfield (1953: ch. 5) and Nadel in Marwick (1970: 264–279).

ready established group',[1] and rules by persuasion, consent and example
rather than political authority. And so on. There is no reason to imagine that
the individuals involved are not cognitively or psychologically beyond intuitive reason, yet the resemblance between such a simple social structure and the
'collective monologue' of intuitive children at play is striking. At the lower
limit one might even find a society that is 'so truly simple that all I could find
was individual human beings'.[2]

Of course, even the simplest social units tend to take some advantage of the
benefits of social organisation, *ad hoc* and episodic though it might be. For example, the hunting of large game is generally organised and disciplined, and
even the least developed social structure has some system of inter-marriage
and exchange, plus periodic gatherings and dispersals, all serving to regulate
the larger social sphere, especially by sharing information on the current state
of the environment, providing access to spouses and economic resources and
conducting warfare. And with or without agriculture, such societies tend to be
sedentary or to move through regular seasonal cycles. Nevertheless, the entire
society may number no more than a few dozen individuals, fragmentation following from purely personal conflicts may be the norm, social occasions may
be literally years apart and at the lower end of intuitive reason such societies
may lack even regular ceremonial or leadership. Ceremony and leaders exist,
and do so in relatively consistent forms, but they are also wholly *ad hoc*, appearing as and when circumstances require. Leadership is by example, ceremony by inspiration, and both are simple, context-specific and spontaneous.[3]

Even more advanced forms of intuitive social and political organisation,
such as 'Big Man' societies, though clearly verging on regular structure and
organisation, still rely on the personal powers and charisma of individuals to
coordinate and direct the activity of society as a whole, especially in war, trade
and inter-clan and inter-lineage politics. They are still vulnerable to the whims
and vicissitudes of personality.[4]

> For in small-scale, face-to-face society the gulf between personal meanings and
> public meanings cannot develop; rituals are not fixed; discrepancy between the
> situation being enacted and the form of expression is immediately reduced by a
> change in the latter. Primitive jurisprudence sees no gap between law and moral-
> ity, because there are no written precedents and because small changes in the law

---

[1] Lévi-Strauss (1984: 407).

[2] Lévi-Strauss (1984: 416).

[3] Lévi-Strauss (1984) paints memorable cameos of such moments, while Johnson and
Earle (1987) provide more extended descriptions and analysis.

[4] Adkins in Strong (1992: 37–8 and 40) paints a comparable picture for archaic Greece,
emphasising the intuitive nature of a successful chief's personal charisma: '"strength-
and-bravery-and-wealth-leading-to-or-deserving-success", the hyphens indicating the
unitary and unanalysed nature of *arete* for Homeric man... Qualities of character, physical attributes, intellect, social position and "external goods"... are all confusedly com-
mended together', not to mention a very literal ability to 'make his presence felt'. Tacitus' *Germania* (Ch. 7) describes a similar state of affairs, which is summarised in *Beowulf*
in the words 'Behaviour that's admired is the path to power among people everywhere'
(transl. Seamus Heaney).

can be constantly made to express new moral situations and because such changes, being unrecorded, are unperceived. The idea of an immutable God-given law is in practice compatible with a changing legal situation.[1]

Conversely, while a recognised Big Man may wield recognised powers, his tenure is informal and limited by personal performance, not by any notion of birthright, legitimate authority or social contract. Furthermore, in contrast to the pre-defined and inherited status, office and powers of the highest forms of intuitive polity[2] (the chiefdom), a Big Man's position depends on personally amassing the necessary resources and following.

It is clear that such societies are clearly not just simple extensions of the family or hamlet, but represent nascent *social* structures. For example, they are usually based on clans which provide for a collective, supra-familial identity, and own collective resources (ceremonial and economic). They are not always co-residential, they often operate through largely nominal groupings whose real membership is defined by social participation (including assorted spirits, demons, and so on), and they contain numerous specialists. Yet these groups still come together and disperse according to the inspiration and powers of their leading lights, reflecting not only individual political and administrative skill but also personal generosity and bravery in battle and personal connections by marriage, exchange and alliance.

In short, the Big Man is a conduit representing the intuitive society as a whole, yet is neither above nor at one with the society itself. Nor can he exercise any more control than the structure of the home economy allows (by virtue of its storage requirements and productive technology, the structure of trade, and so on) or his society is prepared to confer on him. Often he cannot even bind it by his agreements. He is Big Man because he is a big man; he is not a big man because he is Big Man. He stands at the hub of society, not on top of it.

So even a relatively highly developed intuitive society is still a loose affiliation based on inter-personal relations, driven by pragmatic, eclectic and conventional concerns determined by empirical conditions and internal traditions rather than regular collective systems, mechanisms and processes. It is a *nascent* society, but not yet a true society with an independent social structure. Wenke has expressed very clearly how little integrity such a social structure possesses:

> Ethnographic studies tell us that hunter-forager groups often increase to a certain size level, then a fight develops among some members of the group, and the social unit splits, with some members going off into new territory. The long winter nights of north Asia doubtless offered ample opportunity to brood on what a jerk one's cousin was, and by tens of thousands of years of group-fissioning, population growth, and small group interactions, the world was populated.[3]

Of course, populating the planet is an impressive side-effect, but it must be emphasised that it is achieved solely because of intuitive reason's *in*ability to

---

[1] Douglas (1996: 2–3).
[2] Redfield (1953).
[3] Wenke (1990: 201–2).

create a social system that is rich and cohesive enough to maintain anything more than a few dozen individuals in a handful of loosely connected bands.

It must also be emphasised that simply spreading all over the world is not the same as achieving the practical domination (if not true dominion) of the globe we now take for granted. An intuitive level of social organisation tends to be accompanied by intuitive forms of politics, economics, culture, technology, ideology and science, which in turn prevent intuitive reason from achieving lasting or effective control over its natural environment. Although on the cognitive plane one has to wait only a few years before seeing intuitive reason's structural weaknesses overcome, on the historical plane the distance between the onset of intelligence and the final supersession of its intuitive stage must be measured in tens and hundreds of millennia. Hence intuitive reason's limitations explain not only the gradual occupation of most of the globe but also the specific patterns of occupation. To take only examples of truly global importance, why else were so many of the planet's greatest landmasses – including Australia, Russia and the Americas – civilised so slowly? Clearly intuitive reason's lack of scope and range is critical, not only in terms of its lack of social reach and resources but also because of its corresponding inability to overcome natural ecological constraints.

As far as Australia is concerned, the fluctuating width of the surrounding seas prevented any sustained inflow or contact, and the harsh environment kept in check the few human intruders' potential for further development. Or at least, so it did for the aboriginal tribes who first attempted it: as history illustrates, it would prove a substantially less difficult challenge for a society that was capable of post-intuitive levels of technology, economic management and political organisation. The north–south axis of the Americas, with its multiplicity of relatively narrow but sharply differentiated climates and environments, must likewise have inhibited the spread of staple crops, and so the formation of the high cultures for which such an environment would be much less of a challenge. Nor were the available cultivable plants or the very limited range of animals available for domestication in the Americas – the guanaco, the guinea pig and the turkey – capable of supporting urban civilisation on the scale of Old World societies, whose environment consisted very largely of vast east–west sweeps of broadly similar climate and ecology, and was populated by the ancestors of the modern-day pig, goat, sheep and cow.[1] Had the earliest inhabitants of America been more advanced socially, economically and technologically, however, this would certainly have been a less daunting problem.

As for Russia, the natural axis for trade, and so for the formation of settled states, was along the great rivers connecting the immense resources of Scandi-

---

[1] Davis (1987: ch. 6); Crosby (1986: 17ff). Crosby also argues that the near-integration of the world in the early modern period depended radically on the ecological similarity of all the various (but not very varied) 'neo-Europes'. On the environmental damage caused by identifying these neo-Europe with Europe itself, see McNeil (2000). Diamond (1999) describes many of the key issues, especially the ecological differences between the Old and New Worlds and the relative domesticability of their respective fauna and flora.

navia and the northern forests to the southern civilisations of the Mediterranean and Near East. But any political unit formed along this axis would sit astride the natural path of population movement (driven by yet other demographic and ecological forces) pouring westwards out of the steppes of central Asia and eastwards from central Europe. These forces operated along quite the opposite axis to that of any incipient state, and so for centuries horse tribes disrupted incipient Russian polities from the east, while hunters, displaced peasants and others performed an analogous role from the west. Hence the late emergence and precarious histories of substantial settlements and states in this region – again, for want of more than intuitive levels of social, economic, and technological resources.

Nor were these the only ecological factors influencing the occupation of the Earth. Weather conditions become more varied and extreme in rough proportion to their distance from the equator. Different geologies put quite different metals and minerals at the practical disposal of the local population. But the fact that such factors affected human history to the extent that they did is not independent of the level of development of the human beings and human societies involved. More advanced trade networks, more sophisticated mining technologies and a hundred other strictly rational (ie, post-intuitive) structures and controls would have transformed the situation out of all recognition – as, of course, they did as soon as they became available. Generally speaking it is only for less developed societies that most natural forces are critical. But the era of 'less developed societies' is, of course, the era of intuitive reason.

Not that the natural environment is *only* a problem for the least developed societies. Many of the problems described above persisted long after intuitive reason had quit the scene. This in turn reflects the need for even a post-intuitive intelligence to expend vast amounts of time, effort, thought and materials in building up the systems and resources needed to overcome such titanic environmental forces. But the formation of a post-intuitive level of intelligence at least ensures that such a process, which must of necessity take many generations and require the creation of cultural and technological instruments of immense capacity and sophistication, will at least be possible. However, until intuitive reason has indeed been superseded, the specifically *historical* nature of this process will preclude any such accumulation or development, and with it humanity's liberation from the constraints and limitations of its natural environment.

Nor is that historical process complete, even now. So the more radical environmental changes of the kind with which even industrial societies now seem to be faced may defeat us yet, and even without that, the wide swathes of the earth that are dominated by gigantic and impenetrable deserts, jungles and ice-caps remain largely uninhabited and, as far as we are concerned, uninhabitable. Even today few live beyond 55° from the equator – less than two thirds of the way to the poles. Indeed, we were well into the industrial revolution – in most cases well into the twentieth century – before even the most powerful societies ceased to be vulnerable to the natural calamities of failed harvests and epidemic diseases. Even at the opening of the twenty-first century, many of the world's peoples live under an almost daily threat of hunger and sickness. However, this reflects a factor of a quite different order: the sun's radiation and the resulting continental-scale weather systems, whose technological control or effective substitution we have yet to achieve on a sufficiently large scale to occupy the Earth in its entirety.

So we are not out of the woods yet. But then, if such forces could drive the post-intuitive history of continental landmasses, how much more prone must intuitive reason itself be to the natural conditions of its existence, be it at the level of population control or, even more obviously, the body?[1] Having said that, it is important to keep these ecological forces in proportion. Although vast, they should not be regarded as capable of cowing even the most undeveloped intelligence. Human beings have learned to survive in the most hostile conditions,[2] and not even the most primitive intelligence lacks real power and knowledge when compared with even the most capable of non-intelligent organisms. After all, the first humans into Australia and the Americas took only a few thousand years and only intuitive tools, techniques and organisation to slaughter practically every large mammal on three continents: not exactly a positive achievement by our more ecologically-minded standards, but impressive in its own fashion.[3] And yet, like an inexperienced juggler, intuitive reason finds it hard enough to keep everything in the air at once, without having to explain how it does it or putting in place the means to do it better. By preventing intelligence from grasping the full depth and complexity of its situation, this creates ample opportunity and scope for natural factors to play a substantial role.

All in all, one could scarcely imagine a more fertile question than that of how natural factors constrain and unleash the powers of human reason. Nevertheless, as the development of reason proceeds, it will become equally clear that those factors not only cease to trouble intelligence to anything like the same degree, but they quickly come to be dominated in their turn by the growing power of reason.[4]

Conclusions

If intuitive reasoning is not the last word in intelligence (on the contrary, it is literally the first), where does intelligence go next? It is clear that intuitive reason's key weakness is its inability to make explicit the structures, subjective,

---

[1] For the impact of biology on demography in early societies, see Crook (1980: especially ch. 8).

[2] Moran (2000) or, more discursively, Fernández-Armesto (2000).

[3] For a broader review of these mass extinctions, see Goudie (1992: 142–6). As Diamond (1999) points out, this massacre of practically every large mammal (if it is to be laid at the humanity's door) is also, ironically, a key reason for the difficulty human beings had in civilising these continents later, and the ease with which Europeans overwhelmed the indigenous peoples after 1492.

[4] For example, it should be emphasised that the reason why capitalist nations are so deeply obsessed with living space, physical access to remote markets and the control of natural resources has little to do with fear for their own ecological vulnerability, and a lot to do with the inherent expansionism of capitalist economies.

objective or worldly, that determine the nature and circumstances of its activity and the objects on which it acts, its consequent inability to *account for* the things and events it encounters and produces, and so to act in an insightful and critical, stable yet mobile, above all rational, manner. If it had only the least grasp of these structures, it would at least be able to make sense of at least the first tier of obstacles blocking its path, including those it puts in its own way.

On the other hand, lacking this insight, it is debarred from achieving any but purely empirical ends or from acting by any but purely conventional, pragmatic and eclectic means; from achieving true continuity, complexity, consistency; from defining, planning and prosecuting real goals; from verifying and validating its own actions; and so on. Conversely, for lack of the ability to recognise its own constructs *as* its own, its objects participate in its acts either in a purely one-dimensional yet constantly fluctuating manner or as undifferentiated 'things'. Their potential as structures in their own right remains all but unrecognised, except insofar as they can be made to create directly empirical effects or be directly adapted to intuitive reason's established (but largely unstated) custom and practice.

But the solution to all these problems is in intuitive reason's own gift, of course, and so long as it is allowed to develop its own inherent potential, the solution cannot help but be found. If a relationship is a unity of sameness and difference, and more specifically sameness *in* difference, then the first step in solving intuitive reason's problems is simply to externalise the various kinds of samenesses and differences that are implicit in the structures of activity already at its disposal. There is no doubt that intuitive reason will tend to do this, given that even the most mundane problems of everyday existence and of navigating its world will only be solved if it manages to generate further distinctions and refinements and sequences among its (still intuitive) objects. This differentiation and integration of samenesses and differences in the interests of constructing increasingly extended and elaborate objects cannot help but conclude in the internalisation of the relationship between the different kinds of sameness and difference.

The development of intuitive reason's primitive constructs into true relationships is thus the everyday corollary of their everyday application to everyday things and events. It requires no predestination, no 'programme' and no particular experience to make it happen; it happens because intuitive reason has both the specific nature, the general opportunities and the underlying openness that it has. But this development of intuitive reason is also its dissolution, for in constructing relationships proper, the strictly empirical constructs that were furnished by intuitive reason become the *objects* of intelligent activity as well as its subject.

This in turn creates the first intentionally intelligent acts, and thus the first *rationality* properly so called. By not only comprehending the resources at its disposal and the opportunities available to it but also learning to explicitly align things and events with its own interests and appetites, intelligence begins to know explicitly what it wants to achieve and begins to see explicitly how to achieve it; to define real goals and become capable of intentionally assessing its progress towards them; and generally to operate in a manner both advances more single-mindedly and is more sensitive to the content and context of its acts. Hence the fulfilment of intuitive reason in the supersession of intuitive reason's amorphous logic of *identity* with a more definite notion of *concreteness*. With that, *intuitive* reason is replaced by *concrete* reason.

In sum, then, intuitive reason begins with intelligence at a level where it is scarcely distinguishable from, and sometimes (on the individual plane) markedly inferior to, a complex organic structure. But then, empirically speaking, Copernicus' heliocentric model did not perform any better than its Ptolemaic predecessor, yet it contained the germ of a conceptual structure that would eventually supersede geocentrism in every way. What is more, it ushered in a critical and insightful attitude to knowledge (and, indirectly, power) that, in the hands of Bacon, Kepler, Bruno, Galileo and innumerable unsung heroes and martyrs of science, would uproot irrational authoritarianism. Immediate performance is neither the only nor the most significant measure of the value of greater competence.

Meanwhile, intuitive reason begins with intelligence totally oblivious of itself, so totally helpless to guide its own destiny and development that it is only by constantly reminding oneself of the higher reaches towards which it is unwittingly moving that one can feel at all reassured about its future. Nevertheless, intuitive reason marks the parting of the ways for biology and intelligence. At this stage above all, the biological conditions of and constraints on intelligence's existence must be respected, but already the former no longer *explain* the latter in any significant way. There is still, it is true, an immense distance to go before intelligence is entirely freed from all biological limitations (the journey is still far from complete even for the readers of this book), but the road is open, and only intelligence can divert itself from its goal.

3. Concrete Reason

The principle of identity is perhaps, out of all logical 'principles', the one which remains the least identical with itself in the course of development.

J. Piaget and G. Voyat[1]

But now the Great Tao is disused and eclipsed. The world (the empire) has become a family inheritance. Men love only their own parents and their own children. Valuable things and labour are used only for private advantage. Powerful men, imagining that inheritance of estates has always been the rule, fortify the walls of towns and villages, and strengthen them with ditches and moats. 'Rites' and 'righteousness' are the threads upon which they hang the relations between ruler and minister, father and son, elder and younger brother, and husband and wife. In accordance with them they regulate consumption, distribute land and dwellings, raise up men of war and 'knowledge'; achieving all for their own advantage. Thus selfish schemings are constantly arising, and recourse is had to arms; thus it was that the Six Lords... obtained their distinction... This is the period called the Lesser Tranquillity.

Record of Rites[2]

The logic of concrete reason

Piaget: Do you think that Pythagoras' theorem is necessary in our representations in the same way as it was for the first men who thought of it?

Mauss: No. There is a great difference, and it is easy to describe. Human thought has gone from a completely symbolic and empirical representation to demonstration, geometry, and reasoned experience. All knowledge of the first rests on the authority of the symbol; when the authority of reason comes to be added, it is a great stride forward.[3]

With intuitive reason's formation of a sense of identity, one of the central pillars of intelligence is established. However, the specific form of identity actu-

---

[1] Quoted in Smith (1993: 90).

[2] Quoted by Joseph Needham in Porter and Teich (1986: 63). See also Needham (1969: 253–267).

[3] Piaget (1995: 246).

ally available to intuitive reason is so unconvincing that it is all but impossible to see any special merit in it, especially when it is contrasted with the throng of deft and powerful structures offered by organic nature. Although it is possible to make a strong theoretical case for the view that even intuitive reason represents a qualitative advance over any organic structure,[1] the resemblance between them is still too close for comfort. One cannot simply brush aside the claim that, given the practical continuities between the life-strategies of human hunter-gatherers, social primates and more distant species still, such a distinction is merely a nicety: intuitive reason seems to possess scarcely any of that higher vision or spirituality which allegedly marks out human nature from its organic forebears.

Still, the dialectic of structural and functional conflicts and contradictions that drives the development of intelligence as a whole marches on. With the supersession of intuitive reason, the scope of this dialectic now passes beyond strictly implicit controls and into forms of activity grounded in the interplay of subject, object and world as such. From this point onwards, the empirical and somatic planes serve as no more than signs, instruments and opportunities for the interaction of truly abstract intelligent structures such as classes, series, systems, and so on. They embody and are incorporated by intelligence and are certainly more than epiphenomena, but they are no longer the true nexus of intelligent activity properly so called. From this point onwards, except insofar as concrete reason itself extends, revises and enriches them in pursuit of its own agenda, intuitive reason's constructs are now taken for granted. In later stages, even this equivocal attachment to the empirical will be abandoned.

This change of focus radically redefines the nature of activity. Concrete reason's increasingly explicit mastery of the supra-empirical transformations and continuities that informed intuitive reason only implicitly and pragmatically enables it to take active control of a more or less orderly and continuous stream of processes and products, rather than merely juggling a disjointed succession of empirical things and events. That is why concrete reason, unlike intuitive reason, is entitled to be called a form of reason in its own right – because it can give, and is motivated by, reasons. The clash of sameness and difference that so bedevilled intuitive reason is supplanted by an array of structures, processes and mechanisms for which the interplay of sameness and difference represents an opportunity or perhaps a challenge, but seldom a threat.

This is because concrete reason's advance on the raw identity of the intuitive stage is *equivalence.* The concept of equivalence (and its reciprocal, non-equivalence) is far from answering exactly the question of the relationship between things or events, but it does at least offer a framework within which to deal with sameness and difference in a more explicit and orderly way. Likewise for the many other forms of relating that start to be explicated, stabilised and mobilised at this stage, such as boundary, scale, set, part, break, axis and so on: such notions were always available to intuitive reason, but it could never make positive use of them to form, explore and transform its world. Now, however, this interplay forms the very basis of activity, and whole new connec-

---

[1] Megarry (1995: 231ff).

tions start to appear, such as complementarity, conjunction, inversion and classification. Consequently, concrete reason's actions may be both as constructive and as destructive as ever, but now their constructiveness and destructiveness are placed at intelligence's direct and deliberate disposal.

For example, concrete reason is as capable as intuitive reason ever was of anathematising barbarians in the name of civilisation. However, it finds the purely negative definition of barbarism offered by intuitive ideologies (ie, the barbarians' lack of Greekness) increasingly unsatisfactory, making creditable or even effective action increasingly difficult. The higher rationality of relationships demands a *positively* barbarous object to which to relate, rather than just an image to smash out of hand. This in turn requires concrete reason to objectify its enemies before destroying them, to think up good reasons (or at least plausible excuses) for enslaving or massacring them, and so on.[1] The (internal) barbarians may even acquire the status of 'loyal opposition'. In other words, even the most effective action must be seen to be governed by a rule (of some kind) before it can be considered a success.

On the other hand, this higher rationality also permits concrete reason to think up and rationalise the most exquisitely vile means to this particular end. Still, at least it is now necessary to apprehend the barbarians' nature and values for their own sake, to explain in just what sense they are barbarous and in what respects they are the same as and different from oneself, and to show why they merit obliteration, before actually obliterating them. Perhaps the resulting pictures of civility and barbarity are not yet two pictures of a common humanity (a genuinely *systematic* notion, reserved for a still higher stage of development), but at least the simplistic denigration of those who are merely 'not one of us' becomes harder. And so one of the more barbarous aspects of civilisation's treatment of barbary begins to be civilised.[2]

Similar distinctions between empirical surfaces and underlying structures quickly come to be drawn in other areas, although concrete reason does not quite force intelligence from its empirical or functional grounding. The universal concern with divination threw up any number of now explicit methods, tools and techniques for detecting and interpreting patterns and correspondences, but it did not lead to any genuine systematisation operating independently of its empirical content. Horoscopes, alchemy or the geomancy of *feng shui* were as firmly attached to convention, to pragmatism and to empirical experience as to any belief in other-worldly powers. In physics and medicine too, intuitive reason's focus on a balance of static substances (such as Thales' and his successors' identification of fire, earth, air and water) reflects an entirely characteristic failure to distinguish between the *empirical* surfaces of things and events and the *structures* that govern their respective natures and relationships, and when these structures are eventually elaborated by concrete reason, it is by differentiation and integration and by the additional insights to

---

[1] Archer (1988).

[2] On the Greek dramatists' discovery of *humanitas*, see Snell (1960: 124–7, 250–1). On their portrayal of exploitative social relationships, especially slavery, see Wiles in Archer (1988: 53–67).

which this elaboration leads. Hence Anaximenes' focus on diversity and Heraclitus' prioritisation of change itself. This is more than mere complication: it is the injection of a more relational order into the elements themselves. Hence the bifurcation of the classical ontology into an infinitude of empirical *objects*. such as Democritus' atoms, and the various *principles* that explain those objects, such as (in the Greek case) the analysis of fire into 'hot and dry', water into 'cold and wet', and so on. It is this double shift that eventually expresses itself in, on the one hand, the division between scientific systems and methods, and on the other, more sophisticated physical and medical concepts.[1]

A broadly analogous transition that is even more widely observed is the way in which early economic systems obtain their wealth from the possession of specific materials (natural or manufactured), whereas the accelerating and multiplying effects of trade come only once regular trading *relationships* dominate the occasional and *ad hoc* demands for particular articles of trade. Only then – in practice, when not only luxuries but a multiplicity of utilitarian goods and services are routinely obtained through exchange – does the market principle take command and economic activity really take off.[2]

An alternative way of describing this growing command of relationships would be to say that intuitive reason's carefully nurtured but hitherto largely hidden constructs are now placed directly at intelligence's disposal. As a result, they can be either repeated precisely or adapted to circumstances (empirically at least) – both abilities beyond intuitive reason. They become, in Piaget's terms, 'operational'. Or perhaps one should say, intelligence itself is placed at intelligence's disposal, at least in certain limited ways. In particular, the *relationships* whereby concrete reason manages diversity, transformation and change are constructs developed by intuitive reason and internalised *as* concrete reason itself, as the explicit and intentional form of what had previously been the strictly implicit basis of practical activity.

This grasp of relationships allows concrete reason to stand back far enough from its intuitions to deliberate on their execution, to compare and reconcile them, and ultimately to coordinate them all into a single, ongoing process. It also allows them to undo its actions in an intentional and explicit manner – to makes its actions 'reversible', as Piaget has it.[3] In short, by the definition of rationality already given, concrete reason is the first form of intelligence (or of activity of any kind) that is truly *rational*. If a rational act is one that knows itself to be that act and is that act by virtue of that knowledge, here at last is a form of rationality worthy of the name.

The importance of making the forms of activity through which a concrete rational intelligence achieves its results overt, explicit and increasingly articulate is easy to see. For example, the ability to *justify* an action is not necessary if

---

[1] On the development of Greek medical theories, see Lloyd (1979). A modern chemist might be more inclined to liken the Greek 'elements' to the physical phases of matter – solid earth, liquid water, gaseous air, plus energetic fire – than to chemical elements as we now think of them (Williams and Fraústo da Silva, 1996: 3–7).

[2] Hodges (1989). For an extended account of the British case, see Wrightson (2002).

[3] On Piagetian operations and reversibility, see Smith (1993: 58ff and *passim*).

practical success is your highest criterion. But if you cannot say why you acted as you did, then why should I believe that you were not simply lucky, or that you could do it again? Why, for that matter, should *you* believe it? Empirical success does not always require true knowledge, and even true knowledge is not always necessary or even valid knowledge: there is no shortage of truths that are believed for all the wrong reasons. For example, relatively of those who 'believe in', say, Darwinism or Marxism could give a correct exposition of their respective hero's theories. But continued and enduring success normally does presuppose some kind of truth, *guaranteed* success most certainly does require some kind of necessity, and justification is certainly necessary if one is to have confidence in one's abilities, plans and achievements.[1] In short, the intentionality with which concrete reason proceeds is quite different from that of intuitive reason, even if its outward performance is not always markedly superior.

Of course, intuitive reason was already intentional *activity*, for it was based on perfectly valid forms of subject, object and world. But with concrete reason this intentionality extends to the control of these specifically intelligent structures. With that, intelligence becomes capable of comprehending not only the sensory and motor aspects of its objects but also specific aspects of their internal natures, for its relationship to them, for their relationships to one another, for how it constructs them, and so on. Or at least, it can do all this insofar as the objects in question can be comprehended at the level of direct relationships. In comparison with the wealth of abstract, hypothetical, nominal, counterfactual and possible worlds formal reason will later take for granted, this is a decidedly small subset of things and events, so clearly this is by no means activity at its ripest.

Indeed, only during the dialectical stage in the development of intelligence, when the dialectic of internalisation and externalisation itself becomes the direct basis of action, will activity become *intentionally* rational. Only then will intelligence fully apprehend what it means to say that rationality is activity that knows itself to be that activity and is that activity by virtue of that knowledge. Only then will intelligence grasp the real relationship between power and knowledge and proceed in the full expectation that it will constantly transcend itself. Even formal reason, left entirely to its own devices, cannot grasp this level of activity. It is fully capable of intentional rationality in the sense that it recognises that it is employing genuine abstractions of universal application, but it has the greatest difficulty in imagining that the nature of rationality itself is not fixed. And one step further back, concrete reason is capable of *intentional* intelligence as described above – which is to say, of rationality in its simplest sense. But that is only to say that it is only capable of grasping the simplest relationships, and so *in*capable of comprehending them as a totality in their own right. Just as intuitive reason's sense of identity is singularly primitive, so concrete reason's powers of intelligent action (not least its powers of criticism and insight) are singularly limited. All the same, it's a start.

---

[1] On the distinction between empirical, true and necessary knowledge, see Smith (1993: 62ff and *passim*).

All those innovations flow from a single source, namely concrete reason's ability to abstract the internal structure of activity from the crudely empirical level of intuitive things and events, and so to comprehend the relationships that constitute and are constituted by these structures. This allows it to deal with them in a more or less coherent and consistent manner. From the standpoint of intuitive reason, it is a formidable, indeed unimaginable, achievement. On the other hand, this revolutionary constancy is still hemmed in by, if no longer reduced to, the here and now. Even if it is no longer totally dominated by objects it can literally see or get its hands on, neither is it quite able to liberate itself from them. A stable command of particular relationships allows concrete reason to adopt a consistent attitude to a particular object and to construct a process of change as a single, stable object, but that does not yet permit it to reflect on the structures through which it *manages* this feat, as distinct from actually managing the feat itself, or to grasp the yet higher structures that regulate the objective relationships it *can* comprehend. If relationships constitute concrete reason, concrete reason does not constitute relationships. It possesses them, but it is not their direct producer, as formal reason will be. That is a skill it has yet to acquire. To adopt Lévi-Strauss' invaluable term, concrete reason is a natural *bricoleur*.[1] At least at the beginning, relationships occur to it entirely out of the blue.

In that respect, of course, its relationship to its relationships is exactly the same as intuitive reason's relationship to its intuitions, and the metaphor of the juggler can be applied here too, though on a slightly more abstract plane. Although it is much more in command of particular objects, until concrete reason *can* make sense of the relationships it uses to make sense of its objects, clearly it cannot sustain a single coherent, consistent attitude to *all* its objects, and so to its *world* or to objects *as such*. So at that level, intelligence is still juggling. It still lacks a single explicit overarching structure capable of uniting the relationships responsible for all the otherwise perfectly real advances it does achieve. Conversely, it is incapable of unravelling the actual from the essential or particular relationships from overarching principles. So although capable, as intuitive reason never was, of explaining itself, at least within the framework of current conditions, it cannot speculate on matters that presuppose the arrangement of the relationships at its disposal into an integrated system, such as purely hypothetical or abstract or counterfactual cases. There is thus a residue of prejudice, not to say ineradicable structural flaw in concrete reason, which places stringent limits on its grasp of things. Even if it has overcome the fleeting quality of intuitive reason, its world view is still shallow, unbending, episodic and one-dimensional.

So, just as it is its introduction of relationships into its objects that makes concrete reason concrete, it is its inability to transcend particular relationships that makes it *merely* concrete. It might even be said (though I will not labour the point) that, because it cannot quite extricate itself from empirical instances, it can never quite rise above the level of pragmatic 'reasonableness' and arrive at reason proper. Although straightforward actions can generally be repeated

---

[1] Lévi-Strauss (1972: 16ff and *passim*).

precisely, they cannot be repeated *accurately* with contents and contexts whose empirical surfaces are deceptive. The rationality of concrete reason is always obliged to subordinate itself to things and events rather than *vice versa*, so it cannot quite claim the accolade of unequivocal and self-sufficient rationality.

True, its entire development will consist of struggling to overcome this limitation, and left to its own devices it will certainly succeed in this endeavour, little though it is aware of it at the time. Yet, considered *as* concrete reason, it is doomed to failure. On the one hand, it will exhaust concrete reason's entire resources to reach this goal, and on the other, the process whereby this higher structure is developed presupposes a further cycle of internalisation precisely analogous to that performed when concrete reason superseded intuitive reason. But that is only to say that, to resolve the paradoxes of concrete reason requires the transcendence of concrete reason's own essential character. Concrete reason can only realise its inmost potential by abandoning its inmost nature.

So its initial lack of an integrating structure deprives concrete reason of a unified or uniform standpoint from which to assess one relationship in terms of another, or to articulate or rationalise itself. Over and above its ability to maintain a more or less constant perspective on particular situations and specific issues – an ability that follows simply from assimilating things and events to the same relationship over and over again – concrete reason finds it impossible to create a consistent 'world view'. Indeed, as it starts out, it can only just sustain a consistent position of any kind. It can, for example, itemise and enumerate its objects in terms of particular categories and orders, but it has no autonomous grasp of quality or quantity as such: its measures are now vectors rather than scalars, but it lacks the overarching *mathematical* framework that would allow it to explicate and elaborate the vectors as a whole. Likewise it can perform binary comparisons along various dimensions, but this hardly constitutes a general *logic* of things or concepts. That would require it not merely to construe its empirical constructs empirically – the natural upshot of the development of intuitive reason – but also to construct a still higher system of relationships among the resulting relationships.

Like intuitive reason's objects, concrete reason's relationships function, if not strictly in isolation, then certainly in an undifferentiated and unarticulated manner. Certainly they are not truly discrete or distinct. As it cannot grasp them independently of their expression in things and events, they cannot be objectified in their own right. Consequently, they cannot be grasped with real objectivity or placed at reason's disposal until the stage as a whole reaches its climax. At the beginning of concrete reason, they are merely data, known empirically (ie, externally) rather than rationally (ie, internally). Only very slowly will these data be worked up into concrete facts, information, knowledge, wisdom and, at the very apogee of the stage, a kind of concrete truth. To cite just one outstanding instance of a universal issue:

> Thus it seems that a clear acknowledgement of a distinct cognitive ability... seems to be missing in pre-Socratic thought, though we find antecedents of it. Aristotle

repeatedly claimed... that earlier thinkers had not recognised reason as a distinct cognitive ability, to be distinguished from sense and perception. [1]

Still, if concrete reason lacks any logic of activity as a whole, it does not feel the lack at all acutely. Unable to transcend its current circumstances until late in its own development, it cannot positively aspire to anything outside its current framework. From its own point of view, it only needs to grasp – and can only comprehend – the relationships it needs to realise its strictly empirical objectives. By the same token, even where it fails through its own inadequacies it has no urge to formulate what the problem might be, above the level of fixing it in a strictly mechanical manner. It simply has no means of considering any more abstract issue. This in turn only expresses on the methodological plane the episodic nature of concrete reason's everyday existence: it 'fixes' problems as and when they arise, but it is not yet ready to speculate on them. That is why it 'fixes' problems – because it cannot truly *solve* them. It has no principles, no theories, no idea of ideas.

On the other hand, concrete reason can be very adept at compensating for its own systematic deficiencies by means of traditions and conventions, past experience and present expedients, well-worn habit, trial and error, rote learning, and so on. As the termite nest reveals, one can build amazing labyrinths out of the most elementary components. Similarly, concrete reason's operations have a measured aspect that was totally absent from its intuitive or organic predecessors: if an entire plan of campaign, with all its estimates and schedules and priorities and dependencies and milestones and objectives, is beyond concrete reason, at least the next few steps can be foreseen and executed with confidence. Furthermore, concrete reason is responsible for some striking innovations of its own. Not least of these is its fundamental redefinition of 'empirical' itself, which now *includes* the direct apprehension of relationships and may even cause these more profound meanings and significances to supplant the empirical experience altogether.

That is why it is only at this stage that the written word – including these words written on this page – becomes *directly* meaningful. I cannot read these words without also reading what they mean, immediately and spontaneously, and neither could any concrete rational child who was capable of reading them. Indeed, remembering the exact words which transmit this meaning is often a much harder task than grasping or recalling the meaning itself, and registering the text's *perceptual* characteristics – the shapes of the letters, the colour of the paper, and so on – is still more difficult and uncertain. Nor is a given object's relevance to the given problem or its appositeness in a given situation or its affinities or even its implications (within my own frame of reference) apprehended any less directly and immediately. Nor is either the force of an idea or the value of money. For even the most ineluctably empirical object is *constituted* by concrete reason in terms of supra-empirical structures.[2]

---

[1] Frede and Striker (1996: 22). On Aristotle's concept of intelligence (*nous*), see Frede in *ibid.* (pp.157-173).

[2] Ingold makes a complementary point about the real location of technique in the complete, embodied agent rather than in some hypothetical 'cognitive' centre, which formu-

The remarkableness of this first direct intuition of the *form* (over and above the *fact*) of acts, things and events is exceeded only by the extent to which it passes unremarked. In a sense one might reply: of course – after all, the whole point of internalising a structure is to make it transparent. Yet this is also the crux of concrete reason's dilemma, for this transparency is not a function of the practised or articulated nature of the insight it provides. On the contrary, paradoxical though it may sound, although the fact that its objects are constituted in terms of internally articulated and synthesised relationships ensures that they are genuinely concrete, the relationships that make this concreteness possible are themselves *intuited*, and suffer on their own account all the vicissitudes by which intuitive reason's *objects* were haunted. At least at the onset of concrete reason, they are not yet grasped in their own right, and so cannot be appreciated or comprehended or reasoned about for their own sakes. Like intuitive reason's objects, concrete reason's relationships may have names, but they do not have true natures until very late on in their development. So, to an intuitive child, the price of an object is purely nominal, yet the nature of price is treated as quite arbitrary and absolute. That is, it is part of an unconditional (if also, in this case, an unarticulated) identity.[1]

Of course, no form of reason can be understood purely in terms of its internal dynamics, not least because the rather large proportion of the universe it has yet to incorporate declines to leave it alone. On the other hand, whether the universe's intrusions appear as an opportunity or merely as an incomprehensible interruption depends entirely on the maturity of the reason in question, and so on what it can comprehend. Hence not only the general fact of external problems but also their *specific* nature, which in concrete reason's case comes back to the superficiality of its grasp of relationships. In particular, concrete reason is severely content- and context-bound. Of course, in its sensitivity to content and context concrete reason is no different from any other form of intelligence, or indeed any other structure whatsoever, and a good deal more effective than anything that precedes it. Nevertheless, just as the nature of the objects intelligence can construct matures with each passing stage, so does its relationship to and grasp of the content and context of its activity. What is special about concrete reason is the fact that it is the last stage of material relations of *any* kind before the relationship between an action and its content and context begins to inform activity *explicitly*.

This may seem to contradict the previous claim that concrete reason differs from intuitive reason precisely in that its grasp of its objects is explicit, for what is the context of activity but another, perhaps somewhat larger, object? Surely then the context of activity is constructed as explicitly as any other object. As for its content, surely this is synonymous with the object itself. But in fact concrete reason's incomprehension of content and context reflects an important general feature of the development of intelligence, namely that its grasp of con-

---

lates plans in glorious isolation and then issues orders to a passive, subservient body (in Gibson and Ingold, 1993: 429–45). Several of the papers in Marcel and Bisiach (1988) draw similar conclusions, based on various lines of research.

[1] André Hopper, pers. comm.

tent and context must always lie one stage behind its grasp of objects. The context of an activity is an object of a rather peculiar kind, which contains and conditions *all* that activity's other objects. Its construction as an object in its own right must therefore be laboured over rather more than that of any object it might contain, and moreover that labour consists of constructing the conditions for the stabilisation and mobilisation, for insight into and criticism of, *any* particular object it might condition or contain. In short, it is true that, for the context of an action to be comprehended, it must become an object in its own right; however, by being made the object of concrete reason's attention, intelligence then loses sight of the very objects for which it provides that context!

For concrete reason's limitation to simple relationships ensures that the context of a given activity can be either an object in its own right or uncomprehended on its own terms. It cannot, as far as concrete reason is concerned, be both context and object at the same time. For if the context of a given object or activity consists of all the things and events bearing on it, they bear on that object or act in terms of a whole mass of intersecting relationships. Consequently, the context of an object or act can only be grasped as an object in its own right when entire *systems* of relationships can be comprehended, and that is precisely what concrete reason cannot do. So it is not true that context either operates on the same plane as any other object or consists of, say, the sum of the objects it contains. Rather, it is their totality, which is by no means the same thing as their sum, any more than inertia or liberty is the sum of physical objects or rational persons. Indeed, the formation of such a totality is always the signal for the end of one stage in the development of intelligence and the onset of the next. Context must therefore always trail behind the formation of other objects, to the extent that it can only be grasped one degree less well than the objects it contains.

The same is true of a given act or object's *content*, which is not to be confused with a list of its empirical features. Rather, intelligence can only grasp the content of my present action – of this writing with this pen on this paper – by grasping its elements and *their* relationships to one another. In other words, the content of an object or act takes the object itself as *their* context, and comprehending content is essentially applying to the internal structure of an object the same process that comprehending its context applies to its external structure. The object is the framework in terms of which its content exists and functions. As such, as a context in its own right, concrete reason cannot grasp its objects in the same moment or the same act as it grasps their content: its grasp of relationships is simply too slight, too one-sided. In summary, concrete reason may be well versed in *what* the content and context of its objects and activity are – it can discern and list and count and describe them – but it has little separate sense of they are what they are, insofar as that depends on their mutual relationships and collective nature.

So for concrete reason objects are indeed concrete, not least because intelligence can now grasp that objects are more than merely bland, undifferentiated empirical 'things', and must be grasped in terms of the structures and relationships that regulate and inform their precise content and context. Of course, it can take particular aspects of its content and context as objects in their own right, and by the end of concrete reason this problem will have been resolved, with various anticipations and insights being developed as its development proceeds. Nevertheless, generally speaking exactly what their content and context actually are remains a matter of intuition. But at least that is an advance over intuitive reason, which has no sense of content or context whatsoever.

And until content and context are fully explicated, activity must be degraded by both the unanticipated intrusions of the external (ie, external but unexternalised, objective but unobjectified) and the uncontrollable extrusions of the unrecognisably internal (ie, internal but uninternalised, subjective but unsubjectified) structures. That is not to say that concrete reason is left floundering around in the dark. On the contrary, it can be very sensitive to the conditions in which an act is performed. However, this sensitivity is a matter of one-sided flashes rather than steady illumination, and its actions proceed primarily in terms of the *facts* of the situation, and only secondarily in terms of its *nature*.

This chronic weakness is exemplified at every level of concrete reason – even at the broadest levels of history and society. From the point of view of economic and political structure, this one-sidedness leads to severe limits in the ability of concrete rational societies to operate in the strictly systematic manner we now take for granted. It is true that the rise of concrete rational social relationships saw the appearance of many specialists: artisans, soldiers, merchants, priests, and so on. But such groups were never integrated into a single, socially pervasive order of the kind we now take for granted. For example, the crucial limitation on the Greek *demos*, that all eligible citizens had to be able to meet in order to make legal and political decisions, was not the positive product of any principle (though it was frequently rationalised in such terms) but the entirely negative consequence of the lack of any formal structure capable of administering the *polis*.

Likewise concrete reason saw the appearance of huge political agglomerations, yet for all the millennia when concrete rational social systems predominated – from the earliest civilisations until the last absolutist states – it was very much the norm for political entities to combine a wide range of groups (tribes, city states, nationalities, colonies, and so on) into ramshackle wholes of vast proportions and weak sinews. This situation is exemplified by the difficulty of even describing the social structure of ancient Mesopotamia:

> If we want to designate the populations attested in the sources appropriately, we will have considerable difficulty with a terminology that allows for too little differentiation. For lack of a better term, we speak of 'peoples' when the large living-communities of the same language and culture so designated would be better characterised by a neutral term with less content. A term such as 'ethnic group' may fit better, but today this is used primarily in connection with the designation of minority groups in opposition to a people identified with a state. In connection with the political entities of the ancient Orient, we will scarcely have to do with 'tribes'. Similarly the modern term 'nation' is not at all applicable to antiquity… People everywhere were characterised only according to their origin in a particu-

lar land or according to their membership in a social group, insofar as one does not speak merely of 'humankind'.[1]

The problem is not only a lack of differentiation but also a lack of any way of expressing how these social entities were encapsulated into a single political whole. This problem arises not because we lack the necessary *words*; the fact is, it is the social *reality* of concrete reason that lacks either clear differentiation or clear integration. That is what makes it concrete.

Nor were the consequences of this lack of an integrating order merely a political or administrative inconvenience. For the inhabitants of such a society it meant grave limits on their scope and opportunities for individual and collective development. For the lack of a unifying social structure makes it impossible to establish – or in most cases imagine – an overarching form of social activity itself, and so a coherent or consistent conception of one's rights and responsibilities of the kind associated with a concept such as 'citizen'. Instead there was simply a succession of pragmatic, conventional, eclectic connections, incapable of supporting any general social principals. For example, the ancient Near East used the term 'free'…

> …only in the sense of 'free of debts' (ie, freed from certain obligations), rather than in the full sense of the words for 'free' in the Indo-European languages… Thus, one understood under 'liberation' only the release from particular taxes and obligations to service. The members of particularly dependent social groups were also 'free' in comparison with the 'slaves'.[2]

It is hardly a world of constitutions, due process or liberty, equality and fraternity.[3] As Lewontin puts it:

> Western history had, of course, always been marked by civil wars, peasant uprisings, rick burnings, machine breakings, and urban riots, but these were in the name of bread, land, and work. The demand for social and political equality was a creation of the ideologues of modern societies.[4]

This situation continued through a succession of great empires built on equally *ad hoc* arrangements, from the Hellenic world and Rome, through the Carolingians and the medieval church and on to the threshold of the modern day. Even at the hither end of concrete reason – in tsarist Russia, say, or the Austro-Hungarian empire – the same kinds of ramshackle social structure still predominate, all still striving to impose order on diverse groups with no more in common than their Mesopotamian predecessors. Sometimes one even has the strange impression that, politically speaking at least, the last of the Habsburgs ruled over a kind of Babylonia-with-steam-engines.

As this suggests, European feudalism offers a typical example of the limits inherent in concrete reason. Considered purely as a 'concrete' economic sys-

---

[1] von Soden (1994: 14).

[2] von Soden (1994: 74–5). On structures and concepts of dependency in the ancient world, see also Archer (1988); Patterson (1982); de Ste. Croix (1983).

[3] On the extremely limited structure and objectives of famous legal codes of the ancient world, see de Ste. Croix (1983) for Rome and von Soden (1994: 131–44) for the Near East.

[4] Lewontin (2000: 199).

tem, the 'context' of feudalism was its natural environment. Unlike a formal system such as capitalism, which reinvents its natural environment as freely and as faithlessly as it reinvents everything else, feudalism has no power to alter the natural fertility of the soil or the physical obstacles to movement and change, little ability to see into the nature of the plagues by which it is threatened, and so on. So it was very largely as a result of the structural limits of feudalism as a system of social organisation that Europe could still feel the full force of nature's wrath – as it did throughout the fourteenth century. As a population explosion ran up against the natural limits of feudal agriculture, its lack of overall coherence contributed significantly to demographic collapse, which was then massively exacerbated by the calamity of the Black Death, which feudal science and society were equally ill-equipped to fight.

In short, as its essentially concrete logic inevitably entailed, feudalism was chronically lacking in effective command of its context. It was not that it lacked the practical power to do the job; it simply had no idea what the power it needed *was*, and no means of obtaining it even if its leaders had been able to make a good guess. So even at this level there remains a deep residue of irrationality at the heart of reason. Still, in terms of historical development, perhaps the essential advance is that concrete reason *is* historical. Unlike intuitive reason, which is fatally chained to its immediate empirical conditions, concrete reason's mastery of relationships, and so the formation of complex structures and mechanisms, allows it to create a literate society capable of producing complex artefacts. By these means, concrete reason engenders *civilisation*. Like any form of concrete reason, feudalism was at least able to create an enduring order that not only extended beyond the natural conditions of intelligence (environment conditions, lifespan, and so on) – a feat of which intuitive reason is also capable, if only on a small scale – but is also abstracted from, and even turns back upon nature, to begin the immense, perhaps infinite task of ordering and re-ordering that nature in intelligence's own image.

Concrete reason in practice

Like zero, numbers were becoming invisible: no longer descriptive of objects but objects – rarefied objects – themselves. 'Three' was once like 'small': it could modify shoes and ships or sealing wax. Now it had detached itself so far from the rabble of things that instead those ephemera participated briefly in its permanence. Numbers acquired adjectives of their own: positive, negative, natural..., rational..., real... – and in time these adjectives too would become nouns (the Reals, the Rationals)... All that we saw, all that we sensed, was passing from the causes of numbers to their effects... By absorbing ourselves in them – by grasping the equation that governs the fall of a sparrow – we could at last bring all the accidents of living into the theatre of thought.

Robert Kaplan[1]

---

[1] Kaplan (1999: 75–6).

We might ask perhaps whether the state of mind in which an egg-laying cock could be prosecuted at law was necessary in a culture which should later on have the property of producing a Kepler.

Joseph Needham[1]

So the advances concrete reason makes in relation to its conditions are radical and invade every sphere. The change on other levels may be less dramatic, but it is equally marked. Piaget's immense researches and the innumerable extensions and refinements offered by his allies and critics have revealed the huge margin by which concrete cognition (in the Piagetian parlance, 'concrete operations') surpasses its intuitive ('pre-operational') predecessor.[2] Its ability to apprehend the sameness and difference of things and events in a controlled way (which is to say, in a way that is respectful of, yet subsumes, both) leads to attitudes that are both stable and mobile, to reversible trains of thought and action which can be tracked in both directions, to series and to preliminary notions of 'more' and 'less', to an unprecedented sensitivity to content and context, to articulated hierarchies of empirical types (cat, mammal, vertebrate), and so on. All introduce structure, consistency and order into the fragmentation, probabilism and one-sidedness of the empirical world.

Among the most prominent of these cognitive advances is number, and in particular the integers. These form an orderly, dynamic sequence quite distinct from the mechanical numbers of the previous stage, when counting consisted of memorising the name and position of each individual number, without any recognition of the logic of the sequence itself, without which the cardinal and ordinal sequences are simply unconnected.[3] Conversely, true counting only becomes possible with concrete reason, for only then does intelligence's notion of number come to be founded on a *relationship* between these two sides.

> For the symbolism of number is of quite a different logical type from the symbolism of speech. In language we find the first efforts of classification, but these are still uncoordinated. They cannot lead to a true systematisation. For the symbols of language themselves have no definite systematic order. Every single linguistic term has a special 'area of meaning'. It is... 'a beam of light, illuminating first this portion and then that portion of the field within which the thing... signified... lies'. But all these different beams of light do not have a common focus. They are dispersed and isolated. In the 'synthesis of the manifold' every word makes a new start.

> This state of affairs is completely changed as soon as we enter into the realm of number. We cannot speak of single or isolated numbers. The essence of number is always relative, not absolute. A single number is only a single place in a general systematic order.[4]

---

[1] Needham (1969: 37; also 328–330).

[2] For a general account of the nature and development of cognition during this period, see Inhelder and Piaget (1964), or any number of secondary sources.

[3] There have been many effective counting systems that do not even require names for the numbers themselves, resting instead on enumerating the parts of the body (Hallpike, 1979: 240ff).

[4] Cassirer (1944: 211–2).

Contrast this to the strictly intuitive numbering systems that existed in, for example, early Mesopotamia, with its plethora of disconnected tools:

> Each of these systems is context-dependent in that each one is used to measure different kinds of objects: for example, one measures discrete objects, another objects of mass consumption, another grain, etc. In addition, each of the basic systems is organised differently in the sense that each works with a different base value... The symbols used accentuate the quantitative aspect of the objects but also retain some minimal qualitative characteristics, since they stand for specific objects in the concrete world. We might say that this schematisation of objects helps produce a miniature world, a microcosm, which creates its own space of operations by allowing concrete actions with arithmetic meaning to be performed directly on the symbolic objects. Handling the symbols is easier than handling the natural objects, and its main purpose is to keep track in the microcosm of the changes taking place in the macrocosm (ie, the 'real world').[1]

Clearly, a crucial part of what is missing here is any sense of that eminently practical abstraction, number *as such*, to which the various qualitative kinds of object could be made commensurate. By contrast, concrete reason's approach to number allows the fundamental sameness of the integers (ie, the fact that each represents the set of all sets that can be counted by means of the same operation) to be reconciled with their equally fundamental difference (ie, the fact that each number is different); and their difference (ie, that each set of sets represents a different quantity) to be intuited not only at the same time as but also in terms of their sameness (ie, the fact that, as integers, they are all members of a single set). Nor do concrete reason's integers then require some extrinsic force to assemble them into their proper order, as intuitive reason's numbers do, for the differences they embody are already organised in terms of the process of counting whence they arose.

Thus the integers resolve sameness and difference into a single structure – this very 'number as such' – that was previously conspicuous only by its absence. And the way in which concrete reason constructs integers unifies the number sequence as a whole by abstracting away from both those differences that previously separated the individual numbers and the sameness that allowed all lists of numbers to be equivalent in the eye of the toddler, who is blind to their 'inner nature'. In this way, the integers embody the two of the great cognitive triumphs of this stage, namely classification and seriation.[2]

Not that their construction of numbers is immediate. Even long into the development of concrete reason, the quantification of qualities will proceed in a more or less inharmonious manner, especially at the higher social levels. For example, the conflict between the unequivocal conception of status created by a set of basic concrete relationships (ranks, estates, and so on) and a more quanti-

---

[1] Nicolopolou in Cole *et al.* (1997: 212, 219). See Nissen *et al.* (1993) and Ifrah (1998) for empirical details; Damerow (1995) for the relationship between number concepts in prehistory and cognition; and Hallpike (1979: Ch.6) for a Piagetian view of the anthropological literature.

[2] Piaget (1952). On the historical emergence of arithmetic out of the coalescence of series and classification, see Nissen *et al.* (1993: chs 5 and 16).

tative measure of social position and worth such as merely monetary wealth will take centuries to resolve itself.

On the other hand, whatever its success in founding arithmetic (and the construction of integers is by no means the only arithmetical achievement of this stage), concrete reason still has no true mathematics. Mathematics presupposes the ability to reflect on the abstract properties and internal necessities of numbers and other arithmetical structures independently of any actual quantification of any actual content. That is why concrete reason cannot quite grasp pure algebra, geometry or number theory, though it comes tantalisingly close.[1] But this is only to dress in mathematical terms concrete reason's general problem of grasping relationships independently of any particular content or context, and it is, of course, on just this rock that concrete reason founders.

Closely related to the development of concrete cognition is that of concrete science, so to speak, and there are many parallels between the two. Just as concrete reason in general is the first form of intentionally intelligent activity, so concrete scientific reason in particular provides the first formation of intentional knowledge (as opposed to the simple accumulation of isolated facts, of which intuitive reason is entirely capable). Now, instead of simply identifying significant events and endowing them a particular and pragmatic significance as omens of this or that, things and events are to be explained, which is to say, set in some explicit and defined relation to other things and events. Thus the great megalithic observatories of the period at least suggest that, by the beginning of the third millennium BC, ancient astronomers had advanced from interpreting isolated events such as the equinoxes and the rising and setting of particular stars to complete processes such as the circuits and orbits of heavenly bodies,[2] and the kind of interpretation they offered for natural phenomena, though still based on projecting subjective values and intentions onto the natural world, had progressed from isolated omens to the logical acts and purposes of intelligibly motivated divinities. In proportion to the explicitness and articulation of these 'hypotheses' it would be legitimate to attribute such structures with a fundamentally concrete rational order.

Nevertheless, such an infusion of relationships into things and events is not enough to categorise the earliest forms of, say, classification as truly concrete. At the lower bound intuitive reason is perfectly capable of 'classifying' its objects on the practical level, as when it groups things pragmatically into classes, orders them into pragmatic series, and so on. And at the upper bound, classification is only properly stabilised during the latter half of concrete reason, when the child (or the culture) builds its first stable and inclusive hierarchies of classifications such as cat–mammal–animal, and so on (which is to say, classes of classes), capable of true logical quantification (none, some, all). By that point it has clearly risen far above (or rather, penetrates beneath) the level of the Earth

---

[1] Concrete reason's gradual construction of quantification of increasingly complex and subtle kinds is a persistent theme of Piagetians generally. See Hallpike (1979) especially chapters 5 and 6, for a summary and the relevant anthropological literature.

[2] North (1994: 2–6).

Mother imagery, 'pregnant with every kind of embryo'[1] from metals to human beings, which characterised early intuitive reason.

Taken with the shifting and overlapping achievements and interests of succeeding generations, this long, complex process of development, explains the difficulty of categorising some of the earliest forms of, say, biological knowledge as either consistently concrete or intuitive:

> In particular, all known cultures appear to entertain notions of: (i) biological species... of vertebrates and flowering plants that are manifestly and phenomenally salient for human beings, (ii) sequential patterns of naming (eg, 'oak', 'shingle oak', 'spotted shingle oak'), (iii) taxa construction by means of an appreciation of overall patterns of morphological regularity... (iv) overarching animal 'life form' groupings that more or less correspond to modern zoological classes (eg, bird, fish), and (v) overarching plant 'life-form' groupings that have no place in modern botanical taxonomy but are nonetheless of obvious ecological significance (eg, tree, grass).[2]

The rationality of this knowledge may well be doubted. However, once concrete reason has established itself, such folk knowledge may still be being put to ritual or mythological use of the kind so familiar from intuitive reason, but it does seem to be independent of the utility, symbolism or functional value of the thing known – a characteristic feature of concreteness properly so called.[3]

On the other hand, despite its triumphs over the vicissitudes of intuitive reasoning, one should not overestimate the depth or value or power of the structures available to concrete reason. The deployment of even the most comprehensive collection of relationships is of limited value while they remain unarticulated among themselves. That is how, in the case of the Babylonians, concrete reason could know endless practical instances of Pythagoras' theorem (to the point of calculating that $13{,}500^2 + 12{,}709^2 = 18{,}541^2$!), but remain incapable of working out the theorem itself.[4] On the contrary, when the only links between different aspects of knowledge are through the empirical surfaces of the objects they address, arguments will be literally superficial, basing themselves on the slightest analogies and resemblances. From such a method, any degree of confusion may follow. For example:

> In order to know things then, it was necessary to detect the visible signs which nature had placed on their surfaces precisely to permit man to comprehend their re-

---

[1] Eliade (1978: 52).

[2] Atran (1990: 17). More generally on early classification, see Hallpike (1979: 196–235).

[3] On this topic, see Atran (1990: 20); Durkheim and Mauss (1963: 81); and Lévi-Strauss (1972). Although I have relied heavily on their accounts, neither Atran nor Lévi-Strauss analyse their material in terms that are compatible with the present multi-stage model, and Atran's more recent comments are firmly opposed to this approach (Atran, 1998). As a result, it is not always clear where intuitive reason leaves off and concrete reason begins. Given Lévi-Strauss' general conclusions, which tend to interpret as parallel methods what are presented here as different levels of maturity, I think it unlikely that either he or his disciples would want to make any such division. For further references on folk classifications, see Hallpike (1986: 128ff).

[4] von Soden (1994: 168).

lationships. It was necessary to discern the system of resemblances, the network of analogies and similitudes providing access to certain of nature's secrets. For, said Porta, 'divine intentions may be inferred from the resemblances between things'. In order to know an object, none of the analogies by which it is linked to things and to beings should be neglected. There are plants that look like hair, eyes, grasshoppers, hens, frogs or serpents. Animals are mirrored in the stars, in plants, in stones where, said Pierre Belon, 'Nature has taken more pleasure in expressing the shape of fish than that of other animals'. Moreover, resemblances which are particularly difficult to discern carry a mark: they are signed. The signatures help to discover the analogies which might otherwise escape notice. Thanks to similitudes and signatures, it is possible to slip from the world of forms into that of forces. Through analogies, 'the invisible becomes visible', said Paracelsus. For the resemblances are neither useless nor unwarranted. They are not the expression of mere playfulness from heaven. Certain bodies look alike because they have similar properties. Conversely, similarity expresses common qualities. The resemblance of a plant to the eye is just the sign that it should be used for treating diseases of the eyes. The very nature of things is hidden behind the similitudes.[1]

Or more concisely: 'Thus did Divine Providence, by natural hieroglyphics, read lectures to the rude wit of vulgar man'.[2] In other words, the highest aspiration of concrete rational knowledge is a recipe, not an explanation – an *I Ching*, not a *Principia Mathematica*. This is also why the pre-modern diffusion of ideas across the Old World was dominated by mute but directly usable and readily mimicked techniques and devices rather than well structured concepts, theories, methodology or even explicit knowledge. Hence concrete reason's enduring reliance on experience: as Joseph Needham put it:

> Until it had been universalized by its fusion with mathematics, natural science could not be the common property of all mankind. The sciences of the medieval world were tied closely to the ethnic environments in which they had arisen, and it was very difficult, if not impossible, for the people of these different cultures to find any common basis of discourse.[3]

In summary, concrete reason assembles knowledge, but beyond its observation of types and correspondences and similitudes and signs, it is incapable of comprehending it. Conversely, it was only with the seventeenth century's increasingly explicit repudiation of such methods – all methods of 'conjuring' appearances into a merely plausible reality – that magic finally gave way to science. Indeed, it was this turn against analogy, even more than the changing views of nature and society, which justifies the use of the phrase 'the intellectual revolution'.[4]

Of course, no science can exist without an adequately developed concrete basis of this kind. Yet, taken in isolation, not even the most elaborate concrete

---

[1] Jacob (1993: 21–2). See also Huizinga (1924/2001: 192–211, especially p.195).

[2] Jon Heydon, seventeenth-century astrologer and writer on Rosicrucian mysticism, quoted in Harrison (1984: 172).

[3] Needham (1969: 15).

[4] Burke in Teich *et al.* (1997: 119). Needham's massive researches confirm that this limitation is was characteristic of pre-modern Chinese (and other) 'science' (eg, Needham, 1969, *passim*). See Thomas (1983) for extensive historical details of the British case.

knowledge amounts to science properly so called. Merely comprehending particular relationships does not permit one to constitute either a system of scientific knowledge or a disciplined scientific method. On the other hand, in the absence of an independent system of methods and results, proper to its subject matter rather than imposed by virtue of ideological or metaphysical assumptions, it is impossible to avoid injecting a specifically human perspective into knowledge. Of course, it is frequently complained that our own science is unduly influenced by ideological influences, and this is undoubtedly true. But in the case of concrete science, this could not help being the case, and the taint of metaphysics was equally unavoidable. Where it is only through the scientist's efforts that these various relationships can be integrated into a coherent body of knowledge, and a central role is played by empirical plausibility, it is hard to imagine how the ideological components of would-be scientific knowledge could be separated out of the knowledge as a whole, or indeed why anyone would think this ideological perspective is unjustified. On the contrary, it is what gives concrete knowledge its inner meaning, and so its value – 'truly the bond and knot of the universe'.

Conversely, there can be no distinct science of human nature where it is the human agent who is responsible for making sense of everything else, and whose position within that 'everything else' is *be* the essential explanatory principle. After all, the world of concrete reason is one in which human beings not only stand at the physical centre and decide its meaning, but they are the reason for and the meaning of its existence. In such a world, everything else exists for and in terms of human nature, even to the point where disease and wild animals exist to chastise human beings, mountains are seen as a product of the Fall and, according to Aristotelian arguments, it is the human soul that engenders and regulates the most basic of human faculties, right down to nutrition, rather than the body being seen as a biological entity with its own independent laws and processes. In the circumstances, there is neither need nor possibility for a distinct study of human nature: all studies proceed from and end with human nature.[1] And even where the human being does not play quite such an egocentric role (as in ancient China's more expansive but also more modest cosmology), there can be little doubt that subjectivity is the core principle.

This is why early Renaissance science – one of the high points of concrete reason – is not merely the province of polymaths like Leonardo da Vinci but also strongly imbued with ethical and aesthetic considerations. Indeed, 'The systematic extraction of their moral could even be called a paradigmatic act of the Renaissance'.[2] This follows from concrete reason's inability to quite tear its gaze away from its object's empirical surfaces and concentrate fully on the principles that bind it to the universe and give it its singular nature; the contrast between the multiplicity of particular relationships with which it is acquainted and the lack of unifying systems to which these relationships may be

---

[1] On the Renaissance world view see Copenhaver and Schmitt (1992); or Smith (1997: ch. 2) for a summary.

[2] Jaritz and Winiwarter in Teich *et al.* (1997: 99).

subordinated; and its limited self-awareness, which ensures the continued (but now, by contrast with intuitive reason, quite explicit) projection of rational considerations such as divine perfection, morality and aesthetics onto non-rational subject matter.[1] Conversely, there was a constant tendency to subordinate potentially objective systems of knowledge (eg, botany) to subjective and practical needs (eg, medicine) under the cover of metaphysical rationalisations (eg, alchemy, Neo-Platonism, magic, and so on).

Thus concrete reason can be credited with the first scientific tools and techniques, with its intentionally exhaustive and increasingly disciplined observing, collecting, enumerating, cataloguing, arranging, mapping and describing of the insides and outsides (ie, the empirical nature) of everything from geology and gestures to manners and miracles. Yet it is only as it approaches its climax that concrete reason is capable of fully abstracting their internal and external *structures*. And it is that which is the true and essential prerequisite of a truly objective notion of and approach to things, and so of science as such.[2]

Taken on their own terms and treated as isolated functions, concrete cognition and science both tend to emphasise the relationship between appearance and reality. As such their central focus is bound to be on what is to be made of things, on what they 'really' mean, on the conditions and validity of our comprehension of them, and so on. However, concrete reason is no more restricted to problems of appearance and reality than any other stage. It also surpasses intuitive reason in terms of self and other, not least in that it is no longer content to manage this dialectic by means of passive constructs and static tools. These serve to lever intelligence into its world, but they contribute little to its rationalisation that they do not immediately remove again with a subjective, metaphysical or theological rationale. However, once concrete reason is under way, it strives to advance from comprehending the nature of things purely from its own point of view to rationalising the activity of things and events themselves.

Hence, for example, the first machines. The operations of a machine form a complete, independent process, but can do so only because the transformation each component of the machine carries out is part of a larger ordered sequence. On the other hand, the design and construction of concrete rational machinery is strictly a matter of mechanics, which deals empirically, conventionally and pragmatically with the device and its effects. It is not yet a matter of engineering, which rests on abstract principles, of which the machine is merely an implementation. This is entirely because, at the level of concrete reason, everything is an eclectic amalgam of practical knowledge and fragmented concept,

---

[1] On the gradual replacement of 'sacred theories of the earth', which sought to explain the necessity for labour, the fertility of the soil and nature of agriculture 'by tracing their genealogy to God's creative act', see Thomas (1983) or Schaffer in Teich *et al.* (1997: 124–147).

[2] On the culmination of this process in the Renaissance, see Jaritz and Winiwarter in Teich *et al.* (1997: 91–111); Crombie (1994: ch. 9); Thomas (1983: ch. II and *passim*). It is a suitable emblem of this ambiguous position that Erasmus had Paracelsus treat him for gout and a kidney ailment.

in which it is always possible to see directly how the machine works. Thus the characteristic expression of 'concrete' machinery is the astrolabe, the clock or the loom, not the integrated circuit.[1]

As for the dialectic of present and absent, the intuitive form of exchange described by Sahlins in the previous chapter is readily raised to the concrete level. There are various ways of overcoming the limitations inherent in a hunter-gatherer lifestyle, of which two of the most obvious are the development of methods for preserving and storing the fruits of foraging and the hunt, and the domestication of animals and plants to the point where it is no longer necessary to scurry about the landscape at the whim of the seasons.[2] In other words, to the extent that hunter-gatherers can be said to harvest nature, their lot can be improved either by stabilising the harvest by means of long-term storage or by actively husbanding the harvest itself.

Of course, preservation and domestication are common if unintended by-products of just those determinedly intuitive 'Stone Age economies' studied by Sahlins.[3] They should certainly, as Davis says, be ranked in importance with fire and tools.[4] However, at first they seem to have been no more than side effects of purely local and transitory insights, and were probably concentrated on meat, hides and other slaughter products rather than constituting a sustained management programme. Such processes may be ossified in rote, magic and tradition, but they are neither organised nor methodical in a genuinely insightful or critical manner. They certainly are not organised into a regular economic system. Only with yet further development will they come to include the exploitation of beasts of burden, transport and traction or the sustained and integrated management of animals for by-products such as wool, milk or dung.[5] Hence the profound economic and social limitations of intuitive reason.

Still, once the relationships that govern the lives of suitable plants and animals are grasped and techniques for managing these relationships become the very basis of economic activity, intelligence begins to organise the universe around itself rather than just submitting to it. This process takes at least two main (and commonly overlapping) forms: hunter-gatherers organising themselves around focal natural harvests such as salmon runs or seasonal migrations, and domestication *cum* agriculture.

In the former case, it is true that considerable organisational and technical advances are made, but the success of these advances still rests entirely on the naturalness of the events they batten onto. Intelligence has, it is true, begun to redefine the universe on its own terms to a slight degree, but only through the peripheral activities it is obliged to append to the naturally determined 'main event'. This remains almost entirely outside its control. Even herding retains more than a tinge of subordination to events that are fundamentally outside

---

[1] Hill (1984, 1993); Hodges (1971); Landels (2000).

[2] Megarry (1995).

[3] Sahlins (1974).

[4] See also Davis (1987: 127).

[5] Davis (1987: Ch.6); Sherratt (1997: Section III).

the herder's control. To touch on an issue that will reveal its real significance later, in these cases the *conditions* for hunting and gathering are actively produced, but what is actually hunted and gathered is not.

The case of agriculture is quite different: the structure and functioning of plants, animals, soil and fertilisers, not to mention the organisation and equipment of the group involved, are expressly re-arranged and subordinated to the latter's survival. The basic achievement is simple enough:

> In terms of what happened in history, one of the most important things about agriculture is that it produces not just great amounts of food, it supplies *reliable* and *predictable* amounts of food, and thereby allows population densities to rise and people in many areas of the world to live year round in the same place...[1]

---

[1] Wenke (1990: 229). It should be noted here that what is required is a stable, reliable and predictable level of resources. The technology involved is not, in itself, critical. Indeed, at this stage technology is essentially a means of dealing with pre-intelligent nature, so one should not expect the key processes to depend on technological advance. Instead, methods for taking advantage of opportunities for social (ie, intelligent) management should be – and evidently are – paramount. In some especially blessed regions such as the north-west coast of North America (Johnson and Earle, 1987: 161ff) or the Illinois valley of the Hopewell period (Wenke, 1990: 565ff; Fagan, 1995; Fiedel, 1987), equally high levels of social and economic organisation have been based on hunting and gathering. The importance of agriculture is that it introduces social mechanisms for compensating for a lack of natural abundance, and so extends this degree of control to a much wider range or environments.

The reader should contrast the rationality of this whole process with the various ecological explanations of why foraging societies often have population densities of only 20–30 per cent of the land's theoretical carrying capacity (summarised in Johnson and Earle, 1987: 28–9, 72ff and *passim*). Most importantly, both the anthropological and the demographic evidence makes it perfectly clear that Malthus was quite wrong about human population growth, and that he would have been wrong before the industrial revolution made his theories completely irrelevant. As Wenke (1990: 295) observes:

> ... there is no evidence human populations have ever increased at anything approaching the biologically feasible rate. If the world's population 5570 years ago were only one thousand and their annual rate of growth since were four per thousand people – a relatively moderate growth rate – the world's present population would be between 7 and 8 trillion.

It is tempting to reply that this has happened precisely because the Malthusian mechanisms are in place – war, famine, disease, and so on. But real population growth is seldom rapid, and there is ample evidence that the demographic expansion that typically followed the great historical decimations seldom does more than restore the population to its previous unsaturated level. The massive accelerations that characterised the Neolithic revolution and industrialisation are very much the exception, and as the restoration of stable, even shrinking populations in heavily industrialised nations shows, it is not inexorable.

Nor is there anything ineluctable about the urge to procreate, not least because sex and procreation, it turns out, are rather easy to separate. Just as importantly, under mature capitalism people do not starve and their children do not die of hunger because they have no food or because there are too many of them; rather, they starve because someone takes away either the food they produce or the land on which they produce it – an altogether different phenomenon. Meanwhile, all this self-control is very difficult to reconcile with any idea of a continuing selection pressure on human beings, especially

Supplemented by elementary systems of 'staple financing' and other devices for smoothing out seasonal and other extrinsic fluctuations, the immense consequences of this shift will one day reveal themselves, although they remain largely invisible to those involved in the shift itself.

Sophisticated but still concrete economies such as the middle civilisations of Mesopotamia and Egypt, ancient Rome, the pre-Columbian civilisations of the Americas, western feudalism and advanced tribal societies provide a wealth of practical examples of these new forms of economic organisation. There have been many variants on the theme – the relationship between the aristocracy and the state has been particularly diverse – but the theme itself has not varied in its fundamentals.

For example, it is only from the concrete level onwards that a division of labour can become institutionalised and intentionally developed by political authorities,[1] as distinct from the more fluid arrangements that typify previous economies. Tools and weapons can then be made, used and shared to socially defined standards rather than only by individuals for their own use. Leaving aside the resources this liberates, the formation of regular relationships at the social and political level also permits a proto-imperial attitude towards neighbours, with the victors of inter-tribal conflicts permanently conquering and incorporating the vanquished rather than simply driving them from their land. Internally, the establishment of determinate relationships provides at least the practical premises for both regular social power and its legitimation – which is to say, the beginnings of regular political authority. In short, a concretely structured society is capable of defining and institutionalising the requisite relationships, complex and extended though they may be, and quite beyond any intuitive structure. What is more, it defines *itself* in more clearly social terms, with established processes and mechanisms.

For example, whereas the distribution of intuitive social communities was determined primarily by access to natural resources and (other things being equal) tends to arrange itself into a hexagonal pattern of sites that permits equal access, villages at the concrete level are distributed more according to the social frameworks within which they exist – frontiers, trade routes, administrative systems, networks, and so on. Indeed, already in Sumer a more or less comprehensive and orderly system of centralisation, guilds, rations and taxes was in place, supported by a bureaucracy, documented procedure and legality that has seldom been equalled in intensity. Such a system – whose standardisations are also among the few unequivocal conclusions one can draw about the more opaque Mature Harappan civilisation – is already far in advance of even the most complex 'Big Man' system or chiefdom, presupposing as it does not only some kind of objectification and intentional regulation of the basic economic, political and ideological relationships that govern social life but also and the creation of a distinct, articulated and permanent organisational and administrative superstructure overlaying social activity proper. Indeed, so far is concrete reason politically beyond its intuitive predecessor that even an early

---

given Darwin's insistence that excess population is essential to natural selection.
[1] Hodges (1989: 162ff).

city-state such as Sumerian Uruk could occupy more than two square miles, stand at the hub of a four-tiered hierarchy of settlements and support a ten-fold growth in population within two hundred years.[1]

A key part of this process is the development of various kinds of administration, which in some ways provides a kind of social analogue to writing. That is not to say that writing is enough to trigger or support an organised administration (or, as the Incan example demonstrates, that administration presupposes writing of any kind).[2] The clay tablet lists left to us by Sumer, its neighbours and its successor civilisations[3] reveal a decided capacity for objectifying experience externally and then organising it more or less explicitly. However, the earliest lists typically consist of only a single column – is fine for *storing* data (for inventories, audits, and the like) but unlike an arrangement of parallel columns, which converts data into *information* (as in ancient dictionaries, where two or more parallel columns are present), a list cannot be used to make a *decision*, which is the key function of the administrator. Of course, one should certainly not underestimate the power of the data gathered and the summaries scribes generated from them: the interminable counting and lists of the scribes could even be parlayed into strategic decision-making, at least in a limited administration such as ancient Egypt's:

> Even the pedantic lists of all and sundry were far from being the pointless whim of soulless bureaucrats. By giving senior officials oversight of the country's total

---

[1] Nissen *et al.* (1993: 9). For the principles, procedures, methods and techniques – very deliberate but still entirely concrete – whereby ancient cities, especially Greek and Roman colonies, were built, see Chant and Goodman (1999). As the latter reveal, city planning, building and management made little further progress before the early modern period, apart from the gradual elaboration of city management in exceptional cases such as Rome and the occasional intrusion of formal aesthetic, mathematical and cosmological principles in the general designs. In fact such intrusions seem to have been widespread in the pre-modern world, especially China, and are certainly prominent in almost all pre-modern *theories* of urban planning and management. Hence, as ever, the enduring element of subjectivity and projection in concrete reason.

However, such intrusions seldom seem to have had any marked effect on the way real cities really operated except in rare instances such as Beijing, which was rebuilt specifically as the imperial capital, with potentially corrupting forces such as commerce kept firmly at bay. Other outbursts of seeming formalisation, such as the radically geometrical design of many later Renaissance city walls, are more the product of the changing practical demands of defence, and seem to have been implemented, the initial geometrical designs apart, by strictly concrete rational methods, tools and techniques (Chant and Goodman, 1999: 172ff).

[2] Nissen *et al.* (1993) expressly argue that it is administration that creates writing, rather than *vice versa*. As Hallpike notes, 'we should also bear in mind that reading and writing, considered simply as intellectual skills, can be fully mastered by children before they have attained even concrete operational thought, let alone formal operations... [L]iteracy by itself is unlikely to have any decisive effect on cognition, and that a great deal depends on the uses to which literacy is put' (Hallpike, 2004: 161–162).

[3] Goody (1977: Ch.5); Ifrah (1998); Nissen *et al.* (1993). For a summary, see von Soden (1994: 145ff).

stocks it made possible their orderly distribution, the creation of reserves and planning for special projects.[1]

But this still does make the administrative system itself any more structured. Indeed, lists of this kind cannot even begin to compete with a cross-tabulated *matrix*, whose very structure embodies the *relationships* that underpin the data, and so informs the user of the criteria whereby the decision is to be made.

But, like writing, administration does require the structures and functions that constitute the activity being administered – plans, procedures, records, agendas, reports – to be recognised, and so to be stable enough to be recognised. That is, they must be embodied in regular relationships. That is why, like writing, administration is seldom seen before the advent of concrete reason.[2] On the other hand, because many (though by no means all) such systems remained concrete in character, the inherent integrity of the processes they administered and the rationality of the bureaucratic mechanisms they deployed to implement any given policy decision must be doubted. After all, this is Weber's 'patrimonial administration', not his 'rational bureaucracy', and confusion between the administration of state functions and the operations of the ruler's personal life and personal household is as natural at this level as that between the state treasury and the privy purse.

A concrete rational state has any number of other attributes that set it apart from the truly formal administrations that adorn the modern world. As I just noted, it is quite the norm for offices to be converted into the personal fiefs of the office holders, *de facto* if not immediately *de jure*; for the administration to lack most of the usual appurtenances and infrastructure of bureaucracy such as proper archives, specialised offices and facilities, defined procedures or formal training; for connections and influence to take precedence over procedure and expertise; for pomp and ceremony to be used to compensate for and camouflage the limitations of administration; for the powers that be to routinely resort to brute force where due process fails; and for the administrators themselves to be reduced to a social caste rather than a freely recruited and independent cadre of professionals. Given such arrangements, which inexorably bind administration to the practical position and status of the administrator, it comes as no surprise that, like a child writing a story, it would be quite anach-

---

[1] Strouhal (1992: 220). It should be emphasised that new types of document soon came to proliferate among administrators:

> Other documents from the scribe's pen include regulations issued by various bodies, court proceedings and records from private contracts dealing with sale and purchase, loans, hire, financial arrangements between spouses, inheritance, receipts, taxes, accounts and so on.

Goody's account (1977: Ch.5) makes the developmental implications of structured documentation especially clear. However, his (widely shared) emphasis on the importance of writing as such is, I think, mistaken. Writing, like language in general, is only one instrument of objectification, and one whose arbitrary relationship to the world depends for its intelligibility on intelligence's much wider ability to engage not only with that world but specifically *in* that world. In other words, language in general and writing in particular are subordinate to, and the products of, activity in general.

[2] On the role of documentation in the legal systems and administrations of the ancient Near East, see von Soden (1994: 138ff).

ronistic to expect the concrete rational administration to discriminate, let alone keep track of, its main theme.[1]

Nor is all this an issue at the highest levels of society only, where a degree of opacity and unmanageable complexity might be expected. The problem pervades the whole from top to bottom. For example, intuitive reason had already made some attempt at establishing key technical specialisms within the production process through the rise of artisans, while the problem of binding economic activity within and between neighbouring subsistence economies had been at least partially solved by means of barter. However, the specific problem concrete reason then faces (logically, if not historically) is how to manage complex relations of production within its own walls and the economic gaps and conflicts between economies that are neither neighbours nor limited to the subsistence plane. In fact it is the ability to solve this kind of problem – what might be called the problem of reach – that separates concrete from intuitive reason.

In terms of the organisation and transmission of a given society's skills, a characteristically concrete solution to this problem is the apprentice system, which amalgamates technical training, shelter and sustenance, learning one's place and social support within a single undifferentiated concept of service – all without any call for formal tuition, payment, wages, defined roles or any of the other appurtenances of a more formal relationship between master and apprentice. 'The craftsman's special skill and knowledge... was not something which he normally found easy to express. Wages, apprenticeship, working conditions and types of job he could describe to an interviewer; but the heart of the "mystery" often remained veiled.'[2] Indeed, the lack of consciousness of exactly what a skilled craftsman's skill consisted of persisted until the era of mechanisation, which in some industries persisted well up until the Second World War.

The larger problem of the indirectness and complexity of the connections *between* economies demands the positive management of economic activity over historical periods and regional, even continental, spaces. Despite the considerable practical success of feudalism and its kin in this department, it is hard to envisage how this could have been done reliably, efficiently or systematically before a formal management system had been established, and the historical evidence gives ample support to this view.

---

[1] On pre-formal bureaucracy generally, see Kamenka (1989: ch. 1). For how the Roman *imperium* was really administered, see Purcell in Boardman *et al.* (1992). The notoriously bureaucratic imperial Chinese government in fact employed only about 30,000 civil servants in all – about one for every 15,000 inhabitants. This is less than 1 per cent of the concentration in the least bureaucratised industrial state (Chant and Goodman, 1999: 313).

[2] Harrison (1984: 316). On the complicated yet largely implicit structure of apprenticeship, see Wynn, 'Layers of thinking in tool behavior', in Gibson and Ingold (1993: 389–406). On the role played by apprenticeship in personal development in feudal Europe, see Ariès (1973). It is striking that Adam Smith's critique of the pre-capitalist apprenticeship system is as much moral as economic (Smith, 1976: 133ff).

For example, both the management of 'public' finances and trade in luxury goods demand complex, subtle and far-reaching economic tools, of which the most notable were specialised financial 'instruments' such as organised credit, bills of exchange, negotiable bonds, paper money, and so on. Indeed, the transition from intuitive to concrete economic operations demands a striking inversion in economic strategy as a whole. At the earlier stage, trade is used to redistribute goods that happen, through the accidents of the seasons, the environment, local initiative and good fortune, to be surplus to requirements; a concrete economy, by contrast, sees the first organised production of goods specifically for trade. As any student of modern capitalism will be aware, it would be difficult to exaggerate the potential this reversal unleashes, even if realising that potential requires a number of further, very specific changes. All these devices presuppose at least the ability to comprehend the relationships they are designed to serve, independently of the actual exchanges supported – the defining feature of concrete reason.[1]

However, one should not exaggerate the extent or effectiveness of these devices. For example, not only were the majority of exchanges in the earliest concrete rational societies made in kind but so was a great part of economic activity in the Europe at least up to the *ancien régime*.[2] Likewise, a large proportion of the vast unemployed Roman *plebs* was fed by direct rationing.[3] And if one looks at the financial history of feudal economies, it is striking how fragile their financial instruments proved to be and how often they broke down for want of a genuine monetary system, let alone a true formal economic structure of markets, regulation, contract law, and so on. For example, money began to substitute for barter, labour obligations, personal service, and other responsibilities very early on in the history of feudalism,[4] but it never achieved anything like the systematic role we now take for granted.[5]

> That is, although they resemble money, they are not generalised media of exchange but have the following characteristics: (1) the powers of acquisition that they represent are highly specific; (2) their distribution is controlled in various ways; (3) the conditions that govern their issue create a set of patron–client relationships; (4) their main function is to provide the necessary condition for entry to high-status positions, for maintaining rank, or for combining attacks on status;

---

[1] The literature on these topics is immense. For an outline of the development of western European commerce and banking, see Braudel (1982). On the invasion of gold and money, see Vilar (1976).

[2] Braudel (1974).

[3] See Brunt (1986), *passim* and de Ste. Croix (1983: 371–2). Brunt estimates that by 5 BC a total of 320,000 Romans were entitled to free corn. One major function of these doles was to support another part of this concrete system, namely the *clientela* system.

[4] Braudel (1974: 330ff).

[5] On the relationship between the economic development of money and the intellectual transformation of monetary theory from their late feudal to their early modern forms, see Foucault (1970). For the general tone of economic life in this period, see Hale (1971: ch. 4).

and (5) the social systems in which such coupons or licenses function are geared to eliminating or reducing competition in the interests of a fixed pattern of status.[1]

In short, as Karl Polanyi remarked, early money is special-purpose money, and this situation continues to prevail right up to early modern times. The corollary of all this is a characteristically concrete susceptibility to local conditions. This can be illustrated by the precarious position in which moneyed wealth found itself throughout the feudal period. The paradoxes of bi-metallism and Gresham's Law plagued almost every economy of the times, and the same currency could have one value as an official unit of account and another in people's pockets. Money's ideological position was also always equivocal; its economic function was never credibly theorised; the corresponding laws of debt and contract were never more than half-hearted; money never even became a commodity in its own right, as expressed in a strictly economic concept of interest considered as the price of money; there were no institutions capable of defending its status or integrity as an economic tool; and so on. Indeed, money was constantly being forced into ideological, political and economic straitjackets that were quite foreign to its proper nature as *we* understand it. Conversely, innumerable fortunes were laid waste because of the inability of financiers and merchants to gain political power commensurate with the economic resources at their disposal – which meant, among other things, an acceptance of 'the economy' as a formal system of strictly formal relationships, over which interest and status should hold no sway. The same could scarcely be said of contemporary capitalism, not only because, once liberated by true formalisation, money is usually quite capable of buying all the political power it needs but also because the main goal of political power is to preserve and advance an economic system in which money has finally found its true place.

The major reason for this seeming anomaly is, of course, the fact that, in a concrete economic system, a strictly formal structure such as money cannot really embody economic authority. It may exercise real *power* in large parts of a concrete economy, especially among urban, financial and merchant groups, but in the absence of the unquestioned *legitimacy* it now possesses, its *authority* is always equivocal. In a concrete rational economy, limited as it is to empirical forces and relationships, nothing that has no intrinsic and empirically decidable value in its own right – like land, luxuries, gold, and so on – can. The destruction of one feudal bank after another through the refusal of feudal lords to play by the rules of 'pure' money bears brutal testimony to the irredeemably concrete nature of the feudal economy, into which those armed with so strictly formal a weapon as money ventured at their peril. Under feudalism the money economy always relied heavily on the grace and favour of local powers and authorities, especially outside the always more or less monetarised towns. And these authorities were seldom as concerned with 'sound money' or the intrinsic integrity of 'the economy' as they were with manipulating economic power in pursuit of their more immediate social and political interests. Nor could they

---

[1] Appadurai (1986: 24–5). See also Bloch and Parry (1989) or Hodges (1989: 104ff) on the generally equivocal social status of money in pre-formal economies.

have done so, had they wanted: a money economy is an expensive proposition.[1]

The origins of history

I was curious to know how this Prince, to whose dominions there is no access from any other country, came to think of armies, or to teach his people the practice of military discipline. But I was soon informed, both by conversation, and reading their histories. For, in the course of many ages they have been troubled with the same disease to which the whole race of mankind is subject; the nobility often contending for power, the people for liberty, and the King for absolute dominion. All which, however happily tempered by the laws of that kingdom, have been sometimes violated by each of the three parties; and have more than once occasioned civil wars, the last whereof was happily put an end to by this Prince's grandfather in a general composition...

Jonathan Swift, 'A Voyage to Brobdingnag'

The massively enlarged scope of a concrete economy compared to its intuitive predecessors hints at one of the most striking aspects of concrete reason (to which I have already alluded), namely that it is only with the onset of this stage in the development of intelligence that history, properly so called, begins. For the crux of historicity lies in whether our ancestors were not only *in* history but also *of* it.[2] At what point did our ancestors experience their own existences not only as continuous with that of their ancestors but also as integrated with them into an objective *lineage*? When did they first begin not only to *have* ancestors – the prerogative of any organism – but also to act *in terms of* their ancestry, even to the point of choosing which precursors embodied their ideals and their historic legitimacy and should even be treated as their *biological* ancestors?[3] In short, when did societies begin to exist *objectively*, as opposed to merely continuing?

---

[1] For an overview of the infirmities of pre-capitalist monetary systems, see Braudel (1974: 'Money').

[2] The idea that history begins with writing must surely be rejected, if only on the grounds of modesty, at least where the meaning of this criterion is that writing represents the point from which we latecomers are able to decipher what happened in the past through objective artefacts and records. Such a position is only one step away from the progressivist fallacy that the function of history is to lead up to the present. This is a view to which the average Sumerian might well have subscribed too, but that would then place all presents on an equal footing, leaving the entire position in deepest contradiction. There are also massive difficulties in deciding where to draw the line: is a tally stick a written record? See Nissen *et al.* (1993: especially ch. 5) or Ifrah (1998) for examples of transitional forms and pre-literate methods of deliberate social organisation.

[3] White in Breck and Yourgau (1972: 238–9). The artificial creation of pseudo-biological kin in order to maintain social relationships (such as the adoption of unrelated children to ensure the continuity of the family or the creation pseudo-cousins to permit a legitimate marriage) is widely documented in the anthropological literature.

For example, who were the first of the 'twice born' – those who were born once physically and then again into society proper by means of rites of initiation and explicit status? Who were the first people to dream of tracing their ancestry – and their authority – back to the Bharatas, the Sun God, the Trojans or the Lost Tribes of Israel?[1] Which indeed was the first 'people'? And conversely, who were the first to destroy an individual's existence as a rational being through a deliberate *policy* of enslavement, whereby the organic body is retained but all except the most meagre aspects of its subjectivity, its inter-subjectivity and social existence are consciously annihilated? Even if it was for their strictly intelligent capabilities (to understand orders, to apply a skill, to cooperate among themselves, and so on) that slaves were bought in the first place, they were wholly deprived of any distinct historical identity. As the Romans defined them, a slave was merely an *instrumentum vocale*, just as a horse was *instrumentum semi-vocale* and a tool *instrumentum mutum* – and none of them was kin, a member of society, a citizen, or perhaps even a human being.[2]

Similarly, at what point did we begin to translate the sequence of artefacts and symbols into a true *heritage*? When did we start, not only to inherit things from our ancestors but also to interpret and value and treat them in a particular way, *because* they are inherited in a form that gives them inherent meaning? When did we first begin to *need* ancestry, be it to substantiate our social position or (as in the case of the constant search for ancient precursors for alchemy and astrology) to legitimate our beliefs through the authority of hallowed continuity?[3] Whenever it was, it was only from this point on that we are entitled to trace our own history.

Why then is a grasp of the historicity of human nature important? For three reasons. Firstly, historicity means that we have managed to accommodate the most extraordinary diversity of forms and contents to activity, and moreover a completely unprecedented range of developmental levels, within a single invariant basic structure. Secondly, both that history and eventually the fact that we *have* a history figure in and come to regulate our activity explicitly, through anticipation, planning, tradition, ideas of progress, and so on. Finally, this highest form of rational activity (which is to say, of activity that knows itself to be that activity and is that activity by virtue of that knowledge) is the means whereby we transform the world, and so change the very basis of our existence. Thus, it is the historicity of human nature and activity that brings it full

---

[1] On myths of common descent, see Reynolds (1997). On the parallel formation of more global views of history, notably of history as a cyclical or degenerative process, see Janko in Teich *et al.* (1997: 18–36).

[2] On slavery as social death, see Meillassoux (1991) and Patterson (1982). The Romans were anticipated by Aristotle, who considered slaves to be 'living tools' (*Politics*, Book I, ch. 4).

[3] Ariès (1973: 12–6) observes that in order to is only between the fifteenth and eighteenth centuries – the culmination of concrete reason in western Europe – individual and family portraits and other heirlooms were carefully inscribed and dated, apparently 'to give the family greater historical consistency'.

circle, to the point where intelligence is itself the primary condition of intelligence. And much the same can be said for consciousness.

Of course, the completion of this process lies far in the future as far as concrete reason is concerned. Nevertheless, concrete reason does provide history's first forms properly speaking. And the earliest possible basis of this historicity is a concrete grasp of the three sub-dialectics of internalisation and externalisation just reviewed. For both lineage and heritage presuppose the ability to situate oneself in the larger whole, which in turn presupposes an effective grasp, if not yet an objective appreciation, of the relationships that constitute and are constituted by one's situation. They need not quite constitute a totality properly so called, but some sense of time and place is essential.

If, on the other hand, intelligence is still too undeveloped to raise itself above the intuitive plane, it is most unlikely to create anything that will last beyond the passing of its creators, other than by the sheer good fortune on which archaeology relies. And even then the good fortune is entirely the archaeologists', for pre-concrete reason has only a superficial interest in and grasp of lasting consequences, except insofar as they facilitate a recurring cycle of seasonal migrations, support a calendar of ritual events, and other events within the compass of a small group's actively shared world view.

However, once reason enters its concrete stage, with its more intentional sense of self and other, present and absent, appearance and reality, an altogether different order of historicity ensues. For each of these dialectics presupposes precisely that deeper command of the order of things on which both concrete reason and history are built, as I hope the preceding examples of proto-technology, proto-finance and proto-science show. That is not to say that concrete reason *has* a history or even a historiography in the sense of an objective theory and description of what happened in the past. No traditionalist has any sense of history, for the whole basis of history is the recognition not only that things were different in the past but also that they could, perhaps even should, be different in the future.[1]

But history consists of a good deal more than machinery, money and monographs. These are only the outward signs (though no less material or objective or determining for all that) of the history of intelligence, whose inner nature we find determining the deeper struggles and contradictions of 'real' history. So I shall return to feudalism, which I shall take as a typical form of concrete reason on the historical plane. For although feudalism and its equivalents emerged in a variety of times, in many places and under the impetus of a range of forces, their basic logic was consistently concrete, and their history was bounded by the same limits as concrete reason as a whole.[2]

---

[1] On different perspectives on history in classical China, India, Greece and elsewhere, see Needham (1969: Ch. 7).

[2] For the many faces of feudalism and a review of a number of similarly concrete systems, plus a detailed account of the social, political and economic forces (though not the logic) that created and sustained them, see Anderson (1974).

This identification of feudalism with concrete reason does not necessarily imply that, on the historic scale at least, concrete reason must be directly preceded by a phase of

European medieval society emerged out of the simpler forms of Germanic tribalism and the remnants of Roman society. It emerged over a period of centuries, with different aspects of society being increasingly differentiated and integrated at markedly different rates and with quite different effect in different regions, in different strata and at different times. Many aspects of medieval society remained intuitive for centuries after its classic forms had reached their peak, with close-knit communities and strictly parochial forms of organisation, economy and politics the norm for broad swathes of society. And on the highest levels, both monarchs and the Church maintained an equally characteristic position cutting across the more mundane aspects of medieval life.[1] It was also a confused form of social organisation, for reasons that are entirely intrinsic to concrete reason in general and medieval society in particular.

Nevertheless, there seems to have been a kernel of structures and relationships that can be legitimately salvaged from the confusion, one expression of which was feudalism. The original premise of feudalism was an arrangement whereby great lords granted members of their entourage authority over parcels of land in exchange for an assortment of military and administrative services. By this means, large territories could be controlled in the absence of correspondingly large legal, administrative and political mechanisms. This local control could extend not only to direct personal authority over the local population but also to the further partitioning of the land among yet further layers of subordinates.

Hence feudalism's characteristic system of sub-infeudation:[2] land was held by subordinates on behalf of their superiors, who stood in much the same rela-

---

intuitive reason. As I shall argue elsewhere, a logical order does not necessarily translate into a historical order, but that does not render either sequence any less deterministic or the relationship between them any less exact. However, to understand the relationship between concrete reason and the rise and fall of feudalism, one must pose a further question, namely whether the abstract logic of reason is a sufficient as well as a necessary cause of history, or whether other causes might not also condition the concrete unfolding of this logic. In the case of western feudalism, the critical issue is not the logical purity of this particular social formation but rather its origins in, and subsequent articulation and subsumption of at least two previous social formations, the Roman and the Germanic.

The reader will also note that most of the personal pronouns in the paragraphs that follow are masculine. This is not a lapse from political correctness but a reflection of the realities of feudalism, especially in its more militarised medieval phase. Only when approaching its absolutist form could the feudal system be considered self-sustaining, and its supreme governor qualified first and foremost by his or her ability to rule *through* it, rather than personally sustaining and enforcing it through personal leadership in combat and privately held plunder. Hence both the quite legitimate domination of medieval historiography by *kings* and battles, and the later attenuation of this situation.

[1] Reynolds (1997).

[2] The broader European canvass is painted, briefly, by Duby in Cipolla (1976: 175–220). For a summary of the English case, especially the manorial economy, see Postan (1975) and Hilton (1973: 25ff). Hicks (1995) elaborates many of the complexities of this system, primarily for the English case, but many of his qualifications on the classical model apply to other forms of feudalism. Although the present argument takes its evidence pri-

tionship to *their* superiors, and so on. But hence also the many other forms of personal subordination, be they tenancies, households or retinues of various kinds: in each case, the primary relationship was between a master and his dependant. Even where such relationships rested on a cash nexus, it was still just this kind of concrete, bilateral relationship that was created.[1] Conversely, those who stood outside this network of complexly interlocking relationships – not only the vagabonds but also the independent peasants and squires – could generally gain social and political leverage only by attaching themselves to a lord's 'connection' or by creating a retinue of their own. At least at the opening of the medieval period, there was no truly *social* system encompassing these relationships as a whole, no independent framework of laws or regal jurisdiction through which a subordinate could circumvent the authority of his liege.

These relationships came in many different flavours, especially from the point of view of the participants. Under European feudalism, it was an honourable arrangement for all parties:

> By service of greater men they were able to exercise authority delegated to them by their lords and thus partook of their lords' worship and power... It did not disparage the server: an earldom, for example, was compatible with custody of James I's personal privy.[2]

But elsewhere the idea that great aristocrats might offer personal service to their monarch was unthinkably degrading. This led to the formation of many other kinds of concrete rational arrangements, such as the slave administrations of the Roman, Chinese, Byzantine and Islamic empires.[3] In each case the monarch had to be untouchable yet wield tangible power; they could therefore only be represented by someone who existed solely as the embodiment of their authority, such as a personal slave, whose very existence was totally dependent on their master's whim.[4]

Note the superficially formal nature of this hierarchy, whose pseudo-recursive application of the rule of personal subordination can easily create the appearance of a genuine social *system*. But the appearance is deceptive. Firstly, with the partial exception of the church,[5] the basis of feudal allegiance was highly particularistic, depending very largely on the quasi-personal interests of land and lineage it bound together, on the abilities of individual incumbents and on the practical circumstances in which each such relationship arose and continued. Secondly, any formal obligations nominally implied by this chain of

---

marily from European history, my superficial understanding of the histories of India, China and the pre-Columbian Americas supports its principles.

[1] Cf. Hicks account of 'bastard feudalism' (Hicks: 1995).

[2] Hicks (1995: 11).

[3] Purcell in Boardman *et al.* (1992); Patterson (1982: ch. 11).

[4] Patterson (1982: ch. 11).

[5] Hallpike (1986: ch. VI) argues that the separation of Church and state arose as little more than a contingent detail of Indo-European social organisation, yet has had immense consequences for how life is lived in such societies. If this is true then there is no contradiction in treating both this and the very different relationship between religion and state in, say, Chinese society under the same concrete rational rubric.

allegiances – for example, the obligation to protect one's subjects – were largely unenforced and unenforceable. However widely acknowledged, they consisted more of moral and ethical exhortations and platitudes than an effective economic, political or even ideological order. Hence the ultimate opposition between feudalism and truly formal systems of administration:

> A true bureaucrat is free to act only in so far as he is empowered to do so and in the light of the bureaucratic procedures and specified goals, while a feudal lord is free to do all that he is not specifically forbidden to do.[1]

– and, one might add in many cases, all he is not directly deterred from doing by *force majeure*.

It is also thanks to their specifically formal nature that our own government systems can actively sustain themselves without resort to the personal power, wealth or connections of their incumbents, not only in terms of the necessary information and decisions needed for their routine operation but also in terms of the financing and due process needed to preserve their own structure. There was certainly very little in 'the feudal system' that was capable of defining, implementing or policing its own structure effectively. 'The system' was not merely weak; in reality it existed less in any material structure on the ground than in the intentions and personal resources of monarchs, the skills of their ministers and the apologetics of medieval theology and jurisprudence.[2] The mechanisms needed to create, manage and maintain feudalism as a true system were always more or less pragmatic, eclectic and conventional, assuming they existed at all. Consequently, the entire history of feudalism, medieval feudalism especially, can seem like one long dialogue between virtue and whim.

This lack of true 'system' led in turn to what seem, to eyes tutored under more formally structured societies founded on a coherent and deterministic order of 'lower' and 'higher', perplexing consequences. Under feudalism, royal power was by no means merely an alternative to provincial power, but equally well it was by no means its automatic superior, and any contest between them might be settled according to circumstance, opportunity and (often) the clash of arms. In truth, royalty was not yet 'royal' in the unqualified sense a later monarch would recognise. It had more in common with the patron–client systems of Gaul or Rome or the more sophisticated pre-Columbian societies.[3]

---

[1] Kamenka (1989: 3). The Weberian tradition in studying bureaucracy would also confirm this interpretation, of course.

[2] For a summary of some of the relevant parts of feudal administration, political theory and jurisprudence, see Black (1992) and Eccleshall (1978).

[3] For Celtic Gaul, see, Crumley's 'Celtic settlement before the conquest: The dialectics of landscape and power' in Crumley and Marquardt (1987). On the Roman *clientela*, see Brunt (1986), MacMullen (1988), Scullard (1982) or de Ste. Croix (1983); and for a brief review of the wider but equally concrete relationships through which the empire was managed, see Purcell in Boardman *et al.* (1992). On the transformation of ancient Roman slavery into medieval serfdom (which was essentially only a change in the way ongoing concrete rational relationships were managed in changing circumstances), see Phillips (1985). Or, in a more anthropological vein, see Marquardt's 'Dialectical archaeology' in Schiffer (1992). Marquardt also summarises the situation in Gaul and addresses certain

But its lack of truly systematic order and controls notwithstanding, concrete reason can deal with complex, multi-faceted problems by *ad hoc* methods, even though it lacks more abstract, systematic principles through which it might solve them systematically or definitively. For example, the transition from one medieval jurisdiction to another could be controlled more or less seamlessly, even though the whole had no profound regulatory structure. But as the personal basis on which this was achieved implies, there was a constant need for the right person to be at the right place at the right time – a requirement that, as the bloody history of early feudalism especially illustrates, was frequently left unmet.

What is more, there were innumerable paradoxes and lacunae that no amount of personal strength or guile could fill or overcome. For example, a knight might owe allegiance to two different lords at once, who might themselves come to blows. Where then did this knight's duty lie – could he sit on the fence, or was he obliged to choose?[1] Likewise, relatively clear and consistent notions of the principles of justice existed, but its administration resided in the common sense, established practice[2] and ritual gestures of the times. Since these all differed between locations, groups, activities, and so on, no single practice was possible, even in principle. As for the public jurisprudence, due process and formal instruments with which we are acquainted, these were incapable of being implemented even in the rare contexts in which they were recognised. As a result, however clear the facts of the matter, the process of getting to the right answer was often thoroughly arbitrary, unclear and unstable, and the answer itself equivocal, provisional and temporary.

The converse of this lack of a system to hold all these concrete relationships together was a situation in which a society's integrity, operation and direction all relied heavily on the authority, skill and purpose of the individuals and groups who actually stood at the interstices between the particular relationships out of which a given concrete 'system' was composed, and whatever the theoretical structures that allegedly prevailed, most practical action depended on the decisions and decisiveness of key individuals. So concrete societies were always more likely to throw up heroes and villains of truly historic proportions, an Asoka or a Tamerlane, than a strictly formal system such as capitalism, beside which even the most extraordinary individual is likely to seem a rather diminished figure. The paranoia of an Ivan the Terrible or the manipulations of courtiers is equally disruptive, without remedy short of a palace coup. The lack of an impersonal system through which an authority might act was also the main reason why the key skill of the lords of Roman, feudal and other

---

aspects of sixteenth–century Florida tribal communities. For summaries of pre-Columbian American political systems, see Fiedel (1987) or Fagan (1985). See also Johnson and Earle (1987: 282–3). The relationship between personal gods and the great cosmic gods in ancient cosmologies also often seemed to operate on a basis of personal allegiance and petitions (eg, Frankfort *et al*, 1949: 220–3).

[1] See Tuchman (1978) for a case history.

[2] Reynolds (1997).

concrete rational societies was court politics, with all its astute strokes[1] and *ad hoc* judgement rather than systematic administration;[2] why status, deference and the ability to command personal respect and affection[3] and to be personally represented on the spot[4] were so critical to effective rule; why the personal predilections of key individuals so readily transmuted into historical profundities;[5] why personal honour and pride were the pivot of social structure;[6] why legal administration included personal execution and private prisons; why violence was a normal part of the political process at every level;[7] and so on.[8]

This need for personal authority to compensate for the lack of an objective system may even explain why many regimes preferred eunuchs as ministers.[9] As slaves (usually of alien origin[10]) they owed any authority they possessed wholly to their masters, and as eunuchs they were 'genealogical isolates'.[11] Clearly, then, they would be unable to found new dynasties, and so could never replace their masters in enduring ways. But on the other hand, only under a concrete rational regime would either of these considerations be significant: under intuitive reason there was neither enduring authority to be possessed nor dynasties to create, and under formal reason authority will flow from the office rather than *vice versa*, and dynasties will play little part in politics. This conclusion is supported by the fact that slave-based administrations were most likely to break down when the slaves in question were indeed able

---

[1] 'Only the vicissitudes of personality and circumstance can explain how an assertive monarch could squeeze prodigious sums from his subjects without changing the rules under which they were taxed, or how human ingenuity could summon forth huge amounts of borrowed funds for a government whose credit should by all rights have been exhausted' (Tracy in Brady *et al.*, 1994: 563).

[2] Eg, Purcell in Boardman *et al.* (1992).

[3] Reynolds (1997).

[4] On the crucial role played by slaves as representatives of their masters in the ancient and medieval worlds, see Patterson (1982: especially ch. 11).

[5] Regardless of whether he actually made it, the jest attributed to Samuel Pepys – that the Anglican religion 'came out of Henry VIII's codpiece' – stated a fundamental truth of feudalism (Tomalin, 2003: 300).

[6] Huizinga (1924/2001).

[7] See, for example, Riley-Smith (1999) for what, from our standpoint beyond the Reformation, seems an especially paradoxical example.

[8] It also makes it extremely unlikely that formalist approaches to economics – the view that modern economic models and concepts apply universally – will ever make much headway until they take more substantive aspects of social relationships into account. That is not to say that formalism has no place outside the world of strictly formal economies such as capitalism, but its account will always have to be qualified by historically specific explanations of extra-economic meanings, obligations and controls, and by clearly drawn distinctions between strictly formal exchange and more concrete modes of redistribution and reciprocation (Polanyi *et al.*, 1957: 243–70; Sahlins, 1974). On political control over early feudal markets, see Hodges (1989: especially pp. 52ff).

[9] Patterson (1982).

[10] Patterson (1982); Meillassoux (1991).

[11] Patterson (1982: 312).

to develop political allegiances not based on ownership, as in the case of the janissaries. But again, such a change would be of little consequence in a non-concrete political structure, where the state apparatus would either be too rudimentary for this change to matter (as under intuitive reason) or regulated by impersonal processes (as under formal reason).[1]

Conversely, for want of a unitary and comprehensive social structure into which everyone might fit, almost everyone had to have a personal master – as opposed to, say, an employer in the modern sense. So, whether based on slavery, serfdom, peonage or some other arrangement, unfree labour was as central to concrete reason as personal lordship.[2] The abstract unfreedom of the capitalist proletariat was no more conceivable under feudalism than a Bill of Rights: a particular concrete obligation fixing each individual to a particular condition and relationship was indispensable. It is only to bourgeois apologists looking for ancient roots to justify their own revolution that Magna Carta seems to offer guarantees of personal liberty. Even the freedman and freedwoman usually remained more or less forcibly attached 'clients' of the household from which they had been 'freed'.[3]

Nor is the need for much more personalised forms of authority the sole social repercussion of concrete reason. The same lack of an overarching order into which individuals could fit without reference to empirical beacons and badges also explains why time was more shaped in human minds by its social significance than by any objective measure, and was organised around the farming seasons, saints days, festivals, the liturgy, days of ill omen, the crowning of kings and so on – a far cry from the formal, objective time on which puritans, merchants and manufacturers would insist, with its abstract, regular and uniform cycles of work and rest.[4] It is also because of concrete reason's inability to break free of its empirical conditions that sumptuary laws were both necessary and effective means of social control, why transitional social events such as birth, marriage and death were accompanied by such earnest rites of passage, why polytheism (including the effective polytheism of medieval Christianity) was the order of the day, and why objects such as regalia, reliquaries, the sword, the host, and so on were so vital (in both senses of the word).

> Gestures transmitted political and religious power; they made such transmission public, known by all, and they gave legal actions a living image, as for example when a lord received in his hand the homage of his vassals or when a bishop laid

---

[1] It is debatable whether the relationship between master and slave is truly asymmetrical, given that *all* power and legitimacy remains on the master's side: is the relationship between everything and nothing asymmetrical? However, as far as the present account is concerned there seems to be no reason not to treat this as a very refined form of concrete relationship. Both Patterson and Meillassoux (1991) make it clear that the Hegelian version of this relationship is entirely romantic.

[2] See de Ste. Croix's typology in Archer (1988: 19–32); and also Meillassoux (1991: 89ff and ch. 6).

[3] Patterson (1982).

[4] Whitrow (1989: 109–14); Needham (1969: Ch. 7).

his hand on the head of a newly consecrated priest. Gestures bound together human wills and human bodies.[1]

Conversely, the pilgrimages that typified medieval conceptions of penance would be acts of extraordinary (and perhaps hypocritically extravagant) devotion had they only symbolised the pilgrim's contrition, rather than actually constituting it. The crusade and the *jihad* would be unintelligible had they been either purely symbolic gestures or concealed exercises in imperialism and self-aggrandisement (although these and other motives, especially feudal obligation, certainly intrude more and more).[2]

Likewise for intellectual and even apparently proto-scientific activities:

[E]ven the simplest Christian presumably had at least a vague knowledge of the critical events in Christian history. In fact, for most people this timeline remained far more real than the history of their own era: the sequence of the Creation and the events of the Old Testament; the episodes in Christ's life and the lives of the saints. These events needed to be recorded and dated to become valid, and it was this need that motivated time reckoners such as Dionysius and Bede to devise their year-by-year dating schemes in an age when few people cared what year it was beyond year 6 or 10 in the reign of their local king or squire.[3]

The entire alchemical exercise was also designed to put the alchemist in touch with a highly personalised realm of invisible but very concrete spirits and forces, whose supposed subjectivity in turn gave an internal explanation, logic and direction to the mass of otherwise localised, disparate and episodic relationships to which concrete reason is limited. Indeed, the universe as a whole was perceived as a domain (or perhaps one should say, demesne) founded on, explained by and actively ordered by the wishes and commandments of a highly personal deity: not only every*one* needed a master, but every*thing* too. No wonder then that the 'chemical wedding' was one of the most potent images of pre-modern 'science': as Pico della Mirandola put it, 'To work magic is to do nothing other than to marry the universe'.[4] Likewise, to the extent that the notion of 'law' was applied to nature at all, it was in the sense that a monarch creates a law that his or her subjects *ought* to obey as a matter of subjective obligation, rather than a structural necessity inherent in their natures that they were forced to follow by virtue of their objective natures. Conversely, it is only as it starts to approach its own natural conclusion that concrete reason differen-

---

[1] Schmitt in Roodenburg and Bremmer (1991: 60). Huizinga's classic *The Waning of the Middle Ages* (1924/2001) is virtually a catalogue of the cultural effects of this situation, which persisted until very late in the day:

In 1495, during an attempt to settle a demarcation dispute between Languedoc and Provence, a commissioner from Provence (which had been annexed to the crown in 1481) was sent to set up the provincial arms on the Iles du Rhône. In so doing he came across a post to which the royal arms had been fixed. His reaction was revealing. He removed his hat and knelt before this symbol of royal power, then stood up, removed it and left it in the sacristy of a local church 'where relics are conserved' (Hale, 1971).

[2] Riley-Smith (1999).

[3] Duncan (1998: 145–6). On the Chinese case, see Needham, 'Time and eastern man' (1969: 218–298).

[4] Quoted in North (1994: 273).

tiates between cause, force and necessity on the one hand and reason, obligation and will on the other.[1]

Not that all such imputations of a hidden order required that that order be subjective: it was not only in terms of demons and spirits that the hidden world worked. However, the alternatives – generally speaking organic powers and faculties attributed to, for example, rocks, minerals and the physical earth generally – served the same purpose, namely to knit together the morass of relations and series and classifications concrete reason was able to deal with directly, but which it could not integrate through its own resources. That is not to say that this sort of 'explanation' was a matter of choice: as far as I can tell, no one said, 'Let's project a biological metaphor onto things here'. Rather, being unable to systematise their real observations and encounters with the natural world by means of a truly formal logic, concrete reason was obliged to foist onto them the logic that held its own world together. This was, of course, the logic of subjectivity and, to a lesser extent, the metaphor of the organism. The spirits to which concrete reason appealed were likewise only subjects who lacked any physical, chemical and biological existence. They did not lack the ability to *influence* the physical, chemical or biological realms; but the occult (ie, undetectable) nature of their 'means' only reinforces the view that this was a process of projection, not explanation, and the elaborate metaphysical rationalisations that accompanied such projections only reinforce this interpretation. Like any other good marriage, magic was a meeting of minds; and as stars and geological formations generally lack a mind of their own, it becomes necessary to think one up for them. Medieval and Renaissance scholars continued to make fine observations, but they were always liable to be clothed in terms of an imagined subjectivity or life force.

Perhaps in some ultimate sense this mélange of one-sided and ambiguous structures was untenable, and one can easily sympathise with those called upon to account for, justify and administer it. But the dislocations were seldom fatal, and feudalism worked, even thrived, for centuries. In many respects concrete reason's stratagems were very effective, if not always for the best of reasons. If, for example, you conclude that fossils are the spontaneous creations of (literally) living rock, then there is no need to worry about the vast timescales they might otherwise seem to demand.

The resemblance of fossils to living things was not accidental, but nor was it evidence that fossils had once been alive. The earth itself was capable of growth; crystals grow just like a living thing, while many miners believed that the minerals they extracted were perpetually renewed. Nature was full of petrifying influences, as illustrated by pearls, corals and human gallstones. Some Renaissance thinkers even supposed that the 'seeds' of living things could grow by absorbing mineral nourishment, thus producing a stony counterpart to the parent form. Within such a world view the significance of fossils and minerals was bound to be quite different to that which emerged after the foundation of the modern earth sciences. There was no need to postulate great revolutions in the earth's surface, because

---

[1] For a brief comparative review of the transition from concrete to formal rational science, (although not expressed in such terms), including a number of important historical differences, see Needham (1969: Ch. 8).

the organized structures it contained were interpreted as the products of modern processes, not as relics of the past.[1]

But in the long run – if only the *very* long run – concrete reason's fundamentally disjointed character was bound to count against it, and even in the short run crisis was bound to be the norm. Of course, corruption can potentially play a part in any imperfect political system, and demonstrably has throughout the ages. But in the case of concrete reason, there was no all-embracing system in terms of which it would be possible to define 'loyalty', 'corruption', and so on in global terms. So the tendency to disruption by personal and parochial interests is inherent and endemic in concrete reason.[2]

For example, a magnate might owe allegiance to his monarch and be owed it by his barons and his burghers, but what the barons owed the monarch was a troubling and imperfectly unresolved issue, and remained so for some centuries. This left provincial magnates and urban patriciates (who, in western Europe at least, enjoyed remarkable political freedom from feudal interference, not least because of the various monarchs' strenuous efforts to prevent them from being drawn into the orbit of local aristocrats) more or less free to detach the social pyramid beneath them from the centre and, *in extremis*, plunge the realm into civil war. And this is precisely what, when the occasion arose, they proceeded to do. In the end, sub-infeudation, retinues, households, originally instituted to give a workable political structure to an organised society, came to pose a chronic threat to it. Sub-infeudation in particular began to be subverted almost as soon as it was established, with the originally strictly conditional arrangement – land for service – quickly ossifying into *de facto* inheritance and, by degrees, *de jure* ownership.[3] As

But the rise of aristocratic land ownership by no means represented the end of feudalism. On the contrary, not until very late under the feudal regime did this mean ownership in the current sense of the word of alienable property available for sale to anyone with enough money, and these remaining limitations on property rights are directly connected to the *persistence* of feudalism and its fusion of political and economic rights. Tawney put it:

> Property is not a mere aggregate of economic privileges, but a responsible office. Its *raison d'être* is not only income, but service. It is to secure its owner such means, and no more than such means, as may enable him to perform those duties, whether labour on the land, or labour in government, which are involved in the particular status which he holds in the system … The owner is a trustee, whose rights are derived from the function which he performs and should lapse if he repudiates it.[4]

On one side, the aristocracy exercised uniquely protected rights of control which, taken together with a wide range of social, political and ideological

---

[1] Bowler (1992: 83–4).

[2] For the corruption of ancient Rome, see MacMullen (1988); for feudal England, see Hicks (1995).

[3] It may well be that the eunuch ministries of Byzantium and China were created to deal with this problem (Patterson, 1982: especially ch. 11).

[4] Quoted in Hallpike (2004: 53).

rights, gave them a massive preponderance over their subjects. On the other, properties possessed by virtue of specifically feudal ties acted almost as additional personal attributes of their owners, like their height, their hereditary infirmities, and so on. Like personal traits, they could not be disposed of merely because they were inconvenient or because it would be advantageous to their owner to do so. Nobles were as closely identified with this aspect of their heritage as with any Habsburg lip – a fact that was well expressed in the notion that the land inherited its lord as much as the lord inherited the land.[1]

So, although this dependence was resisted from the first, feudal property was in principle inalienable. What is more, it *had* to be so, not because of the will of monarchs or the arguments of the lawyers, but because any other property system would have been unmanageable by the concrete means available to feudal society. Feudal property rights were merely the institutionalisation of structural limitations that could only be overcome when feudalism itself was overcome. Although one should neither understate the variability of its expressions nor overstate the consistency with which this principle was conceived or enforced, the arbitrary yet inalienable nature of feudal property made it the antithesis of ownership in its later, more strictly formalised sense.

Just how concrete reason deals with this intrinsic instability and immobility its very concreteness produces depends very much in the plane on which they are met. Any ambitions concrete reason (or immature form of intelligence) may harbour beyond its immediate range are readily realised where a more advanced intelligence is on hand to manage the broader supra-concrete conditions of its activity. Children can achieve goals far beyond their personal abilities when adults are on hand to draw their attention to the otherwise unrecognised reaches of their own acts. Conversely, it is the absence of analogous guidance that compels a concrete social formation like feudalism to rely on history itself to usher it to *its* conclusion. For example, the threat posed by subinfeudation and its concomitants could only be overcome by the systematisation of political and economic relationships that was capable of locking local lords into a general system within which the interests of individuals would be served only insofar as they collectively supported the whole. In practice this meant the gradual development of an organised central power and the concomitant suppression of all opposition through a wide range of legal, political and even military means.

Of course, as the development of feudal thought at all levels revealed, concrete reason is perfectly capable of posing at least a veiled version of the problem. The growing tendency for the same relations to fall into regular conflict with one another pointed the way, if not to a valid solution then at least to a correct formulation of the problem. Unlike intuitive reason, concrete reason at least finds its own problems thinkable, and with that the possibility of organised change. Nevertheless, no feudal system could make the necessary leap

---

[1] See, for example, Marx (1975: 175). As late as the eighteenth century Samuel Johnson observed that in some parts of Scotland the greater dignitaries expect to be addressed by the name of their place of residence, whereas 'the meaner people' are addressed by their forenames (*Journey to the Western Islands of Scotland*, 'Inch Kenneth').

without passing through a long drawn-out agglomeration and organisation of
political power, whether in the abattoir of civil war or by some other, equally
brutal process.

Eventually, however, even the rhetoric of personal fealty and sub-
infeudation was exhausted, and a true feudal system and a truly systematic
feudalism were established, in the form of the absolutist state.[1] In very general
terms, absolutism was founded on royal monopolies of force, taxation and
right supported by a standing army, a centralised civil service, a closely super-
vised legislature and the gradual subjection of local autonomy to the royal prerogative. Where once the monarch stood in fear of his dukes and in need of the
extra-territorial powers of the military orders[2] and the Church, now the royal
court became the nexus – sometimes more like a merry-go-round – of political
life, where entrenched local interests could fight, corrupt and inveigle one another under the more or less benign (but also more or less unconditional) authority of a more or less united monarchy. *L'état c'est moi* indeed.

So, for the first time a systematic concept of public order was transferred
from political theory to political practice, with profound and widespread effects on the entire population, from the greatest aristocrat and financier to the
most exploited serf and the most destitute vagrant. What is more, this systematisation changed not only how each particular individual and group lived their
life but also every kind of relationship between these groups. The impact of the
enclosure movement on rural society is too well known[3] to need any explanation here, except to observe the extent to which it was made both possible and
necessary by the systematisation of agriculture, commerce and politics. Rather
less widely known is the transformation of the urban environment, which saw
revolutionary changes in city planning, building and management, once again
essentially because the city came to be treated as a genuine system that required a systematic response.

Popular images of pre-modern urban life notwithstanding, medieval Europeans were by no means insensitive to the filth and pollution that infected their
towns (although the standards and medical lore that informed their perceptions were undoubtedly different from our own). On the contrary, their ideals
and urban laws often aimed explicitly at the kind of control familiar from the
modern world.[4] Nevertheless, it was only in the early modern period that
complete systems for the organisation and control of town life became possible.
Hence the relatively late rise of city-level planning and designs that aimed to
solve the real problems of the city's real inhabitants. This in turn transformed
the built environment, including not only city-level designs and plans but the

---

[1] What follows is based mainly on the development of absolutism in feudal Europe.
However, most of the same general points could be made about the more highly developed concrete rational societies throughout history.

[2] On the decline and (sometimes) fall of the military orders in the face of ascendant absolutism and nationalism, see Luttrell in Riley-Smith (1999: 323–362).

[3] See, for example, Harrison (1984: *passim*), who also summarises one of enclosure's key
concomitants, the system of public relief.

[4] Laures (1992).

explicit integration of support systems (city police forces and fire brigades, open spaces, street lighting, organised food supply, carefully planned sewers, and so on) – a change that could only come about once the whole urban landscape was regarded *as* a whole. Likewise the parallel creation of appropriate political powers (effective city authorities, national-level royal and parliamentary support and properly enforced laws and decrees) and administrative instruments (building and zoning regulations, compulsory purchase orders, specialised and dedicated administrators). Even the greatest and longest established cities of the ancient world could boast more than a superficial acquaintance with any of these.

As one might expect, all this only came about in the early modern period and the reconstruction of cities such as London after the Great Fire of 1666, Paris under Louis XIV, Colbert and their successors and Amsterdam in its Golden Age.[1] These examples can all be contrasted with the city management of the medieval city or the *ad hoc*, parochial and, from a business point of view, very distracting role played by the guilds in pre-industrial China, where the management of the city was essentially localised, episodic and incoherent and the basic process of city growth was one of only weakly controlled influxes. As so often, there seems to be a good deal more similarity between ancient and medieval forms – the historical poles of concrete reason – than between either and any modern city built and managed by means of formal rational principles, systems and methods.

The changes systemisation brought about were extraordinarily pervasive but highly contradictory. Especially at the upper and lower extremes of society, where the principal beneficiaries of the unified state and the principal victims of the 'Great Confinement'[2] were to be found, the pragmatic order of medieval politics, economics, ideology and even science was first augmented but then vigorously suppressed by the new rationality. In between those extremes, a plethora of stubbornly concrete interests and increasingly formal organisation reigned, often in what seem to observers from our own times the most unlikely places:

> Luther lived in dread of witches. Pico della Mirandola wrote what is now regarded as a classic of rational humanism, *On the Dignity of Man*, in the service of a Neo-Platonic philosophy according to which man's power reaches its climax in the *magical* manipulation of the spirits of the world. Jean Bodin, one of the founders of the modern conception of the state, himself a secret heretic, argued for the relentless legal persecution of witches. The astronomer Johannes Kepler, a leading force in the revolution which established the new heliocentric astronomy, remained committed to astrology and drew horoscopes. Only by means of extensive and judicious 'editing' can the leading intellectual figures of the Renaissance and

---

[1] Chant and Goodman (1999: 186–234).

[2] The great theorist of the disciplining of society during this period is, of course, Michel Foucault, whose work complements – and differs from – the present account in many ways. See also Hirst and Woolley (1982: Part III, but pp. 172ff and pp. 255ff especially).

Reformation be made to serve as exponents of modern humanism, rationalism and empiricism.[1]

These were not just leftovers from the previous regime or concessions to popular prejudice by intellectuals who were 'really' above such naïveté. After all, 'We have 800 horoscopes from Kepler's pen that could be put down to a need for ready cash, but this does not explain why he drew up so many horoscopes for himself'.[2] Concrete relationships continued to prevail even under absolutism. In the political sphere this was not least because it was the intention of absolutist monarchs that they should, and in this sphere at least absolute monarchs wielded the power needed to make their will felt. In some cases, what had been marginal views under the previous regime – such as belief in witches – were greatly exacerbated and popularised by the birth pangs and uncertainties of absolutism.[3] And it is no great surprise that so many early attempts at urban planning and design were at least partially subverted by the aristocracy creaming off the benefits of city-wide management. For example, the great schemes to provide Paris with a reliable water supply were routinely diverted to feed the fountains of Versailles.[4]

Formal organisation and concrete interests do not make happy bedfellows, of course. However, the paradox they present is solved by noting that absolut-

---

[1] Hirst and Woolley (1982: 214). See also Kamen (1976: 263–78 and *passim*). For the view of Newton as the last alchemist, see Westfall (1980) or White (1997).

[2] North (1994: 313–9). But the transition to a more strictly naturalistic world view was clearly under way: as North goes on to add, Kepler was interested in the stars' potential contribution to the physical, metaphysical and psychological causes of things, and expressly rejected astrological interpretations couched in terms of 'signs'. Bacon and Descartes were somewhat more explicit in rejecting signs and other Renaissance methods of explanation, but even Newton harboured a (now notorious) sympathy for alchemy.

[3] For surveys of the changes wrought by absolutism, see Rabb (1975) or Kamen (1976). Regarding witchcraft, Hirst and Woolley (1982: Part III), following many others, make a strong case for the rise and fall of witch beliefs being a function of the decline and restoration of social order. This tension was heightened by the use of witchcraft as an issue in ecclesiastical and civil politics (Hirst and Woolley, 1982: 229ff). It is important to recognise that much persecution took place in marginal areas (eg, the Alps and the Pyrenees) just being assimilated to the mainstream of European society and many accusations were directed at 'wise women' and other representatives of the out-going tradition (Spierenburg, 1991: 113–8). Likewise, witch hunting in England seems to have peaked with the Civil War rather than any transition to absolutism as such (Sharpe, 1996: 105ff), which suggests that it is not necessarily disruption of the social order as a whole that is the cause of persecution. See also Alland (1972: 112–6), Trevor-Roper (1969: 28ff and 37–38) and various papers (especially Macfarlane's) in Marwick (1970) for discussion and examples of the relationship between witchcraft and the breakdown of social order. Similar explanations have been offered, not only for the historical persecution of gypsies, Jews and other groups of 'aliens' and for cargo cults, millennialism, Ghost Dances and various other tribal phenomena, but also for racial and political persecution in our own century, not to mention our own 'folk devils and moral panics' and fundamentalism (Armstrong, 2000).

[4] Chant and Goodman (1999: 218–9, 223). On modern water supplies, see also Petroski (1996).

ism's systematisation of feudal relationships was only systematic in the sense that state management was controlled by officials applying regular and more or less integrated processes to the fulfilment of well-defined policy, and so on. This quasi-formal method and architecture should still be contrasted with the *content* of this policy and the implementation of this system, both of which remained self-consciously concrete and relentlessly eclectic, conventional and pragmatic respectively. 'What we have at this point is a picture of a central government that was weak and yet was capable of acting in an arbitrary and tyrannical fashion'.[1] For neither state nor administration was ever truly formalised under absolutism, in the sense of operating on pervasive and strictly abstract principles standing above any concrete interest. There was no equality before the law, even within the individual estates, nor were offices separated from their holders. The *lettre de cachet* could never be anything but the instrument of arbitrarily concrete power. Neither could absolutism have operated indefinitely through formal mechanisms such as a fully monetarised economy or an independent tax system,[2] since that would have forced power out of the hands of the particularistic interests absolutism was supposed to further. One could even define absolutism as a disciplined, centralised socio-political machine for managing an intrinsically undisciplined, decentralised social formation, namely feudalism itself.

This machine proved itself an immensely powerful device for reproducing feudalism's basic economic logic in higher, much more efficient and effective ways. However, it achieved this result by shifting feudalism's central political focus. Having begun with the monarchy's assault on the independence of the great magnates, absolutism's subsequent reinstatement of the nobility was based on their subordination to a monarch who stood above all particularistic concerns and whose goal was not so much the preservation of the nobility as a group of *individual* magnates as the maintenance of the noble *estate*. Maybe individuals were less likely to stand out in proportion to their personal qualities, but persons of quality could rely on the vigorous support of the state, as a group if not as individuals.

On the other hand, although, taken as a whole, their particularistic privileges and authority were transformed (and, with the creation of a permanent *noblesse de robe*, somewhat reallocated), the power of the nobility as a whole was by no means expunged. The degradation of a more or less large number of individual nobles did not entail or lead to the elimination of the nobility itself, and still less to the displacement of its highly concrete collective interests from the centres of power. So, after a painful interlude of humiliation, exile and execution while the mechanics of feudalism were upgraded, the nobility returned to full power, possessed of comprehensive political, legal, economic and ideological privileges.[3] This resurrection is the key to the real logic of the transition

---

[1] Wooton (1986: 27).

[2] For a brief but illuminating summary of absolutism's financial arrangements, see Braudel (1982: 519ff).

[3] On feudal privilege in general, see Bush (1983). On the humbling and restoration of the nobility, see Anderson (1974). On the final fate of privilege and the collapse of concrete

from medieval to absolutist forms of feudalism: whether or not individual no-bles or even lineages survived was a matter of secondary importance – the critical question, whether or not it was explicitly articulated, was whether feu-dalism as a whole would be preserved.[1]

But even absolutism could only offer a temporary respite (assuming, that is, that 'temporary' can be stretched to mean 'for a century and more'), and feu-dalism's inherent contradictions quickly found new avenues through which to express themselves. Indeed, the ultimate incoherence of this ramshackle sprawl of perspectives, interests, ambitions and conflicts underlying this superficially satisfying formality is the key problem faced by concrete reason in all its forms. What is more, it is the logic of absolutism specifically as a form of concrete rea-son that ensures feudalism's ultimate downfall. For if absolutism served to eliminate the contradictions of medieval feudalism by replacing a failing as-semblage of sub-infeudations with an organised state apparatus, this process soon began to press feudalism beyond mere systematisation and on to the true *formalisation* of the entire social edifice.

This is a shift of the first magnitude, for this quite unintended change in-jected a formal and formalising logic into the historical realm that was not merely inimical but profoundly contradictory to the concrete interests absolut-ism was supposed to perpetuate. By organising and polarising the previously incoherent estates, the social system as a whole quickly came to be mediated by increasingly strictly formalised relationships exemplified by bureaucratic power, commodity relations and the universal solvent of money. With that, the conflict between particularistic feudal rights and interests and the universalism of the rising political and economic systems took an increasingly urgent, fo-cused, strident and comprehensive turn.

Most especially, for most of Europe it was largely absolutism that brought the long drawn out progress of commercialisation and formal roles throughout the medieval period to the fore. Long before the rise of absolutism, money had established itself as the universal medium in the economic and political spheres and the quasi-personal relations characterising the local manor and the affairs of court had long since been tainted by the consequent equivocations.[2] Nevertheless, this did not lead to the formation of a new *system* of relations connecting economic and political tasks. That had to wait for the development of the corresponding economic and political structures, namely capitalism and the nation state.[3]

---

reason, see Fitzsimmons (1987).

[1] There are broad similarities between this process and the attempts to preserve the pharaonic basis of the ancient Egyptian state during the Third Intermediate Period. For a summary, see Trigger *et al.* (1983: 226–9, 238–40).

[2] Spufford (1988).

[3] To draw an analogy with another aspect of praxis, tool-making is already a qualitative advance over even the most sophisticated forms of tool *use*, but it is only when the mak-ing of tools is itself subordinated to a definite mode of *production* that the revolutionary forces implicit in radically new technology come to fruition. Likewise, money and roles always revolutionise the logic of barter, apprenticeships and the like, but it is only when

Nor was this a purely external intrusion into the absolutist system: 'reasons of state' and the personal interests of many of the old nobility were also increasingly aligned with the ideals, objectives and methods of the rising bourgeoisie, with their entirely formal notions of economy, power, interest, propriety and method.[1] So it was only a matter of time before absolutism found itself submitting to the forces of formalisation. The revolution took decades, even centuries to complete, encompassing not only the formation of the nation state and the rise of the bourgeoisie but also, in their different ways, both Renaissance and Reformation. Nevertheless, the writing was on the wall from the day the first *intendant* was despatched to the provinces.[2]

Like sub-infeudation before it, absolutism was established to protect feudalism, but soon became its nemesis. The increasing differentiation of the powers and interests of the monarchy from those of their subjects both permitted and necessitated the flourishing of structures that could bestride the feudal world, if not like a colossus (and in the case of Louis XIV, more like a dwarf on stilts) then certainly on an altogether more abstracted plane from that inhabited by most individual aristocrats. Hence the formalisation of absolutism, for formalisation surpasses simple systematisation in that it expresses what the system would become if it were indeed abstracted away from the concerns of, yet increasingly precisely and forcefully imposed upon, either its actual content and context or the interests and intentions of its controllers. And ultimately it was the specifically formal nature of this plane rather than the altogether concrete intentions of its increasingly isolated ruling caste that would decide the fates of nations. Having defeated over-ambitious and insubordinate individuals by means of the absolutist *system*, that same system's *formalisation* meant that it could not remain content with serving another concrete individual or even group, no matter how exalted they might be and no matter that they were the system's nominal owners.

---

they find themselves integrated into a strictly formalising mode of production that their own formalising power can be manifested truly and to the full.

[1] For the British case of the 'financial revolution' that fuelled the larger political economic and revolution, see Dickson (1967) or Roseveare (1991). It is important to recognise that the fall of feudalism came about through its internal logic, and that the bourgeoisie was itself a creation of feudalism, not some glorious epiphany of the human spirit released from the thrall of religious superstition and wicked barons. The argument that the bourgeoisie was somehow the product of the separate urban civilisation is empirically correct, for the bourgeoisie certainly originated in the towns and there was a fundamental antipathy of interests between rural and urban communities from the first. Nevertheless, as an account of the underlying structures and genesis that created the bourgeoisie, it assumes a false premise, namely that towns were somehow extra-feudal. In reality, many were directly founded by local nobles, and were founded specifically in order to milk the revenues that might accrue from trade, commodity production and other altogether non-rural activities. For further argument and references, see Robinson (1987). For a sweeping account of the historical interconnection between absolutism and capitalism, see Braudel (1981, 1982, 1984).

[2] Kamenka (1989: 91ff).

So, the formal machinery of the absolutist state (ie, the formal political instrument for preserving feudalism from its own concreteness) supplanted the machinations of the royal court (the apogee of concrete political organisation), the monarch's finance became increasingly state finance,[1] and a formal economy based on commodities, markets and taxes overwhelmed the feudal economy of entailment, subsistence and tithes. Simultaneously, the attitude of the leading elements of the social formation as a whole to feudalism of any kind became first one of indifference and then open hostility. So even absolutism went under, with a violence proportionate to the local regime's arrogance and rigidity, the monarch slipping from *roi proprietaire* to *roi bureaucrate*[2] and thence more or less suddenly to constitutional monarch or private citizen. Or if monarch or nobility or even peasants should demur, the tumbrels stood waiting.[3]

As the many parallels with both psychogenesis and the history of science show,[4] the development of feudalism is only one expression of the development of concrete reason generally. But this is more than a matter of parallels, for the decline and fall of absolutism also provide the arena where all these aspects of concrete reason and more came together, at least as far as Europe was concerned. Whatever its initial frailties, concrete reason culminates in the first intuition of the totality of relationships that completes concrete reason as a whole, and indeed determines the sum of human activity and human nature. If the onset of concrete reason sees the onset of history and the historicity of human beings, then its conclusion offers at least to its most sophisticated participants a vista of history as the history of reason *itself*. It is no accident that absolutism culminates at almost the very moment that Saint-Simon advocated temples to Reason and making Newton the patron saint of a new religion.[5] Formal reason was, after all, the crown of creation.

Yet in another sense this is not an achievement at all.

The fateful inevitability of this process was not then apparent to the men who… directly participated in it. To them, it seemed to be a deliberate effort of reform, directed against dangerous survivals from the dark past, the rubbish of decaying political and religious establishments, and the superstitions which had for too many centuries enslaved mankind. Their ideal was a renewal of society through the application of scientific methods and a return to moral health, in other words, through reason and nature, twin aspects of one great reality before which the old errors would vanish like a dream. The program which was to bring about this

---

[1] For example, Roseveare (1991: 30–2).

[2] Shennan (1974, 1986).

[3] For an account of the last days of the French *ancien régime* which brings out the element of formalisation especially clearly, see Fitzsimmons (1987). It is notable that the most conspicuous counter-example to this seemingly implacable process of formalisation and revolution, namely Imperial China's extraordinary endurance, seems to have been based on the ability of the dominant political class (the mandarinate) to suppress any challenge to its authority and to undermine all other aspirants to power, including both hereditary aristocrats and wealthy merchants, and all alternative ideologies (Needham, 1969).

[4] Piaget and Garcia (1989); de Caprona *et al.* (1983); Strauss (1988).

[5] On Newton's apotheosis by the Enlightenment, see Gay (1969: Ch.3).

secular salvation... rested on the optimistic assumption that careful planning, general education, and improved institutions could produce a universal advance. The reformers envisioned an ideal society which would function with the regularity and predictability of a vast machine, working in harmony with the even greater mechanism of nature.[1]

For the leading revolutionaries, the premises and prejudices of concrete reason were already things of the past, more undead than alive. They had already crossed the threshold into the Promised Land of *formal* reason, on the intellectual, scientific and (to a lesser extent) political planes at least. With that, their notion of human nature and human activity shifted from *submission* or *reaction* to the conditions of human existence – the gods, fate, the 'natural order', and so on – to a demand for the participation of reason in all things and the right and responsibility of reason to control its own destiny. At every level reformers and revolutionaries promulgated their visions of humanity and a new world-order, all more or less faithful to the formalisation of the world that preceded, engendered and surrounded them and to which they desired nothing so much as to contribute their efforts. For the revolutionaries, revolution had no more ultimate logic than that of formalities such as science, as liberty, equality and fraternity, indeed as 'pure' reason itself. All unreason would be swept away and a New World built to the specifications of formal rights and responsibilities. All would be empowered through this regeneration of the human spirit.

But just as one should expect of a new stage in the development of reason, especially when at its most naïve, there was no grasp of the real origins or consequences of the ideals the reformers advocated so fiercely, nor that this entire process was predicated on the development of economic and political structures that would not be tamed quite so easily or even be widely recognised until long after this 'salvation' had been achieved. Most revolutionary manifestos of the day were free not only of the superstition and corruption of the old order but also of any recognition of the real forces that had brought humanity and the world to this pass, or of practical programmes to create a real society that actually realised their aspirations. It is true that there were those who perceived the dire consequences of the bourgeoisie being allowed to take command of the revolution, not only among the reactionaries and the revolutionary petty bourgeoisie but also among the more imaginative and critical members of the bourgeoisie itself. *The Wealth of Nations* even expressly cautioned that the interests of those who lived by profit were contradictory to those of the nation as a whole. The great captains of a formal economy were, says Adam Smith,

> ... an order of men, whose interest is never exactly the same with that of the public, who generally have an interest to deceive and even to oppress the public, and who accordingly have, upon many occasions, both deceived and oppressed it.[2]

---

[1] Eitner (1971: 3).

[2] Smith (1976, vol. 1: 278; see also pp. 144, 519–20; vol. 2: 264–5, 280–2). Even landlords, who are otherwise roundly criticised by Smith, are seen as being in greater harmony with society as a whole than capitalists, and he presents the state of wage labour as a sensitive barometer of the state of society in general (vol. 1: 276–8; see also p. 88).

However, the critics were in no position to act on their presentiments, either because they were devoured by the revolution or because their presentiments led to equally romantic programmes. Or, in some of the most important cases – notably Smith, Mandeville's *Fable of the Bees* and many *philosophes* – they were simply unable to foresee the long-term consequences of industrial capitalism with the same acuity with which they observed its spectacular beginnings. But that is hardly a criticism. As Tawney observed:

> The creed which had exorcised the spectre of agrarian feudalism haunting village and *chateau* in France was impotent to disarm the new ogre of industrial capitalism who was stretching his grimy arms in the north of England, for it had never conceived the possibility of his existence.[1]

All the same, the sweatshops, imperialism and self-congratulatory hypocrisy of nineteenth–century Europe and America were by no means betrayals of the Revolution; on the contrary, they were its most perfect fruit.

Conclusions

> If you say that God has established Laws, to be executed by Beings capable of knowing them, it follows that animals, plants and in general all bodies which act conformable to these Universal Laws, have knowledge of them, and that consequently that they are endowed with understanding, which is absurd.[2]

If, as I claimed at the end of the previous chapter, intuitive reason begins with intelligence at a level where it is scarcely distinguishable from a complex organic structure, concrete reason ends with intelligence reaching a peak at which comparisons with any organic structure become patently irrelevant. If intuitive reason begins with intelligence totally oblivious of itself, and so totally helpless to guide its own destiny and development, concrete reason ends with intelligence at last coming to grips with its own nature and its first glimpses of where it might fit into the order of things.

But the idea that the concept of concrete reason can explain so much about the history of human reason must raise the suspicion that, by trying to explain so much, it seems to deny that there is any real difference between the many phenomena for which I have tried to account. In particular, it seems to suggest that there are no significant differences between, say, the earliest post-tribal state systems and the absolutist monarchies of the last few centuries. At the very least it implies that practically the whole of human history from Gilgamesh to the Winter Palace can be explained by a single concept. This is a proposition that, were I confronted with it for the first time, I would not criticise but simply laugh at.

There are many reasons for denying that I am making any such claim. First and foremost, the concept of intelligence itself only explains the outlines of

---

[1] Tawney (1921/1943: 21). For a summary of how the bourgeois revolution was stabilised in Europe, see Beaud (1984); for Britain, see Saville (1994).

[2] D'Argens, writing in 1737, quoted in Needham (1969: 308).

human nature – an important service, and a much greater one than most accounts of intelligence seem to realise, but still a limited one. Explaining so many social systems in terms of concrete reason no more implies that all such societies are somehow 'the same' than the Piagetian claim that everyone can be located at one of a small number of *cognitive* stages implies that all people have pretty much the same *personality*. Likewise, one should certainly expect considerable differences between Hopewell, Babylon, republican Rome and Tsarist Russia.

Furthermore, as I shall argue in a later chapter, the major stages in the development of intelligence are definitely *not* vast, undifferentiated scenes of uniformity. On the contrary, every stage has it sub-stages, and one should expect there to be many substantial differences between the opening of a given stage and its conclusion. In addition, there is no reason to assume that a given stage will unfold smoothly. The likelihood that a given stage will be completed successfully is directly proportionate to its distance beyond intuitive reason, and the reason for this is the persistence of non-intelligent factors at the earlier stages.

On the other hand, I certainly am claiming that there is an important sense in which all these societies – the societies that make up the bulk of written history to date – are indeed characterised by a single logic, even if that logic does operate at a very high level. This is the logic that is expressed in the Treaty of Verdun of 843, in which Charlemagne's heirs partitioned most of western Europe among themselves, and agreed that 'all men should have a lord'. It is just this logic that governs the relationship between a Chinese aristocrat and his tenants, between a Roman senator and his *clientela*[1] (or the emperor and his client states), and between a medieval baron and his tenants and retinue: a personal or quasi-personal relationship of obligation and service on one side and protection on the other. Even within that relationship there are, of course, innumerable variations; but that fact does not detract from the equally valid fact that the logic controlling all these relationships is the same.

Likewise, although, from a political point of view, many such societies featured extensive bureaucracies with extensive holdings, and many generated an overall structure akin to absolutism, as far as the great majority were concerned the predominant social relationship was of this strictly concrete kind. And within this whole epoch there were remarkably few even nearly successful attempts to change this fact.[2] Even more importantly, this relationship was the basis on which society's surplus product – and so the real power to accomplish anything – was distributed. Hence not only the legitimacy but also the importance of choosing to describe this vast swathe of societies in such apparently simplistic terms.

---

[1] On the obligations and ceremonial that marked the day-to-day relationship between Roman patrons and their clients, see Carcopino (1956: 191–3) or MacMullen (1988).

[2] On the absence of revolutionary change throughout the Greco-Roman period, see de Ste. Croix (1983) or Finley in Porter and Teich (1986: 47–60). On the lack of revolutionary change in China, see Needham (*ibid.*: 61–73).

But concrete reason is only the beginning of reason's adventures, for having *recognised* and *taken up* the reins of its own destiny, it still has to carry that destiny to its conclusion. This adventure is the special responsibility of the concluding stages in the development of intelligence, namely *formal* and *dialectical reason*. By the time it has completed its own development, concrete reason has finally prepared a subject, object and world for which not only relationships but also relationships between relationships can be grasped and even, at the concrete plane, be taken for granted. However, exactly what they grant is a different matter, and it is the task of formal reason to determine this.

4. Formal Reason

Now what is to guarantee that I *am* a subject of this kind, capable of exercising pure practical reason? Well, strictly speaking, there *is* no guarantee; the transcendental subject is only a possibility. But it is a possibility I must *presuppose* if I am to think of myself as a free moral agent. Were I wholly an empirical being, I would not be capable of freedom, for every exercise of will would be conditioned by the desire for some object. All choice would be heteronomous choice, governed by the pursuit of some end. My will could never be a first cause, only the effect of some prior cause, the instrument of one or another impulse or inclination.

Michael J. Sandel[1]

The originality of formal reason

Sweet Analytics, 'tis thou hast ravished me.

Christopher Marlowe, Doctor Faustus

Intelligence enters intuitive reason in a form few would consider intelligent and none should think rational. By the culmination of concrete reason, with its synthesis of innumerable pragmatic, conventional relations, virtues and forms into strictly formal systems, it has moved beyond superficial forms of rationality such as merely empirical constancy or the exhaustive enumeration of instances and is beginning to establish an explicit, insightful and critical grasp of the true nature of rationality. Not content with well defined relationships, it is beginning to shore up and integrate their relations with one another in the form of relationships of complementarity, compensation, consistency, and so on. That is, formal reason is *intentionally* rational.

It is a remarkable evolution, from a shallowness and dependence that would embarrass any thinking being to a union of power and confidence that outstrips any non-intelligent structure by literally infinite orders of magnitude. For when intelligence steps over the threshold of formal reason, it finds itself stepping out onto a stage that is more than merely cosmic in scope. Formal reason's 'niche' is not just very large, or even its entire environment. It is not limited to intelligence's actual world or even to the entire physical, chemical, biological, intelligent universe. Its home is any *possible* environment, any *possible* world, any *possible* universe.

---

[1] Strong (1992: 83).

Like all previous forms of intelligence, formal reason's synthesis of all pre-existing structures allows it to take for granted all the relationships developed by concrete reason. On the other hand, its formality ensures that their piece-meal and empirical sensitivity is transcended by an integral perspective that abstracts away from any actual content or context of activity, even while imbuing all content and context with a unitary, universal perspective. Its synthesis of concrete relationships ensures formal reason's circumspection, and their formalisation ensures that any enterprise it does undertake will be pursued in a disciplined and orderly manner. In this way, formal reason frees itself from the particular, specific and even universal conditions in which it acts, without at the same time omitting to take them fully into account.

Nor is this creation of an independent order, based on the properties of a system of relationships considered *as* a system, simply a more indirect or more sophisticated means to the pragmatic ends that dominated its concrete and in-tuitive predecessors. On the contrary, the formal notions of propriety, form and principle that flow from its specifically systematic nature cause formal reason to denounce as naïve, cynical or dishonest the best-intentioned motives and perspectives which characterised its precursors. For example, it is only at this level that a grasp of natural laws (which concrete reason seems to find per-fectly congenial taken one at a time but impossible to comprehend when con-sidered as an independent system) can be set in the broader context of a scien-tific theory. But this is more than simply the addition of a new layer of reason-ing, for the very creation of a new layer is to release a potential that natural law as such lacks. In particular, a natural law allows one to investigate individual phenomena, whereas a scientific theory properly so called provides a pano-rama of infinite possibilities.

> Specifically, a theory should embody an abstract calculus, a model or interpreta-tion, and correspondence rules. The abstract calculus is a formal skeleton, which can be mathematical or logical. The model is an inventory of the notions that give content to the abstract descriptions. Correspondence rules relate theoretical enti-ties to observational procedures... Thus a theory is never equivalent to any finite set of laws, still less to a set of observational predictions.[1]

Such a structure – and its counterparts are to be found in every department of activity, especially social activity – proliferates endless new tasks and endless new responsibilities for self-regulation, many entirely non-practical and often complicating even the most simple practical tasks. For formal activity must make sense to an unprecedented degree, and moreover must explicitly *make sense* – a criterion that was only implicit during concrete reason, and whose total absence was the very reason why intuitive reason was so childish.

So formal reason's formality is by no means aloofness. On the contrary, it is only with the subordination of activity to truly formal systems that such famil-iar, elementary and entirely practical axioms of rationality as coherence, consis-tency, completeness and even correctness can be formulated and enacted prop-erly. Intuitive reason was incapable of making explicit judgements of any kind, so appeals to it to 'make sense' in these terms would fall on deaf ears. Concrete

---

[1] Smith (1993: 100), drawing on Nagel (1961: 79–80 and 90–105).

reason might manage to check that, as a matter of fact, this or that set of actions or objects is coherent, consistent, and so on, but only insofar as this can be judged empirically. Given the ease with which an empirically correct but logically invalid argument can be constructed, concrete reason is always threatened with being undermined by its own limitations.[1]

Formal reason, by contrast, can not only track and verify the full range of both empirical and logical possibilities, and do so explicitly and systematically, but can also check its logic quite independently of whatever happens, empirically speaking, to be the case. Indeed, as any basic course in formal logic will readily prove, when formal reason is concerned solely with logic, it is very largely a matter of indifference how imaginary, abstract, hypothetical, obscure, bizarre, extravagant, improbable, incorrect, impossible or even absurd an argument is from a narrowly empirical point of view. As Piaget put it, 'The adolescent is the individual who commits himself to possibilities...'[2] Or, just as often, to impossibilities, or, at the very least, to a position that is independent of any external consideration, be it social convention, personal interest or even natural forces. But in either case, 'nothing that actually occurs is of the smallest importance'.[3] By this measure, concrete rationality cannot help but seem a very superficial prelude to formal reason proper.

This chapter will describe a number of the key structures that make up formal reason, and analyse the aspects of the latter that bear on the further development of intelligence. This will not include much about such obvious candidates as scientific method or formal logic and mathematics, whose formality has been amply assessed and diagnosed over the last century or two. Instead, the main focus will be on elements of formal reason that are even more abstract than logic and mathematics, such as the intellect, and even more concrete than science, such as happiness. The purpose of this selection (apart from a natural desire to avoid the tedium of yet another critique of formal logic, scientific method, and so on) is to account for the structures that not only dominate everyday life directly but will one day drive formality to its demise.

The nature of formal reason

> Unlike the two women shouting from their Edinburgh windows at one another, who would never agree (says Sydney Smith) because they were arguing from different premises, Newton and Leibniz would never agree because their premises were the same: God needed the greatest glorification. Absolute empty space, Newton thought, implied God's continual governance of all within it; this read, to Leibniz, as God always having to wind up a faltering clock.
>
> Robert Kaplan, *The Nothing That Is*[4]

---

[1] Smith (1993).

[2] Inhelder and Piaget (1958: 339).

[3] Oscar Wilde.

[4] Kaplan (1999: 183).

Sleepy, obsessed, almost happy, I reflected that there is nothing less material than
money, since any coin whatsoever... is, strictly speaking, a repertory of possible
futures. Money is abstract, I repeated; money is the future tense. It can be an eve-
ning in the suburbs, or music by Brahms; it can be maps, or chess, or coffee; it can
be the words of Epictetus teaching us to despise gold; it is a Proteus more versatile
than the one on the isle of Pharos. It is unforeseeable time, Bergsonian time, not
the rigid time of Islam or the Porch. The determinists deny that there is such a
thing in the world as a single possible act, id est an act that could or could not
happen; a coin symbolises man's free will.

Jorge Luis Borges, The Zahir[1]

So deeply are the vast majority of readers of this book embedded in formal reason that it may seem superfluous to do more than mention this stage in passing. Certainly they are likely to find much of what follows obvious. But even if
the formality of, say, money, bureaucracy or commodity relations were as
transparent as that of formal logic or hypothetico-deductive method, its significance for the development of reason as a whole might not be so clear. Most especially, it would not be clear that formal reason had any deficiencies, that it is
open to criticism or that it is capable of replacement. On the contrary, one of
the most celebrated attributes of formal structures is their alleged self-
sufficiency, or at least the irreducibility of their limitations to non-formal terms.

For example, few mathematicians interpret Gödel's proof of mathematics'
limitations as evidence of its immaturity. Given the propensity of many recent
mathematicians to see mathematical propositions ambiguously, as 'in one
sense, ... as true as anything could possibly be true; in another, ... as no more
than marks on paper, which led to mind-stretching paradoxes when one tried
to elucidate what they meant',[2] the problem has perhaps not been as pressing
as it seems to outsiders. If Gödel's proof is generalised at all, it is usually
treated as a reflection of the tragic limitation of reason in general. But as I shall
argue below, formal reason's recurrent crises, its internal contradictions and its
constant need to be managed out of new difficulties support a rather different
view. The illusion of self-sufficiency is really only a reflection of the limitation
formal reason shares with all other stages, namely its inability to recognise any
alternative to itself, let alone a higher perspective. Consequently, none of its
essential problems can be identified if one insists on operating strictly on formal reason's own terms, and none will be solved by shoring it up or reforming
it from within.

That I am able to make such a negative claim about formal reason is itself
the result of one of its most important and (largely) positive achievements – the
creation of the intellect. Of course, there was *mental* life before formal reason,
but it was never strictly *intellectual*. Concrete reason always required the support of empirical objects to sustain or complete a given train of thought. Because its component structures were limited to more or less isolated relationships, they had no general access to each other except through empirical activity.

---

[1] Borges (1970)
[2] Hodges (1992: 85).

So concrete reason could never establish a single Archimedean point from which to move its own world, let alone the universe. True, it was perfectly capable of discoursing logically on things and events in their presence, but that was only because empirical objects provided the scaffolding needed to support otherwise disjointed reasoning. Consisting as it did of somewhat disjoint relationships, concrete reason was incapable of *breaking free* of this presence, and so of an *intentional* objectivity that could, for example, take account of things in their complete absence. Without having something empirical to think about, its thoughts were bound to be fleeting and fractured.

Nor could it abstract purely formal constructs, such as inertia or virtue, and certainly it could not, say, verify a proposition's validity (or even its factual correctness) by systematically exhausting every logical alternative.[1] That would presuppose insight into the purely internal nature of and connections between structures and relationships – an insight that is only available to those capable of abstracting away from any actual instance. True, it is concrete reason's task to overcome all these limitations, but it is formal reason's privilege to embody them.

Hence the absence of a purely intellectual sphere to concrete reason. As for intuitive reason, here the 'mental' consists of nothing more than fleeting images and gestures – perceptual images, expressive looks, appeals to nearby adults, self-regulatory speech, and so on.[2] However, once intelligence can relate all structures of activity to one another without recourse to empirical things or events, it can create *purely* internal objects, synthesised entirely out of previously internalised symbols and images. Its mental life then takes on a purely internal dimension capable of independent expression and development on its own terms – intellectual, in fact. And, of course, it is the same independence from empirical conditions that liberates the orderliness that also characterises formal reason and the rigours of the intellectual life. Hence the seemingly paradoxical character of the intellect: it combines the most free-flowing and abandoned activity combined with the strictest discipline. But hence also the characteristic danger of intellectualism: the proliferation of false yet compelling notions through a combination of *anti*-empiricism and idle speculation.

Not that this pursuit of an objective internal order for its own sake is limited to the specifically intellectual aspects of intelligent activity. On the contrary, it is the norm for all forms of rationality. Even Socrates chose the skill of the artisan as his model of knowledge.[3] On the historical level too, it is the formalisa-

---

[1] Inhelder and Piaget (1958, 1964).

[2] See, for example, Leontyev (1981), Luria and Vygotsky (1992: 75–109), Luria and Yudovich (1966), Piaget (1951), Vygotsky (1962, 1978 and 'The instrumental method in psychology', in Wertsch, 1981: 157–65) and the post-Vygotsky school generally (Wertsch, 1985). See also Dennett (1991: 193–9) and Goldin-Meadow in Gibson and Ingold (1993: 63–85). There is evidence that chimpanzees also use sign language in this way.

[3] Snell (1960: 185–6). On the role played by simple technologies in development, see also Hallpike (1979: 95ff).

tion of concrete political and economic structures – the creation of just such an objective internal order – that permits their elevation from tools of highly particularistic (which is to say, highly concrete) groups and interests to independent, universally accessible structures such as markets, exchange, property, the state, and so on. At the same time, formalisation gives such structures remarkable resilience, not only because of the practical powers they accrue but also because of the independence and capacity for self-regulation that flow from their commitment to formal rationality.

That is why, as the emergence of the nation state out of the absolutist court demonstrated, the formal deconcretising of the previous concrete systems is also, paradoxically, their definitive practical institutionalisation. Even so, an institution's practical services and empirical success are no longer quite enough to vindicate it; rather, there are formal requirements of lawfulness, administrative rigour, accountability, and so on, to which even the most powerful formal state must submit. These requirements have only been slowly and incompletely met by even the most advanced formal organisations, but they represent a definite strand in the organisation and self-consciousness of society itself. This exposes such institutions to objective scrutiny. In the relations of authority and responsibility, policy and process embodied in a formal system's constitution and programmes, in the light of its official ideology and official *raison d'être*, in the events that throw it into conflict and disarray, in the evidence this affords and the analysis it permits, in all these things it exposes itself to the most detailed and trenchant criticism.

Of course, these criticisms are unlikely to impress the system's apologists and those whose interests the system serves, even when embodied in the most massive dysfunction and resistance. It is always possible to blame the ineptitude of the previous administration, the moral turpitude of the victims or the madness or criminality of those who resist, or simply claim that the problem is out of their hands. Indeed, precisely because they constitute the very premises of the historical situation, the great institutions in which many formal systems are embodied have a way of presenting themselves as forces of nature or acts of god it would be foolish, if not downright wicked, to resist.

All the same, the most radical problems a formal system faces can usually be best understood in terms of the essential inadequacies of the system itself, considered *as* a formal system, rather than in terms of any particular policy, action or result. Formal systems are often so powerful that the problems that arise from their day-to-day operation in the external world are quite slight and easily corrected within the system itself. But for the same reason, any problems that arise from fundamental problems with the system will be infinitely harder to define or resolve. Likewise, formalisation makes it easy to understand and attack any particular empirical state of affairs, but as one delves deeper and deeper it becomes harder and harder to comprehend and truly criticise the underlying processes and the basic laws of the situation. So it is fortunate that, in the long run, just as formalisation of absolutism eventually rendered the absolutist monarchy irrelevant, so the further development of a formal system can only end by empowering its victims and inspiring its critics. As at every other stage in the development of intelligence, the perfection of formal reason is the touchstone for its conservation and its revolutionisation alike.

Universal though the impact of formalisation has been, not even the most imposing list of examples could reveal its ultimate nature. What is required is an account of its structure. What is the nature of the formal subject, object and world?

One key problem any system that possesses its own independent order is bound to face is the validity and maintenance of its internal integrity. It might even be said that it is its only indispensable concern, for formal criteria of integrity such as coherence and consistency cannot be altered by empirical success or failure.[1] By contrast, the most glowing success can be vitiated by residual *in*coherence and *in*consistency, and the most dismal failure lightened by the formal purity of its motives, its methods, its consequences, and so on. Or at least, it can for a formal system, where formality is necessarily regarded as an indispensable virtue. At the same time, integrity certainly *is* an objective condition of objective effectiveness. Consequently, integrity now becomes both a primary end in its own right and a means to every other end.

As far as formal reason is concerned, this concern with integrity always extends a good deal further than the merely subjective. Not only its activity but also its objects and its world are to be fully formalised, so they too must be coherent and consistent. That is not to say that either its objects or its world can seek their own integrity – it is only subjects that have an *interest* in integrity. Nevertheless, with formal reason the development of intelligence as a whole has now reached a stage where each object and each world is an independent system in its own right and participates in its parent and child objects and worlds in a systematic manner. Consequently, each poses itself as a problem for the formal subject in a way that no previous object or world ever did, for they demand to be grasped *as* existing in their own right, on their own terms and quite possibly for their own sakes. Unlike intuitive reason's strictly implicit attitude to its object's intrinsic order or concrete reason's pragmatic, conventional, eclectic approach, for formal reason the problem of integrity explodes into a universal issue. It is helpless to control or evade this problem, so it is left with no choice but to solve it.

Perhaps the formal subject need not fully reconcile the tensions these concerns bring. It may reach an acceptable level of stability by adopting an expressly pragmatic or agnostic or fatalistic view of things. It may conclude with a dualistic universe of truth and falsehood, good and evil, divine and profane, and so on, and so apparently come to a final conclusion, but the residual contradiction continues to haunt the feast. For example, Christianity is nominally monotheistic, but by carefully isolating its divinity from responsibility for temporal evil, it has effectively made the Devil God's equal, at least until the Last Trump.[2]

But while it lasts, any such resolution, partial and imperfect though it may be, absolves formal reason of the obligation to face ultimate questions of ra-

---

[1] Lloyd suggests that the Greek founders of science were often more interested in mathematical purity than empirical correctness, even in specifically empirical studies (Lloyd, 1979: 121–2).

[2] On the historical origins of the Christian Satan, see Pagels (1996).

tionality, such as the meaningfulness of existence or the defensibility of its principles (not to mention truth, freedom, being, eternity, and so on), while still creating the impression of a principled, if tragic or submissive, resolution. Only obeying orders, perhaps. But even then it is difficult for a formal subject to create a defensible position without also formalising the very intractability of such problems and giving pragmatism or agnosticism a formal style. On the other hand, formal reason is an unprecedented opportunity for the subject to create a whole range of artificial assistants for the task of making sense of things. For there is another sense in which the problem of integrity is not only subjective. Being always an independent system of (more or less) coherent and consistent relations governing activity, the subject is perfectly capable of objectifying that system.

This leads to two consequences. Firstly, it can say exactly what it means by integrity. Secondly, it can mimic and reproduce that objectified system in the form of real objects. For example, computer systems that can check their own integrity or check the integrity of other objects are not really concerned with integrity itself. The order they embody derives from external sources, and they literally don't know what they're doing. Nevertheless, the more advanced such systems become, the clearer the notions of integrity are made, the more fully they can be implemented artificially and the more completely the artefact will replicate the subject's concern with and approach to integrity.

Nor is this process limited to the sphere of artificial intelligence. On the contrary, it has been the norm in the development of organisations for at least the last century or two. No strictly formal organisation, no policy, no programme can expect to succeed if it does not accept, approximate and in some sense internalise in its processes and procedures basic mechanisms for defining, establishing, maintaining, validating and extending its own formal integrity. Unlike the methods, procedures and techniques created during previous stages, formal organisations are designed to operate above the level of either pragmatic effectiveness or the interests of their incumbents. In many cases it is as much the function of an activity (eg, auditing and accounting) to preserve the system as to further any operational objective.

Naturally, this may lead to various kinds of 'goal displacement', whereby means are substituted for ends and the operational goals of the system are subordinated to its interests *as* a system. After all, the smoothness of an organisation's internal processes is often much easier to come to grips with than its external effectiveness, and much more likely to remain a stable target. Still, that is no more a vice than unfettered pragmatism, and it shows how readily even limited forms of formal reason can inject quasi-subjective qualities into strictly objective structures of activity, so creating a huge set of transitional objects to an artificial intelligence properly so called.

As for the formal object in general, perhaps it is a little too paradoxical to say that its main attribute is its objectivity. Nevertheless, this is what follows from its construction as an independent system in its own right. During previous stages in the development of intelligence, its objectivity resided in intelligence as a whole, in the interplay of subject, object and world rather than in the object alone. For example, the concrete subject relies on the empirical content of its activity to support and complete its attempts at constructing objects, which is effective only where the context of its activity can be taken for granted. Such success as concrete reason does achieve in the creation of objects relies heavily on the inertia of the things and events by which it is surrounded, not to mention the assistance of other, more developed intelligences. As for intuitive reason, its objects' lack of *independent* objectivity is even more conspicuous.

But as I have already said, with the coming of formal reason, subject, objects and world are all reconstructed into systems in their own rights. Consequently, the objectivity of formal reason's objects is independent of the objectivity of its subject and its world, just as their subjectivity is independent of the presence of any actual objects or the nature of its world, and so on. That is why Newton could hypothesise a totally empty time and space[1] and medieval physicists could speculate about what a uniformly accelerated body *would* do, if only they could find one.[2] These were the true progenitors of modern science, for in both cases the focus is on objectivity as such rather than any particular knowledge.

This is not objectivity in the narrow and trivial sense of collecting empirical data (a notoriously subjective business) but in the sense of constructing objects by whatever methods are needed to free them *from* their empirical content and context and render them intelligible to any possible audience under any possible circumstances. Formalisation, in fact. In the case of Newton and the medieval physicists, of course, their objects may have been independent, but they were also strictly intellectual. Even their experimental apparatus and results were only means to the end of creating purely intellectual objects. But as the practical uses to which science has been put have subsequently shown, the formal object can make its independent existence felt in much more imposing ways, from medicine to germ warfare and from power stations to nuclear weapons.

So formal objectivity is by no means merely a matter of epistemology. The difference between the raw 'things and events' from which an intelligent act may proceed and the 'objects' in which it culminates is not that the former are things of substance of which the latter are pale subjective reflections of one kind or another. This may be the limit of any single intelligence's activity (and with the institutionalisation of the intellect, never before has this outcome been either more possible or more likely); however, 'making sense' of things and events also consists of making and remaking them *in themselves* until they conform to an ideal, can be assimilated to some larger plan or programme, or otherwise embody the requirements formal reason imposes on them. On this plane it is only too obvious what a formal object's objectivity really amounts to, especially when it fails and our reliance on a given object – a bridge, an economic system, a teaching method, an ideology – proves to have rested a little too much on the *merely* subjective imagination of its enthusiasts (however coherently and consistently articulated) and a little too little on the intrinsic validity of the object in itself.

---

[1] Newton's basic definitions of formal time, space, place and motion are to be found in the Scholium to the Definitions of his *Principia Mathematica*.

[2] Lindberg (1992: 290–301). Contrast this with the state of theoretical knowledge among the ancient Greeks (Landels, 2000: Ch.8).

But formal reason has cures even for these ills. The obverse of its notions of internal coherence and consistency is a system of formal methods for verifying its empirical achievements, especially its *completeness* and *correctness vis à vis* the relevant range of plans and specifications, aims and objectives. In particular, the ability to *prove* that an object is objectively complete and correct is quite different from the ability to empirically *enumerate* and empirically *check* its various empirical facets – a skill of which concrete reason is fully capable. For just as it is only with formal reason's identification of each object as an independent system of relationships in its own right that its internal coherence and consistency can be determined, so it is only with the ability to work through the implications of that system *as* a system *vis à vis* the empirical conditions in which it is expected to operate that it can be demonstrated to be complete and correct.

The practical implications of these developments could scarcely be greater. For example, they explain the growth of models and formal analysis that underpin the whole of contemporary engineering, which rely at least as much on demonstrating the formal validity of systems as on confirming any particular facts. These techniques are completely indispensable in the face of the intractable complexity of even quite modest computing systems, the intrinsic dangers of many modern technologies and the impossibility of testing most space and military systems in real conditions.[1] How far even the simplest formal mechanism is from concrete technology, with its pulleys, lock gates and looms![2] Indeed, hence engineering itself, which supersedes the work of the mechanic solely by virtue of its ability to abstract a comprehensive system of independent principles and then synthesise them empirically, so bypassing the latter's pragmatic, eclectic and conventional methods.

Formal reason's objectivity clearly relies on the fact that all its objects have a much more developed non-empirical order, even in comparison with the expanded notion of the 'empirical' developed by concrete reason. Indeed, given the abstraction of formal reason's systems from any actual content or context, a formal object can clearly be totally non-empirical. It may be entirely abstract, hypothetical, counter-factual, imaginary, and so on. On the other hand, the same strictly formal character of a formal object also implies that it is only a *possible* object. If formal systems operate independently (though, as ever, not regardless) of any particular object, their operations clearly have a degree of freedom that permits formal reason to accept or reject any particular object independently of the empirical evidence for or against it. That is why formal reason can concern itself with issues such as validity, but also why it finds it so difficult to draw firm conclusions about what is and what isn't *actually* the case,

---

[1] For the intrinsic intractability of some computer systems and related problems, see Harel (1987). For the more general principles of computability (with its implications for verification and engineering), see Boolos and Jeffrey (1980).

[2] On the limitations of pre-industrial technology and the built environment, see Hill (1993), Hodges (1971), Landels (2000) and Chant and Goodman (1999). On the concrete rational form and limitations of even the most advanced pre-modern scientific instruments and the supporting observation techniques, see North (1994).

and always experiences a lingering scepticism about the ultimate status and even the reality of the empirical world.

Despite this rather equivocal conclusion, the formal object inspires the formal world with a doubly powerful character. Firstly, now that intelligence consists of a system of truly independent objects, they can be relied on to pursue its empirical objectives without its direct intervention. With that, even the remotest corners of its world are either rationalised or capable of rationalisation without much further ado. Conversely, the content and the context through which formal reason exists and on which it acts inform it, not from an invisible but omnipotent position off stage, as with intuitive reason, or even vaguely visible through the half-light of concrete reason, but as an acknowledged guest and even as an explicitly constitutive part of intelligence itself. In other words, formal reasoning is no longer at the mercy of implicit pragmatic, empirical and conventional *conditions*, but rather acts explicitly and in terms of practical, synthetic, normative *considerations*.

Conversely, formal reason's construction of its world as a *system* of independent objects gives that world a universality and integrity that vastly exceeds the merely empirical comprehensiveness and continuity that was the pinnacle of concrete reason. But that is only to say that, with formal reason, the world itself and the world as such become the arena of action, not only by virtue of *force majeure* (as with intuitive reason) or as a matter of practical effect (as in concrete reason) but as a matter of policy. If, with formal reason, intelligence is for the first time freed of any particular empirical time, space, substance or causality, and so from the empirical as such, that is not to say that it slips off into some mystical 'beyond'. On the contrary, the more intelligence develops, the more clear (which is to say, more intelligible) its empirical world becomes.

I suspect that it was this formalisation of subject, object and world that inspired the emergence of classical Greek philosophy. Of course, Greek society and culture as a whole were not formalised in the manner of, say, capitalism – too many of their key features, from their popular religions to the administration of justice[1] and even ancient Greece's vaunted approach to reason[2] or natural science,[3] betray a pre-formal order – but large sweeps of the Greek intellect were. By proceeding from neither the empirical concerns of concrete reason nor the mythopoeic patterns of intuitive reason but from subject, object and world as they are in themselves, entirely new forms of explanation emerged. These explanations were also cast in terms of origins and causes, but not in the form of a progenitor or a divine creation or mythical Eden. Rather, they sought an immanent and lasting ground of being, an enduring principle and system from which things would spring not only *in* themselves but also *of* themselves. Even their First Causes and Unmoved Movers had to be accounted for in strictly logical terms, which is to say, in terms of their intrinsic properties. When the arguments of Plato and Parmenides, not to mention Zeno's paradoxes, are scrutinised, they turn out to be heavily formalised in just this way. Even their

---

[1] Cf. Cohen (1995).

[2] Frede and Striker (1996).

[3] Lloyd (1979); Sorabji (1988).

superficially peculiar assignment of primordial powers and status to earth or water or fire or air can reasonably be treated as an attempt to find grounds for the complete system.

Only then, of course, could the intellect proceed by insight and criticism rather than simple acceptance by the faithful. Only then could knowledge begin to grow and spread and have a history from which lessons could be learned. Only then could knowledge be analysed, evaluated and improved. Only then could it even dream of coherence, consistency, completeness and correctness. And at the bottom of all this lay an unwarranted yet revolutionary assumption, so totally different to that of concrete or intuitive reason and so fundamental to formal reason – that the universe made sense in its own right, on its own terms and for its own sake.[1] Unfortunately for the Greeks, the basis for grounding knowledge outside purely speculative arguments would not be established for another two thousand years, until Grotius and the scientific revolutionaries of the seventeenth century renewed the shocking proposal that the natural world, including human beings, might perhaps be accounted for on their own terms, without reference to will or purpose.

The emergence of formal reason

> The old society concentrated the maximum number of ways of life into the minimum of space and accepted, if it did not impose, the bizarre juxtaposition of the most widely different classes. The new society, on the contrary, provided each way of life with a confined space in which it was understood that the dominant features should be respected, and that each person had to resemble a conventional model, an ideal type, and never depart from it under pain of excommunication.
>
> Phillipe Ariès, *Centuries of Childhood*[2]

To the extent that formal reason's systems are formal, they embody enormously powerful systems of abstraction. However, these systems are by no means merely tools to reduce the universe to intelligence's own private categories. That would be to reduce the universe to the world, and so formalisation to paranoia. Rather, having leavened the eminently pragmatic achievements of concrete reason with systematic order, formal reason is normally far freer from delusions than its predecessors (although its vastly greater reach means that such faulty imaginings as it does entertain are much more likely to have disastrous consequences). Furthermore, it can turn its sights in a direction in which no previous structure has been able to look steadfastly, namely onto itself. Not content with making an entirely new sense of the world of objects, formal reason also obliges *itself*, as self as well as subject, to acknowledge systematic values that stand above and beyond its own particularistic concerns. Even concrete reason, which possessed the ability to look inwards to some degree, was helpless to impose order there. But once everything must be vindicated in

---

[1] Frankfort *et al.* (1949: 248–262).

[2] Ariès (1973: 398). On the organisation of space in the transition to the modern world, see Sennett (1977).

terms of formal, systematic precepts, it is clear that this 'everything' should include both formal reason as such and this particular intelligence considered as a complete personality – an unprecedented inclusiveness.

So formal reason obliges itself to explain and justify and amend and reform itself in terms of the very formal structures it has just established. Now this can indeed induce a degree of paranoia, especially in its early stages, for its lack of experience leaves it helpless to discover anything that meets such lofty standards. It strives in vain to construe its still minuscule identity in terms of the echoing labyrinths of infinite possibility its own structure proclaims, or to gain a foothold for its own apparently arbitrary contingency on the icy surfaces of abstract necessity. In short, having begun with such enthusiasm, formal reason soon finds that it has constructed a world into which it does not – and cannot – fit.

The reason for this contradiction is straightforward: although a truly new level of comprehension has been initiated, the world has yet to be made sense of in terms of formal reason itself. The self-evidence that reconstruction into a formal world-system would confer has yet to be extended to more than the surfaces of formal reason's actual universe. Consequently, practically every matter of fact still appears 'merely' empirical, pragmatic, conventional, and so on, without any sense of the profundity of those terms, and so only in a most pejorative sense. Conversely, nothing that actually exists is worth any effort to a naïvely formal system, because nothing yet exists *within* formal reason, in terms formal reason recognises. There is interminable fact but practically nothing of any value. No wonder that an inexperienced formal reason so often responds to its own existence with nausea, disgust and icy disdain.

Of course, in general terms this is the position from which every new stage of intelligence proceeds. However, what distinguishes formal reason is the fact that it is a form of rationality that can think and speak for itself. Why then is it mute now? Again, its lack of experience – its lack of a properly formalised grasp of the content or context of its new spheres of activity – leaves it speechless, empty mouthings and denunciations apart. It lacks the insights needed to translate its abstract requirements into programmes or even policies; or, where a policy can be promulgated, it is hopelessly naïve, and the systems it creates to implement it are likely to prove reluctant to follow its dictates.

This leads to formal reason's peculiar mixture of modesty and immodesty during its formative phase. On the one hand, from Eleatic paradox to Protestant submission to the ineffability of God, it speaks out, plainly and volubly, against its own inherent inadequacy. But on the other, it may thrive on this revelation, mistaking its lack of significance and conclusions for a lack of boundaries and constraints. That is why so many of its most vigorous growths – adolescent idealism, the Parmenidean horror of change, revolutionary purism, existential vertigo, bureaucratic sclerosis, Calvinism, free market economics – proselytise an awful barrenness. As Diderot put it: 'Frighten me, if you will, but let the terror you inspire in me be tempered by some grand moral ideal'.

Perhaps Diderot would have been less sanguine about terror had he lived to see the Terror. Or perhaps he would simply have translated this high-minded boldness into self-consciously tragic sacrifice to 'Revolutionary Necessity' –

that 'devout willingness to be damned'[1] so perfectly illustrated in Camus' *Myth of Sisyphus* or Koestler's *Darkness at Noon*. In this way formal reason vindicates its abstract principles without being required to grow up. As the fall of absolutism demonstrated, naïve formal reason is all for the wholesale replacement of unreason with something more suited to its own universal, ineffably superior yet astoundingly simplistic aspirations:

> Let the individual, when a creed is presented for his belief or a work of art for his admiration and enjoyment, consider whether there be anything in it which he cannot suppose to be accessible and obvious to every rational mind through the 'unaided light of nature' or through those modes of experience which are everywhere the same. If such a non-universalisable element be found in it, let him reject it as a false religion or as unsound ethics or as bad art, as the case may be.[2]

But formal reason is less able to say, lofty generalities and exhilaratingly clarion calls apart, exactly what should replace the particular religion, artistry and ethics it rejects in this off-hand manner, other than that it should be intrinsically valid and abstract. In its own mind, so to speak, this is not a mistake but the acme of reason, for has not Kant shown that *no* contingent goal, not even happiness or the will of God, could satisfy formal reason's demand for a truly *categorical* solution? Hence formal reason's search for eternal truths as well as concrete realities, its preference for rights over any particular conception of the good,[3] its unprecedented concern with notions such as liberty, citizenship, justice, individuality and fairness,[4] and its perennial enthusiasm for the market, the state and property, as though they were capable of creating genuine solutions to human problems.[5] But then, it does not really know what 'human' means, but instead seeks the abstract, the formal, the immutable, and so on – all those things a human being is not. That is why even its accounts of such truly formal structures are so removed from the realities it claims to portray with especial insight, acumen and rigour: formal abstraction is not an adequate basis for portraying even formal abstractions! Even formal reason's notions of truth and freedom are totalitarian in their undiluted abstractness and empty universality.

---

[1] Lovejoy (1964: 211).

[2] Lovejoy (1964: 289). As well as this synopsis of one Enlightenment attitude, Lovejoy also provides an excellent summary of the equally abstract, consciously anti- yet never quite trans-formal, Romantic backlash in favour of difference, originality and plenitude.

[3] Sandel in Strong (1992). See also Hallpike (2004) for a general critique of Kantian, Rawlsian and other formal notions of moral and ethical understanding.

[4] Rawls in Strong (1992). Note that the formal conception of liberty and citizenship is only distantly related to that espoused by the ancients, and the differences between the former and the latter are generally the differences between concrete and formal reason.

[5] The gulf separating ownership of property by the few and freedom for the many has always been more or less clear to the unpropertied majority, and the question apologists of formal liberty who confuse the two seem determined to ignore is, as Christopher Hill puts it, 'Liberty for whom?' (Hill, 1996). This shortcoming of formal reason will be come more evident as the present argument unfolds.

So an adolescent stepping out into the adult world of a formal society is likely to find most things too sophisticated to comprehend immediately, and a society taking its first steps into formality is likely to find that its own inexperience generates more complication and *dis*order than the prophets of formalism had bargained for. One has only to recall the embarrassments of early adolescence to see how little one understood then. During this early phase, formal reason has yet to face up to the subtlety or concreteness of things, to the need to make sense of the world on its own unyielding terms, or the possibility that the only tool fully at its disposal from the start, namely the intellect, is only a small part, and by no means a valid microcosm, of reason as a whole.

Hence the characteristic vulnerability of early formal reason, with its inability to transcend a *merely* formal choice between, on the one hand, purely verbal games and, on the other, a legalistic obsession with formal correctness. Because it is already subject to the demands of its own systematic nature, but lacks power or knowledge, it comes to premature conclusions – that its primitive vacuity is an ineffable fact of nature (its own or its world's); that it must either accept or reject its world wholesale, perhaps in a typically cynical (and always crass) gesture to 'realism' or an equally emphatic stand on behalf of principle; that either there is no truth whatsoever or the only truth lies in some kind of other-worldly wisdom, in devotion to a tyrannical yet abstract notion of democracy, the state or anarchy, and so on. In short, existentialism, conservatism and navel-gazing, ennui, traditionalism and idle speculation are natural, if rather unexpected and unwilling bedfellows.[1] It is a painful set of alternatives.

Even though we are still only at the birth of formal reason, this brings me to my fundamental criticism of its as a whole: that although this initial abstractness is something with which formal reason will eventually come to grips, it remains its Achilles' heel. Formal reason can scarcely be authentically formal and still avoid an ultimate sense of distance between, on the one hand, its actual existence, including its self, its circumstances and its world, and on the other, the abstracting, formalising, systematising dictates of the values and systems it holds dear. For from the point of view of strictly formal reasoning, the actual is at best an instance, at worst an epiphenomenon. Conversely, the formal order is formal reason's sole absolute necessity, yet in itself it achieves absolutely nothing.

This distance between the actual and the formal is created by the very act of formalisation whereby formal reason makes sense of the actual in the first place. Formal reason can find no consolation in either the facticity of the situation or the ideals by which it lives: the one will always tend to discredit and rebuff the other, and do so with the full authority of formal reason itself. Consequently, the twin illusions of infinite possibilities and irreducible contin-

---

[1] On other-worldliness, see Lovejoy (1964: 25–9). For contemporary political conservatism's synthesis of trivial content, crass one-sidedness and empty formality, see any Marxist critique of post-1848 bourgeois apologetics. However, the shelves of any supermarket provide tacit, yet more than adequate, comment. The latter will also provide some insight into the appeal of existentialism. For existentialism itself, see its literature and its psychiatrists rather than its official philosophising.

gency cannot be cured with the medication of formal reason, no matter how large or sustained the dose. Whatever the content with which experience may fill them, the axioms and inferences in which formal reason grounds itself can only really be satisfied by other formal structures, of which the intelligence in question, considered as that *actual* intelligence in all its concrete and existential reality, is *not* an example.

One consequence of this contradiction between the actuality of any given formal rational intelligence's existence and the strictly formal tools it has at its disposal to grasp that existence is the fact that formal reason is both the fount and the victim of metaphysics. Precisely because it is formal, formal reason cannot comprehend the ultimate basis of actual existence or grasp the essential nature – the actuality – of the actual. This includes both myself (as an actual individual rather than the instantiation of innumerable concepts, models and systems) and the universe I inhabit (considered not as an abstractly physical, chemical, biological and even intelligent structure but rather as both content and context, ground, origin and explanation of my own actual existence). As a result, formal reason is doomed to an often urgent sense of unreality, of having only glimpsed existence, of existence lying just beyond its fingertips, never quite in focus, its meaning always on the tip of its tongue but never shouted out loud. On the other hand, the formal structures which constitute it and which it cannot gainsay are perfectly capable of having a stab at the answer. Indeed, they cannot help themselves.

Hence the emergence of metaphysics, and hence also metaphysics' characteristic forms and conclusions. Both being concrete, no abstract solution can be found within either the universe or itself, and so formal reason must look outside both. The fact that 'outside the universe' is a contradiction in terms does not deflect it, since it is obliged by the nature of its own internal order to postulate a solution of this general kind, and there are many forms, from Platonism to agnosticism, which can disguise the contradiction by dressing it up as an enigma. Hence also the two basic forms of metaphysics: formal accounts of actual existence (eg, cosmogony and cosmology); and actualistic accounts of formal existence (eg, existentialism and revelation).

In short, although capable of pursuing any train of reasoning to any lengths, formal reason cannot come to any conclusion about any actual thing or event. Its unprecedented power over the conditions of its own activity should not blind us to the fact that the systematisation constituting and constituted by formal reason is achieved by not only abstracting but also isolating the internal structures of intelligence from any actual content or context. This is a necessary precursor to its eventual reconstruction on a higher, dialectical plane, and in the mean time permits intelligence to preside over any possible event, relationship or activity with equal and identical disinterest even where its most vital interests are directly concerned.

So formal reason is marvellously sensitive and responsive to whatever meets its rigorous specifications – and awful in its annihilation of whatever does not. It does not mean to destroy what it does not comprehend, any more than an amoeba 'means' to dismember the animalcules it assimilates; it simply fails to notice that anything untoward has happened. Or, where it does notice its own failure to respect the content and context of its own activity, it can (unlike an amoeba) provide a host of entirely plausible rationalisations as to why it has done so, and how this was for the greater good, it was a lesser or a necessary evil, and so on. In every case this turns out to mean that the formal solution conformed to an entirely formal notion of the situation – a valid proof, the 'greater good', and so on. So it comes as no surprise that the critics of formal reason are not silenced. Of course, non-formal protestations are hardly likely to be heard, while those who remain within the formal canon may get elected but they can never do more than ameliorate the worst excesses.

That is not to say that formal reason cannot see the contradiction inherent in its 'solution'. On the contrary, I hope the reader is seeing it right now. However, as often as not its response to this contradiction is to accept it, and then draw one of a small number of possible conclusions: that there is no solution to the riddle (the universe is a freak, life is meaningless, and so on); or, by positing a 'cause' that is really an imaginary hybrid of the actuality demanded by the nature of the problems at hand (*my* existence and the existence of *this* universe) and the formality demanded by the nature of formal reason. In its petty form, the latter is typified by the later Olympian or Norse pantheons, where imaginary persons are infused with formal roles (eg, *dike* and other divinities of justice and fate, and perhaps also the Egyptian *ma'at*[1]). One may postulate cosmic *cum* abstract forces such as fate, destiny or Plato's 'necessity'. Or, where the process of formalisation has all but eliminated the psychological and naturalistic elements, one may posit an individual yet not quite personal deity in the manner of the Judaeo-Christian-Islamic tradition. Not that the conflict of the formal and the actual is resolved by this approach: formal reason can *never* comprehend actuality, and the formal rational individual cannot give up looking for an answer.

Innumerable structures analogous to metaphysics abound in the world of formal reason, but all have the same more or less hidden pitfalls. No matter how thoroughly embedded in the factual content and context of its immediate activity, formal reason will always have one foot in 'pure' abstractions. And *vice versa*. Unfortunately it cannot resolve the tension between them, so formal reason's independence of its own activity, which is its ultimate strength, cannot quite avoid turning into isolation from it. So, in Albert Camus' bitter words: 'His exile is without remedy since he is deprived of the memory of a lost home or the hope of a promised land'.[2]

---

[1] On the syncretistic transformation of Babylonian mythology into a quasi-formalised theology, see von Soden (1994: 179ff) and Frankfort *et al.* (1949). On the gradual transformation of the Olympians, see Kirk *et al.* (1983); for *ma'at* Trigger *et al.* (1983). For the progressive development of *ma'at*, *dike*, and similar terms, see Hallpike (2004).

[2] Camus (1975: 13).

Roles, commodities and money

Our culture is an avalanche of obsolescence hurling itself into the Sea of Non-existence.

Jules Henry

It isn't necessary to imagine the world ending in fire or ice – there are two other possibilities: one is paperwork, and the other is nostalgia.

Frank Zappa

Silver and gold have been denied them – whether as a sign of divine favour or of divine wrath, I cannot say.

Tacitus, *Germania*

Nowhere is formal reason's uneasy amalgam of universal ambition and inherent self-destruction revealed more clearly than in the key structures for the social organisation of subject, object and world in our times – roles, commodities and money. These structures, more powerful and pervasive than any others in the entire history of intelligence to date, seem to offer everything, yet must always confound the very subject, objects and world they embody so effectively and develop so well. Nor should this paradox be seen as narrowly social: although social in origin and peculiarly dominant in contemporary society, roles, commodities and money are, to repeat, forms of subject, object and world, considered in their most general sense. They also have specifically psychological roots, rather than simply being imposed by social structure, as much theorising in this area seems to assume.[1] Nevertheless, once they invade the central logic of the social system, nothing can remain aloof from their engulfing power. Their most obvious expressions may be on the social, political and economic levels, but their influence, and eventually their direct expression, pervades reason from top to bottom.

It is clear that money, roles and commodities determine many of the main forms of action in the formal world, and their influence is constantly growing. The commercial urge to commodify the world, the administrative advantages to be had from managing society in terms of formal roles and the technical benefits of using money to quantify all objects, and so make the incomparable at least commensurable, are obvious enough. However, even in the absence of such pragmatic benefits there would still be an inexorable and accelerating tendency to reduce other structures to monetary, commodity and role-based terms. For the natural corollary of these structures' ability to comprehend everything is their logical inability to deal with anything that is not structured in their own terms. They will therefore always tend to remake other structures in their own image. And the further this process is extended, the greater the impetus it will have. When, as in the case of capitalism, they have usurped all the

---

[1] On the psychic roots of roles, see Piaget (1928), Watson (1984) and Watson and Fischer (1980). For a summary of research on the analogous abilities of great apes, see Parker and McKinney (1999: 129ff).

central structures of activity, they become truly inexorable.[1] They can therefore be treated as a test-bed for formal reason as a whole.

Roles are by no means unique to formal reason. On the contrary, there is evidence a role-like the social ordering of activity in earliest stages of social and psychic development.[2] Indeed, they are not even peculiar to human beings.[3] Yet there no lack of preliminary tasks needing to be completed before *formal* rational roles become possible. The subject must be able to recognise and represent themselves and others as objective agents; learn routines and 'scripts'; grasp that individuals can substitute for one another, with all playing the same role; synthesise appropriate patterns and suites of activity into role-specific functions and responsibilities; appreciate that social relationships are independent of psychic relationships; coordinate diverse but related roles to one another; and so on. Many social and psychic factors, from imitation to play to cultural demarcations between childhood and adulthood all affect how (if at all) roles emerge and what exactly they entail.

On the other hand, formal reason elaborates and makes explicit many aspects of roles that were previously hidden or missing. In particular, for formal reason there is no such thing as a discrete role. A particular role is only one element in a larger system of complementary roles that collectively constitute a formal social system as that system. Although its actual performance is subject to its incumbent's personal foibles, desires and perceptions, and certainly must be made sense of to some extent by its incumbent if it is to be executed properly,[4] a role remains what 'one' does, not what 'I' or even 'we' do. It is the larger system that defines and enforces the various statuses, functions, rights and duties to which we are literally subject – as members of this or that organisation, as holders of certain social positions with more or less defined expecta-

---

[1] See Robinson (1987: 13–4) for the critical requirements of this process. The greatest exponent of the radical formalisation of the modern world (although he might not have described it in those terms) was undoubtedly Max Weber, especially in *The Protestant Ethic and the Spirit of Capitalism* and *Economy and Society*. Nevertheless, Weber's analysis is inadequate because it insists on an exogenous original impetus for rationalisation (the 'Protestant ethic'), which emerges without plausible explanation. Nor is the empirical evidence for any *simple* connection between the rise of capitalism and the rise of Protestantism compelling (a sample of contrary evidence is provided by Elton, 1963, 311-318). Still, Weber does take the evident processes of formalisation inherent in a capitalist economy into account. On the other hand, because he largely ignores the major structural contradictions inherent in a capitalist economy, he fails to identify the fundamental developmental consequences of rationalisation, which include not only extensive and growing social conflict (which certainly does play an important role in Weber's account) but also the resolution and supersession of the process of rationalisation itself (on which see the next chapter). See Brubaker (1991) for a comprehensive exposition and analysis of Weber's position.

[2] On the psychic origins of roles, see Bretherton (1984: 32-41); *Introduction* to Case and Okamoto (1996); Fischer *et al* in Wozniak and Fischer (1993: 93-117); or Watson and Fischer (1980).

[3] Parker and McKinney (1999: 129-160).

[4] Horrocks and Jackson (1972: 93–122).

tions and obligations, as owners of property with defined rights of access, usage and disposal, as citizens with legal and constitutional rights and duties, and so on.

So, in principle, a role determines relationships not between people but between yet more roles. All the same, once roles have become integral to the organisation of activity, they can scarcely fail to take control of a good deal of our relationship to other people. What am I to make of this person? Simple: ask them what their job is, whether they are a parent, who they vote for. How am I to relate to this person? That depends on the social stance predicated by the role they are playing – and by the role *I* am playing too. The answers to such questions may not exhaust their social being, but they will usually (one should perhaps say 'normally') account for an extraordinarily large proportion of their preferences, beliefs, decisions, actions, and so on. Of course, neither the concept nor the system of roles is foolproof;[1] however, as most important roles are limited to (indeed, create) differentiated spheres and demarcated episodes, any cracks or conflicts between them are seldom dangerous to the system itself.

On the other hand, it is important to recognise how far such a system is from its concrete rational predecessors. Far from merely replacing one set of parochial positions and personal interests with another in the manner of a feudal rebellion, or even the thoroughgoing mobilisation of all personal relationships by absolutism, capitalism's reconstruction of society into a system of formal roles creates structures of activity that reject the notions of parochialism and personality altogether. Thus, before the advent of industry (an archetypal formal system), work was not organised into a continuous system that operated independently of the concrete conditions in which it took place and independently of the views or interests of the individuals that operated it. For example, when a task was complete, there was nothing more to be done. Although there were many tasks that involved a good deal of preparation and follow up, there were few that were simply repeated and repeated in the way that 'work' is under capitalist conditions of (in particular) mass production.

I should emphasise that, although the clock and the machine are clearly the key instruments through which this discipline was implemented, understood

---

[1] Having begun my study of sociology not too long after the demise of classical role theory, I am well aware of its historical prominence and eventual debacle. Looking back on the rise and fall of this critical concept, I doubt that its eventual abandonment was caused by any intrinsic weakness. Rather, academic sociology seems not to have recognised well enough that the main determinant of roles is the division of labour, and that they can only be understood in terms of the structure and function of economic systems, in the broad sense of general systems for the reproduction of society as a whole.

Sociology's failure to grasp this essential point was exacerbated by its equally false expectation, linked to its inadequate conception of capitalism especially, that the system of roles should somehow be logically sound and should be in some sense good for people, or at least that a given collection of roles should be manageable by the individuals in question. However, the fact that the system of roles depends on a scarcely acknowledged economic system, that neither that system nor the ensuing system of roles quite makes sense and that roles need not be intelligible, let alone good, for anyone in no way reduces their reality.

and enforced, it was never machines that provided the rationale. It was only because capitalist production is production for the market, and not production for any current need, that a strictly formal code of work made any sense at all. Once one produces for a remote, invisible market, the motivation for production is the generation of profit and the key indicator of productivity is cash flow, then work itself can have equally abstract goals, motives and indicators. Thenceforth work found itself organised, if not in terms of the clock, the factory and production *as such*, then certainly in terms of the *functions* of the clock, the *organisation* of the factory and production *process*. And what is the typical synthesis of controlled activity, organisation and process but the role? Of course, all roles are always subordinate to the real logical nexus of capitalism as a whole, namely the pursuit of profit through production for a market rather than for use. But then profit itself embodies a completely abstract and formal notion of economic accomplishment – certainly far more so than any possible *practical* outcome.

The formality of the systems that replaced concrete reason's more naturalistic rhythm is evident at every level:

> ... there is a universal culture of organisations that transcends political or economic ideologies of the left or of the right... control, rewards, punishment, careers, promotion, corruption, errors and fear exist anywhere modern bureaucratic structures are established... there is a universal culture of organisations that stresses task orientation and goal attainment (making a profit or fulfilling plan objectives)... which emphasises what is systematic, thorough and painstaking; which rejects amusement, pleasure, and delight for their own sakes; which endorses verification, control and formalisation; which applauds risk-taking but rarely encourages it; which rejects hedonism in the organisation as sheer fantasy; which assumes that organisational survival is the only relevant goal to be pursued.[1]

Conversely, it is easy to see how difficult it would be to mobilise and stabilise as vast a social system as our own using only the congelations of administrative caste and sinecure that abound among the patrimonial administrations of pre-formal societies.[2] Although pre-formal systems did not lack practical skill and experience in dealing with large-scale public works, warfare, regional administration, managed production, religious ritual, long distance trade, and so on, their lack of true formality (and so of explicit and inherent order and self-regulation) precluded the dynamism and flexibility demanded by formal goals such as totalitarian power or the maximisation of profit – or any notion of democracy, civil rights or personal freedom that we would recognise today. More generally, as with all the overriding motives of a formal society, not only is effective organisation a matter of formality but it can only be optimised by adopting a strictly formal attitude towards it. This means being willing to dis-

---

[1] Guy Benveniste, quoted by Kamenka (1989: 5).

[2] Kamenka (1989) assesses the extent to which historical administrations – Chinese, Egyptian, Roman, Indian, Mesopotamian and Inca – met the criteria of strictly formal bureaucracies. Some comments on how the existence of a formal administration might be reconciled with a pre-formal social system are presented in Chapter 7.

pense with *any* particular or actual reality that may stand in the way of the system's higher objectives.

Hence the new paradox at the heart of activity. True, it would be difficult to name any technical advance apart from (perhaps) fire, writing and the wheel that has benefited humanity more than bureaucracy. Certainly the computer is not a candidate, if only because a computer is only an electronic bureaucracy. Nevertheless, an organisation like the one described above may well be created to serve a particular group and to achieve a particular purpose, but as described it surely has no interest in any actual authority, right, efficiency, human need or any other concrete end. Nor is this simply a shortcoming of the above description, for the prominence, even pre-eminence, of formality in the thinking of managers, administrators and other functionaries is frequently denounced as 'merely' bureaucratic by those whose main concern *is* authority, right, efficiency or human need.

Like roles, commodity relations provide a powerful and startlingly simple structure for organising relationships between a vast, indeed indefinite, range of objects. How is an apple like three pencils? Even the most superficial glance provides a kind of answer: they sell for the same price. Of course, comparing prices fails to provide any comparison between apples and pencils as such, but it is hard to imagine any valid comparison that did otherwise, and from the point of view of a formal system that is no loss anyway. Indeed, it is not even a detectable omission: as with roles' independence of their incumbents' personal concerns, it is only because commodity relations abstract from and formalise the actual things they bind together that they can regulate relationships between them in the first place. All the commodity relation asks is that both sides respond to its mechanism for establishing coherent, consistent relationships across the economic system as a whole.

Given the minute attention Marxists and others have paid to commodities over the last century, it is not necessary to dwell on this topic in any great detail here. However, it is important to understand the relationship between commodities and roles. In particular, it must be understood that, notwithstanding the validity of the conventional Marxist insistence on the centrality of commodity relations to the *objective* dynamics of a capitalist society, even the most complete account of commodity relations would still leave us a long way short of the actual organisation of real people. Commodity relations determine how *objects* are connected, whereas roles are concerned with how the *subjects* who operate such a formal social system make sense of it – a perspective without which it is quite impossible to grasp how they develop *through* it.

Nor can one simply subordinate the one to the other: from the point of view of its inhabitants, both commodities and roles mobilise and stabilise society to an unprecedented extent and at the most fundamental level.[1] Indeed, it is

---

[1] But only at a terrible price. During capitalism's period of 'primitive accumulation', during which it became the dominant mode of economic activity, the major instruments of this process were the enclosure movement (Hill, 1975) and the manufactories, mills and factories (Berg, 1985). They all created the utmost suffering. Nor have more recent attempts to industrialise by capitalist methods been any less painful: the Factory Inspec-

through their *joint* operation that the need from which this whole account proceeds – intelligence's need to make sense of the world and to make the world make sense – is raised to an unprecedented level. On the one hand, the system of roles is increasingly embodied in rigorously enforced and quite objective social relationships, and as such is obliged to come to terms with the laws that govern intelligent activity in general; and on the other, the system of commodities must respect the laws governing all levels of matter, from the physics of the things it commodifies and the processes it exploits to the independent and objective rationality of the economic system through which they pass. And between them, in the organisation of the whole range of activities through which they are produced and reproduced, roles and commodities create a vast range of profoundly new structures and relationships.

The ability to abstract from actual objects is also the basis of the third key structure of formal rational activity: money. However, unlike roles and commodities, which serve primarily to establish relationships, money is the very embodiment of the capitalist *system*. For money is the commodity whose function is to mediate the relationship between other commodities. This in turn is possible only because the commodity relation itself is indifferent to its own content. It makes no difference which object's production, distribution and consumption it controls; all that is required is a genuinely formal process of exchange. Hence both the necessity for and the possibility of money – the completely abstract medium of a completely abstract form of exchange.

But money is not merely a matter of commodities: increasingly it mediates roles too. This is obvious enough in the case of economic roles, increasingly many of which exist solely for the sake of the capitalist economy. For these roles, the primary condition of their performance is the transformation of the concrete capacity a concrete individual possesses to perform the activity in question into yet another abstract commodity, namely labour power. However, even private roles increasingly rely on money. Firstly, fewer and fewer roles can be performed without resort to commodities, which in turn presuppose money. Secondly, private roles are constantly being socialised, through public provision and private service organisations alike, or are accessible only through direct payment, taxation or social and work-related entitlement programmes. For example, even as mundane an activity as shopping is swiftly being transformed from a private chore into a commercial service supplied by transnational corporations. These all presuppose some kind of money relation. And so on.

The ascendancy of money, roles and commodities is no historical accident, but a direct expression of the nature of formal reason on the social plane. For-

---

tors' reports on British mills and factories, quoted at length in *Capital* (Marx, 1954: ch. 10), read exactly like today's reports on working conditions in the Third World. Capitalism's recent attempts to colonise the defunct Soviet system also seems to have created mass misery, in this case precisely because the institutions involved, flush with a decade of 'success' in the West (millions more unemployed, vast debts, ever-growing gaps between rich and poor), have tried to apply the same abstractions to a group of societies in a totally different economic situation (Stiglitz, 2002).

mal systems are by their very nature systems of relationships abstracted from content and context, so it is unlikely that *any* formal system could ever develop without establishing a mode of subjectivity akin to the role, a mechanism for coordinating objects in the manner of commodities, or a structure like money for integrating the system as a whole. And through the enormously powerful forces the establishment of a formal social system inevitably releases, humanity undergoes an equally enormous spurt of development. However, that is not because human nature is cherished by such a system or even compatible with money or commodity relations or roles as such. Although by no means anarchic (the view from the bottom notwithstanding), formal reason is intrinsically nihilistic with regard to the actual people and things it so successfully organises and drives. If a Socrates or a Jefferson is able to find a positive place for humanity within such a system, it is no thanks to the system itself.[1]

That is after all what makes a system like capitalism a *formal* system: its capacity to abstract from any particular content, empirical, normative or otherwise. Such a system has its own values, of course, but they are not the values of the participants. Indeed, a formal system respects *no* interests other than those of the system itself – not social agreement, not moral right, not technical efficiency, not environmental sanity, and certainly not human need.[2]

> Through wasting design talent on such trivia as mink-covered toilet seats, chrome-plated marmalade guards for toast, electronic fingernail-polish dryers, and baroque fly-swatters, a whole category of fetish objects for an abundant society has been created. I saw an advertisement extolling the virtues of diapers for parakeets. These delicate unmentionables (small, medium, large, and extra large) sold at $1 apiece. A long-distance call to the distributor provided me with the hair-raising information that 20,000 of these zany gadgets were sold each month in 1970.[3]

As countless bankrupt capitalists and distressed gentlefolk have discovered, capitalism does not even respect the interests of those it seems to serve most directly. Ultimately, the logic of money, roles and commodities can no more be modified to suit human ends than the laws of mathematics. On the contrary, the intrinsic natures of the people and things it controls are of no significance to a formal system, so long as the requirements of the system itself are met.

Unfortunately for the people and things concerned, if they are of no significance then they are also of no importance. At the very least there is constant practical pressure for people and things and events to fit in with formal systems rather than *vice versa*. New roles are quickly promulgated, becoming mandatory personal postures in their own right, despite their frequently dire consequences for the individuals in question. If a given economic system contains functions x, y and z which translate into jobs a, b, c, d and e, then so long

---

[1] On Socrates, see Snell (1960: 187–90).

[2] On the subordination of the design profession to the demands of marketing and profitability, and the general divorce of commercial design from suitability, efficiency and effectiveness, social responsibility, elementary morality, its own consequences and reality in general, see Papanek (1985).

[3] Papanek (1985: 221).

as someone with formally appropriate attributes and qualifications is doing those jobs, exactly who it is matters very little. In fact, even the job is entirely secondary, a means to the system's larger ends, and the job's incumbent, considered as a person, is not even visible to the system.[1] Consequently, the system may be stable and successful and the necessary roles performed efficiently and effectively, but the people who live in it may be isolated, fragmented and depressed.

That is not to say that individuals cannot find more or less authentic self-expression through their various roles. Especially for professionals, their role is sufficiently rich in content, authority and alternatives to meet most of their personal needs and desires. There is also no shortage of workers with no higher aim than just to get on.[2] Nevertheless, constant formal reassurances of personal liberation notwithstanding, opportunities for real development are increasingly restricted to those determined, structured, supplied and disciplined by the formal system itself. So there are degrees of commitment, there is direct and indirect resistance, there are local subversions and deformations of 'the system', there are various forms of therapy, from irony to encounter groups to dinner party radicalism to shopping, to help manage the mess an ill-fitting assemblage of roles can make of human existence; and so on. And much the same might be said of money and commodities.

All of which is bound to leave any account of formal reason in a characteristic contradiction. Capitalism is without doubt the single most powerful force for the development of human nature ever to appear on this planet. Yet its capacity to vitiate and undermine its own achievements is equally unrivalled. This contradiction is the subject of the remaining sections of this chapter.

A critique of happiness

Now [Tantalus] hangs, perennially consumed by thirst and hunger, from the bough of a fruit-tree which leans over a marshy lake. Its waves lap against his

---

[1] This picture of the formal organisation's unremitting indifference to the individual may seem to be refuted by the increasing attention organisations pay to personnel. This is a valid comment, but not a true objection. Firstly, as I shall argue below, the eventual amelioration of the conflict between individual and system inherent in any immature form of praxis, capitalism included, is part of its own praxis, though it follows from a deeper logic than any capitalist is likely to acknowledge. Secondly, such issues are only raised within a formal organisation to the extent and in the terms that they affect that organisation, rather than for the sake of the individual concerned.

[2] Of course, there is nothing new in that. The following summary of a book of etiquette comes from the Old Kingdom of ancient Egypt (quoted in Frankfort et al., 1949: 109):

The ideal picture is that of a correct man, who wisely avoids impulse and fits himself by word and deed into the administrative and social systems. An assured career as an official awaits him. No moral concepts like good or bad come into discussion here; rather the standard lies in the characteristics of the knowing man and the ignorant man, perhaps best given in the words 'smart' and 'stupid'. Smartness can be learned...

But then, this is a period when the Egyptian state was highly systematised, if not strictly formal (Kamenka, 1989).

waist, and sometimes reach his chin, yet whenever he bends down to drink, they slip away, and nothing remains but the black mud at his feet; or, if he ever succeeds in scooping up a handful of water, it slips through his fingers before he can do more than wet his cracked lips, leaving him thirstier than ever. The tree is laden with pears, shining apples, sweet figs, ripe olives and pomegranates, which dangle against his shoulders; but whenever he reaches for the luscious fruit, a gust of wind whirls them out of his reach...

Sisyphus was now given an exemplary punishment. The Judges of the Dead showed him a huge block of stone... and ordered him to roll it up to the brow of the hill and topple it down the farther slope. He has never yet succeeded in doing so. As soon as he has almost reached the summit, he is forced back by the weight of the shameless stone, which bounces to the very bottom once more; where he wearily retrieves it and must begin all over again, though sweat bathes his limbs, and a cloud of dust rises above his head.

Robert Graves, The Greek Myths[1]

The previous section gave only a literally superficial account of capitalism. This is quite deliberate: if I were trying to explain the forces and interests which drive contemporary economies, I would certainly have looked far more closely at profit, class, markets, the accumulation of capital, the extraction of economic surpluses, and so on. But for present purposes that is not necessary, because I am concerned here with the structures through which human beings come to grips with their world, independently of any underlying nature that may lie out of sight and, for the moment, out of mind. For it is here that the structural and functional overlaps through which the development of individual intelligences actually takes place are to be found, and little of the substrate of human activity will force its way into the main stream of human development except by this route. And, in any case, it takes very little thought to see how profit, class and markets are themselves increasingly structured in formal terms.[2] Meanwhile, money, roles and commodities represent a new, specifically formal and genuinely revolutionary world. It is therefore well worth inspecting them a little more closely, especially in terms of their contribution to human happiness.

The structure of happiness

The humanities and their neighbours have always had great difficulty defining happiness. But natural science has not fared any better. For example, the following is a representative biological definition of happiness:

We may therefore suppose that in Man a feeling of happiness is registered when behaviour is broadly within the guidelines that lead to the achievement of a biological goal of high inclusive fitness.[3]

---

[1] Graves (1981: 74, 139). See also Lefebvre (1991: 159ff). Any account of Sisyphus should be measured against Camus' interpretation (Camus, 1975).

[2] Eg, Marx (1954: 46–7 and *passim*).

[3] Crook (1980: 153). Crook's whole chapter provides a clear account of the basic biological issues surrounding this approach.

Fortunately for biology, such a definition is so imprecise, cast so wide and based on so little credible empirical assessment of what actually makes people happy that practically anything from sky-diving to reading *Pride and Prejudice* to martyrdom could be made to fit the bill by one *Just So* story or another. On the other hand, this evolutionary definition is not significantly weaker than most of the concepts of happiness that have dominated the humanities over the last century, such as 'reinforcement' or 'utility'.[1] Perhaps happiness has never been defined properly; but it certainly never will be in the absence of an adequate theory of human nature.

As the approach taken in this book suggests, the first criterion of a valid definition of happiness is that it should be stated in terms happy (and unhappy) human beings recognise. Although it is notoriously difficult to grasp happiness directly, that does not mean that it happens entirely behind people's backs, as the above definitions all imply. Indeed, the very idea that the development of intelligence consists of intelligence being progressively more self-conscious implies the importance – not to mention the possibility – of defining happiness in such terms. Part of the specifically developmental nature of intelligence is the result that people become increasingly capable of saying what makes them happy and unhappy. So we should not assume that a profound analysis must lead to an obscure result.

Based on this assumption, I shall define happiness as the unity of pleasure, satisfaction and contentment. Starting from the triad of subject, object and world standing at the heart of intelligence, satisfaction consists of the establishment of a non-contradictory subject, pleasure consists of the creation of non-contradictory objects, and contentment consists of the maintenance of a non-contradictory world. Given that the entirety of human consciousness and history to date is constrained by its current developmental level, clearly happiness is likely to pass through transitory and transitional stages, but equally clearly they become more autonomous, more permanent and more universal as subject, object and world themselves become so. More precisely, having defined happiness in this way, it should be clear that the pleasure, satisfaction and contentment of any actual person is tied, closely if not irredeemably, to the level of development of the social structures in terms of which they live their lives. Hence, at the formal level, the intimate yet also strained relationship between happiness on the one hand and roles, commodities and money on the other.

Roles are satisfying to the extent that they organise our activity along lines that are coherent, consistent, complete and correct, at least as far as the situation at hand demands. They satisfy in proportion to their ability to allow us to overcome the specific internal contradictions that role-based activity engenders in the first place. Satisfaction follows from the successful execution of the corresponding structure of activity, which restores the subject to a stable, mobile state. In more concrete terms this may mean the successful execution of a deliberate act, a task, a plan, a programme, and so on, for its own sake, independ-

---

[1] The notion of reinforcement probably no longer requires criticism; for some of the shortcomings of utility, see Sen in Strong (1992).

ently (though, as ever, not regardless) of the actual result of that action. It may even consist of resolving a contradiction of which the subject was not aware, at least so long as the fact of its resolution *is* recognised.

Hence the potential of formal roles: they break down the complexities of social life as a whole into clearly circumscribed, often explicitly articulated, socially supported and so potentially satisfying patterns of activity. Of course, it is not only roles that offer satisfaction in this way; however, as the underlying formal system matures, it is increasingly difficult to avoid the reduction of activity to roles, even if those roles are simultaneously richer, more versatile and reflect a more generous interpretation of human nature.

Commodities complement roles in that they are pleasurable only if they give us coherent, consistent, complete and correct objects. These are objects that, if not perfect by all possible criteria, at least approximate to the expectations of the consumer. An object is pleasing to the extent that it is objective and it is what it should be. However, just as there are certain subjective conflicts that are satisfying, this definition of pleasure does not completely exclude the possibility of a pleasing contradiction. Still, this contradiction must be one required of that particular object.

That this definition also accounts for bodily pleasures is shown by the fact that a pleasure is greatly accentuated by the thorough objectification of the relevant appetite. For example, a truly satisfying meal articulates the hunger as it feeds the diner. And precisely because it is always finding ever newer and more sophisticated appetites to feed, capitalism creates a more refined and demanding consumer. An objectively worthless commodity is equally little a problem, either for capitalism or for the present account. Within the terms of reference of capitalism itself, a commodity can be legitimised by nothing more than the existence of a demand for it, and creating demand for useless objects is not usually a serious obstacle, ethical or technical, for modern advertisers.[1]

Finally, money offers contentment by offering to let us create for ourselves a coherent, consistent, complete and correct world. It offers to create for us a world that will endure on *our* terms, and so allow *us* to endure without causing us constant concern or demanding our constant intervention.[2] Contentment follows from the realisation that there are no insuperable problems lurking beneath the surface of pleasure and satisfaction, no precipitate curtailment in the offing, and so no lurking suspicion that our current happiness is short-lived or ephemeral. Money permits its owner to possess in the present the means of ensuring that the future will be under control, almost regardless of its content or context. It lets us be happy with our happiness. Of course, money is not the only source of contentment, and in periods of crisis not even money can allay a profound sense of unease and even active malcontentment. Nevertheless, just

---

[1] Lasch (1980: 71–4).

[2] At least on the phenomenological plane, money precedes even property, for property is always a risk and a source of care, whereas money, by its very abstractness, liberates one from the uncertainty and burdens of ownership. On the other hand, the precedence of money is precisely what follows from Marx's formula for the core capitalist process, M-C-M'.

as money is the universal solvent, so it is the closest we have yet come, on the social plane at least, to universal reassurance.

Critique of roles, money and commodities

I do not hesitate to assert that, taken together, roles, commodities and money take satisfaction, pleasure and contentment to unprecedented heights, and that the capitalist[1] system as a whole provides powerful instruments for the most felicitous development of subject, object and world. The only remaining question is whether they also produce happiness, which presupposes the *unity* of pleasure, satisfaction and contentment rather than their mere co-presence. Taken in isolation, they soon create the very opposite. Hence the key question in any contemporary critique of happiness is whether the bourgeois equation:

$$commodities + roles + money = pleasure + satisfaction + contentment$$

is equivalent to the human equation:

$$capitalism = happiness$$

This is not a trivial question. Even taken separately, money, commodities and roles cannot be considered simple matters, and they are naturally connected in a huge range of human activities. For example, a work of art is not merely satisfying to the artist and a pleasure to the onlooker (in the sense that the tensions between its various elements are resolved or stabilised within it) but also, by revealing and allowing us to resolve unsuspected tensions in our own existences, a potential source of the most profound satisfaction to the onlooker too.

The creation of a work of art can likewise be both a pleasure and a satisfaction. Similarly, despite defining satisfaction in terms of the internal structure of the activity, regardless of its results, it is clear that satisfaction is not totally unaffected by the outcome of a given activity. A plan may be carried out correctly without being successful – an operation may be a success even though the patient dies – but the satisfaction this affords is likely to be vitiated by the fact that, for intelligence, the plan was itself part of a programme to achieve a still higher objective, namely the health of the patient. In both cases, the problem is that both pleasure and satisfaction presuppose both structural and functional aspects. Conversely, a surprisingly low level of pleasure or satisfaction may be

---

[1] It is possible to imagine a non-capitalist formal socio-economic system that does not rest on money, commodities or roles. However, because of their close connection with subject, object and world, it is clear that such a system would include both their counterparts and the same logic. In what follows, the finger is pointed at capitalism, but the aspect of its guilt with which I am concerned here is a function of its formality, so the same criticisms would apply to any formal system. Just as it is often easier to write about human nature than about praxis or intelligence, so it is both easier and more cogent to write in terms of capitalism than a formal economy. Nevertheless, the reader should not assume that my critique is restricted to even the truly planetary unhappiness capitalism is capable of causing. A non-capitalist but still formal 'solution' might turn the capitalist world upside down, but it would not solve any of its essential problems.

accepted if accompanied by long-term security, but this does not make you happy.

Nor should one ignore the possibility that roles, money and commodity relations will eventually engulf *every* aspect of human existence. Increasingly many of the devices we use to defend ourselves against the emptiness of mere roles and mere consumption – hobbies, community festivals, 'making your own entertainment', even conversation – are being usurped and subverted as increasingly many modes of human intercourse are reduced to roles, commodified or suppressed by the isolation of the consumer that accompanies the formalisation of the division of labour. Hence the great difference between the equations set out above. For example, pleasure is doubly divorced from satisfaction: firstly in the production of commodities themselves, and secondly in the gradual elimination of the possibility of producing anything *but* commodities. Hence both the perfect blandness of consumerism and the bourgeois life and the conclusion that the commodity is not a possible source of happiness.

Nevertheless, as commodities, roles and money are rapidly becoming the only vehicles for pleasure, satisfaction and contentment capitalism affords, we must hope that the equations posed above are indeed equivalent. Unfortunately, the gist of the argument that follows is that they are not – that the logic of capitalism is anathema to the achievement of happiness, and the reason for this is precisely the formal nature of money, commodities and roles. Indeed, capitalism has submerged human existence in a bubble bath of activities and experiences that creates the impression of an inexhaustible supply of bright, shiny, immaculate and neatly encapsulated moments of happiness, each of which unfortunately explodes on contact with real human beings.

The potential independence of pleasure, satisfaction and contentment can easily be grasped by imagining a world of pleasure without satisfaction, or *vice versa*, or a world that offers either in abundance but sets them in an unstable, transient, threatening world. The decadence of the ruling class of the later Rome empire, whose self-indulgence seems to have been matched only by their boredom and resignation, comes immediately to mind here: boundless opportunities for amusement, but entirely dependent on slave and plebeian classes for all productive activity, and often under threat from predatory emperors. (It is a measure of the spiritual destitution of this class that it eventually embraced Christianity.) More generally, did society *ever* lack hedonists or martinets or plutocrats, who have one of the means to happiness but lack – or even shun – the others? And how many of them were happy? Is not the miser 'as much in want of what he has as of what he has not'?

But Rome's combination of fabulous wealth, rapacious exploitation and precarious politics is not the only possible route to the fragmentation of pleasure, satisfaction and contentment, and neither is any other permutation of these forces. If, in an era of advanced capitalist production, we regard it as the norm for *all* products to be produced for universal distribution via the market, and almost all distribution is effected through the exchange of goods and services for money, then *all* access to *all* the things one might want will be by routes determined by a formal system that actively divorces the three elements of happiness. The formal character of the systems and relationships in question ensures that there is no direct connection between production (satisfaction), consumption (pleasure) and wealth (contentment). If everything can be bought and sold, this may well create a generalised system for the delivery of pleasure on a scale beyond the dreams of any Roman sybarite, but this arrangement also divorces pleasure from satisfaction completely. At the same time, if the very formality of the system makes it disinterested towards *every* interest, then contentment is only available to the especially undemanding or the pathologically short-sighted.

Of course, everything that is to be consumed also has to be produced, so *in general terms* the link between money, the production of commodities and the playing of formal roles is crystal clear to everyone. However, no one actually exists 'in general terms', and the actual process of production, which is the only strictly satisfying activity directly linked to particular commodities, is entirely divorced from their enjoyment. Factory and offices workers do not, by and large, consume what they produce.

Of course, from a social and historical point of view, this is just as well, since it is only through capitalism's acceleration of the division of labour to its logical, functional and historical limits that we have achieved the sheer breadth and depth of experience to which almost everyone in a formal rational society can lay claim to some degree. Nevertheless, the situation of the individual human being in such a society is far from being so promising. On the contrary, the pleasure of consuming a given commodity is firmly divorced from the satisfaction of producing it. The absence of happiness – not its overt or active denial, only its persistent absence and undermining – is the very hallmark of the commodity, even when the pleasure it offers is the greatest imaginable. Its consumption may leave a memory but, not having engaged it in any productive way, there is no sense of anything significant having taken place.

There can equally easily be satisfaction without pleasure. For example, the formalisation of the division of labour raises the organisation of activity to unprecedented heights. However, as Adam Smith's exquisitely appalling example of the manufacture of pins so famously illustrates,[1] it does so by first fragmenting the overall structure of activity (of the task, the enterprise, the state, the institution, the market, and so on) into a million sub-structures of activity – which is to say, a million roles – any of which may be significant in the context of the structure as a whole, but none of which makes much sense in its own right. It is always on behalf of another role, a larger function, some external goal that they are deployed. It is therefore only for impersonal reasons – known to the system alone, so to speak – that roles are exercised. As often as not there is no specific, let alone significant, product in whose production the immediate producer can take personal pleasure, and only satisfaction on a minute scale. From the point of view of the participants, roles (economic and non-economic) are almost entirely arbitrary, lead to no outcome they might personally desire, and often have no significance at the level of the work in which they personally engage. So roles cut actual individuals off from taking pleasure in their task from both ends, as it were. They are driven by external motives (eg, earning a living) whose satisfaction is, in itself, entirely incapable

---

[1] Smith (1976: 8ff).

of affording them pleasure, and they conclude their activity without have created anything that *they*, considered as more than functionaries in the larger machine, might want or might feel that *they* have created. From their own point of view, the best they can hope for is 'a job well done'.

This mutual independence between pleasure and satisfaction does not prevent their connection from becoming very complex. For example, the self itself can become a commodity and the possession of the right commodities the only socially valid index of selfhood. The trappings of beauty and power have always had this quality but, as Covey has observed, the last century has seen an increasing tendency for the self itself to be invaded, in the form of the substitution of 'personality' for authentic character. Under this regime, 'self-improvement' is increasingly directed towards creating an impression of the right kind of self, or where genuine change is sought, it is in the form of a shiny, glib, barren *persona* aimed at seduction and performance at the expense of integrity and authenticity; it aims at re-engineering the self to meet the specifications of social roles, which in turn will ensure its viability as a commodity.[1] Sincerity, that's the thing: anyone who can fake that has got it made.

Finally, contentment under such a system must remain a moot point. Although one may have enough money to guarantee a lifetime of pleasure, there is nothing one can buy that will overcome the rift between satisfaction and pleasure, nothing that can translate money's apparent omnipotence into a real command of all the means needed to ensure substantial happiness. After all, what can money buy other than more commodities? It may well be that, as Byron once remarked, ready money *is* Aladdin's lamp, but what is required here is more than magic; it is revolution. And even leaving aside the reservations already entered above, the very logic of commodity relations and roles makes it impossible to be sure that one's pleasure or satisfaction is not merely a passing moment of good fortune. Firstly, it is extremely difficult to comprehend the system as a whole, as the multiplicity of competing theories of capitalism testifies. Secondly, even if any of these theories are correct, their strictly formal character – universal, abstract and one-sidedly devoted to a particular system of concepts or interests – offers the individual no practical power over capitalism. Indeed, not even the most powerful player seems to have a decisive influence, as the ineffectiveness of attempts to manage capitalism out of its periodic crises demonstrates. Thirdly (although this is a matter of constant dispute between capitalism's apologists and critics), these crises show every sign of being inherent in the normal operations of the system. So the population at large remains unassured. Nor do they seem much more confident of its promises of life or liberty, each of which could be subjected to analogous criticisms. Indeed, for a system of such unmatched promise and power, it is truly amazing how little enduring confidence capitalism inspires.

---

[1] Covey (1989). See also Lasch (1980) or Handy (1995). Sennett (1977) draws out many of the factors that have paid a role in creating this predicament, while Sennett (1998) elaborates the deleterious effects of the organisation of modern work.

The revolt against formality

The true divide between God and Nature had to be insisted upon; typically, in the mechanical philosophy, all activity was attributed to God, but a God who was increasingly distant, and Nature was reduced to a machine, inert and passive. Similarly, man and Nature were also demarcated, most extremely in Cartesian dualism in which nature became merely extension (matter in motion) and man alone possessed consciousness ... If Nature were not after all alive but just an object, it could be taken to pieces, anatomised, resolved into atoms... 'tortured' into revealing its truth.

Roy Porter[1]

'What're you rebelling against, Johnny?'
'Whaddya got?'

The Wild One[2]

The critique of formal reason's attempts at happiness is scarcely the exclusive province of intellectuals. On the contrary, even if all the above were not the case, even though for long periods capitalism only creates a level of uncertainty which most people can at least tolerate,[3] the most ordinary experience of capitalism is still one of exploitation. In most cases this is a relatively neutral process, in the sense that human beings are exploited in the same impersonal and generic way as any other resource – a mine, a machine, and so on. So, we go to work, we come home, we get paid, we watch TV and see the advertisements – not without a sense of the situation, but with little feeling of being exploited or any accompanying sense of anger or grievance.

Of course, human beings are different from other 'resources': unlike a mine or a machine, we are capable of recognising an exploitative relationship, not to mention taking exception to such repulsive expressions as 'human capital' and being reduced to 'assets'. All the same, this situation is so taken for granted that it is difficult to adopt any more radical form of resistance than welfarism, reformism, the privatisation of personal life, or simple resignation. We all know our place, the system is by no means totally barren or irrational, and it is difficult to imagine a serious alternative, if only because of the effort its apolo-

---

[1] In Porter and Teich (1986: 302–3).

[2] Columbia Pictures (1954). Written by John Paxton, directed by László Benedek.

[3] Though as Sennett notes, 'Through most of human history, people have accepted the fact that their lives will shift suddenly due to wars, famines, or other disasters, and that they will have to improvise in order to survive... What's peculiar about uncertainty today is that it exists without any looming historical disaster; instead it is woven into the everyday practices of a vigorous capitalism' (Sennett, 1998: 31; also pp.80ff). On the other hand, as Bernstein has argued, the modern world has also equipped us with better means of dealing with uncertainty. Where once the future was perceived entirely in terms of fortune, fate, the will of God, and so on, the emergence of probability theory, risk management, psychologies of choice and innumerable side-disciplines has transformed our view of the future into something we can chose on the basis of a rational, if not exhaustive, calculus (Bernstein, 1998).

gists put into 'proving' that capitalism represents the natural order, the best of all possible worlds, and so on.

But from time to time the predatory nature of the system comes to the fore. And for those at the bottom of this sorry heap, it is self-evident at every moment, although generally speaking only in the inarticulate forms of resentment and despair. Whatever the passing pleasures and satisfactions offered by capitalism (or any other embodiment of formal reason) there is little reason to feel wholly contented. So it comes as no surprise that formal reason in general is plagued with a constant undercurrent of criticism, occasionally erupting into open revolt: it is the natural corollary of its failure to comprehend the world in the first place.[1] But revolt is not revolution; in fact it is only rebellion, until at least two closely connected things happen. Firstly, the rebels must recognise the true nature of their enemy, and as with any other form of intelligence, the nature of a formal rational system will only be intelligible to its inhabitants as a whole in proportion to its own maturity. Secondly, the rebels can only transform their actions into true revolution when they recognise that the terms on which they rebel are the product of formal reason itself.[2] Until then, they are doomed either to fail or to achieve no more than isolated adjustments to the system as a whole.

Indeed, they are just as likely to sanctify as to attack the moments of crisis that reveal a formal system's shortcoming. For example, romantic and existentialist critics of formal reason often simply insist on the primacy of subjective experience and the present moment that, for them, validate the individual and the irreducibility of choice, contingency, decision, responsibility, and so on. But such experiences and moments are only troublesome and contradictory to the dehumanising nature of the system as a whole because no formal structure is capable of capturing them. That is, they represent the points at which formality fails. Consequently, to insist on their intrinsic significance and irreducibility is to hallow the symptom, and so perpetuate the cause. Indeed, it does not address the real disease at all. Hence formal reason's long history of internal revolt and the almost total absence of genuine revolution.

Whether at the level of the philosophical speculation they have occasioned or the titanic world-systems they have sired, it is surely the inability of formal structures to truly comprehend the *actual* world that leads so many of their leading exponents to profoundly unhappy conclusions, be they agnosticism,

---

[1] 'It is significant that the thought of the epoch is at once one of the most deeply imbued with a philosophy of the non-significance of the world and one of the most divided in its conclusions. It is constantly oscillating between extreme rationalization of reality which tends to break up that thought into standard reasons and its extreme irrationalization which tends to deify it' (Camus, 1975: 48).

[2] Armstrong (1993, 2000) argues that contemporary Christian, Jewish and Islamic fundamentalism arises out of the attempt to perpetuate traditional and mythical religious beliefs, to justify religious and mystical experience and to resist the encroachments of the barren and threatening rationalism of the modern world by quite inappropriately 'modern' means such as logic, evidence, proof, and so on, and by the conversion of mythical insights into ideological and political programmes.

relativism, withdrawal, reductionism, scepticism, sophism, pragmatism, eclecticism, cynicism (in both its original and its contemporary senses), nihilism, hedonism, decadence, asceticism and even self-mortification.[1] Historically speaking there has always been a struggle between the overweening claims of formalisation and the nuggets of actuality it cannot quite comprehend. Hence, for example, the irreducible distance within so many religions between the exoteric, kerygmatic knowledge designed for disciples and debate, and the true, esoteric dogma accessible only to initiates.[2] From the latter point of view, formal reason itself offers nothing more convincing than increasingly elaborate formulae, blunt assertions and pious hopes that one day all the pieces will fall into place.

The poverty of this attitude was recognised even as formal reason stepped up to take over the reins of society, for this was surely the crux of Romanticism:

> The black-and-white terms these neo-scholastics use to describe man – an inexhaustibly complex organisation – seem... wilfully absolute and arbitrary. Instead, for example, of asking themselves how free men are, free from or for what, and where and when and in what respects, or what renders them more or less free, these thinkers dogmatically pronounce man to be free, wholly free in some absolute sense... They speak of man as distinguished by his possession of reason (not as being more or less rational), and define him in terms of selected properties that one must either possess wholly, or not possess at all; they describe him in terms of sharp, artificial dichotomies that arbitrarily break up the interwoven, continuous, at times irregular, fluid, shapeless, often unanalysable, but always perceptible, dynamic, teeming, boundless, eternal multiplicity of nature, and so provide distorting lenses both to philosophers and historians. Attempts to bring manifestations so complex and so various under some general law, whether by philosophers seeking knowledge, or by statesmen seeking to organise and govern, seemed... no better than a search for the lowest common denominator – for what may be least characteristic and important in the lives of men – and, therefore, as making for shallowness in theory and a tendency to impose a crippling uniformity in practice.[3]

Naturally, our view of what the Romantics said and wanted is much simplified by two centuries distance and fascinated hindsight,[4] but one could as eas-

---

[1] Leaving aside the prevalence of these positions among modern thinkers, see Nakamura (1986: Ch.2), for a comparative history of Indian, Greek and other positions, and Kirk *et al.* (1983), on the rapid progression of these modes of thought among the earliest western thinkers.

[2] Armstrong (1993).

[3] Berlin (1976: 175; also 2000). See also Hegel's parallel critiques of Enlightenment rationalism and pietism (1977: §§ 527–81). Rather more eloquently, see Lovejoy (1964: 28–9). See also Engelhardt in Teich *et al.* (1997: 195–208).

[4] See, for example, Radkau in Teich *et al.* (1997: 228–239) for the really rather equivocal nature of the Romantic attitude to the great northern forests to which they now seem so attached. Thomas' (1983) account of the progressive romanticisation of nature by the English shows that it too was most ambiguous. It also suggests that a great deal of its apotheosis of animals, the countryside and even plants can be traced to the very formalisation of our views of nature to which Romanticism in general seems so opposed: nature was romanticised in direct proportion to the 'dethronement of man' and the setting

ily quote *The Rime of the Ancient Mariner*, Hesse's *Glass Bead Game* or even
Frankenstein and *Dr Jekyll and Mr Hyde* – all consciously dire warnings against
the hubris of abstraction, technology without compassion, mechanistic systematisation without values, and gratuitous formalisation.[1] Even *The Wealth of
Nations* was written in full consciousness of the wealth of moral and political
implications of what would soon be sterilised into formal economic arguments.[2]

It is true that sometimes formal reasoning seeks out and confesses its own
inadequacies, often with a frankness and an alacrity that astonish. Mathematicians queue up to prove that mathematics cannot prove itself coherent or consistent or complete or correct.[3] However necessary they may be on their own
terms, even such seemingly omnipotent structures as formal logic usually
claim to be truths only in the abstract (although Pythagoreanism and Platonism
persist among mathematicians). They help us manipulate, investigate, interpret
and rebuild our world once we are in it, but their application to that world remains arbitrary and superficial, to be defined by their users' practical concerns
rather than by the methods themselves. But where does that leave us when we
must face up to the great existential issues which follow from the actuality
even the most powerful formal systems cannot address? Nowhere.

So, not even the most assiduous devotion to the formalities of fashion can,
by itself, confer taste; no matter how meticulously or felicitously framed, law
cannot, by itself, deliver the justice that the uniqueness, circumstances and individuality of human action demand; and so on. As Aristotle put it, equity 'is
the rectification of law in so far as law is defective on account of its universality... An irregular object has a rule of irregular shape... And sympathetic
judgement is correct judgement that decides what is equitable; a correct
judgement being one that arrives at the truth'.[4] Nor is this simply an occasional

---

up of an increasingly articulated, systematised and formalised picture of nature.

Romanticism itself seems to be largely a contradictory reaction to the contradictory
features of this gradual emergence: on the one hand, the recognition that nature exists
independently of human beings set up nature as a separate realm, but on the other, until
the real relationship between animals and human beings had been established (a transition that has yet to be completed), a tendency to project human attributes onto everything from 'Mother Nature' to individual trees established nature as humanity's equal,
if not its superior, even in areas such as morality and wisdom. It is therefore no surprise
that a growing sensibility to animal feelings and rights coincided with the struggle
against slavery, corporal punishment and other social evils (Thomas, 1983: 181–91). This
confusion also goes a long way towards explaining how it is that so many animals are
traditionally attributed degrees of gluttony, murderousness and carnal passion that are
only properly found in human beings. As Coleridge noted, to call human vices bestial is
to libel beasts.

[1] On *Frankenstein*, see Gould (1996: 'The monster's human nature').

[2] See Brewer (2000).

[3] For a relevant critique of mathematical formality, see Pankow in Jantsch and Waddington (1976).

[4] Aristotle, *Nicomachean Ethics* (1137b24–1138a11; 1143a16–32). On the social and historical development of equity, see Hallpike (2004). On Aristotle's theory of equity, see

nuisance: rather, 'the general case, the one all our legal rules and formalities are designed for and the one on the basis of which they're all worked out an written into the legal text books, simply doesn't exist, for the very good reason that every case, every crime, ... as soon as it takes place in reality, turns into a thoroughly special case...'[1] And of course, the essential difference between formal principle and the reality to which that principle must be applied is one of the most compelling reasons for having judges as well as legislators. On the other hand, although equity is intended as a principled corrective to any formal system needs in order to dispense justice, it is notoriously difficult to state exactly what the principle of correction actually is, and appeals for equity frequently degenerate into lists of exceptions, *caveats* and mitigating factors, and useful but imprecise nuggets of advice. More often than not, 'We are dealing with an inventory of ways an advocate can ask for the indulgence of the judges, not with an inventory of principles which permit the judge to know whether they should acceded to this kind of request'.[2]

Which is, of course, exactly what one would expect of formal reason.

Thus, in arena after arena we raise new formal edifices of ever-growing scope and power, yet these abstractions continue to fall short of or even belie and distort the reality they were supposed to deliver into our hands. Not that the romanticism alluded to above offers a solution to this problem, and neither does the existentialist's 'project'. On the contrary, central to both is surely their insistence on what theories, abstraction and formalism *cannot* do, rather than any positive alternative. A demand for authenticity may be an entirely valid aspiration, but it is not a programme of the kind in which formal reason abounds. Hence the pivotal role Kant plays in the intellectual history of formal reason: in many respects the epitome of Enlightenment rationalism, it was nevertheless he who, in the *Critique of Pure Reason*, finally shut and bolted the door between formality and reality. Kant himself famously remarked, 'Enlightenment is man's release from his self-incurred tutelage. Tutelage is man's inability to make us of his understanding without direction from another'; but he went on to add, 'Self-incurred is this tutelage when its cause lies not in lack of reason but in lack of resolution and courage to use it without direction from another.'[3] In other words, Kant had no quarrel with the *nature* of formal reason, only with its capabilities and use.

This is perhaps why the most positive contribution of which formal reason's critics seem capable has often been to exhort its enthusiasts to integrity, faith, individuality, even irony.[4] In that respect these critics are only *alter egos* of the Enlightenment, scientific method, industrialism and so on, with their central focus on the things of which formal reason is most eminently capable – measure, proportion, process, method, and so on. Hence the fabulous diversity of

---

Brunschwig in Frede and Striker (1996: 115–155).

[1] Dostoyevsky, *Crime and Punishment*, translated by D. McDuff.

[2] Brunschwig in Frede and Striker (1996: 151).

[3] Kant (1963: 3).

[4] On irony, see Enright (1988).

the various definitions offered for romanticism itself.[1] But hence also the wholly inadequate attitude romantics share to the separation and antithesis of self and other, present and absent, and appearance and reality, that formal reason brings into such sharp focus: to denounce them as illusory, to announce their 'revolutionary' overthrow, or bemoan them as inexorable tragedies. In no case does romanticism, existentialism or any other anti-rationalistic philosophy contribute to a genuine resolution.

On the social plane too, social democracy is notorious for pretending to reconcile profit with human need while actually offering nothing more than to manage capitalism in the interests of abstract principles such as 'social justice'. This liberal–romantic–existential axis will long retain a persuasiveness in the face of formal reason, but as first and foremost a direct reflection of formal reason, it cannot expect to overcome it. So in the long run it is irrelevant for Romantics and existentialists and liberal-minded social democrats to exhort us to personal integrity or authenticity or social responsibility in the face of 'the system'. The modern obsessions with originality and romantic love are equally misplaced (as are most of the criticisms they provoke). On the other hand, the only other alternative seems to be to evade, leave or abolish the system itself. The rest is idle defiance and self-defeating reformism.

Hence the question of just how the limits imposed by formal reason can be overcome. This question cannot be answered until the profundity of formal reason is grasped. Formal reason does not fall short of perfection in a purely negative sense. No other material structure has ever reached a state one could call 'perfect', so a merely negative outcome – a lack of power and knowledge – could hardly be held against formality as such. However, even if this ultimate practical fallibility is not enough to condemn formal reason, it must surely count for something that the negative shortcomings of formal reason are *not* merely the renewed expression of some universal tragedy of the human condition. On the contrary, as the above arguments regarding roles, commodities and money have, I hope, demonstrated, the instruments of human disappointment are actively produced by formal reason, and produced by its most basic logic.

Nor, given the all-pervasive nature of money, roles and commodity relations, can one say that all this is limited to the social and economic levels. To repeat, a role is merely a socialised mode of subjectivity, and as such perfectly capable of invading the most personal recesses of subjectivity as a whole. Likewise, the abstractness of the commodity relation enables it to dissolve absolutely any object, and money shrinks the infinite world to an infinitesimal cipher. Furthermore, not only roles, commodities and money but absolutely all formal modes of subjectivity, objectivity and worldliness undermine the individuality they seem to promote, for they let reason bring together an infinitely rich complex of talents and experiences, but only on the condition that the intelligence in question does not take possession of them and mould them into a truly individual form. On the contrary, the system must retain its formal integ-

---

[1] Berlin (2000: 14–18).

rity, and no individual thing or event is reducible to even the sum of all possible formal systems.

But surely one could still argue – a little pathetically, it must be said – that somewhere in the nooks and crannies of the personality, of imagination, of morality, of belief, one still has that irreducible iota of vision and liberty that no amount of formalisation can take away? Regrettably this is not so, if only because formal structures such as roles, commodities and money are not external conditions to which intelligence must adapt, but are the very structures and mechanisms through which the formal subject, object and world are constituted in the first place. And far from reconciling everything, as the apologists and ideologues of markets, the state and citizenship claim, once they have finished their handiwork there is *nothing* left of value or meaning, and actual existence is reduced to a shadow of itself.

Indeed, formal reason is constantly setting up irreconcilable antitheses such as (formal) liberty and (formal) equality, and seeks to defuse the inevitable civil war that follows by exhorting us to the mutual kindliness of fraternity. By means of money, roles and commodities all reasons and all reasoning are eventually co-opted and reshaped by formal reason itself, so there is no material basis for this fraternity, and every attempt to kindle it is forced into an equally formal mould. Consequently, there is every reason to set it aside. Like justice, quality or common humanity, under the complex and incoherent system of interests set up by formal reason, the notion of fraternity is as hollow as it is grand.

Of course, one should not expect otherwise. The preliminary apotheosis of reason effected by formal reasoning is boundless in its diversity, versatility and, in principle, power. But at the same time it is infinitely tantalising in its monstrous emptiness. It establishes a universal order of the utmost sophistication and disinterest, and thereby frees itself from interest and uninterest in content and context alike. Yet it does so only by placing itself outside them. Its infinities are the 'bad' infinities against which Hegel railed: the infinities of a hall of mirrors, of vicious circles, of theologies that begin by expelling God from the universe and philosophies that eject the subject from the body, of economic formalisms that despoil whole societies.[1]

Indeed, in the shadow of Gödel, formal reason even annuls the significance and meaning and purposefulness of its own constructions, without ever realising that it has delivered up the most damning judgement on itself imaginable. For all its infinite reach, the infinite multiplicity of its possible worlds, its subsumption of the seeming contingencies of existence into increasingly abstract yet rich and powerful frameworks, the infinitude of formal reason is the infinitude of infinite regression, not infinite fulfilment. The more formality is piled

---

[1] I should emphasise that the main exponents of formal reason are seldom unaware of the paradoxes to which this leads. For example, no one except Newton contributed more to defining formal reason on the intellectual level than Immanuel Kant, yet he insisted on the need to transcend false infinities of merely quantitative extension. See, for example, 'The end of all things', in Kant (1963). But note also that Kant failed to resolve the paradox he identified.

on formality, the more clearly (or perhaps only the more brilliantly) our doctors and politicians and economists and pundits and lobbyists identify the latest means and ends of our most profound needs, wants and desires – and the more entirely they escape our grasp. Indeed, the more certain we are that they have escaped, even though our grasp has become that much more certain. The more refined the means, the more equivocal, evasive and illusory the ends – and *vice versa*. The more powerful formality's tools, the more ephemeral its results.

Not that the value of formal reason is to be doubted. Nor are its achievements to be discounted or evaded. Yet it is clear that this formality is not *enough*. For formal reason promises everything, and promises it with the utmost sincerity, yet on the plane of ultimate fulfilment, it fails to deliver anything at all. Like any other adolescent, it is full of amazing energy, achievement and potential, but that does not make it grown up. Though capable of orchestrating an infinitely varied medley of deductions, it is incapable of coming to any *actual* conclusion. Although capable of constructing any 'possible world', it fails totally to construct the world before its eyes. Its results – more correctly its by-products, for there is no end to this process – are qualified by interminable possibilities and intimations, its necessities lead to no necessary outcome, its potency and vigour are squandered in reflections on reason's reflections on reason.

So formal reason proves itself the most powerful and imposing form of reason to date, but only at the price of being the most banal, for the seeds of futility lie in its very heart. Whether in the vacuity of the commodity, the vapidity of roles or the venality of money, the arena formal reasoning creates for itself to exercise and prove its powers turns out to be the most impenetrable vale of impotence, delusion, insignificance and self-betrayal. Although every possibility is explored, it proves impossible to actually find anything except more possibilities. I think, therefore I am... I think.

Meanwhile, formal reason may manage to crowd the unresolved contingency of its existence into a tiny space, but it cannot eliminate it altogether. How could it? – it is of its own making. At best it will recognise the havoc it wreaks, but it will never do more than devise a new system for coping with the problems that ensue:

> The practice of organising capitalism creates a mass of contradictions; and for each particular case a sociologist is put to work. One studies juvenile delinquency, another racism, a third slums. Each seeks an explanation of his partial problem and elaborates a 'theory' proposing solutions to the limited conflict he is studying. Thus, while serving as a 'watchdog' our sociologist will be at the same time making his contribution to the mosaic of sociological 'theories'.[1]

---

[1] Daniel Cohn-Bendit *et al.*, quoted in Dews (1987: 172). As Richard Sennett adds, 'The "dull science" – as Michel Foucault calls American sociology – legitimates dissociation from the entanglements, contradictions, and difficulties of actual social experience... Sociology in its dumbed-down condition is emblematic of a society that doesn't want to know too much about itself.' (in Lewontin, 2000: 270-1). Papanek (1985) makes an analogous case from the fragmentation of one of the core functions of any industrial

Even the problems it does acknowledge are likely to be reduced to problems *for the system* – of performance, of reliability, of efficiency, and so on – rather than for the individuals and societies involved. And so powerful are those who place formality above substance – which is to say, who place the formality of formal reason above its rationality – that it might well be centuries, if not millennia before the demands of rationality in the wider sense gain the upper hand.

The tragedy of formal reason lies not in not yet having arrived at a correct account of its own existence, or even in the impossibility of any such account. It lies in the fact that it can do no other. It can have existence only by reducing it to an untenable mix of abstraction and contingency, cannot even touch on entity without first turning it into non-entity. In short, although the necessities of formal reasoning are as compelling to reason as gravity is to the planets, the one thing whose necessity proves to be totally inaccessible is that which merely is. No matter how convincing or compelling, formal necessity can never quite touch the actuality of things. Nothing of substance can be comprehended without necessity, yet nothing within formal necessity seems quite substantial.

So it is the actuality of the actual that defeats formal reason. This renders actual individuality – and therefore the lives of individuals – unintelligible, and thus both subjectively and objectively meaningless. From a formal point of view (which must always reduce actual things and events to functions of some or other formalism), we are discrete but intersubstitutable, if not in ourselves then by virtue of the very process whereby we are reduced to the parameters of the system. This leaves us unique without being true individuals. We have unique concatenations of attributes, but they serve only to compare, if not equate, us with everyone else. To the question, 'Why me?', the only answer formal reason can manage is something like, 'Because you are an instance of...'. How infinitely further is it then from even posing the still more radical question, 'Why *I*?'

It is only to be expected that this reduction will be resisted, for it is the nadir of existence. But although formal reason can intuit this, it cannot fully comprehend it. This restricts its efforts to overcome this dreadful fate to denial and evasion, to dwelling on the paradoxes in which any formal system abounds, seducing itself with the perfectly crafted surprises and distractions of consumerism, and so on. In more existential mode, it can resist the lack of principle in its actual existence through a principled acceptance of the nullity of principle. But that only reduces the authenticity of the actual to the obviousness of the merely immediate.

That is why that ultimate exercise in trivialisation, consumerism, although apparently the acme of personal fulfilment, is in truth only the reciprocal of

---

system, namely design, and the fragmentation of other elements of capitalist industry is well known. More generally, the lack of direction in formal systems is captured by Bowler in his history of the environmental sciences, when he observes that 'The unity of the environmental sciences is not created by the sciences themselves; it is imposed by the public's growing awareness of the threat posed to the environment by our own activities' (Bowler, 1992: 2).

existentialist despair. Both declare that the only solution to the human condition is to look the other way for a while, and then die. The culture of formal systems is thus littered with the anti-formal, anti-rational rebellions sometimes aimed at proclaiming the emptiness of formal reason, sometimes yearning to fill that awful, self-emptying void, at least in some tiny corner of private reality, but never quite managing to do so. What else could explain the triumph of gardening and gambling, soap operas and fan clubs, not to mention the first great renaissance of pet-keeping since hunter-gatherers occupied the whole inhabitable world?[1]

Conclusions

> I observed here and there many in the habit of servants, with a blown bladder fastened like a flail to the end of a short stick... With these bladders they now and then flapped the mouths and ears of those who stood near them... This *flapper* is... employed diligently to attend his master in his walks, and upon occasion to give him a soft flap on his eyes, because he is always so wrapped up in cogitation, that he is in manifest danger of falling down every precipice, and bouncing his head against every post, and in the streets, of jostling others or being jostled himself into the kennel.

> Jonathan Swift, 'A Voyage to Laputa'

> Man never is, but always to be blest.

> Alexander Pope, *Essay on Man*, I, 95

Whether formal reason's ever-renewed cycle of promise and achievement, betrayal and revolt can be brought to a positive conclusion is the critical question not only for our understanding of intelligence but also for our survival as intelligent beings. Before it shuffles off, not without vigorous protests and many premature final curtains, formal reason is still capable of causing incalculable harm, not to mention inadvertent suicide. For unlike its predecessors, formality means not only a universal vision but also a universal determination to reduce the universe to that vision.

How beneficent the consequences of its realising this ambition are likely to be can be suggested by repeating that the characteristic mode of the formal psyche is adolescence. Even now formal reason stands at the close of half a century of brinkmanship between its two most powerful expressions, with victorious capitalism wading knee-deep in a range of interconnected social, political and ecological crises it is barely able to register, let alone resolve.

So is there no end to formal reason, which is to say, to the failure to grasp existence without first pulverising it? It happens that there is, though it will not be achieved by means of the characteristic style of revolt created by formal reason itself. Indeed, exactly what the successful supersession of formal reason would mean cannot be judged from the standpoint of formal reason itself at all. The final truth can only be grasped at the pinnacle of reason. Below that, what-

---

[1] Serpell (1996: 149–50 and *passim*); Thomas (1983: 110–20).

ever is yet to come must seem cloudy, utopian, trivial or preposterous. But there really is a sound of one hand clapping, although it cannot be heard by those for whom this is simply a queer or silly or gratuitous enigma.

On the other hand, we can certainly say what contradictions must be resolved if we are to reach this higher stage. The shortcomings of our present social and psychic order are plain enough: Gödel and Heidegger pronounce them as clearly as each new crisis of capitalism. As to whether there is a mechanism capable of raising human beings to the next level, this can also be answered positively. After all, we are dealing with intelligence here, and the structural and functional overlaps and negations and contradictions that have driven its development from the first cannot be denied now.

So what is the final conundrum formal reason cannot overcome, whose solution will mark the supersession of formal reason itself? As I have already said, ultimately, formal reasoning is forced to address itself to the *actual*, to that which merely is, and to ask itself one last formal question. For the actual, simply because it is the actual, is nothing more that the one *really* necessary possibility and the one *really* possible necessity. So what is this one necessary possibility, this one possible necessity? The gradual development of ever more sophisticated modes of formalisation notwithstanding, the deployment of precisely the right combination of structures in any actual case remains a fundamentally pragmatic problem. A formal system can neither answer nor avoid the question of which of the infinite possibilities it is capable of generating can actually comprehend any actual case or situation or event in all its actuality.

Indeed, the answer to this conundrum is that *no* formal system or systems can do this, any more than a list of relationships defines a system or a single intuition can comprehend even a single static event. In fact it is only an entirely new stage of intelligence, namely dialectical reason, that can finally supply this level of structure, and so put formal reason out of its misery. Under formal reason, one is compelled to proceed *ad infinitum*, yet never achieve infinitude. Under dialectical reason, by contrast, nothing proceeds *ad infinitum*, yet everything is constructed in all its actuality, and thus infinitely. The infinities of formal reason remain infinitely bad infinities, negative yet unable to comprehend even the value of negativity as the impulse to advance yet further. They annihilate without residue, yet reality declines to be annihilated. The infinities of dialectical reason, by contrast, abolish conditionality, and so finitude, by synthesising *all* the systems needed to comprehend *all* conditions into a single, unconditional totality. Thereby it raises them to a greater height, establishing the infinity of things in a positive sense.

However, this transformation cannot be undertaken until the necessary, systematising structures are in place, and the only candidate for this task is formal reason itself. Conversely, once its plethora of systems is in action, where can their mutual integration under the pressure of their own mutual overlaps and contradictions go but to their mutual synthesis? So even while it is elaborating its own mode of rationality into the most overwhelming economic, political, ideological and scientific apparatus ever seen, even while creating the most sophisticated and articulated forms of personality, imagination, ethics and judgement, formal reason is also nurturing its own successor, whose focal interest is not on the system at all, but on the actuality which defeats the most intensive and extensive systematisation.

Of course, there is little love lost between formal and dialectical reason, and formal reason will resist this upstart, treating it as its rival rather than its heir, and not only because, like any structure, it lacks the wisdom to recognise and submit to its superior. On the contrary, formal reason is unique among pre-dialectical structures in its ability to grasp, on a certain level, what its own logic, pitfalls and history portend. But such insight does not make the transition any less painful. In particular, any actual formal reason is as unevenly developed as any other structure, and so incorporates a mass of interests, institutions and other impediments that are more or less contrary to its ready dissolution.

But in the long run, just as concrete reason was ultimately helpless before formal reason, so formal reason is helpless to resist dialectical reason. It is moreover helpless for exactly the same reason: that the higher form is neither usurper nor invader but, on the contrary, is precisely what the lower form will become if only it is allowed to take itself to its own logical, natural and historical conclusion. So, intuitive reason ends in the first intuition of the relationships it needs to control its initially blind intuitions, and concrete reason concludes by constructing systems by establishing relationships between relationships – in each case the fundamental contradiction with which each lower form of intelligence begins is resolved through the application of the fundamental principle of that form to itself.

What then should be expected of the development of formal reason, other than that it should take the naïve systems on which it was founded and, systematising them among themselves, overcome their potentially disastrous contradictions – assuming, that is, that they do not bear fatal fruit first? Assuming that my readers are themselves at the stage of formal reason, this leaves us at the threshold of the unimaginable. Occasional moments of enlightenment in the upper reaches of formal reason aside, dialectical reason remains for the inhabitants of formal worlds as inaccessible as calculus is to a babe in arms.

Or at least, *direct* experience of it is out of the question. But formal reason is not quite blind. Firstly, unlike its predecessors, it possesses the means to grasp the basis and status of its own rationality and the nature of its development, and so to pose the question of where it is going next. Hence the promise of Marxism (and, in its tiny way, of this book): to the extent that the resulting analysis incorporates the key factors in the production and reproduction of the formal world, they put at the analyst's disposal an insight, if not into the positive nature of dialectical reason, then at least into the specific contradictions formal reason has yet to overcome, and whose absence will define dialectical reason, negatively speaking at least. Nor are these anticipations purely intellectual. Just as formal systems such as capitalism create powers and interests that resist the flowering of higher forms of order, so they also create groups and forces whose fundamental interest is precisely the establishment of a dialectical reality.

Secondly, there are ways of gaining at least a glimpse of this new world. In particular, there is mysticism, through which the world of formal reason can indeed be superseded by a truly dialectical world. However, apart from some tangential participation in a larger historical tradition (sacred scriptures, 'transmitting the lamp', and so on), this world is entirely personal and phenomenological. The methods of creating it are likewise entirely implicit and restricted to the cognitive plane. As a result, mystical insight remains incommunicable, the conventions of the community (monastery, *sangha*, etc.) notwithstanding. Consequently, the dialectical world mysticism creates is of no *historical* significance, for it contributes nothing to the *explicit* development of the *social* systems on which the yet higher development of intelligence as a whole and intelligence as such depends. That is why, when confronted with the social, political and economic evils of the world, mystics are forced to resort to the same irritating combination of principled resignation and moral exhortation as formal reason's own romantic and religious enthusiasts.

That is not to say that the cognitive achievements of mysticism are less profound than its defenders claim. Nor, given its revolutionary impact on the lives of those who take this route, can one criticise them for taking an ahistorical option: it is not as though the strictly historical alternatives are either obvious or immediately feasible. Furthermore, the conclusions mystics have reached regarding the nature of identity are essentially correct, at least once intelligence has completed its development. Then there is no *ego*; the identity of self and other is absolute; reality is precisely as it appears; all existence is present before the eyes; and so on.[1] Nevertheless, each purely personal Nirvana is a historical dead end. For what is at issue here is the possibility of other, non-mystical, historical routes along which humanity *as a whole* may be 'saved'; the real nature of the developmental process through which this collective conclusion (devoutly to be wished) is to be achieved; and the metaphysics and other collateral issues surrounding the whole process. For a real answer to these questions we must look elsewhere.

---

[1] The exact meaning of such seemingly contradictory phrases itself only becomes clear as the appropriate degree of enlightenment is reached. For a brief comparison of mysticisms, see Goleman (1978), who also summarises the deleterious consequences of trying to capture through formal structures the mystical experience, with its fundamentally dialectical mode of consciousness:

> These transcendental states inspired churches, monasteries, and orders of monks and have spawned theologies. But too often the institutions and theologies outlive the transmission of the original states that generated them. Without these living experiences, the institutions are pointless, the theologies empty (1978: p. xv).

5. Dialectical Reason

Eternity is in love with the productions
of time.

William Blake, *Proverbs of Hell*

The emergence of dialectical reason

If thought discovered in the shimmering mirrors of phenomena eternal relations capable of summing them up and summing themselves up in a single principle, then would be seen an intellectual joy of which the myth of the blessed would be but a ridiculous imitation. That nostalgia for unity, that appetite for the absolute illustrates the essential impulse for the human drama. But the fact of that nostalgia's existence does not imply that it is to be immediately satisfied.

Albert Camus, *The Myth of Sisyphus*[1]

Formal reason is not the first phase of reason proper, and neither is it the last.[2] Which, given its contradictory character and potentially catastrophic consequences, is just as well. And the general logic of development, already rehearsed so often above, makes it obvious where intelligence must go next. Formal reason's own history consists of the formation and reformation of systems and of systems of systems, each accompanied by a new explosion of systematic necessities and possibilities, the ruthless reduction of all contingency, and the corresponding all-round development of intelligence in all its many facets. All this culminates in the final question of which formal reason is capa-

---

[1] Camus (1975: 23).

[2] Within the Piagetian canon, of which the present theory is a natural first cousin, post-formal stages of development have been proposed by Arlin (1975), Basseches (1984), Buck-Morss in Silverman (1980: 103–143), Commons *et al.* (1982), Riegel (1973, 1975), and others, often in expressly dialectical terms. However, none of these writers adopt an approach close to the one advocated here, not least because their approach either remains essentially cognitive or only addresses the larger historical issues in the most general terms. In many cases the supposedly *post*-formal forms of thought and reasoning a model identifies are more truly only *late* formal – they do not imply a qualitatively new stage. That Piaget's personal position (1971a, 1980) could not be extended to encompass the present account is made clear by the fact that, like Colletti and others, he wants to formalise even dialectics, which would be like trying to restating calculus in baby-talk. For other papers on post-formal stages of development, see Alexander and Langer (1990) or Commons *et al.* (1984; 1990); and Lourenço and Machado (1996) or Marchand (2002) for comment and references. For more general discussions of the relationship between formal and dialectical schemes, see p. 5, note 350.

ble: what is the one necessary possibility, the one possible necessity, which will finally comprehend the one thing formal reason cannot grasp, namely that which lies before its very eyes? It is this question that will not only draw formal reason to its close but also establish a new stage in the development of intelligence – dialectical reason.

The theoretical inevitability of this transformation is, I hope, clear. After all, it presupposes only the combined operation of the general logic of the development of intelligence and the more specific logic of formal reason. What it means in practice is another matter, for however effective the previous chapter may have been in explaining the role formal systems such as capitalism play in the elaboration of formal reason, it did not even begin to explain their part in the passage to dialectical reason. Over and above unpleasant snapshots of the plight of the formal subject, object and world, one must also consider the changes that flow from capitalism's internal dynamics. This is the problem that occupies the first section of this chapter.

The second section then reviews dialectical reason's central achievement: its grasp of the actual. To anticipate the argument somewhat, the developments outlined in the first section bring reason to such a pitch that intelligence *can* finally grasp what is before its very eyes. This may seem a peculiarly glib definition of the culmination of reason, but it really is as simple as that. However, simplicity is always organised complexity, and the process described in the opening section will show just how vast and complex a structure must be before it really can comprehend the actual.

In particular, because grasping the here and now adequately depends on grasping all the structures that mediate its content and context (otherwise our sense of the here and now would be inherently unstable and contradictory), one must also grasp all the structures that determine how that content and context operate. This naturally leads one off into both higher and higher levels of abstraction, to account for more and more abstruse aspects of the here and now, and also into more and more detailed and concrete issues, lest the actual collapse into incomprehensible noise.

The section on actuality is primarily concerned with the theoretical competence of dialectical reason. However, it ends with a few paragraphs on more practical approaches to actuality. But this raises an obvious problem, for if it is formal reason that defines the present level in the development of intelligence (at least as far as most readers will be concerned), dialectical reason will only be found in its full form in the future. So what can be said about the future of the actual (whatever that may mean) that is of any practical value in the here and now? The answer lies in a topic that will be, for many readers, less than respectable – mysticism.

As I have already suggested, mysticism has never offered more than a partial transcendence of formal reason, with no enduring effect on the larger social and historical world in which the vast majority of human beings live. That is because it may achieve dialectical reason on the cognitive plane, but it achieves this by disengaging almost entirely from the social and historical content and context of 'real life'. Indeed, the more mysticism becomes embroiled in the wider world of economics, politics, ideology and science, the more it reveals its ignorance, naïveté and even irrelevance. This leaves a vastly larger task than the mystics have ever addressed, let alone solved, namely the transcendence of formal reason as a historical force. So why should I include any account of mysticism at all? The answer is, because it is the only direct anticipation of dialectical reason we have.

The pursuit of profit

Despite the rationalisations of its apologists, capitalism's only coherent ideal is to maximise profit. From a developmental point of view, this is an absolutely crucial fact. Because the search for profitability is entirely indifferent to how profits are generated and entirely uncontaminated by commitment to any standards, methods or interests other than those of profitability itself, the development of capitalism is completely unfettered.

Having characterised capitalism in such brutal terms, one feels an immediate urge to qualify such a sweeping description with a whole range of political, philanthropic and ethical equivocations. Certainly that is what business people tend to do when confronted with such a blunt statement of their effective purpose in life. Yet such reservations are increasingly put aside by capitalism itself, not so much by the supposed greed and wickedness of individual capitalists as by the nature of the capitalist system itself. The self-sufficiency, and hence the abstract attitude of any formal system – intellectual, economic, cognitive, political, and so on – will always tend incline that system towards the peripheralisation of all concerns other than those of the system itself. As a formal system, capitalism's primary law lies with the higher, specifically abstract logic that defines it *as* capitalism. This is the logic of profit.

It is the very abstractness of this logic that affirms capitalism's independence from any actual content or context. From raw materials to scientific discourses to human beings to nation states, real things exist more as supports and opportunities for its activity than as the primary drivers of activity in their own right. They are indispensable, but only in the sense that *some* such means must exist for a formal system to achieve its larger ends. As soon as they can or must be improved upon, they are discarded with the same alacrity with which they were previously espoused. Nor will they be able to resist for long: although, as material structures in their own right, a structure such as 'the nation state' is as capable of determining events as any other structure, the specifically systematic character of capitalism will eventually enable it to transform, circumvent or simply eject it. With that, capitalism re-establishes its internal equilibrium (or at least the pristine and meticulous indifference that passes for equilibrium in a formal system) and the authority of its own 'primary law', the maximisation of profit. Like any formal system, capitalism will always pursue its own agenda, until it too can be transcended, subverted, or overcome by *force majeure*.

In short, even if all capitalists were relentlessly ethical and philanthropic, the capitalist *system* would undermine any such admirable personal stance. This relentless treachery is embodied in a number of persistent trends. First and foremost, there is the permanent pressure created by competition for, on one side, investment, and on the other, a return. Nor is this just any return or even a 'reasonable' return, for there are no reasons within capitalism itself for seeking anything but the highest possible return. There being, from profitability's point of view, no special merit in any particular kind of economic activity, even in the medium term profitability is not merely the sole enduring measure of success but also the only effective defence against competition and the only means to further ends.

It is true that in seeking to maximise returns, it is necessary (or at least prudent) to exercise a little judgement, if only to the extent of balancing the short- and long-term consequences of alternative policies and plans. There is also a tendency to cultural and technological inertia that characterises any social system, even in the face of its own most urgent or profound economic interests. And, of course, capitalism is not a single system but a network of interpenetrating systems that only partially integrates the great mass of diverse capitalist groups, structures and interests. So there are few moments in the history and development of 'capitalism as a whole' – whatever such a phrase might mean – when all capitalists are of one mind as to what it is that capital as a whole actually needs.

In addition, in periods of boom the scope for intruding personal and *ad hoc* qualifications to the naked maximisation of profit may be greater, and a more expansive and speculative interpretation of 'profit' and the wider interests of the owners of capital may hold sway. However, it is striking how little of this philanthropy there is even at the best of times (how many OECD countries have *ever* contributed to Third World development even the 0.7% of their gross national product proposed by the United Nations?[1]), remarkable how often ethics can be twisted to coincide with self-interest, and inevitable that the succeeding slump will eliminate most of the humanitarianism which surfaces during the good years.

That is not to say that capitalism must always revert to the naked savagery of its early industrial history. On the contrary, it is undoubtedly the most powerful force for civilisation the world has ever seen. Still, there is nothing like a higher rate of return to bolster shareholder confidence. And behind all these structural necessities, innumerable other factors conspire to disarm all but the most critical: the legitimacy of profit, the distance separating legal ownership from day-to-day operations, the owners' own financial commitments, and so on. Nor does the pressure created by the search for profit concern only the owners and directors of the capitalist enterprise. The secret of capitalism is, as Voltaire put it, '...the secret of forcing all the rich to make all the poor work',[2] regardless of who the rich and poor in question actually are or whether the wealth in question is corporate, propertied or personal. All its 'stakeholders' find themselves more and more embroiled, and not a few of its victims are forced to acknowledge it as a least evil.

---

[1] For summary figures, see United Nations (1997). According to the UN, 'the developed world as a whole has reached only 0.2 per cent.' (United Nations: 2001.) On the recent history of official development aid, see Martens and Paul (1998).

[2] Quoted in Beaud (1984: 56).

The managers

This is also why it makes so little difference that, in practically all capitalist organisations of any size, ownership is separated from control. It is the managers who have practical, operational control over the strategy, methods, resources and systems that actually generate an organisation's profits, and it is the managers who define how, in practical terms, key performance indicators such as customer satisfaction, delivery, value for money and quality are defined and realised. This, it has often been argued, creates a cadre of managers capable of imposing technocratic values, objectives and direction on the organisation, effectively superseding the profit-seeking of its capitalist owners.

But even if such an independent and articulate cadre actually existed – and there seems to be little empirical evidence that it has any substantial presence in existing organisations – and the managers were no longer obliged to deploy their own power and knowledge in the interests of the owners, they would not have escaped the primary condition of the existence of their organisations, namely capitalism itself. For capitalism is not a conspiracy of capitalists, but rather a system of relationships to which not only capitalists but all organisations and individuals on which it impinges are forced to submit. These relationships are entirely independent of who controls such organisations, of what their personal or collective interests or perspectives or motives may be, and so of whether this control is based on strictly personal property, corporate organisation or managerial authority. As far as capitalism is concerned, they are merely alternative ways of arranging the cogwheels driving its unchanging mill. Whoever is in charge, their charges continue to be capitalist organisations and the same logic of investment and return continues to apply.

So capitalism imposes its system of property relations, but exactly how these relations are managed is largely a matter of indifference to the system as a whole. At least in the long run, specifically managerial interests and ideals will always tend to be implicitly excluded from consideration, even by the most empowered managers, except insofar as they contribute to the pursuit of profit, and will be explicitly and vehemently excluded where they actively oppose it. Like human need, technical efficiency, legitimate authority, environmental responsibility and elementary ethics, any separate interest the managers may have is circumvented, co-opted, bribed, transmuted or destroyed. Perhaps only common sense has as permanent and pervasive a grip on the capitalist imagination as the pursuit of profit, but even that is only because, as Gramsci observed, common sense is the practical ideology of the ruling class.

In fact the managerial 'class' is so far from being the enemy of capitalism as to be its epitome, and it is this epitome precisely because of the formal nature of its role. The managers' role is to build and operate the system that will meet the demands of capitalism, and management includes all those activities that are needed to interpret, organise, plan and implement the formal aspects of profit maximisation. However, just as one would expect of so contradictory a structure as formal reason, the special centrality of their position within the system as a whole also gives managers a paradoxical subversiveness. For if the specific form in which capitalism develops is through the continuing refinement of the formal systems whereby profit is maximised, then it is through the lens of management – which is to say, through the controllers of those systems – that all such advances are focused.

What is more, for reasons that will become clear shortly, management will eventually enter into virtually all actual labour under capitalism, and all occupations tend to become managerial, at least in the general sense of being concerned primarily with the flow of information and decisions rather than direct manual labour. At the same time, precisely because this becomes one of the *normal* forms of labour under advanced capitalism, management ceases to command special attention or respect. In the terminology of conventional Marxism, the proletariat is gradually raised up to perform managerial functions, even as the entire caste of managers is proletarianised. So the fate of the managers also focuses the opposition between formal processes such as the maximisation of profit and human interests. This gives them a crucial role in the development and fate of capitalism as a whole.

The entrenchment of capitalism

This inexorable subordination of all comers to the rules of the capitalist *system* should not be taken to imply the subordination of all other groups to an omnipotent class of capitalist *owners*, either directly or via the state and the managers. The capitalist class, considered as a discrete group of personal owners of capital, is as vulnerable to the transforming powers of the capitalist system as any other group. For the other side of this mass formalisation of capitalist organisations is the elimination of the personalised ownership of property by the wealthy few, and so the dissolution of the link between capitals and capitalists. Indeed, the trend of capitalism is to the definitive replacement of a capitalism of capitalists by a 'capitalism without capitalists', led by executives and run by the managers. Just as feudalism's natural path of development was from a soup of individual seigneurial interests and domains to the suppression of the individual lord in the name of the feudal *system*, so the mass of autonomous capitalists is ousted through the systematisation of their own capitals and interests.

Even now wealthy individuals and families own a relatively small fraction of the mature capitalist economies. Most have long since been replaced either by massive institutions or by the legion of private individuals who, through personal savings, employee share options, small share holdings and indirect methods of ownership, own their iota of the system as a whole but exercise no control over it.[1] Neither group of *nouveaux riches* threatens the logic of capitalism as a whole. Indeed, both the institutionalisation and the dispersal of ownership help to loosen the remaining fetters on capitalism's formalising tendencies. At the same time, both the abstraction of ownership from personal control and the integration of the system as a whole beyond the powers of any single body tend to embed the entire population ever more deeply in the system, even while implicating them, as individuals, less and less.

---

[1] For a practical capitalist's view of share options as 'cuckoos in the capitalist nest', see Plender (1999).

This trend is amplified by others. The simultaneous concentration and extension of capitalism tend not only to free the system from external controls but also to make capitalist organisations less and less tolerant of extrinsic interests. In that respect capitalism is only doing the same as any other formalism, of course – one would be equally hard pressed to interpolate an informal proposition into any logical, mathematical or scientific system merely on the grounds that it happened to be true!

This entrenchment of capitalism has at least three main aspects. Firstly, the interests of capitalism are increasingly conflated with those of society as a whole, and relationships based on money, roles and commodities identified with political and social values such as democracy and liberty. This confusion has been a persistent theme since the birth of modern capitalism. For example, early drafts of the US Declaration of Independence set up 'life, liberty and property' as its ideals, rather than 'life, liberty and the pursuit of happiness' – a distinction the bourgeoisie has always had difficulty in grasping. Nowadays, capitalist notions such as 'free enterprise' and 'the market' are directly equated with freedom and democracy.

Secondly, with the extension of capitalism to all spheres, there is less and less scope for alternative views. As I argued in connection with the revolt against formality, the very possibility of a genuinely alternative view is severely restricted by the capitalist system's position as both the major producer and the major product of the education process, popular culture, information media, the political system, and other ideological forces. As a long line of (largely scorned or neglected) critics has argued, even science, the *ne plus ultra* of formal reason, is contaminated by its relationships to capitalism. This in turn leads to the increasing identification of capitalism and the bourgeois worldview with the 'natural order', and so the curtailment of effective criticism from any external point of view.

Thirdly, there is the relationship between capitalism and the external conditions of its existence, particularly the natural environment. Both its burgeoning scale and the intimacy of the functions it performs for its consumers ensure that it is increasingly capitalism itself that defines our relationships with the rest of nature. What is more, the same factors that drive the development of capitalism as a whole also ensure that the scale and intensity of its relationship to the environment grow greater and greater. It does this not solely by confronting and crushing nature but also by incorporating ever broader tracts of the natural environment into capitalist processes. In that respect, of course, industrial capitalism is only the highest point yet reached in a more general process:

> ... the human race... embarks on 'conquering nature' by taking into itself the very properties which were once hers and remixing them in ever more effective permutations. Against this strategy, no ecological check could work in the long run... Rarely can the planet have seen such an unstoppable and sustained explosion of a single species, now deploying abilities with a potential for affecting events at the climatic and geophysical levels. We swarm like flies in the wake of the retreating ice. Only by our own understanding of our situation from this perspective will we

come to be able to do what no other force can now do: get ourselves under control.[1]

At first sight, capitalism offers little prospect of fulfilling this last, final hope. Although, under capitalism, the environment is focused on more intensively than ever before, it is also perceived in far narrower terms. In contrast to the wealth of many pre-formal peoples' grasp of the natural environment and the corresponding symbolism, modes of interpretation and so on,[2] for capitalism the environment is just one more opportunity for profit, to be treated as little more than a collection of raw materials, tourist traps, backdrops for nature films, and the general basis for commodifying nature as a whole. Consequently, we seldom encounter the natural world other than through a production process to which we are largely indifferent and which we certainly do not control, and through the consumption of commodities whose genuinely 'environmental' qualities (whatever they may be) are all but obliterated. This broadens immensely the 'environment' any inhabitant of a capitalist system can expect to encounter in a single lifetime, but it is achieved by reducing these encounters to a series of shallow, one-sided, distorting formalities.

Meanwhile, the scale of a mature capitalism is such that its impact on the natural environment makes it a force of ecological proportions. The damage this can lead to is now evident. However, as material beings, we have to have *some* kind of commerce (literal or metaphorical) with the natural environment, and sheer numbers mean that we cannot withdraw to some kind of agrarian ideal. Of course, the more entrenched capitalism becomes, the easier its ecological impact will be to identify and criticise. Even now it is so large as to be inescapable. However, the greater the sheer scale and intensity of that impact becomes, the harder it will be to develop less harmful methods of carrying out elementary ecological functions such as feeding, protecting ourselves from natural disaster or just keeping warm, without simultaneously deranging the basic economic mechanisms without which capitalism as a whole cannot operate.

All these trends not only free 'the system' from both human and natural constraint; they also tend to make the preservation of the system the precondition of all human activity and natural systems alike. Hence not only the irrelevance of reformism (which can never do more than ameliorate the system in the name of its victims) but also, apparently, the potentially catastrophic effect of a genuine revolution. So it seems that we can look forward to more of the same, only more so, until global eco-catastrophe returns us all to the alleged pleasures, satisfactions and contentment of hunting, fishing and gathering. Apart from that, the only hope seems to be that capitalism could perhaps be sustained indefinitely. Two dead ends.

It is hard not to find such logic bleak. And as far as the present argument is concerned, surely it completely contradicts the basic premise of this chapter, that there *must* be a yet higher, post-formal stage in the development of intelli-

---

[1] G. Richards (1987: 315–6). See also Crosby (1986: 273 and *passim*).

[2] Appadurai (1986); Atran (1990); Bloch and Parry (1989); Lévi-Strauss (1972).

gence. And in fact, there is another, quite different side to the development of formal reason, signalled by one of the most impressive features of modern economies, namely their staggering success, amidst all the filth and violence, all the 'absurd and slimy bloatedness of modern capitalist society',[1] in civilising humanity. Leaving aside the near-miraculous system of culture and technology through which these very words were transmitted from my mind to my reader's, practically every valuable expression of modern life is the product of formal reason's other, more beneficent side. For example, not only is it hard to imagine Beethoven writing the *Eroica* without the formalisation of the society around him – for it is surely the sound-track of the French Revolution – but what other system would let me put the *Eroica* straight into my ears, any time I choose, simply by pressing a few buttons? Surely one can forgive capitalism a great deal for such achievements?

Nor is this an exception to capitalism's basic logic. For the very processes that entrench and propagate roles, commodities and money also promote another, quite opposite trend. And it is this trend that comes to fruition in the formation of a genuinely dialectical reason. Or rather, this trend is not directly opposed to the pursuit of profit – this is not another form of adolescent rebellion. Rather, it increasingly transforms the pre-conditions of profit itself, even if it cannot, while formal reason endures, supplant profit altogether. So it is still an open question whether the logic outlined above can only promote profit as the ultimate rational value and universal measure of success, or whether any countervailing processes could tame capitalism. With any luck, we may not need to choose between saving our souls and gaining the whole world.

The apotheosis of money, commodities and roles

As one would expect of any dialectic, the mechanism whereby this paradox is resolved is the mechanism whereby it was raised in the first place. Most especially, the process whereby all extrinsic alternatives to and external controls over capitalism are relentlessly expunged is matched by a reciprocal process whereby capitalism is compelled to take command of an infinitely expanding range of forces and factors. At every level of nature, from the great oil shales to human performance management to the waiting world of nanotechnology, capitalism increasingly finds itself needing to command ever broader swathes of nature. For the first century or two, industrial capitalism achieved this by trampling the natural environment underfoot, but in the long run, nature, to be commanded, must be obeyed. There simply comes a point where the sheer scale of the natural forces through which capitalism (or any other industrial economy) operates obliges it to take the power, systems and balances of nature into account. Furthermore, these forces of nature include the latent capacities of intelligence itself, whose vast potential even formal reason has barely begun to tap.

Of course, this transfiguration is a long time in the making, but it can be summarised. To begin with, most new commodities tend to originate in more

---

[1] Beaud (1984: 229).

sophisticated economies, and at first they require a high level of training, culture and resource to produce them at all. Gradually, though, as the techniques of production are developed, the forces and relations of production are simplified, standardised and generally reduced to a level where they are, on the one hand, capable of routinisation and mechanisation and, on the other, more reliable, predictable and generally controllable than they ever were when they were the exclusive province of highly trained and richly experienced specialists. Eventually they become things practically anyone can do. But that is only to say that such commodities can be produced efficiently and effectively by much less sophisticated economies, and inevitably are, with all the concomitant reductions in cost to which this transfer to poorer societies leads. As a result, it is no longer possible for the most advanced economies to extract even a minimally acceptable profit from them.

Hence the constant stream of mass-produced products that can be produced to an equal standard and at lower cost in relatively undeveloped parts of the capitalist world. Eventually they can be made by even the least developed regions and organisations, exploiting the very cheapest labour power. The only prerequisite is the importation of appropriate capital. And every time a new product or service is perfected, the same thing happens: some take longer than others (especially in the service sectors), but the trend is universal and inexorable.

This leaves little respite for the more advanced to rest on their laurels. On the other hand, their greater experience and sophistication with the processes involved allow the more advanced groups to make routine many operations that were previously the exclusive province of the especially skilled, experienced and adept, so there is usually a plane, between production for very exclusive markets (luxury, high technology, and so on) and fully developed mass production, where large numbers of people of the major capitalist economies can be profitably employed.

This period of routinisation also allows the more advanced to improve their goods and services in a number of different directions, and so to maintain their overall competitiveness. Many of these improvements are purely quantitative – in power, performance, precision, and so on, heightened durability, availability, maintainability, reliability, and so on. However, commodities are also becoming more and more sophisticated, more comprehensive in the benefits they offer the consumer and more tailored to the individual consumer's requirements. The processes whereby products and services are created, developed, elaborated and maintained also grow ever more sophisticated, with mysterious notions such as re-use, scalability, portability, and so on, becoming more and more prominent for the effective management of commodities. And in all these cases, the more things advanced economies can find to commodify, the longer they can fend off the competition of the less advanced.

All this is paralleled by increasing sophistication in industry. On the technological plane, production lines are designed to respond to the individual buyer's precise specification and to rapid shifts in design. Culturally there is growing attention to the spontaneous professionalism and competence that can be liberated within the work force if control-oriented methods of management can be replaced by 'vision', 'leadership', 'teamwork', 'empowerment' and the like. Strategically, the notion of 'partnership' between buyers and sellers, based on joint strategy, intense functional coordination and mutual commitment, is beginning to evolve. And so on. Although they have few successes to boast of so far (and they have a tendency to degenerate into verbal replacements for real action), such developments seem to be both irreversible trends in modern industry and harbingers of yet more radical change in the near future.

This new phase in capitalist management, the natural and necessary successor to mass production, goes by many names: total quality, process re-engineering, business integration, the 'quality revolution', and so on: the consultants add a new twist and a new term every now and again. And in one sense it is indeed a revolution, for it represents an escape from the problem of sustaining profit levels in a mature production system by replacing quantity by quality. But in another sense it is only a palace coup, for the ultimate motivation is the same, as is the underlying approach: find out what makes an exceptional (or even a reliable) profit, and make that. Sometimes the revolution lies solely in the violence with which organisations are forced to transform the methods whereby they pursue what is, in fact, a constant objective. However, from the present point of view, the key to this constant pressure to change is that precisely what makes a profit is not merely constantly *changing*; much more importantly, it is also continually *developing*. Indeed, the ultimate commodity would be one that touched every human sensibility, every rational consideration, every desire, every need, without residue or excess. But that is only to say that (as befits its role as the standardised object of formal reason in its capitalist guise) the ultimate commodity is simply the perfect object.

Nor is it solely the production of goods and services that is transformed by this process. Not only does the proliferation of commodities broaden and deepen their consumers' general experience but the repeated exhaustion of new avenues of profitability means that the only way to sustain profit is to tap more sophisticated needs, wants and desires. So, considered as consumers, we are driven to new heights, not because we want it but because capitalism demands it. But by the same token, as consumers become more experienced, they become more discerning, setting higher and higher standards for their own satisfaction. This is not only because all human beings have a propensity to discriminate by quality, to pursue the reality behind appearances, to make sense of each new experience in the light of experience as a whole, and so on. In addition, the quest for ever more lucrative sales will oblige capitalism itself to make us as conscious as possible of whatever it is that differentiates a commodity from its competitors.

Often the difference between competing commodities will be trivial or even illusory, of course. All the same, once every avenue of illusion has been exhausted and competition is forced to address objective need, efficiency, ethics and other human and rational values, capitalism is entirely capable of rising to the challenge. After all, it is not as though capitalism *objects* to being genuinely valuable to human beings; it is only that human value is not its real goal. On the other hand, the very success with which it does enhance the human value of its offerings hoists it by its own petard, for this will surely make consumers increasingly aware of what they might require of a given commodity and of what they are no longer obliged to accept. This is tantamount not only to 'educating' consumers in applied scepticism but also to positively goading them into rejecting whatever falls below an ever more rapidly rising par. If, as Tawney observed, the fallacy of simplistic consumerism is that it is 'like a man who, when he finds that his shoddy boots wear badly, orders a pair two sizes larger instead of a pair of good leather',[1] it is capitalism itself that will teach us better. In the long run it will even raise the question of whether the commodity relation is itself a fundamental obstacle to the consumer's ultimate pleasure, and whether the role of 'consumer' is a suitable vehicle for human satisfaction.

So it seems eminently possible that the spontaneous development of capitalism, leading as it does to the commodification of everything, may itself lead consumers to reject the commodity relation, and with it one of the central tenets of capitalism. Recent history abounds in examples of this kind of organised practical criticism, although so far it has usually been limited to single-issue campaigns, consumer boycotts, and so on. The ideological and political implications of the licence the commodity relation creates may half-surface in isolated cases – apartheid, baby milk, whale hunting, deforestation – and the amorality of profit may occasionally disgust, but its generally contradictory and inhuman nature has not yet been widely recognised. All the same, this process can be expected to intensify, spread and accelerate, and to take on more sophisticated and comprehensive spheres of existence as capitalism itself develops.

As producers too we are under constant pressure to raise our level of development, again not because we wish it but because the future of capitalism depends on it. The replacement of skills by routines and procedures, of living labour by dead capital, of people by machines, are constant themes in the development of capitalism, driven by opportunities to reduce costs and raise prices through advances in technology, organisation, methods, resourcing, and so on. That is, capitalism is constantly replacing subjects with objects.

Not that capitalism prefers things to people, or *vice versa*. The problem is rather than the profit motive simply cannot tell the difference between the costs and benefits associated with human workers and those offered by any other 'factor of production'. There can be few terms in the capitalist lexicon that are more offensive than 'human resources' and 'human capital', but there are also few that express its real viewpoint better. It would not be enough for any capitalist enterprise that replacing people with machines should liberate human beings from labour of stunning harshness or stupefaction; this amelioration must be accompanied by improvements in the 'bottom line'. Still, it does mean that there is a constant drive to discover areas of activity that could be performed more economically by a thing than by a person; after all, things do not require holidays, pensions, sick leave or a life outside of work. So capitalism is constantly enriching the systems and resources and methods and strategies at its disposal, and just as constantly eliminating human beings.

So why should all this lead to the development of humanity at large? It is true that those who are required to manage this rapidly swelling mass of systems and structures will benefit in all sorts of ways, but who will these fortu-

---

[1] Tawney (1921/1943: 5).

nates be? Surely not the displaced workers – they are no longer qualified even for the work of the machines that replaced them. Is anyone needed at all? Are the displaced workers not redundant in the most absolute sense? Yet there are forces at work insisting that redundant workers be reabsorbed. On one side, workers, as intelligent beings, are capable of learning new skills. On the other, the increased efficiency and effectiveness of the new machinery, systems, and so on generally leads to the same old commodities now being made at lower prices, which effectively reduces the price of the labour power that could be supported by those commodities.

For example, if I can halve the price of electricity, I can pay workers less for the same work without reducing their standard of living. Even allowing for the cost of retraining, this reduction in the price of labour power may well create an incentive to re-employ previously redundant workers in new capacities elsewhere in the system. And by the same token, the whole purpose of replacing these human beings was to increase profits. So, to the extent that this objective is achieved, it will tend to increase the total amount of fresh capital in search of resources to exploit, for which, given that it must compete with other capital, it must be prepared to pay a premium – such as the cost of retraining and re-equipping redundant workers. Hence the same mechanism that encourages capitalism to replace living workers with dead capital also encourages it to take the same workers back – eventually.

So, the long timescales and the fundamental rapacity of capitalism notwithstanding, even recurrent recessions can be regarded as preludes to new heights in the development of the workforce. It may be a distressing thought that today is the bright new tomorrow we were promised yesterday, but it takes a very distorted memory to recall any time in the last few decades when most people living at the hubs of capitalism were economically worse off than even the rich were at *any* other time in history – even allowing for the great capitalist recessions, the dishonesty of bourgeois apologetics about the 'good life' and the supposed quality of life of unsophisticated societies.[1]

And the content of these advances will, like that of consumption, tend to involve development in an ever-fuller sense, which is to say, the increasingly all-round development not only of the economy as a whole but also of the individual. For the reorganisation of capital implicit in the above cycle is by no means a purely economic process. Its success, even by the crudest measure, requires the integration of larger and larger structures, a process that in turn presupposes an increasingly extreme elaboration and coordination of the system's structures and functioning. So even the most exploited position under an advanced capitalism is increasingly sophisticated. On the other hand, the continuing displacement of workers by capital will leave the lower tiers of capitalism populated almost entirely by one kind of mechanism or another. This will place human workers atop an ever-growing mountain of structures that is only governable by means of ever more advanced strategies, methods, resources and systems. The sophistication of these systems will require their 'operators'

---

[1] Few anthropologists seem to accept Sahlins' claims about the 'original affluent society' now.

to build and operate more and more elaborate, comprehensive and responsive tools and techniques.

Such methods and systems could only be mastered through equally advanced capacities for insight and criticism, so one precondition of workers being able to perform their roles is that they develop a many-faceted view of things corresponding to the multi-faceted structures they are required to manage. They will also require working conditions that allow them to carry out their tasks: it may be possible to carry out simple manual labour in a sweatshop, but it is quite impossible to meet the intellectual challenges that face the management of a large organisation in such an environment.

Not that every worker needs to become a new Newton, but they can take their position, if not on the shoulders of giants, then on top of a millions-strong pyramid of machines, systems, processes, organisations, markets, communications systems, technical resources, and so on. That is why any moderately well educated individual now knows more than Aristotle ever did. Of course, this leaves them completely reliant on a mass of systems, resources, processes and strategies they would be helpless to re-invent for themselves. Nevertheless, the increasing sophistication of the systems they build will create a far richer individual out of the same raw material. So the development of the producer is proportionate to the development of capitalist production itself.

And just as the world view of the consumer cannot remain oblivious of the contradictory character of the commodity relation that produced it, so these increasingly sophisticated producers can scarcely be forced to accept the contradiction between a one-sided role as producer and their existence as actual individuals. It ill becomes intelligent beings to worship their maker, especially when the latter espouses the doctrine of free will with such enthusiasm. In the case of capitalism, the very experience of an increasingly complex and powerful production process will make it obvious that the first condition of participation in the labour process is the reduction of the producers to an abstract, formal role, with all that this entails for any individual producer's sense of themselves as actual individuals.

Hence the history of labour under industrial capitalism. Step by step, the initial trivial, totally one-sided and subordinate formal role that made the worker into an 'appendage to a machine' is supplanted by increasingly broad and many-sided skills and responsibilities and by more individualised forms of labour that exploit (still) the potential all-round abilities of the individual concerned to the full. Industrial capitalism's natural 'command economy' gradually takes a more 'professional' form, in which individuals are employed not as cogs in a machine but, on the contrary, to hone and use their individual abilities, training and experience to build and drive the machine themselves.

So, just as the development of consumption leads to the development of the consumer and the rejection of the commodity as the basic condition of consumption, so the development of production leads to both the development of the producer and the exposure of roles as the irreducible – and unacceptable – condition of capitalist production. Just as the perfect commodity is also the perfect object, so the increasing articulation and integration of roles leads to the

fect object, so the increasing articulation and integration of roles leads to the ultimate role, so to speak, which actually consists of being the perfect subject.[1]

As for money – 'in whose absence we are coarse but in whose presence we are vulgar' – at first its universality and indifference towards any actual human concern makes it a double-edged sword. On the one hand, its ability to store and convey economic value (only perfected with the rise of capitalism) makes it the ultimate formal tool for organising a world of infinitely expanding frontiers and completely unforeseeable denizens. On the other, its complete neutrality renders it just as suitable for drug smuggling, gun running and political corruption as for any more benign purpose. Money has no smell. Nevertheless, just as it is through delving into the most abstract physical and chemical principles that the most revolutionary technological advances are made, so it is through the elaboration of money into every sphere and its technical elaboration into a million forms that the world as a whole is united. So again, the ultimate expression of money is the world, for money cannot complete its development until the world too is perfected.

But what will become of money when we have the whole world, when we have not just the abstract model of contentment but its real concrete basis? Will we not then be inclined to put money itself back into the accounting systems where it belongs, declining to let it lead us by the nose any longer?

Economy and ecology

Finally, there is question of how capitalism deals with the external conditions of its development. Here the major question is, again, its ecological impact.[2] All

---

[1] I believe that this argument reconciles the conflicting positions on routine adopted by Adam Smith and Denis Diderot, namely that routine is deadening and enlightening respectively (Sennett, 1998: Ch. 2). As Sennett summarises the conflict, 'routine can demean, but it can also protect; routine can decompose labour, but it can also compose a life' (*ibid.*: 43).

[2] The natural environment is by no means the only external condition on the development of capitalism. However, there seems to be little reason, and less evidence, to suppose that the other main group, namely other modes of production, will have any further impact on its development. The Soviet system, the only serious historical challenger to its hegemony, has been dismembered by a plague of politicians, entrepreneurs, advisers and consultants, who succeeded in persuading the successor regimes of the old communist bloc that capitalism was the sure and instant recipe for democracy, peace and plenty (Stiglitz, 2002). The locals were not all convinced, of course: as a manager in a Polish paint factory put it to me shortly after the end of communism, 'Under communism we were poor and miserable; under capitalism we will be rich and miserable instead'.

As for the various pre-industrial societies capitalism has overrun, they have provided powerful and affecting images of the devastation and inhumanity of which capitalism is capable, but it is hard to believe that they will still exist (as independent hunter-gatherers, that is) a century from now, or that they will have had any effect on capitalism, notwithstanding all the anger of radicals, the guilty consciences of liberals and the fantasies of romantics.

major forms of activity that have played any significant part in the development of reason have done at best a haphazard job of sustaining the ecological matrix within which this development has taken place. It is true that we are a good deal more respectful of our environment than any non-intelligent species, whose apparently balanced lifestyles rest on organic controls operating entirely outside their own command or concern. We at least worry about whether the last white rhino is worth saving, which is more than white rhinos do. Nevertheless, at first sight there appears to be little in the profit mechanism to protect the natural environment.

But as I have already argued, capitalism needs the natural environment as much as any rhino does. What is more, the larger the scale of capitalism itself, the larger the proportion of the natural environment it incorporates directly within itself and the more forcibly it is obliged to acknowledge and attend to the ecological systems it engages. Unlike human beings, the natural environment is incapable of being persuaded to do anything but follow its own inclinations. No amount of public relations will mend a hole in the ozone layer. Since the long-term development of capitalism cannot help but embrace all the major ecosystems of the world, its own logic of profit will compel it to make their maintenance, integration and coordination as effective and efficient as possible, for in the long run capitalism can afford only a minimum of waste and disruption.

To the extent that this requires capitalism to force nature into its own mould, so much the worse for nature. However, to the extent that the advancement of capitalism, with all its concomitant problems of sustainable systems and controllable processes, requires the integration of more and more systems on a larger and larger scale, sensitivity to the objective needs of ecosystems will become an integral feature of capitalism itself. Capitalism may expand to fill the whole world, but it will only be able to achieve its objectives where it allows the whole world to inform capitalism with a whole set of values, conditions and goals belonging to nature itself.

Consequently, even though capitalism has no *direct* interest in preserving the beauty of the Earth (except perhaps as a tourist attraction), the filth and trauma it visits on the planet cannot be kept out of mind precisely because, even from the point of view of the annual accounts, they cannot be kept entirely out of sight. Inefficiency, pollution and dislocation are all objective facts that are perfectly capable of forcing themselves into the minds not only of ecologists but also of investors. And once these facts start to impinge on profits, an increasingly large part of the development of industry (capitalist or otherwise) will consist of finding new, simultaneously more *economical* and *ecological* links in the cycle of production, circulation, exchange and consumption. So the *logos* of the world of nature and the *nomos* of the world of human beings converge.

Whatever the outcome of this process, its connection with the development of intelligence as a whole is clear. With the emergence of intelligence, matter's most general formula – the dialectic of internalisation and externalisation – is itself internalised. With that, internalisation and externalisation change from strategic *consequences* for matter – through, say, natural selection, or the dispersal of the opacity of the radiation-shrouded early universe by the formation of stable physical structures – to matter's intentional stratagem. Whether by purely symbolic representation or by the comprehensive fusion of human beings with technology, we take command of the universe by making it part of ourselves. As the subsequent history of intelligence demonstrates, this leads to unprecedented success in the further organisation of activity.

Unfortunately, until intelligence reaches complete maturity, its errors and omissions will also grow in scale and scope, and nowhere is this more obvious than in the ecological damage inflicted by capitalism. But at the same time, it is only through formal reason that intelligence can create either the scientific grasp of the threats posed by uncontrolled proliferation or the capacity for political organisation and direction needed to reverse the damage of which capitalism has been guilty. Similarly, only through the thoroughgoing formalisation of the universe will we develop an economic system capable of responding to, let alone solving such problems, and the ideologies needed to justify and motivate the necessary changes.

So, just as it was the very indifference of formal structures such as capitalism to any particular content that created these crises in the first place, so it is their disinterest towards any particular content – towards any particular constellation of needs or interests or roles or resources or processes or strategies or methods – that makes such a profound development possible. That is why the creation of a world system capable of superseding the capitalist caricature of rationality represents not only a task of Herculean proportions but also the maturation of humanity as a whole. We have always been doing this to some extent – ever since farmers started putting manure back into the soil in fact. Not only all agriculture and all industry but also all the more deliberate forms of hunting and gathering are attempts at rationalising nature. However, through the increasing development of formal reason in general and capitalism in particular, the pre-rational ecology of Nature is gradually supplanted by a rational ecology in which the desires of reason and the integrity of the physical, chemical, organic and intelligent realms are not merely balanced but become one and the same. Of course, while capitalism prevails, this is a precarious process, and we remain appendages of some machine or other; but what a machine!

The end of formal reason

Just how far a strictly formal system such as capitalism can take this process is another matter.[1] In all likelihood it will only be up to the point where the conjunction of economic, ideological, political and scientific crises drives us to take the next step. Again, this is not out of any special respect for or awareness of

---

[1] Pearce (1995) and van Dieren (1995) employ conventional economic concepts to connect ecology and economy. The problems with this approach will be obvious to any critic of bourgeois political economy, but these sources demonstrate the ability of the dismal science to engage with ecological issues, even if only with the usual dismal results. See Gustafson for doubts about the ability of economic theory to do this job completely (in Teich *et al.*, 1997: 347–363).

any higher rationality: formal reason is entirely capable of destroying Nature, and so itself, first. Rather, the timing of the transition will be determined by capitalism's own internal dynamics. As far as the general logic of this process is concerned, however, for as long as capitalism prevails, the ecosystem we end up with will be fashioned in capitalism's own image; but at least it will also express capitalism's attempts to comprehend the environment at the least cost and to the maximum profit. But both these terms will tend to be defined in increasingly rational, and so human, terms.

In that limited respect, the general logic of capitalism leaves one hopeful for the viability of human existence, even in the long run. But at the same time, there are limits to capitalism's capacity for amelioration. Although it creates endless new vistas of the good life, the only real lives capitalism permits are the ones it can force into the matrix of profit, property, money, consumerism and all the other gilded banalities of contemporary life. Its truth and freedom prove to be illusions – or rather, they are the purely formal truths of scientism and idealism and the equally formal freedoms of rights and property.

All this remains a superficial review of the development of formal systems. It ignores much of the specific content of their future development; even more of their history to date; the interaction between the development of the actual individual as consumer and the development of the same individual as producer; the interplay between the development of the individual and that of the system as a whole; the radical socialisation of the relationships between the individuals involved; the struggle and oppression that characterises so much of existence within formal structures; and many other important questions. Nevertheless, recalling the original concepts of role, commodity and money and their status as archetypal formalisms, I hope it is clear how formal reason drives itself to its own historical, natural and logical conclusion, and what that conclusion is.

Formal reason achieves its objectives by constituting subject, object and world strictly in terms of its own logic, yet this seeming subordination consists of raising subject, object and world to new pinnacles, from which the inadequacies of formal reason itself are plain to see. Proceeding from indifference to anything but profit, the development of production, consumption, its external relationship to the environment, and so on all compel capitalism to attend to, respect and finally espouse such values as efficiency, need and ethics, and indeed value as such. Proceeding from a position where the pursuit of profit is the increasingly exclusive precondition of human and rational values, human values, and reason above all, become the precondition of all profit. Having begun as the very epitome of Wilde's definition of cynicism – knowing the price of everything and the value of nothing[1] – capitalism is forced to accept not only that the creation of value is the precondition of price, but also, finally, that price is nothing but an accounting tool, a means to larger, more completely 'profitable' ends.

In terms of the passage from formal to dialectical reason, the process through which all this change is effected consists precisely of the synthesis of

---

[1] *Lady Windermere's Fan*, Act III.

all formal systems, culminating in the final formation of a single, totalised and totalising structure capable of constructing anything, and through which anything that is actually constructed is created in a form that is free of all contradiction. With this, the actual forms of subject, object and world in terms of which we actually exist are freed from the endless possibilities and necessities of formal reason, as the actual becomes the single necessary possibility and the final possible necessity that defines the highest form of undivided, indivisible individuality. For the emergence of this final outcome (final as far as a formal system such as capitalism can make it, that is) consists of the replacement of all particular, specific and even universal structures – social and symbolic, economic and political, human and natural, and all the rest – by a single, completely totalised successor, integrating all its predecessors and capable of anything of which they were capable, without succumbing to their errors and contradictions.

By this means, all possibilities and contingencies are eliminated, in the sense that they are totally accounted for, because the last word in formal systems is a 'system' that recognises and anticipates every contingency and every possibility, and recognises and anticipates them at every point. Such a 'system' comprehends each eventuality in all its actuality, either directly or through some internal capacity to construct it from first principles.

The actual

> Zen does not confuse spirituality with thinking about God while one is peeling potatoes. Zen spirituality is just to peel the potatoes.
>
> Alan Watts

The problem of the actual

> Seeing God in a midge is not so difficult. What is really difficult is to keep one's eye fixed steadily on the insects, and not let God usurp their divinity.
>
> R.H. Blyth[1]

The idea of the actual is very simple: first and foremost actuality is this, right here, what you are doing now. It is your reading these words, as you are reading them. It is also the conditions in which you are reading, independently of whether or not you are subjectively aware of their existence. It is any other activities you are performing right now too, and *their* conditions. And it is the conditions of those conditions, and their conditions, and so on, out to the furthest reaches of the universe.

That is not to say that the actual is simply identical with the universe, especially when one considers how limited in scope and impact any human act is or how much about the universe could be quite different without it impinging on

---

[1] Blyth (1994: 39).

our local here and now. The spatial and temporal horizons set by physical (and other kinds of) relativity qualify what constitutes a condition of the here and now. But in proportion to the development of intelligence, both of the individual and of all rational beings, so the here and now bears on greater and greater breadths and depths of the universe as a whole. So ultimately the actual is *all* that exists – absolutely all.

The problem of the actual is equally straightforward. It is that, in everyday life, *experience* of the actual is quite unusual. It is not that we are not constantly actually doing something or other; on the contrary, we could scarcely be doing anything else. But that is not the point. Rather, we are not really interested in the actual *as* actual – not even the actuality of our own actions. To take the case of formal reason, it is more often a role, commodity or just money that we pursue than the moments of existence we pass while pursuing them. But neither role nor commodity nor money is either wholly actual in itself or encompasses actual things or events in their full actuality. Rather, in adopting a role or consuming a commodity or dealing with money we operate on an altogether more abstract plane, complexly social and psychic, historical and phenomenal, but only incidentally here and now. It is true that, through the processes described in the previous section, the elaboration of money, roles and commodities will eventually raise subjectivity, objectivity and worldliness to a level at which the actual is the natural sphere of intelligence, but that is scarcely necessary or typical of roles, commodities and money in their original, their historical or their current forms.

So before dialectical reason, we seldom look at any actuality in its own right, on its own terms or for its own sake, and it is certainly not the actuality of things and events that we *seek*. Unless we are playing serious jazz or meditating or engaged in some other altogether exceptional activity, the actual is simply something we pass through. It may provide interesting scenery but it is not to reality that we really aspire. We don't seem to pay much attention to the journey either. The chances are, the actual moment is regarded as merely 'on the way', a means to the desired outcome. As when we make a journey for purely instrumental reasons and travelling as such becomes merely a tedious but necessary interlude before we reach our goal, we are intent on actual things and events only to the extent that they let us track our progress and accomplishments, or provide a venue for our activity: our focus is on the map, not the journey. So we only attend to it to the extent that it relates to whatever we happen to be doing, by confirming our plans or presenting milestones along the way – or perhaps by showing warning signals or threatening to undermine our purposes with unplanned or otherwise untoward obstacles. We navigate by actual things and events, but the actual itself is practically never our goal, and absolutely never our home port.

Nor has it ever been, not since the first formation of a truly intelligent subject, object and world and the first inklings of tradition, thought, myth, barter and imagination, and all those other structures that extend our existences beyond the empirical surfaces of things and bridge successive moments of actuality, without however providing us with the completeness of reason that would allow us to be untroubled in the here and now. In that respect, the only thing that distinguishes formal reason from its predecessors is that formal reason has perfected this abstraction from the actual to the point where it doubts the value, meaningfulness and even existence of actuality itself. And finally, even when we reach our destination, we seldom linger; much more likely we will move on – to the next goal, to Phase II, or just get on with something else. We are always passing through the actual, but we are never simply *here*; most of the time we don't even notice that the actual actually exists.

It is tempting to ask whether this lack of interest in the actual matters. If we are not constantly at one with the actual, if there are always aspects and details of the totality of things we do not understand, might this not simply mean that we have better things to do than navel-gazing? If – as I would readily agree – it is one of the defining features of intelligence that it exists on a plane which extends beyond the moment, why should it be a problem that we don't always notice all the details of our lives or that some things have to be ignored or not taken fully into account? Surely one is not being unduly modest in admitting that one can neither know nor do everything?

There are three problems with this reply. Firstly, who is it that is being so modest here? It is formal reason, whose very limited ability to live a sensible life even by its own standards was reviewed in the previous chapter. Formal reason could not attend to the full actuality of things even if it wanted to, and it is congenitally incapable of truly wanting the actual and still being true to itself. It would always be deflected into some kind of abstraction – a rule, an attitude, perhaps a passing thought (or an entire disquisition) *about* the actual; but the actual itself? – not at all.[1] Nor is it likely to reach the actuality of things by speculating on the possibility of some kind of phenomenological reduction or 'raw feel'; on the contrary, these are merely more symptoms of formal reason's desperate urge – and inability – to come to grips with things! Everything is constructed, and 'reductions' and 'feels' are no exceptions: they simply reflect formal reason's characteristic belief that, if we only take the process of abstraction far enough, we will surely arrive at the concrete. And if I jump quickly enough, I can escape from my own shadow, not to mention know pure Forms and look on the face of God.

Secondly, why should one assume that the triviality of everyday life needs to *conflict* with formal reason's grander dreams? What could be more everyday than formal reason dreaming of higher things? And is the actual so trivial? On the contrary, is there not a natural and necessary connection between the actual and our most imposing ambitions such that, the more extensive our grasp of reality as a whole becomes – and so the more likely our chances of succeeding in any of our endeavours – the more intensive our grasp of the things which stare us in the face would be? Is it not (again) formal reason itself, with its irreducible abstractness, that conceals this link from us? After all, only if we grasp the conditions of our existence fully can we expect our plans and strategies to succeed fully. Conversely, if we could grasp all the conditions of our existence

---

[1] As Fodor remarked, 'Scholarship is the process by which butterflies are transmuted into caterpillars' (Fodor, 1983). Or a little more poetically, 'Writing is the ash of the experience' (Leonard Cohen).

fully, the actual (which is after all nothing other than the nexus of those activities and conditions) would be self-evident.

It is tempting to reply that this is merely an abstraction, if not downright childish: there is always dirt and noise and luck in any situation, all quite capable of derailing us but too random and too trivial to be totally anticipated. The world is an untidy place. But again one can only note that dirt and noise and luck are only the surfaces of structures we have yet to grasp. At the very worst dirt is only misplaced matter, noise is only the signal for uncontrolled elements in the communications channel, and luck can be amplified and even summoned by a combination of attention, care, diligence, skill, knowledge and insight – all of which are more or less under our own command. Indeed, not only should we not have to chose between actuality and the larger view claimed by formal reason, but the twin facts that the actual is not self-evident and that we do not find it possible to settle down in actuality are surely *prima facie* grounds for doubting that we are going to succeed in anything else either.

This leads to the final problem, for what else, in reality, is there other than the actual? If we do not even plan to fetch up in reality, where do we think we are going? It is true that formal reason has always had a predilection for denouncing the world in the name of some allegedly higher ideal or realm, even to the point of utter other-worldliness. But from the point of view of any theory of reason's place in the universe, can this be considered anything more than reason temporarily preferring its own rationalisations to the actuality they are too weak to rationalise?

The structure of actuality

Actuality has three aspects: the here and now; content and context; and the mediate and the immediate. All three aspects are constantly in play in intelligence: not only are they always expressed in all intelligent acts but the successive stages in the development of intelligence as a whole can be defined in terms of their growing maturity, which is to say, in terms of the growing maturity of our grasp of the actual.

Of the three, the actual is probably most obviously connected to the first, the here and now, which is the part of the actual that exists for me, from my point of view in space and time. This may seem a very simple idea, but the connection is not as straightforward as it may seem. As the subject of the here and now, I possess knowledge, powers, experience, assumptions, abilities and resources that effectively extend far into the elsewhere and elsewhen. This ensures that whatever grasp I may have of the here and now, it already implies that – and how – it will unfold into the unseen elsewhere and elsewhen of the next moment of actuality.

So my earlier definition of the actual, which seems to define it exclusively in terms of time and space (which is to say, defines it phenomenally), is every bit as much a matter of substance and causality, and so of the processes and mechanisms that define the inner structure of things and events, and the structures that determine how the present moment will generate its successor. In other words, if the here and now is a phenomenon, it is a historical phenomenon. Conversely, there are elements of actuality that impinge on my existence –

on those very same powers, experience, resources, and so on – in ways of which I am *not* aware and over which I have no control. So the here and now is not only more richly but also more insidiously embedded in the actual than a naïvely phenomenal conception of the here and now might easily suggest.

The link between the actual and its content and context is almost equally obvious. Both what an object actually is and what effects it might have on its neighbours depend on its content and context, given that the latter jointly determine the how and why of things and events. They also determine what will become of that object, be it as a result of its relationships to other objects or as a result of its own spontaneous tendencies. What is more, the *sense* in which an object exists for its subject here and now depends specifically on how its content and context are construed. Without some sense of its content or context, an object may be present for me but I would find it impossible to make out what it was, what it might do or what bearing it might have on anything I have in mind. Without an idea of its content and context, it would be impossible either to tell what such an object means or to keep it under control, even at the level of simple surveillance, for I would be oblivious of the factors that might set it into action. It would make no sense to me, and could only barely be said to actually exist from my point of view. It would be there on the periphery of my vision, my eyes might skim over its surface, I might touch it accidentally, incidentally, it might lie out there in the misty edges of my imagination, but for want of any notion of its content or context, it would have no actual existence or implications from my point of view. However much sound and fury it may generate, it would signify nothing.

To make this same point in a somewhat different way, the actual is the locus of *meaning*. Things exist and events occur without asking our permission, but they acquire a meaning only to the an extent to which they are actually constructed by an intelligent being – which is to say, constructed as actual objects, here and now. For it is only intelligence that is capable of construing things and events as meaningful (which is to say, as objects). In terms of the ancient conundrum, yes, a tree falling in forest does make a sound even if there is no one there to hear it, at least insofar as 'sound' is a physical phenomenon. But no one will care, for a sound signifies nothing without anyone to hear and give it a meaning.

That is not to say that all the components of meaning come into existence only in the actual moment or that they cease to be meaningful when they are passed. We arrive in the here and now well equipped with a great range of structures through which various kinds of meaning can be constructed, and the range and nature of the possible meanings are conditioned by the social and psychic, historical and phenomenal conditions in which both the here and now and the structures at our disposal developed. We are all creatures of our times. What is more, the things by which we are confronted and the events in which we participate are themselves imbued with pre-existing significance, at least to the extent that they are the products of previous intelligent acts and we are able to detect the significance in question. They also have purely objective properties that massively limit the kinds of meaning they will bear. The meanings the *Titanic*'s passengers attributed to its sinking were no doubt many and various, but they were, I suspect, severely constrained by the objective fact that they were all on the point of drowning.

Nevertheless, meanings are not merely imported into the moment, to hang up on any objects that can be found to fit them. The act, the object and the meaning are one and the same, just as the sound and the meaning of speech are identical. The meaning of what I say no more exists before I say it than water is hidden in the hydrogen and oxygen atoms out of which it is composed.[1] The ability to construct objects *is* the ability to construct meaning. So it is in the here and now in which I construct my objects that my meaning first comes into existence and only here and now that it has literally objective validity. Thereafter, that meaning may imbue my entire subsequent existence with a new significance, but any such meaning only continues because I reconstruct it over and over again in each new moment.[2] So, given that each new moment is anything but a simple replica of its predecessors, it is not surprising that old meanings are constantly (but largely implicitly) adapted to new conditions, or, therefore, how disappointing or treacherous assumed meanings can be when the original conditions are replicated and all the accommodations made to later conditions are subsequently exposed.

To contrast the subjective and objective aspects of content and context and the here and now in this way is only to repeat for the actual what I have already said elsewhere about intelligence in general. For these are the very complexities of the dialectic of internalisation and externalisation, with its component dialectics of appearance and reality, self and other and present and absent. Given that each of these is also a distinction between how things exist in themselves and how they exist for me, plainly a sizeable portion of the problem of actuality lies in the contrast – and frequent contradiction – between these three somewhat broader oppositions. I also suggested examples of how these rather abstract relationships are expressed on the concrete level – through experimentation, reflexivity and means–end relationships – and the nature of these examples implies that our relationship to the actual is not only active but also tends towards the gradual resolution of the underlying tensions by means of just the kind of growth in knowledge and power that was described in still less abstract terms in the first half of this chapter.

As far as the actual is concerned, though, the more general opposition between the subjective and objective facets of the here and now and content and context can be best expressed in terms of the third pair introduced above: the mediate and the immediate.

The significance of the mediate and the immediate can be explained by considering how one actuality succeeds another. Certainly there is nothing in the concepts of here and now and content and context as such that explains this

---

[1] This analogy was used by de Saussure, and the same existential view of meaning was upheld by Merleau-Ponty (1973). It is also the view taken by authors writing about such esoteric matters as *haiku* poetry (eg, Blyth, 1994). The point being made here should not be restricted to linguistic meaning.

[2] However, note also my remarks on the formation of implicit and enduring structures, including implied meanings, in Ch. 7.

transition. All that has been said in that direction is that both pairs imply some kind of link between the here and now and elsewhere and elsewhen. And in the absence of a structure capable of comprehending just this connection, capable of grasping that *this* actuality, here and now, should be succeeded by another, equally sensible actuality, linked to this one in some sensible manner, why should anyone think that one actuality is *not* in fact being constantly replaced by an infinite succession of completely random, unrelated actualities? And even if it weren't, in the absence of such a structure, how would you know?

Hence the importance of the mediate and the immediate. For it is specifically reason's grasp of the structures which *mediate* the content and context of the here and now to one another that allows it to grasp the 'deep structure' of the actual – the increasingly wide and deep structures whose functioning determines how any given concrete actuality 'works'.

> Activities are not short-lived events or actions that have a temporally clear-cut beginning and end. They are systems that produce events and actions and evolve over lengthy periods of sociohistorical time. The subject and the object are mediated by artifacts, including symbols and representations of various kinds. The activity system incessantly reconstructs itself through actions and discourse.[1]

This in turn allows the subject to infer – and perhaps directly determine – where the here and now will go next, so to speak, and so sustain its grasp of the actual even through what are, from the narrowly phenomenal point of view that would be enjoined by the lack of such a deep structure of actuality, the radically disjointed sequences of paradox and contradiction. It is moreover its grasp of this deep structure – expressed through experimentation, reflexivity, means–end relationships, and so on – that reason actively *resolves* the complications created by the difference between the subjective and objective aspects of actuality.

As with the here and now and content and context, the mediate and the immediate make up a natural pair. Given that there are no unmediated processes or mechanisms in the universe, this is just as well – otherwise it would be impossible to make sense of even the simplest thing or event. And as a good deal of this book has been devoted to showing, intelligence is certainly up to the task of grasping the mediate. The relationships that define concrete reason, the systems of which formal reason is (more or less rightly) so proud and the totalities informing dialectical reason's radical grasp of the actual all represent massive advances in intelligence's capacity to identify, organise and control the mediations needed to control both its own actions and the universe on which it acts. What is more, the same process of historical development from intuitive reason to formal reason sees these mediations develop in every sphere of activity, from purely intellectual sophistication to the tremendous elaborations of industrial societies. The actual is as much mediated by flints and lathes and global communications networks as by logic, thought and philosophy.[2]

---

[1] Cole *et al.* (1997: 4).

[2] For a practical demonstration of the subtleties introduced by even the simplest mediations, see Hutchins in Cole *et al.* (1997: 338–53). For a systematic account of the devel-

Because the relationship between the mediate and the immediate is continually developing, the boundary between them is not only continually shifting, but the mediate is increasingly incorporated within the immediate. The sum of our power and knowledge not only grows (generally speaking) to include more and more structures, resources and so on, but its nature matures, in the sense that objects that once could be grasped, if at all, only by the most painstaking application of difficult and poorly comprehended devices, come to be dealt with simply, straightforwardly, even automatically. The structures in terms of which new tasks are constructed generally come to be so thoroughly mastered and made so completely predictable and reliable that they can be taken completely for granted.

Thus, as a baby I did not realise that objects exist independently of the sense I made of them at the time when I made it; now it is perhaps the most important feature of my grasp of objects that they continue to exist regardless of the sense I make of them. That is why, for example, I can now step out into a social world of unprecedented depth and breadth, yet still navigate it with (relative) ease: I know that I can (usually) count on other actors and social systems to play their part. The mediations I once struggled so hard to grasp are now integral parts of the way I make even the most superficial sense of the world. They begin as unintelligible, pass on to being highly mediated and culminate by directly constituting what I find most immediately obvious about things.

To take what is perhaps the most obvious example, I cannot look at these words without also reading them. I do not look at their shapes and colours and only then see what they mean: to look at them at all is to read them, and to read them is to read their meanings. I suspect that I could not *not* read them, even if I wanted to. Likewise, my world is full of similar technological and cultural elements that I take completely in my stride, and I could not *not* interpret them in cultural and technological terms. Not only are there no 'raw feels' and no phenomenological reductions, but the theories in which such notions are grounded are some of the most intensively and extensively constructed things formal rational cultures have produced to date.

So, every object in my current here and now was created by means of fantastically rich and elongated chains of natural and intelligent processes. Even at the cognitive level I only find them intelligible by virtue of a mass of assumptions, experiences and logico-mathematical structures of the kind on which this book has already dwelt at such length. Not only is this teacup only present on my desk because human beings discovered how to fire clay, because at least one large American industrial conglomerate operates in the teacup business, because Bloomingdale's exists, because a global transport system took my mother-in-law to New York and because I possessed the subtle interpersonal skills needed to persuade her to 'lend' it to me all those years ago, but its presence only makes sense to me because I am acquainted with and make certain assumptions about thirst, tea, western culinary tradition and the kettle in the kitchen next door.

---

opment of mediation on the cognitive plane, see Piaget (1978, especially chapter 3).

Nor are these exactly abstruse achievements, at least not in their most general form. The very first intelligent mediation – the object permanence by virtue of which I recognise that objects continue to exist even when outside the here and now – is there at the very start of intelligence. For what is object permanence but our first insight, our first tool for grasping that the real extends beyond mere appearance, that things are still somehow 'there' even in their absence, that an object exists in all its objective otherness even when I myself have nothing to do with it?

The closure of actuality

I have often been asked what I thought was the secret of Buddha's smile. It is – it can only be – that he smiles at himself for searching all those years for what he already possessed.

Paul Brunton

However, there is a more critical point to be made here about the process of mediation and the role played by the actual in the development of intelligence as a whole. As I have already suggested, the ambiguity of the concepts of the here and now and content and context can only be reinforced by the planetary scale and scope of the mediations that place me in my current relationship even to as trivial a thing as this teacup. How then can the actual ever do anything but torment me with doubt and uncertainty about what anything really is or what even my personal existence could possibly mean?

Yet there are compelling reasons for believing that, however things may be in this actuality – the actuality of a limited individual standing at a relatively lowly point in the history of reason – there will come a time when an intelligent being's grasp of the actual will be not merely much broader and deeper and more rational than the one I take for granted, but will actually be infinite. When that happy day dawns, the vast processes of historical development outlined in the previous section will not only be complete but their results – a totality of mediations whose extent and intent is literally universal – will be the normal form of every intelligent being's activity and consciousness. Then reason's grasp of actuality will be complete in every sense of the word.

Of course, there are many problems with the idea that all actuality, everything that exists, could be grasped immediately by reason, such that the entire content and context of the actual could be made to coincide with the here and now. Firstly, even if there is some sense in which the content and context of my here and now could be made to embody my entire world, surely I am not so vain – or solipsistic – to imagine that my world encompasses the whole universe? Secondly, no matter how extensively or intensively structured my world might become, there are surely many elements of the world that are simply not – and never will be – in the here and now. In the terminology of the general model of intelligence I am assuming here, there are things that are real but not apparent, absent and not present, other and not self. Perhaps all could become part of the here and now at some time or another – a doubtful proposition in its own right – but surely those that exist for us at any given moment can only make up a tiny fraction of the whole?

Finally, even if all absence, reality and otherness could be incorporated into the present, the apparent and the self, my relationship to much of this remarkable world will surely be highly qualified, in the sense that many things are only contingently present, apparent and self. Things might be otherwise, and might become yet more 'otherwise' at any moment, without my noticing or understanding the change. And even if by some Cartesian miracle things stay perpetually in line with my beliefs about them, what I know about them is only a matter of fact. At the very least there are many features of this teacup and the kitchen next door about which I might easily be mistaken, let alone industrial corporations, New York shops and my social skills. Object permanence does not extend to the unconditional necessity of Bloomingdale's.

In fact it is extremely difficult to circumscribe the contingent: after all, what is there outside the realm of pure abstractions such as logic and mathematics that is *not* contingent to some degree? Isn't some degree of contingency intrinsic to the concrete? Indeed, isn't there a powerful case for seeing logic and mathematics themselves as necessary *for us* but contingent on the conditions of human existence (at whatever level), and so as contingent *in themselves*? So the contingency that afflicts so many things qualifies my grasp of the actual rather fundamentally.

But none of these problems is insoluble.

Firstly, my world could indeed encompass the universe. From our current point of view the universe is incomprehensibly large, but then so far human beings have only had a culture and technology capable of looking beyond our most pressing biological problems for a few decades.[1] On the other hand, we have (on current expectations) at least fifty billion years to get to grips with the universe. Of course, it is difficult to demonstrate that this process could really come to any conclusion, such that the universe *as a whole* is encompassed by intelligence, especially if we take the limits set by relativity theory seriously, and even more especially if we assume that the completion of dialectical reason and the complete identification of our world with the universe both depend on colonising space as a whole.[2] However, for my world to comprehend the universe it is no more necessary to conquer every galaxy than working this computer requires that I control every atom in it. The closure of actuality does not mean freezing the universe into a kind of Parmenidean nightmare: all that we need is the knowledge and power needed to remove any limits to rational activity. That requires altogether less than either omniscience or omnipresence.

Nor does the universe's evident complexity set any bounds to this process. Although it may well be endlessly *complicated*, in the sense that its different *empirical* expressions are indefinitely many, the number of, and possible relationships between, the *structures* that determine the universe's empirical forms must be finite. Or rather, if they were infinite, everything in the universe would also be infinitely complex, and *no* finite structures or processes would exist,

---

[1] On the biological limitations on human life up to the industrial revolution, see Braudel (1974: 37–54). On the cognitive limits set by agrarian societies, see Gellner in Teich *et al.* (1997: 9–17).

[2] On the really quite large complexities of this process, see Barrow and Tipler (1986).

intelligent or otherwise. Infinite complication does not presuppose infinite complexity. On the contrary, there is an infinite variety of integers, but the rules for constructing them all could scarcely be simpler. And our ability to comprehend finite amounts of structure, no matter how large, is surely not in question. Given the progress we have made in four centuries of serious science, it seems short-sighted to imagine that any finite set of structures that may determine how the universe works will not be understood in, say, the next four *million* centuries – a timespan that would itself take us less than one per cent of the way to the universe's earliest expected end. My own expectation is that it will all fall into place a little sooner than that – four more centuries, perhaps four millennia, is probably a little closer. So the empirical complication with which the universe confronts us may never be grasped directly and in every detail – why would anyone want to do that? – but an intelligent world can reconstruct the universe to the point where the difference between them makes no actual difference.

Nor can the final structure be too difficult for us to grasp just because intelligence is too puny to grasp anything so vast. Grasping the universe is not the same kind of problem as multiplying a hundred hundred-digit numbers in your head. On the contrary, if the idea that making sense of the universe includes making the universe itself make sense, then our heads are the last things whose limitations we need to worry about. For intelligence is an abstraction from its own physical, chemical and biological precursors; as such its very structure is a synthesis of all the levels of material activity that preceded it, and its own activity is automatically and inherently appropriate – on some level – to all forms of physical, chemical and biological matter. That is why logic and mathematics are so unreasonably effective, and why Einstein was wrong to claim that the intelligibility of the universe is its most inexplicable feature. On the contrary, its intelligibility to intelligence follows directly from the very way intelligence came into existence in the first place.

That is not to say that intelligence somehow intuits the laws of physics, chemistry and biology, and still less that it immediately understands everything about any actual physical, chemical or biological thing or event. There is no still small voice whispering the answers, if only we would but listen attentively enough. Indeed, the process of abstraction by virtue of which intelligence embodies the highest principles of physics, chemistry and biology is also a process of abstraction *away from* physical, chemical and biological reality. Nevertheless, any intelligence's concrete development as a rational being is simultaneously the accumulation of knowledge of and power over the physical, the chemical and the biological (not to mention other intelligences), and the elaboration of the physical, chemical and biological structures from which it emerged – the two processes that are fulfilled in dialectical reason. Somewhere in my knowledge and experience, not to mention my technological and cultural reach into the world I inhabit, there will one day be structures that take into account all the conditions and modes of expression of even universal complexity. Well, perhaps it won't be me, but reason of some kind or another.

And the way in which this mutual closure of my world and the universe in the actual comes about also removes the second objection cited above: that there are many aspects and elements of the actual that will never be in the here

and now, because the real will never be wholly apparent, the absent will never
be wholly absorbed into the present, and there are some kinds of other that will
never be included within the self. Even if my world could be made to encompass the entire universe, that scarcely guarantees any resolution to these oppositions. Indeed, I have just claimed that my world need not enclose the entire
universe to encompass it for all real purposes. But it is far from obvious that
the development of intelligence can really be completed in even this limited
sense, given that the gap between a dialectical rational world and the universe
must presumably include enduring differences between appearance and reality, present and absent and self and other.

Nevertheless, the relationships between self and other, appearance and reality and present and absent are dialectical, and are therefore relationships
whose intrinsic oppositions are both superficial (though by no means illusory)
and capable of resolution. It is moreover only intelligence that is capable of carrying out that resolution, for intelligence alone is capable of abstracting from
any particular, specific or even universal paradox, and so seeing the larger totality that gives it its true meaning, force and solution.

In more concrete terms, the process whereby the universe is encompassed
by the world of intelligence consists precisely of the formation of this totality.
Insofar as the two poles become identical, reality is made apparent, the absent
is fully absorbed in the present and the other is fully incorporated into the self.
More generally, the mediate is internalised, and so made immediate. This may
happen purely intellectually or by the forces of production, organisation and
control made available by industrialism, but happen it will. And insofar as
each of these oppositions must remain unresolved, it is only at the level of empirical complication, not structural complexity. Perhaps that sounds like mysticism (or science fiction); but then how long is it since the computer would have
seemed like witchcraft?

As for the final problem mentioned above, it is certainly true that there is
nothing necessary about the connection between the here and now and the
many structures I have mentioned in connection with this teacup. Even if everything I believe about clay deposits, American industrial conglomerates and
my silver-tongued powers of persuasion were true, I could not take them for
granted. And in most cases, of course, I would be well advised to be a lot more
circumspect and modest than that. The fact is, the content and context of the
here and now may not be as limited as the previous objections suggested, but
they certainly seem to be infected with an irreducible air of mere possibility, if
not utter contingency. Even if the highest level structures that make up my
here and now – the ultimate formulae of physics, chemistry and biology, for
example – were *necessarily* valid, surely the more concrete structures that enter
in at the lower levels are increasingly suspect?

But not even this objection is insuperable, although in this case the critical
issue is the objectivity of intelligence. That is, the problem is not to make more
sure of the assumptions from which I proceed or the knowledge I hold, as a
conventional interpretation of certainty and (to a lesser extent) necessity would
suggest. Rather, it is to make necessary the objective connections that actually
regulate the here and now and its content and context, rather than merely pos-

sibilities and contingencies. As ever, for the universe to make sense for me, it must sometimes be made to make better sense in itself.

And here the question is one of control of the concrete through the synthesis of abstractions, and the answer is again the relationship of industry to intelligence on the one hand and to the universe on the other. Here the key point that needs to be made is that the development of intelligence consists of two simultaneous processes: the embodiment of intelligence in the world and the incorporation of the world in intelligence; and the ever greater rationalisation of both to which this leads. In both cases what emerges is, on the one hand, the ever-greater mediation of the actual by remote factors, and on the other, intelligence's increasing rationalisation of these factors, such that they support and augment reason rather than operate indifferently or at odds with it.

The crucial role of labour in creating value (in every sense) in the face of indifferent nature has been a recurring theme in social and economic thought at least until the rise of neo-classical economics. One need not go quite as far as Mandeville (in *The Fable of the Bees*):

> There is nothing Good in all the Universe to the best-designing Man, if either through Mistake or Ignorance he commits the least Failing in the use of it; there is no Innocence or Integrity that can protect a Man from a Thousand Mischiefs that surround him: On the contrary everything is Evil, which Art and Experience have not taught us to turn into a Blessing.[1]

On the contrary, one may be fairly pessimistic about the short-term prospects for the environment under current regimes. But the long-term trend has been clear enough ever since the great 'hydraulic societies' of antiquity, if not since the Neolithic revolution itself. By one means or another – a chapter of accidents culminating in the industrialisation of the world – necessity has played an increasing role not just on the most abstract levels of intellectual activity but also through the increasingly structured form of the most concrete elements too. Already the organisation of information is creating necessity in realms where ignorance and uncertainty once prevailed; soon an analogous structuring of the physical, the chemical and the biological (through scarcely imagined forms of nuclear, molecular and organic engineering) will extend such control to all levels of matter.

So the ultimate conclusion of these complementary processes – a conclusion the first readers of this book will not live to see – is the formation of an actuality which is so richly informed by and so richly implies all the other structures that affect that actuality that even the most remote structures operate as necessary parts of that actuality. And there is no limit to the structures this might involve.

This rather dramatic conclusion is in fact only the logical and historical implication of the very first tool intelligence developed for dealing with the actual, namely the permanent object. All that later developments do is to extend and intensify the kinds and degrees of certainty the intelligence in question achieves by means of the yet greater abstraction of itself through successive

---

[1] Quoted by Herlitz in Teich *et al.* (1997: 168).

intuitive, concrete, formal and dialectical levels, and its progressive (and still scarcely begun) concretion into more powerful, more knowledgeable forms of subject, object and world. It may be that Bloomingdale's and my social skills are relatively contingent things right here and now, but what links might exist between culture, communication, technology and consumption a few millennia into the future? I am not suggesting that there will in practice ever be a system of mediations, cultural and technological, literally embodied in human person-hood, consciousness, imagination or wherever, that will allow human beings immediate knowledge of everything to do with teacups and kitchens, but why not? If it will not come to pass in the next hundred years, how about the next million?

This may seem a peculiar idea, perhaps silly or pointless, closer to gratui-tous speculation than a serious account of the development of reason should ever be. But as the example of the cup and the kitchen shows, it is an idea that, on a smaller scale and infinitely less certainly, we take for granted every day. All that I am suggesting here is that, developed to its logical, natural and his-torical conclusions, there are no real limits to how far this process could be ex-tended, and so no real limits to the depth or scope of actuality we might come to comprehend. Conversely, how can we ever expect to be absolutely sure of what we are doing without constantly pushing back the current limits of the actual towards those infinite (but not infinitely remote) bounds? Is that not what the logic of dialectical reason implies?

The development of actuality

There are many steps in the formation of an infinite actuality. This is because, although all forms of reason reason about the here and now, they do so with very different degrees of success. The problem with most stages in the devel-opment of intelligence is that, where their attempts to make sense of the here and now fail, they often direct attention to the things which matter to the struc-tures through which they were trying to get to grips with the actual, rather than to the actuality with which they are confronted. That is not very surpris-ing, of course: what else could they possibly use to guide their next steps?

Much more insidious, though, is the fact that, when they manage to explain, compensate for or otherwise adjust to this failure by means of some kind of rationalisation, inadequate forms of intelligence are often perfectly satisfied with the result. Indeed, the need to add such a rationalisation is seldom seen as a failure at all. At the lower levels intelligence simply moves on to the next task, and by the time formal reason has made its appearance, it treats its ra-tionalisations (which it calls philosophy, theology, and so on) as its highest ac-complishments.

For example, intuitive reason is (initially) limited to the empirical surfaces of things, and literally cannot see the real depths controlling the apparent behaviour of things and events. So it is bound to the here and now, but has no sense of what the here and now really is, or means. It recognises the identity of particular things and events, but its ability to deal with either precise content or wider context, and so to have enduring consequences, is limited to *ad hoc* adjustment. Wandering through the here and now with only the most superficial sense of direction, its grasp of the distinction or relationship between the mediate and the immediate is neither substantial nor exploited in the way it will be later. Intuitive reason may pursue them from one level to another, from the smallest surface details up to the widest perspective, but it cannot knit them together into even an appearance of a stable actuality. Both socially and psychically it reveals a slight and fragile grasp of the actual. A wider order may occasionally be stamped by means of some kind of superstition or ritual, but this does not resolve anything in any enduring sense. Indeed, the very nature of this apparent ordering of things and events reveals an inability to penetrate the surface of things to the relationships that really control them. In each case, each new moment is a new object in its own right, without either connection to its neighbours or any clear focus on or attention to the nature or sense of this moment as this moment.

Concrete reason can certainly see particular relationships, so its view of the actual is much richer than that of intuitive reason. For example, it includes explicit mediation between each here and now and its successor. Or, more simply, concrete reason knows where it is and how it got there, which is more than intuitive reason can usually claim. However, as soon as there is a discrepancy between these relationships and actuality – some aspect of the actual it cannot explain, some failure of the actual to live up to concrete reason's expectations – it is forced to choose. Either it can break off these relationships – which means it loses track of why the current activity makes sense – or it can follow the structures it is currently using to their conclusion – which means losing track of the here and now. Either way, it can't win: the mechanisms which mediate its activity, and so make it strong, divorce it from the here and now, which is to say, from the only thing which has unequivocal actuality. Nevertheless, it too can rationalise its failure by asserting the divine ordination of its 'principles'. This certainly allowed absolutism to fight a long bloody rearguard action against the rising formal systems and structures of the bourgeoisie.

Compared with its predecessors, formal reason has the great advantage that its activity is regulated in terms of complete systems – which is to say, in terms of relationships between relationships. Concrete reason can always say a great deal about these relationships, but only in a discursive manner: it is always rationalising, even when it is in the right. Only with the arrival of formal reason can intelligence explain its objects (or its world or its own subjectivity) in terms of systematically ordered disciplines, be they physics or metaphysics. Only then can it explain the connections that bind an object to its content or context (which is to say, its relationship to the relationships that define and determine it), from equations for the acceleration of point masses in a uniform gravitational field to rigorous proofs of the transmigration of souls.

Conversely, only with the onset of formal reason can intelligence build the technical methods, tools and techniques, from spectrometers to interest rates, through which some element of its conceptual armoury can be deployed and the results of that deployment fed back into the various intellectual disciplines that designed the tools in the first place. More generally, formal reason can understand why carrying out complete actions is sensible, regardless of the distractions of the here and now: if it breaks off merely to admire the view, so to speak, it will lose track of both the larger totality and the more intimate indi-

speak, it will lose track of both the larger totality and the more intimate individuality in terms of which actuality operates.

This self-seeking can be taken to such extremes that every single one of the major expressions of its relationship to the universe may be denounced, be it as trivial appearance, brute reality, vulgar selfhood, alien otherness, mere presence or abyssal absence. On the other hand, formal reason is equally capable of appreciating why the actual should be the ultimate arbiter of activity, since it can reason that the only infallible proof of its grasp of both totality and individuality is its effective synthesis of the full range of mediations needed to construct the object that would satisfy its current purposes. To do that, it must be able to handle all aspects of that object's content and context, and moreover do so in the form of a single, unitary immediacy. But that is only to say that its object must have the coherence, consistency, completeness and correctness of the actual. Hence formal reason's passion for, among other things, the scientific experiment, with all its commitment to testing hypotheses by their empirical manifestation in the here and now.

Nevertheless, the actual remains an insoluble conundrum for formal reason. As I argued at such length in the previous chapter, these same extraordinarily powerful systems oblige formal reason to reduce everything to figments of formal systems. That is, it has no alternative but to mediate the content and context of the actual by means of abstract formal systems. But no formal system can grasp the here and now by this means, since the here and now is not an 'instance' of anything, and 'instances' are all that formal structures know how to recognise. Hence the fate of its scientific experiments is not to create a new, better actuality, but only to receded from such a truly great accomplishment into – another hypothesis. So formal reason's ambition to create truly satisfactory objects is inevitably thwarted. Conversely, its ideologies and rationalisations absorb enough resources, facilities and energy to make the theory of divine right look like a child's excuse.

Indeed, formal reason's relationship to the actuality of its objects, its world and its own subjectivity are always somewhat tortured. Not only is its view of the actual both abstract and negatively tinged but it has long since unmasked Stevenson's aphorism that it is better to travel hopefully than to arrive. For even the milestones and way-stations on its itinerary are cursed with transience. Here we are – but why here, after all? Why not there? Why anywhere? Indeed, why travel at all: there is no satisfaction in travelling in the company of the Flying Dutchman or the Wandering Jew, unable either to come to rest or to take pleasure in the journey. So formal reason can neither stay nor go, and is thus perhaps infinitely farther from the actuality of things and events than any of its predecessors, even when it is quite certain – as it so often is – that it is on the verge of realising them directly. So instead it either drifts into mysticism or rushes off in endless pursuit of a typical formal structure such as a role, money or the latest commodity.

If a formal system consists of relationships between relationships, what about a system of all systems? This would allow intelligence to comprehend the actuality of things, since it would bring to bear all systems simultaneously. As a result, it could be in the here and now and yet be sensitive to all the necessary mediations that brought the here and now into existence and enable intelligence to remain there. This, of course, is dialectical reason: a complete comprehension of the content and context of activity, based on a comprehensive set of mediations, and so arriving immediately at the here and now. Such a here and now would not, of course, be different from any other here and now; its originality lies instead in the fact that a pre-dialectical individual has very little idea what the here and now, considered in all its actuality, looks like in the first place.

This rather large obstacle notwithstanding, I hope that the previous section has made it clear how the limitations of formal reason are overcome by the formation of dialectical reason. Formal reason's radical development and synthesis of all the strategies, processes, resources and tools needed to carry out any given activity can only conclude with the subject in the fullest, most internalised, and so most immediate command of all these mediating factors. Its objects and world are likewise constructed in a manner that progressively resolves all outstanding conflicts and contradictions, so dialectical reason is not forced off into the kinds of detour and distraction that are so typical of all previous modes of reasoning. Dialectical reason is not *capable* of constructing the here and now: it simply *is* here and now.

So the subjectivity whereby dialectical reason reasons must be clearly distinguished from the tragic, faintly pathetic and ultimately illusory homunculus-cum-marionette of formal reason, whose subject's autonomy is paid for by every form of radical isolation from Cartesianism to consumerism. Nor do its objects sit like bell jars over actual things and events, encapsulating, suffocating but never quite touching the here and now, in the manner of formal reason's permanent but also inert arrangements.

On the other hand, given that the readers (and the writer) of this account are in all likelihood overwhelmingly formal rational individuals, it is crucial to make the difference between a formal and a dialectical grasp of the actual completely clear. As I have already argued, formal reason is quite capable of distinguishing between the empirical content and context of an object and the methods whereby that content and context were revealed. In other words, it can grasp the *distinction* between actual things and events and the structures in terms of which they are constructed – the very distinction I have already claimed leads pre-dialectical levels of reasoning through a whole series of quite fallacious attitudes to reality.

This then poses the question of the specific sense formal reason makes of this distinction. For there is nothing to stop formal reason from developing a well-defined *notion* of the actuality of empirical things and events, even if only as the negative of its own abstract and systematic structures of activity. Indeed, it can hardly avoid doing so, for intelligence, unlike other, strictly biological life-forms, must treat the kind of negation with which actuality sometimes greets its efforts as a *positive* failure that must make sense in its own right. So formal reason must push on to a positive answer and, if necessary, fill in the cracks in its picture of the actual with metaphysical and ideological 'solutions'. Or books on the history of human reason, perhaps.

Given the fundamental incompetence of the means at formal reason's disposal to bring it to actuality, it is not surprising that it quickly begins to speculate on the irreducibility of phenomena, the transcendental nature of things and events, and all the other phenomenological, idealistic and mystical notions alluded to above. These speculations are often made with a quite extraordinary confidence, considering they are founded solely on formal reason's inability to draw any positive conclusions. But inevitably, formal notions of actuality are still abstractions from actuality – even its concept of that least abstract aspect of reality, the empirical – and as such negate the actual's most fundamental property.

Occasionally formal reason's sense of the actual tries to escape this abstractness, frequently by way of existential questions of the 'Why do I exist?' variety. Since formalisation cannot go very far beyond 'Because you are an x' (where x is an organism adapted to a particular niche, a sinner cowering before the majesty of God, a finite observer in an infinite universe, or just a victim of 'the human condition'), the best it can achieve is to situate its objects at the intersection of many systems, derive them from a logical multiplication of types, and so on. Or it may simply recoil from the contingency (ie, the still unintelligible actuality) of things and events, resorting as often as not to a more or less profound version of 'Because life's like that'. Ultimately, it simply cannot tell us why we, considered strictly as actual individuals, exist, or what the things and events we encounter, considered in strictly actual terms, mean. The formality of formal reason ensures that it experiences all actuals as logically conditional and intersubstitutable, even where their identity and differences proclaim the very opposite. After all, it takes formal reason a long time even to hear the voice of actuality, let alone understand what it is saying.

But should one really be so sceptical of formal reason's approach to actuality? First and foremost, isn't it odd that a theory of the history of human reason should try to judge one enormously successful stage in the development of intelligence by standards defined in terms of an abstract model of the hypothetical achievements of an equally hypothetical future? Secondly, should one really discount completely the possibility that formal reason is right to discount the actual as the mere surface of reality? In a world governed by formal reason, it is only through structures such as money, commodities and roles that anything of any consequence happens at all, or that the actual itself comes into existence in the first place. In a formal world, many aspects of our existence have no authentic actuality, at least in the sense that their meaning or value lies in their actuality, except insofar as that actuality reflects these formal structures. Why then is formal reason wrong to address actuality in this way?

Of course, the answer lies in the fact that formal reason does not succeed even by its own criteria. Take, for example, the concept of freedom that, explicitly or implicitly, plays an absolutely central role in formal reason's view of itself. From consumer choice to civil liberties to the existentialist condemned to freedom to artistic licence to due process to money to scientific discovery to moral responsibility, there is no aspect of formal reason that does not require or assume the existence of freedom of some kind. Yet even this most profound of formal reason's aspirations – rivalled only by its natural counterpart, truth – exists for formal reason only to account for the arbitrariness and contingencies of existence formal reason cannot account for or come to terms with in any other way.

For reasons already set out at great length, a system constituted by money, roles, commodities and other formal structures must always be, from the point of view of any actual here and now, radically underdetermined. To be legitimate within the systems in play, the outcome must always 'work' in terms of those formal systems, but exactly which outcome is actually chosen – which commodity is consumed, which decision is made at this point in playing this role – will always be left to the moment.

Formal reason itself likes to call such moments of arbitrariness moments of 'freedom', 'choice' or even 'faith', but all this really means is that the actual basis for the choice in question, be it psychological preference, social prejudice, tradition or whim, simply makes no sense within the prevailing formal system. That may make sense to *me*, here and now, but that is a quite separate issue. In terms of the formal rational structures whereby formal reason itself makes sense, they appear not as free but as arbitrary. But formal reason cannot progress beyond this point and still remain formal. Conversely, they may be formally modelled, but a model simulates only the external states and transitions; it does not need to represent actuality in itself. That is why our dominant ideologies – which must *compensate* for formal reason's failings – are obsessed with the alleged specialness of the actual – consumerism's act of choice, Romanticism's devotion to the moment, and so on – yet our entire science – which is bound to *reflect* those failings – is about the actual's complete lack of specialness.

Nor are formal reason's fallacious attempts at grasping the actual restricted to the intellectual sphere. On the contrary, they have left a terrible trail of suffering behind them. By projecting their internal abstractness onto the world, they engender literally endless illusions of the reality of essences and Forms[1] and races and principles and the like, or even simple yet disfiguring notions of propriety. These notions may be false (and indeed self-contradictory) but, answering as they do the inmost needs of formal reason, the conception of existence they impose is always liable to seize precedence over real existents, who find themselves subjected to one or other fanciful metaphysic rather than being accepted as actual realities worthy of respect in their own right. Hence formal reason's perennial marriage of piety and murder: although it likes to think that it inhabits a world of ideals to die for, the reality is more often ideals to kill for. And why not? In the words of Arnauld Amaury, Papal Legate to the Albigensian crusade: 'Kill them all. God will know his own'.[2]

Mind and body

But perhaps the most obvious expression of formal reason's inability to grasp the actual is the mind–body problem. My mind is in here, my body is out there, and the more closely one inspects their apparent relationship, the more

---

[1] On what exactly Plato meant by 'Forms', see D. Frede in Frede and Striker (1996: 29-58).

[2] See also Victor Frankl's account of the reduction of human beings to numbers in Auschwitz in Frankl (1959: 73).

ephemeral it seems. For all the immediacy with which intention or desire to perform a given act is followed or accompanied by the appropriate movement, it often takes only a little reflection for my body to appear to me as simply another object, inhabiting the same sphere as all the other objects now before me. Thus, my hands pass over this keyboard, and if I take appearances seriously, my hands and the keyboard are clearly much more of a kind than my hands and the mind that is thinking the words they are typing. If there is a more direct link between mind and body, it is not obvious.

Indeed, there had better not be, otherwise the progressive differentiation of action and consequences from motive and intention that is indispensable to any moral reasoning will turn out to be a delusion. Without this critical distinction, Moses' injunction against adultery would only be muddied by Jesus' injunctions against lust. Or again, Matthew's assault on 'the scribes and Pharisees' for mere 'observance' in place of the divinely enjoined love of God and neighbour would be completely unintelligible.[1]

Insofar as the body is simply another object, the solution to the problem of why it is so difficult to comprehend is simple enough. Certainly it is no grand metaphysical conundrum. On the contrary, it is a direct expression of the most ordinary operations – and so also of the limitations – of formal reason. The body appears as an external object because that is how formal reason treats all actual objects. The body is simply the object whose unusual relationship to the mind – the fact that it is *my* body in much the same sense as this is *my* mind – has made it especially problematic, and the very emblem of mystery.

But being able to state why there is a problem does not solve it. On the other hand, surely stating the problem in this way – treating the body as just another object – ignores the special relationship between mind and body that I demonstrate every time I walk down the street? Whatever its other resemblances to objects generally, my body is not 'out there' in quite the same sense that its other objects are. Apart from this peculiar linkage between this particular object and its subject that enables me to make it do things just by wanting to, my body is the basis on which my intelligence – including the very subjectivity that is trying to grasp that body – developed in the first place.

It is true that, once the sensorimotor stage is completed and intelligence proper takes the stage, the body recedes a little, but it is no less both the original fount and enduring foundation of intelligent activity. Even if the body is reduced to a kind of communications channel *cum* tool kit, it remains the basis of my ongoing relationship with all these other objects in the world. Even if this ceased to be the case and my natural body were replaced *in toto* by artefacts and prostheses, that would only be to replace one body with another: given the intrinsic abstractness of subjectivity, an equivalent connection would still be required. Finally, my body is peculiar in that my experience of it is unique: it is nothing more or less than *my* body. Although it may exist as an object in many other worlds than my own, it is only in my world that it appears to its subject by such oddly private channels. This may not, as is some-

---

[1] On the significance of these distinctions in the formation of Christianity, see Pagels (1996).

times suggested, amount to *privileged* access, but it certainly is peculiar to me. So there really is a special mind–body relationship, and even if formal reason cannot grasp objects in general in their full actuality, the same can only be partly true of the body. The body is not simply another object, and if the link is not obvious, this may be solely because it is transparent.

But unfortunately the existence of this special relationship only makes the problem worse. If my mind is linked more directly to my body that to other objects, why does this fact not alter the equally irreducible fact that my hands and this keyboard are also both equally 'out there'? If there is some deeper genetic and developmental link, why is it completely hidden to the point of mystifying most of humanity ever since we began thinking about it? Why was the mind–body problem a problem – and a different problem from that of objects in general – in the first place?

The answer to this problem comes in two parts. Firstly, there is the question of why it is that mind and body operate on quite different planes, in different times and spaces, with difference forms of substance and causation. In short, if the existence of the body is straightforward enough, where does the mind come from? And secondly, how does the relationship between mind and body actually operate to create the vertiginous regression into which formal reason retreats every time it tries to make sense of actuality, its body included?

At risk of circularity, mental life is the part of activity that is purely internal to the cognitive subject, and the construction of mental objects and a mental world is carried out by means of structures lying solely within that subject. The closest it comes to the world of empirical phenomena is in its use of the sensorimotor structures (to create images, thoughts, memories, and so on). These structures certainly arose from the sensory and motor organs and mechanisms through which the infant first encountered the world, but their link to mental life is not through some irreducible dependence of intelligent activity on the body (or any other organic structure). Rather, just as it was their internal synthesis and abstraction that led to the origins of intelligence proper in the first place,[1] so now they allow that intelligence to simulate or reproduce internally various aspects of the world. But there is nothing sensory or motor about mental life's proper structure or functioning.

So mental objects are the objects the subject can construct solely through the mutual implication of its own structures, without empirical content. The mental world is likewise the totality of mental objects and the relationships that arise from their mutual implication – which, like the implications of any other object and any other world, are at least partially determined by their subject's intentions, assumptions, expectations and desires, even if, in this case, that subject is peculiarly placed to control them. But they have their revenge, for the subject's mental existence is as much determined by the independence of the relationships between its mental objects and its mental world as its empirical

---

[1] Piaget (1953, 1955). The vast body of criticism to which Piaget has been exposed seems to have done nothing to dislodge this fundamental conclusion. For a general defence of Piaget, see Smith (1993).

existence is determined by the independence of the relationships between its empirical objects and its empirical world.

Inevitably, the formation of the mind has a fundamental developmental aspect. The extent, scope, integration and capacity of the growing child's mind is directly determined by the cognitive stage the child has reached. An intuitive child – Piaget's pre-operational subject – can never quite free itself of the empirical content and context of the here and now – including the here and now of its mental life – so elementary are the forms of mediation available to it. And although the concrete rational child is capable of articulating the transformations, series, categories and other structures in terms of which it mediates its various forms of expression and representation, he or she can still only fully break free of the empirical content and context of its here and now under carefully managed conditions. So in both the opening stages in the development of intelligence, the child is always more or less embedded in the practical exigencies of its day-to-day existence.

Regarding the origins of the strictly formal mind, however, the fact that formal reason's operations take the form of closed, self-sufficient circuits enables the formal mind to operate independently of any input from or concrete relationship to the 'outside world'. That is, after all, how it arrives at independent structures such as logic and mathematics: by objectifying and then reflecting on its own internal structures, independently of the concrete content or context through which they happen to be expressed. This in turn is only possible because the circuits in which the formal mind runs really are systematic and self-sufficient: otherwise even formal reason could not establish a separate or distinct set of disciplines, principles and methods without constantly conflating them with the particular things and events to which they are applied, as concrete reason is wont to do. Even when its mental activity takes on a more concrete character – in the routine, half-realised thoughts and images of everyday mental life – formal reason only requires the mind to make use of some of the sensorimotor structures through which it deals with the world. As these were rendered largely independent of any concrete content by the same developmental process that created the highest level logico-mathematical structures, this is not a great new demand. So formal reason has a uniquely well-structured, uniquely independent mental apparatus.

As I was at such great (perhaps excessive) pains to argue in the previous chapter, the process of formalisation prevents formal reason from quite engaging actuality, and this is as true of mental life as of the most powerful structures of global industrial capitalism. The formal mind is always thinking *about* something, always feeling *that* something else, and so on. All the same, it is a uniquely powerful instrument for dealing with the world, not least because it enables formal reason to construct a complete alternative mental world, fully populated with hypotheses, possibilities, theories, belief systems, methods, and so on, with their own peculiar modes of time, space, substance and causality and their own dictates regarding the phenomenal world of empirical things and events.

As for the second component of the mind–body problem, the relationship *between* mind and body, it is clear that formal reason has no difficulty managing this relationship in practice. There has never been a structure comparable in scope and power to formal reason, not least in terms of its mental ability to turn these mental powers to practical, empirical effect. Of course, it has its own vicissitudes, but there is nothing of which any non-intelligent structure was capable that it could not repeat or surpass if it (literally) put its mind to it. The real problem of the mind–body relationship lies in formal reason's ability to theorise this relationship. But this is by no means a purely intellectual issue, for the independence and power of the mind are among the hallmarks of formal reason as a whole. As I have already argued, the theoretical divorce between the formal mind and its body and the pervasive sense of doubt this can create are insignificant only to the shallow. And it is from this problem that the mind–body problem really flows.

Here the key problem is not the mind–body relationship in the abstract: if mind and body truly paralleled one another, their mutual existence would not be a problem. Rather, the problem lies in the formal mind's attempts to grasp the thing that actually binds mind to body, that actually *is* this relationship, the thing through whose mediation my mind does indeed have this exceptional relationship to my body. This thing is the activity I am currently carrying out. And here again the chronic contradiction between formal reason and the actual reappears.

However it may be instantiated, both this activity and its products (ie, the content of the formal mind) must be structures that the mind must be able to comprehend if it is to grasp the body through which its own intentions are implemented. This structure is the activity formal reason means to carry out. That structure is as actual as any other, and can only be grasped fully if it is grasped in its actuality. Hence the mind–body problem, for how can we resist the conclusion that even the actuality of the structures through which mind and body are actually related is as unintelligible to formal reason as any other? All formal reason can manage is to turn its fabulous powers on this very special component of the here and now – and fail as completely to grasp the actuality of this component as it fails to grasp the actuality of anything else.

To complete the paradox, is this inability to grasp the actual not the reason why the mind–body problem can be extended into the mind itself? After all, if we turn our attention from our bodies to the very thoughts that embody the independence of our unprecedented minds – if, that is, we project our own thoughts as actual phenomena in their own right – what do we find but that our very thoughts recede as we try to grasp them. They may be completely private thoughts and images, but they are also actual objects whose actuality resists formal reason as much as that of any other. In other words, the problem is not the relationship between the mind and the body as such, but between the mind and any actuality – even, absurdly, its own.

Anticipations of actuality

> I regard 'haiku' as *fundamentally* existential, rather than literary. Or if you will, as primarily an experience, rather than a form of poetry. Bashô's statement that: 'Haiku is simply what is happening in this place, at this moment', shows that he regarded intuitive experience to be the *basis* of haiku. And Now, his criterion, is my own.
>
> J.W. Hackett[1]

What, then, is 'real' actuality? It is not any particular or privileged existent, be it God or History or Consciousness or whatever. Nor is it the irreducible empirical reality of things towards which reason should somehow strive like a good positivist. Rather, it is *existing*, known to us through the successful mediation of the content and context of the here and now, but not requiring any such support in itself. Its meaning can only be found in itself: it is not an example or expression of anything, or rather, its point is independent of its relationships to any external consideration, including the purposes and significance its creator intended it to have. Its meaning lies in the totality, intentional or inadvertent, it actually realises, not in the structures or the functioning of which it is the totalisation.

So it is no surprise that aesthetic experience has sometimes been proposed as a prototype, and jazz and certain forms of Japanese classical music in which the next note is determined solely at the point of playing make equally strong candidates. As such, the actual subject, object or world is the incommensurable and the irreplaceable – as, in its more metaphysical and existential moments, formal reason knows only too well, and as all its most spontaneous tendencies actually deny.

So for reason to reach the actual, it is not enough merely to repeat or ossify the conclusions of formal speculation, which are, after all, only corollaries of formal reason's *in*comprehension of actuality. Rather, dialectical reason raises intelligence to a level where to think of replacing or comparing one thing with another is to lose sight of what makes it that thing in the first place. If the actual is incommensurable or irreplaceable, this is purely because the actual is itself and not something else. Just as formal reason would never accept its objects' empirical surface at face value, or even the specific relations they incorporate and embody as a substitute for 'real' objects in all their formal, systematic 'essence', so dialectical reason would never confuse the formal (or, *a fortiori*, concrete or intuitive) object with the truly actual object. It would not even accept the *idea* of 'a dialectical object' – the actual is simply there, and needs no theorising to justify or explain it.[2]

---

[1] Quoted in Blyth (1994: 138).

[2] It is not always clear how authors who address this topic perceive the relationship between formal and dialectical logic. Depending on one's source, they may be presented either as logical contemporaries or as developmental parent and child; as purely intellectual tools or as ideological weapons wielded by contending classes; as alternative philosophies or as competing guides to revolution; and so on. With the exception of simplistic (though still illuminating) theories that present dialectical and formal logic as

Thus, the dialectically actual possesses its actuality by virtue of its synthesis of all the structures that constitute and bear on it, uniting them in a single, integral structure. This actuality is realised not by the onlooker or the dialectical philosopher, but by the thing itself. Conversely, unlike the pre-dialectical subject's experience of its object, dialectical reason's grasp of its objects is not conditional and does not consist of knowing 'about' this or that. Having resolved all the gaps and contradictions that haunt formal reason, all conditions on the dialectical subject's apprehension of its objects disappear, all mediations become transparently integral to the subject–object relationship itself. With that, all conflicts between appearance and reality, self and other and present and absent dissolve. Subject, object and world encounter one another as a single, infinitely profound, infinitely articulate, infinitely sensible existence. Insofar as reason needs to create mediating structures for the purpose of managing unresolved contradictions – including the mind itself – they can now all fall away.

It is a fascinating and exhilarating notion, and not a little unnerving. On the other hand, as the reader will have noticed, despite some hopefully informative observations on exactly what it is about formal reason that must be overcome for dialectical reason to emerge, plus some brief comments on how this may perhaps be accomplished, very little has been said about dialectical reason itself *beyond* these very speculative notions. Discussing dialectical reason from the strictly formal standpoint of an essentially theoretical book is obviously problematic, if not downright contradictory. Standing no closer to this culmination of reason than the concrete rational child stands to calculus, there is something slightly preposterous about presuming to go beyond pointing out the necessity of such a phase: the only thing one can guarantee about such speculation is that it will be wrong.

Nevertheless, there are pockets of existence where dialectical reason has already found practical expression, even institutionalisation, and those cases can be used to illuminate, in a very limited way, what a world governed by dialectical reason might be like. In particular, we can look to mysticism of various kinds and to specific cultural forms such as *haiku*.

Regarding mysticism, it is instructive to consider some of the classic techniques teachers have devised to engender discipline and insight, and in particular to grasp directly and immediately the actuality of things. This grasp may be spoken of in many more or less religiously coded terms such as grace, the Third Eye, god-realisation, and so on, but the goal itself seems to be quite consistent. The goal of an absolute and unconditional apprehension may be pursued by means of a huge range of techniques from the simple contemplation of a candle flame to the ascetic's many years of self-denial.

---

reflexes of economic structure (typically of the labour process or commodity relations), they are seldom related to any more profound process. Although this is not my main concern, I hope the present volume contributes something to our understanding of this relationship. For alternatives, see Colletti (1973), Ilyenkov (1977), Lefebvre (1969), Lévi-Strauss (1972), Lukács (1978), Novack (1971), Piaget (1980), Riegel (1973, 1975), Schmidt (1971), Sohn-Rethel (1978), Thomson (1961) and della Volpe (1980).

Such techniques serve to train the would-be mystic to track in a simple yet structured way both the continuity and the fluctuations of a single simple object. The fragility of the flame, flickering with every least breath of air, ensures that it cannot be grasped at all if it is not tracked from moment to moment. No thought, no speculation, no theory *about* the flame will improve one's grasp of it by one iota; no method, no skill can be applied without achieving precisely the opposite effect, namely distraction *from* the flame.

Anyone who has tried this exercise will be aware of how quickly, at first, one wanders away from it, and how little ordinary awareness is really focused on the here and now. On the other hand, those who persevere with the task discover that a more immediate awareness of the flame does not exclude an equally immediate and complete awareness of its setting, or of themselves. Progress with the task also intensifies one's awareness of the nature of the flame, so complementing context with content. This is only to be expected, of course: any object is what it is by virtue of both its internal and its external structure, and the flame can only be comprehended to the extent that its setting is comprehended too. The focus on the flickering transience of the candle flame is only a ploy to establish basic technique and discipline, and to provide a lever on the ultimate truth of the world – its actuality.

Many mystical methods have a comparable logic, though their content can be very different. A Japanese acquaintance was made to sit under a waterfall, no doubt helping to ensure that his attention was focused fully on the task at hand. Some schools require extended attention to a particular aspect of activity or surroundings. The twin techniques of 'and that, and that' and 'not that, not that' are simply two techniques for preventing fixity on any particular object, without at the same time denying the objects themselves. It does not matter whether this fixation is on a single object of contemplation, a particular perspective on the world or even a commitment to a particular means to enlightenment: it is fixity itself that is fatal to dialectic, and so to a grasp of the actuality of things in all their absolute and unconditional immediacy. If you meet the Buddha on the road, kill him.

To achieve this immediacy is also to achieve the most misunderstood of mystical goals, namely the end of consciousness. Not having mentioned the problem of consciousness before in this book, this is certainly no place to try to solve it; however, in the context of mystical method it can be observed that to be conscious of an object is to have an attitude towards it, and this is the key to the idea of its dissolution through the achievement of a higher state. 'Attitude' presupposes limitation, for it implies a partial and self-centred interest in the object in question, a fixed, one-sided and phenomenal perspective, and so on. At the very least it implies a difference between consciousness and that of which one is conscious, be it an idealist's concern with the *imperfection* of consciousness or a materialist's distinction between one's consciousness of a cat and the cat itself. All previous states in the development of intelligence (including the present theory) are characterised by attitude in this sense, are 'about' their objects rather than appropriating or bespeaking them directly and immediately. Nowhere is this more so than with formal reason, which, by perfecting the self-sufficient system, sets itself over against even the objects of which it is the author. Its relationship to its objects is therefore inherently external, conditional, partial – an attitude.

To overcome this partiality, the subject of consciousness requires not isolation from its object but harmony, even identity, with it. However, the only durable basis for such harmony or identification is total comprehension. This in turn presupposes at least two things, namely the actual possession of all the structures required to comprehend the object through all its transformations, and the internal organisation required to maintain a constant comprehension regardless of changing conditions or perspective. With that, the challenge of content and context would be met and overcome. With that, all partiality, fixity, one-sidedness and attitude would be abolished. What is more, so would all resort to anything outside the object in question, including all thought, all reference, all meaning. Insofar as these are present at all, it is because they are implied by the object taken on its own terms.

And this is precisely what dialectical reason – and dialectical reason alone – offers. A similar case can be made for the supersession of the self, which is, of course, another goal of mysticism. Just as it abolishes the opposition of appearance and reality on which attitude is built, so the totalisation achieved by dialectical reason posits self and other as no more than the complementary poles of a single unified field, and perhaps not even as distinct as that. The antinomy of present and absent is equally fragile.

This singular commitment to the absolute significance of actuality has had a considerable impact on a number of Asian cultures. It is certainly one of the major differences between Oriental and Occidental world views (insofar as such gross distinctions help more than they hinder). While the West has taken formal reason to far greater lengths than the East, it leaves little room for actuality. The same cannot be said of Eastern societies, though their historical lack of development at the formal level, especially in the political, economic and scientific spheres, forcibly restricts entry into actuality to a small segment of society, to specialised settings such as monasteries, and to highly controlled rituals.[1] Nevertheless, its accomplishments in relation to actuality as such far outshine those of the West.

Hence, for example, *haiku*, a form of Japanese poetry. The goal of *haiku* is to present the present *as* present, to present the actual as no more and no less than itself. A *haiku* is not 'about' its topic, and its topic is not merely an excuse for a poem. Nor is the verse a description of the *experience* of its subject matter, or the state of the subject of that experience. Rather, like all dialectic, it strives to recrystallise the totality, the individuality, the *truth* of the moment directly. One might even say that the *haiku* cares nothing for the *original* moment, but rather uses that moment as a lever for crystallising the *present*, by focusing the audience on a self-sufficient, here and now. As far as the poet is concerned, this focusing is no doubt assisted by the insight provided by the original experience,

---

[1] See in Suzuki (1970b: 332–66). Okakura (1993) provides a classic, if brief, account of the inner meaning of the tea ceremony, while Herrigel (1985) discusses archery in similar terms.

but for the audience – and therefore from the point of view of a successful *poem* – ultimately it is grounded in this new moment, here and now.

In short, *haiku* is not a literary form in the sense that it constrains the poet to a particular kind of message or technique. On the contrary, perhaps the only rule regarding content is that there must be *no* message or technique:

> Demands for a special kind of content – ideological, moral, doctrinaire, modern, etc. – are generally based on the assumption that content is separable from form, and that indeed art itself is only a prettifying of some practical point of view to make it acceptable to the masses or to explain some aspect of the world of confusion in which we are said to live.[1]

Instead of using the content of the poem to convey some 'deeper' meaning, the *haiku* poet aims at something infinitely more difficult and precious, namely to present the content itself. The old pond, the galaxy over Sado Isle, the snowy heron – how much easier to abstract from these things, to say something 'about' them, than to evoke them directly.

Similarly for *haiku* technique: for true evocation, the *haiku* poet must observe many 'rules', but all of them are entirely negative. There must be no analysis, no judgement, no commentary and no sentiment, no emotion or embellishment, no metaphor or allusion or personification or simile. In short, there must be no space between representation and expression, in the poem and its recitation any more than in the original encounter.

> When Bashô looked at an onion, he saw an onion; when he looked at the Milky Way, he portrayed the Milky Way; when he felt a deep unnameable emotion, he said so. But he did not mix them all up in a vague pantheistic stew or symbolic potpourri. In poetry as in life itself, distinctness, the individual thing, directness is all-important.[2]

In short, *haiku* is not 'much in little' but merely enough in little.[3] The objective is precision, not decoration or allusion. Indeed, the objective is objectivity – not the objectivity of the isolated thing, but the objective expression of the objective existence of the object. Just say it as it is – if you can. Then, in proportion as the structure of the experience is replicated within the poem, in proportion to the attentiveness and maturity of poet and audience, the thing itself will appear.

This is, after all, all that intelligence has been up to ever since its inception: when we, as adults, hear a child strive to express something beyond its comprehension, we too use language to make explicit the child's intuition, and so to point directly to the thing.[4] Of course, operating as we do at a higher level than the child, the insight we are able to convey is as likely to mystify the child as to enlighten it. Conversely, our insight is limited to the current level of our own development – a magical realm to the child, no doubt, but not necessarily adequate to the demands of *haiku*. Indeed, what distinguishes our attempts to

---

[1] Yasuda (1957: 28).

[2] Blyth (1994: 63; see also pp. 68–72).

[3] Blyth (1994: 120).

[4] Blyth (1994: 51ff).

grasp the works of Bashô and Issa and Buson[1] from our own attempts to shepherd the child along is the fact that we are not the adult to their child. On the contrary, we are the child, and now it is our turn to feel a certain obscurity and humility. Yet, just as the child can sense and be satisfied that there *is* a higher meaning intimated in our words, even if they cannot explain or even repeat them, the *haiku* may convey some kind of intuition of actuality even to formal reason, even if it is not yet ready to comprehend it by its own means.

In all this, the *haiku* is only the corollary of a larger element of Japanese culture in general and of Zen in particular. If the goal of *haiku* is to present the present as present, this is no more than the goal of Zen itself. Not that the unity of *haiku* and Zen is complete: for example, unlike Zen, *haiku* seldom acknowledges the ugly, the deceitful or mere brute power.[2] Nevertheless, in matters of method they are all but identical: the presence of things is not achieved by isolating the tea room or the archer or the painting from the world or by denying the world beyond, but rather by creating a moment, a focus, at which disharmonies may be momentarily reconciled and conflicts balanced. The *haiku* is limited to words, but even here the presence it creates relies not on its artistic merit or its rhetorical power but on the self-sufficiency of the object in evokes. This is created not regardless of its subject (the meaningless ideal of so much of formalising) but only independently of it. And again, this independence demands not the abstraction of the one from the other, but rather their identity as mutually constituting and constituted structures.

All these examples of dialectical reason and actuality in practice come from a very narrow range of activity: cognition, transient cultural forms, and so on. They are precious portents, perhaps, but still only portents. As with all other aspects of experience, the duration of the moment is proportionate to the depth *and breadth* of the action of which it is part. By that standard, an experience that is limited to transient subjective illumination must be considered a very limited moment of activity, even if it does manage to encapsulate Blake's world in a grain of sand and heaven in a wild flower. However, as with every other stage in the development of intelligence, dialectical reason must ultimately extend itself across the entire range of activity, from the immediacy of the candle flame to the furthest reaches of nature, history and consciousness.

So the brevity of the events on which even the most sophisticated cognitive and cultural forms such as the *haiku* and the tea ceremony focus is also a measure of the distance between such forms and a truly dialectical *world*. In terms of the preceding argument, the basic condition for completing the development of reason, namely the actual formation of *all* the structures needed to construct and comprehend a truly dialectical world, is by no means fulfilled by such achievements. Indeed, they tend to be antithetical to a social or historical per-

---

[1] For a summary and examples of these three masters of *haiku*, see Blyth (1994: 29ff).

[2] Blyth (1994: 66). Since the 1960s there have been successive more or less convincing discussions of Zen in connection with practically every aspect of everyday life, from flower arranging to motor-cycle maintenance. In some cases the centrality of the actuality of things, of their absolute and unconditional being, seems to be understood, though the quality of the insight offered by such books is extremely variable.

spective. Whatever the enlightenment undoubtedly offered by various forms of mysticism, their lack of an adequate method – theoretical or practical – for dealing with the wider human world, with all its economic, political, ideological and scientific dimensions, precludes their creation of anything more socially expansive than the monastery, the *sutra*, the tradition, the *sangha*, and so on. It is possible to trace exactly how dialectical reason expresses itself in these realms, but it is extremely doubtful how relevant such an exercise would be to grasping the nature and completion of intelligence as a whole.

Conclusions

Although they may seem to address completely different issues, the two sections of this chapter aim to solve a single problem. On the one hand, the massive social and historical developments described in the first half are necessary to grasp the actuality described in the second. On the other, it is only our ability to grasp the actual that proves the maturity and completeness of those social and historical revolutions. Of course, no matter how valid this account may be, it is still inherently inadequate. It is, after all, an account – a theory, a collection of statements *about* history and consciousness, which must – if the present theory is correct – be transcended in the real conscious, historical existence of those who participate in it if it is to be anything more than another philosophical excuse for thinking about existence in place of actually existing.

It is possible to circumvent this to some extent by pursuing a mystical solution, but one does so at the expense of losing any sense – in any sense of the word – of the larger structures, functioning, processes and mechanisms through which the actual comes into existence. Insofar as one constructs one's own private actuality – the most optimistic upshot of any form of mysticism of which I am aware – one will undoubtedly arrive at profound revelations about the nature and meaning of existence; but one will also divorce oneself from the larger ebb and flow of human life that gives it its human richness and flavour. Failing such a 'solution', the answer to the question of when the development of intelligence is complete is as this chapter has implied: when the structures that inform both intelligence and the universe generally are united. Again, this is not quite the paranoid definition it appears to be, given that control of all the complexity, dimensions and scale of the universe is not the same as controlling all its complexities and empirical details. No rational act has ever been based on bean counting. But neither can this development end by retreating into navel-gazing: even our navels are unlikely to put up with that kind of approach, as anyone who has ever suffered from appendicitis would be only too willing to agree.

The other side of this developmental process is equally important, and very easy to miss. It is easy, in principle at least, to see how many structures impinge on the here and now. What is less easy to see is that all activity aims at making sense of the here and now in all its actuality. The diversions, protests and denials of metaphysics notwithstanding, the actual is what activity is about. As, given the definition suggested above ('this, right here, what you are doing now' and all the conditions that currently apply to that activity), one should expect it to be. But more than that, dialectical reason's abolition of so much that formal reason considers *sine qua non* of rational existence – not least metaphysics, and even mental activity – should be considered not so much a sacrifice as a triumph. After all, one does not regret the passing of a child's interest in how words are spelt once the child has learned to spell. In fact, everything we think about (metaphysically or otherwise) we think about solely because it is not self-evident. Likewise, we ponder the grander issues of truth, freedom and existence only because it is not yet self-evident what they mean. We think about them only because, for want of the necessary grasp of structures that inform the here and now, the here and now itself protests that it is not understood. If that were not so, intelligence would be entirely at home in the here and now. But it isn't, so clearly the here and now doesn't work.

Having reached what seems to be the end of the development of intelligence – a curious claim from someone who plainly is nowhere near such exalted heights – it might be sensible to stop here. But there are still many things to be said about this process, not so much to amplify it as to ward off some of the many objections this view of reason is likely to provoke. In particular, there are two main areas of concern.

Firstly, although the reader may be convinced by the broad developmental sweep of the major stages of intelligence defined so far, there seems to be little holding them together. In particular, there must be a suspicion that they express some kind of unfolding biological programme. This would be anathema to the entire sense of the present model of intelligence, for which intelligence's independence of the specificities of any underlying biological structure or functioning is fundamental. Without this independence, it would be impossible to account for intelligence's very ability to deal with the specifically existential character of its existence, which is itself only one part of intelligence's view of actuality in general. Given the centrality of this aspect of human life, not least to dialectical reason, it is important to be able to show that the underlying processes and mechanisms that explain each major stage in the development of intelligence as a whole are themselves rational. This is the topic of the next chapter.

Secondly, there are always many complications to any developmental process, and the development of intelligence is no exception. Indeed, its special unity, rigour and pursuit of consistency notwithstanding, intelligence has a more complicated trajectory than any other structure. As a result, it can easily seem not only as though this single process is really many overlapping processes (thus defeating any notion of intelligence as a single structure) but also that large swathes of human activity are entirely irrational. This impression is, as I shall argue in Chapter 7, largely illusory, and even where the irrationality is real enough, it still does not confound the present account of intelligence as a whole.

6. The Developmental Process

If one compares, for example, the music of Bach and Mozart, you can take a small section of Bach and all the voices in the music will be observing the same kind of movement. That is to say, if the movement is chromatic all of the voices will be moving so; or if the unit or the module is rhythmically the sixteenth note, then if you add up all the voices you get steady movement to the sixteenth note. This brings about a state of 'wholeness' or 'unity'. Which is a great contrast to Mozart. In Mozart, taking just a small section of the music, you are very apt to see not one scale, but I would myself see three. You would see one of the large steps made by arpeggiation of the chords; you know – thirds and fourths; then you would see diatonic scales, making use of the combination of whole steps and half steps; and you would also see chromatic passages; all within a small area sequence. They would generally be going together so that you have differences working together, in Mozart's case, to produce what you might call a harmonious wholeness.

John Cage

The problem of development

In the last few chapters I have tried to show how the development of intelligence proceeds through a sequence of stages that are regular in order, logically progressive, consistent between intelligences and structured as a whole. The factors controlling this process are entirely internal to intelligence itself, and as such they meet the requirements of a theory of maturation without invoking biological factors. Our biology creates the abstract *capacity* for intelligent action – much, I might add, as physics and chemistry provide our bodies with the mechanical and metabolic capacities on which our biology rests – but the *ability* to act intelligently follows solely from the concrete organisation of this capacity through the dual process of abstraction and concretion described at various points in this book.[1]

As such the development of intelligence also relies entirely on the activity of the individual intelligence. This development is driven, not by an organic programme or instinct for clarity or insight, or a semi-innate, semi-automatic maturational process, but by each individual intelligence stumbling about in its

---

[1] Ashley Montague (Montague, 1976: 72ff) provides an analogous argument for a range of specific aspects of human nature such as aggression and territoriality.

own incompetence. At the same time, the developmental process is isolated from any definite motivation by the original separation of sensorimotor techniques from their corresponding affects. Consequently, it does not latch on to any particular train of activity or development, and can be driven by any contradiction that may happen to follow, directly or indirectly, from its initial structural and functional overlaps.

It all sounds like a recipe for developmental chaos, or at least complete arbitrariness. But juxtaposed to the right model of intelligence itself, this is precisely what ensures development's ultimate orderliness. Where there are no constraints whatsoever on the content or context of development, there are no limits on the structures that might result. Conversely, where development can feed on anything that disturbs its equilibrium, it can continue until it has resolved every contradiction in every aspect of subject, object and world, and so realised the full potential of both intelligence and the universe.

It is a startling thought. However, the problem it faces is immediately obvious. Human beings are not the marvellous beasts of infinite power and resource this seems to call for. On the contrary, they are decidedly limited in capacity – a problem that, as the reader will have long since noticed, haunts this entire account. For does not finite capacity necessarily imply finite ability? Unfortunately for the pessimists, no, it does not. We are surrounded by infinite abilities derived from strictly finite capacities. At the level of formal reason in particular, iteration and recursion happily spin infinite series out of the most meagre resources. Any formal equation does as much, given only a little input for its parameters. So does the number system, and so could even the most basic bureaucratic procedure or the simplest computer program. Once a complete system of self-regulating structures is in place – which is to say, once formal reason has been attained – the ability to conjure infinite results from finite resources can be taken for granted, even if, in formal reason's case, they are the 'bad' infinities of the infinite regression and the black hole. As for the 'good' infinities of dialectical reason, I hope the previous chapter made it clear that these arise not from the construction of innumerable instances but from synthesis of a decidedly finite suite of nevertheless all-embracing structures.

Of course, apart from black holes and other physical singularities, all these examples are restricted to intelligence and its more direct products. Does that mean that intelligence's infinite abilities are simply formal intelligence feeding on itself? If so, does that mean that, whatever its triumphs over itself, reason is ultimately making little headway against the *non*-intelligent universe? Fortunately, there is every reason to believe that the same potentially infinite ability extends to intelligence's command of the physical, chemical and biological structures it encounters.

Firstly, there is the evidence of history. We have changed the world beyond recognition, and done so precisely through our command of the full range of physical, chemical and biological structures, processes and mechanisms. We may not be very good at this yet, but there is also ample evidence of our ability to correct mistakes (although not, at the moment, as quickly as we make them). Secondly, there is the evidence of science. Or rather, where is the evidence (liberal relativism, reactionary pessimism and romantic fantasy notwithstanding) of an area of reality science *cannot* comprehend?

It is tempting to respond that we only grasp what we are adapted to grasp, as though science and history were an immense exercise in biological solipsism. Certainly this is a very widespread view. But it still isn't a credible argument, for even if we were positively programmed to ignore the immense tracts of reality that have no bearing on our biological interests, reality is not programmed to ignore us. We do not live in an anthropocentric bubble, with the rest of the universe politely obliging us by keeping well clear. On the contrary, every time we venture out into a wider reality – which is to say, every time we move a muscle – we risk stumbling into a new conflict with uncomprehended reality and into new chasms of error and incompetence. If there are errors and omissions in our grasp of the universe, they are simply bound to generate contradictions in any action they happen to relate to – as our actual experience of history, science and everyday life proves in abundance.

Of course, this proves only that intelligence is very sensitive; it does not show that it is even potentially omnipotent. Nevertheless, there is a third argument that does indeed imply that we have a potential for omnipotence, even if we never realise it. This argument (which has already been mentioned in passing) follows from the logic of intelligence itself and its place within nature and the universe as a whole.

Intelligence is an abstraction from physical, chemical and biological structures and entities.[1] More particularly, it embodies the progressive reconciliation of a huge range of fundamental physical structures and functioning into stable, mobile chemical elements, the reconciliation of a huge range of highly ordered chemical structures and functioning into adaptive, organised organisms and, through the triumph of organic adaptability and individuation, the reconciliation of the most powerful organic structures and functioning into intelligence itself.

So the logic of intelligence already synthesises the logics – the generic internal structures – of all preceding forms of matter and activity. Of course, that does not mean we can see directly into these preceding levels. However, it does mean that the logic of activity is not only compatible with but also capable of embodying and re-incorporating their logics. We may not be able to deduce physics, chemistry and biology from first principles or by navel-gazing, but they are certainly capable of being comprehended by rational activity, given enough opportunity to pursue this task through history, science and everyday existence.

So in principle at least there is no limit to what this finite thing, intelligence, can do. Given the right starting point, one can progress from the extremely limited capacities available to the sensorimotor neonate and conclude with the infinite abilities of dialectical reason. On the other hand, unlike the infants of adapted and particularising species, intelligence's offspring can only realise their potential by passing through a true developmental process of the kind outlined above: there can be no program or instinct for capabilities of this kind, and no side-stepping the need for a thoroughgoing developmental process. And that process can be extremely long and convoluted, as the historical

---

[1] The assertions that follow are defended at length in Robinson (in preparation).

growth of intelligence, whether from infant to sage or from the Pleistocene to the emergence of a totally artificial intelligence, reveals.

In the absence of the conditions needed to *complete* this process – conditions that have been absent in all human societies to date – this may mean no more than that intelligence makes better and better mistakes. But even mistakes are not entirely negative things – would that more of us could make mistakes like a Kant or a Newton. And in the long run, there seems to be no reason to assume that the final completion of intelligence can be put off forever. On the other hand, the very regularity with which the stages of intelligence succeed one another places any account of intelligence in a somewhat paradoxical position. At first glance it looks like a strength, as though it confirmed the account I have presented of intelligence as a great unitary structure. Yet the differences between the stages in its development can be startling. For example, intuitive reason is literally as primitive as it could be and still be intelligent at all. So why should an adult, or even the formal rational adolescent, accept kinship with the toddler? All stages may exhibit the same general logic of subject, object and world, and so agree on the fundamentals of intelligence, but subject, object and world could surely be considered as so abstract a set of structures as to signify almost nothing in the way of substantive continuity. Are they really any more clearly linked to one another than to different kinds of organism, stimulus and environment?

Again, even if the sequence were completely unvarying, regularity does not, in itself, entail any deeper resemblance between the major stages. The stages in a butterfly's development are equally rigid but its underlying mechanisms are the very antithesis of reason's increasingly deliberate and sophisticated rigour. So is the development of intelligence itself any less organically determined than an insect's? Or perhaps they are merely a matter of persistent environmental conditions? Are its stages really the necessary product of a truly profound process of self-regulating change? Or does so insistent a constancy amidst the staggering complexity and variability of human experience, activity and systems betoken precisely the kind of external control over development the present theory is supposed to refute?

In the absence of a more specific argument to the contrary, it is tempting to write off the sequence of intuitive objects, concrete relations, formal systems and dialectical actuality as only superficially rational. In response to this threat, in the present chapter I shall review the inner workings of the major stages themselves, and try to show that their regularity stems from a recurrent, spontaneous and distinctively rational process analogous to the sequence of major stages. This process, far from being in any way external to the workings of intelligence itself, only expresses on the micro-developmental level the functioning of subject, object and world themselves.

In this way the major stages will be shown to consist of dialectical returns to the same basic structure of subject, object and world – the set of structures that defines intelligence itself – even while superseding the limitations of each preceding form of subject, object and world themselves. This analysis will by no means disregard the ox-bows and cataracts of activity and development, though equally it will not deal with them in all their gratuitous complication. It certainly will not imply the pacification of history, so to speak, by denouncing perfectly real forms of disorder and stupidity as illusory. Indeed, no valid theory of rational activity could fail to raise the persistent empirical facts of upheaval and resistance to the level of a rational necessity for periodic violence and revolt. After all, each stage in the development of intelligence consists of the construction of a new world, a completely new attempt to come to terms with the universe. Within such a process, revolutionary change is not so much a natural component of the process as its defining attribute. I hope this chapter will show how simply the whole process is handled – even if not, as history and psychopathology demonstrate in abundant, bloody and sometimes sordid detail, how easily.

The sub-stages of development

When looking at the development of intelligence, it is tempting to regard its major stages as qualitatively different from one another (which they are), and therefore as arising from quite different origins (which they do not). In particular, it is tempting to look for a 'primitive mentality' among children, simple societies, impoverished social classes and others who do not seem to measure up to the onlooker's idea of rationality; to contrast it with more 'advanced' forms of reasoning; and then to assume that each of these forms of thought has a different source, be it as distinct adaptations, as the products of a more or less advanced culture, and so on.

It is certainly the case that there are stages in the development of intelligence, each revealing a different *kind* of reasoning. However, a multiplicity of kinds entails neither multiple sources of reasoning as such nor the existence of insurmountable barriers between the different kinds. These are, after all, *stages* in the development of intelligence, not different kinds of intelligence *as such*. But this still raises the basic paradox of development, namely how anything can become something different by doing no more than persisting in being itself. In the case of non-organisms the answer is relatively straightforward, for many aspects of organic development are controlled by essentially exogenous factors: rather than the organism relying on its own efforts, an environmental trigger activates a dormant control, the expression of a particular suite of genes diverts a basic biological process, and so on. In that respect, the organism does not in fact develop difference out of sameness, but to a very large extent relies on other 'differences' doing the job for it. For intelligence the answer is not so simple or mechanical: there seems to be nothing other than the normal activity of a lower stage available to explain the emergence of the higher.

The solution to this paradox seems to lie in the notion that the development of intelligence is basically *recursive*. The relationship between stages is that each is equivalent to its predecessors, but operates on a higher level; and it reaches this new level of the structures made available at the lower stage embodying themselves through that intelligence's own activity in the world, reflecting on the resulting objects – which are of course also objectifications of those structures of activity – and using the very same structures to construct a yet higher version of itself. As such, each new stage *does* essentially the same things as its predecessors, but does them on a higher plane. In particular, each new stage both overcomes the omissions, conflicts and contradictions to which previous stages were subject and opens up a new potential of which all previous stages were oblivious.

On the abstract plane, this recursiveness can be illustrated by any number of familiar distinctions. For example, it is useful to distinguish between what we know and what we know that we know. Unrecognised knowledge may inform intuitive knowledge with implicit assumptions and perspectives, but only when we can state these assumptions explicitly can we start to use that knowledge actively. But then, being able to use knowledge *actively* is not the same as being able to use it *creatively*, in the sense of being able to deploy it in new circumstances for new purposes. Nor is it the same as being able to use that knowledge rationally, in the sense of being able to explain, articulate, communicate or justify it – or, *a fortiori*, to use it to explain, articulate, communicate or justify anything else. On the other hand, the relationship between all these distinctions is recursive: we establish each new ability by reflecting on its predecessor, using the tools with which each previous ability furnished us, which come to us in a distinct order. What is more, the creation of a completely new stage – and with it, a qualitatively new world-view – is only the culmination of this process.

The complexity the presence of sub-stages adds is developmentally important, as it means that the logical superiority of the later stages over the earlier does not translate directly into functional superiority. From a strictly practical point of view, the earliest sub-stages of a given stage are often out-performed by the last sub-stages of the immediately previous stage. This is because the new principles on which the new stage is based need substantive experience before they can realise their potential. This takes not only time but also the very changes to which the recursions referred to above (and detailed below) give rise. That is why, for example, both a four year-old and an eight year-old child will perform some tasks better than a six year-old: the four year-old has a relatively superficial insight into the problem, but at least they have a good deal of practical experience. The eight year-old has both, of course. But although the six year-old has a better 'theory' than the younger child, he or she has too little experience to turn their superior theory into superior practice.[1]

More concretely, the vehicle for this recursiveness is the developmental *sub-stage*. Each of the major stages in the development of intelligence is divided into six sub-stages. The sub-stages are always and everywhere the same, recapitulated in identical order, repeating the same broad types of strength and weakness, success and failure, even while raising intelligence to new heights. It is therefore impossible to treat even such distantly related forms of intelligence as intuitive and dialectical reason as anything but different levels of the same structure and functioning. These sub-stages are (to adapt a very apt Buddhist terminology) *impulse, doubt, awakening, enlightenment, wisdom* and *certainty*.[2]

---

[1] Eg, Karmiloff-Smith (1992: 84–6).

[2] The origins of this nomenclature notwithstanding, the model that follows is actually a re-interpretation of Piaget's six sub-stage account of sensorimotor development. It differs from Piaget's model in that, by taking the model on to the development of intelligence as a whole, it deals with subject, object and world as the content and context of

Each modulates intelligence's relationship to the things and events it encounters, and so determines the kinds of object it constructs, the world it inhabits and the kind of subject it is.

To summarise this sequence, intelligence starts each new major stage of development with the potential for wholly new forms of activity, and so of producing whole new levels of object. As a result of these new powers, intelligence becomes capable of making an entirely new – and higher – sense of its world and its existence. However, the potential to do this is still unfulfilled at the onset of the stage as a whole, and the task that faces intelligence is to realise that potential. So, at the start of the new stage, things merely exist for the intelligence in question, events merely occur, and so on, without any more specific appearance, selfhood or presence – or, therefore, intelligibility. In other words, intelligence is oblivious of everything definite about its object.

Development then proceeds to a second sub-stage during which it positively recognises that there *is* something there, that something is happening, but it is limited to meagre, one-sided ways of relating to the object, and so of grasping the problems it presents. The second-stage intelligence perceives many different aspects to things and events, but it cannot assemble those aspects into a single coherent picture. In short, there are many forms of activity available to it as an intelligent being, but they have yet to be organised into a single subjectivity (at that stage of development). The second-stage intelligence knows *that* its object exists, but what kind of object or in what sense it exists is another matter.

So, it is in the third sub-stage that intelligence begins to establish an autonomous and integrated control of all the different dimensions of its activity. Hence the emergence of the subject properly so called, with the capacity to

---

development, and not merely as its result. As apparently no more than an extension of an existing process it might easily be taken for granted, but in the present chapter I intend rehearsing some of the features of subject, object and world that cannot be addressed by any account of sensorimotor development.

Unlike its predecessor, the present model is also generalised to all stages and all aspects of development, from the cognitive to the historical. The reader should also note that, given their provenance, it is inevitable that both the semi-Piagetian names for the main stages and the Buddhist names for the sub-stages (which have no Piagetian titles) tend to emphasise the subjective and phenomenological aspects of reason. I hope that my own emphasis on the objective and worldly aspects not only of the developmental process but also of intelligence itself goes some way towards correcting this imbalance. Social structures such as economics, politics, ideology and science are every bit as much a part of intelligence as psychic functions such as judgement, imagination, morality or personality. Gödel and Gautama under the Bodhi Tree may represent peaks of reason, but so do the stirrup, the symphony and the communications satellite.

The Buddhist terminology also understates the constructive nature of development: 'awakening' especially suggests pre-existing structures just waiting to be summoned from their slumbers, which is quite wrong. The structures produced during development are not awakened but constructed by their predecessors. In many respects Piaget's own account is derived from Baldwin (whose intentions were as broad as my own) and Hobhouse, for whom see R.J. Richards (1987) and Langer in Strauss (1988: 68–85).

ask just *how* any given object exists. However, creating a coherent subjectivity does not, in itself, permit the subject to come to terms with the object as such, considered as an object for its own sake. A subject may be able to synthesise the various ways in which its object can be acted upon without yet being able to grasp what the object is, considered independently of the subject's own point of view, interest, purpose, actions, and so on. Indeed, it is still not an object properly so called.

It is only in the fourth sub-stage that the object is grasped for its own sake and the question of *what* it is can be raised. With that, it is as much the object that regulates the subject's attitude and actions as *vice versa*. However, this still does not amount to the ability to grasp an object's detailed content or context explicitly (without, that is, being distracted from or losing track of the object itself). As a result, the intelligence in question has little sense of *why* its object exists, either in the sense that the object's part in a larger picture is grasped or in the sense that the object's detailed inner workings are comprehended well enough to reveal the logic of its own proper actions.

Only in the fifth stage is the object grasped on its own terms, for it is only then that the internal and external order of its object existence is finally comprehended, and only then that the changes and the possibilities of which it is capable are realised. On the other hand, not even the most thorough grasp of these *dimensions* of an object's existence and activity can lead to the ability to construct that object as a genuine totality.

However, once the various dimensions on which any given object exists have been synthesised, the resulting totalisation of all forms of activity and existence provides a functional and structural matrix within which any given object can be grasped in its own right. What is more, those dimensions and relationships being the same for all objects of the same general kind, it becomes possible to assemble whole swathes of previously disconnected objects into a more comprehensive totality. And that is precisely what the sixth stage of development accomplishes. With that, objects finally become self-evident (at this developmental stage), and the subject can let out a triumphant 'it is'. The process of reconstruction is complete, the new stage becomes truly self-evident, and the need to act out, test or even justify its new axioms disappears.

However, the construction of such a larger, more or less self-regulating totality of subject and objects can only be described as the creation of a new world. And that in turn can only mean the appearance of totally new forms of structure, and so the onset of a complete new stage.

Impulse

The primary characteristic of the first sub-stage, impulse, is not merely not knowing; it is not knowing that one does not know. Unaware even of our impulsiveness, we encounter things and perform acts, but take no account of them except to respond glibly to their most egocentrically construed and immediate appearances. We experience them – if this level of encounter can be called an 'experience' – solely to the extent that they happen to come our way. However, to stride out into this cloud of unknowing, as any active but impulsive intelligence is bound to do, is to invite conflict: conflict between what we take for granted and how things really stand; conflict between the different skills and schemata we implicitly bring to bear through our impulsive actions; conflict between the higher contradictions of an implicitly incoherent subjectivity, inconsistent objects and our lack of even the slightest sense of how to reconcile the two sides; and so on.

Our ability to overcome such contradictions, be it by detour, by compensation, by anticipation or, best of all, by raising our world to a level where they simply do not occur, is the essential practical yardstick of maturity. At the stage of impulse, when we suffer from, yet disregard, the pitfalls and blind alleys we get ourselves into, there is no possibility of avoiding even the most superficial trap or illusion. What is more, being too impulsive even to detect our problems, we are ensnared not only by illusory objects but also by the delusion that our objects are unproblematic. If our impulsiveness were acted out in a vacuum, there would, of course, be no escape. But even the most self-satisfied impulsiveness is eventually forced to go beyond itself. For the impulsive intelligence is impulsive only from the point of view of the major stage this intelligence is just entering; from the point of view of the stage it has just left behind, it is fully armed with a comprehensive system of subject, object and world. Even intuitive reason proceeds from the elementary intelligence synthesised during sensorimotor development. There is therefore always ample scope for further development, not only in the negative sense that intelligence still has much to make sense of but also in the more positive sense that it has ample resources to carry out that task.

From the point of view of this new, higher stage then, the achievements of the old, lower stage may be fundamentally flawed – that is after all why intelligence finds itself emerging into the vast echoing chambers of a new stage of development. But however immature they may be, the skills and experience inherited from the previous stage also ensure a continued active overlapping of structures and functioning even while intelligence is still too ignorant to realise it has a problem.

Doubt

The resolution of the structural and functional overlaps between the structures with which a new stage begins creates a synthesis of at least local structures of activity. Such local structures are effective within their own realm, but this realm is not defined in any way, and its own overlaps with the realms of other second-level structures leads to routine but still unintelligible conflicts between the very structures that emerged from the resolution of the previous round of conflicts. Hence the primary characteristic of this new era: *doubt*.

As its name suggests, the onset of doubt does not signal a complete end to impulse. Although objects and events have only to persist in being themselves (which is to say, to persist in being more than figments of the impulsive subject's trivial imagination) to drive our various impulses into contradiction with one another, they do not call attention to themselves directly. Indeed, in the sub-stage of doubt the contradiction remains external to and unrecognised even by the activity currently in progress. From the developing intelligence's point of view, the only problem it faces is that things keep disrupting work in progress. They are not problems in themselves; they simply generate local dislocations as incidental as they are accidental. Consequently, even when the developing intelligence has overcome its impulsiveness far enough to *continue* its activity, the multiplicity of the local structures this overcoming engenders may create a wide range of more or less stable sensitivities and skills, but they remain entirely local. The purely parochial grasp of *aspects* or *instances* of objects this advance confers still cannot guarantee the effectiveness, stability or mobility of activity *as a whole*.

So the doubting intelligence may notice that there *is* a problem – which is more than impulsiveness could manage – but because it has only a one-sided grasp of things, it is a problem without determinate content, significance or solution. The only approach open to doubt is pragmatic, conventional and eclectic, based on trial and (as often as not) error. There are simply certain things that one does or one fails to do, but little sense of how this happens and none at all of why.

Of course, it could hardly be otherwise: given that they assume a grasp of the relationship *between* different kinds of structure or functioning, *disequilibrium* and *contradiction* are necessarily unintelligible (ie, incapable of objectification, internalisation and rationalisation) from a strictly parochial point of view. So any of the second sub-stage's locally effective but globally incoherent structures are naturally stymied. If they were not, doubt would consist of no more than a brief hesitation while intelligence took its bearings, whereas at this stage it represents a straightforward breakdown in activity. So, although in doubt the fundamental problem of the current major stage has begun to express itself, the actual contradiction that defines it has yet to materialise. Indeed, the problem has yet to crystallise enough even to have a name. All that is guaranteed is that the doubting intelligence will be doubtful, accompanied perhaps by unease and malaise, frustration and evasion, depression, even rage.

This severely constrains the doubting intelligence's abilities. Even with systematic guidance from a more advanced intelligence, it cannot get beyond cobbling together locally effective but parochially conceived and globally unsustainable tools and techniques for handling isolated problems, as and when they present themselves. What is more, having been assembled without reference to one another, these temporary measures are more than likely to fall into turmoil among themselves. Like intuitive reason's interminable juggling, a doubting intelligence may know enough to keep things in motion but it knows nothing of the things juggled as they exist in themselves.

Indeed, even its own activity has no enduring order to it. And for lack of even the clear systematic organisation of its own activity, intelligence hasn't even a clear sense of its own activity, over and above the succession of acts in which it is engrossed. A doubting intelligence is plunged into circumstances that may be managed but not comprehended. Its earnest efforts to produce a stable and mobile solution of the kind it was accustomed to producing at the previous stage not only fail frequently but it is its own incoherence that immobilises and destabilises it.

Awakening

However, the structural and functional overlaps from which the development of intelligence began continue to ensure that, by bringing these quasi-solutions into opposition with one another, they inject their mutual incomprehension directly into the heart of intelligence itself. Hence the rapid formation of larger and larger super-structures out of these initially very confused and isolated elements. Gradually, the dissonant and amorphous monomaniacs with which doubt begins synthesise themselves into a more harmonious community.

Finally, by assembling a single integrated structure of activity out of all the diverse ways it has learned to express itself, intelligence establishes a new, higher form of *subject*. With this development of a single internal structure capable of handling complete sequences of activity, intelligence *awakens* to the larger 'how' of things rather than merely responding to them through piecemeal adjustments and manipulations. That is not to say that this subject has any grasp of the *nature* of its objects: at this sub-stage 'how' is limited strictly to its objects' ability to support intelligence's now unified internal inspirations. It does not include any consideration of the objects themselves. A single structure of activity may now be in place, but the unity and integrity of action and experience are strictly limited to their subjective aspect, ensuring the coherence (and so, to a great extent, the continuity) of activity without constructing or conserving objects properly so called. Still less can objects be justified, in the sense of being accorded a place in a yet larger scheme of things – the world of which the subject and its objects are only moments. In other words, although the question of 'how' can now be posed, not only the answer to the question 'why' but the question itself continue to elude intelligence.

But at least the awakened intelligence confronts the multiplicity of things and events from a unitary point of view. So now, instead of being limited to merely dealing with one thing after another, intelligence can engage in activities that extend well beyond the empirical limits of the here and now. But by the same token, it is forced to deal with the fact that things have their own systematic complexities, which may not manifest themselves all at once or in a completely transparent way. Many may never reveal themselves to intelligence at all without being actively rooted out. As a result, the syntheses the awakened intelligence will develop through its encounters will gradually be moulded around real objects of various kinds – even if, as is inevitably the case for the lower stages of intelligence, the intelligence in question has no explicit category either for 'object' or for the structures that regulate the relationships between objects or categories or relationships.

Enlightenment

So intelligence enters the fourth, enlightened sub-stage of intelligence, when it recognises the *objective* nature of events and things. In contrast to the instrumentalism and pragmatism that the merely awakened intelligence adopts towards its objects, the structures with which intelligence now begins to acquaint itself are based not on what it can handle (or get away with) but on a grasp of the existence of things in their own right. That is, intelligence's previously egocentric sense of the 'how' of things is enriched by a more permanent conception, based on *what* they are, independently of how they can be exploited, evaded or otherwise manipulated. In this way the awakened intelligence's pragmatic prejudice that things are true because they work begins to be transformed into the realist premise that they work because they are true.

This is still not a definitive solution to the problem of subject, object and world, of course. It is not even a complete articulation of the puzzle posed by objects. In particular, to grasp something in its own right (ie, to recognise that it has its own proper existence, in itself, independently of the grasping or of the subject that grasps it) is not quite the same as grasping it on its own terms (ie, *as* it exists in itself). As the purely preliminary character of Buddhist enlightenment suggests, this sub-stage represents no more than a glimpse of this particular object at this particular point in time and space – a glimpse that is lost again as soon as the situation changes. Although the object may be subject to a kind of accounting, this account is purely empirical.

So an enlightened apprehension of particular things is only a promise of the certainty with which all things will be viewed at the end of the current stage, and the promise is still far from being fulfilled. Indeed, it is highly conditional (though intelligence does not yet recognise this fact), for it is limited to isolated, dimensionless experiences of objects of indisputable objectivity, but the precise nature of their objective character is still imponderable. The object exists, but the subject's sense of that existence is undifferentiated beyond lists of descriptive attributes. It is apprehended but not yet comprehended.

So even enlightenment is crucially superficial. In particular, neither the internal nor the external relations that determine its actual existence have yet been grasped. Consequently, any least change in content and context may push the object out of the subject's grasp, and the enlightened intelligence lacks the insight into its objects that it needs to bring them back into line. So the enlightened intelligence is confined to the empirical plane, at least as far as the current stage in the development of intelligence is concerned, even though its premises are far from empirical in the usual sense of the word. Because the total matrix of objects and object relationships, at once broader and more profound than even an enlightened intelligence realises, remains unrecognised, particular objects can be sustained only through vigilance and effort. The enlightened intelligence only *establishes* the new level of object that corresponds to the current major stage; it cannot yet reflect on or comprehend objects at that new level.

Wisdom

But as everywhere else in the development of intelligence, it is most surely revolutionised by persisting in being itself. In applying its new enlightened standard of reasoning in terms of its empirical objects to the entire range of activity, a great range of new events and things is encountered, established and synthesised. The same things and events will support different forms of objectification when required to support the same kinds of activity in different contexts, in connection with different objectives, and so on. However, managing the structural and functional overlaps this creates requires more than the empirical grasp that comes with enlightenment. On the other hand, it is only a

little more, and can be comprehended by comprehending the overlaps themselves by means of the normal cycle of objectification and internalisation. With
that, the intersections between objects, reflecting both the internal and external
relations of the corresponding things and events, also come to be comprehended in the form of the dimensions on which they collectively exist and operate.

This has a double benefit. Firstly, it becomes possible to actively track, sustain and control a single object through all its manifestations, or, conversely, to
actively alter it as required. Secondly, by establishing definitions, criteria and
methods for establishing and managing functional, conceptual and other
equivalences, a group of related objects can be managed jointly by virtue of
their mutual relationships, rather than each single object having to be managed
separately. And it is only necessary to ask persistently enough 'what' something is – the key question of the fourth sub-stage – and how the various answers for different objects relate to one another to eventually identify all the
different ways these benefits can be realised. Hence not only the generation of
many more enlightening glimpses of and insights into particular objects but
also the formation of a systematic skill in achieving and sustaining a stable and
mobile vision of things, whatever the prevailing conditions. When we are
enlightened enough to truly seek the 'why?' behind all these 'hows' and
'whats', we are rewarded with the fifth sub-stage in the development of intelligence, namely *wisdom*. In particular, by developing the capacity to transform
and coordinate objects wisely, intelligence gains control not only over the objects it encounters but also over the conditions of its own existence. For the first
time it becomes capable not only of positing itself as an object (already
achieved during the sub-stage of enlightenment) but also of positing itself as
one object among many, existing not only as the author or observer of other objects but also in a positive relationship to them, and even existing on the same
terms.[1]

Conversely, as soon as the wise intelligence gains access to the relationships
governing its objects (and so its relationships to them), it begins to apprehend
new dimensions to activity, be it its objects' or its own. For example, since its
objects can now be sustained even when they take on new forms and enter into
new relationships, intelligence acts for the first time (during the present stage,
that is) in terms of dynamic processes rather than static outcomes. Otherwise
mutually external sequences of products and processes can be coordinated into
projects capable of being planned and executed in an organised and controlled
manner. Constancy of perspective and approach become the norm, and what
were once moments of pure contingency and arbitrariness may remain puz-
zling, but at least now they take the form of explicit dilemmas definable in
terms of distinct options and alternatives. Hence the calm mastery of events,
the exuberant but never manic games, the experimentation and the deepening
self- and other-knowledge, through which the wise intelligence revels in its
world.

---

[1] Hence also the first possibility of a number of ethical qualities, notably (as Nagel, 1978,
demonstrated) prudence and altruism.

Nor is it only the subject's attitude to its objects that is changed by its entry into wisdom. The subject itself is changed, adding what can only be termed an ideal aspect. Not that wisdom leads to idealism in the metaphysical sense; however, because wisdom permits the construction of objects in terms of explicit relationships, including relationships to ideal but previously isolated objects such as norms and values, intelligence takes yet another step towards freeing itself from domination by either empirical things and events or its own transient position, status or mood. Without sacrificing the empirical, wisdom's abiding attention to transformation and coordination permits it to produce objects that conform to definite standards and procedures. During the intuitive and concrete stages these will be limited to empirical exemplars, prototypes and the like, serving as practical paragons of the object as it should be rather than offering the purely abstract index of adequacy that emerges at this point in the development of formal reason. Nevertheless, even the meanest wisdom allows comparisons and analogies between the actual and the ideal that are capable of generating notions of 'ought' and 'might' and 'should', and thus a vast range of rational tools with which to guide activity.

Certainty

Yet not even wisdom is final. In fact it has a definite negative aspect. Although the fifth sub-stage permits the wise intelligence to address the question of the content and context of the world, it still does not really consider the world *as* a world. However easily wisdom formulates and resolves individual conundrums concerning the conditions of its existence, the world itself – the condition of all existences and the existence of all conditions – remains a mystery. The answer to any single problem may have become obvious, even the object of idle jest, experiment and play, but why are things problematic at all? Beyond reason's now explicitly insightful and critical comprehension of this or that particular aspect of existence, what is the nature of the world, considered not only as the empirical *sum* but also as the structural *totalisation* of this's and that's, of objects and aspects, structures and relationships? How, in short, can intelligence achieve the level of comprehension where such questions simply fall away, restoring the certainty and assurance with which the stage began, but on a new, higher, plane?

Fortunately, reason at the stage of wisdom already possesses the resources needed to solve this mystery, and it has only to elaborate itself to the full to achieve that certainty. The same *abstraction* of internal and external relations will also, by permitting wisdom to *concretise* these relationships back into every corner of its world, provide the conditions for the eventual totalisation of all objects in all their relationships. Within this final totality, objects and events no longer present any difficulties, at least not at the level of the present major stage. To say 'it is' is no longer an assertion of external fact, apparently true but actually supported by nothing more than empirical evidence and *ad hoc* inferences, but rather the self-expression of a fully internalised, and therefore absolutely unconditional, reality.

The 'it is' of the sixth sub-stage is therefore infinitely more necessary, infinitely more obvious and infinitely more compelling than that of any predecessor. For it is now intelligence's world itself that embodies the definitive solution to all the problems with which the stage as a whole began. There is no doubt as to intelligence's own place in its world, nor regarding the structures or functions of any of its objects (again, as far as the present stage in the development of intelligence is concerned). So the problems from which the need and drive for a new stage of development originally issued are not so much solved as abolished. Where there was once ignorance even of one's own impulsiveness, now there is not only certainty but also self-certainty; which is to say, a certainty grounded in the internalisation within intelligence of all the conditions on which its activity and existence, and so the possible conditions of its confidence in itself, in its actions and in things and events, rest.

That is not necessarily the end of the matter. This new world may have rendered self-evident all the problems out of which the newly completed stage originally arose, but can we not now pose a new form of the original question, more appropriate to the new insights accrued during this stage, namely, what does that new, higher self-evidence *itself* mean? It is correct to describe it as *self-evidence*, and there is also a sense in which it is completely self-sufficient, so long as one does not push it beyond its own proper logic. Yet intelligence is not likely to be left to 'its own proper logic' for long. When describing it as 'self-sufficient', the self in question is no more than the current totalisation of intelligence, which is to say, subject, objects and world, and this totality cannot be guaranteed to be *absolutely* complete or correct by the standard of the *universe* – the presumptive ideal of the development of intelligence. Has the universe still further depths to reveal? Have subject, object and world themselves still more profound implications to unleash? What higher impulsiveness is it that this new certainty expresses? In short, is there yet *another* stage to development?

On the other hand, should a new stage ensue, one should not expect the entry into it to be quite the same as the transition between any other two sub-stages within a single stage. This is not because of any mysterious difficulty in transferring between two stages: this is after all only another transition between sub-stages, even if it is between the last sub-stage of the lower stage and the first of the higher, and the mechanism and process is certainly the same as for other transitions. However, there is an important difference in the content. The final product of the last sub-stage is a new world, whereas the problem that confronts intelligence during the opening sub-stages of the next stage is the general inadequacy of this world to the next level of reality. Unlike the transition between two sub-stages of a single stage, *this* situation can only be considered as a major crisis, and the transition revolutionary, regardless of whether this expresses itself in the form of 'the terrible twos' or tumbrels in the streets.

Practical implications

One child drew a (stick-like) figure of her mother. I asked her what the drawing was and she told me that it was her mother in the dining room. Then she immediately went back to the paper and drew a little square with a small line in it, near the figure's head. This later addition was the light switch in the dining room, she said. In this example, one can imagine how the separate representative schemata (her mother, light switch) and the context of the dining room were kept separate but, in the child's mind, came into 'contact' with one another through the external medium of the paper (the drawing). Thus, this child was composing, on the paper (ie, 'out there'), a composite representation more significant than the hitherto separate representations that she was capable of in a more mental, or internalised, manner.

André Hopper[1]

Development as dialectical recapitulation

A number of points can be made about this progression from impulse to certainty. Firstly, as the recurrence of the same sub-stages demonstrates, each major stage is in many ways a reworking of its predecessors and an anticipation of what is still to come. For example, it is always instructive to watch how ancient writings are 'reinterpreted' as not only the parochialism and irrelevance but also the logical immaturity of their literal message becomes more and more obvious, leaving metaphor and fundamentalism the only options.

This process of recapitulation also explains two otherwise peculiar and apparently deeply irrational manifestations of reason. Firstly, a child who asks for an explanation of something beyond its cognitive reach may be strangely satisfied by an adult's response, even when the answer is plainly beyond their understanding. Is this mere childishness, or perhaps submission to the adult's authority? Not wholly. Differences in maturity notwithstanding, the structural correspondences between successive levels enable the child to assemble out of the adult's reply a message to which they can attach some meaning. It is not, of course, the adult's intended meaning, as a few pointed questions to the child will quickly establish, and the child is soon lost in the ramifications of what they have only superficially 'understood'. Rather, a resemblance to things the child *does* find intelligible is detected. Nevertheless, the original acceptance is a legitimate cognitive act, however quickly the child's own efforts to remember what it has heard dismember it instead.

The reciprocal of this recapitulation can be found in the seeming wisdom in the child – out of the mouths of very babes and sucklings indeed. However, such flashes of apparent wisdom are again only misapplications of a lower level insight to a higher level problem. This time the result is at least potentially more positive, since the ability of the adult audience to supply, elaborate and sustain the higher level interpretation the real explanation requires is infinitely greater than the child's own. If the child is pressed, its 'wisdom' soon turns into nonsense, yet the original 'insight' is no less a clue to the truth, once it has been shored up with the scaffolding of a higher form of reason.

On the other hand, the same appearance of maturity beyond its years can encourage a romantic cult of the innocent, be it fool, child or noble savage. Children especially have gone in and out of fashion as icons of innocence, but more recently they have been ousted by hunter-gatherers. These peoples are

---

[1] Hopper, pers. comm.

supposed to be in closer touch with reality, nature, the Earth, themselves, and so on than we industrial savages.[1] Yet hunter-gatherer cultures typically rest on totemism, suffer appalling rates of infant mortality, have depressing life expectancies[2] and frequently employ an incendiarist agriculture, often practised on an astounding scale.[3]

In fact everyone seems to be credited with more 'maturity' of one kind or another than the peoples of industrial societies. Nevertheless, if 'indigenous peoples' are close to nature, nature probably does not always enjoy their proximity quite as much as modern 'noble savage' mythology supposes. Magellan did not name Tierra del Fuego for its volcanoes, the salinisation of Mesopotamia and the Indus valley began millennia before the first hint of industrialisation, and it is perhaps no accident that the virtual extinction of large land animals in the Americas, New Zealand, Madagascar and perhaps Australia coincided with the arrival of the very peoples we now eulogise for their sensitivity to nature.[4] Of course, later invaders have scarcely been innocent, but from a strictly ecological point of view we have operated...

> ... not simply as adversaries, with the indigenes passive, the whites active, but as two waves of invaders of the same species, the first acting as the shock troops, clearing the way for the second wave, with its more complicated economies and greater numbers.[5]

If this is the work of innocents, it is not a form of innocence one would expect to stand up in a court of law. Indeed, if their romantically inclined apologists are right about the special insights provided by a hunter-gatherer existence, they certainly cannot plead ignorance. More generally, the cult of the innocent is usually mistaken, even if *we* have no grounds to plead not guilty.

A further apparently contrary manifestation of reason this recapitulation explains is the frequency with which forms of activity that are supposed to be reserved for a higher stage seem to appear during the previous stage. Leaving

---

[1] Even at its height the cult of the noble savage was less than universal: for a brilliant (and equally ill-informed) drubbing, see Dickens' 1853 essay, 'The Noble Savage', quoted at length in Carey (1999: 239–45).

[2] Johnson and Earle (1987).

[3] For further comments of the deliberate and routine nature of pre-colonial incendiarism and its ecological consequences, see Crosby (1986) and Goudsblom (1992). Pyne (2001) provides a wide ranging review of our relationship to fire. Goudsblom also emphasises its social and psychic impact on the incendiarists and their neighbours. Note that, despite its unsavoury reputation, slash-and-burn agriculture is typically a skilled and carefully applied technique, and a potentially sustainable agriculture system (Goudsblom, 1992: 47–54). Nevertheless, it is always liable to end in the exhaustion of the soil, from which springs the need for more intense forms of exploitation, and so violence and oppression.

[4] Davis (1987: 99ff). It should be emphasised that alternative interpretations are at least equally compelling. For a summary, see Goudie (1992: 142–6) or Megarry (1995: 256-265). On other aspects of the damage done by pre-industrial cultures, see Goudie (1990: 323; also pp. 28, 107–8 and 125–6).

[5] Crosby (1986: 280).

aside the many spurious cases, this is still a widespread phenomenon, and taken at face value clearly refutes the idea of well-structured stages in the development of intelligence.

For example, Piaget's genetic epistemology – on which the present model of development is, of course, partly based – has often been criticised on the grounds that many of the developments that supposedly typify a given stage actually make their appearance significantly earlier than the standard Piagetian timetables prescribe. But this is only a legitimate criticism if, for example, all strictly concrete activity were strictly limited to the stage of concrete reason – as, at first sight, it clearly should be. But the stage of concrete reason (in Piaget's terminology, 'concrete operations') consists of the gradual *working out* of the implications of a concrete subject, object and world taken as a whole. As such it presupposes the presence of the complete suite of intelligent structures right from the beginning of the stage, even if, as the previous section showed, they are only present in the most primitive form.

But where do concrete reason's subject, object and world themselves come from? As Chapters 2 and 3 show, they are constructed by intuitive reason, and are more or less present as intuitive reason unfolds. In fact that is what, in a sense, intuitive reason *is* – the development of concrete reason. If the previous section of this chapter is correct, then by sub-stage three of intuitive reason intelligence has created concrete reason's basic form of subjectivity; by sub-stage four its form of object; and by sub-stage six a concrete world is in place, though with all the limitations the previous section implied. So it is only to be *expected* that the abilities attributed to concrete reason should be foreshadowed by intuitive reason. Of course, each sub-stage also *lacks* many things that will be routinely available when the stage is truly complete. Mostly notably, it is only very late in the development of a given stage that the child can not only *know* things and *solve* certain problems but also *justify* that knowledge and those solutions. And so on for each stage and sub-stage in the development of intelligence, with each stage being anticipated – if only superficially – by its predecessor. They are in an important sense *all* analogies of one another, but at the same time they are *no more than* analogies; anticipation is therefore as natural as it is deceptive.

Hence the problem with the of the experiments that seem to refute Piaget. Very often they consist of seeing whether pre-concrete children can carry out standard concrete rational tasks if provided with various ways of simplifying them – by reducing their logical complexity, by *not* asking for explicit justifications for the subject's conclusions, by setting them in a more familiar cultural context, by coaching the subjects in the relevant language, and generally by providing helpful cultural or psychological scaffolding. But don't these techniques also provide the means intuitive intelligence would need to carry out the required tasks if they were already armed with one or more of the basic structures of concrete reason? So these experiments do not refute Piaget; rather, they illustrate how the developmental process works by a process of recapitulation – and, by showing how much practical assistance a child at a previous stage actually needs, how limited the various anticipations really are.[1]

---

[1] For a comprehensive defence of Piaget against a huge range of criticisms, especially

The practical expression of intelligence

Clearly, the sequence of sub-stages should not be identified with merely asking bigger or more sophisticated questions (beyond the strictly metaphorical sense in which all rational acts pose questions). The resolution of purely verbal or even intellectual conflicts is not the acme of reason. In this context, impulse, doubt, awakening, enlightenment, wisdom and certainty are not to be seen as purely cognitive states: the same sub-stages and features are equally present in organisations, disciplines, industries, methodologies, institutions and all other embodiments of intelligence. Although intelligence certainly commits itself to a certain degree of intellectualism, it does not oblige itself to become an academic. Marx's famous thesis, that 'The philosophers have only interpreted the world in various ways; the point however is to change it',[1] could as easily be the motto of intelligence as of revolutionary socialism. Furthermore, this need for practical expression (which is really only an expression of the drive towards externalisation) is true not only of the *results* of intelligent development – machines in factories are as much the product of reason as the scientific theories behind them – but also of the developmental *process*. Even strictly cognitive development relies on practical expression, especially in its intuitive and concrete phases.

This brings me to the main point of the present section, which is that the logical coherence of the sequence of sub-stages described in the previous section would be worth very little were it not for the fact that the same sub-stages show themselves in all kinds of rational activity. For example, it does not seem to me coincidental that the emergence of great empires often seems to follow the same sequence of six sub-stages as children developing a knack for solving jigsaw puzzles. In the former case, the sequence is from city states to transient confederations to a more or less permanent central power based on military and political but not economic force, to an integrated 'nation state', which then adds a web of interconnected colonies and eventually becomes a full-scale empire – a new world. The sequence for jigsaws is explained below, but as the reader will see, it is essentially the same, at least from a logical point of view.

It is true that, in most cases, the imperial sequence does not unfold quite as evenly as skill with jigsaw puzzles (although in the cases of ancient Mesopotamia, Rome and the British empire, it came remarkably close), but the differences are largely traceable to the fact that empires are subject to rather greater practical constraints, such as insuperable structural or functional limits set either by nature or invasion by neighbouring societies. These factors seldom upset the development of an aptitude for jigsaw puzzles. In fact, examples proliferate in every sphere of human activity.[2]

---

the relationship between justified and unjustified knowledge, see Smith (1993).

[1] Marx, *Theses on Feuerbach*, no. 11, in Marx (1975: 423).

[2] For example, Jarman (1976) has suggested what seems to be a characteristic sequence of six functional sub-stages in the exploitation of animals. Goudie's five-stage sequence of human interference in the natural environment may, with some modification, provide another instance (Goudie, 1990: 25–6). MacDonagh's account of the British gov-

As the following paragraphs will show, this sequence is repeated again and again across the entire spectrum of intelligent activity. However, I shall limit myself here to just a few sketches. I hope that readers will treat them purely as illustrations, and overlook the rather eclectic mixture!

The development of knowledge

My first example comes from the development of knowledge. Like all other rational structures, knowledge seems to proceed through the same six sub-stages (within any major stage), and these sub-stages are then repeated at each subsequent stage. Initially, our impulsiveness prevents anything but the most elementary, unacknowledged *data* from being registered. Things are noticed, but they make no sense and what is noticed generates neither insight nor criticism. This is the stage of the most naïve *empiricism*, if not quite in the philosophical sense then certainly in the sense that our approach to things is completely uninsightful and uncritical.

Of course, a combination of the same kinds of activity carried out on various objects and the application of a variety of structures of activity to the same object quickly allow a second level of knowledge to emerge, namely knowledge of *fact*, when a certain sense can be made of this or that isolated particular. This is the stage of *positive* knowledge. As with the parallel sub-stage of doubt, 'the facts' permit intelligence to register its own impulsiveness, but the latter's notorious fragmentation, heterogeneity and slippery one-sidedness prevent the doubting intelligence from sustaining a consistent or coherent position.

Hence the characteristic difficulty of fitting raw facts into a larger framework. Indeed, taken by itself, even the largest assemblage of facts would not enable intelligence to verify the completeness or even the empirical correctness of its 'world view', such as it is. Fortunately, the subsequent period of awakening allows reason to transcend particular things and events, and so to make a broader sense of these facts. This is the sub-stage of *information*, of *systemic* knowledge, when all branches of the subject's activity can be informed of the mutual implications of previously isolated facts for the whole range of things and events on which intelligence acts.

But even at this sub-stage, when its knowing as a whole begins to be properly regulated, reason cannot be said to have knowledge properly so called, even with regard to things and events taken one at a time. It can be very knowing, yet there is nothing in particular about which it can be said to know anything in particular. A consistent awareness or way of knowing is not the same as knowledge of any actual thing. Hence the eventual emergence of a fourth

---

ernment's typical response to 'social evils' during the nineteenth century has a similar ring (quoted in Kamenka, 1989: 123; see also p. 124 for a further instance). I suspect that different forms of humour also represent different levels of maturity. Even the process of the empirical observation and analysis of micro-social activity can be organised into a broadly similar sequence (Erickson and Schultz, in Cole *et al.*, 1997: 26–9). Karmiloff-Smith (1992) presents a model for the transformation of implicit into explicit knowledge that is broadly similar. And so on.

sub-stage of empirical knowledge: the sub-stage of *apprehension*, of knowledge of discrete things and events rather than merely a unified perspective. This is knowledge in its *definite* form. But even the apprehension of defined objects is scarcely adequate, as its link to the very partial and transient achievements of enlightenment implies. In particular, such knowledge is limited to the definition of the object regarded as an undifferentiated whole; not only its content and context but also the specific dimensions of its existence and activity remain undefined, indeed indefinable.

On the other hand, the eventual synthesis of the various ways in which single things and events can be apprehended ensures that isolated definitions are soon superseded by genuinely relational knowledge, of *relativity*, from which the wisdom of the fifth sub-stage proceeds. But relativity is also the counterpart of scepticism, reflecting its fundamentally undecidable character. So, although entirely capable of informing an indefinitely extended stream of activity, even relativity hesitates in the face of the world as a whole.

In fact, that is precisely the problem: relativity can do no better than treat the world as such as a *whole*, of which it may have a general sense but whose integral character still eludes it. Intelligence may travel its world with the utmost facility and aplomb, but it is still obliged to take only the highways and byways it has managed to chart. That is, it knows the dimensions of every particular thing and event, but it cannot comprehend their *totality*, which alone gives the world unity on its own terms and frees intelligence to travel precisely as it wishes. But as ever, intelligence presses on, feeding on the very gaps and conflicts to which preceding sub-stages were prey. Eventually it recognises that its world really is a totality, and not just a latticework of relations and dimensions. But what could be the counterpart in knowledge of a final, spontaneous, certain activity? Surely it can only be *dialectic*, which is to say, *truth* itself, for surely only that which is true can possibly proceed with completely warranted certainty and spontaneity? All else would surely fall foul of its own hubris.

The history of software engineering

A second example comes from the history of software engineering, past and future, particularly the structure and functionality of software languages, which also seem destined to pass through all six sub-stages.

The first form of software – barely recognisable as such – was machine code. From the point of view of the problems it was designed to solve, machine code could not be more like the first sub-stage in the development of intelligence: completely focused on pragmatically manipulating isolated elements of the machine at the lowest level of detail, such 'software' provides not even the simplest tools for even completely parochial tasks. Insofar as any functional consequences followed from this manipulation, they were entirely the achievement of the individual programmer. With the appearance of 'assembly languages', the direct manipulation of registers and addresses is replaced by commands from which sequences of machine states could be executed automatically, but as with the second sub-stage of any form of intelligent activity, the software is still limited to discrete functions such as arithmetic operations and data transfers, and it is still tied to particular kinds of hardware.

However, once complete sets of assembler instructions can themselves be routinely assembled, the aptly named 'third generation' languages ('3GLs') emerge, capable (in principle) of solving any computational problem and of running on any machine. Indeed, at this third sub-stage, knowledge of underlying technology is theoretically irrelevant.[1] As one would expect at this level, such software is still incapable of operating directly in terms of the objects – that is, on real information and decisions – on which the solution to 'real' problems rests. This must await the appearance of 'fourth generation' and 'object-oriented' languages. But even at this fourth sub-stage, when the functional building blocks of the solution are given by the development environment rather than produced by the developer (in the form of generic 'frameworks' of reusable compatible components, for example), this is all that is given. It is still up to the developer to produce the solution itself, particularly the complex dimensions that define and regulate the content and context of the data and processes needed to achieve the result. The pre-defined information and control may be suited directly to the problem set, but not the wisdom needed to solve any but a strictly circumscribed set of 'boiler-plate' problems. What is more, the developer must still complete all the remaining stages in building the final solution. This includes not only defining the functions whose execution would solve the original problem but also creating those functions out of the building blocks available and implementing them in a physical system.

However, the fifth stage in the development of software languages sees even these problems overcome. Here true functional languages appear, creating in one direction sophisticated 'office' suites capable of performing complete multi-functional tasks seamlessly, and in the other, more 'dimensional' and matrix-based methods, tools and languages that permit IT systems to shift the focus of software engineering from the individual units of information and decision to variants and relationships between such units. This allows the developer to operate rather like a manager, who solves problems by assigning them to the relevant specialist. So, just as I do not need to understand dentistry to know how I can solve my dental problem, but only that this is the kind of problem dentists solve, so developer-managers do not need to understand the 'skills' offered by each function in a programming language, just so long as they understand how each function is *used* and what can be *achieved* by invoking it.

Finally, at the sixth and final stage (final because this is the point at which software begins to merge with artificial intelligence), the developer only has to state the problem correctly for the software to derive the solution. Of course,

---

[1] As one would expect of such a pragmatic and results-oriented activity as software development, there are exceptions to this rule. For example, the 'C' programming language and its popular offspring tend to include both second and third generation controls. But C's hybrid character is recognised by software engineers themselves, who frequently refer to it as only a '2½ GL'. On the other hand, it is equally striking how cleanly the break between second and third generation languages has been made, no doubt because each level represents a stable 'equilibrium point' in the development of programming languages, independently of the views, theories or intentions of language developers.

that assumes that the problem can be stated, which will be precisely the problem. Up until this point, software engineering has always been concerned with solving problems with which we were already reasonably well acquainted through pre-existing manual processes, partial computerisations, and so on. In the case of a sixth level of development, with its formation of a new world of activity, it is more likely that software engineering will pass from being primarily an instrument of activity to a leading force in determining what is to be done. At that point, the ends will necessarily need to be defined in parallel with the means, and with little clear conception of the order of precedence between the two. But then, the problem of defining problems and stating requirements has also been developing, not least because these very developments in – and failures of – software engineering have freed both the engineers and those whose problems they try to solve to concentrate on defining more precisely exactly what they are trying to achieve.[1]

The history of the machine

In many respects the history of software engineering only repeats that of machinery in general, which has its own six-step sequence. In the first, there were no machines, only tool kits, with an assortment of disparate tools and other useful bits and pieces. At that point, the artisan's ability to fix a problem or create a product lies entirely in the skills they learned through their apprenticeship, in their personal experience, and so on. The form, fit and function of the end product are all in the hands of the tool *user*. In the second sub-stage, the situation has improved somewhat: the tools form a matching set, and produce components of interlocking shapes and sizes. Now at least some of form, fit and function are the product of the properly organised tool*maker*, and the tool *user* has much less need to manage all three at once.

In the third sub-stage, things have moved on still further: the precision tools of the previous stage have been still further refined, augmented and integrated to form the first machines properly so called. Placed in suitable chassis; linked

---

[1] Owing to the different semantics which characterise each layer, there appear to be irreducible logical obstacles to completely automating software engineering, or engineering of any kind. However, that is not the issue here, since that kind of problem is just as likely to be effectively eradicated through the development of expert systems and their successors, which will no doubt do at least as good a job as human engineers one day. Rather, the issue is the sequence of *historical* stages through which software languages have passed, considered as a logical sequence. This history has indeed reflected the sequence of sub-stages proposed here.

I should also add that there is another dimension to the maturing of software engineering, which has revealed itself in parallel to the strictly technical sequence reviewed in the main text. This sequence is reflected in the gradual retreat of the software engineering *problem-solving* process from direct manipulation of the machine back through increasingly high levels of design before writing any code, to modelling the required solution before even beginning to design, to systematic capture and analysis of the overall requirements, to feasibility studies to the organised evaluation of initial concepts. I suspect that this sequence would yield a similar logic.

and driven by cogs and belts and levers; powered by animal and natural forces; each fed with the output of its predecessor; and now only minded by human beings, the operator can only be said to 'use' the machine in the most general sense. On the other hand, the first machines move in unchanging clockwork cycles – as one would expect of the third sub-stage of any aspect of intelligence. But soon a new sub-stage begins, when self-regulating machines pre-dominate. By means of centrifugal governors, temperature regulators and other feedback devices, the machine is protected from outward disturbances while it gets on with its job.

It is significant that both Adam Smith's 'invisible hand' and natural selection were expressly compared with self-regulating machines. But such a machine is still very limited. It can do the particular job it was designed and set up to do, so to speak, and can only do another with significant modification. The scope of any such machine is also very limited, in the sense that there are in practice relatively few steps in the production process that a single machine can execute. Hence the importance of sub-stage five, when individual machines are made more versatile and more or less complete production lines are organised, allowing complete products to be produced in a single process. And so on to the factory, in which multiple integrated production lines organise a complete flow of resources, processes and products.

What is the relationship between the history of machines in general and of software in particular? In general terms, the development of machines requires no more than a concrete rational grasp of the processes involved, although as any acquaintance with factories will confirm, the processes in question are fairly thoroughly concealed in the factory. But that is the whole point of developmental processes: through an increasingly extensive and intensive acquaintance with things and events, by acting on and by means of objects, we gradually construct higher level structures of activity. In this case we proceed from an artisan's tool kit to an aircraft factory.

As the example of an aircraft factory already implies, it would be absurd to say that the above account exhausts the history of machinery. Machines, factories and complete industries must operate on much more sophisticated principles to make modern products. However, the passage to a higher, truly formal level of control is characterised less by changes in the hardware and more by the systems through which they are operated. These are increasingly characterised by, on the one hand, more and more abstract physical, chemical and biological principles, and on the other, more and more effective simulations of a rational operator. Hence the link to software, for the upshot of both these processes is the identification, organisation and embodiment (in yet more machines – in this case, computers) of the *principles* through which machines (and non-mechanical processes) are controlled. In that respect, software engineering is the archetypal form of formal rational engineering.

Jigsaw puzzles

My next example is taken from a quite different level and kind of activity, namely child psychology, and in particular from the child's developing strategy for solving jigsaw puzzles.[1] Here the sequence begins with the child ignorant of what a jigsaw puzzle is: at first, intuitive children are not simply ignorant of what sort of thing is called a 'jigsaw puzzle' (a shortcoming that is easily remedied) but more importantly, they cannot grasp what the 'puzzle' is. Indeed, lacking any notion of relationships, they have no explicit notion that anything could be a problem of *any* kind.

That is why intuitive reason responds to problems so impulsively – with force, with dismissive rejection, by evasion and avoidance, and so on. It is not merely a matter of temperament: although the intuitive child has an effective and orderly grasp of the whole world at the sensorimotor level, that grasp is limited to the perceptible surfaces of things. Once it becomes necessary to delve beneath empirical surfaces in order to grasp things, the intuitive child is lost. Even the fact that the protrusion on one piece of the puzzle fits into the recess of another or that there could be any alignment of the picture fragments each part represents is a mystery to it.

But this initial period passes, and the second sub-stage sees the child aligning neighbouring pieces, though they rely entirely on local adjustments to do this. What is more, these adjustments are directed solely by the physical act of fitting protrusions into recesses; the picture counts for little or nothing. This reflects the localised character of activity at this second sub-stage: the child can only carry out one local activity at a time, so (at least at the point where they are actually joining pieces together) the child must concentrate on the strictly physical compatibility between them. It may be able to make use of the fact that all the pieces of a given colour go together, but it is easily misled by even quite gross similarities. Since the image any given pair of pieces reveals is extremely partial and fragmented, it cannot be used to guide the alignment between pieces. The child will therefore be satisfied to jam pieces together, looking for nothing more than an approximate fit.

In the third sub-stage, when these local processes have been integrated into the single subjective perspective on the problem, the simultaneous alignment of partial images and pieces of the puzzle becomes possible and the child begins to appreciate that both must be achieved to do the puzzle correctly. However, this method is only stabilised in the fourth sub-stage, when each area of the puzzle (as defined by the visual blocks that make up the picture) can be grasped as an object in its own right. The size of parts assembled will depend on the size and complexity of the puzzle, and with practice, a simple puzzle and favourable circumstances, it may even extend to the whole puzzle. Furthermore, having grasped the main areas as objects in their own right, the child will begin to compare them with the picture of the finished puzzle. Before this sub-stage, the child does not grasp the relationship between the parts it assem-

---

[1] I owe much of the following account to André Hopper's unpublished research (pers. comm.).

bles and the picture on the box, at least not in the sense that the one is used to determine the other. On the other hand, because the fourth sub-stage is limited to isolated objects, the child's ability to proceed from a clear conception of discrete local assemblages to completing the puzzle is crude and easily exhausted. In fact, to complete jigsaw puzzles in a systematic way actually requires two further sub-stages. In sub-stage five, the child may progress by continually extending and combining local assemblies by means of increasingly well-orchestrated overlaps, but only at the final sub-stage does the child adopt systematic and global solutions such as assembling the outer edge of the puzzle first or pre-grouping pieces according to their colour before beginning.

The history of management

It may seem a far cry from the ability to complete jigsaw puzzles to the ability to manage an organisation, especially if you have seen how obscure and poorly structured a puzzle the average contemporary management system is. Nevertheless, their respective developments show a more than passing resemblance. Management systems operate at a quite different level from the intuitive child, of course. In fact, no explicit system of any kind is possible before formal reason, and none is necessary, at least not in the same sense, once dialectical reason has been achieved.

In addition, unlike jigsaw puzzles, management systems are one of the major forces in shaping the contemporary world, their influence and power spreading through practically every organisation that exceeds a certain critical mass. So their development can be considered a paradigm case of the development of formal reason. For each sub-stage I shall concentrate on certain key things: what is inherited from the previous sub-stage (and therefore what can be taken for granted in the present one); what the new sub-stage can normally achieve (and therefore the new level of routine operations); what can still only be done through personal skill, experience and effort (and therefore defines the manager's job); and what will be learned in the course of the new sub-stage (the seeds of the next stage). This in turn will show what is possible at each sub-stage and what is not – yet.

All kinds of organisation face the same basic strategic problem. Slightly embarrassingly, this can be illustrated with an image from Lewis Carroll. This is not embarrassing because it comes from Carroll but because the same image has been adopted by biology to express one of the central questions of evolutionary theory. In both cases the problem is, how can any structure that is operating as efficiently and effectively as it can prevent itself from being overtaken by competitors? The Red Queen is relevant here because, at a certain point in their conversation, the Red Queen unexpectedly takes Alice firmly by the hand and starts to run. Yet 'the most curious part of the thing was that the trees and the other things around them never changed their places at all: however fast they went, they never seemed to pass anything'. When told 'Well, in *our* country... you'd generally get to somewhere else – if you ran fast for a long time, as we've been doing', the Red Queen uttered her famously paradoxical reply:

Now, *here*, you see, it takes all the running *you* can do, to keep in the same place. If you want to get somewhere else, you must run at least twice as fast as that![1]

If the structure in question is already doing the best it can, the problem is obvious. There is no tactical solution – you are already at the limit of your resources. All you can hope for is a genuinely strategic breakthrough. And in that respect, of course, the intelligent solution is quite different from, indeed frankly contradictory to, any of its predecessors. For an organic structure, the solution requires externally induced (ie, 'random') variations in structure, validated by an equally external (ie, 'natural') process of selection between the available candidates. The specifically rational solution, by contrast, is an internally induced (ie, intentional) change created by the intelligence in question *itself*. In the specific case of strategic change to management systems, the solution is to be found in the ways that they are restructured through a sequence of levels corresponding to the six sub-stages of formal reason.

Management begins in a form that probably all contemporary managers have experienced and probably all contemporary managers fear. This is the stage of permanent 'fire fighting', when there is in fact no management system, nor even any regular processes. At this stage – which we may politely refer to as the sub-stage of 'personal' or 'intuitive' management – nothing can be taken for granted, work is unfocused and undirected beyond the immediate task, and the managers are making the job up as they go along. It is not that they are constantly faced with new problems; on the contrary, the very same problems come back over and over again.

I suspect that most managers at this sub-stage would echo Edna St Vincent Millay's remark that 'It is not true that life is one damn thing after another – it's one damn thing over and over'. On the other hand, through continual effort managers develop enough skill and experience to begin to stabilise isolated facets of their work, and begin formalising at least the basic mechanics of work. Basic tools such as plans, distribution lists, local records and regular local checks begin to appear. Nevertheless, they are only used because individual managers chose to create and use them or a vague dictum descends from above enjoining them to do so. There is neither consistency between managers or processes nor coherence within the work as a whole. Indeed, it remains unclear what 'the work as a whole' actually is, unhelpful (and at this stage usually disregarded) 'job descriptions' and 'terms of reference' notwithstanding.

Having established some discrete, localised control, the second, 'tactical' sub-stage in the development of management systems is a little less frantic than the first, but the whole is still less than the sum of the parts. No matter how apt the instruments they create or how strenuous the managers' efforts, the level of waste and rework that follows from the lack of overall structure is still immense. The existence of local procedures, standard formats and the like ensures that basic tasks can certainly be at least partly taken for granted; indeed, a manager can now perform any isolated task such as planning or calibration fairly routinely. However, because they still do not constitute a management *system*, individual tasks are still vulnerable to local dislocations, in-

---

[1] Carroll (1968: 166–8).

consistencies between managers, failures in the flow of information and decisions and the impossibility of verifying an action's correctness in terms of the
overall system or validating even favourable results against the organisation's
objectives. After all, the 'overall system' exists only in the management's
imagination (or occasionally in unread company manuals), and its objectives
remain almost as obscure and unstable as before.

Nevertheless, the managers' collective efforts to use their disparate tools to
manage complete operational functions and to keep the work process as a
whole on track also provides them with the insights and experiences they need
to integrate those instruments. It is the ensuing system that defines the next
sub-stage – the sub-stage of genuinely 'systematic' management. This system
integrates all processes and products, all resources and tools, all structures,
elements and relationships, into a single structure. As any practising manager
will confirm, this process of integration demands much more than the mere
collating of standards and procedures into a manual. It requires the complete
rationalisation of the parts into a coherent, consistent, complete and correct
whole. However, the effort is generally a sound investment, for it allows the
managers to take the *entire* process for granted. For example, scheduling becomes a more exact science, to the point of permitting 'just in time' supply
chains. This allows costs and effort to be reduced by the elimination of ware-
housing, waiting time and 'emergency' deliveries. In this way, a huge range of
previously skilled and effortful management tasks are relegated to established
and actively maintained suites of processes and procedures.

Not that the managers are now redundant. Rather, the appearance of this
third sub-stage in the development of management provides the management
with a kind of collective subjectivity, namely this very system for defining, coordinating and solving their collective problems. However, just as naïve subjectivity is insensitive to the proper nature of the objects before it, so a purely
systematic management system is insensitive to the special requirements of
particular products, processes and projects. In other words, the system may be
able to do the particular things it was designed for to perfection (or at least to
within the tolerances set by the management system itself), but even quite
small variations can only be handled successfully by either informal (and so
formally illegitimate) adjustments or by a formal but disproportionate redesign
of the management system itself. And this in turn defines the manager's job at
the third sub-stage: to tailor the formal system to the job at hand, and thereby
to steer the work to its unique goal. But as before, the experience this generates
permits management to develop yet further tools and techniques, this time for
routinising this very task.[1]

Once the process of adapting the management system to each new content
and context is itself part of that system, the manager may now be reasonably
confident that each individual job will be carried out correctly (at least to the
extent that correctness can be achieved through any management system).
Unlike a systematic management system, which can only check that a given job

[1] For a practitioner's view of the difficulty of achieving this degree of flexibility, see
Agrawal et al (2001).

conforms to its entirely generic definition of good quality work, by the end of the fourth sub-stage (the sub-stage of 'adaptive' management) it can positively assure its quality by the job's own unique standards and the conditions in which it is carried out. For example, the 'just in time' systems that were established during the previous sub-stage will soon show the limitations of a systematic system, which is unresponsive to *ad hoc* changes in traffic conditions, price fluctuations, and so on. Under a truly adaptive project management system, however, the mechanisms for detecting, analysing and responding to such changes are built into the system, as are the means of optimising the system to both the job and external conditions.

However, this same advance also presents the manager with a new kind of task. This is no longer focused exclusively on the job at hand, whose effective control can be largely delegated to the system, but consists of looking outwards and setting that job in the context of *all* work. The purpose of this new attitude is to make sure that, however well it may be done in itself, the task at hand both benefits from past experience and benefits related work in the future. But as my previous references to setting things in context indicate, this can only be achieved when it is complemented by an explicit grasp of the unique requirements imposed by a given task's *content*. That is, the management system must itself develop generic methods for making sense of each new piece of work, and then adapting itself to that work's individual needs.

At first sight this approach may seem to contradict the fourth sub-stage's emphasis on treating each job on its merits, which surely implies that no such comparisons can be made. And while management is still in its fourth sub-stage, this is correct, for the first attempts to sensitise the management system to individual tasks is bound to be a relatively haphazard and *ad hoc* process. This creates a singular problem that was well expressed by the White Queen in *Through the Looking Glass*: 'What's one and one and one and one and one and one and one and one and one and one?'[1]

But the paradox is not insoluble. Although each task or product may be unique, the process of individuating it may have its own generic characteristics. These will be discovered during the sub-stage of responsive management, and their integration into the management system will signal the onset of fifth sub-stage, that of 'programme' management. During this sub-stage, all individual pieces of work – projects, functions, and so on – are aligned and then regularly re-aligned to a single corporate strategy. Furthermore, this goal is designed to effect radical change in the organisation and its environment, rather than just the localised change that was typical of the previous sub-stage.

Conversely, because of the standardisation carried out during the previous sub-stage, each individual project, function, and so on can be defined in terms of a single (if flexible) set of standard dimensions that allow the key management issues to be translated into a set of parameters. This in turn allows the systems and processes used to carry out the work to be pre-set to the task at hand, without having to be redesigned in any significant way. Likewise, the results of the work can be analysed, interpreted and communicated in an un-

---

[1] Carroll (1968: 262).

ambiguous yet generic way which is positively and directly meaningful to all the other tasks in the programme, rather than providing the merely indicative clues that the results of less mature management gave.

So managers can now explain, control and predict activity and so manage progress with unprecedented ease, precision and confidence. Consequently, the manager can focus on larger objectives – the development of the organisation as a whole, supporting the customer's larger business goals as well as their immediate needs, and so on. The individual manager benefits from the shared experience of the entire organisation, and the entire organisation benefits from the unique experience of this manager. This reduces almost all new work to routine, whilst simultaneously raising managers above the level of routine of any kind.

Of course, programme management is an immense advance on any previous level of management. Nevertheless, it still leaves the manager with the task of implementing the new insights this larger perspective provides. But for the same reason, it also suggests yet another sub-stage, based on the synthesis of the results of this stage. As channels of communication for transmitting this information are perfected they also become capable of routinisation and automation, as can any special implementation tools and techniques. But if this process is taken to its conclusion, what is left of management itself? The answer, quite clearly, is: nothing. Or rather, as this revolutionary outcome is limited to those spheres of activity that lie within the management system's current scope, the answer is nothing, so long as the system is never applied to situations of which it knows nothing and if the existing conditions of activity never change. This, of course, is as improbable a steady state as any other, but still, to the extent that the corporate situation does remain stable, all management is now absorbed into the management system itself. In this truly 'strategic' management system, all experience is communicated and used immediately and directly. Because of this, constant improvement, prevention and development are the norm and the organisation as a whole can do anything, can do it expertly, and can do it immediately.

As I have already suggested in connection with the passage from adaptive management to programme management, the relationship between sub-stages can appear contradictory. Each clearly subsumes its predecessor, the higher absorbing the achievements of the lower while abolishing their limitations. But at the same time, they also seem to conflict with one another. For example, the third sub-stage's introduction of a universal perspective on activity seems to replace the locally focused approach of the second with homogenisation, even indifference. The fourth seems to resolve this by restoring the focused approach, and seems to further contradict the adoption of a systematic perspective by insisting on a distinct approach to each new object. But the focus comes from the coordination of the system as a whole, so the contradiction is not as substantial as it seems. The fifth then denies this in the name of a new, higher form of commonality even while preserving the fourth sub-stage's individuation of tasks, while the sixth installs a truly universal system capable of both articulating and subsuming the achievement of any single one of its predecessors.

In summary, as with any dialectic, the contradiction, if not more apparent than real, is certainly not irreducible: each new sub-stage simply externalises the unrecognised internal structure of the preceding sub-stage and re-internalises the results. It is this dialectic of internalisation and externalisation that creates the impression of contradiction, but it is also the key to the effective subsumption of each sub-stage by its successor.[1]

The development of capitalism

Managing an organisation is a somewhat larger enterprise than solving a jig-saw puzzle. However, set beside capitalism, even the most extensive contemporary management system shrinks to tiny proportions. Can the same logic that regulates the development of children solving jigsaw puzzles also regulate history on the grandest scale? As the history of capitalism illustrates, it certainly can. The same sequence of sub-stages is present, although many complexities arise from its relationship to the feudalism that gave it birth and nurtured it, constrained and distorted it and was eventually done to death by it.

The first inklings of Western capitalism are seen when early medieval Europe's feudal economy becomes stable enough and mobile enough to support money transactions.[2] However, as this is only the first sub-stage, there is

---

[1] Other aspects of management have developed in a similar manner. The Carnegie-Mellon Software Engineering Institute's 'Capability Maturity Model' (Humphrey, 1989) reveals something of developmental sequence, although its pragmatic origins and residual logical shortcomings are evident, even to the point where it can be doubted whether it provides a model of *maturity* (as opposed to a sequence of steps of broadly equal maturity) at all. Pressman (1993) has proposed a comparable sequence of steps, from crisis management to the elimination of root causes.

[2] It is important to note at the start that the history of capitalism is by no means identical with the history of money or money economies. Practically all stable economies of any sophistication at all have used a form of money, not to mention engaging in various forms of trade and limited production for the market. But money is not, in itself, a form of capital, and the systematic properties of capitalism are not the same as those of money. The reader should also note that capitalism emerged from a feudal system that was in different states and at different stages of development in different parts of Europe. In addition, it was always subject to internal and external distortions and restrictions of its own, especially in its earlier sub-stages. So the discussion which follows is highly schematic.

For example, the market towns that I portray as emerging only as capitalism itself begins to take shape were never actually absent in southern Europe, and in eastern Europe played a much less formative role than in the south and west of the continent. The role of the state was likewise very mixed. Neither do I take any account of the complicated changes in direction that took place as a consequence of, for example, the seismic up-heavals of the fourteenth century. Finally, no account is taken of non-European intimations of capitalism. As a result, many of the generalisations I make here are unsafe from a strictly historical point of view. However, what follows is only intended as a semi-ideal history of capitalism, abstracted from its actual history and re-generalised to the hypothetical world where no such complications exist. And even in the real world, it is doubtful how significant they have been for the long-term development of capitalism as

no recognition at the time that anything new is afoot. There is certainly no question of stable capitalist *structures*, political, economic, ideological or otherwise. The key issue is the tentative possibility that there might be some other method of mobilising an economic surplus by extra-feudal methods, based on independent exchange. Occasionally economic transactions – pure exchanges of surplus agricultural and craft products, speculative investments, local trading fairs (though not yet permanent market *towns*), and so on – take place outside the normal round of subsistence farming and feudal obligations, but like particles emerging from a quantum vacuum, they come and go as opportunities arise and circumstances dictate. This activity is not only entirely parasitic on the feudal economy but is to a large extent the direct and deliberate product of the feudal aristocracy's desire to find outlets for its economic surplus and more flexible monetary instruments to support its often peripatetic lifestyle.[1]

Like the first sub-stage in any new development, those who experience this process are entirely unaware that they have advanced beyond the boundaries of their 'native' stage, and the advances themselves are purely provisional, episodic and conditional on the efforts and enthusiasms of their progenitors. Nevertheless, as such transactions become more regular, specialists begin to emerge and a second sub-stage, consisting of localised but established capitalist structures and processes, begins. Again it is not the use of money as such that defines this sub-stage but the intimation of a way of diverting an economic surplus out of the concrete relationships that define feudalism and into the formal relationships the use of money implies. Although still far from making up a capitalist system properly so called, permanent market towns begin to appear, merchants and professional financiers traverse the land in numbers and landless labourers begin to gather in the towns. This is reinforced by the continuing substitution of money payments for labour obligations and rents in kind and the growing tax demands of emerging regional and state administrations.

All this activity is still parasitic on feudalism, and during this sub-stage even the most powerful merchants and bankers operate in the interstices and at the behest of feudalism. Yet clear differences are beginning to appear between the principles and interests driving each group. Nor does the feudal system show its offspring any mercy when their interests collide, as the collapse of more than one great medieval banking house testifies. Nevertheless, even though it would still be more correct to regard the figures on the capitalist side as burghers rather than bourgeois, and apprentices and journeymen were far from proletarian, the first independent capitalist structures are beginning to come to life.

Even without the exceptional opportunities and impetus afforded by the crusades and other national and international crises,[2] this process could not have continued for long without the various local capitals coming into close juxtaposition, through both political and ideological realignments and straight-

---

a whole.

[1] Hodges (1989). See Robinson (1987) for further discussion and references.

[2] Vilar (1976).

forward economic concentrations. This in turn supports the development of the absolutist state, which, although still devoted to the notion of aristocracy, is relatively indifferent to the means it uses to achieve its ends. Absolute monarchs like bourgeois money just as much as any other kind. This places capitalism in a much more favourable position *vis à vis* feudalism than previously, not least because it is much more able to provide the sizeable financial infusions absolutism requires than any strictly feudal economic apparatus. With the new lease of life this gives, plus its own spontaneous growth and the capitalists' ability to profit from the colonial empires and global trade that feudalism only squandered,[1] a capitalist *system* now takes shape, and with it a capitalist *class* that can be properly termed bourgeois. Though not yet a completely independent mode of *production*, this situation does permit capitalists both to organise independently and to penetrate the feudal system to an unprecedented extent, with massive economic, political and ideological benefits to the bourgeoisie.

The immediate economic benefits notwithstanding, in the long term the most important of these benefits are the legal right, political power and ideological authority to operate on its own terms. This is critical because, in the long run, the principles that control feudal and capitalist economies are not merely different, they are radically contradictory. Consequently, capitalism's effective liberation from feudal restraint not only permits it to absorb wide tracts of the economy as a whole but also puts it into a collision course with feudalism as a whole. Hence the importance of the legal, political and ideological levers to which the entrenchment of a capitalist *system* leads. Then, having disposed of its feudal opponent, the capitalist system evolves into a full blown and completely autonomous *economy*, with a unified process of production, circulation, exchange and consumption, unhampered by effective political or ideological opposition.

To the extent that it faces any competition, it is only from the workers it exploits and the peasant farmers and indigenous colonial peoples whose economies it invades and subverts. But they are quite incapable of forcing capitalism to respect their interests or politico-economic practices. Indeed, they were long since shackled and burdened, even before capitalism triumphed over feudalism, by legal, political and ideological chains. From enclosure movements and Poor Laws to the slave trade and the forcible dismantling of the Indian textile industry, the entire apparatus of authority seems to have been determined to make it a crime to resist incorporation into the growing capitalist system: as late as 1823 the British Parliament could pass a Master and Servant Act that treated breach of contract on the employer's side as a civil issue, whereas a breach on the employee's side was a criminal offence punishable by up to three months in prison.[2]

All this characterises capitalism in its fourth sub-stage, when clear and distinct economic 'objects' are created, usually in the form of national economies

---

[1] On the role of colonialism in the development of the capitalist system and economy, see Davis (1973) or Wallerstein (1974).

[2] Saville (1994: 21–3).

run on the basis of a capitalist mode of *production*. In Marx's words, this is achieved through:

> a systematical combination, embracing the colonies, the national debt, the modern mode of taxation, and the protectionist system. These methods depend in part on brute force… But they all employ the power of the State, the concentrated and organised force of society, to hasten, in hothouse fashion, the process of transformation of the feudal mode of production into the capitalist mode, and to shorten the transition.[1]

This unit is large and rich enough to support a complete system of production and incorporate the full range of economic enterprises and institutions needed for each of its participating capitals to operate freely and effectively. On the other hand, it is only one national economy among many, and many diverse, uncoordinated forms of capitalism spring up even within a single national unit.

This unharnessed complexity decides the next step to be taken. Just as any equivalent object of any fourth sub-stage is undifferentiated, so the national economy does not define explicitly how any individual capital operates, internally or externally. Indeed, internally national (and nationalist) capitalism rampages largely uncontrolled, producing mass commodities and mass immiseration in equal measure.[2] Even the major exceptions to this, such as the politi-

---

[1] Marx (1954: ch. 1).

[2] The idea that capitalism immiserates the proletariat has a long and unhappy history, largely the result of the failure of most of its exponents to distinguish between the economic notion of impoverishment and human immiseration proper. The myth that even the mature Marx predicted the perpetual and increasing impoverishment of the workers (and that, therefore, consumer capitalism refutes Marxism) can be disposed of by consulting *Capital* (Marx, 1954: ch. 25, s. 1). Marx also demolished the 'iron law of wages' on which much of the myth is based.

To put the matter in a nutshell, you can make people wretched without making them poor. As Marx himself put it, 'just as little as better clothing, food, and treatment, and a larger peculium, do away with the exploitation of the slave, so little do they set aside that of the wage-worker' (Marx, 1954: 579). Indeed, as I hope have already shown, a wealth of commodities can be the principal instrument of existential suffering. During capitalism's ascendancy the situation was straightforward, and Braudel (1981) reports research suggesting that between the start of the sixteenth century and the end of the nineteenth, the standard of living of the 'common people' halved while that of the ruling classes rose markedly (see also Clay, 1984: 28ff).

Later, when industrial capitalism is more mature, the case for systematic impoverishment is extremely hard to sustain, even allowing for the massive and systematic impoverishment of the Third World, on whose backs the wealthy nations spread their gargantuan feasts. However, only the most naïve utilitarian could believe that wealth is to be measured exclusively (or even primarily) in commodities, especially when human happiness, not to mention the very intelligibility of the capitalist world and the ability of human beings to control it, are all increasingly thrown into doubt.

A fall in the standard of living after revolutionary social change is certainly not peculiar to capitalism. Leaving aside all the recent examples, such as the attempts to revolutionise Soviet and Third World agriculture, it seems highly likely that the first great economic revolution of all, the rise of Neolithic agriculture, may have allowed a larger population to be fed and to be fed more securely, but for individuals the quality of life

cal direction of the German economy under Bismarck and the Japanese economy after World War II, are expressly designed to serve the 'national' interest (which is to say, a form of 'enlightened self-interest' for the ruling class), not the interests of the population at large. And externally, capitalism operates freely throughout the colonies acquired during the previous era, even to the extent that these colonies are re-arranged into a vast investment and trading system for the benefit of the domestic economy rather than the development or well-being of the colony. Simultaneously, the whole drive to colonialism, now clothed in the allegedly enlightened rhetoric of imperialism, is renewed.[1]

This brings capitalism to its fifth sub-stage, namely the *transnational* economy.[2] Internally this leads to a greater articulation of economic activity, both with itself and with the prevailing political and ideological systems. This is exemplified by massive vertical and horizontal integration, successful political rebuffs to a homogenising national identity, an elaborately mixed (though still more concentrated) economy, the taming of unions and social democratic parties, and even the general acceptance[3] of a genuinely social ideology of sorts. Its multilateral economic agreements and institutions are mirrored on the political plane by a variety of multi-national organisations[4] and alliances and, less convincingly, the United Nations.

During this sub-stage, the nation state remains nominally in control of national economies, but it becomes harder and harder to control the operations of global markets, corporations and regulatory bodies. Occasional, perfectly sincere ideological nods may still be made in the direction of a residual patriotism, state powers are regularly invoked when required, multilateral political

---

fell, with more disease, a lower life expectancy, reduced stature and chronic malnutrition (Cohen and Armelagos, quoted in Wenke, 1990: 264). Conversely, Johnson and Earle (1987: 96) report cases of members of pre-agricultural societies who deliberately reject opportunities for social development because it will reduce their own personal quality of life. However, Redfield (1953: ch. 5) is very sceptical of the general ability of relatively undeveloped societies to carry out positive reform – a more exacting capability. It would appear that sometimes development is obliged to creep up on intelligent beings and take the form of an immediate impoverishment – the cunning of history, of course.

[1] I think Mark Twain showed the right attitude towards imperialism with his splendid back-handed compliment to one of its greatest exponents, Cecil Rhodes: 'I admire him, I frankly confess it; and when his time comes I shall buy a piece of the rope as a keepsake'.

[2] van der Wee (1987).

[3] This acceptance can be highly conditional on support for the overall objectives of a capitalist system. Most notably in the so-called 'Anglo-American' model, in which social welfare is seen as strictly the result of more or less unbridled capitalism, but also to an extent in the so-called 'Rhine' or 'Scandinavian' model, where welfare is seem as an independent ideal or even precursor of economic advance, the welfare state is increasingly reduced to an ideal and social and political cooperation are conditional on specific 'business' goals. In other words, the whole of society is even more explicitly subordinated to the economy than during previous sub-stages.

[4] Reinalda and Verbeek (1998).

and economic ties are ruthlessly manipulated in the interests of the more powerful nation states, and each crisis generates its own brand of jingoism and protectionism.[1] Nevertheless, all such appeals are diluted by increasing migration (driven by economic development and desperation in equal measure), the globalisation of communications and the mass media, and the predominance of the import and export components of economies. Even pollution, from acid rain to the depletion of the ozone layer, is a transnational business, and the United States, which has not seen a case of polio in two decades, currently spends hundreds of millions of dollars on polio vaccination, purely because it might so quickly enter from literally thousands of different points of the compass.

In the end, only the most powerful and most ideologically committed nation state can now influence the international economic system to any great degree, and even then it requires a larger and larger economic crisis to rein in the transnationalising tendencies of the great corporations. Even the 'realistic' rhetoric of national politicians, who increasingly find themselves relegated to riding the coat-tails of transnational processes far beyond their control, confirms that the transnational capitalist economy is rapidly subsuming its national predecessors.[2]

Once the passage from a national to a transnational economy is complete, the sixth and final sub-stage ensues. Now that capitalism has raised itself to the global level – the universal empire to which so many pre-formal systems aspired but never had the means to create – it abolishes the national economy altogether, and with it the (already faintly pathetic) nation state. Hence the truly global economy. With that, all components of the human world – all economic, political, scientific and ideological activity, all culture and technology – are marshalled to capitalist ends. But the same process also brings the war between capitalist interests and economic democratisation to a head, for the globalisation of economic development means that there is no longer a Third World to exploit and groups that were once destined for exploitation by their gender, race, nationality or other defunct criteria have used the very economic development and powers they acquired through their integration into the economy to overcome their exploiters. With that, even the most global and remote of truths offered by formal reason are embodied and implied in the most local of presents: a world political system is accompanied by the most local of democracies; economic union finds that the most individualised of producers and production processes are its most indispensable condition; the abstractions of formal rational ideology are driven to their final articulations; and the universal truths of science are inscribed in the most intimate details of quotidian existence. In short, the processes described in the previous chapter come to a head, and capitalism, the premier formal system on the planet, is abolished.

---

[1] On the ambivalence of one of the most powerful transnational organisations, the European Union, see Carchedi and Carchedi (1999).

[2] On the forms of personal experience created by this sub-stage, see Sennett (1998).

Conclusions

As far as I can tell, such a conclusion is still far in the future. However, to return to the issue with which this chapter began, it is even further from any possible biology. The processes and mechanisms described above, whether for solving jigsaw puzzles or for the creation of the world, have nothing in common with biological structures or functioning. Far from being either the outward expression of a natural process of maturation, the product of learning, or a succession of variations and selections, such sequences of sub-stages only occur because each single sub-stage throws up its own problems and opportunities, to solve which the intelligence in question requires no further experience than the problem and opportunity itself.

Each solution then defines the next sub-stage, and the mechanisms whereby the problem is determined and the solution realised are entirely the products of that individual intelligence. There is no necessary unfolding, no 'evolution' in any biological sense of the word, and certainly no pre-programming of solutions. If there were, it would be impossible to trace the logic of the solution in the activities themselves, any more than the way a chrysalis becomes a butterfly could be said to express the nature of chrysalidhood.

Nor does the fact that all such developmental processes pass through the same sequence of stages and sub-stages imply that there is something more profound than the solution of particular problems going on, something concealed beneath the operations of intelligence itself (something to be found in our biology, no doubt). Or rather, there certainly is something beyond the unique experience of single intelligences, but that something is the regularity, integrity and universality that follow from the identical abstract and abstracting character of all individual intelligences, through which all particulars are synthesised.

Having transcended any particular form, content or context of activity (a transcendence that is even more complete than the organism's transcendence of any particular chemical reaction), intelligence is not distanced from concrete activity; rather, it simply becomes radically independent of it. There must be activity of some kind, but the stabilisation and mobilisation of intelligence as a united and increasingly uniform structure of activity provides it with a universal perspective on any particular act or object. This permits it both to comprehend any particular activity or object in all its individuality, but also to regulate all individual acts in terms of the structure of intelligence as a whole. Hence its independence and its abstractness. And hence also the uniformity of the developmental process, regardless of content or context.

Furthermore (to step back a little further still), the stages in the development of reason constitute a single process in the strongest possible sense of the word. Their succession is not only universally observable but also inherent in the internal logic of the stages themselves. This point is critical to the entire argument for intelligence's independence from biology, of course: the development of reason makes no appeal to external forces of any kind, be it divine *fiat*, a particular organic substrate or special empirical conditions.

That is not to say that biological conditions in which intelligence develops make absolutely no impression or that there is something immanent in reason that ensures its successful completion of a predetermined programme. On the contrary, without a pre-intelligent infrastructure and substrate, intelligence would be as impossible as an organism without a chemistry – whatever that might mean! Similarly, with no empirical opportunity to act, intelligence would simply wither away. But by the same token, almost any opportunity to act suffices for the development of intelligence, and so does almost any organic substrate and infrastructure that is capable of supporting sensorimotor reflexes and the rudiments of sensorimotor development.

In that, as in everything else, intelligence is fundamentally different from any possible biology.

7. The Bounds of Reason?

She said: What is history?
And he said: History is an angel
Being blown backwards into the future.
He said: History is a pile of debris
And the angel wants to go back and fix
    things,
To repair the things that have been broken.
But there is a storm blowing from Paradise,
And the storm keeps blowing the angel
Backwards into the future.
And this storm, this storm
Is called
Progress.

Laurie Anderson
'The Dream Before (For Walter Benjamin)'

The dimensions of irrationality

In this book I have tried to present convincing grounds for accepting a particular conception of intelligence as the basis of human activity. If it is to deal with human nature adequately, a proper science of human nature not only should but must take human beings' loftiest aspirations and achievements completely seriously. Which is all very well, except for one rather large fly in the ointment. If there are limits on, say, human biology's power to intervene in human activity, surely the same can be said – perhaps with even greater justice – of reason itself? Grand theories of human nature notwithstanding, human beings are not always very bright, let alone rational. So what is the point of proposing an 'explanation' of human nature that is couched exclusively in terms of reason? Conversely, where else are we to look for the explanation of the conspicuously irrational aspect of human existence, if not to our biology or (perhaps even worse) to intrinsic limitations in the powers of intelligence itself? This is the problem to be addressed in the present chapter. It is dealt with in several parts.

Firstly, there is the preliminary problem, not of irrationality as such but of the absence in much of our activity of any visible or active rationality. Leaving aside intelligence's avowedly pre-rational phase during intuitive reason, its later stages also harbour vast reservoirs of plainly spontaneous, even automatic control. How can this be accounted for if intelligence itself is defined as 'activity that knows itself to be that activity and is that activity by virtue of that knowledge'? Even when intelligence is at its most effective, it plainly does not always know what it is doing. This elementary functional paradox is linked to a genetic paradox of equal difficulty, which is itself a version of the well-known Red Queen paradox to which I have already alluded. How can an intelligence, which is already working at full stretch, raise itself by its bootstraps into a qualitatively superior form, not once but three times – from intuitive reason to concrete reason, from concrete reason to formal reason, and from formal reason to dialectical reason too?

Both these paradoxes share a single solution: that the creation of higher level structures of activity is based not only on the accumulation of skills and experiences and concepts and powers and institutions but also on the organisation and re-organisation of all that knowledge and power into more and more profound and compelling structures. That is, the *extensive* accumulation of structures is complemented by their increasingly *intensive* synthesis among themselves. Of course, there are restraints on our capacity to grasp the world that no amount of synthesis or abstraction can overcome, and there are many changes, from brain growth to cultural and technological advance, that are needed to realise the potential intelligence offers. However, the particular problem I am concerned with in the first section of this chapter is to show how the knowledge and power embodied in intelligence take the form of a vast *infrastructure*, on which the higher stages of that development rest.

The second section is concerned with a quite different problem. If intelligence develops in a well-defined sequence of stages, how is it that so many aspects of human nature exhibit such confused degrees of maturity? How could the mighty and (in some respects[1]) highly organised Roman *imperium* have existed side by side with the most primitive superstition and fetishism, not just briefly but for centuries on end? How could Aristotle's logic have been so commanding but his physics so weak? But here again the problem is not to decide the limits of intelligence but to extricate the logical potential of intelligence in general from the implications imposed by the successive stages in the developmental logic outlined in the previous chapters. As I shall argue below, far from conceding that its unevenness reflects either any insuperable fragmentation within intelligence or an unacknowledged closeness between biological conditions and rational actions, such fragmentation is exactly what the present theory predicts for the development of intelligence, even if it were wholly unaffected by external forces, be they biological, ecological, historical or otherwise.

The basic reason for this is that, if intelligence is activity that knows itself to be that activity, and so on, this is only possible for intelligence as a whole if it is also true for each individual act. There is after all no objectivity except in the here and now. Consequently, although shortcuts are possible and insights are readily shared between different areas of intelligence, not only each intelligence but also each distinct aspect of an individual intelligence must be developed in its own right. Otherwise it is hard to see how each aspect of each act could be seen (even potentially) as an attempt either to make sense of things as

---

[1] For an overview of the Roman 'art of government' that makes its structural limitations very clear, see Purcell in Boardman *et al.* (1992).

that individual intelligence encounters them, in the here and now, *or* to make a sense of them that is indeed objective, which is to say, in terms that are adequate to its object's own proper nature. We are not born with concepts such as 'glue' or 'tautology', and to deal with glue and tautologies objectively we must make sense of both. To do this demands that each be developed in its own right, on its own terms and for its own sake.

In short, the mere fact that intelligence *is* individual, and so a multi-faceted but integral synthesis of many structures, guarantees that its development will be complicated, paradoxical and noisy. Even if the developmental processes for inventing glue and establishing tautologies are broadly the same, the development of even a single individual is all but bound to be a very mixed and uneven affair. Indeed, the only reason that reason does not degenerate into chaos is because of the complementary process of abstraction and concretisation whereby each individual intelligence coordinates and regulates its overall activity and development, and so resolves all these different encounters and experiences into a single, increasingly coherent, consistent, complete and correct point of view.

Then there are the effects of intelligence's immaturity, while it lasts – the topic of the third section. Quite apart from the inadequacy that necessarily typifies any immature structure, a certain genuine irrationality results from the facts that, firstly, intelligence has little sense of its own immaturity until it approaches the very highest reaches of development; and secondly, it cannot help but use that immature structure, however immature it may be. These structures are after all the basis on which it not only does anything but also wants to do anything. So, insofar as being immature means that I must act before I can resolve all the conflicts between the various facets of myself and between my world and myself, this leads me into irrational acts, including not only irrational methods, tools and techniques but also irrational intentions, goals, and solutions. In the absence of the self-knowledge and self-control that immaturity by definition lacks, I have little propensity to restrain myself and little capacity to see that restraint is required. This is, I think, why Malinowski attributed magical acts to the tension created by the need to act even when achieving an effect by more direct means is clearly out of the question, and myth to the need to shore up magic in intelligible terms.[1]

And in every case, if the alternative to doing something immature is to do nothing till I grow up, just *how* am I supposed to do nothing – or, for that matter, to grow up? An intuitive child can no more wait until it has grown up before it takes action than a feudal baron could have waited for the formation of representative democracy before he decided how to deal with his serfs. Nor would either see any need to wait: from their own point of view, the situation is already clear enough. Nor do I feel that *I* need to wait until humanity at large has reached the end of dialectical reason before I start speculating about how intelligence will end. Not only are all three of us almost equally incapable of imagining such remote possibilities, but it is only when children and barons and writers act out the implications of their respective situations that higher

---

[1] Quoted in Marwick (1970: 210ff).

level structures such as adulthood and representative democracy and (hopefully) a better theory of human nature come into existence in the first place.

Finally, there is the fact that, precisely because of the transient limitations to which a group of intelligent beings is exposed, some kinds of action that are rational at the individual level have collective consequences that are not only contrary to what was intended but also actively conceal the processes and mechanisms through which they come about, even creating the impression that everything makes perfectly good sense, and that the irrationality of the situation is either illusory or the unavoidable outcome to which we should, as mature beings, resign ourselves. This is the problem of alienation, which is dealt with briefly.

Given all these forms of irrationality, real and apparent, we cannot eliminate even the illusion of irrationality, let alone the substance, until we have expressed it not only in thought and theory but also in practice – however indirect or partial that expression may be. In Hegel's famous image, the owl of Minerva flies only at dusk. So a final, unequivocal rationality can only be established by intelligence occasionally falling short of its own ideals, not only apparently but really too. But even that does not mean that intelligence is ever quite irrational. After all, even when our acts are profoundly mistaken and self-defeating, at the very least we are trying to make sense of our world – a notion completely beyond any non-intelligent organism. Even Nazism was an attempt to make sense of the world – and, through a regime of delusion, lies, terror, war and mass murder, to make the world make sense.

Meanwhile, taken together with the pathologies to which all intelligence, like any structure, is inevitably exposed, these forms of irrationality, real and apparent, are quite enough to preclude a neat linear development, even if all the other complexities outlined in this book were not. In summary, intelligence remains a fundamentally rational structure, but our full capacity for rationality takes time to emerge. And while that potential has yet to be fulfilled, one should not expect such rationality as we do possess to resemble maturity, health or neatness.

The infrastructure of intelligence

> [C]onsciousness : awareness :: map : itinerary :: memory : recollection (and, possibility, :: collectivity : individual)…
>
> Anthony Cohen and Nigel Rapport[1]

The active and the passive

> [A] belief constantly inculcated during the early years of life… appears to acquire almost the nature of an instinct; and the very essence is that it is followed independently of reason.[1]

---

[1] Cohen and Rapport (1995: 16).

There is a fundamental paradox any stage-based theory of intelligence must face: if it takes an early stage of intelligence such as intuitive reason all its time and effort just to be intuitive, what is left over to support additional layers of intelligence, from concrete and formal to dialectical reasoning? Fortunately the solution to this problem is simple, for the problem itself is illusory. *Adding* new layers is precisely what is *not* happening in the development of intelligence. Rather, this is a classic dialectical *Aufhebung*: each new stage is a reworking, synthesis, correction and elaboration of its predecessor, including not only the realisation of its potential but also the elimination of its many incoherent, inconsistent, incomplete and incorrect elements. By this means, the *quality* of reason improves without there being any special need for a greater *quantity* of resources. It may be that the sheer mass of resource available determines just how far the process can be taken, but in principle at least, qualitative advances flow from reorganisation rather than growth.

> Such developments are distinct from something like the biological development of a butterfly… It is not true to say that the butterfly still retains or even supersedes the caterpillar – it is a different form. In the development of intelligence's qualitative structures, by contrast, each subsequent level supersedes its predecessor and surpasses it in *every* way. Each stage of intelligence's development involves the *retention* of the accomplishments of earlier stages (without those earlier accomplishments being retained separately from the higher level structures), which is synonymous with the *conservation* of the relations being developed.[2]

That this supersession is possible without the acquisition of massive new resources reflects an aspect of intelligence I have not yet detailed. So far my account has concentrated exclusively on the *activities* through which intelligence formulates, shapes and implements its many and varied strategies, solutions, precautions, tools, resources, innovations and goals. It has taken the structures that implicitly support this activity almost entirely for granted. But there is more to rational activity than activity alone, and the structures that constitute rational activity actually and directly are themselves informed by an increasingly powerful, sophisticated and comprehensive *infrastructure* of established systems, captive resources, routine methods and copybook stratagems – not to mention unresolved prejudices, unnoticed implications, unacknowledged assumptions and unstated *a prioris*. In other words, before it makes even the slightest move, intelligence is already constituted by a *passive* order from which its actions will emerge and that forms one of the major conditions of any activity.

This infrastructure expresses itself in every aspect of activity from personal quirks to factory floor plans to international treaties. It is the skeleton of past experience incorporated in the flesh of the present moment, created and reformed as development proceeds in different directions, passing in and out of focus as action moves now this way, now that, more and more deeply buried as it proves itself increasingly capable of handling the less interesting parts of

---

[1] Darwin (1901: 187).

[2] Hopper (pers. comm., slightly modified with the author's permission).

the world effectively and efficiently. Collectively it dictates what the intelligence in question can assume, grasp and achieve directly, without reflection or effort, because its existence ensures that all the conditions of a given activity are already to hand as that activity unfolds, even to the point that it dictates how intelligence experiences itself.

> This is an awareness of self in action (driving, etc.) where the inspection of self as an object of consciousness is absent. This is a task rather than a self-oriented mode of being. In this state highly elaborate decision-making and information monitoring processes may be carried out in which the consciousness of self as agent is an implicit rather than an explicit awareness.[1]

For example, what do you get if you add two and two? How do you ride a bicycle? What is the name of the child on my left in this 30-year-old school photograph? How should I approach a roundabout in France? When shouldn't I press that button, and why not? How do you spell 'accommodation'? Or build a skyscraper or dig a mine? Or organise a football team? What is $e^{i\pi}$? How do I strike this flint to create a chopper? How does one go about dismembering a giant ground sloth? Should I stand when another country's national anthem is played? Or my own? Which clothes count as 'casual dress'? How do I make a pun out of this person's name? Should I try a flanking movement? What is the correct procedure for purchasing a new computer at the office? Should we use Spearman or Pearson's correlation coefficient? Who's in charge of this? Is this a good painting? In what sense? Of what disease is this a symptom, and what is an acceptable prescription under current health service regulations?

More to the point, how do you and I *know* any of these things, such that we should do and know them completely without thinking? Expressed in more positive terms, the infrastructure of intelligence embodies a mass of tacit knowledge, automatic processes and unnoticed objects, all of which pass completely unremarked because its owner finds them completely unremarkable. I do not need to think about how to spell these words; it just comes naturally. And just in case what comes naturally does not come correctly, there is a spelling checker built into this computer – both are equally embedded and routine parts of the culture and technology in which I live and whose control I have internalised. Such knowledge is clearly not innate, but neither is it immediately available for unfettered inspection and change, at least not in its everyday usage. It is seldom obvious where or how we learn this kind of thing or how it comes to be expressed so easily: it just seems to come out. But out of where? The answer is, out of the infrastructure of intelligence – a deeply personal yet increasingly global system of virtual systems, methods and judgements, by virtue of which we benefit from the explicit rationality of the experiences and accomplishments of others without needing to recapitulate them explicitly in the here and now.

Conversely, what happens when intelligences collide who do not share much infrastructure? This is common enough, not only for individuals but for entire societies, as the history of migration, colonisation and the formation of

---

[1] Crook (1983: 13).

new languages all show.[1] When the 'other' is neither aided nor constrained by the skills, meanings, symbols, knowledge and so forth that I take for granted, they are likely to be seen as stubborn or wily or wise or stupid or mysterious or impure, but above all else they will seem to be alien. Their otherness may seem to be a qualification or a curse or just neutrally different, but it will seldom fail to set them in a quite different world, often quite literally so.

Not that it usually requires any special experience of the other to judge them. Difference alone is often enough, especially differences that are important to our own world view and sense of ourselves. This is especially true when that sense and that world view are relatively undeveloped and we are still unaware of how it comes into existence, and so unaware of the general equivalence of different infrastructures, or of the fact that difference marks anything but a natural or a God-given boundary between us. But then it only requires such intuitively felt differences and a little crass rationalisation and suddenly we are on the road from the enlightenment offered by Darwin to apartheid and even Auschwitz, across bridges furnished far more by imaginations poisoned by social warfare than by the theory of evolution.

It is important to note here that even the most passive aspects of such infrastructure are still specifically intelligent. Unlike the structure of a leg or a nesting instinct, which cannot be changed by the organism that possesses (or rather, is possessed by) it, the beliefs and powers at an intelligent being's disposal are all open to insight, criticism and transformation. Or if they are not, then this is serious evidence of a pathological derangement. Often, of course, we don't actually use that ability, and altering some of structures on which we rely would be inordinately demanding and inadequately rewarding, and perhaps simply impossible in practice. I doubt that I personally could invent an alternative to the English language if I felt that it lacked the subtleties I needed, let alone persuade the rest of my linguistic community to adopt my innovations. Nevertheless, it could be done if that community put its collective mind to it. The point about the infrastructure of intelligence is that, where a nonintelligent organism is not *able* to address its environment in terms of fully explicit, completely articulated schemes, intelligence does not (normally) *need* to address explicitly great swathes of its own existence, precisely because of the rationality (objectivity, and so on) of what has been accomplished in its past.

Embedded structures

Returning to intelligence: we find potential intelligence not only in brains and minds but also in books and tools. Tools contain ready-made answers to practical problems. Given a pair of scissors, you do not need to solve the problem of how to cut cloth. This problem is already solved in the design of the scissors. Scissors were developed through many generations by steps of kinetic problem-solving intelligence, to produce the potential intelligence that is built into their present design. Apart from the invented basic feature of pivoted knives, all manner of problems had to be solved, such as techniques of metallurgy and how to form their

---

[1] Bickerton (1990), Cavalli-Sforza and Cavalli-Sforza (1995).

shapes and sharpen them. Each step required some kinetic intelligence to solve the problems: now these are stored as useful potential intelligence solutions built into every pair of scissors.

Richard Gregory, 'Seeing intelligence'[1]

The infrastructure of intelligence does a great deal more than provide a repository for past experience. For example, the mass of implications created by the gradual maturing of intelligence – implications that may incorporate any degree of intension without entailing any explicit intentions at all – makes it unnecessary for intelligence to actually *acquire* many, perhaps most, of the capacities it needs to make sense of the universe. The very process of embedding a new structure is enough to create a great range of new connections. For example:

> The inclusion of a tool in the process of behaviour (a) introduces several new functions connected with use of the given tool and with its control; (b) abolishes and makes unnecessary several natural processes...; and (c) alters the course and individual features (the intensity, duration, sequence, etc) of all the mental processes that enter into the composition of the instrumental act.[2]

By the same token, far from being limited to a particular set of conditions, a newly embedded structure of activity is liable to apply itself to any circumstances to which it is (or even seems to be) applicable. A lesson learned from an apple falling on your head can, given the right connections, be applied to the motions of planets. More generally, it is this omnipresent but subterranean web of implications that explains why it is perfectly possible to be insightful and original without any previous experience of the problem at hand – and also why it is often so hard to break free of a particular set of prejudices. After all, it was the same capacity for unspoken assumptions that allowed the ancients to ascribe circular orbits to the planets: their overt reasoning may have been based on the logical perfection of the circle, but it is hard to see how such conclusions could have been drawn without both a mass of presuppositions and large gaps in their reasoning, of both of which the Greeks seem to have been largely unaware.

From the present point of view, the most important consequence of this increasingly massive infrastructure is the impression it creates that human beings are pre-programmed to perform a wide range of functions. After all, what could such an infrastructure contribute to activity other than the sense that, however *correct* it might be, it is automatic, unreflecting, uncritical and generally not rational at all? This impression is exacerbated by the occasional unpredictability and apparent arbitrariness of human acts: on the one hand, the full implications of this infrastructure may not come out until the appropriate content and context are actually present; on the other, shortcomings in this infrastructure may come out in completely unexpected circumstances, revealing blind spots and misconceptions of the most surprising kind.

---

[1] Gregory in Khalfa (1994: 14).

[2] Vygotsky, in Wertsch (1981: 139).

This passive yet vital aspect of reason grows and changes continually, creating new levels of self-evidence and automation with each new stage of intelligence as a whole. It permits intelligence to *not* take things into account, at least not explicitly, without ever losing control of them. That is not to say that the entire infrastructure is wholly or directly at intelligence's direct or even effective disposal. Indeed, to the extent that the intelligence in question fails to internalise a given structure of activity in its entirety, any actions that rely on that structure will always be more or less subordinated to it, and so to some external locus of control. If the tool referred to by Vygotsky above is *not* fully internalised – if some aspect of its form, fit or function is superficially or incorrectly grasped or their latent implications are not recognised – then a good deal of the work it should facilitate may in fact be hampered by its actual use. Nor is this is a minor problem: most social structures are accompanied by at least a degree of disharmony, yet must be submitted to if one is to participate in social relationships.

In the case of ingrained habit or tradition it can also be very hard to gain full control over one's own actions, not least because the structure in question actively resists proper internalisation and rationalisation in the first place. For example, a religious mystery may be invalidated by insufficiently respectful execution, so no objective test can lead to a devotee losing their faith in it, because 'objective' testing shows a lack of proper respect. As Evans-Pritchard observed of magic, it may also be embedded in a comprehensive but circular system of reasoning.[1] And so on.

Nevertheless, given the opportunity and the occasion, intelligence is capable not only of changing its mind but also of apostasy against its most heartfelt beliefs. It may even (collectively) transform the whole structure of social relations in which it is embedded. It is impossible to imagine a non-intelligent organism executing such an about-face: biological structures are simply incapable of supporting self-knowledge, self-criticism or self-development of this (or any other) order.

Nor is this infrastructure dead to the world, invisible, incorrigible or inaccessible; indeed, there are whole organisations, from families to schools to global corporations to the United Nations, dedicated to its maintenance and operation, for which what the rest of us take for granted is the focus of the most explicit and vigorous attention. For example, there is a mass of laws relating to my social rights, to contract and to due process, and a mass of institutions on which I can call should a dispute arise. These laws and institutions are not neutral, and they are routinely used as weapons in the struggle between different elements in a given society; but for present purposes at least, that is not the point. The point is that they exist as a constant potential in my existence, and moreover do so without my having to do anything about it, once I have tapped into the requisite structures and relationships. They are not, in themselves, part of my personal infrastructure, but the ability to understand, address and perhaps make use of them is.

---

[1] See also Polanyi (1958: 286–94).

What is more, there are various processes whereby we seek out and take control of ever more aspects of that infrastructure at every level. This is one of the main consequences of market forces, not to mention basic research in the sciences or the more radical elements of politics, though they clearly exhibit very different degrees of deliberateness. Furthermore, at least part of the benefit offered by these processes is the increasingly rational control they give us over these very processes. Not that this is an unmixed blessing: I doubt that the subtle use of sophisticated social and psychic pressures by advertisers is a completely unalloyed blessing for consumers. Nevertheless, the general trend seems to be clearly towards an increased internalisation and rationalisation.

Obviously, then, to describe this infrastructure as passive does not mean that it was not created by intelligence or that it is inert. It is passive in much the same sense that my skeleton or even much of my nervous system is passive: it operates without prompting and is sustained without appreciable attention or reference to any external source, even if it is perfectly capable of taking such externals into account. Its passivity represents the inertia of structures that are anything but inert, the real activity of only apparent inactivity, an absence implicit in the present, a link to a kind of subterranean otherness constantly constituting and reconstituting the self.

The development of passivity

Given the way in which it complements the active aspect of intelligence, it will come as no surprise that the infrastructure of intelligence develops, and that there are intuitive, concrete, formal and dialectical forms of passivity as well as of activity. Furthermore, each main stage in the development of this infrastructure can be divided into a sequence of sub-stages exactly equivalent to activity's passage from impulse to certainty, with the single *caveat* that the complete internalisation on which the formation of an effective infrastructure relies is inevitably delayed *vis à vis* the creation of the ability to solve the original problem, so to speak. After all, if the objectification of a problem and its solution is a precondition of its subsequent internalisation within the subject, then its active construction *as* an object must necessarily precede its entry into the infrastructure.

The sub-stages of passivity are *ignorance, uncertainty, integrity, engagement, scepticism* and *spontaneity.*

As the nature of these sub-stages can be inferred from their active counterparts, they need only be sketched out here. Thus, while impulse can be considered the wholly *ignorant* form of activity – unheeding, unaware – *uncertainty* can be seen as impulsiveness that at least intuits its own ignorance, and as such corresponds directly to doubt. Uncertainty and doubt may be blind, but they are not altogether oblivious in the manner of ignorance and impulse. Similarly, just as awakening centres activity on assembling the parochial, one-sided forms of reasoning constructed during the previous sub-stage into a single *integral* intelligence, so the bare integrity that follows from this synthesis suffices to gather every mode of awareness to itself, to the extent that coherence becomes a minimal standard of activity – a decided advance on its predecessors.

However, taken by itself, integrity is a self-absorbed virtue, as indifferent to its objects as its newly awakened status would suggest.

On the other hand, precisely because it insists on the integrity of its own point of view, the integral intelligence cannot help but encounter different things and events in a regular manner. Conversely, precisely because it has yet to grasp that even the simplest, most compliant object still exists on its own terms too, its lack of enlightenment as to the nature of individual objects means that the integral intelligence will regularly encounter the same things in different ways as different facets of its own infrastructure are brought to bear on them. As a result, if it tends to do things purely on its own terms – as at the present sub-stage, it must – it can scarcely help but be rebuffed, and can scarcely escape the conclusion that it must address things and events more wholeheartedly on their own terms. And because the rebuffed activities arise out of the fact that even the integral intelligence already possesses multiple overlapping types of structure and functioning, it can scarcely help coming to see that it is through their synthesis that it will be able to create a sustainable grasp of the confounding object.

With that, intelligence begins to make *engagement* with its objects on their own terms the natural framework of activity. And beyond even engagement, the playful, experimental character of wisdom may support a certain attitude of confident, easy mastery, but it is also fated to harbour a niggling *scepticism*, if not downright denial of any possible finality. The intentional ambiguity (not to say occasional unintelligibility) of the present 'post-modern' trend in cultures,[1] with its deliberate re-introduction, if not of noise then certainly of contradictions, into the pure forms (of music, of argument, and so on) with which the preceding sub-stage was obsessed, is a case in point. So is the increasingly multinational (though not yet truly global) character of markets, corporations and state organisations. Nevertheless, a wise scepticism and a sceptical wisdom are the only road to either spontaneity or certainty. And once they are reached, 'passivity' reaches its apogee, and a whole new mode of reasoning *a priori* is established.

As with the developmental sequences detailed in the previous chapter, the outward appearances of this process can be paradoxical. At the extremes, both ignorance and spontaneity are self-sufficient and proceed confidently. However, this confidence and self-sufficiency are not equally well founded at each pole. An impulsive intelligence is merely indifferent to, because unaware of, its real situation and proper nature, whereas a spontaneous intelligence is genuinely disinterested in, because in full command of, a fully internalised situation and a fully totalised nature, at least as far as the present stage is concerned. In other words, their equal confidence flows from mutually contradictory wellsprings.

In the interregnum between ignorance and spontaneity, intelligence can neither completely ignore nor completely comprehend its situation, but acts with

---

[1] Jameson (1997: Introduction). See also Gellner (1974: 47ff) for the particular case of contemporary Anglo-Saxon philosophy, or Sokal and Bricmont (1998) for a splendid savaging of some of the worst excesses.

prejudice moderated by circumspection, wishfulness constrained by ambivalence. During the more mature sub-stages, it will apply its preconceptions across objects because it recognises that two objects are, for the purposes of this particular generalisation, the same; but before this there must be a less mature period while it generalises across objects because it does not realise that they are different. Similarly, by abstracting from context at a relatively advanced sub-stage we raise our awareness above the limitations of the here and now; but at an earlier sub-stage we lack the power to comprehend the richness and complexity of the concrete situation precisely because we cannot transcend the impoverished and schematic abstractness of the undeveloped object.

Hence the seductive yet treacherous power of tradition, of ideology, of received wisdom, of established practice: one day they stand in the vanguard of reason, and the next they are sinks of reaction.

The infrastructure of consciousness

> Vision is the art of seeing things invisible.
>
> Jonathan Swift

So large parts of intelligence, even of rationality, are hidden from sight, not least because they provide the very preconditions of seeing. And that is precisely why they should not be underestimated, taken for granted or considered secondary to the 'real' business of intelligent *activity*. Returning to the *terminus ad quem* of all intelligent activity, namely the actualisation of the world, it is clear that it is overwhelmingly by virtue of the infrastructural character of most of the means at intelligence's disposal that it can even begin to approach the actual. It is after all scarcely ever because we are explicitly *articulating* our grasp of reality that we are able to *grasp* it. When the real is at its most obvious, the ideas, concepts, plans, models, principles, methods, tools, techniques, machinery, systems through which it is constructed are least in evidence.

Insofar as these structures are truly internalised within the infrastructure of intelligence, they are as much features of rational activity as the steps in a mathematical proof: you do not need to be aware of them all at once to be able to take advantage of them or to be able to infer when some of their implications are invalid for your present purposes. A skilled artisan knows when they are using the wrong tool for the job without having to think why, and may well never have thought about it explicitly. Indeed, the internalisation of such structures means much more than increased efficiency or effectiveness. For example, it is only because the infrastructure is the embodiment of the intelligence in question's past experience and conclusions about existence that there is no conflict between actuality being wholly objective and its being filled with meaning for the individual subject.

All the same, precisely because it harbours a vast and growing range of means for taking the world for granted, the infrastructure of intelligence is a double-edged tool. As well as providing an immediate insight into things, it also creates the illusion that this immediacy is created without mediation – the exact opposite of the truth. That is, it creates the impression that experience is not in fact *constructed* at all. This is particularly clear from the history of epis-

temology and of ideas generally, although it is by no means a purely philosophical fancy. Ideas such as free will have a clear and profound impact not only
on the predominant scientific and political climates of our time but on many a
homespun morality too. So, by operating completely spontaneously and transparently, an effective infrastructure can easily create the impression of a kind
of empiricist immediacy, of 'direct perception', 'natural talent', 'the facts', 'raw
feels'[1] or 'the natural order'.

The existence of such an infrastructure also has a critical bearing on much
more practical problems. For example, it explains why many activities that are
apparently based solely on primitive sensorimotor and perceptual-behavioural
structures turn out to be impossible without the guiding hand of this more profound but wholly implicit framework. For example, conditions such as blindsight and cortical blindness are pathological not because the sufferer's sensory
or perceptual abilities are damaged but because the sufferer cannot *make sense*
of – objectify, cognise, recognise, rationalise, and so on – the content these sensory and perceptual systems offer. The problem is not that sufferers cannot see
but that they cannot look. The *mediations* needed to *actualise* the relevant sensorimotor and perceptual content and context are not themselves sensorimotor
or perceptual. So even where there are clear sensory and perceptual deficits, it
is clear that, taken by themselves, these fall far short of explaining the higher
level problem.[2] Without the infrastructure of intelligence, the senses make no
sense.

But if the evidence suggests the existence of some kind of superordinate
structure regulating how things and events are made sense of – and there have
always been those for whom the empiricism of 'sensory' or 'perceptual' knowledge always was obviously flawed – there is nothing about the way in which
so much human activity is actually grounded in this infrastructure that gives
any clue as to what the alternative is, and critics of the empiricist idea of the
self-evidence of data often simply fall into their own characteristic mistakes. In
particular they are prone to inferring from the same apparent lack of construction that we are hosts to 'innate ideas', or 'reflexes' and 'instincts', or 'fatalism'
or a rather different kind of 'natural order'. The problem with such postulates
is equally clear – that they can only be accounted for in terms of equally

---

[1] As the reader will recognise, the present account has clear implications for Dennett's
well-known critique of *qualia*, though its larger thrust lies in a quite different direction,
to say the least. See Dennett (1991) and his paper, 'Quining qualia', in Marcel and
Bisiach (1988), as well as Marcel's 'Phenomenal experience and functionalism' in that
volume; and Edelman (1992: 111ff and 151ff).

[2] On the significance of blindsight, see Dennett (1991) Humphrey (1992), or Edelman
(1992). On the impossibility of performing many apparently primitive perceptual-
behavioural and cognitive tasks without the support and direction of higher level cognitive processes, see the papers by Marcel, Weiskrantz, Gazzaniga and Kinsbourne in
Marcel and Bisiach (1988). For a variety of essays on related themes, from the consciousness of childhood to the civil rights of multiple personalities, see Cohen and Rapport (1995). See also Hirst and Woolley (1982: 23ff and *passim*) for a general account of
how still higher order social and historical structures determine and regulate organic
structures.

unlikely notions such as the inheritance of concepts or some kind of divine spark.

Nor, finally, does it make sense to lump these two positions together, as though as vague a notion as 'learning' – the most subtle concept to which any combination of empiricism and innatism can aspire – could account for the qualitative differences that arise between the successive stages in the development of human nature or the fundamental shift away from any possible heritage of experience a structure such as mathematics represents. Indeed, I suspect that even a concept as simple as 'not' is quite beyond either. If seeing is indeed believing, this is not because of the primacy of the perceptual or the verisimilitude of the empirical but because of the profound but implicit order the infrastructure of intelligence injects into even the most 'superficial' act, be it perceptual, empirical, phenomenological or otherwise. The 'self-evidence' of the senses merely expresses the perfected – and therefore invisible – stability and mobility of the structures through which intelligence controls them.

The idea that intelligence has a profound infrastructure is also relevant to the recent debate on the relationship between human and non-human experience. There is a school of thought[1] that rightly observes that the greater part of human activity requires no thinking, being characterised by a kind of bare consciousness. However, from this lack of correlation between thinking and consciousness the same school infers, wrongly, that the apparent absence of thought in animals does *not* imply that animals in general are *not* conscious.

Hopefully the arguments explain presented here why this conclusion is false. As intelligent beings, we are able to do so much without thought – without overt reflection, without explicit plans, without defining any special expectations in advance – not because the link between consciousness and thinking is unnecessary but because each stage in the development of consciousness (in my terms, the formation of the passive infrastructure of reason) internalises previous modes of reasoning to the point where it is no longer necessary to articulate them explicitly. Once mastered, we no longer need to think at their level.

So it is not true that there is no correlation between thought and consciousness; on the contrary, the link could scarcely be closer, and it is precisely because of the closeness and nature of this link that the higher forms of consciousness render the lower forms of thought redundant. It is true that we are conscious even when we are not thinking, but that does not mean that if we had *always* lacked thought we might still be conscious in some bland, undifferentiated sense. As I write these words I do not need to think *how* to write, as I did when I was a small child. I just know. But I could never 'just know' if I had never thought about it *at all*. Since pre-intelligent animals not only do not think but have *never* thought, whatever consciousness they may have can bear little relation to the consciousness we possess – whatever such a contradictory phrase may mean.

---

[1] See, for example, Griffin (1981, 1984), Midgley (1978) and various papers in Ingold (1988).

At the same time, the fact that it is possible to advance such an argument at all reflects the fact that so many psychologists, biologists and philosophers treat consciousness as an unstructured field, which can therefore be freely attributed to anything. If that were an accurate reflection of the nature of consciousness, then consciousness would, as Griffin, Midgley and others have asserted, be a more parsimonious explanation of the more elaborate forms of 'instinctive' activity than a billion years of evolution.[1] But then the same would apply to the activities of plants, rocks and neutrinos, which leaves us with the monstrous postulate of pan-psychism.

However, if a serious analysis of consciousness is undertaken (and although I have avoided this issue, I believe that such an analysis is implicit in the account of intelligence given here), it soon becomes clear that it has a structure and functions that are so critical to rational action, so immense in their implications and so different from those characterising any other kind of activity that it would be all but impossible *not* to notice that another organism was intelligent, or to *not* conclude that an intelligent being – and only an intelligent being – is simultaneously a conscious being. The possession of, for example, objectivity has such massive and obvious consequences for the organisation of activity – through planning, representation, symbolism, social organisation, means–end relationships, reflexivity, and so on – that one could scarcely be mistaken about such a thing.

This false approach to consciousness finds echoes in all sorts of places. For example, it seems to typify the kind of phenomenology that entertains the notion of 'pre-reflective experience'. It is true that 'In the silence of primary consciousness can be seen appearing not only what words mean, but also what things mean...',[2] but this 'primary consciousness' is itself the product of extended effort and development. Both its veridicality and the apparent absence of reflection required to create it are the results not of any 'immaculate perception' but of an extended history of construction and reconstruction, to the point where the significance and implications of an object are (more or less) self-evident. This is confirmed by the fact that, once intelligence has come into existence, its objects are not merely *capable* of being named, classified, ordered, systematised, and so on, but positively *call out* for active comprehension in this way. This is why a 'phenomenological reduction' is only possible for the most sophisticated intelligence – because only then can it take such an extraordinary range of concepts and structures for granted that it can even imagine that the world might be grasped directly, and so affect to rise above them.

---

[1] For example, Midgley in Ingold (1988: 40–1). For Lloyd Morgan's original canon of parsimony, see Morgan (1903: 54ff), where Morgan explicitly refutes precisely this version of parsimony. Of course, Morgan was by no means the originator of this criterion of good method. Newton postulated that 'We are to admit no more causes of natural things than such as are both true and sufficient to explain their appearances' (*Principia Mathematica*, 'Rules Of Reasoning In Philosophy'). Equally famously, William of Ockham asserted that '*Entia non sunt multiplicanda praeter necessitatem*' – entities should not be multiplied unnecessarily. No doubt he too had many predecessors.

[2] Merleau-Ponty (1962: xv).

On the other hand, for want of any sense of the constructed or constructive nature of its methods, that kind of phenomenology is left with no solution at all – a condition it then passes on to its ethical cousin, existentialism. This leaves both completely incapable of achieving their objective, namely to give the world a sense, be it a content, a structure or a direction. Hence the exotic intellectual flora that has sprung up on this well-rotted soil. As Lévi-Strauss observed:

> Instead of doing away with metaphysics, phenomenology and existentialism introduced two methods of providing it with alibis.[1]

Such an approach is unlikely to provide reason with much nourishment.

That is not to say that phenomenology and existentialism have nothing to tell us about reason. On the contrary, the phenomenal and existential character of consciousness and the intimate link between consciousness and intelligence ensure that the development of a suite of phenomenological and existential tools will be an indispensable step in the creation of a true science of human nature. But the ideas of pre-reflective experience and phenomenological reduction are not likely to be among the things a full theory of intelligence needs to preserve, except perhaps in a museum.

The obvious

> 'And you think things will be better in San Lorenzo?'
>
> 'I know damn well they will be. The people down there are poor enough and scared enough and ignorant enough to have some common sense!'
>
> Kurt Vonnegut, *Cat's Cradle*

To summarise all these points under a single rubric, the infrastructure of intelligence deals in the *obvious*. However, the obvious is only obvious to an intelligence who is at the level at which it is constructed and who accepts the assumptions on which it rests. That is why what is obviously factual to me may be obviously fatuous to you. Isn't it obvious that the Earth is flat, stands still and the Sun goes around it once a day? Isn't it obvious that private property and the 'free' market are the guardians of democracy? Isn't it obvious that any science of human nature must be based on biology? Isn't this just common sense? But with a single simple change, it can all become common nonsense after all. The change in question can be one level of development, one different fact or assumption, one shift in social or psychic perspective, or any of a hundred other changes, large or small. But until that change actually comes about, the world retains its own peculiar obviousness and we our common-sense credulity. That is why intelligence finds it so hard to escape from its own standpoint in the here and now or to take seriously other conditions, other interests and other perspectives.

Returning to my original account of the organisation of intelligent activity, the obvious means that the infrastructure of intelligence is in permanent thrall

---

[1] Lévi-Strauss (1984: 71).

to the present, the apparent and the self, which may make it all but impossible to grasp that the absent, the other and the real may not only differ from but also flatly contradict our most profound beliefs and assumptions. From where you and I are sitting, the Earth obviously is flat, stands still and the Sun goes around it once a day, but from the surface of the Moon – the location, for most historical purposes, of other generations, other classes, other genders, other cultures – the Earth is plainly round, in constant motion, and its movements have no bearing whatsoever on those of the Sun – which, incidentally, looks very different from up there. Even when we are wise enough to incorporate a little scepticism into that infrastructure, often it either consists of a blanket denial that anything is quite as it seems or simply substitutes a socially organised and approved common sense for the more private variant. In neither case is this likely to be a significant advance.

Likewise, being limited to what it can literally take for granted, common sense lacks the ability to overstep the bounds of sterile generalisation into fruitful abstraction. Nor can it ever dig beneath the merely empirical and arrive at the genuinely concrete. Consequently, it is incapable of either genuine originality or true authenticity. But then neither could things be otherwise, given that common sense is what you think when you are not thinking. Even when, at more advanced levels of development, it becomes common sense to concede that, realistically, the absence and otherness of large parts of reality ought to be taken into account, it is almost always an ineffectual concession, because the sheer effectiveness of an advanced infrastructure usually makes it unnecessary, in practice, to do any such thing. At the very least, common sense commands a huge range of excuses for not doubting the obvious just *now*.

Hence the first aspect of the apparent bounds of reason: we take altogether too much for granted. But I hope it is clear that, precisely because it is possible for us to note and face up to the fact that we do this, and even to institutionalise our defences against taking too much for granted in the form of scientific method or revolution, it is not an absolute boundary while reason continues to reason.

The unevenness of development

> An analysis of Trobriand behaviour and language shows that the Trobriander, by custom, focuses his attention on the things or act in itself, not on its relationships... he deduces no causal connexion from a sequence... The Trobriander has no linguistic mechanism for expressing a relationship between events or acts. Culturally, causality and teleology are either ignored or non-existent... By this I mean, not that the individual Trobriander cannot understand causality, but that in his culture, the sequence of events does not automatically fall into the mould of causal or telic relationship.[1]

A second aspect of the apparently limited role played by reason in human activity is the unevenness of individual intelligences. Even the greatest and most

---

[1] D. Lee, quoted by Kluckhohn in Marwick (1970: 221n).

deliberate exponents of reason in one field can show remarkable backwardness in another. To mention only one example (of which more will be heard shortly), Aristotle's logic was the acme of formal rationality for more than two thousand years, yet many of his views on biology or physics could be spontaneously refuted by a modern school child.[1] Indeed, whole eras have passed in which the philosophical sophistication and scientific knowledge of a society's élite exceeded the society in question's technological or cultural grasp in just this sense. Medieval Islam and Christendom provide obvious examples, as does ancient Greece.[2]

This unevenness, which is entirely real and far more widespread than we, in our complacent modernity, usually recognise, poses a double threat to the present theory's claim that all aspects of that individual are governed by a single universal structure of subject, object and world, and that its development is determined by a single universal process of abstraction and concretion. One would surely expect such alleged unity to lead to a consistent level of development across the whole of any individual intelligence, whereas the actual unevenness we find seems to suggest both a multiplicity of uncoordinated developmental processes and perhaps the need for an extra-intelligent explanation of how each local facet of reason really develops. What else could account for the startlingly modern use of proportion and perspective by the stone-age artists of Lascaux, Chauvet and Altamira or the coincidence of the most primitive technology with the most elaborate lineage systems among Australian aborigines?

In a way this is a problem of my own making. The preceding chapters presented the development of reason as an all but automatic programme of almost unalloyed progress, yet real history and consciousness are notoriously messy things – awash with distractions, breakdowns, diversions and stases, abounding in rationalisations and alienations, complications, errors and omissions. Occasional asides to the effect that the development of intelligence can be pretty convoluted scarcely explain the convolutions themselves. There is clearly a case to be made for the view that, whatever their hypothetical rationality may suggest, in practice human beings do not seem to be very interested in acting intelligently, let alone rationally. Nevertheless, as I hope to demonstrate in this section, this perfectly real unevenness is just what one should expect from intelligence, not *despite* its striving for objectivity but precisely *because of* its aspirations and tendency to such lofty rational goals.

---

[1] For a summary of Aristotle's scientific principles, methods, achievements and limitations, see Lloyd (1979: 200–25). Lloyd shows that, although Aristotle was the first to advance systematic methodological principles or to follow a systematic research programme (and the Greeks were the first to insist on logical and mathematical *proofs*), his real methods were quite different, as a result of which his results were substantially contaminated and undermined.

[2] Hill (1984, 1993); Hodges (1971); Landels (2000).

Intersecting developments

> We're all of us, every one of us without exception, when it comes to the fields of
> learning, development, thought, invention, ideals, ambition, liberalism, reason,
> experience, and every, every, every other field you can think of, in the very low-
> est preparatory form of the gymnasium! We've got accustomed to making do with
> other people's intelligence – we're soaked in it!
>
> Dostoyevsky, *Crime and Punishment*

Each aspect and product of intelligence is a structure in its own right. An art
form, an idea, a belief, a technology, a method, an institution, an estate or a
class, a practice, a value: each has its own necessities, its own possibilities, its
own proper logic, its own propensities, its own dynamics, its own internal order, its own residual contingencies. It must therefore be developed in its own
right – Nature no more makes leaps here than anywhere else. This is the fundamental reason why, its natural (if unintentional) pursuit of coherence, consistency, completeness and correctness notwithstanding, any immature intelligence will always tend to be unevenly developed, with frequent errors, omissions and consequent conflicts. For to be grasped in all its many-sided complexity, any given object must be grasped in all these different aspects, and to
grasp each aspect the subject must come to terms with each of them independently of (though not necessarily in isolation from, and certainly not regardless
of) all the others. Hence the uneven development of each individual intelligence is the reciprocal of its need for objectivity.

To return to my teacup and the tea it contains, to treat it objectively I must
be able to deal with it as a physical object located in time and space and existing within a distinctive framework of substance and causality. Otherwise I
shall spill the tea, or perhaps leave it for so long that even I would find it too
cold to drink. I must also grasp its chemical aspects. For example, when deciding how full to fill it or whether to carry it across the room, I need to bear in
mind tea's ability to stain the carpet. Of course, I am not conscious that this *is*
chemical knowledge, but it is certainly a quite different aspect of the objective
significance of drinking tea, about which I must learn independently of its
strictly physical aspects. And biologically too, I must recognise not only tea's
power to refresh and its propensity to go mouldy if left around for a week or
two, but also the fact that it contains drugs that I will regret imbibing to excess.
And as the object of specifically intelligent activity, it is still richer. For example, as a object located in the very different world of social and symbolic conventions and processes such as 'having a nice cup of tea', it resonates with all
the peculiar rules and preconceptions with which contemporary English society imbues this odd ritual. As for the unspoken significance and nuances of
sharing this cup of tea with this individual in these singular circumstances…

Given the very different demands made by trying to grasp so many different aspects of even a single object, it is no wonder that the development of intelligence is so uneven and that the relationship between more and less sophis-

ticated aspects of a single object can become so convoluted.[1] Sometimes the higher leads to lower, as when a Greek temple embodies concrete rational technology and formal rational aesthetics; and sometimes the lower commands the higher, as when the Nazis subordinated the formal economy of a great nation to an ideology of extraordinary primitiveness. And sometimes the two simply co-exist, side by side, often mediated by a combination of common sense, *ad hoc* ritual and indifference. That is not to say that every single aspect of intelligence develops in isolation, any more than it acts alone. After all, I did not learn about tea and teacups by studying each facet in turn; I just drank a lot of tea. Of course, the less mature a given intelligence is, the harder it is for it to actively make use of its intelligence to ensure that the unification of its knowledge and powers is actively pursued. Conversely, the apparent simplicity and ubiquity of the experiences by virtue of which I acquired my grasp of tea does not alter the independence of each of its different aspects. Nevertheless, the completion of each successive stage – of intuitive objects, of concrete relationships, of formal systems and then the final dialectical totalisation and actualisation of all structures and functions – is also the completion of a new form of organisation of intelligence as a whole. Hence the great countervailing force preventing the highly localised need for accuracy and precision from exploding objectivity into chaos: the process whereby the higher and higher levels of integration are constructed ensures not only that larger and more complex objects may be composed but also that they are structured in terms of more profound and subtle connections.

And given that common internal structure relating all its different modes of activity to one another, why should insights and criticisms garnered in one field not be applied, in the right translation, elsewhere and elsewhen? If a link can be established between otherwise distinct topics – an analogy, a correspondence, a resemblance, a metaphor, an equivalence, or whatever – then it should be possible to solve or even pre-empt later problems almost purely on the basis of the insights gained in solving earlier ones, even where the latter are not entirely the same. The only question is whether a given structure is mature or experienced or skilled enough to take advantage of the opportunities offered

---

[1] That it is objectivity that is developing here, as opposed to the kinds of functional skill and sophistication any bird or mammal can be expected to achieve with experience, is shown by the fact that, to master a simple physical task such as walking along without spilling a very full cup, one must be able to apprehend the objective properties of the liquid in the cup independently of one's interest in it. After all, merely wanting to 'not spill' something is certainly not enough to ensure that one does not actually spill it. That presupposes the ability to deal with the object in question in its own right, for its own sake and on its own terms. Simple though such a task sounds, it is extremely difficult to elicit evidence that any organisms other than primates – the sole serious candidates (so far) for the status of intelligent beings – can accomplish this feat, or in any other way grasp any aspect of the environment they inhabit independently of their organic interest in it. Even the largely sensorimotor mammals and birds that are capable of using tools seem to be restricted to exploiting them only when they fit in with their current appetites. I don't think anyone has seen a chimpanzee build a tool shed, let alone devise a research programme.

by changing circumstances.[1] This might create the appearance of direct insights and long distance saltations, seemingly in violation of any consistent notion of a consistent developmental *process*, but the reality is simply the exercise of the routine capabilities of intelligence in general.

So, despite the fact that each new form and aspect of intelligence must have its own development, the abstract need for each aspect to intelligence to be developed in its own right does not preclude the elimination of huge amounts of redundant experience. There is no need for each and every intelligence to take each and every facet of every possible object through every possible phase and nuance. In fact it is quite startling what links intelligence can create, given a sufficiently rich mix of individual talent, knowledge, principles, clues, coaching and opportunity, and a sufficiently powerful social and symbolic matrix within which to operate. Of course, it would be a great deal harder for a Neolithic society to assimilate fully the germ theory of disease or the idea of equality before the law than the proper use of a steel axe, but ultimately it is only *absolutely* necessary that the right structures be effectively appropriated developed from somewhere – a strangely unconcrete postulate, but entirely in keeping with intelligence's abstractness and unprecedented combination of resources and resourcefulness.[2]

Nevertheless, whatever promises of cross-fertilisation the unity of intelligence as a whole may hold out, the concrete reality is unlikely to live up to this promise fully. The developmental process can scarcely be made to shrink almost to vanishing point merely because it is theoretically redundant; the practical exigencies of the daily life of an immature being militate against it. For example, the ability to compartmentalise knowledge and experience may hamper any process of cross-fertilisation.[3] There is also ample evidence to show how mature adults drop a good way below their usual level of competence when confronted by a new task.[4] This may even reach the extreme of having to recalibrate the body's sensory and motor expectations (when, for example, coming to terms with massive neurological damage or a zero-gravity environ-

---

[1] Eg, Cole, Gay and Glick in Berry and Dasen (1974: 159-195).

[2] One of the main areas of interconnection is that between culture and various aspects of intelligence. On this, see 'Culture and intelligence', from the Laboratory of Comparative Human Cognition, in Sternberg (1982: 642–719), which also discusses some of the conceptual, methodological and theoretical complications of studying the effect of various 'levels' of activity on intelligence, and *vice versa*. For an extended practical instance, see Luria's study of the industrialisation of Uzbekistan under the Soviet regime (Luria, 1971, 1976). Luria's account of the relationship between cognitive and social development seems to assume a very close connection between cognition structure and the concrete social, cultural and linguistic conditions in which it develops, whereas I would argue only that changing historical conditions facilitate the emergence of universal forms of reasoning. This may only be a matter of emphasis: Luria focuses on a much more concrete level of reasoning, whereas my goal is to account for reasoning at its most abstract. See Hallpike (1979: 117ff) for a relevant critique of Luria's position, and related cases. For a range of related issues, see Cole (1996).

[3] Eg, Jahoda (1970)

[4] Fischer and Bidell in Lerner and Damon (1998).

ment). More generally, there are presently more than six billion intelligent beings on this planet, but it cannot be said that humanity as a whole makes six
billion years progress each year. On the other hand, it makes a good deal more
progress, and makes it more quickly and more securely, than evolution has
ever managed.

This unprecedented combination of simplicity and complexity and its impact on development have often been noted, from Hegel's 'cunning of history'
or Lenin's 'combined and uneven development' to Piaget's concept of *décalage*.
Any such concept is bound to take account not only of the evident empirical
unevenness of human development but also of the logic that makes this
unevenness necessary and the forces that eventually resolve the whole into an
evenly developed totality characterised by the coherence, consistency, completeness and correctness to which I have alluded so often. However, until that
resolution is brought about, all such models also entail that any given intelligence is at more than one level of maturity at the same time, depending on
which aspect of it one has in mind.[1]

For example, the members of a society whose social structures are intuitive
are unlikely to be limited to intuitive levels of cognition. In fact they could not
be: childish intelligences could not sustain a society of any kind without the
constant support and guidance of much more advanced caretakers. So I have
no doubt that cognitive testing of members of Sahlins' 'Stone Age economies'[2]
or Levi-Strauss' 'savages'[3] would quickly dispel any idea of simple societies
being populated by individuals with simple minds. So does the simple fact that
their technology is strictly intuitive, yet they often have a well-articulated tax-
onomy of literally hundreds of species[4] and are generally sensitive enough to
the internal order of their natural environment to avoid over-harvesting or
over-hunting it at least as well as we avoid despoiling our more artificial environment. None of these achievements would be open to cognitively intuitive
individuals.

In more social and historical terms, what constitutes a 'higher' level of development in strictly economic terms may not be 'higher' as far as the ideologies and values of the individuals involved are concerned. As a result, there
may be serious unrest at the prospect of change, regardless of the agreed benefits, even before the change is any more than an aspiration. For example, it has
been observed that the members of intuitively structured hunter-gatherer societies may be aware of the potential benefits of higher levels of social and economic organisation can bring (eg, through trade or other association with local

---

[1] Cole (1996: 86–92).

[2] Sahlins (1974).

[3] Lévi-Strauss (1972).

[4] Atran (1990 and in Sperber *et al.*, 1995: 205–33); Lévi-Strauss (1972). I should emphasise
that these taxonomies are not specifically formal. In particular they lack both objective
principles and an overarching abstract structure, and they are the products of occasional
observation, not the systematic research to which formal reason would naturally resort.
Finally, they lack organised technical methods for investigating phenomena and wield
only vague and inconsistent conceptual methods for incorporating new exemplars.

town-dwellers), but they are unwilling to make the investment needed because they foresee no benefit to themselves as individuals.

This does not indicate either a natural individualism or a determined adherence to the *status quo* for its own sake or a lack of real foresight, but only a rational comparison of short- and long-term costs and benefits at various levels.[1] Again, this is scarcely what one would predict, given nothing more than the intuitive nature of their social system. Indeed, only with the emergence of global social systems at the formal rational level has it *ceased* to be commonplace for either individuals and the society of which they are members or different segments of individual societies to operate on quite different levels.

The relative independence of, say, social and cognitive development is especially clear where intellectual issues are at stake, for intellectual development can be much more self-contained and self-directed than others spheres of development, especially where the requirements of intellectual development do not include significant apparatus (as demanded by the natural sciences, for example). In such circumstances, thought and argument can ascend to a far more sophisticated plane than the social order within which it arises. It is also clear that many important cultural structures routinely operate on a higher level than the economic and political structures with which they are historically associated. Yet they are by no means radically separate, as even the most striking cases of the independence of the intellectual from the social illustrate.

Jaspers' proposed 'Axial Age' (c. 800-200 BC), for example, seems to exemplify the growing independence of thought from things, in the sense that a very great part of our subsequent intellectual methods and concerns were laid down at that time, and have continued in recognisably similar form ever since.[2] And although there were corresponding social changes, it is by no means obvious how the specific forms of thought that arose during the Axial Age were determined by the prevailing social conditions, except in the very general sense that the societies in question were able to support a regular élite that possessed the leisure and opportunity to develop new ideas for their own sake. Nevertheless, this apparent declaration of intellectual independence is by no means complete. In particular, it is striking that most of the systems developed then are less than optimistic about human existence, if not directly then certainly in the sense that they see little merit in living for its own sake, as contrasted to the universality of human suffering and the notion that the 'real' rewards of life were achieved through submission to a wholly external authority (ie, God), and generally obtained only in a hypothetical afterlife. This persistent negativity surely cannot be unrelated to the fact that none of the societies in question possessed either the economic resources or the social sophistication to translate an intellectual enthusiasm for respect for the individual, the relief of suffering, morality and justice into social realities. There is no shortage of similar contradictions in history. The Renaissance, the great cultural efflorescence during the sixteenth century of the Ottoman, Safavid and Moghul empires, and so on – it

---

[1] See, for example, Johnson and Earle (1987: 96).

[2] Hallpike (2004: Ch.7).

is far from unusual for the cultural and intellectual achievements of a society to outstrip its material capabilities and social arrangements.

To the extent that the great accomplishments of such periods imply that the members of economic, political and cultural élites must have achieved a level of cognitive development that was largely denied to the social strata these élites exploited, they embody in the most practical manner the distinction to be drawn between the specifically cognitive level of development individuals actually achieve and the developmental forces and resources different societies make available for cognitive development. On the other hand, such limits clearly do not doom the members of such societies to a child-like existence. Individuals may be quite limited in their capacities in the sense that they do not progress significantly beyond concrete operations,[1] but as folk taxonomies and folk biology demonstrate, the practical knowledge that the members of a relatively undeveloped society routinely acquire will greatly exceed what any single individual might discover on their own. Indeed, it may even be far beyond anything a more advanced culture or technology could quickly construct. After all, the Parthenon and the pyramids were built without the least knowledge or application of formal engineering methods, but we would be hard pressed to find their equals among modern architecture.

On the other hand, not only may a culture not require an individual to make use of their higher cognitive capabilities in terms of participate successfully, but it may also provide positively approved 'answers', structured at the lower level than that at which the individual in question would spontaneously operate. It may even punish the 'wrong' answer, by ostracism, juridical sanction or a thousand other measures. In such a case, the individual's cognitive competence would be hidden by their compliance with the cultural norm. There are, for example, several known cases of individuals in pre-formal societies seeming to develop from one cognitive stage to the next in the course of an experiment or a specialised game or activity, apparently because they were perfectly *competent* to reason at a higher level than they would usually *perform*.[2]

Hence the link, but also the difference, between the cultural and technological sophistication of a given society and the cognitive competence and performance of the individuals who inhabit it. Hence also the fact that development is a function of opportunity and compulsion as well as innate potential, structures and forces. That is why it is possible to accelerate the developmental process (be it through advanced social structures or direct education), even if it cannot be radically diverted. Even when one correctly rejects the view that the development of the individual is wholly determined by the social system they inhabit, the latter is certainly a major factor in determining the depth and complexity of experience and activity that is open to that individual. This is true even for our experience of the natural world, whose subtlety and independence of social relationships are otherwise widely underestimated.[3] So, given that

---

[1] Hallpike (1979, *passim*).

[2] See, for example, Bovet in Berry and Dasen (1974: 311–334); or Hallpike (1979: 190–191).

[3] Hallpike (1979: 95–102).

until recently no large-scale society had reached a formal level of structure, where would the impetus come from for individuals to rise to the level of formal reason? There may well be *opportunity* to develop that far, especially among educated élites, but it requires an exacting historical analysis to identify real instances and to demonstrate their real effects. Certainly there can be no simple reading from one level to another in either direction.[1]

A similar argument applies to the otherwise curious fact that when western societies invented childhood a few centuries ago, they made much more of this distinction for boys than for girls. As Ariès says, 'boys were the first specialised children'.[2] This does not mean that boys were objectively or apparently more child-like; rather it reflects the different ways in which childhood related to adulthood for the two sexes in pre-modern Europe. The different roles played by men and women meant that the formal schooling of boys began to demand specialised institutions and processes long before that of girls, whose education continued to be overwhelmingly domestic. During the same period, songs and dances and games that were once common to all ages and classes came to be abandoned by the adults of the upper classes but retained by their children and by working people of all ages – again because of the quite different trajectories of personal and cultural development that were created by their different social lives.[3] In each case, it seems to be the interplay between differently developed structures that explains the otherwise inexplicable inconsistencies between the individual cases, with all the social and psychic repercussions this must have had.

This multiplicity of parallel and overlapping developments also tends to make a people's account of their own existence strikingly complex and many-layered. For example, a social group that has apparently been assimilated to a more sophisticated social system may frequently retain less sophisticated rites and values, or its maintenance of ancient ways may be completely misunderstood by the dominant society.[4] Likewise, the somewhat concrete and even intuitive arrangements that characterise private life in many modern households seems to belie the formal nature of industrial society as a whole, and advanced societies are commonly littered with small groups who have refused the formal paraphernalia of society at large in the name of the concrete rituals of a particular sect or creed. The official tenets of Catholicism laid out in successive Papal encyclicals are overtly magical, and many of the conflicts within contemporary Catholicism are traceable to the difficulty many individuals in a formal rational society have in accepting them.[5] Conversely, the internal logic of the events described by ancient, classical and most Biblical mythology is often plainly in-

---

[1] Piaget himself concluded that 'in numerous cultures adult thinking does not proceed beyond the level of concrete operations' – a view shared by a variety of anthropologists and comparative psychologists (in Berry and Dasen, 1974: 309). An extensive analysis of the relationship between social and cognitive structures is provided by Hallpike (1979).

[2] Ariès (1973: 56; see also pp. 357ff).

[3] Ariès (1973: 60–97).

[4] See, for example, Layton in Coote and Shelton (1992: 137–159).

[5] Douglas (1996: 46ff and *passim*).

tuitive or concrete, yet the interpretations placed on them by later generations were generally cast well above that level.[1] The content of a given story may remain as intuitive as ever, but the interpretation the storyteller uses to mediate between the text and its audience might be more or less formalised. On the other hand, the very fact that events need expert interpretation in order to convey their 'real' meaning shows that there remains a schism between the original events and the audience to whom they are interpreted. For example, the ancient Egyptians provisioned the departed for their journey, and when this practice started it was real bread that went into the grave. But it soon came to be replaced with a more theological substitute:

> This is an easy concept: the physical man was formerly here; now the spiritual man is over there; we must project over to him spiritual, not physical bread, so that the absolute is not necessary; the name or the idea or the representation will be enough.[2]

But if this distinction between the physical and the spiritual had been obvious to the originators of this rite, why would the dead have required bread of any kind? Is this consistent with any notion of a *purely* spiritual life beyond the grave? Clearly the original content – the provisioning with bread – has been shifted into a more formalised mode to accommodate this distinction, but only at the level of its practical implementation, so a paradox remains.

Nor is it likely that the apparently intuitive and concrete themes of the art that decorates the tombs of the monarchs, nobles and high functionaries of ancient Egypt reflect an intuitive or concrete level of thought among those buried there, those they left behind and the artists who created them. Like any other kind of art, it had only to symbolise much more highly developed forms of reasoning, at which the ancient Egyptians were indisputably adept; it did not need to keep up with them or correspond to them at all directly.

This is a common phenomenon. In part the reinterpretation of fairy tales over the last few centuries reflects changes in taste and attitudes towards children. Most English-speaking parents have stopped regaling their offspring with macabre tales of torture and martyrdom from John Foxe's *Actes and Monuments*, the prince does not rape the Sleeping Beauty in our version of her tale, and Red Riding Hood isn't generally eaten by the wolf. But as the content of the stories has become more tailored to current views of the child's sensibilities, the *form* of the tales has also become more sophisticated, and as more advanced literary forms take hold, the old tales are given more polished structures, complete with coherent plots, uplifting morals, dramatic tension and a beginning, a middle and an end – all features that were frequently omitted from, say, the folk-tales gathered by the Jacob and Wilhelm Grimm.

Likewise, appeals to some kind of Golden Age or Kingdom of God treat the distant past or future as periods with divine properties that are completely incompatible with historical continuity with the mundane present. Yet that continuity is asserted. Nor is it really explained just how either this infinitely re-

---

[1] Frankfort *et al.* (1949: 11–36 and 237–63).

[2] Frankfort *et al.* (1949: 72).

mote future will suddenly arrive or past glories will be restored, at least not in terms that are compatible with current reality as experienced by their audience. Indeed, if the Last Days could be explained in such comfortably familiar terms, they would lose their specifically eschatological status. But then neither is any such explanation called for, as the *normal* consciousness of time during this period was in terms of religious meanings, even to the point where the main motive for such apparently scientific activities as establishing the precise length of the year were actually to ensure that religious rites are performed at the right times.

A parallel streak of utopianism is visible in the political sphere (especially in concrete rational societies), with similar implications for the realisation of the fundamental changes to which would-be revolutionaries aspired. There is a persistent harking back to a bygone world of natural nobility, egalitarianism, collectivism and benevolence – the era 'when Adam delved and Eve span' and no one was a gentleman. And whereas its religious counterpart was flawed by the very fact of being religious (and therefore only capable of being resuscitated by the Will of God), so the political ideal was rendered utopian (in the negative, quasi-eschatological sense) by its specifically *naturalistic* character, even though it disregarded the specific historical quality and position of human nature. That is, because the ideal to which this utopianism aspired was widely assumed to be an intrinsic feature of human nature that had somehow been lost or betrayed rather than the product of determinate social changes, its proponents were incapable of putting forward a social or political programme that was likely to restore it. General calls for redress of grievances, the reduction of dues and services and the abolition of the landlord's monopolies – the normal aspirations of ancient and medieval peasant revolts – could never lead to genuine revolutionary change, and the mystical and magical practices and rites that were frequently adduced to help achieve these ends were unlikely to make much of a difference, their latent meanings and capacity to enthuse their participants notwithstanding.[1] Consequently, it would have required a miracle for any such Golden Age to be restored, and in practice it generally resulted in nothing more productive than bloody rebellions, *coups d'état* and changes of dynasty.[2] It is no surprise that 'utopia' translates as both 'a good place' and 'nowhere'.

As far as the conventional *cum* official line is concerned, the relationship between past, present and future bears all the hallmarks of intuitively grasped (ie, unarticulated) succession, yet the very act of hypothesising such an absolutely removed time is precisely the kind of imaginative leap of which an intuitive intelligence would be completely incapable. Again the original has been infused with more mature elements as each generation found the original imagery less and less satisfactory, but the unevenness with which different aspects of intelligence are developed never disappears altogether.

---

[1] For example, Needham in Porter and Teich (1986: 61–73).

[2] The cult of the Noble Savage, the utopianism of medieval peasants and other European expressions of this phenomenon have all been widely documented. For a brief account of its Chinese counterpart, see Needham in Porter and Teich (1986: 61–73).

This need to bridge the gap between the original tale and the terms the audience finds intelligible can eventually become too great to be sustained. For example, neither miracles nor the Will of God qualify as explanations to modern believers in any field other than religion, and belief in miracles is a notorious stumbling block for modern religions in industrial societies. Nor is this a purely modern phenomenon brought about by the rise of scientific reasoning, the consumer society or any other familiar scapegoat. No doubt they all play their part, but the fundamental problem is the extreme distance that separates the simple social condition in which the tale originated and the sophistication of later audiences – a pervasive problem in all civilised societies. Many, perhaps most, more or less advanced societies have difficulty convincing themselves of their own received mythology, no matter how official or sanctified it may be, leading to both a pervasive scepticism among the educated and the forcible repression of public agnosticism and atheism.

In short, by injecting a contemporary literary form and an up-to-date 'moral', the contradictions that make it so hard for contemporary audiences to understand what the traditional story means may resolved, but only at the price of depriving the tale of its original significance. It thus becomes possible to retain the tale as a valued part of the canon without doing too much literal violence to the original, as there is now a well-understood and accepted 'interpretation' to hand. Its re-telling may even enhance the original in its new audience's eyes, as the now strikingly 'metaphorical' nature of the actually crude and inconsequential original and its ability to transcend time and place can now be hailed as proof of its genius! In this way a worn out old story is turned into a statement of a profound 'mystery' – precisely what its original was not.

Nor is this solely a matter of intellectualising cultural traditions; on the contrary, it is an integral part of every struggle to make decisions of any significance. Persistent primitive residues and unevenness in the development of reason can be found even in those forms of reason such as science that are famous for their sophistication and maturity. To show how long essentially intuitive modes of reasoning endured, one has only to consider Jacob's summary of the rise of biological knowledge in Europe, when intuitive reasoning, with all its insistence on the interventions of a pure divine will, remained the norm for orthodox pre-Darwinian thought. Of course, the more primitive forms Jacob describes were left behind centuries before, and the theology and metaphysics on which Darwin's opponents based themselves were anything but intuitive in themselves. Yet there are echoes:

> At this time, it was not even conceived that natural phenomena, the generation of animals as well as the movement of heavenly bodies, could be governed by laws. No distinction was made between the necessity of phenomena and the contingency of events. For if horse was obviously born of horse and cat of cat, this was not the effect of a mechanism that permitted living beings to produce copies of themselves, somewhat as a printing machine produces copies of the text. Only towards the end of the eighteenth century did the word and concept of reproduction make their appearance to describe the formation of living organisms. Until that time living beings did not reproduce; they were engendered. Generation was

always the result of a creation which, at some stage or other, required direct intervention by divine forces...[1]

Science, mathematics and problematics

Another especially striking example of how different conditions influence the development of different aspects of intelligence can be found by contrasting the development of what are undoubtedly the most overtly and intentionally rational achievements of intelligence, namely science and mathematics. These are indisputably the most determinedly coherent, consistent, complete and correct forms of activity, and their respective careers are as radically intertwined as any. Nevertheless, in many ways their respective developments could hardly be more different. Of course, there are parallels and influences operating in both directions. Mathematical innovations and refinements have always been at least partially motivated by practical problems originating from every possible source, including accounting, surveying, gunnery, logistics, architecture, painting, navigation, astrology and astronomy; and some of the most remarkable of physical discoveries, especially in the twentieth century, flowed almost directly from possibilities implicit in the mathematics brought to bear.[2] Yet in many respects their careers have been extraordinarily different.

To see how great the dichotomy is and how powerfully affected their respective developments were, one only has to reflect on the paradox that classical Greek science seldom rose above the intuitive and concrete levels, yet Aristotle, its greatest single exponent, produced a logic that stood as the epitome of formality until long after intuitive and concrete reason had ceased to be the norm in either science or society, to the point of positively obstructing further development for centuries.[3] Not that science and mathematics have developed along *qualitatively* different routes; rather, each has been faced with very different obstacles and opportunities for development. In particular, as far as logic, mathematics and other more narrowly intellectual disciplines are concerned, their development is largely under direct internal control, whereas that of science is beset with any number of practical problems, organisational, disciplinary, technical and methodological, all of which had to be solved (often over and over again) before science could establish a canonical approach, let alone a body of credible knowledge. Geometry can be done with a stick in the sand; meteorology demands a little more.

Hence the relatively free and rapid development of Greek logic and geometry, whereas the Greeks' meagre scientific achievements illustrate only too well the restraining power of external obstacles. Greek astronomy in particular was

---

[1] Jacob (1993: 19).

[2] Ifrah (1998); North (1994); von Soden (1994).

[3] Piaget and Garcia (1989). See pp. 83–87, for some illuminating examples of the independence of different levels, and the forces which bring them into line; pp. 253-254 for comments on the contrasting history of Chinese science; and pp. 235–267 for a general summary. De Caprona *et al.* (1983) present a wide range of related arguments and observations. See also Carey in Strauss (1988: 1–27).

characterised by advanced mathematical models, but also by *ad hoc* and poorly supported technical skills and tools and, at least until Hipparchus and Ptolemy, few credible observations, let alone research programmes. Only at this late date – centuries after the Greeks' first attempts at astronomy and millennia after the first organised observations in Mesopotamia – did astronomy progress from identifying isolated phenomena and detecting patterns and correspondences – the archetypal forms of intuitive and concrete rational 'method' – to producing geometrical models of the motions of celestial bodies and formally deriving predictions from the independent totality of relations of an independent body of knowledge. And even then, the fully integrated system of observations and technical methods (such as of a formal coordinate system) and the supporting apparatus of conceptual criticism and justification one would expect of a fully formalised structure can scarcely be said to have been in place. On the contrary, attempts at physical explanation were flimsy and far between, and the whole floated on rafts of philosophical speculation. Meanwhile, the mathematics that supported this cosmology from the other end, so to speak, grew ever more florid and sophisticated.[1]

More generally, even leaving aside the many social, ideological and historical factors that often militate directly against it,[2] the internal complexities of any scientific discipline always make it a great struggle to establish science on a proper footing. Partly for want of suitable techniques of research, partly for want of a workable organisation or concept of science itself and partly because of the inadequate social and symbolic organisation of experience in general, early science especially was doomed to a series of massive and often catastrophic detours, and later sciences are often encumbered by the prejudices and preconditions set by existing systems and methods. That is the main reason why Aristotle failed to solve scientific problems school children today find relatively straightforward: not because of some personal blind spot but because the problems with which he was dealing had yet to find a suitable form. Although his logic is exactingly formal, his physics, with its concentration on sequences of static states rather than dynamic processes, is scarcely more advanced than one would expect from intuitive reason. Regardless of the genius he brought to bear on these particular problems, the relevant *problematic* had yet to be developed to the proper degree.[3]

That is not to say that the development of mathematics has been entirely uncontaminated by externally imposed content and context. On the contrary, some of the conditions on which its development depends are far from being under the control of mathematicians alone. The lack of a suitable notation, us-

[1] North (1994).

[2] See, for example, Needham (1969: Ch. 2 and *passim*) on the radically different impact the same technology had in China and Europe, largely as a result of the very different social, cultural and technological conditions.

[3] Lloyd (1979) traces the history of Greek thought with just this issue in mind, while Landels (2000: Ch.8) concludes his survey of engineering in classical antiquity with the same point. Analogous factors that affected the resolution of a number of more recent debates in the sciences are analysed in Engelhardt and Caplan (1987).

able numerical symbols or any means of signifying zero hampered western mathematics for centuries.[1] In fact it appears that many ancient and classical number systems operated at an intuitive level. This is indicated by the fact that the choice of symbol depended on the nature of the thing counted, a single symbol could refer to different amounts depending on what was being counted,[2] large numbers are symbolised by simply adding and subtracting the values of smaller valued symbols such that 1848 is signified by, say, MDCCCXLVIII, and so on. Unfortunately for such a system, even simple arithmetic requires something like the multiplicative *structure* that is provided by zero and a true positional notation (in which 1848 is constructed by adding the results of 8, 4 x 10, 8 x 100 and 1 x 1000), and very large numbers are usually completely inexpressible.[3] And how would one express the value of *pi* beyond a handful of places?

Nor was this a problem restricted to purely intellectual endeavours: the lack of a medium capable of supporting even semi-abstract arithmetical operations hampered the development of administrative systems in the ancient world.[4] Furthermore, by hampering the accurate calculation of time, it was impossible to agree definitive dates for major religious events such as Easter and saints' days,[5] which naturally perpetuated discord among those concerned with the timely performance of ritual. Nevertheless, the salience, persistence and power of these problems is still quite limited by comparison with those faced by even the simplest science, and in any case any obstruction of mathematics by the lack of suitable externalities only reinforces the point that conditions can make very heavy weather of development.

As for the relationship between science, mathematics and everyday life, that is equally conditioned by the circumstances in which each kind of intelligent activity actually develops. And again, the disjunctions are stark: objectively speaking, we inhabit a world imbued with science and mathematics, and a vast range and volume of scientifically established and mathematically structured knowledge informs everyday life, often quite explicitly; yet our personal knowledge and reasoning about the world around us are only very imperfectly characterised by the formality on which its informants rest.[6]

---

[1] Ifrah (1998). For an engaging account of the history of zero, place-holders, the number system and related matters, see Kaplan (1999).

[2] For example, 'the S' system... was apparently used exclusively either for the recording of slaughtered or perished cattle of the current accounting year or for denoting a specific type of produced or distributed beer' (Nissen *et al.*, 1993: 27).

[3] The place value system on which this method rests has been invented at least three times, by the Babylonians, the Chinese and the Mayans. For the limits of non-place value systems – 'practically unusable for any purpose save writing numbers down' – and the earliest examples of place value, see Ifrah (1998: ch. 23 and *passim*), or Nissen *et al.* (1993: 142ff).

[4] Nissen *et al.* (1993); Damerow in Strauss (1988: 125–52); or Nicolopolou in Cole *et al* (1997: 205–25).

[5] Duncan (1998).

[6] See Atran in Sperber *et al.* (1995: 211–6 and 228–30); and Polanyi (1958: *passim*).

Nevertheless, the reasons for this discrepancy are perfectly intelligible without hypothesising fundamental differences between, on the one hand, the scientific and mathematical mind and, on the other, everyday mental life. One does not need to be a giant of the sociology of knowledge to understand the gap between the two sides or to acknowledge that the intentional *creation* of knowledge by means of science and mathematics faces very different conditions from the *use* of the same knowledge for decidedly non-scientific and non-mathematical purposes.

Bergson and biologism

The question of problematics is doubly important in the present context, for not only is their growth a clear example of how the development of intelligence is complicated by the conditions in which that development takes place, but the problematic of human nature is itself immature. It is moreover to a very large extent the immaturity of that problematic taken as a whole rather than any paucity of factual knowledge about human beings that explains why human nature remains so impervious to scientific explanation.

For present purposes a problematic can be defined as the sum of conditions that allow the problem in question to be solved. These conditions include not only an adequate definition of the problem and the technical and conceptual tools needed to solve it but also suitable organisational and disciplinary factors, problem solvers with the right skills, the experience, the ethical willingness, the resolve and the leisure to look for a solution, and so on. It also demands access to the necessary raw materials, be they the infinitesimal particles generated by a linear accelerator or the tiny and fast evaporating pool – perhaps already gone – of societies still untouched by industrial culture and technology.

Not that all the elements of a particular problematic need to be in place before a problem can be solved: we should never underestimate the power of human ingenuity. An adequate problematic is one in which *enough* of the conditions needed to solve the problem at hand are present for those who wish to do so to solve it. On the other hand, the mere presence of all the right factors is not enough for a solution to appear. A quite distinct (and generally quite separate) act of construction is also necessary, without which the pieces of the solution may well lie about the intellectual landscape for a long, long time, waiting for someone not only to arrange them correctly but also to realise what they mean.

As even this imprecise definition suggests, a problematic is very much a historical construction. As such, it is not only unevenly developed on its own terms but access to it varies from one place and situation to another. For example, it may well be that Mendel's seminal researches – 'conclusive in their results, faultlessly lucid in presentation, and vital to the understanding of not one problem of current interest, but of many'[1] – were ignored because few scien-

---

[1] R.A. Fisher in Stern and Sherwood (1966: 171).

tists of his day were 'mentally prepared' for his ideas, as R.A. Fisher put it.[1] Clearly Mendel was in full possession of an adequate problematic, but it would not become available to his fellow scientists for decades to come.

The fates of such brilliant biologists as D'Arcy Thompson and Hans Driesch[2] also stand as stark yet tragic warnings to those who would go too far too fast, although for the opposite reason. Mendel was moving too quickly for his professional colleagues, but he was moving in the right direction; others have tried to solve legitimate problems without having the appropriate problematic at their disposal, and consequently have been led on a wild goose chase. Although it is not at all clear that Driesch and Thompson have deserved the vilification to which they have been subjected, it is clear that the absence of credible biological concepts forced Driesch especially to resort to non-scientific concepts, and for many years Thompson also stood far outside the pale, although he has been somewhat rehabilitated.

The fate of Henri Bergson and his famously heretical treatise, *Creative Evolution*,[3] is especially instructive. For among the key features of a problematic are the assumptions a discipline makes about the nature of the problem at hand, and so about the kind of solution it calls for. In Bergson's case, he assumed that, to explain human nature, he had to address the full range of phenomena it presented, including its 'spiritual' dimension; and that the only kinds of solution that were possible were evolution or vitalism. Bergson chose vitalism, and paid the price.

But that is not the moral of this particular tale. Although mainstream biology has successfully disposed of Bergson's *élan vital*, its own solution is only acceptable if one makes quite the opposite assumption about the kind of solution that is needed, and takes it for granted that one does *not* have to account for the 'spiritual' aspects of human nature. At the very least the allegedly higher reaches of human nature may be treated as secondary, derivative or epiphenomenal, if not wholly illusory. However, given that one must surely define a scientific solution in terms of its adequacy to the reality it is trying to explain, one can scarcely even begin to describe what is specifically human about human nature without reference to a whole range of characteristics of which biology knows nothing. Consequently, this is no solution at all. Indeed, Bergson's work is relevant here not only because of his attachment to these problems but also because his approach to them stands as a warning biology would also do well to heed.

There is no question that vitalism is a dead end. But Bergson's remarkable book did hit on three vital problems any credible theory of human nature must

---

[1] Fisher also points out that Darwin's similar breeding experiments during this period were also largely ignored. Regarding the claim that is sometimes made, that the journal in which Mendel's work was published was too obscure to be noticed by those who might have appreciated it, in London it was received by the Royal Society and the Linnaean Society. Mendel was also in regular, if frustrating, correspondence with Carl Nägeli (Fisher in Stern and Sherwood, 1966: 56ff).

[2] For example, Thompson (1961) and Driesch (1908).

[3] Bergson (1947).

surely address. These are the limits of human reason (in particular the inability of certain forms of reasoning to grasp the realities of existence); the difficulty of making either mechanism or finalism account for evolution, especially the evolution of human nature; and exactly what, if anything, is so special about human beings.

Unfortunately, Bergson's preferred solution was far less promising, consisting as it very largely did of imposing archaic and artificial methods on the problem, and so arriving at conclusions that were as wide of the mark as Aristotle's and Plato's (and for very similar reasons). Had he been writing after the stabilisation of Darwinism or the advent of systems theory, field theory or structuralism, or had he even been better acquainted with other models of development available in his own time, his evident intellectual powers might have brought him closer to the truth. But this being no more the case for Bergson than for Aristotle, his ideas remain quaint curios, a testimony to the impotence of even the most powerful sympathy and imagination once it has encumbered itself with an immature problematic.

But Bergson is only notorious for a sin for the inverse of which almost all recent would-be biologies of human nature should also be notorious. Bergson imagined that the biological could be explained in terms of the spiritual, and this was a mistake; however, biologism sins every bit as grievously by asserting the reverse. Bergson erred because he supposed that the stunted combination of overt mechanism and covert finalism he diagnosed in the biology of his day represented the *terminus ad quem* of science, so science itself had to be discarded if human nature was to be comprehended. But biologists have erred in turn by supposing that the undoubted power of contemporary biology entitles it to claim authority over human nature too, and that it is unnecessary – and unnecessary *a priori* – to look too deeply into human nature itself before deciding how to deal with it. Bergson failed to grasp human nature because he grasped too little of biology; and biology fails to solve the same problem today because it grasps too little of human nature.

However, Bergson's sin was the more forgivable of the two, for he set out on his expedition before biology had achieved the maturity we now take for granted. Modern biology, by contrast, has not only fundamentally underestimated the nature of its human object, but the territory it claims for itself is not the virgin land it imagines it to be. For example, not only are concepts such as culture, altruism and territoriality simply reduced to entirely imprecise and inappropriate biological analogues, but the general lack of discussion of existing uses of such terms by philosophy, the humanities and the social sciences only illustrates either how little respect many biologists have for other disciplines or how ignorant they are of the vast amount of discussion that preceded biology's contributions by two and a half thousand years.

At the same time, because biology's conceptual inadequacies prevent it from going beyond the most elementary features of human nature – the structure of the central nervous system, the features that hunter-gatherer societies supposedly share with baboons, wolves or whatever, and so on – it achieves no more than Columbus achieved when he first stepped ashore in the Americas and claimed a continent for the Spanish crown. It is, of course, a marvellous achievement, but it does not do justice to the hinterland, which such an expedition can scarcely detect, let alone explore. Even now, unable to tell that they have discovered a truly New World, many biologists persist in the fantasy that human nature really is just another province of the animal kingdom. But then, Columbus long believed that his new lands were really only the approaches to the Spice Islands or Japan. Of course, many biologists are happy to acknowledge that human beings are rather exotic by the standards of plants, ants or fish and even practically all birds and mammals, but deny that they could possibly be *fundamentally* different. So human nature is to be ruled by the same methods as biology's other provinces. Like good conquistadors, biologists claim everything for their sovereign, and take practically no notice whatsoever of their involuntary subjects. Like any imperial power, biology assimilates its human subjects to its own preferred system of rules and regulations. After all, have they not been proved over and over again with innumerable other species? Is it not the case that, as Richard Dawkins has put it:

> ... when you are actually challenged to think of pre-Darwinian answers to the questions 'What is man?' 'Is there a meaning to life?' 'What are we for?', can you, as a matter of fact, think of any that are not now worthless except for their (considerable) historical interest? There is such a thing as being just plain wrong, and that is what, before 1859, all answers to those questions were.[1]

So much for everyone from Buddha to Marx, not to mention well known passages from Darwin himself denying that biology had anything at all to say about questions of this kind (although most of these, it must be admitted, date from after 1859). And if others protest that there is more to human beings than the categories biology can muster, then we explain (*very* patiently) that they are being unscientific, or that the phenomena they insist on are illusory or superficial, or that they are only romanticising and refusing to face up to the biological facts of life, or that science will only be able to address these things when it has dealt with allegedly more 'fundamental' issues such as how the brain works and how we 'process information', when it has worked out what conditions prevailed on the savannahs of east Africa three million years ago, and so on. After all, no self-respecting scientist would try to understand the architecture of a modern building before they had understood the molecular structure of concrete, worked out how the bowerbird makes its nests and established a workable model of Neolithic campsites. By these means biology remains above the superficial foibles of *Homo sapiens*, such as technology and culture, history and consciousness, love and hate, humour, existential *angst*, doing scientific biology and all the rest of these inconsequential distractions.

But this apparent (and in many quarters apparently triumphant) culmination also reveals the flaw on which the whole enterprise rests, at least as far as any possible biology of rationality is concerned. The reason why biologists look to concepts such as adaptation, insist that understanding the brain will explain

---

[1] Dawkins (1989: 267). Dawkins is only one recent (and especially clear, direct and honest) exponent of a position that has been a constant theme among evolutionists from T.H. Huxley and Haeckel onwards (Haeckel, 1883, 1913; Huxley and Huxley, 1947; see also Simpson, 1969: 80ff, and Darlington, 1964: 217). Edelman provides a very similar, if much more supple and sophisticated case (eg, 1992: 174–5).

the mind and are constantly seeking continuities between rational and non-rational activity is because they believe that this allows them to deal with human beings objectively. But this claim is actually self-defeating, for biology has no concepts capable of explaining the capacity for objectivity itself. So biologists are studying organic life by means of abilities that have no apparent biological explanation. That is not to say that objectivity is not adaptive. On the contrary, it is hard to imagine anything more guaranteed to enhance adaptiveness. Nevertheless, the adaptiveness of objectivity, once it exists, tells us nothing about how it came into existence in the first place, or whether it can be understood as an adaptation properly so called. As I have already observed, it would be adaptive to be able to perform miracles too, but that would not explain how miracles could happen, make 'performing miracles' a biological function or show that this ability as an adaptation in any meaningful sense.

But in what sense could objectivity *not* be an adaptation? As I shall argue elsewhere,[1] objectivity (like intelligence in general) is indeed the product of normal organic processes, including adaptation, but once it exists it forsakes ordinary biological forms and functions as completely as life itself transcends the chemical reaction. For objectivity includes the ability to deal with things and events independently of one's interest in them. Without such objectivity, all science's claims and ambitions would be in vain. But such an independence of perspective is the very antithesis of adaptation in the normal biological sense, even allowing from the relative indirectness that accompanies many more sophisticated adaptations. Nor is there any other biological concept that can account for objectivity's simultaneous detachment from, yet also insight into, the conditions and facts of our existence; on the contrary, the basic model of adaptation precludes both. Nor is it any happier when confronted with a structure capable of reconciling the two sides of the process of natural selection out of which adaptations grow. Yet that again is exactly what objectivity (and intelligence in general) offers. For our objectivity allows us to identify, predict and control the very forces of variation and selection through which adaptation arises. Hence its ability to short-circuit evolution, which presupposes the inability of organisms to achieve precisely this insight. And nowhere is this expressed more clearly or explicitly than in evolutionary biology itself.

In short, although the capacity for objectivity certainly arose through ordinary biological processes, its actual operations do not appear to be organic. And the corollary of this position is that, insofar as it insists that human nature must be accounted for in biological terms, science cannot help concluding that objectivity is either impossible or unintelligible. Given that objectivity is an indispensable element of science itself, biology's 'scientific' account leads inevitably to the conclusion that science itself, biology included, is a fraud, a mystery or a very large mistake. There is indeed such a thing as being just plain wrong, and self-contradiction is the very best way to prove it.

The same argument can be extended to biology's inability to grasp other aspects of human nature. For example, given the current tendency to emphasise the (perfectly real) continuities between human beings and our primate cous-

---

[1] Robinson (in preparation).

ins,[1] I should also emphasise that even if other species are tool-makers, self-aware, language users, and so on, and even if those capabilities are plainly adaptive, that would not mean that normal biological concepts are capable of explaining how they are possible. Indeed, it would not make any difference if *every* existing species on planet Earth showed all the features sketched out in this book, if they spent their days discussing the secret names of God, and only concealed their intelligence from us as part of an amazingly successful, if somewhat surreal, joke. All it would prove would be that they were indeed intelligent: the question of whether biological concepts could explain these abilities would still be open.

Indeed, to the extent that human nature is 'understood' by biology, it becomes unrecognisable to any moderately self-conscious human being, biologists included. Whatever biology's merits in its own sphere – and I do not contest them for a moment – by forcing intelligence and reason into the straitjacket of biological categories, biology deprives them of their most essential features: on the one hand, their meaning, and on the other their intelligibility. Ultimately biology can no more conquer human nature than Ferdinand and Isabella could have conquered the animal kingdom. It is not a new 1492 that the biology of human nature needs, but a new 1789.

So why has this happened and what has it to do with the uneven development of intelligence? First and foremost, it has happened because of an obvious but dubious feature of the prevailing scientific problematic of human nature, namely the assumption that human nature will – indeed must – ultimately be found to be a biological nature. For the purposes of understanding human beings, science and biology are simply conflated. Not that this is entirely culpable. Not already having at their disposal the means of grasping human nature on its own terms, scientists cannot avoid starting by applying the most promising methods, tools and techniques they *do* have. For many scientists, that means the methods, tools and techniques of biology. This is a universal feature of activity of all kinds: as babies, we reach for the moon with our bare hands. But we have to wait a long time before the moon can really be reached – not least until we have taken the trouble to investigate what the moon really is.

Likewise, the problematic of human nature – the concrete conditions on which a solution to this great mystery rests – is too immature to be solved, and an arrogant biologism is certainly not the answer. Science must be willing to abandon its first thoughts and pay human nature the attention and respect it deserves. If it ever does that, it will be able to set in place another of the conditions on which the final conquest of human nature – a prize science is perfectly capable of winning – depends.[2]

---

[1] For example, Gibson and Ingold (1993); Parker and Gibson (1990); Antinucci (1989); Russon *et al.* (1996).

[2] For an illuminating analogy from the early history of scientific biology itself, see Eiseley's account of Lord Kelvin's understandable but misdirected attack on evolution and the damage this did to Darwinism (Eiseley, 1961: 234ff).

Alfred Russel Wallace

One final example from the annals of biology: the career of Alfred Russel Wallace.

It was, of course, Wallace, who not only prompted Darwin publish his theory of evolution but did so by presenting Darwin with an account of evolution quite the equal of – and extraordinarily like – his own.[1] Although Darwin's account was far more elaborate and he had spent decades substantiating it, Wallace has every claim to share priority with Darwin. Yet strangely, while Darwin's is a household name around the world, only among those with an active interest in evolutionary theory is Wallace at all well known. Part of the explanation for Wallace's eclipse is the disproportion between the two men's contribution: publication date alone is not enough. But it is probably at least as important that, when Darwin and Wallace began to address the problem of human evolution, they came to fundamentally different conclusions. Superficially the difference is simple enough: Wallace drifted into mysticism, whereas Darwin remained staunchly scientific. But that is not quite how it happened, and the real story provides yet another – in this case extraordinarily important – case study of how an immature problematic can betray a great idea.

The rift between Wallace and Darwin began to show when, in 1864, Wallace published what should have been one of the seminal papers of evolutionary theory.[2] He begins with a remarkable paradox – the stability of the human body in the face of substantial changes in other mammals – and then offers an equally remarkable solution:

> We must... look back very far in the past to find man in that early condition in which his mind was not sufficiently developed to remove his body from the modifying influence of external conditions, and the cumulative action of 'natural selection.'[3]

That is, Wallace's explanation for our unusual anatomical stability was that our exceptional mental faculties allow us to deflect the forces of evolution as understood by conventional evolutionary theory. Our bodies do not change because we can think our way out of the kind of predicament that normally allows natural selection to operate.

The clear implication of this argument was that *Homo sapiens sapiens* marked a fundamental break in the nature of evolution itself. Notwithstanding the quasi-Lamarckian strain of Darwin's work on human beings,[4] the difficulties

---

[1] Claims to priority over Darwin have been made on behalf of various theorists such as Patrick Matthew (Dempster, 1983).

[2] Wallace (1864).

[3] Wallace (1864: 167).

[4] Despite the fact that the inheritance of acquired characteristics is usually said to be a secondary mechanism for Darwin, my own reading of his *Descent of Man* is that, had I not already known of *The Origin of Species*, I would have taken natural selection for the secondary mechanism and habit, reason and the inheritance of acquired characteristics for the primary motors of human evolution. Indeed, Darwin says as much himself. For example, he expressly denies the primacy of natural selection for morality (Darwin,

offered by the apparent gaps in the fossil record, the mystery surrounding variation and heredity, and so on, all non-human evolution showed a reasonable fit with Darwin's original account. But as far as human beings were concerned, there seemed to be little that is specifically human that could be made to fit conventional ideas of variation and selection. One could still account for isolated features of human nature in terms of variation and selection, but this hardly seemed to explain the specifically human character of human beings.

Darwin's reaction to Wallace's argument was one of surprise and caution, but initially at least he could not resist its logic:

> I have now read Wallace's paper on Man, and think it most striking and original and forcible... I am not sure that I fully agree with his views about Man, but there is no doubt, in my opinion, on the remarkable genius shown by the paper. I agree, however, with the main new leading idea.[1]

Nevertheless, whenever Darwin discusses any substantive aspect of human activity (in his major works at least), he ignores Wallace's key point altogether. Although verbally he accepted many of Wallace's arguments to the contrary, Darwin was more or less content with conventional evolutionary processes and happy to treat human evolution as yet another accumulation of incremental and localised changes over long periods – which is to say, as an extension of the same evolutionary processes that came up with fins, flowers and flagellae.

It is not my concern here to support Wallace. It is clear that the problem he had identified can be solved in various ways, including in terms of a strictly Darwinian intra-specific competition between human social groups and similar pressures. Nor am I concerned with the extent to which Wallace's widely noted intellectual foibles and inconsistencies contributed to his subsequent eclipse. I only raise the subject in order to make a single, very brief point connected with what Wallace did next. It was clear that, for Wallace as for Bergson, no solution to the problem of human nature could come from evolutionary theory as it stood at that time. But neither was there any scientific alternative. In particular, there was no account of human intelligence comparable to that which has developed over the last three-quarters of a century. Conversely, Richard Dawkins' claim that the only alternative to evolution is God was much more compelling in Wallace's time than it is in ours.

As a result, even the dean of Darwinians, T.H. Huxley, was capable of some extraordinary contradictions. In 1858 he was maintaining simultaneously the view that 'the mental and moral faculties are essentially and fundamentally the same in kind in animals and ourselves' and the view that, by virtue of our capacity for speech (which Huxley distinguished from any 'spiritual' qualities), human beings are 'the only organic being in whose very nature is implanted

---

1901: 945–6). As Adam Kuper has observed, 'even Darwin found that he could be a Darwinian only intermittently when he reflected on the course of human history' (in Teich et al., 1997: 278).

[1] Quoted by Eiseley (1961: 305). Eiseley claims that Wallace later managed to dispel most of Darwin's remaining reservations. Contrast Darwin's reaction to Wallace's later spiritualism (eg, Darwin, 1901: 72–3; see also pp.195ff). On Darwin's later attitudes to Russel, see Desmond and Moore (1992, passim).

the necessary condition for unlimited progress'. Hence the cultural and ethical gap between human beings and other primates is 'infinite'.[1] As I shall argue elsewhere,[2] this is not a complete contradiction: there are material processes and mechanisms that are capable of creating an infinite difference out of a finite evolutionary change. But apart from pointing vaguely towards speech (which has, in itself, no moral properties whatsoever and is not an especially important part of the real answer), Huxley contributed no more to our understanding of them than any of Wallace's other contemporaries, from Darwin downwards. True, it is striking how many early evolutionists were much more sensitive to the *problem* of human nature than most modern biologists, especially neo-Darwinians. Yet there seems to be no acknowledgement by Huxley that the very notion of an 'adaptation', with all its inherent pragmatism, eclecticism and functionalism, is completely contradictory to any notion of indefinitely sustainable progress, or the infinite difference Huxley noted between the ordinary run of adaptations and human ethics.

So as far as the problematic of human nature was concerned, the only credible road open to Wallace was towards spiritualism. Precisely because he wanted to grasp human intelligence *objectively*, Wallace felt obliged to introduce the idea of a higher Intelligence guiding our development. Nor was this such a peculiar conclusion in Wallace's own time. Unlike spiritualism today, many late Victorian scientists with eminently materialistic credentials regarded mediums, séances and the like as serious topics of research (though few shared Wallace's enthusiasm or conclusions). For example, Robert Chambers, author of the scandalous *Vestiges of the Natural History of Creation*, was a convert, and it is striking that he only prompted T.H. Huxley to take on Bishop Wilberforce at their famous confrontation at Oxford *after* his conversion from a notorious materialism. Romanes likewise investigated spiritualism extensively, Francis Galton touched on the matter, and Darwin (who had previously allowed his fatally ill daughter Annie to be diagnosed by a clairvoyant, albeit reluctantly[3]) was disturbed by the issue. It was also considered a fit topic for letters and articles in *Nature*, the *Spectator* and other serious journals.[4] In short, although Wallace's conclusions may have seemed regrettable to many of his fellow scientists and Darwin, Huxley and others were sceptical (if not downright rude[5]), spiritualism was a respectable topic for research and many contemporaries shared his interest. This was, after all, the epoch of mesmerism and hydropathy too, and any number of other semi-respectable 'cures' straddling the border between medicine and quackery.

Nor did Wallace himself see his approach as contradicting Darwinism's authority regarding other species.[6] In many respects it was no more than a thread

---

[1] Quoted in Desmond (1994: 241)

[2] Robinson (in preparation).

[3] Desmond and Moore (1992: 379).

[4] Oppenheim (1985: 267–96).

[5] Desmond and Moore (1992: 607-608).

[6] For example, Wallace (1908), published in his eighty-fifth year, contrasts 'the vast range of subjects which the Darwinian theory explains' with 'the inadequacy of any

in a larger scheme to save the more spiritual aspects of human nature (especially religion and ethics) from being reduced to brute adaptations, with all the catastrophic repercussions that would have for the Victorian world view. This goal was shared by most of the founders of Darwinian evolutionary theory, but in the absence of a science of human reason they could scarcely reach that goal without introducing a range of profoundly unscientific elements. The same process has continued ever since in endlessly different and equally inconclusive religious, metaphysical, sociological and existential guises.[1] The only difference is that resorting to spiritualism has not only ceased to be an alternative to science but is widely seen as a catastrophic failure of reason. But that that difference is very largely a difference in context rather than goal is seldom taken into account by modern biologists. So, by accepting what was then the only alternative to the shortcomings he perceived in Darwinism, Wallace effectively discredited himself in the eyes of future generations of scientists. Perhaps his reputation will never recover. But he really had very little choice at the time.

So once again, the unevenness with which intelligence develops led to a great intellect being betrayed, and betrayed precisely because he wanted only to remain true to the ideal of reason. Like Oedipus, Wallace was destroyed not by stupidity or cowardice or venality or hubris, but by his commitment to doing what was right. His conclusions may not, with hindsight, seem very clever but, unlike those of many biological 'explanations' of human nature, they were motivated by a genuinely intelligent approach. Meanwhile:

> It is lucky for us that we don't make mistakes any longer; those who do so clearly have little to expect from history or from the intellectual charity of their professional colleagues.[2]

The rationality of unreason

History is often portrayed as a tale told by an idiot, as a comedy of manners concealing an inner core of folly, cunning, bestiality and darkness. Although this interpretation scarcely seems to square with the present account of history as the progress of reason, not only are these views compatible but any account of the progressive development of reason positively predicates a history of unreason as its corollary. To see this, it is only necessary to recall the first fact of development – that any developing structure is by any standard weaker and less able in its earlier incarnations that it will be later. That is what development means. So if history is the history of reason, for most of it there must be significant vestiges and dark pools into which intelligence can neither see nor reach, where 'unreason' prevails by default. At some point, in trying to deal with these aspects of existence, intelligence will be forced into some kind of ultimately non-rational compromise, from idiosyncrasy and pragmatism or

---

other explanation of the whole series of phenomena yet made public'.

[1] R.J. Richards (1987).

[2] Fodor (1983: 23).

convention or eclecticism to a savage impulse to force the world into an acceptable shape by the most violent means. Whether this means the over-
generalisation of incompletely understood concrete experience or the imposi-
tion of arbitrary but expedient abstractions, intelligence is always obliged to at
least *try* to deal with the lingering (but by no means incidental or peripheral)
contingency of complex and profound things of which it can make no convincing sense.

Add to this the inevitably uneven development of so many aspects of human activity, plus the fact that an immature and inexperienced intelligence will
find much of its own private infrastructure difficult to comprehend, and it is
not surprising that intelligence's undeniable achievements are laced with
equally undeniable failings, almost as though they were joined by some kind of
regrettable but inexorable genetic linkage. Hence the juxtaposition within a
single world of passion and nihilism, science and nostalgia, the lowest sensa-
tionalism and the highest principles. Although the present theory portrays
human activity strictly in terms of the development of reason, it does not imply
that we are always reasonable, or even that we always aspire to rationality. On
the contrary: if the emergence of intelligence is the universe saying to itself,
'Let there be light', then that light begins as a diffuse and precarious flickering.

Having conceded that intelligence is not just occasionally irrational but often leaps into irrational acts with terrifying alacrity, it is important to state exactly what that concession really means. There are, I think, two fundamentally
different interpretations of the relationship between rationality and irrationality. The first is that they are flatly opposed, locked in eternal struggle, as incapable of overcoming one another as they are of disengaging from the struggle
itself. This interpretation comes in innumerable flavours, from the Manichaean
struggle between darkness and light or Good and Evil to contemporary oppositions between body and spirit or art and nature. The recent trend for biologists and biologically-minded social scientists to see irrationality as an irreducible fact of human nature is only its latest, most scientifically respectable
expression.

But this is not the concept of the irrational I am trying to convey here. From
the present point of view, irrationality is a transient and localised form of
reasoning, indisputably flawed (if not downright catastrophic) but fully
capable of being completely dispelled by further development. This sense of
irrationality can be explained in terms of a range of analogous phenomena to
be seen on the organic plane. For just as an organism may be young, mistaken,
sick or ineffectual without being any less alive on that account, so intelligence
has its own special forms of immaturity, error, inexperience, illness and
ineffectiveness, yet they do not render that intelligence in any sense
unintelligent. Just as the sickness, immaturity, and so on to which organisms
are susceptible are themselves specifically organic in nature and reflect the
character of that organism as an organism, so the various forms of irrationality
found among rational beings express their fundamentally intelligent character.

For example, Yahweh's instruction to Abraham to sacrifice his first-born son
is at first sight a characteristic act of Old Testament savagery (though by no
means exceptional in the ancient Middle East). Yet it is possible to detect in the
story's *dénouement* the first rejection of the idea that human beings can relate to,

and perhaps influence, the gods by means of a form of magical participation. This rejection becomes even more explicit in Isaiah, where God is made to express his disgust at sacrifice even more vehemently.[1] Likewise it may seem that the painstaking genealogies of the gods Hesiod set out in his *Theogony*[2] only compound the irrationality of previous beliefs in nymphs and heroes. But in fact they marked an important step – more specifically a concrete rationalisation of the previously intuitive myths and beliefs – towards the identification of key cosmological principles (embodied in the Olympian deities, Fates, and so on), and so an important stepping stone towards the formation of a more strictly formal world view in which justice, fate and order might preside. 'One might almost say that mythological classifications, when they are complete and systematic, when they embrace the universe, announce the end of mythologies properly speaking.'[3]

So if reason does not always appear to make sense, even of or to itself, the nonsense it does make is peculiarly rational nonsense, and nonsensical precisely because its proper measure is the same as that of the highest forms of reason. An act is irrational because it is *in*coherent, *in*consistent, *in*complete or *in*correct – a set of criteria with no meaning on any other plane, and which it would be meaningless to apply to the functioning of a physical, chemical or biological structure. Or rather, there may be some sense in which, say, an adaptation is incoherent, inconsistent, incomplete or incorrect, but that would hardly make it *mal*adaptive in the same sense that its incoherence, inconsistency, incompleteness or incorrectness makes an intelligent act irrational.

Conversely, where the opportunity for rational management of their world is, for whatever reason, closed to the individuals involved, they do not become irrational in the sense that they cease trying to make sense of things. Rather, they strive to create a coherent, consistent, complete and correct order of things within the limited resources and within the limited horizons they *can* control. So there is no need to appeal to any countervailing force of irrationality, subverting or even directing our aspirations to reason, any more than we need evil spirits to explain disease. However, if irrationality *is* a transient and remediable state, what is the process whereby reason remedies it?

Rationalisation

Like atoms, molecules, and waves, then, the gods serve to introduce unity into diversity, simplicity into complexity, order into disorder, regularity into anomaly.

Robin Horton[4]

---

[1] Isaiah, 1: 1 – 17.

[2] Summarised in Kirk *et al.* (1983: 34–43), and more familiarly in Graves (1981).

[3] Durkheim and Mauss, (1963: 79).

[4] In Marwick (1970: 343).

It has been judged more pious and reverent to believe in the alleged exploits of the
gods than to establish the true facts.

Tacitus, *Germania*, 34.

Although the previous chapters have already illustrated the major stages
through which intelligence passes, for present purposes it may be useful to
generalise one of the key processes underpinning their emergence. Each stage
has its own unique way of unfolding, but when trying to grasp as general a
notion as irrationality, it is legitimate to be equally general about the process
whereby it comes and goes – and all too often, comes back again. In this area,
one key mechanism is *rationalisation*.[1]

The idea and process of rationalisation both link directly to the picture of intelligence set out in Chapter 1. There it was suggested that intelligence is always and everywhere structured in terms of real objects and a real world, as
opposed to (but also complemented by) an intentional subjectivity; that all relationships between the intentional and the real were mediated, on both social
and psychic planes, by social and symbolic relations; and that history and consciousness are the products of the resulting dialectics, the former as the reality
and the latter as the intentions we create. From a developmental point of view,
the construction of each new historical reality or conscious intention becomes
the springboard for further action and development. Given the infinite possibilities this raises, the complexity and unpredictability of consciousness and
history come as no surprise.

In this account, rationalisation then becomes the process of resolving the errors, omissions and conflicts – in short, the contradictions – that arise from this
process, leading to 'the substitution of increasingly general and articulate rules
and categories for those of a more particularistic and idiosyncratic type'.[2] But
this is by no means always a positive, progressive and constructive process. On
the contrary, it may well be evasive or hypocritical, not to say horribly brutal,

---

[1] It is important to distinguish between, on the one hand, structures and concepts that
only come into existence as development proceeds and, on the other, modal principles
that are always operative within intelligence, which development only articulates. For
example, an empirical concept such as density appears only at a certain point in cognitive development, whereas principles such as identity, necessity, consistency, non-
contradiction, and rationalisation itself, are key factors at all levels of maturity, and development itself serves only to render them more explicit, more articulate, more expansive, more supple, and so more stable and mobile. They are not created by intelligence,
but rather are facets of intelligence wherever it is found, just as much (and for the same
reason) as subject, object and world. Indeed, for intelligence to come into existence is for
all these things to come into existence too, and intelligence's subsequent development
consists of the transformation of these functional universals into structural features. As
Leslie Smith has put it, 'The key question is not whether consistency is present but
whether it can be maintained through irrelevant transformation' (1993: 57; also 167ff).
There will likewise be no end to the refinements wrought by intelligence to these functions, even when, in all essentials, they are complete. Smith provides comprehensive
analysis of this point.

[2] Hallpike (2004: 155).

regressive and destructive. In its positive sense, to rationalise something is to enhance some aspect of its coherence, consistency, currency, completeness and correctness by reconstructing it either into or in terms of yet more powerful structures. As such it requires only the routine forms of reasoning – insight, criticism, abstraction, generalisation, organisation, reconstruction, and so on – to make things make sense. A rationalisation doesn't always succeed,[1] but it is an attempt at success – something it is hard to account for in non-rational terms. This book is, I hope, a rationalisation in this positive sense. And in many cases, even the strange arguments children offer to explain things can be said to be attempts to rationalise the world in this positive sense, even when they plainly do not succeed.

> … children may respond to… questioning in at least five different ways. Their an-
> swers may be due to guessing, to romancing, to belief fabricated on the spot, to
> triggered belief, or to spontaneous belief. Using normative rationality as the stan-
> dard, only the latter could meet the standards whereby an individual can reason
> productively and deductively in the absence of self-contradiction.[2]

This kind of rationalisation could no more be called malign than a game of Chinese whispers. In fact what makes the child's approach so interesting is the innocent and unwitting yet also ready and spontaneous nature of their explanations.

But rationalisation can have more negative connotations too. To rationalise negatively is to create the appearance of rationality by forcing reality into a mould to which it is unsuited; to suppress the other in the interests of the self; to deny the absent by manipulating the present; and so on. In many contexts, rationalisation is all but a synonym for prejudice, hypocrisy and self-interest. Perhaps most generally, in terms of the logic of coherence, consistency, completeness and correctness on which I have insisted above, the imperfection and immaturity of our respective social and personal world views mean that we quite often have to choose between social and personal ideals. In the modern world there are vast ideological paraphernalia to rationalise the gap between rich and poor, exploiters and exploited, but these are often only a more sophisticated version of the public baths Roman emperors would bestow upon their people. Being forced to choose between moral integrity and success or between logical integrity and plausibility is especially common, and it is striking how individuals and organisations try to have both even when they are clearly incompatible: one would be a great deal more impressed by

---

[1] Hallpike (1986) provides ample examples of weak and contingent rationalisations that are nevertheless very durable, and points out the radical implications of this fact *vis à vis* biological explanations of social organisation and 'evolution'. As Hallpike puts it, 'Quite apart from mistaken ideas, social institutions, especially before the emergence of the state, can be organised on very different principles, *all* of which are viable, with the result that it is extremely difficult for a society's world view, by which it interprets both nature and its own institutions, to come into those conclusive confrontations with the facts envisaged by Durkheim' (1986: 127) – or by adaptationist and functionalist theories of society.

[2] Smith (1993: 57). Smith provides a comprehensive Piagetian treatment of the child's development of valid and justifiable knowledge and the empirical, epistemological and methodological issues that surround this process.

compatible: one would be a great deal more impressed by corporate charity if it were as anonymous as the contributions of private citizens. In fact it is often as a result of forcing such unstable compromises that the most destructive forms of negative rationalisation arise.

In more familiar cases too, a degree of negative rationalisation is present. Indeed, a huge range of research illustrates how subjects strive to make sense of things around them by reference to largely contrived and imaginary arguments and evidence: Bartlett's famous studies of the decay of memory and the growing child's confabulation of new memories based on what it can understand *now*; research on eye-witness testimony; the pathetic attempts of Korsakov's sufferers to come to terms with their appalling predicament and of commissurotomy patients to explain away the conflicts between what the two sides of their split brains experience;[1] the medieval map-makers whose twin passions for godliness and order persuaded them to place Jerusalem at the centre of the world, allot Africa, Asia and Europe equal sizes and surround the earth with the great stream of Ocean;[2] and so on. So do the more brutal forms of negative rationalisation, from populism to totalitarian ideologies, theories of natural slavery[3] and witch-hunts to the self-justification that follows so closely on betrayal.

Some of the most conspicuous rationalisations are to be found in politics and ideology, which inevitably reflect their times, for better or worse. As we all know to our collective cost, a good deal of modern 'democratic' political discourse relies on mythology, manipulation, 'image management', 'spin', and downright lies. But then, great swathes of modern thought still rely on myths of one kind of another, be they the myths of national identity and social welfare that until recently predominated in Europe or myths of frontier individualism, community spirit and benevolent capitalism that once dominated American ideology. Nor is it less striking how failed revolutions quickly revert to traditional themes as soon as they are shown up by historical events, as both Stalin's need to describe the Nazi invasion of Russia as the 'Great Patriotic War' (a title that would be anathema to any Marxist) in order to galvanise popular support, or recent Chinese chauvinism, amply illustrate.

In fact all the major changes in recent history have been accompanied by highly romanticised (and largely self-serving) versions of events, with notions such as 'the Dark Continent', 'the Yellow Peril' and 'the White Man's Burden' on one hand and assorted Promised Lands and Manifest Destinies on the other, standing in for either real knowledge or rational analysis.[4] Indeed, whole patterns of rationalisation can be linked to specific historical conditions: for example, half a millennium ago, the struggle for political power in Europe was ex-

---

[1] Cf. Gazzaniga in Marcel and Bisiach (1988: 218–38).

[2] Boorstin (1984).

[3] Eg, Archer (1988).

[4] On the rationalisation of the American frontier, see Strohmeier in Teich *et al.* (1997). Strohmeier recalls Truettner's description of the American West as 'A dream world in which personal greed and the national good became magically associated' – which is to say, the Promised Land of Adam Smith's 'invisible hand'.

pressed in terms of religion, whereas modern rebels prefer to speak of democratisation, socialism, populism, nationalism, and so on. In none of these cases is this a matter of pure propaganda or self-deception – there is no such thing as an absolutely negative rationalisation – even though neither the Reformation nor modern revolutionaries have come very close to attaining their goals. On the contrary, the floodgates were really opened by the much wider political and economic changes these eras brought to a climax. But they were partially negative rationalisations all the same, and in all such cases the need for vindication became (for many of the participants) a more important consideration than the truth of what they had done.

Of course, because a negative rationalisation is used to manipulate appearances, to satisfy one's self-image and banish the unacceptable rather than to effect a change of any substance, nothing fundamental need actually be done. Sometimes it can be achieved by the simple expedient of annihilating or hiding all alternative interpretations with a barrage of propaganda or denouncing those who decry the witch-hunt as servants of the devil. Or perhaps a few lame excuses will do. But at least the conflict – or at least the *sense* of conflict – is eliminated, if only temporarily. And if denial is not enough, there are more practical methods for removing troublesome details, from lying and cheating to mass deportation, genocide and war.

However, it is usually only an illusory stability that can be achieved in this manner: even the most artfully concealed reality is unlikely to stay hidden for long, and supposedly annihilated objections (and objectors) have a knack of resurrecting themselves in direct proportion to the scale and profundity of the original crisis. For example: we probably know far more about pre-Holocaust Jewish life in eastern Europe than we would have known had the Holocaust never taken place; although an independent Jewish state was probably in gestation anyway, the creation of Israel was almost certainly greatly accelerated by the Nazis' very attempts to annihilate European Jewry; the orthodox Jewish suspicion of a return to a worldly Promised Land[1] was greatly attenuated by the Jews' suffering at the hands of their Diaspora 'hosts'; and Israel began its existence with a mountain of moral capital that can only be understood in terms of their Nazi enemies' dreadful actions. No rational individual would have *chosen* such events as their means to create a modern Jewish state, but there is a hideous irony in the way in which the most violent anti-Semitism in history has created the ultimate secular bastion of Jewish power.

Whatever one may conclude about the wisdom or morality of negative rationalisation, its intelligence cannot be in question, however perversely it may be expressed. And in every case, a negative rationalisation is not always – or even usually – an intentional falsehood. By and large, the need to rationalise simply reflects the limited resources and resourcefulness of the intelligence in question – a constraint that inevitably means making sense of reality by reducing and demeaning it. One knows, one remembers, one justifies in terms of one's position, what one understands, and so on. Where these are not only inadequate to the subject matter they claim to address but actively undermine

---

[1] Armstrong (2000).

the coherence, the consistency, the completeness or the correctness of our actions, a negative rationalisation results. And this is so, *whatever* the intentions of the individual or group from which it originates. Consequently, to be the author of or a party to a negative rationalisation is more often a misfortune than an act of wickedness.

Nor is the intelligence in question guilty of hubris in trying to make sense of the world; it is not as though it has a choice. On the contrary, no entity cursed with even the most meagre objectivity could fail to look for the sense even of things that are quite outside its personal sphere. Whether haunted by the possibility that one's existence makes no sense, enthused by the delusion that one's personal views constitute a privileged and universal vision, or simply caught lying, one must make some kind of sense of the situation, however unconvincing or provisional that sense may be.

Despite the vivid contrasts that can be drawn between positive and negative rationalisation in their pure forms, in practice they tend to be closely linked. Not only do world views combine both but any given rationalisation may only start to appear in a negative light – as, perhaps, incompetence, anachronism or ideological sleight of hand – after a long career of historic achievement and universal acclaim. What starts out as a positive rationalisation – as a valued and effective tool for revealing and even creating great truths – degenerates into a negative rationalisation – a mean and vicarious weapon for fending off reality. That is why even the most successful rationalisation, positive or negative, is as often the target of savage assault as of keen approbation.

This inherent ambiguity is exacerbated by the unevenness of intelligence during most of the term of it existence, and its reliance on a larger and growing infrastructure that, although always open to revision in principle, often finds itself cast in forms that are quite capable of rebuffing all attempts to change them, if not indefinitely then certainly for a very long time.

For example, a key problem faced by the medieval founders of modern natural science was the immense gulf that lay between the loftiness of their intellectual standards (embodied above all in their devotion to logic and mathematics), and the poverty of their empirical knowledge, methodological discipline, institutional arrangements and technical resources.[1] Faced with these discrepancies, medieval intellectuals – like their ancient Greek predecessors[2] – chose to compensate for the poverty of their knowledge and the crass-

---

[1] For a summary of the growth of early modern scientific method, see Crombie (1994: 313–423 and 499–680). On the decline of anthropocentrism, see Thomas (1983). Lovejoy's classic, *The Great Chain of Being* (1964), documents yet another instance of the gradual development, normalisation and eventual supersession of one of the central problematics of western philosophy and proto-science, with many insights into the interplay of the different intellectual and social components.

[2] See Lloyd (1979), 'The development of empirical research', and especially Aristotle's criticism of the Pythagoreans' doctrine of a counter-earth, the sole justification of which seems to have been the 'desire to make the number of moving heavenly bodies total ten, the perfect number' (p. 173).

ness of their practical methods – intolerably flawed to minds accustomed to strictly formal notions of necessity, certainty and validity – by adopting a wider range of assumptions, arguments, methods and observations from theology, folklore, metaphysics, alchemy, and so on. But this also created a double contamination, since it led not only to the shoring up of correct scientific conclusions with invalid justifications and meanings but also to unwarranted compensation for the real inadequacies of intuitive and concrete structures by means of their formal intellectualisation.

For example, no rationalisation could possibly have successfully formalised astrology, which is inexorably concrete not only in content but also in intention, yet the intellectuals of the day saw no conflict between that formalisation and the material to which it was applied.

> The unity of universal life, which flows everywhere and gives life to everything, speculatively justifies the universal sympathy, and the multiplicity of operations which man, an abbreviated image of the cosmos, comes to fulfil. So then the link between the totality, object of metaphysical intuition, and the multiplicity of things and events, in which magic operates, presents itself as something fantastic and arbitrary, the logical consequence of that metaphysical and theological vision... In an animated and consentient universe, connected and working together, in an all-understanding sympathy, one speaks with the stars, the plants, the stones: they pray, they command, they constrain, making more powerful spirits intervene through prayers and appropriate speeches. 'Science' becomes a magical formula, not a mathematical one; its methods and its instruments are incantations, talismans, amulets, not machines. The word... rises to the stars or to the stellar divinities or reaches the 'spirits' of things...[1]

On one side stood a universalised subjectivity in the form of an interventionist divinity, providing the abstract order, sense and dynamism formalisation required but could never find in the concrete rationality of the feudal world. And on the other stood an imagined world of microcosm and macrocosm (a kind of fractal cosmology), demons and divinities, entelechies and sympathies, angels and intelligences, each with its own role in the cosmic theatre, within which human beings played a more or less significant but, without astrology, unconscious role. Thus the strictly concrete structure of the real world was successfully concealed by formalising its content, processes, mechanisms, and so on – but only at the price of the most massive negative rationalisation imaginable.

Not that the results of this process were exclusively negative. By constantly elaborating and refining the theoretical and empirical framework by means of which horoscopes were cast and almanacs drawn up, astrological adepts such as Kepler found themselves deriving better and better models of the astronomical heaven too. Indeed, as Kepler's constant striving to fit the orbits of the planets into various philosophically prescribed shapes (most famously Plato's regular solids) showed, huge advances towards reality could be made by individuals and disciplines seemingly heading in the opposite direction. Not for a moment, I suspect, did most astrologers imagine that discovering the instruments that *really* made the music of the spheres would destroy the entire foun-

---

[1] Garin (1990: 54–5).

dation of astrology itself. But it was in just this way (reinforced by a growing literary taste for cosmic and astrological allusions[1]) that the astrological method of rationalisation was thrown into disrepute – by revelations about the truth about its astronomical tools.

Alchemy incorporated a similar logic of analogy, projection and anthropo-morphism designed to corral a huge range of real and illusory phenomena into a semblance of order, but its intentions were often expressly rationalistic.[2] And, as with astrology, these flaws were by no means merely bizarre foibles of ab-surd and now defunct pseudo-sciences. In their heyday, astrology and alchemy were in many ways the most accomplished and widely respected of disciplines and arguments of this kind were all but universal. After all, Newton thought alchemy valid[3] and practically all of medieval and Renaissance philosophies ran in the same vein, not to mention the rites that surrounded the crafts and industrial processes such as mining and smelting.[4] And so had the cosmogo-nies, rites and daily routines of all previous concrete rational societies from Sumer, Egypt and Babylon onwards.

What was true of medieval science was equally true of early modern politi-cal philosophy, which strove to shore up the irremediably concrete nature of the feudal state with imaginary social contracts, states of nature, theological justifications and ideological prejudices, all tricked out in the most exacting – and inappropriate – formal dress and grounded in imposing axioms drawn from Roman law, Biblical exemplars, the Ten Commandments and *ius gen-tium*.[5] Bizarre, self-seeking and inconsequential though many of these argu-ments seem today, it cannot be doubted that they performed the important so-cial function of giving ideological shape and direction to the re-normalisation of feudal life around changing political realities. But later, as even absolutist feudalism began to wane, it became harder and harder to conceal the conflicts between the concrete goals and mechanics of the absolute state and the ideals and aspirations to which it continued to cling. This drove apologists to increas-ingly forced, one-sided and even irrational explanations, and in particular to appeals to an entirely speculative order of reality, incapable of being grounded in an intelligible world. Hence another crucial example of rationalisation: the theory of divine right.[6]

The theory of divine right was based on the strictly theological notion that God personally anointed individual kings and queens. So it is fitting that it was James VI and I who stated the theory most succinctly:

---

[1] For the use made of astronomy and astrology by Chaucer, Dante and others, see North (1994).

[2] Eliade (1978: 9–13 and *passim*). Eliade also argues for a similar structure to yoga (ch. 12). See also Nakamura (1986).

[3] Westfall (1980); Eliade (1978: 231–4).

[4] Eliade (1978: ch. 5).

[5] See Black (1992) for a summary.

[6] For an example of still greater historical import, see Pagels (1979, 1996).

The state of monarchy is the supremest thing upon earth. For kings are not only God's lieutenants upon earth, and sit upon God's throne... And the like power have kings: they make and unmake their subjects; they have power of raising and casting down, of life and death; judges over all their subjects, and in all cases, and yet accountable to none but God only. They have power to exalt low things and abase high things, and make of their subjects like men at the chess: a pawn to take a bishop or a knight, and to cry up or down any of their subjects, as they do their money. And to the king is due both the affection of the soul and the service of the body of his subjects...[1]

Of course, divine right was not simply an idea whose time had come. Or rather, its time had come mainly because of the changes in feudal society as a whole, described elsewhere in this book. For the practical everyday basis of this loosening of Sun Kings from earthly constraints was the vast increase in the reach of society as a whole, and so of the monarchy that controlled it. Whether in its vast finance and commerce, state undertakings without precedent since the functional of the Roman Empire or its massive cultural efflorescence, the absolutist era signalled an unprecedented extension of the monarch's power and legitimacy, of whose successful consolidation the theory of divine right was both an important expression and a major ideological instrument. Consequently, so long as this system remained in force and the monarchy retained effective control over it, the monarch was safe from almost any threat.[2]

However, the *systemic* character of absolutism, on which its massive power rested – which is to say, the organised linking of its parts to support a series of centrally promulgated policies – soon began to turn into true *formality* – which is to say, the organisation of that system *as* a system. This required no special concern with formality as such – only an interest in eliminating explicit incoherence, inconsistency, incompleteness and incorrectness, and the consequent empowerment of the state and political apparatuses to deal with any *possible* policy. But as I have already observed, this transition from system to formality meant that this machinery became increasingly suitable for promulgating non- and even anti-absolutist policies too – a change that naturally began to undermine the absolutist monarch's claims to exclusive control. As with any formal system, it is essential to the nature of a mature absolutism that it can be controlled by anyone with access to the right levers.

Then the role of divine right changed from triumphant celebration of God-given authority to the concealment and resolution (in the monarchy's favour) of the tension between the monarchy's concrete rational claims and objectives

---

[1] *A Speech to the Lords and Commons of the Parliament at White-Hall* (1610), quoted in Wooton (1986). See also *ibid.*, p. 102 on the reciprocal powerlessness of the monarch's subjects. Wooton collects a wide range of contemporary writings, for and against divine right. For a more general summary of the major contemporary views of absolutist political philosophy and divine right, notably the advocacy of Hobbes and Bossuet and the criticisms of Algernon Sidney, Locke, Montesquieu and Rousseau, see Doyle (1992: 231ff) or Morrow (1998).

[2] For an analysis of why James I and his successors has such difficulty in carrying out their divine mission in Great Britain, to the point of James' son being executed by Parliament, see Stone (1972).

to which the state was officially dedicated and the formal rational economic and political order burgeoning beneath, which was falling more and more into the hands of a bourgeois class rather better disposed to formal systems, ideals and methods, in politics as in every other sphere. It is no coincidence that absolutism was both perfected and abolished in parallel with the rise of stock exchanges, central banks and national debts:[1] the world was already moving on to strictly formal considerations such as property, equality and representation.

It is important to understand exactly why absolutism's apologists could not sustain its rationalisation, even though they included some of the most powerful thinkers and institutions of the day. Any state organisation, indeed any explicitly organised political structure is open to usurpation. The difference in this case is that the strictly formal character of the state apparatus actively conflicted with the concrete rational goals of its creators. This conflict and the resulting decay intruded into every corner of politics and ideology:

> The process of destruction is very complex. What occurs is a slow erosion of the old symbols, a wasting away of the things they once evoked, an increasingly disjointed and inconsistent expression of political ideas, a nervous insistence upon the old units and references – all this accompanied, willy nilly, by a more and more arbitrary and extravagant manipulation of them – until finally the units cease to be accepted as intellectual givens and the references cease to be meaningful.[2]

This left it open to usurpation by forces who, like the revolutionaries who overthrew Louis XVI, had every intention of installing a completely different *kind* of regime. Instead of a series of dynastic coups, the creation of a more or less formalised state left absolutism open to full-blooded revolution. In fact it is hard to see how a regime devoted to concrete rational goals could have retained control of a formal rational system for any length of time.

So what had begun with the more or less plausible notion of the divine anointment of a particular individual degenerated into the vanity of claims to personal authority where authority had become a formality in every sense. Like Protestantism's attempts to safeguard the faith by formalising theology from first principles, which ended with God's effective expulsion from the universe, the practical formalisation of the absolutist state left the absolutist monarch – the theoretical *primum mobile* of society as a whole – disconnected from society itself. If the rupture between Louis XVI and the increasingly bourgeois state was hardly as radical or complete as that between the Protestant god and his universe, Louis was just as much in need of a miracle to prove his continuing relevance.

---

[1] For general accounts of this process in Europe, see Doyle (1992) and Braudel (1982). For a summary of the British case, see Roseveare (1991). I should emphasise that other factors were much slower to make their presence fully felt. For example, even in England banks only achieved joint stock status after 1826, limited liability only became the norm after 1856 and a workable bankruptcy law took longer still.

[2] Walzer in Strong (1992: 69)

The perpetuation of rationalisations

As this succession of rises and falls demonstrates, the process of rationalisation is not wholly irrational. But the link is not automatic: negative rationalisations are bound to lead to contradiction in the long run, to manage which reason may resort to a seemingly endless string of further negative interconnected rationalisations.[1] Nor will all these rationalisations necessarily even pretend to preserve a kernel of rationality. Sometimes the situation becomes so devoid of intelligible meaning that I will even proclaim my lack of principle to be a matter of principle – that my might is right, for example, that I aspire only to the triumph of my will, that I only serve the dictates of my genes, and so on.

But as these examples show, even the most profoundly irrational world view seeks its own rationalisation in essentially the same terms as the most rational. Regrettably, few demagogues of irrationalism have found twiddling their thumbs – the last resort of one of Greek philosophy's more consistent sceptics – a satisfying conclusion. The fundamental difference between the rational and the irrational is not that the former aspires to coherence, consistency, completeness and correctness and the latter does not, but that the latter does not grasp the role of these rationalist ideals in giving their irrationalism what little sense they have. From Hamann to Hitler, irrationalists have always expended hundreds of pages rationalising their faith in the irrational.

Hence the next aspect of irrationality I shall deal with here, namely the perpetuation of rationalisations not merely through the creation of more and more layers of self-justification but through the organisation of rationalisations into complete world views, within which positive and negative rationalisations cannot be told apart. By this means intelligence puts a final layer of veneer of reason on unreason. And it does this not because it is willing to forego its commitment to rationality but precisely in the name of that commitment.

Of course, this is never a stable situation, but one may have to go to great lengths to expose such frozen reason (surely the perfect contradiction in terms), and still further to supplant it. Reason's always burgeoning vocabulary of metaphors, analogies and connotation also makes it hard to extricate the rational from the rationalised, as does its regular resort to convention, pragmatism and eclecticism within which a choice may be correct even though it is incapable of rational justification.[2] Nor does intelligence find it hard to invent pseudo-rational traps and obstacles by means of which the most grotesque unreason can be made to seem the paragon of self-evidence, especially where it has been institutionalised and powerful interests are at stake. One has only to

---

[1] Familiar examples include the use of parallels between the divinely ordained structure of the universe and the absolutist monarchy or between the abstract principles and structure of the Newtonian universe and bourgeois order of laws and rights. See Walzer in Strong (1992) for a summary. See also Needham's view on the influence of Chinese social relations on the development of science in China and elsewhere (Needham, 1969: Ch. 8 and *passim*).

[2] On the relationship between beliefs that are factually correct and beliefs that can be justified, see Smith (1993).

consider the history of politics to find endless instances of such self-serving 'reasonableness'.

It is important to appreciate the source of such mechanisms for the perpetuation of the irrational. On the one hand, there is the impossibility of an immature structure being able to function completely effectively. But that does not explain why the intelligence in question does not simply turn away from its own failures and get on with something else. After all, that is what would happen if it were genuinely indifferent to the unintelligibility of things in the manner of, say, a non-intelligent organism. Precisely because it is capable of objectivity, the contradiction that unintelligibility reveals will continue to nag it long after it has ceased to have any pragmatic significance. That is why rationality tends to dress up both the smallest mistake and the deepest incomprehension in some kind of rationalisation. Reason simply cannot *not* come to some kind of conclusion or infer 'first principles' of some sort, even about errors and omissions it could easily work its way around and even though its very immaturity, inexperience and impotence preclude its reaching conclusions or principles that really are coherent, consistent, complete or correct.

Although in practice intelligent beings can adopt any number of approaches to this situation, they all represent some kind of compromise between just two alternatives. On the one hand it can recognise that it *is* only rationalising its predicament (in the negative sense of 'rationalise'), and perhaps opt out of the (explicit) pursuit of sense, meaning and direction altogether. Note that this is a principled decision in its own right, and has the kind of global consequence one would expect. In particular, once intelligence starts to believe that it is *incapable* of arriving at an unconditional sense, it cannot help but draw the conclusion that *all* its meanings and beliefs and sense of direction are incoherent, inconsistent, incomplete and incorrect to some degree.

This naturally leads to a kind of institutionalised scepticism. *In extremis*, it may conclude not merely that there is no truth but even that everything is a lie. It may expel the comprehensible or the real themselves: after all, if experience teaches the unintelligibility of existence – that reality is concealed behind an impenetrable veil or that our finite natures prevent us from beholding it directly – why not treat the appearance of intelligibility as itself the hallmark of illusion? How many otherworldly philosophies already preach this argument? How difficult would it be to set up a complete theology on this basis? Did not Tertullian insist that 'it must be believed, *because* it is absurd'?

Fortunately, reason does not usually retreat as far as full-blown nihilism. But it can go a long way towards it. For example, it may easily retrench to a position of least commitment, setting strict, explicit and minimalist limits on what it is prepared to entertain, based on unconditionally constituted authority and unconditional defence. That is, at least within a closed situation, a sustainable position to which many a defeated party has retreated, be it a millennialist movement or a casualty of more everyday disasters. Conversely, one may decide to vigorously expel the exotic and the alien from one's world as intrinsically incomprehensible, if not inherently wicked – another form of the closure to which rational beings have often resorted to preserve the intelligibility of their own (now constricted) world.

But even this kind of explicit denial and abnegation does not really divest intelligence of its commitment to rationality. It is not as though it can side-step the need for the rational, even if it cannot see where that rationality lies. Rationality is a fact of intelligence, not as a free choice but by virtue of its own basic structure. Even the most committed agnostic has to grasp the many-layered logic of teacups, and does so using the same tools as the most rigorous logician. Indeed, one of the most striking proofs of the indispensability of rationality is the enthusiasm with which solipsists will explain their position to anyone who will listen. The most devout pragmatic and eclectic defender of convention is likewise keen to prove that their anti-philosophy makes sense (or at least, is put out by a proof that it does not).

Hence the perpetuation of rationalisations through their synthesis into complete systems, within which positive and negative rationalisations are inextricably fused. For once assembled, the conclusion intelligence arrives at will be as smooth and seamless as any, with no obvious or unequivocal distinction between the objectively necessary, valid and certain aspects of the matter and the speculation, the metaphysics, the ideology and the prejudice. Once properly integrated, all the different elements become equally necessary components of the same truth. So are they not also, from the intelligence in question's own point of view, all equally necessary truths in their own right? As such, are they not all equally worthy of perpetuation? And as such, is the perpetuation of each not the precondition of successfully perpetuating the whole?

Indeed, isn't the logical tendency likely to be to treat the parts that have been deduced and inferred as *more* convincing than those that have arisen from, say, experience? After all, if an immature intelligence has any capacity for insight or criticism, isn't the weakness on which it is most likely to alight the contingent character of empirical experience? If there is anything at all to the dialectic of internalisation and externalisation, it is clear that the *internal* frailties of any given position will only confront its adherents *after* the flaws in its empirical surface have been dealt with fairly thoroughly. With that, any irrational methods such as magic, mysticism and fantasy that were originally introduced in order to *support* this 'rationality' will seem to be *vindicated* by it.[1]

Conversely, having constructed these methods from its own innermost dictates, reason naturally finds it hard to see how they can be exceeded or even questioned. In fact, once they have 'proved' their value, it is naturally inclined to appoint them the chief guardians and servitors of reason as such – a tactic that can only delay the further development of reason. Hence the extraordinary and disproportionate power of *conviction* – one of the aspects of rationality that differentiates intelligence most completely from any of its precursors – to sub-

---

[1] Nowhere is this principle more forcefully embodied than in the period classical and pre- classical Greek philosophy, which created the first great edifices, Platonic and Parmenidean, to be powered primarily by the power of deduction. During this startlingly condensed and productive period (summarised by Frede in Frede and Striker, 1996: 1–28), not only did formal reason finally come into its own but it demonstrated in the clearest manner possible the authority the internal structure of reason can claim over empirical experience.

vert rationality itself. After all, to possess a conviction, any conviction, is not merely to have discovered another fact, as though facts were discrete, neutral records of events, accessible to yet neither constituting nor constituted by reason, and therefore expelled one by one as easily as they were acquired. Even the meanest fact is convincing only because it informs and confirms reason on a more abstract plane than its factual content, taken at face value, seems to warrant.[1] Likewise, the conviction of having remembered a single fact correctly is inherently conditional on the sense that is made of it:

> Remembering is not the re-excitation of innumerable fixed, lifeless and fragmentary traces. It is an imaginative reconstruction, or construction, built out of the relation of our attitude towards a whole mass of organised past reactions or experience, and to a little outstanding detail which commonly appears in image or in language form. It is thus hardly ever really exact, even in the most rudimentary cases or rote recapitulation, and it is not at all important that it should be so.[2]

On the other hand, the absence of this integrating capacity is disastrous, no matter what specific intellectual skills may be available to the individual:

> It is characteristic of the savant memory (in whatever sphere – visual, musical, lexical) that it is prodigiously retentive of particulars. The large and the small, the trivial and momentous, may be indifferently mixed, without any sense of salience, of foreground versus background. There is little disposition to generalise from these particulars or to integrate them with each other, causally or historically, or with the self. In such a memory there tends to be an immovable connection of scene and time, of content and context...[3]

That is, intelligence's ability to generalise from experience is grounded in a capacity for abstraction rather than for creating direct reflections, correspondences or copies of experience, and so proceeds by the true generalisation of the original experience rather than its mechanical repetition in like situations. That is, it generalises by *recreating* the applicable aspects of the original experience as they relate to the situation to which it is generalised. That is why intelligence needs the tools of modal reasoning (could, should, and so on) to perform even the simplest act – and why modal reasoning cannot be explained as the product of experience. So, in proportion to its success in internalising particular experiences, intelligence is liberated from their content and context, yet can still profit from the lessons they teach. On the other hand, it is able to be convinced by this process only because (and to the extent that) it takes for granted the structures of activity through which it accomplishes this feat.

The ubiquity of the process of abstraction within intelligent activity has a profound effect on our attitude towards experience, on the sense of conviction

---

[1] The purely epistemological case for this assertion is not yet won. However, a scientific case can also be made: see Keil in Sperber *et al.*, (1995: 239–40) for empirical references, and almost anything by the Geneva school of genetic epistemology for massive argument and evidence.

[2] Frederic Bartlett, quoted in Sacks (1995: 164). See also Edelman (1992).

[3] Sacks (1995: 190–1; see also pp. 217ff). Sacks is at pains to point out that a savant's experience is anything but a faithful copy of the original encounter, but rather consists of the identification, replication and variation of key features (pp. 196, 212ff).

experience conveys and on the threat the refutation of experience poses. In fact, without this process of abstraction our experience would signify nothing at all; we could not even be said to *have* any experience, any more than a rock does. That is why the meaning of even the simplest fact always extends far beyond the content and context of its original acquisition. Indeed, this latent significance may commit us to preserving an apparently minor fact far beyond its intrinsic meaning, value or certainty. Of course, while intelligence is very immature, it can only manage the most simplistic forms of internalisation, such as mimicry. This will often cause the original event to be trivialised or overly rigid conclusions to be drawn from superficially grasped experience. Nevertheless, it is the higher forms of the same process that provide us with, for example, the very basis of most contemporary scientific method, in the form of falsificationism, *modus tollens* and so on.

Conversely, it is because of its internal structuring in terms of abstractions that the refutation of a single fact may require the recuperation of far more than the fact in question, and which makes it so hard for us to give it up. Consequently, not only may a single fact's place in the scheme of things be far more profound than seems realistic (even to the intelligence that holds it) but attempts to justify and preserve it may seem – and truly become – deeply neurotic. In more straightforward terms, this is why it is often so hard to change one's mind – a notoriously irrational aspect of human nature.

This is not an exclusively negative process, however. In the first place, this is clearly the same process whereby intelligence raises itself from intuitive to dialectical reason, so it can scarcely be completely destructive. And secondly, abstraction is a fine shield against the precariousness of many of the lower level structures on which intelligent activity relies. For example, it is true that specific faculties may, for lack of exercise, decline in efficiency and effectiveness, and even wither altogether, and one might well expect whole areas of understanding and ability to wax and wane in tandem with these changes. And in a superficial sense this is just what happens. However, the contributions to *experience* and *development* made by even the most obsolete structures of activity are unlikely to be lost altogether, even when the structures themselves are. An individual blinded in adulthood does not forget all the lessons of vision, especially the ones relating not to sight alone but to, on the one hand, space, time, substance and causality, and on the other, the particulars of things and events that can be inferred from, yet do not rely on, their visibility.

In summary, insofar as it is preserved at all, each element of a given intelligence is an *abstraction* from the original experience, and its internalisation consists not of the creation of an image or a habit or a passive 'record' but of a change to the structures through which it was constructed and on which its stable comprehension depends. And beyond that, the experience may also contribute to yet higher and wider structures, not only through its original sensorimotor or perceptual-behavioural form but also through the modifications it induces in those structures. And so on, both 'horizontally' across the whole gamut of everyday structures and 'vertically', up to the very highest echelons of reason.

By this means, an intelligence may continue to register the *significance* of the original experience even when the experience itself is forgotten and even though the intelligence in question might now be incapable of having that experience again, even though the original conditions were replicated exactly. Indeed, so remote is the *content* of experience from the centre of the intelligence in question's subsequent world view that the details of the experience are in constant need of rehearsal and recalibration to the actual circumstances in which they are newly invoked,[1] and are constantly threatened with simple confusion and forgetting. By contrast, the structures of which the experiencing intelligence is composed (including those that only came into existence as a result of this experience) may well be so commonly in use that it is impossible to lose them without a disproportionate distortion of the intelligence in question.

So the rationalisation of experience is by no means an inherently pathological process. Indeed, it only reinforces the assumption that nothing can succeed that does not establish a solid foundation, even if improving that foundation later does demand an inordinate amount of effort. In fact, all of science's greatest triumphs seem to have come about in just this manner. For example, *The Origin of Species* and *The Descent of Man* lay great emphasis on the mass of empirical evidence they contain. For many of Darwin's original readers, this must have added great weight to what would otherwise have seemed not only unsubstantiated but entirely counter-intuitive speculation. However, the theory of natural selection having now established itself, its tentacles spreading not only to all corners of biology but to all aspects of scientific thought, its influence is no longer based on empirical evidence. Nowadays at least half the significance of Darwinism lies not in Darwin's original writings or even in vast achievements of evolutionary biology but in the theory's transformation of the whole of scientific culture:[2] there can be few corners of scientific reason – or of reasoning of any kind – that have been left untouched by Darwinian models and arguments.

But that is precisely why, even if Darwin were to be completely refuted as an *empirical* account of organic evolution, it would still be immensely difficult to weed it out of our intellectual *Zeitgeist*. But then, for most disciplines this might not matter, since the general model of variation and selection can be applied to a huge range of non-organic systems too. Not that there is much risk of Darwinism being eclipsed in the foreseeable future, not least because it would now be extremely difficult to *formulate* any refutation of Darwinism without seeming to disregard the basic canons of scientific reason. After all, for many scientists these are now constituted, in part, by Darwinism itself.

How long this situation will last it is impossible to say, but I suspect that Darwinian theory of evolution has at least as much staying power as the theory of divine right! On the other hand, the massive over-generalisation of Darwinism by recent sociobiologists, evolutionary psychologists and the like has not been a completely unmixed blessing, and the durability of Darwinism proper can only be improved if its limitations are also acknowledged. For example, it might enhance Darwinism's standing in the non-biological sciences if it were

---

[1] Eg, Lee in Pick and Saltzman (1978: 159–170); Smyth and Marriott (1982).

[2] R.J. Richards (1987).

explicitly recognised that chemical elements or cultures 'evolve' only in a strictly metaphorical sense.

To put the same point more generally, this three-cornered relationship between experience, rationalisation and reality ensures that for a mature intelligence, fact and truth may be one and the same, but, for an immature intelligence, facts can be the enemies of the truth. At any given stage, facts (which is to say, constructions placed on objects that are correct and undistorted at the current level of reasoning) are invaluable as far as they go. However, 'as far as they go' is only as far as the abilities implicit in the present stage and sub-stage of development are able to take us. Beyond that point, they become positively reactionary, for insofar as we continue to cleave to them, we also cleave to the declining standards of a disappearing age. To the extent that established facts are used to abort or suppress new arrangements of the kind that abound at the edges of each new stage of development, and reason trusts too uncritically in that which is merely convincing, to stick to the facts is to threaten progress itself. In seeking to bolster and rationalise our partial knowledge by reference to metaphors, analogies and unstated presuppositions, we betray the intelligibility of our world by the very devices through which we strive to make it intelligible in the first place. Conversely, to the extent that 'facts' are defined by their compliance with established modes of rationalisation, we risk turning what are immensely powerful and positive rationalisations in one field into fatally destructive negative rationalisations in another.

Alienation

> But only the other day Mr Lebezyatnikov, who follows the latest ideas, was explaining that the science of our day has actually declared compassion a social evil, and that this notion is already being put into practice in England, where they have political economy.
>
> Dostoyevsky, *Crime and Punishment*

Although intelligence's achievements may often interfere in its subsequent development, even the worst error or prejudice can be exposed, in principle at least. But there is another process that, if less conspicuous than the institutionalisation of error, is much more powerful. It is moreover an entirely inescapable feature of intelligence right up until the beginning of dialectical reason, intrinsically difficult to grasp and peculiarly rational in its own dire way. Deeper even than error, ignorance, incompetence, disease, abnormality and sub-normality, there is at the very heart of intelligence the betrayal of everything of which reason should be most certain. Central to the entire enterprise of development, growing in power and treachery as reason ascends, is the most powerful of all engines of irrationality, namely *alienation*.[1]

---

[1] The key sources on alienation are, of course, Hegel (1977) and Marx, especially the *Economic and Philosophic Manuscripts* (Marx, 1975) and *The German Ideology* (in Marx and Engels, 1976). Marx's *Grundrisse* (1993) is also littered with references to alienation. For histories and exegesis, see Taylor (1975) and Kolakowski (1978). Ernest Mandel's 'The

The basis of alienation is quite straightforward. All intelligent beings are also social beings. Through their capacity for objectivity, they share the same world with all other intelligent beings, though this sharing is rendered both partial and conditional by the differing maturity, experience and circumstances of the individuals involved. But more than that, they are social by virtue of the relationships into which they are thrust at birth, through changes in social structure and through their own actions, and it is through these relationships that they experience and act on the world and one another.

Intelligent beings are at once more detached from and more embedded in their mutual relationships than non-intelligent organisms. For example, they are capable of both insight into and a critical attitude towards the connections that bind them – something of which non-intelligent beings are quite incapable. But they also depend on their relationships with one another much more than other organisms. Partly this is because, considered in isolation or in purely biological terms, we are extraordinarily puny creatures, so we depend on one another not simply to accomplish anything of any consequence but also to survive. But more than that, we are constituted by our social relationships in a much more active and defining sense, because once we have begun to relate to one another, increasingly many of the forms of activity on which we rely come to be mediated through those relationships.

The best known (and most important) example of this is probably the division of labour. To accomplish anything beyond the immediate abilities of any single individual, we work collectively. This combines our abilities not only additively, in the sense that two people are twice as strong as one, but also in the multiplicative sense that a group of individuals can be a group of specialists, can organise themselves to execute successive and parallel parts of a complex process, can control mechanisms that would be beyond the capabilities of a single individual, can learn from one another, and so on. By these means, we add not only to our collective efficiency and effectiveness but also to our average competence and performance as individuals.

But social organisation is more than just an aid to efficiency or effectiveness. Once human beings are organised socially, they begin to know and act in the world through their social relationships as well as – and increasingly instead of – any direct or strictly personal psychic perspective. Of course, even the most socialised viewpoint relies on the individual who holds it to make a psychological sense of things. But its social mediation makes an immense difference to what one sees of the things and events one must comprehend. Furthermore, just as there never was a time when human beings were not socially organised, so there never was a time when the very perspective from which we make sense was not itself, to some extent, socially organised. Because we are all embedded in a social matrix from the moment of conception, even the most 'psychic' aspects of our development are socially structured from the first. So even if there was an age of asocial 'innocence', we have long since passed the point

---

causes of alienation' (in Mandel and Novack, 1970) is a sympathetic brief introduction to some of the key phenomena.

where it was fruitless to try to differentiate the psychic from the social on any but the theoretical plane.

But the fact that our intelligence makes us all social is not the problem with which I am concerned here. In fact there is no reason, in principle at least, why being social in this general sense should not be a marvellous bounty. The problem is rather that, as incompletely developed beings on both social and psychic planes, we no more grasp the full extent and implications of the social relationships in which we stand and through which we act and develop than we know ourselves psychologically. So for long millennia we have couched our explanations in terms of God and Destiny and other ineffable but imposing metaphysical reasons, or perhaps 'blood', 'race' and other naturalistic yet imponderable causes. Nor is it obvious that the contemporary enthusiasm for finding genes for ever human feature and foible is so very different – although, given the level of social and historical knowledge to which we have access, we have far less excuse.

Nor is this situation helped by the fact that, as well as direct social relationships between individuals, the entire history of social organisation has consisted of its self-expansion into new domains and layers of structure and function that not only distinguish organisations from their members but also generate organisations of organisations, organisations of organisations of organisations, and so on. What is more, since these higher level structures do indeed *organise* their subordinate members and sub-organisations (as opposed to simply housing them), they also modify the effects of their actions, alter the consequence and significance of those effects and even determine them directly.

As a result, it is quite the norm for individuals and lower level groups to regard the higher level structures in which they participate as remote, unknown and uncontrollable as forces of nature – if, that is, they are aware of them at all. In such conditions, even if an act's latent consequences do not massively distort its author's objectives, its original conception is at least partly the brain-child of social structures of which its author may be only hazily aware. Or at least, it is until the structures in terms of which socially organised intelligent agents act and experience are fully totalised with and among themselves – a concept whose *meaning* is far from straightforward, let alone its realisation.

But until this ideal is realised, the very fact that individual actions, not to mention interactions between individuals (and organisations of individuals and organisations of organisations), generate results that lie at least partially beyond the reach of any of the individuals or organisations involved means that such results cannot be in every respect what their instigators intended. Their consequences must bear the marks not only of their agent's intentions but also of the unintended and unrecognised implications of the larger structures and processes through which they were also created.[1] So things are never quite as they seem – not even the claim that things are never quite as they seem.

---

[1] For a compendium of 'revenge effects' of this kind, see Tenner (1996).

Of course, this is just as true of actions that do not rely directly on the participation of other individuals. In fact the whole process of social alienation has its counterparts on the cognitive level, and in many respects the consequences are just as radical and just as dire. But alienation properly so called differs from general incomprehension in that the agency executing a social action is quite different from the individual agent who must grasp that action if they are to take real control of it and its products. For the 'agency' of a social act extends beyond the individual, whereas only individuals are capable of comprehending anything; and the agency of an alienating activity makes the nature and consequences of the action as a whole incomprehensible to the individuals who are involved in it. That is why every kind of human activity and artefact from neuroses to menus to global economies has its specialists and interpreters and schools of thought, all eager to tease out their specialism's latent order on every level from class warfare to etiquette to neurotransmitter levels. But that is also why so much human activity goes so far astray, and why so many intelligent acts need rationalisations of one kind of another.

However imperfect these interpretations and rationalisations may necessarily be, the need to seek out and take control of deeper structures beyond our present control is perfectly real. If all the connections they created were completely straightforward, mastery of an object or an action would be simple indeed. But unfortunately, precisely because they are embedded in a complex of larger structures, all but the highest forms of intelligence include the active, if unintended, *production* of discrepancies, distortions and discontinuities, of gaps and barriers between self and other, appearance and reality, present and absent. That is what, for an immature intelligence, the whole being greater than the sum of the parts means.

But in addition to that simple truism, alienation means that the whole is so structured that both the nature of the parts we come into contact with and our view of both parts and whole are actively distorted. That is why alienation is not identical to, say, a system of commodities, roles and money, although one could scarcely imagine a better vehicle for alienation than a system consisting of a mass of one-sided, superficially defined relationships mediated by a pure abstraction – which is to say, roles, commodities and money. Nor is the advent of an industrial Leviathan the issue, or the coming of an information technology that often seems to have deprived us of the freedom to decide for ourselves. On the contrary, it is a very ancient problem indeed: as the historian Josephus observed two thousand years ago:

> But if any people were tempted to rebel by its peculiar advantages, that people is the Gauls, provided as they are with such marvellous defences.... Yet in spite of these immense obstacles, in spite of their huge total of three hundred and fifty tribes, in spite of the prosperity that wells up from their soil and enables them to flood the whole world with their goods, they submit to being the milch cow of Rome and receiving from her hands what they themselves have produced![1]

It is not the fact that roles or machines control or decide anything that is the problem, but rather the nature of the control they exercise over human beings

---

[1] Josephus (1981: 159).

and the criteria they use to make decisions – little of which relate to human needs. What an alienating system such as capitalism adds is to embed all this in a system that fragments, and then invert the real relationships and results of human activity and the real power that is conferred by the division of labour, to the point where everything not only *appears to be* but *really is* what it is not.

So reason's failure to comprehend, totalise and internalise all the structures involved in an action actively wrests ultimate control of both the action and its results from that intelligence. This may take the form of *mystification*, in the sense that the very process whereby an object is produced ensures that its *appearance*, at least from its producers' perspective, belies its *real* origin, nature and consequences. The angle of incidence is different from the angle of reflection, so to speak. In addition, alienation can mean *estrangement*, in the sense that the process of production takes the product out of the hands of its producers and places it either in the hands of others or in no hands at all. Thus, instead of enlarging freedom, these uncontrollable powers increase human servitude and strip human beings of the capacities for self-determination and self-direction that have raised them above the animals.[1]

The classic exemplars of alienation are still hard to beat:

> Money is the jealous god of Israel before whom no other god may stand. Money debases all the gods of mankind and turns them into commodities. Money is the universal and self-constituted *value* of all things. It has therefore deprived the entire world – both the world of man and of nature – of its specific value. Money is the estranged essence of man's work and existence; this alien essence dominates him and he worships it.[2]

So our work builds and rebuilds the world, but as individuals, we work for the money and discount the time we spend on these colossal feats as the price we pay to be able to do what we *really* want to do. The very system that harnesses us to remake everything turns us into superficial, self-seeking individualists. As for any higher aspirations we might entertain, so great is the distance alienation sets between each of us as subjects and the objects we 'own' and 'consume' and the world we inhabit that even such notions as truth and freedom are reduced to impotent ideals and abstract speculations. Feuerbach's interpretation of theology as anthropology standing on its head is an equally well-known use of the concept of alienation. Nor is the theory of religion as a form of alienation a wholly recent invention:

> God created humanity; [but now human beings] create God. That is the way it is in the world – human beings make gods, and worship their creation. It would be appropriate for the gods to worship human beings![3]

I should emphasise that alienation is only partly a question of *feeling* mystified or estranged. It is always possible to establish *some* subjective awareness of any aspect of intelligent activity, so it would be very surprising if alienation had no phenomenal impact whatsoever. Nevertheless, the objective facts of

---

[1] Mandel and Novack (1970: 7).

[2] Karl Marx, *On the Jewish Question*, in Marx (1975: 239). See also Marx (1954: ch. 1, s. 4).

[3] From the gnostic *Gospel of Philip* found at Nag Hammadi, quoted in Pagels (1979: 122).

alienation are not faithfully translated into subjective perspective or experience. On the contrary, the faithlessness of their translation is what makes alienation both so important and so hard to see. As the brief summary given above shows, alienation is not primarily a psychological phenomenon, and its psychological consequences are neither straightforward nor simple. For example, the typical alienated individual is not much like the heroes and anti-heroes of Dostoyevsky, Kafka, Camus, Beckett or Sartre, or the 'lonely crowd'. On the contrary, alienation is just as likely to express itself in anything but 'feeling alienated'. When Marx described religion as the opium of the people, he was referring not least to the positive interpretation religion can place on the direst of situations, with all its attendant reassurance and exultation.

Furthermore, critical aspects of alienation are characterised precisely by the fact that they are actively concealed from view. And again, Marx's account of the relationship between capital and labour shows how a grossly inequitable exchange can be made to seem both fair and natural: the relationship is perfectly visible to both participants in the exchange, but it is only seen through distorting lenses.[1] So even the most powerful intelligence can be left helpless not only to manage but even to recognise the consequences of its acts. This situation is survivable, even tolerable, only while intelligence's ambitions are so parochial, its standards so low and – most importantly of all – its reach so restricted. Conversely, it can only be overcome when all perspectives are coordinated and reconciled – a task of historical proportions, which we are far from completing.

But in the mean time, at least until intelligence reaches its full flowering, what is produced turns out as it should only to the same extent that it is also what it is *not* supposed to be. As I argued at length in Chapters 4 and 5, the vast scope and comprehension offered by formal reason, with its rigorous knowledge, formidable industries and vast organisations, is matched by its incomprehension of its situation and the most comprehensive system of alienation of all.

Alienation has been implicated in practically every form of human activity, from economics and politics to art and religion.[2] However, it is too familiar a notion to need analysing in any detail here. At each stage, intelligence achieves a more comprehensive grasp of its world, yet does so only by building more massive, more profound machinery for its own alienation. Still, it is this same process which propels development forward. For the unintended realisation of the unrecognised relationships to which alienation leads is also the process whereby those relationships are made visible and material. It is also the process whereby the forces that turn these structural chasms and conflicts into human misery are tamed and placed at the disposal of members of society, and so the process whereby the necessary conditions for superseding this alienation comes to fruition.

---

[1] Marx (1954: ch. 1).

[2] For the further implications of alienation, see Ollman (1976) and Mészarós (1970).

So pessimism regarding the future of capitalism is as misplaced as enthusiasm for its formal orderliness and equivocal liberties. Although the immediate consequences of alienation may be largely destructive to all involved, they also drive the structures that create this alienation into the mutual overlaps, interference and negations – in short, into the contradictions – that are needed to force their mutual reconciliation, synthesis and totalisation, and thus the abolition of the conditions that brought about this alienation in the first place. In short, although intelligence's every immature achievement is transformed by alienation into its nemesis, that nemesis is not only the portent of a more hopeful future but also the motor for its creation.

Conclusions

It was not the purpose of this chapter to deny that human beings are ever irrational. Far from it. Human irrationality is perfectly real. However, it *was* its purpose to suggest that many, perhaps most aspects of that irrationality are by-products of failed, immature, partial and misdirected attempts to be rational. No amount or degree of intelligence can guarantee either omniscience or omnipotence, any more than the its inherent adaptiveness can confer immortality.

Of course, much of what seems, if not actually irrational then certainly not rational, can be explained in terms of the great infrastructure of intelligence I referred to in the first section, through which much of the rationality of our actions is effectively obscured even from ourselves. One consequence of this is that we are often right in what we do, and began to do that kind of thing for good rational reasons, but we cannot quite put our finger on its justification. This situation is always exacerbated by the fact that, as creatures of history, our rationality always tends to be limited by our immaturity and inexperience. However, that does not mean that we are not trying to be rational, that we are not using the tools and criteria of rationality to overcome our ignorance or that there is no end to this process, even when there is no end in sight. Finally (and at risk of stumbling backwards into the great philosophical debate on 'weakness of will'), when we rationalise our follies, how often are we really trying to make legitimate sense of them – if only as a least evil, as a trifle or as an excusable lapse of judgement? Even when we are guilty of cynical manipulation, how often is that, in its perverse way, a sincere expression of a distinct and would-be objective world view?

All in all there seems to be little reason to believe that there is any completely irreducible residue of irrationality in human activity. Indeed, it is striking how great the scope of rationality is in our own time, even when compared with a century or two ago. Nevertheless, the age of negative rationalisations is not quite dead, even for science. For example, one might say that the ancients' projections of the higher – the rational, the animate – onto the lower – the mechanical, the inert – is only the obverse of the present-day error of reducing the higher to the lower. Their belief in the spontaneous perfectionism of nature and the role of the alchemist and astrologer as midwives of that perfection[1] is like-wise mirrored – in much more sophisticated forms – by our own tendency to deny the possibility of perfection in the name of brute mechanism, and to define the role of the scientist as that of chief apostle of futility.

---

[1] Eliade (1978: 51–2).

Conclusion

We have given you, Oh Adam, no visage proper to yourself, nor any endowment properly your own, in order that whatever place, whatever form, whatever gifts you may, with premeditation, select, these same you may have and possess through your own judgement and decision. The nature of all other creatures is defined and restricted within laws which We have laid down; you, by contrast, impeded by no such restrictions, may, by your own free will, to whose custody We have consigned you, trace for yourself the lineaments of your own nature. I have placed you at the very centre of the world, so that from that vantage point you may with greater ease glance round about you on all that the world contains. We have made you a creature neither of heaven nor of earth, neither mortal nor immortal.

Pico della Mirandola, *Oration on the Dignity of Man*[1]

A thought experiment

The stages through which the development of intelligence passes can be summarised by means of a kind of thought experiment. At the stage of formal reason, it is possible for me to imagine that the present is only a dream and that in a moment I will awake to find that things are in fact quite different from how I think they are. Changes in matters of fact might be of any scale: that I am really writing in Pali, not English; that the world isn't flat after all; that (for any Freudian's looking in) my mother's middle name is not Jezebel but Mary. As the famous conundrum of whether I am a human being dreaming that I am a butterfly or a butterfly dreaming that I am a human being shows, entire philosophies can be built out of this kind of uncertainty. Similarly, concrete reason can (in an episodic, empirical way) wonder about alternatives and options, and even intuitive reason can discriminate between same and different, playing with this relationship through jokes, games and rituals. In short, the basic fact of imagination of any kind is the capacity to act as though experience can be not only disregarded but also intentionally subverted.

But it is an equally essential feature of the development of intelligence that its current level of maturity also circumscribes the *nature* of what can be imagined. There are always certain aspects of my present existence I find it impossible to imagine would be different, even if I did suddenly awake into a quite different reality. However, just which particular aspects these are depends on

---

[1] Pico della Mirandola (1956: 7).

my level of development. At the stage of formal reason, for example, it seems to be impossible to imagine a world in which elementary propositional arguments are invalid. If I am not merely dreaming that Socrates is a man or that all men are mortal, then it is literally inconceivable that I am only dreaming that Socrates is mortal. However, it probably would be possible to induce concrete reason to act as though this were the case, for concrete reason lacks the formal controls that insist that this inference must be invalid. But even concrete reason seems to be incapable of acting as though the number system and basic arithmetic could be violated, whereas intuitive reason is always more or less willing to allow this. And again, although intuitive reason may act as though structures such as number series were infinitely malleable, the simple permanence of objects – the fact that they continue to exist even when we are not directly aware of them – seems to be inescapable, even for a small child.[1] In short, as personal experience, research into the consciousness of the child and the history of all previous epochs testify, the fact that we find some things inconceivable is not merely a negative phenomenon, reflecting our incompetence, ignorance and immaturity, but also a positive expression of the structures that *are* at our disposal. In each case, both the range and bounds of our imagination are determined by the structure and consequent relationships of necessity, possibility and contingency implied by out current level of development.

However, once intelligence is raised to the level of dialectical reason, its totalisation of all structures of activity and its corresponding recognition of the absoluteness of the actual make it literally inconceivable that *anything* might be otherwise than that which simply – infinitely simply – *is*. The absoluteness of a totally comprehended actuality presupposes the abolition of all conditions on both its existence in itself and its existence for us, and where nothing is conditional, nothing is optional. With dialectical reason, what is, is absolutely, both in itself *and* for us. At the final stage in the development of intelligence, therefore, everything is finally both constituted and recognised as being absolutely determinate.[2]

---

[1] One must distinguish here between our assumptions and our ability to criticise and justify those assumptions. Bishop Berkeley may have had difficulty in *explaining* how or why things exist apart from our awareness of them, but he does not seem to have *lived* as though he really thought they might not. I assume that both Parmenides and Zeno of Elea ate and slept and changed many things, themselves included, even though they felt they could prove that real change was illusory. On the cognitive and epistemological significance of this distinction and its development in the individual, see Smith (1993). On Parmenides, Zeno and others, see Lloyd (1979: 68ff); Waterfield (1989: 42–5).

[2] Whether dialectical reason is really the final stage is another question. That it might not be is suggested by two arguments, one positive, the other negative. The positive argument is that there are striking analogies (to put it no stronger) between the sub-stages into which a single stage is divided and the overall sequence of major stages. In certain fundamental respects, intuitive, concrete, formal and dialectical reason resemble the opening sub-stages through which they each proceed. But as I have argued, there seem to be only four major stages, as opposed to the 6 sub-stages. Might it be that further major stages await us beyond dialectical reason? As for the negative argument, I have argued that an intelligence at one stage would be unable to grasp the nature of its

So dialectical reason has no need of imagination. But this is not the tragedy one might easily take it to be: imagination, like thought or the nation state, is just as much an expression of intelligence's inadequacy as of its strength. Just as, at the stage of formal reason, we should think it childish to imagine that Socrates might live forever anyway, despite his being a man and all men being mortal, so dialectical reason finds the enthusiastic speculations of formal thought the very hallmark of its immaturity. After all, what could be more marvellous than that which absolutely, unconditionally *is*?

As one should expect of so vast yet so simple a thing as the development of reason, the process of getting to actuality may be infinitely convoluted and revolutionary, yet it is also essentially straightforward. Its implications are likewise simultaneously obvious and astounding. Each new stage offers a new mode of activity, of construction, of existence, and of the impossible, the inconceivable, the indispensable and the incontrovertible. The convergence of subject and object engendered by this process, the unconditional abstractness of the former and the absolute concreteness of the latter, the extension of reason to every sphere of existence – all these help dissolve the previously impenetrable oppositions in which the world was cast, of appearance and reality, self and other and present and absent. For where world and universe are finally one, where subjects exist solely in their objects and every object exists solely as the expression of its subject, it is literally meaningless to even hypothesise the differences from which these distinctions are bred.

A strong conception of human nature

One essential benefit this account of the development of intelligence offers is that it allows an extremely strong conception of human nature as a distinct and specific reality, without identifying the intelligence that underlies it with any of its concrete features. However paradoxical it may seem, the only enduring basis for a truly strong conception of human nature is in the most abstract of all structures, namely subject, object and world, and in the equally abstract kinds of activity and consequence that follow from their nature. After all, in asking for a definition of human nature we are not looking for something like a definition of 'ant nature' or 'wildebeest nature'. Insofar as defining human nature is equivalent to defining intelligence – and as I have argued elsewhere, it is our intelligence that makes us human – to define human nature is more like defining 'life' or 'chemical reactions'. And what, one might ask, could be more abstract than that?

It is true that such a nature is, by the standards of non-intelligent structures, a little peculiar, yet humanity is as much a part of nature as bacilli or quasars. It is moreover a good deal less peculiar, in its way, than any of the things by which it finds itself surrounded. For example, it can wonder what a notion such as 'peculiar' might mean and, if it wants, do something about it, so

---

successors in any but the most superficial terms. So, if there are indeed stages beyond dialectical reason, how would we – how *could* we – know?

amending any untoward strangeness it may find in itself. That does not mean that intelligence finds itself easier to comprehend than the non-intelligent. On the contrary. But our greater facility in comprehending other structures is a function of our position at the zenith of matter: from that perspective, all other structures are necessarily easier to grasp than our own. As the historical order in which the major sciences were established suggests, our own intelligence is the last thing we come to grips with.

That does not mean that intelligence is the last thing intelligence has on its mind, though. As the histories of both science and philosophy illustrate, not only is it the first thing on intelligence's mind but our initial attempts to grasp the physical, chemical and biological levels of matter were all thoroughly imbued with projections of intelligence, and our interpretations of our essential nature were constantly coloured by the accidents of our current world. Only once we had worked our way through these lower forms of matter were we able to distinguish or differentiate ourselves from them, or raise ourselves to a level of maturity needed to bring ourselves into focus. We were therefore forced to rely on what we had learned from lower levels of matter to account for our own proper nature, leading us to exacerbate our tendency to anthropomorphise nature with our repeated reduction of our own intelligence to pre-intelligent terms. So we have always appeared to ourselves as essentially apes, angels or hybrid beings – all equally unhelpful models. The inadequacy of the ensuing metaphors has always been more or less clear, so human nature is bound to appear more than a little odd, even to ourselves. So at least until the essentials of the problematic are all in place, intelligence always seems a good deal more peculiar than the non-intelligent structures by which it is surrounded.

The reader may find it tempting to reject the argument I have presented in this book on the grounds that it too presents human beings as something outside the normal run of nature. I hope that my demonstration that intelligence is formed through a developmental process that begins with intelligence itself on the very verge of non-intelligence anticipates this objection. One of the reasons why strong accounts of human nature – and so of human beings as *sui generis* – have usually seemed so implausible is that those who propose them generally fail to grasp the analogous achievements and nature of intelligence's predecessors and the role they play in preparing for intelligence itself. The nature of reason is remarkable only for the same reason that the view from the peak of a mountain is remarkable: it may only be at the peak that the triumph is obvious and complete (and the view so panoramic), yet it would be a small triumph were it not for the enormity of the supporting mass.

I hope I have not fallen into that trap. Even if it is not clear from the present volume how intelligence achieved its privileged position, I hope that have I shown that, whatever the lofty peaks from which it looks out at its pinnacle, this is the culmination of a quite natural process that begins from a level of structure and functioning we would willingly concede at least to our nearest primate neighbours, and perhaps to other species too. And I hope that I have also shown that intelligence's capacity for genuine objectivity and its ability to organise its own development allow human beings to decide their own destinations and the vehicles they need to get there. Conversely, whatever the starting point of human development, one day we will discard even the last remnants of our organic nature – that we sleep, that we do not photosynthesise, that our frames are mortal – and whatever forms we create in order to replace our present bodies, the principles guiding our actions and those choices will continue to be guided solely by the abstractions of subjectivity, objectivity and worldliness.

In the meantime, any conception of human nature that persists in seeking a fixed concrete content and context for our humanity rather than regarding particular conditions as the necessary yet transient paraphernalia of a more profound and fundamental process, implicitly denies everything that flows from subject, object and world and the dialectic of internalisation and externalisation – including, of course, the underlying rationality, and therefore intelligibility, of its own concept of human nature. If there really are irreducible concrete constraints on human nature, especially of the kind usually proposed by either biology or the humanities, then it is not hard to see why the same constraints would force us to doubt that we can know what human nature is. If our ability to know is an organic adaptation, then that ability is broadly limited to knowing in a way that, far from objective, is limited to functional interests, specific environment conditions, current states, and so on. However broadly this may be interpreted, it certainly means that there is no question of objective knowledge. The humanities likewise offer us only a view filtered and refracted through definite historical or phenomenological prisms – ultimately an equally limiting condition on objectivity. To limit human nature to any set of particularities, specificities or even universals, without then going on to produce true actuality out of them – and so both fulfilling and transcending any given concrete character – can only diminish and eventually corrupt.

Of course, that does create a rather shifting picture of human nature, but then which single frame is it that tells us the 'real' nature of a complete moving picture? It turns out that Machiavelli was right to say that to be rational was to be Machiavellian; some adolescents are right to have a romantic faith in a pure and idealistic human nature, just as others are right to be cynical; Hamlet and Sartre were as right to philosophise the futility of human existence as Hegel and the Buddha were right to find life full of significance. Each is an equally valid concretion of human nature at that point in its progress. It is natural for the rulers of Renaissance city-states to be Machiavellian, for adolescents to be both idealistic and cynical, for certain kinds of philosopher and princeling to be futile. Each is a true statement of human nature in its place. The error lies in promoting any of these transient images to the status of a universal truth, valid for every individual in every society in every age. There are no concrete definitions of 'human nature' as such. It is natural for reason to take such forms, but only to the same extent that it is natural for it to abandon them again. Indeed, it is natural for different human natures to co-exist, and to be different precisely because of their different positions and mutual relations within the larger totality. It is therefore no surprise that theorists of human nature have come to the most relativistic and the most rigid, the most rabid and the most inert conclusions.

Successive forms of human nature are more than merely contingent responses to changing conditions, however. Cataloguing the stages in the development of human nature is not a branch of stamp collecting, nor is it simply a record of prejudices or *aperçus*. Although it is perfectly capable of standing still or even going backwards, the formation of intelligence is indeed a developmental process, in the strong sense that each successive form is more mature than any of its predecessors. A formal cognitive structure such as Piaget's formal operations or a formal economic structure such as capitalism is by no means merely bigger or more comprehensive than concrete operations or feudalism. Each completely abolishes the contradictions that plagued its predecessor, and so eliminates a whole swathe of previously uncomprehended constraints on rational action. So whatever intelligence may make of formalism in hindsight, it represents not only an immense leap forward but also a profound transformation of the nature of intelligence itself – and so of human nature as such.

And so on, through each successive stage in the development of intelligence. What each new stage abstracts from its predecessors is a new structure that is infinitely more powerful than any simple re-arrangement or enhancement of its previous elements. This is no 'mere' abstraction, abstraction as vagueness or intellectualisation; rather, it is abstraction as transcendence, as revolution. This has a double effect: to make human nature ever more full, but also to make it ever emptier. Human nature is increasingly filled with its own achievements, but the growing independence each new level of achievement creates, including independence of its own current state and position, mechanisms and processes, simultaneously empties it of anything fixed or opaque, anything that could be called a self in the conventional psychological or metaphysical sense of the word. It is therefore impossible to identify human nature with any given set of instincts, propensities or even sensibilities, except on a plane which is so obviously historically contingent or so abstract as to defeat any attempt to circumscribe humanity at all.

It is true that there exist universal and perfectly real structures of human nature. As I have already argued, intentionality and symbolism, politics and economics, imagination and personality, sociality and technology and culture all follow directly from the central triad of intelligent structures, subject–object–world. But these structures are scarcely more concrete than subject, object and world themselves, and to the extent that they are concrete, it is only in the sense that they determine the forms of concreteness. They do not place concrete limitations on human nature themselves. To be precise (if also, as so often, paradoxical), they are the abstract forms of concreteness. To have a determinate technology is indeed a determinant form of human nature; however, no particular technology is forever, whereas saying that technology *as such* is forever is only to say that one particular aspect of the intrinsic relationship between subject, object and world will always exist – which is scarcely a constraint on human nature! The omnipresence of such structures says nothing about what actual human beings feel or know or do; all they guarantee and express is the fact that we exist, and that we are aware of that fact.

Even the terms that seem to predicate a definite nature most clearly – for example, that intelligent is inherently social – imply little more than that the world is very largely composed of other subjects, that we exist in relation to these other subjects, that it is commonly other subjects that stand at the interstices of shared objects, and that these relationships between subjects have their own implications and higher structures. As I argued in Chapter 1, insofar as human activity can be described as 'economic', this merely reflects the fact that the world of intelligence includes the social organisation of reality and the real organisation of society. The political is no more than the social organisation of intentions and the intentional organisation of society. As for 'intention' and 'reality' themselves, these turn out to be no more than reciprocal aspects of subject and object. And so on, for each of the basic terms of human nature: in each case what seem to be highly charged and highly concrete terms turn out to be grounded in nothing more concrete than inherent, indeed tautologous, relationships between subject, object and world – the most abstract terms of all.

Defining human nature in this way leads neither to empty generalities nor to insuperable constraints. Rather, it points to ever-increasing wealth, openness and diversity; not to closure or convergence on some more or less arbitrary 'mature' form but to the increasing enrichment of intelligence's potential and its confrontation by ever greater challenges and opportunities. Of course, we do not always have the strength or resources to go on. Yet the alternative to activity and development is invariably anger or despair (rationalised away, perhaps, in terms of a higher faith or a principled irrationalism), banishing all insight, criticism and intelligibility and declining to play any active part in the further development of reason. A line is simply drawn, a false circle enclosing the frontiers of current usage, experience and convention. Beyond this lie only madness, the void, dragons, and whatever else is needed to keep reason from acknowledging its current contradictions. Yet even here it is surprising how swiftly the elaboration and defence of solemn unreason makes appeal to rational arguments and proofs. The deity of faith reappears as a cosmic watchmaker and his existence and actuality are proved by theorems of mathematical rigour and niceness; private utility justifies itself in the universal felicific calculus of economic theory; astrology, numerology and all the dreams of a philosophic magic – every anti-, non- and irrational form spawns its codifiers and scholastics; Nirvana itself proves to be the realm of a rationality far more tyrannical than mere formal logic or mathematics can conceive.

A real conclusion: truth and freedom

> In that mythic age, man was no freer than he is today; but only his humanness
> made him a slave. Since his control over nature remained very limited, he was
> protected – and to some extent released from bondage – by a cushioning of
> dreams. As these dreams were gradually transformed into knowledge, man's
> power increased and became a great source of pride; but this power, which gears
> us, as it were, to the universe, is surely little more than our subjective awareness
> of a progressive welding together of humanity and the physical universe, whose
> great deterministic laws, instead of remaining remote and awe-inspiring, now use
> thought itself as an intermediary medium and are colonising us on behalf of a si-
> lent world of which we have become the agents.
>
> Claude Lévi-Strauss, *Tristes Tropiques*[1]

What last picture can give a final, compelling impression of what intelligence
really is? To dwell too intently on the abstractness of intelligence would be to
risk neglecting the concrete nature of any actual intelligent being, reducing intelligence's unique and defining abstractness to a mere abstraction. On the
other hand, to concentrate on intelligence in the concrete would risk creating
the opposite impression, that intelligence is no more than a clutter of semi-
contingent historical and phenomenological accretions. Such a summary might
be very vivid and much more obviously human, yet it would only conceal the
essential abstractness on which I have insisted, so depriving it of all conviction
by the very attempt to render it more convincing.

Fortunately there is another approach to summarising intelligence, more in
keeping with the logic of intelligence itself. This is to ask in what ways intelligence summarises itself, not only theoretically but in practice too. Precisely
because of its abstractness and its consequent disinterestedness towards any
concrete embodiment, there is no end to the development of intelligence until it
reaches the point at which it has both constructed every possible abstraction
and implemented those abstractions in every possible concrete form. Of course,
whether or not such a point can actually be reached is an important question,
but as I have already suggested, there is no insuperable limit to intelligence's
ability to grasp the universe as a whole. You do not have to comprehended
everything in detail for every detail to be immediately comprehensible.

Clearly the construction of all abstract and concrete structures is also the
point where intelligence reaches its most perfect development. What is more,
since this point is necessarily the same for all possible intelligences, it is here, at
the culmination, fulfilment and terminus of dialectical reason, that all intelligences become identical. Not only are they the same in terms of their abstract
structures, but their most concrete forms are also totally intelligible to all other
completely developed intelligences. For a truly complete world would be one
that embraced all the universe, so all complete worlds not only possess the
same structure and content (which would still allow them to be distinct and
separate) but are actually *the same world*.

---

[1] Lévi-Strauss (1984: 512–3).

This unification of the abstract and the concrete into a single totality also offers reason a practical goal and a theoretical ideal towards which it may realistically strive, even though it cannot yet plot a direct course towards it and may know in advance that it will never be achieved during any existing intelligence's individual existence. Indeed, once detected on even the most remote horizon, this goal has always provided the highest aspiration and most profound inspiration for humanity.[1] This is intelligence as it appears when all the transformations sketched out over the last few chapters are finally brought to fruition. Hence the approach of this final section: to define reason in terms of the ultimate (highest, most mature, final) structure it (or matter in general) can attain, in terms of the ultimate (most powerful, most comprehensive, most faithful) forms of activity of which it (or any material structure) is capable. In short, the final image of intelligence I propose here is the image of *truth* and *freedom*.

The reader will have gathered by now that the truth and freedom I have in mind are not the pale simulacra of bourgeois ideology. A completely developed intelligence needs neither philosophers nor politicians to expound or defend them on its behalf. Truth and freedom are things that dialectical reason lives. To have to explain, proselytise or justify them at all serves only to emphasise just how far they are from being realised. For truth and freedom that are not self-evident, self-sufficient and self-sustaining are not true or free in and for themselves, cannot be true or free with any necessity or conviction or justification, and so cannot be true or free at all. The same lack of realisation also entails that their ultimate significance must remain somewhat opaque to those who have realised neither fully. Still, to be able to address these issues at all, even in corrupt and naïve terms, indicates a high level of development.

A completely developed intelligence would clearly have no limits. The uniquely rational forms of activity and development the appearance of intelligence unleashes – history, consciousness, production, judgement, personality, technology, culture, conscience, imagination, politics, science and so much else – allow intelligence not only to build a completely rationalised world but also to transcend any concrete substrate or ancestry out of which it might have developed. Taken all in all, the developmental process described in the opening chapters of this book gives intelligence access to every corner of the physical, chemical and biological universe, not to mention the worlds of every other mature intelligence. Its progressive formation of more and more powerful structures permits it not only to organise and control ever broader sweeps of activity but also to see more profoundly into the workings of its objects, its world and itself. It is therefore only a matter of time before each particular, specific and universal aspect of the conditions it inherits and encounters is comprehended. Conversely, intelligence is perfectly capable of resolving not only all experiences and actions and all tensions, lacunae and conflicts between its experiences and its actions, but also all tensions, lacunae and conflicts between its resolutions of these tensions, lacunae and conflicts, all tensions between these tensions, and so on and on, until all contradictions of all kinds are resolved. That in turn can only be accomplished when all possible

---

[1] Cassirer (1944: 54–5, 62).

That in turn can only be accomplished when all possible contents and contexts have been embraced by the intelligence in question.

In short, when the actualisation of intelligence is complete, our actual objects and our actual world exist for us as they exist in themselves – which is to say, absolutely. But how can something exist for us as it exists in itself except when we and it are one? Where else could this convergence be accomplished except within intelligence, which alone of all material structures exists *for* as well as *in* itself? Hence the connection between actuality on the one hand and the totalisation of all structures of activity on the other, and between both of these and truth and freedom. This totality is the condition of our ever comprehending the actual, and the state and status of the actual is the sole incontrovertible index of the validity of that totality. But to say that we have achieved either that totality or that actuality is only to say that we have achieved this identity of the *for us* and the *in itself*.

What then does it mean to say that we, our objects and our world are one? By internalising our objects, our world and ourselves in the most literal and material way, as I suggested in connection with the higher stages of intelligence, not only we but our objects and our world come to exist in themselves not only in the same way but also in exactly the same sense that they exist for us. Not only do we know all *about* our objects and our world, but the structures out of which we are composed as subjects and agents come to be the very structures out of which our objects and our world are composed. That is what technology ultimately means: the identity of our intentions with the reality to which they relate. And to the extent that that technology is perfected, so is our identity with our world, and with the physical, chemical, biological and intelligent reality through which that world exists. Conversely, to the extent that we as subjects are united by the social and symbolic relationships through which our objects and world are constructed, we are united among ourselves. That is what a shared culture ultimately means: the unity, and ultimately the identity, of the social and symbolic orders through which we act.

Hence the relationship between the development of intelligence and the development of truth and freedom. Regardless of whether the 'other' to which or to whom we relate is a neutron, an ant or another intelligent being, if that other is grasped as it is in itself – which is to say, grasped in all its actuality – then it is grasped truly. And if in grasping the other we incorporate it within ourselves, if we make its actions our actions and the conditions of its existence are the conditions of our existence, then it both imbues us with its implicit wisdom and places its intrinsic powers at our disposal. By this means its incorporation within ourselves (through the adequate cultural organisation of an adequate technology) frees us from the conditions it would impose upon us, even as we adjust ourselves to the processes and mechanisms its activity presupposes. Thus we realise Bacon's ambition of mastering nature by submitting to it: our comprehension of the other both liberates us from it and liberates us through it. Truth and freedom, precisely because they are the products of actuals and actuality, are thus corollaries of one another, the spontaneous goals and measures of the totalisation of reason. And once they are brought to fruition, they are self-evident.

Of course, not all intelligent activity is directly liberating or enlightening. Its objective consequences may or may not be as purposed. The result may even transcend that intelligence's ability to grasp it at all. To the extent that this is so, it will be experienced as an absurdity rather than a lesson, as a catastrophe rather than an accomplishment, as a threat rather than a power. Nor are such outcomes rare or insignificant. Any revolution is a case in point: not even the most profound revolution realises all its goals, and not even the most superficial revolution can fail to surprise the revolutionaries. Still, if at least some of our activity did not lead to genuine development, it is hard to see what sense could be made of the otherwise fantastic changes intelligent life has brought about in the last ten thousand years, not only to itself but to the planet itself.

Not all change is development, of course. However, as matter moves closer and closer to intelligence, not only are the scope and power of change altered but the very locus of its various determinants shifts too. In the case of the purely external determinacy of physical structures, matter may be completely determined as a whole (which is to say, at the level of the universe as a whole), but no part of it constitutes a totality of determinations in its own right. So no single physical structure (other than the universe itself) determines its own activity entirely, and no assemblage of physical structures can guarantee its own continuity or deal with every possible intrusion from outside. At the opposite extreme, that of purely internal determination, activity is not only determined *as* a single totality but also *by* that self-same totality, which is to say, by itself. At that point, activity includes all its own opportunities and limitations, potential and constraints, and nothing can intrude whose implications and consequences cannot be anticipated, controlled and, if necessary, forestalled. It is at this extreme that dialectical reason stands, with a truly complete range of ways of making sense of the world and making the world make sense, from mystical contemplation to industrial society to planetary management and beyond. At that point, which comes only at the completion of intelligence, the determined and the determining structures of activity are one and the same.

This view of the development of intelligence permits me to reconcile the two great axiomatic yet antithetical languages of action: the language of freedom and determinism, and the language of fatality and arbitrariness. Until the completion of intelligence, each of these pairs of terms is a pair of antonyms, but at its conclusion they reappear as synonyms. All four terms also come to converge on a single meaning. For that which includes within itself all the determinants of its own activity, resolving them into a single coherent, consistent, complete and correct totality, is still as fully determined as the most trivial mechanism. But by the same token, it knows what there is to be known and knows it as it is in itself. Likewise, a mature intelligence has reached the point where it knows all the determinants of its activity by virtue of the very process whereby it internalised them in the first place – by making sense of them, and by making them make sense. Conversely, if intelligence fails to penetrate them to the very core, they will make it pay for its hubris the moment it presumes too much upon their acquaintance. And this in turn will initiate yet another round of making sense of things.

Likewise a mature intelligence wills and desires entirely on its own terms, not because it forces all nature to dance to its tune but because it has learned that it can only succeed in proportion to its willingness to learn nature's songs and retune its instruments accordingly. So, having internalised all the determinants of its own activity, it not only knows but actively incorporates – it *is* – every instrument, resource and capability necessary to its endeavours. So it commands every occasion and opportunity for activity, directly and without effort. Its actions may be strenuous and its experience stressful, but they are without strain, without distress. In short, it is totally determined but, having internalised all the conditions of its own activity, it is also the sole determinant of its own activity. In other words, it is free because it is determined and as determined as it is free.

On the other hand, until intelligence reaches that happy condition, there always remains an element not only of external control – of fate – but also of ignorance and incomplete control over its own order and dynamics – of arbitrariness. These are the natural corollaries of the incoherence, inconsistency, incompleteness and incorrectness that immaturity of any kind inflicts, and regardless of the *potential* for truth and freedom it confers, to trace the development of intelligence is also to trace the history of *actual* fatality and arbitrariness. The structures making up an immature intelligence could not (by definition) include all the conditions of their own existence, and its lack of a proper perspective creates a constant temptation to conflate the actual with the natural and the normal. Consequently, during all but the last stage of development, intelligence's very notions of truth and freedom are inevitably constrained and undermined by the illusion that either external determination or a kind of metaphysical freedom from determination is inherent in the human condition.[1]

Nor is this illusion a delusion. However determinate the structures involved, from the standpoint of an immature intelligence a degree of arbitrariness is entirely necessary to it taking any action at all. The illusion of 'free will' created by the recognition of, yet inability to account for, oneself as a knowing, capable and responsible agent is likewise indispensable, even though it is bound to be confounded by the sense of fatality engendered by the simultaneous intimation that wider, deeper, unresolved forces are at work behind the scenes, not least within oneself. As Darwin observed, the natural conclusion of this is likely to be a kind of predestinarian atheism.[2]

Yet by gradually making sense of, and so internalising, this arbitrariness and fatality, intelligence shows how they harbour the seeds of their opposites, which is to say, freedom and determinism. However, to arrive at a final truth and freedom it is also necessary to grasp that truth is not merely the last word

---

[1] Penrose's 'explanation' of consciousness in terms of quantum uncertainty (Penrose, 1989, 1994) seems to be essentially just such a mistaken attempt to locate free will by finding some remaining locus of arbitrariness. This is precisely the opposite of the approach required for a theory of freedom. As Waddington noted of the alleged indeterminacy of quantum processes, 'The experience of free will is not that of some rolling of dice within our minds; it is, exactly, that we *choose* one result rather than another' (Waddington, 1961: 117). In other words, the only person who can benefit from quantum freedom is Maxwell's Demon.

[2] Darwin (1974: 19).

in knowledge, any more than freedom is merely unconstrained power. As Lévi-Strauss has put it:

> Knowledge is based neither on renunciation nor barter; it consists rather in selecting *true* aspects, that is, those coinciding with the properties of thought. Not, as the Neo-Kantians claimed, because my thought exercises an inevitable influence over things, but because it is itself an object. Being 'of this world', it partakes of the same nature as the world.[1]

But in that case, truth is not an epistemological category at all. Indeed, like freedom, it is not a *intellectual* structure of any kind of any kind. If intelligent activity is activity that knows itself to be that activity and is that activity by virtue of that knowledge, then the culmination of intelligence must surely come when knowing and doing are one. At that point, truth belongs to neither the empiricists nor the rationalists, is neither consensus nor convention, is neither eclectic nor pragmatic, is neither a function of some natural capacity for 'reflection' nor an issue of correctness and precision, of the endless accumulation of 'data' or the achievement of 'correspondence'. It is neither purely internal (in the manner of, say, speculation), and thus lacking independent verification, nor purely external, like trial and error, whose implications are as arbitrary and obscure as its method and whose only consolation is the depressing certainty of error offered by falsificationism. Freedom is likewise the possession of neither the politician nor the anarchist, neither the stoic nor the existentialist, neither the nihilist nor the mystic or the moralist. It is not a question of election, divine or popular, not a matter of either seizing power or abjuring it. It is neither subjective nor objective nor worldly; rather, like freedom, it is the totalisation of all three.

But what would the completion of truth and freedom really mean? In part this question has already been answered, in the earlier accounts of dialectical reason, actuality, infinitude, and so on. Here I need only repeat that the dialectic of internalisation and externalisation, and with it the structure and function of intelligence, culminates in the transcendence of all limits and the inclusion of all existence, be it in terms of time, space, substance or causality. In each case one can observe that the problem facing intelligence is not that of coming to terms with the alleged unknowability of the thing in itself or the interminable expanses of existence so much as making sense of the here and now. For that to occur, the contingency and conditionality of activity and experience must be raised to, and abolished by, the absolute.

Firstly, the internalisation of space – initially the formation of subjective structures capable of comprehending an actual space, but increasingly the creation and arrangement of objects in space and then intelligence's grasp of space itself – concludes in the absorption, and so the abolition, of all external conditions on the spatial existence of the intelligence in question. In other words, the external, extensive structure of space within which intelligence first finds itself is replaced by the internal, boundless, intentional order of *infinity*. Such an infinity is no longer the logical yet contradictory, irresistible yet imaginary attribute of space 'as such'; rather, because it comprehends the totality of all ac-

---

[1] Lévi-Strauss (1984: 68).

tual structures and unites them at every point in their existence, it becomes the true and immediate nature of each and every actual thing and event. The internalisation of time likewise transposes *eternity* from theology and metaphysics to the presence, the selfhood and the immediate appearance of every action. With that, the infinite and eternal are extended out from the private realm of the intellect and the imaginary Kingdom of God to the most ordinary, everyday structures of common sense.

As for causation, intelligence's eventual construction and incorporation of all relations controlling activity of all kinds leads to the replacement of causation itself, with its latent sense of an external relationship between cause and caused, by a true *totality* of mutually determining, defining and generally implying relationships. Finally, with the simultaneous incorporation of all intelligent and pre-intelligent structures within reason and the rationalisation of all the intelligent and pre-intelligent structures that make up its world, mere substance is transformed into true *being*. After all, how else could any of intelligence's solipsistic demons be assuaged without also reconciling ourselves with the demiurge of the world, who demands equal respect? Thus reason totalises intelligence and universe together, rendering intelligence and universe identical.

So, to achieve truth and freedom, intelligence must prove itself through external confirmation as well as internal affirmation. The unity of this dual process is, I hope, clear. Were it based solely on the purely transcendent rationality of isolated and *a priori* abstractions, lacking any grounding in the ordinariness of everyday existence, intelligence could raise itself no higher than lofty inspiration. Then, failing to grasp its actual existence, it would fall back, mired and corrupted in the incidents and accidents of contingent experience and impulse of every kind. Transcendent values remain necessary, but to give free rein to the merely formal values of the academic or the bureaucratic or to money or 'the market' would be as viciously utopian as relying on the 'pure' immanence of the empirical, the pragmatic and the conventional would be idealistically meretricious.

So it is again fortunate that intelligence cannot help transcending mere functional approximation, overcoming the contingency of the moment and rising above the literally worthless concatenation of empirical skills and opportunistic impulses. Yet it is equally incapable of settling for the thin gruel of ideals. Only by surpassing both immanence and transcendence can such basic processes as abstraction and concretion remain viable, for in the absence of intrinsically abstract values such as coherence, consistency, completeness and correctness, not even the most utilitarian, venal or opportunistic act would be intelligible, even to its author. On the other hand, such abstract values quickly become unintelligible when they do not allow us to comprehend even the most minor and ordinary of actions. Over and above functionality, expedience or economy there must also be objectivity, integrity and validity. But at the same time, objectivity, integrity and validity must be capable of creating concrete value, in every sense and on every plane.

Only intelligence, by uniting the intangible world of ideals, goals, methods, skills, functions and principles with the droning empirical world of problems and solutions, departments and organisations, materials, people and tools, can reconcile and unite these two antithetical utopias. However, intelligence can only do this when it has perfected itself too – and can only perfect itself to the extent that it does all these things.

These are only logical consequences of the nature and development of intelligence, of course. To the extent that my sketches of the relationship between intelligence and other, pre-intelligent forms of matter are correct, they are their natural consequences too. Whether they will also be their historical consequences, in the sense of actually being brought to fruition, is another matter. However, it is already clear that the routine formation of dialectical reason on this planet is only a matter of time. So is the full rationalisation of the conditions of intelligent existence for as far as human existence currently extends. On the other hand, this simultaneous liberation and validation of intelligence is not only beyond all non-intelligent beings but also a matter of indifference to them. For intelligence it comes as a matter of course, though the course in question may be long, twisting and hard. To be human may be to make existence up as we go along, but it is also to make it up by means possessing increasingly intrinsic necessity and validity, making existence increasingly lucid and compelling. At the limit, intelligence is constrained only by the irreducible actuality and absoluteness of the universe itself. But they, of course, not only provide an unconditional goal but also confirm the incontestable absoluteness and actuality of the highest expression of intelligence, namely reason itself. To achieve truth and freedom is therefore not to achieve a grasp of the absolute; it is to *be* absolute.

Exactly what all this means, what revelations (and catastrophes) intelligence will visit upon itself on the way, and how much further intelligence can extend itself into the universe cannot yet be known. One has only to recall how the future looked to sophisticated scientists and politicians only a century ago to appreciate the absurdity of even guessing. On the other hand, so long as intelligence continues, its ultimate goals cannot help but be attained, for with the rise of intelligence, matter passes from the age of fate to the epoch of destiny. If there is a difference between what, for intelligence, is logically possible, what is naturally possible and what is historically possible, this difference grows smaller and smaller as intelligence itself unfolds. The profoundly logical nature of the process through which reason liberates itself even from its own conceptions of itself tells us that this conclusion will be reached, and even, in general terms, how it will come about. Yet the revolutionary nature of the process involved means that it cannot be said just what the conclusion will be. As the greatest of all exponents of human liberation observed:

The man who draws up a programme for the future is a reactionary.[1]

---

[1] Karl Marx. Letter to Professor E.S. Beesly.

Bibliography

Agrawal, M., Kumaresh, T.V. and Mercer, G.A. (2001). The false promise of mass production. *McKinsey Quarterly*, 3.

Alexander, C. and Langer, E. (eds) (1990). *Higher Stages of Human Development*. New York: Oxford University Press.

Alland, A. (1972). *The Human Imperative*. London: Columbia University Press.

Anderson, P. (1974). *Lineages of the Absolutist State*. London: NLB.

Antinucci, F. (ed.) (1989). *Cognitive Structure and Development in Non-Human Primates*. London: Lawrence Erlbaum.

Appadurai, A. (1986). *The Social Life of Things: Commodities in Cultural Perspective*. Cambridge: Cambridge University Press.

Archer, L. (ed.) (1988). *Slavery and Other Forms of Unfree Labour*. London: Routledge.

Ariès, P. (1973). *Centuries of Childhood*. Harmondsworth: Penguin.

Arlin, P.K. (1975). Cognitive development in adulthood: a fifth stage? *Developmental Psychology*, 11, 5: 602–606.

Armstrong, K. (1993). *A History of God*. New York: Random House.

Armstrong, K. (2000). *The Battle for God. Fundamentalism in Judaism, Christianity and Islam*. London: HarperCollins.

Atran, S. (1990). *Cognitive Foundations of Natural History: Towards an Anthropology of Science*. Cambridge: Cambridge University Press.

Atran, S. (1998). Folk biology and the anthropology of science: cognitive universals and cultural particulars. *Behavioral and Brain Sciences*, 21: 547–609.

Barrow, J.D. and Tipler, F.J. (1986). *The Anthropic Cosmological Principle*. Oxford: Oxford University Press.

Basseches, M. (1984). *Dialectical Thinking and Adult Development*. New York: Norwood.

Beaud, M. (1984). *A History of Capitalism*. London: Macmillan.

Bekoff, M. and Jamieson, D. (eds) (1990). *Interpretation and Explanation in the Study of Animal Behaviour*, vols. I and II. Oxford: Westview Press.

Berg, M. (1985). *The Age of Manufactures*. London: Fontana.

Bergson, H. (1947). *Creative Evolution*. New York: Random House.

Berlin, I. (1976). *Vico and Herder: Two Studies in the History of Ideas*. London: Chatto and Windus.

Berlin, I. (2000). *The Roots of Romanticism*. Edited by Henry Hardy. London: Pimlico.

Bernstein, P.L. (1998). *Against the Gods. The Remarkable Story of Risk*. New York: John Wiley.

Berry, J.W. and Dasen, P.R., (1974). *Culture and Cognition: Readings in Cross-Cultural Psychology*. London: Methuen.

Bickerton, D. (1990). *Language and Species*. Chicago: University of Chicago Press.

Black, A. (1992). *Political Thought in Europe 1250–1450*. Cambridge: Cambridge University Press.

Bloch, M. and Parry, J. (eds) (1989). *Money and the Morality of Exchange*. Cambridge: Cambridge University Press.

Blyth, R.H. (1994). *The Genius of Haiku: Readings from R.H. Blyth*. British Haiku Society.

Boardman, J., Griffin, J. and Murray, O. (eds) (1992). *The Oxford History of the Classical World*. Oxford: Oxford University Press.

Boolos, G.S. and Jeffrey, R.C. (1980). *Computability and Logic*. Second edition. Cambridge: Cambridge University Press.

Boorstin, D.J. (1984). *The Discoverers*. London: J.M. Dent and Sons.

Borges, J.L. (1970). *Labyrinths*. Harmondsworth: Penguin.

Bowler, P.J. (1992). *The Fontana History of the Environmental Sciences*. London: Fontana.

Brady, T.A., Oberman, H.A. and Tracy, J.D. (1994). *Handbook of European History 1400–1600. Vol. 1 Structures and Assertions*. Grand Rapids, Michigan: William B. Eerdmans.

Braudel, F. (1974). *Capitalism and Material Life 1400–1800*. London: William Collins Sons.

Braudel, F. (1981, 1982, 1984). *Civilisation and Capitalism* (vols 1–3). London: William Collins Sons.

Breck, A.D. and Yourgau, W. (1972). *Biology, History, and Natural Philosophy*. London: Plenum Press.

Bretherton, I. (ed.) (1984). *Symbolic Play: The Development of Social Understanding*. New York: Academic Press.

Brewer, A. (2000). Adam Smith's two invisible hands. Inaugural Lecture, University of Bristol, 25 January 2000.

Brubaker, R. (1991). *The Limits of Rationality. An Essay on the Social and Moral Thought of Max Weber*. London: Routledge.

Brunt, P.A. (1986). *Social Conflicts in the Roman Republic*. London: The Hogarth Press.

Bush, M. (1983). *Noble Privilege*. Manchester: Manchester University Press.

Butterworth, G. (ed.) (1982). *Infancy and Epistemology: An Evaluation of Piaget's Theory*. Brighton: Harvester Press.

Byrne, R. (1995). *The Thinking Ape: Evolutionary Origins of Intelligence*. Oxford: Oxford University Press.

Caprona, D. de, Ducret, J.-J., Rod, O., Rosat, M.-C. and Wells, A. (1983). *History of Science and Psychogenesis*. Geneva: Fondation Archives Jean Piaget.

Camus, A. (1975). *The Myth of Sisyphus*. London: Penguin.

Carchedi, B. and Carchedi, G. (1999). Contradictions of European integration. *Capital and Class*, 97: 119–154.

Carcopino, J. (1956). *Daily Life in Ancient Rome*. Harmondsworth: Penguin.

Carey, J. (ed.) (1999). *The Faber Book of Utopias*. London: Faber and Faber.

Carroll, L. (1968). *Alice's Adventures in Wonderland and Through the Looking Glass*. London: Macmillan.

Cassirer, E. (1944). *An Essay on Man: An Introduction to a Philosophy of Human Culture*. London: Yale University Press.

Cavalli-Sforza, L.L. and Cavalli-Sforza, F. (1995), *The Great Human Diasporas: The History of Diversity and Evolution*. Harlow: Addison-Wesley.

Chant, C. and Goodman, D. (eds) (1999). *Pre-Industrial Cities and Technology*. London: Routledge.

Childe, V.G. (1963). *Social Evolution*. London: Collins.

Cipolla, C.M. (ed.) (1976). *The Middle Ages*. London: Harvester Press.

Clay, C.G.A. (1984). *Economic Expansion and Social Change: England 1500–1700. Vol. II, Industry, Trade and Government*. Cambridge: Cambridge University Press.

Cohen, A. and Rapport, N. (eds) (1995). *Questions of Consciousness*. London: Routledge.

Cohen, D. (1995). *Law, Violence and Community in Classical Athens*. Cambridge: Cambridge University Press.

Cole, M. (1996). *Cultural Psychology. A Once and Future Discipline*. Cambridge, Mass.: Harvard University Press.

Cole, M., Engeström, Y. and Vasquez, O. (1997). *Mind, Culture and Activity*. Cambridge: Cambridge University Press.

Colletti, L. (1973). *Marxism and Hegel*. London: NLB.

Commons, M., Armon, C., Kohlberg, L., Richards, F., Grotzer, T. and Sinnott, J. (eds) (1990). *Adult Development: vol. 2. Models. Methods in the Study of Adolescent and Adult Thought*. New York: Praeger.

Commons, M., Richards, F. and Armon, C. (eds) (1984). *Beyond Formal Operations*. New York: Praeger.

Commons, M., Richards, F. and Kuhn, D. (eds) (1982). Systematic and metasystematic reasoning: a case for levels of reasoning beyond Piaget's stage of formal operations. *Child Development*, 53: 1058–1069.

Coote, J. and Shelton, A. (eds) (1992). *Anthropology, Art and Aesthetics*. Oxford: Oxford University Press.

Copenhaver, B.P. and Schmitt, C.B. (1992). *Renaissance Philosophy*. Oxford: Oxford University Press.

Covey, S.R. (1989). *Seven Habits of Highly Effective People*. New York: Simon and Schuster.

Crombie, A.C. (1994). *Styles of Scientific Thinking in the European Tradition*, vol. 1. London: Gerald Duckworth.

Crook, J.H. (1980). *The Evolution of Human Consciousness*. Oxford: Oxford University Press.

Crook, J.H. (1983). On attributing consciousness to animals. *Nature*, 303: 11–14.

Crosby, A.W. (1986). *Ecological Imperialism: The Biological Expansion of Europe, 900–1900*. Cambridge: Cambridge University Press.

Crumley, C.L. and Marquardt, W.H. (eds) (1987). *Regional Dynamics: Burgundian Landscapes in Historical Perspective*. San Diego: Academic Press.

Damerow, P. (1995). Prehistory and cognitive development. Invited Lecture to the Twenty-Fifth Annual Symposium of the Jean Piaget Society, Berkeley, June 1–3, 1995.

Darlington, C.D. (1964). *Genetics and Man*. London: George Allen and Unwin.

Darwin, C. (1901). *The Descent of Man and Selection in Relation to Sex*. London: John Murray.

Darwin, C. (1974). *Metaphysics, Materialism and the Evolution of Mind: Early Writings of Charles Darwin*. Chicago: University of Chicago Press.

Davis, R. (1973). *The Rise of the Atlantic Economies*. London: Weidenfeld and Nicolson.

Davis, S.J.M. (1987). *The Archaeology of Animals*. London: B.T. Batsford.

Dawkins, R. (1989). *The Selfish Gene*. Oxford: Oxford University Press.

Deacon, T. (1997). *The Symbolic Species*. London: Penguin.

Dempster, W.J. (1983). *Patrick Matthew and Natural Selection*. Edinburgh: Harris.

Dennett, D.C. (1991). *Consciousness Explained*. Boston: Little, Brown.

Dennett, D.C. (1996). *Kinds of Mind*, New York: Basic Books.

Desmond, A. and Moore, J. (1992). *Darwin*. London: Penguin.

Dews, P. (1987). *Logics of Disintegration: Post-Structuralist Thought and the Claims of Critical Theory*. London: New Left Books.

Diamond, J. (1999). *Guns, Germs and Steel: The Fates of Human Societies*. New York: W.W. Norton.

Dickson, D.B. (1990). *The Dawn of Belief: Religion in the Upper Paleolithic of Southwestern Europe*. Tucson: University of Arizona Press.

Dickson, P.G.M. (1967). *The Financial Revolution in England: A Study in the Development of Public Credit 1688–1756*. London: Macmillan.

Dieren, W. van (ed.) (1995). *Taking Nature into Account: A Report of the Club of Rome*. New York: Springer-Verlag.

Douglas, M. (1966). *Purity and Danger*. London: Routledge and Kegan Paul.

Douglas, M. (1996). *Natural Symbols: Explorations in Cosmology*. London: Routledge.

Douglas, M. and Isherwood, B. (1996). *The World of Goods: Towards an Anthropology of Consumption*. London: Routledge.

Dover, G. (2000). *Dear Mr Darwin. Letters on the Evolution of Life and Human Nature*. London: Weidenfeld and Nicolson.

Doyle, W. (1992). *The Old European Order 1660–1800*. Second edition. Oxford: Oxford University Press.

Driesch, H. (1908). *The Science and Philosophy of the Organism*. London: Adam and Charles Black.

Duncan, D.E. (1998). *The Calendar*. London: Fourth Estate.

Durkheim, E. and Mauss, M. (1963). *Primitive Classification*. London: Cohen and Paul.

Eccleshall, R. (1978). *Order and Reason in Politics: Theories of Absolute and Limited Monarchy in Early Modern England*. Oxford: Oxford University Press.

Edelman, G. (1992). *Bright Air, Brilliant Fire: On the Matter of the Mind*. London: Penguin.

Eiseley, L. (1961). *Darwin's Century: Evolution and the Men Who Discovered It*. New York: Doubleday.

Eitner, L. (1971). *Neoclassicism and Romanticism 1750–1850*, 1. London: Prentice-Hall International.

Eliade, M. (1978). *The Forge and the Crucible: The Origins and Structures of Alchemy*. Second edition. London: University of Chicago Press.

Elton, G.R. (1963), *Reformation Europe 1517–1559*. London: Fontana.

Engelhardt, H.T. and Caplan, A.L. (1987). *Scientific Controversies. Case Studies in the Resolution and Closure of Disputes in Science and Technology*. Cambridge: Cambridge University Press.

Enright, D.J. (1988). *The Alluring Problem: An Essay on Irony*, Oxford: Oxford University Press.

Fagan, B.M. (1995). *Ancient North America: The Archaeology of a Continent*. Revised edition. London: Thames and Hudson.

Fernández-Armesto, F. (2000). *Civilizations*. London: Macmillan.

Fiedel, S.J. (1987). *Prehistory of the Americas*. Cambridge: Cambridge University Press.

Fitzsimmons, M.P. (1987). Privilege and polity in France. *American Historical Review*, 922: 269–295.

Fodor, J.A. (1983). *The Modularity of Mind*. Cambridge, Massachusetts: MIT Press.

Foucault, M. (1970). *The Order of Things: An Archaeology of the Human Sciences*. London: Routledge.

Frankfort, H., Frankfort, H.A., Wilson, J.A. and Jacobsen, T. (1949). *Before Philosophy: The Intellectual Adventure of Ancient Man*. Harmondsworth: Penguin.

Frankl, V. (1959). *Man's Search for Meaning*. New York: Simon and Schuster.

Frede, M., and Striker, G. (1996). *Rationality in Greek Thought*. Oxford: Oxford University Press.

Garin, E. (1990). *Astrology in the Renaissance*. London: Penguin.

Gay, P. (1969). *The Enlightenment: An Interpretation. Vol. II: The Science of Freedom*. New York: Alfred A. Knopf.

Gellner, E. (1974). *Legitimation of Belief*. Cambridge: Cambridge University Press.

Gibson, K.R. and Ingold, T. (1993). *Tools, Language and Cognition in Human Evolution*. Cambridge: Cambridge University Press.

Godelier, M. (1972). *Rationality and Irrationality in Economics*. New York: Monthly Review Press.

Goleman, D. (1978). *The Varieties of the Meditative Experience*. London: Hutchinson.

Goodwin, B.C. and Saunders, P. (1992). *Theoretical Biology. Epigenetic and Evolutionary Order from Complex Systems*. Baltimore: Johns Hopkins University Press.

Goody, J. (1977). *The Domestication of the Savage Mind*. Cambridge: Cambridge University Press.

Goudie, A. (1990). *The Human Impact on the Natural Environment*. Third edition. Oxford: Blackwell.

Goudie, A. (1992). *Environmental Change: Contemporary Problems in Geography*. Third edition. Oxford: Oxford University Press.

Goudsblom, J. (1992). *Fire and Civilisation*. London: Penguin.

Gould, S.J. (1984). *The Mismeasure of Man*. London: Penguin.

Gould, S.J. (1996). *Dinosaur in a Haystack: Reflections on Natural History*. London: Jonathan Cape.

Gratzer, W. (2000). *The Undergrowth of Science. Delusion, Self-Deception and Human Frailty*. Oxford: Oxford University Press.

Graves, R. (1981). *The Greek Myths*. London: Cassell.

Griffin, D.R. (1981). *The Question of Animal Awareness: Evolutionary Continuity of Mental Experience*. Revised and enlarged edition. Los Altos: William Kaufmann, Inc.

Griffin, D.R. (1984). *Animal Thinking*. London: Harvard University Press.

Haeckel, E. (1883). *The Evolution of Man*. London: Kegan Paul, Trench.

Haeckel, E. (1913). *The Riddle of the Universe*. London: Watts.

Hale, J.R. (1971). *Renaissance Europe, 1480–1520*. London: Fontana.

Hallpike, C.R. (1979). *The Foundations of Primitive Thought*. Oxford: Oxford University Press.

Hallpike, C.R. (1986). *The Principles of Social Evolution*. Oxford: Oxford University Press.

Hallpike, C.R. (2004). *The Evolution of Moral Understanding*. Prometheus Research Group: www.prometheus.org.uk.

Handy, C. (1995). *The Empty Raincoat*. London: Arrow Books.

Harel, D. (1987). *Algorithmics: The Spirit of Computing*. Reading, Massachusetts: Addison-Wesley.

Harrison, J.F.C. (1984). *The Common People. A History from the Norman Conquest to the Present*. London: Fontana.

Hegel, G.W.F. (1977). *Phenomenology of Spirit*. Oxford: Oxford University Press.

Herrigel, E. (1985). *Zen in the Art of Archery*. London: Routledge and Kegan Paul.

Hicks, M. (1995). *Bastard Feudalism*. Harlow: Longman.

Hill, C. (1975). *The World Turned Upside Down: Radical Ideas During the English Revolution*. Harmondsworth: Penguin.

Hill, C. (1996). *Liberty Against the Law: Some Seventeenth Century Controversies*. Harmondsworth: Penguin.

Hill, D. (1984). *A History of Engineering in Classical and Medieval Times*. London: Croom Helm.

Hill, D. (1993). *Islamic Engineering And Science*. Edinburgh: Edinburgh University Press.

Hilton, R. (1973). *Bond Men Made Free: Medieval Peasant Movements and the English Rising of 1381.* London: Methuen.

Hirst, P. and Woolley, P. (1982). *Social Relations and Human Attributes.* London: Tavistock.

Hodges, H. (1971). *Technology in the Ancient World.* Harmondsworth: Penguin.

Hodges, R. (1989). *Dark Age Economics: The Origins of Towns and Trade AD 600–1000.* London: Duckworth.

Horrocks, J.E. and Jackson, D.W. (1972). *Self and Role: A Theory of Self-Process and Role Behaviour.* Boston: Houghton Mifflin.

Huizinga, J. (1924/2001).. *The Waning of the Middle Ages.* Transl. F. Hopman. London: Penguin.

Humphrey, N.K. (1992). *A History of the Mind.* London: Chatto and Windus.

Humphrey, W.S. (1989). *Managing the Software Process.* New York: Addison-Wesley.

Huxley, J.S. (1912). *The Individual in the Animal Kingdom.* Cambridge: Cambridge University Press.

Huxley, T.H. and Huxley, J. (1947). *Evolution and Ethics.* London: Pilot Press.

Ifrah, G. (1998). *The Universal History of Numbers: From Prehistory to the Invention of the Computer.* London: Harvill.

Ilyenkov, E.V. (1977). *Dialectical Logic: Essays on its History and Theory.* Moscow: Progress Publishers.

Inhelder, B. and Piaget, J. (1958). *The Growth of Logical Thinking from Childhood to Adolescence.* London: Routledge and Kegan Paul.

Inhelder, B. and Piaget, J. (1964). *The Early Growth of Logic in the Child: Classification and Seriation.* London: Routledge and Kegan Paul.

Jacob, F. (1993). *The Logic of Life: A History of Heredity.* Princeton, N.J.: Princeton University Press.

Jahoda, G. (1970). Supernatural beliefs and changing cognitive structures among Ghanaian university students. *Journal of Cross-Cultural Psychology,* 1 (2): 115-130.

Jameson, F. (1991). *Postmodernism or, The Cultural Logic of Late Capitalism.* London: Verso.

Jantsch, E. and Waddington, C.H. (eds) (1976). *Evolution and Consciousness: Human Systems in Transition.* Reading, Massachusetts: Addison Wesley.

Jarman, M.R. (1976). Early animal husbandry. *Phil. Trans. R. Soc. Lond.* Series B, 275: 85-97.

Johnson, A.W. and Earle, T. (1987). *The Evolution of Human Societies: From Foraging Group to Agrarian State.* Stanford: Stanford University Press.

Josephus (1981). *The Jewish War.* London: Penguin.

Kamen, H. (1976). *The Iron Century.* London: Weidenfeld and Nicolson.

Kamenka, E. (1989). *Bureaucracy.* Oxford: Basil Blackwell.

Kant, I. (1963). *On History.* New York: Bobbs-Merrill.

Kaplan, R. (1999). *The Nothing That Is: A Natural History of Zero.* London: Allen Lane.

Karmiloff-Smith, A. (1992). *Beyond Modularity. A Developmental Perspective on Cognitive Science.* London: MIT Press.

Kauffman, S.A. (1993). *The Origins of Order: Self-Organization and Selection in Evolution.* Oxford: Oxford University Press.

Khalfa, J. (ed.) (1994). *What is Intelligence?* Cambridge: Cambridge University Press.

King, M.C. and Wilson, A.C. (1975). Evolution at two levels in humans and chimpanzees. *Science,* 188: 107-116.

Kirk, G.S., Raven, J.E. and Schofield, M. (1983). *The Pre-Socratic Philosophers*. Second edition. Cambridge: Cambridge University Press.

Kolakowski, L. (1978). *Main Currents of Marxism*, 1. Oxford: Oxford University Press.

Landels, J.G. (2000). *Engineering in the Ancient World*. New revised edition. London: Constable and Robinson.

Lasch, C. (1980). *The Culture of Narcissism*. London: Sphere.

Laures, R. (1992). A medieval response to municipal pollution. Paper presented to the Mid-America Conference on History, 17–19 September 1992, University of Kansas, Lawrence, Kansas.

Lefebvre, H. (1969). *Logique Formelle, Logique Dialectique*. Paris: Editions Anthropos.

Lefebvre, H. (1991). *Critique of Everyday Life*. Vol.1. London: New Left Books.

Leontyev, A.N. (1981). *Problems in the Development of the Mind*. Moscow: Progress Publishers.

Lerner, R.M. and Damon, W. (eds) (1998). *Handbook of Child Psychology: Vol. 1. Theoretical Models of Human Development*. Fifth edition. New York: Wiley.

Levins, R. and Lewontin, R. (1985). *The Dialectical Biologist*. London: Harvard University Press.

Lévi-Strauss, C. (1963). *Structural Anthropology: Vol. 1*. Harmondsworth: Penguin.

Lévi-Strauss, C. (1972). *The Savage Mind*. London: Weidenfeld and Nicolson.

Lévi-Strauss, C. (1984). *Tristes Tropiques*. Harmondsworth: Penguin.

Lewontin, R.C. (1991). *Biology as Ideology: The Doctrine of DNA*. New York: Harper-Collins.

Lewontin, R.C. (2000). *It Ain't Necessarily So. The Dream of the Human Genome and Other Illusions*. London: Granta.

Lindberg, D. (1992). *The Beginnings of Western Science*. Chicago: University of Chicago Press.

Lloyd, G.E.R. (1979). *Magic, Reason and Experience: Studies in the Origins and Development of Greek Science*. Cambridge: Cambridge University Press.

Lorenz, K. (1977). *Behind the Mirror: A Search for a Natural History of Human Knowledge*. London: Methuen.

Lourenço, O. and Machado, A. (1996). In defense of Piaget's theory: A reply to ten common criticisms. *Psychological Review*, 103, 1: 143–164.

Lovejoy, A.O. (1964). *The Great Chain of Being*. Cambridge, Mass.: Harvard University Press.

Lukács, G. (1978). *The Ontology of Social Being. 2. Marx*. London: Merlin.

Luria, A.R. (1971). Towards the problem of the historical nature of psychological process. *International Journal of Psychology*, 6 (4): 259–272.

Luria, A.R. (1976). *Cognitive Development: Its Cultural and Social Foundations*. Cambridge, Mass.: Harvard University Press.

Luria, A.R. and Vygotsky, L.S. (1992). *Ape, Primitive Man and Child*. Orlando: Paul M. Deutsch Press, Inc.

Luria, A.R. and Yudovich, F.Ia. (1966). *Speech and the Development of Mental Processes in the Child*. London: Staples Press.

MacMullen, R. (1988). *Corruption and the Decline of Rome*. London: Yale University Press.

Mandel, E. and Novack, G. (1970) *The Marxist Theory of Alienation*. New York: Pathfinder Press.

Marcel, A.J. and Bisiach, E. (1988). *Consciousness in Contemporary Science*. Oxford: Oxford University Press.

Marchand, H. (2002). Some reflections on post-formal thought. *Genetic Epistemologist*, 29 (3).

Martens, J. and Paul, J.A. (1998). The coffers are not empty: financing for sustainable development and the role of the United Nations. Global Policy Forum.

Marwick, M. (ed.) (1970). *Witchcraft and Sorcery*. Harmondsworth: Penguin.

Marx, K. (1954). *Capital*, I. London: Lawrence and Wishart.

Marx, K. (1975). *Early Writings*. Harmondsworth: Penguin.

Marx, K. (1993). *Grundrisse: Foundations of the Critique of Political Economy*. London: Penguin.

Marx, K. and Engels, F. (1976). *Collected Works*. Vol. 5. London: Lawrence and Wishart.

Mason, S.F. (1991). *Chemical Evolution*. Oxford: Oxford University Press.

McNeil, J.R. (2000). *Something New Under the Sun. An Environmental History of the Twentieth Century World*. London: Penguin.

Medawar, P.B. and Medawar, J.S. (1978). *The Life Science*. Frogmore: Granada.

Megarry, T. (1995). *Society in Prehistory. The Origins of Human Culture*. New York: New York University Press.

Meillassoux, C. (1981). *Maidens, Meal and Money: Capitalism and the Domestic Economy*. Cambridge: Cambridge University Press.

Meillassoux, C. (1991). *The Anthropology of Slavery: The Womb of Iron and Gold*. London: The Athlone Press.

Merleau-Ponty, M. (1962). *The Phenomenology of Perception*. London: Routledge and Kegan Paul.

Merleau-Ponty, M. (1973). *Consciousness and the Acquisition of Language*. Evanston: Northwestern University Press.

Mészarós, I. (1970). *Marx's Theory of Alienation*. London: Merlin.

Midgley, M. (1978). *Beast and Man. The Roots of Human Nature*. Hassocks: Harvester.

Montague, A. (ed.) (1962). *Culture and the Evolution of Man*. Oxford: Oxford University Press.

Montague, A. (1976). *The Nature of Human Aggression*. Oxford: Oxford University Press.

Moran, E.F. (2000). *Human Adaptability. An Introduction to Ecological Anthropology*. Boulder, Colorado: Westview Press.

Morgan, C.L. (1903). *Introduction to Comparative Psychology*. New York: Walter Scott Publishing Co.

Morrow, J. (1998). *A History of Political Thought. A Thematic Introduction*. New York: New York University Press.

Nagel, E. (1961). *The Structure of Science*. New York: Routledge and Kegan Paul.

Nagel, T. (1978). *The Possibility of Altruism*. Princeton, N.J.: Princeton University Press.

Nakamura, H. (1986). *A Comparative History of Ideas*. New York: Kegan Paul International.

Needham, J. (1969). *The Grand Titration. Science and Society in East and West*. London: George Allen and Unwin.

Nissen, H.J., Damerow, P. and Englund, R.K. (1993). *Archaic Bookkeeping. Writing and Techniques of Economic Administration in the Ancient Near East*. Chicago: University of Chicago Press.

North, J. (1994). *The Fontana History of Astronomy and Cosmology*. London: Fontana.

Novack, G. (1971). *Introduction to the Logic of Marxism*. New York: Pathfinder Press.

Okakura, K. (1993). *The Book of Tea*. Boston: Shambhala.

Ollman, B. (1976). *Alienation: Marx's Conception of Man in Capitalist Society*. Second edition. Cambridge: Cambridge University Press.

Oppenheim, J. (1985). *The Other World: Spiritualism and Psychical Research in England, 1850–1914*. Cambridge: Cambridge University Press.

Pagels, E. (1979). *The Gnostic Gospels*. New York: Random House.

Pagels, E. (1996). *The Origin of Satan*. London: Penguin.

Papanek, V. (1985). *Design for the Real World* (second edition). London: Thames and Hudson.

Parker, S.T. and Gibson, K.R. (1990). *Language and Intelligence in Monkeys and Apes*. Cambridge: Cambridge University Press.

Parker, S.T., and McKinney, M.L. (1999). *Origins of Intelligence: The Evolution of Cognitive Development in Monkeys, Apes and Humans*. Baltimore: Johns Hopkins University Press.

Patterson, O. (1982). *Slavery and Social Death: A Comparative Study*. Cambridge, Mass.: Harvard University Press.

Pearce, D. (1995). *Capturing Global Environmental Value*. London: Earthscan.

Penrose, R. (1989). *The Emperor's New Mind*. Oxford: Oxford University Press.

Penrose, R. (1994). *Shadows of the Mind*. Oxford: Oxford University Press.

Pepperberg, I.M. (1999). *The Alex Studies. Cognitive and Communicate Abilities of Grey Parrots. Cambridge, Mass.: Harvard University Press.*

Petroski, H. (1996). *Invention by Design*. Cambridge, Mass.: Harvard University Press.

Phillips, W.D. (1985). *Slavery from Roman Times to the Early Transatlantic Trade*. Manchester: Manchester University Press.

Piaget, J. (1928). *The Child's Conception of the World*. London: Routledge and Kegan Paul.

Piaget, J. (1951). *Play, Dreams and Imitation in Childhood*. London: Routledge and Kegan Paul.

Piaget, J. (1952). *The Child's Conception of Number*. London: Routledge and Kegan Paul.

Piaget, J. (1953). *The Origins of Intelligence in Children*. London: Routledge and Kegan Paul.

Piaget, J. (1955). *The Child's Construction of Reality*. London: Routledge and Kegan Paul.

Piaget, J. (1966). Nécessité et signification des recherches comparatives en psychologie génétique. *Journal International de Psychologie*, 1 (1): 3-13.

Piaget, J. (1971a). *Structuralism*. London: Routledge and Kegan Paul.

Piaget, J. (1971b). *Biology and Knowledge*. Edinburgh: Edinburgh University Press.

Piaget, J. (1977). *The Grasp of Consciousness*. London: Routledge and Kegan Paul.

Piaget, J. (1978). *Success and Understanding*. London: Routledge and Kegan Paul.

Piaget, J. (1980). *Les Formes Élémentaires de la Dialectique*. Paris: Editions Gallimard.

Piaget, J. (1995). *Sociological Studies*. London: Routledge.

Piaget, J. (2001). *Studies in Reflecting Abstraction*. Hove: Psychology Press.

Piaget, J. and Garcia, R. (1989). *Psychogenesis and the History of Science*. New York: Columbia University Press.

Pick, H.L. and Saltzman, E. (eds) (1978). *Modes of Perceiving and Processing Information*. Hillsdale, New Jersey: Lawrence Erlbaum.

Pico della Mirandola, G. (1956). *Oration on the Dignity of Man*. Washington DC: Regnery Gateway.

Plender, J. (1999). Share options: Cuckoos in the capitalist nest. *Financial Times*, 11 November 1999.

Polanyi, K., Arensburg, C. and Pearson, H.W. (eds.) (1957). *Trade and Markets in the Early Empires*. Chicago: Free Press.

Polanyi, M. (1958). *Personal Knowledge*. Chicago: University of Chicago Press.

Porter, R. and Teich, M. (eds) (1986). *Revolution in History*. Cambridge: Cambridge University Press.

Postan, M.M. (1975). *The Medieval Economy and Society*. Harmondsworth: Penguin.

Pressman, R.S. (1993). *A Manager's Guide to Software Engineering*. New York: McGraw-Hill.

Pyne, S.J. (2001). *Fire. A Brief History*. Seattle: Washington University Press.

Quiatt, D. and Itani, J. (eds) (1994). *Hominid Culture in Primate Perspective*. Niwot, Colorado: University of Colorado Press.

Rabb, T.K. (1975). *The Struggle for Stability in Early Modern Europe*. Oxford: Oxford University Press.

Rappoport, R.A. (1967). Ritual regulation of environmental relationships among a New Guinea people. *Ethnology*, 6: 17–30.

Redfield, R. (1953). *The Primitive World and its Transformations*. Ithaca: Cornell University Press.

Reinalda, B and Verbeek, B. (eds) (1998). *Autonomous Policy Making by International Organizations*. London: Routledge.

Reynolds, S. (1997). *Kingdoms and Communities in Western Europe 900–1300*. Second edition. Oxford: Oxford University Press.

Richards, G. (1987). *Human Evolution*. London: Routledge and Kegan Paul.

Richards, R.J. (1987). *Darwin and the Emergence of Evolutionary Theories of Mind and Behaviour*. Chicago: University of Chicago Press.

Richardson, K. (1999). *The Making of Intelligence*. London: Weidenfeld and Nicolson.

Riegel, K.F. (1973). Dialectical operations: the final period of cognitive development. *Human Development*, 16: 346–370.

Riegel, K.F. (1975). Towards a dialectical theory of development. *Human Development*, 18: 50–64.

Riley-Smith, J. (ed.) (1999). *The Oxford History of the Crusades*. Oxford: Oxford University Press.

Robinson, R.J. (1987). 'The Civilising Process': Some remarks on Elias's social history. *Sociology*, 21, 1: 1–17.

Robinson, R.J. (in preparation). *The Birth of Reason*. Prometheus Research Group: www.prometheus.org.uk.

Roitblat, H. and Meyer, J.-A. (1995). *Comparative Approaches to Cognitive Science*. Cambridge, Massachusetts: MIT Press.

Roodenburg, H. and Bremmer, J. (eds) (1991). *A Cultural History of Gesture*. Cambridge: Polity Press.

Rose, S., Lewontin, R.C. and Kamin, L.J. (1984). *Not in Our Genes*. London: Penguin.

Roseveare, H. (1991). *The Financial Revolution 1660–1760*. London: Longman.

Rouland, N. (1994). *Legal Anthropology*. London: Athlone Press.

Russon, A.E., Bard, K.A. and Parker, S.T. (1996). *Reaching into Thought: The Minds of the Great Apes*. Cambridge: Cambridge University Press.

Sacks, O. (1995). *An Anthropologist on Mars*. London: Macmillan.

Sahlins, M. (1974). *Stone Age Economics*. London: Tavistock Publications.

Ste. Croix, G.E.M. de (1983). *The Class Struggle in the Ancient Greek World from the Archaic Age to the Arab Conquests*. Second impression, corrected. London: Gerald Duckworth.

Saville, J. (1994). *The Consolidation of the Capitalist State, 1800–1850*. London: Pluto Press.

Schiffer, M.B. (ed.) (1992). *Archaeological Method and Theory*. Vol.4. London: University of Arizona Press.

Schmidt, A. (1971). *The Concept of Nature in Marx*. London: NLB.

Scullard, H.H. (1982). *From the Gracchi to Nero: A History of Rome 133BC to AD68*. Fifth edition. London: Routledge.

Sennett, R. (1977). *The Fall of Public Man*. New York: Knopf.

Sennett, R. (1998). *The Corrosion of Character: The Personal Consequences of Work in the New Capitalism*. New York: W.W. Norton.

Serpell, J. (1996). *In the Company of Animals*. Second edition. Cambridge: Cambridge University Press.

Sharpe, J. (1996). *Instruments of Darkness: Witchcraft in England 1550–1750*. London: Hamish Hamilton.

Shennan, J.H. (1974). *The Origins of the Modern European State 1450–1725*. London: Hutchinson.

Shennan, J.H. (1986). *Liberty and Order in Early Modern Europe*. Harlow: Longman.

Sherratt, A, (1997). *Economy and Society in Prehistoric Europe. Changing Perspectives*. Princeton, N.J.: Princeton University Press.

Silverman, H.J. (ed.) (1980). *Piaget, Philosophy and the Human Sciences*. Brighton: Harvester.

Simpson, G.G. (1949). *The Meaning of Evolution*. New Haven: Yale University Press

Simpson, G.G. (1969). *Biology and Man*. New York: Harcourt Brace Jovanovich.

Smith, A. (1976). *An Inquiry into the Nature and Causes of the Wealth of Nations*. Chicago: University of Chicago Press.

Smith, L. (1993). *Necessary Knowledge: Piagetian Perspectives on Constructivism*. Hove: Lawrence Erlbaum.

Smith, R. (1997). *Fontana History of the Human Sciences*. London: HarperCollins.

Smyth, M.M. and Marriott, A.M. (1982). Vision and proprioception in simple catching. *J. Motor Behaviour*. 14: 143–152.

Snell, B. (1960). *The Discovery of the Mind: The Greek Origins of European Thought*. New York: Harper and Row.

Soden, W. von (1994). *The Ancient Orient: An Introduction to the Study of the Ancient Near East*. Grand Rapids, Michigan: Wm. B. Eerdmans.

Sohn-Rethel, A. (1978). *Intellectual and Manual Labour. A Critique of Epistemology*. London: Macmillan.

Sokal, A. and Bricmont, J. (1998). *Intellectual Impostures*. London: Profile Books.

Sorabji, R. (1988). *Matter, Space and Motion: Theories in Antiquity and their Sequel*. London: Duckworth.

Sperber, D., Premack., D. and Premack, A.J. (1995). *Causal Cognition. A Multidisciplinary Debate*. Oxford: Oxford University Press.

Spierenburg, P. (1991). *The Broken Spell: A Cultural and Anthropological History of Pre-Industrial Europe*. New Brunswick: Rutgers University Press.

Spufford, P. (1988). *Money and its Use in Medieval Europe*. Cambridge: Cambridge University Press.

Stern, C. and Sherwood, E.R. (eds) (1966). *The Origin of Genetics. A Mendel Source Book*. San Francisco: W.H. Freeman.

Sternberg, R.J. (ed.) (1982). *Handbook of Human Intelligence*. Cambridge: Cambridge University Press.

Stiglitz, J. (2002). *Globalization and its Discontents*. London: Penguin Books.

Strauss, S. (ed.) (1988). *Ontogeny, Phylogeny, and Historical Development*. Norwood, New Jersey: Ablex.

Strong, T.B. (ed.) (1992). *The Self and the Political Order*. New York: New York University Press.

Strouhal, E. (1992). *Life of the Ancient Egyptians*. Norman, Oklahoma: University of Oklahoma Press.

Suzuki, D.T. (1970a, 1970b). *Essays in Zen Buddhist*. First and second series. London: Hutchinson.

Tawney, R.H. (1921/1943). *The Acquisitive Society*. London: G. Bell and Sons.

Taylor, C. (1975). *Hegel*. Cambridge: Cambridge University Press.

Teich, M., Porter, R. and Gustafson, B. (1997). *Nature and Society in Historical Context*. Cambridge: Cambridge University Press.

Tenner, E. (1996). *Why Things Bite Back: Predicting the Problems of Progress*. London: Fourth Estate.

Thomas, K. (1983). *Man and the Natural World: Changing Attitudes in England 1500–1800*. London: Penguin.

Thompson, D'A.W. (1961). *On Growth and Form*. Abridged edition. Edited by J.T. Bonner. Cambridge: Cambridge University Press.

Thomson, G. (1961). *The First Philosophers*. Second edition. London: Lawrence and Wishart.

Tomalin, C. (2003). *Samuel Pepys. The Unequalled Self*. London: Penguin.

Trevor-Roper, H.R. (1969). *The European Witch-Craze of the 16th and 17th Centuries*. Harmondsworth: Penguin.

Trigger, B.G., Kemp, B.J., O'Connor, D. and Lloyd, A.B. (1983). *Ancient Egypt: A Social History*. Cambridge: Cambridge University Press.

United Nations (1997). Sources for the financing of development. Report of the Secretary-General. A/52/399. 8 October 1997.

United Nations (2001). Opening statement at the special event on the challenge of eradicating poverty for sustainable development: international community response. Third United Nations Conference on the Least Developed Countries. Brussels, 14 May 2001.

Tuchman, B.W. (1978). *A Distant Mirror*. Harmondsworth: Penguin.

Valen, L. van (1974). Two modes of evolution. *Nature*, 252: 298–300.

Vauclair, J. (1996). *Animal Cognition: An Introduction to Modern Comparative Psychology*. London: Harvard University Press.

Vilar, P. (1976). *A History of Gold and Money 1450–1920*. London: NLB.

Volpe, G. della (1980). *Logic as a Positive Science*. London: NLB.

Vygotsky, L.S. (1962). *Thought and Language*. Cambridge, Massachusetts: MIT Press.

Vygotsky, L.S. (1978). *Mind in Society: The Development of Higher Psychological Process*. Cambridge, Mass.: Harvard University Press.

Waddington, C.H. (1961). *The Nature of Life*. London: Allen and Unwin.

Wallace, A.R. (1864). The origin of human races and the antiquity of man deduced from the 'Theory of Natural Selection'. *Journal of the Anthropological Society of London*, 2: 158–187.

Wallace, A.R. (1908). The present position of Darwinism. *Contemporary Review, August*.

Wallerstein, I. (1974). *The Modern World System*. New York: Academic Press.

Waterfield, R. (1989). *Before Eureka: The Pre-Socratics and Their Science*. Bristol: The Bristol Press.

Watson, M.W. (1984). Development of social role understanding. *Developmental Review*, 4: 192–213.

Watson, M.W. and Fischer, K.W. (1980). Development of social roles in elicited and spontaneous behaviour during pre-school years. *Developmental Psychology*, 16, 5: 483–494.

Wee, H. van der (1987). *Prosperity and Upheaval: The World Economy 1945–1980*. Harmondsworth: Penguin.

Wenke, R.J. (1990). *Patterns in Prehistory*. Third edition. Oxford: Oxford University Press.

Wertsch, J.V. (ed.) (1981). *The Concept of Activity in Soviet Psychology*. Armonk, New York: M.E. Sharpe.

Wertsch, J.V. (1985). *Vygotsky and the Social Formation of Mind*. Cambridge, Mass.: Harvard University Press.

Westfall, R.S. (1980). *Never At Rest*. Cambridge: Cambridge University Press.

White, M. (1997). *Isaac Newton: The Last Sorcerer*. London: Fourth Estate.

Whitrow, G.J. (1989). *Time in History*. Oxford: Oxford University Press.

Whyte, L.L. (1968). *Aspects of Form*. Second edition. London: Lund Humphries.

Williams, R.J.P. and Fraústo da Silva, J.J.R. (1996). *The Natural Selection of the Chemical Elements*. Oxford: Oxford University Press.

Wooton, D. (ed.) (1986). *Divine Right and Democracy*. London: Penguin.

Yasuda, K. (1957). *The Japanese Haiku*. Tokyo: Charles E. Tuttle.

Index